MW01011591

Fullmetal Alchemist (*Hagane no Renkinjutsushi,* 2001-2010) is a long-running *manga* by Himoru Arakawa, a masterwork of narrative art of recent times which led to the production of two truly magnificent *animé* series in 2003-2004 and 2009-2010.

MEDIA, FEMINISM, CULTURAL STUDIES

The Sacred Cinema of Andrei Tarkovsky
by Jeremy Mark Robinson

Liv Tyler
by Thomas A. Christie

The Cinema of Hayao Miyazaki
Jeremy Mark Robinson

Stepping Forward: Essays, Lectures and Interviews
by Wolfgang Iser

Wild Zones: Pornography, Art and Feminism
by Kelly Ives

'Cosmo Woman': The World of Women's Magazines
by Oliver Whitehorne

The Cinema of Richard Linklater
by Thomas A. Christie

Walerian Borowczyk
by Jeremy Mark Robinson

Andrea Dworkin
by Jeremy Mark Robinson

Cixous, Irigaray, Kristeva: The Jouissance of French Feminism
by Kelly Ives

The Erotic Object: Sexuality in Sculpture
From Prehistory to the Present Day
by Susan Quinnell

Women in Pop Music
by Helen Challis

Detonation Britain: Nuclear War in the UK
by Jeremy Mark Robinson

Julia Kristeva: Art, Love, Melancholy, Philosophy, Semiotics
by Kelly Ives

Luce Irigaray: Lips, Kissing, and the Politics of Sexual Difference
by Kelly Ives

Helene Cixous I Love You: The Jouissance of Writing
by Kelly Ives

FORTHCOMING BOOKS

Death Note	*Naruto*
Hellsing	*Vampire Knight*
Mushishi	*One Piece*
Tsui Hark	*Harry Potter*
Legend of the Overfiend	*The Twilight Saga*
Bleach	*Nausicaä of the Valley of the Wind*

FULLMETAL ALCHEMIST

THE *MANGA* AND THE *ANIMÉ*

FULLMETAL ALCHEMIST

A Critical Study

Himoru Arakawa
The *Manga* and the *Animé*

JEREMY MARK ROBINSON

Crescent Moon

First published 2023.
© Jeremy Mark Robinson 2023.

Set in Book Antiqua 9 on 14 point.
Designed by Radiance Graphics.

British Library Cataloguing in Publication data available for this title.

ISBN-13 9781861714978
ISBN-13 9781861719102
ISBN-13 9781861719133

Crescent Moon Publishing
P.O. Box 1312, Maidstone, Kent
ME14 5XU, U.K.
www.crmoon.com
cresmopub@yahoo.co.uk

CONTENTS

PART FOUR ✷ *FULLMETAL ALCHEMIST*: THE MOVIES AND
ORIGINAL VIDEO ANIMATIONS

ACKNOWLEDGEMENTS

To Arakawa Himoru.
To the authors and publishers quoted.

PICTURE CREDITS

Illustrations are © Square Enix. Hachette. Yen Press. Kodansha. Dark Horse. Studio Ghibli. Toho. Tokuma Shoten. Hakuhodo. Geneon. Dark Horse Comics. Optimum Releasing. Tokuma International.

Images are used for information and research purposes, with no infringement of copyright or rights intended.

LET US READY THE HORSES WITHOUT DELAY.

Manga: Hiromu Arakawa x Original Script: Yoshiki Tanaka
(published by Kobunsha Kappa Novels)

I SEE WE'VE OVERSTAYED OUR WELCOME.

NO GOOD WOMEN HERE, ANYWAY.

His trustworthy companions! Arslan's force prepares for action!!

THE HEROIC LEGEND OF ARSLAN
CHAPTER 22: FOR ONE'S LORD

Armor Design Assistance: Daisuke Niizuma

Resumes Serialization!!!!

THE MOUNTAINS ARE HUGE!

BUT OF COURSE, IT WAS AN INVITATION TO WORK, NOT THE OTHER KIND... ♥

AND LATER I'M SUPPOSED TO DISCOVER THE TWIST THAT YOUR GRANDPARENTS WILL BE THERE OR SOMETHING, RIGHT!?

YEAH, THEY'LL BE THERE.

SERI- OUSLY!? I'LL DO IT!

WELL, IF YOU DON'T HAVE ANYWHERE TO GO, WHY DON'T YOU COME STAY AT MY PLACE?

SUMMER VACATION BEGAN AND HACHIKEN DIDN'T WANT TO RETURN HOME. THAT'S WHEN HE GOT AN UNEXPECTED INVITATION FROM AKI.

THE STOR UP UNTI NOW

WOULD YOU LIKE TO TRY

BUT- CHE- RING THIS FELLER!

AND IN A STRANGE TURN OF EVENTS, ENDED UP BUTCHERING A DEER WHILE AT KOMABA'S HOUSE.

WHY WOULD ANYBODY HAVE A FARM IN SUCH A DANGE- ROUS PLACE!?

HE WAS FOUND BY HIS CLASS- MATE, KOMABA.

HACK TOOK UP O OFFE WORK ENDE GET LO IN WOO

WHAT THE HECK IS THIS!?

WOAH!

ASSEMBLY LINE SYSTEMS INCREASE EFFICIENCY AND LET US MILK ALL THE COWS QUICKLY!

IT LETS THE WORKERS DO THEIR JOB WITHOUT SHUFFLING FROM COW TO COW AROUND VERY MUCH.

IT'S A MERRY- GO ROUND FOR COWS!

IT LOOKS LIKE THOSE ROTA- TING TABLES YOU SEE IN CHINESE RESTAU- RANTS.

IT'S CALLED A ROTARY PARLOR. IT'S A SPECIAL TYPE OF ROTATING MILKING EQUIP- MENT.

IT'S AMAZ- ING!

WHEN HE FINALLY GOT A BREAK, HE WENT TO VISIT TAMAKO AT HER PLACE, GIGA FARM.

OH.

AFTER T HACHIKEN ACT TOGETH BEGAN WO HARDE

HACHIKEN SURE SEEMS TO BE WORKING HARD.

Part One

Himoru Arakawa

01

HIMORU ARAKAWA: BIOGRAPHY

Himoru Arakawa (born May 8, 1973, Tokachi, in Hokkaido) grew up on a dairy farm in Hokkaido, Northern Japan. She has three older sisters and a younger brother. Arakawa's experience on the farm[1] directly influenced her *manga*, including *Silver Spoon*, and her short *manga* about farming (*Noble Farmer*). She is married with three children (born 2007, 2011 and 2014), and lives in Tokyo (Arakawa's *manga* output slowed in the 2010s, as she looked after her husband and son who were ill with a blood disease). Like other *mangaka* such as Masamune Shirow (*Ghost In the Shell,   Appleseed*) and Tsugumi Ohba (*Death Note, Bakuman*), Arakawa protects her privacy, and prefers not to do many public appearances (actress Romi Pak, who plays Edward Elric in the animated versions of *Fullmetal Alchemist*, often appears in Arakawa's stead).

Himoru Arakawa moved to Tokyo (as thousands of *manga* artists tend to do) in 1999, and was an assistant to Hiroyuki Eto (b. 1971, *Magic Circle Guru Guru, Gadget*). An early job was drawing 4-*koma* for the magazine *Garnest*. Arakawa has acknowledged the influence of Suiho Tagawa (*Norakuro*), *Kinnikuman* (*Muscelman*, 1978-1987, by Yudeta-mago[2]), Hiroyuki Eto, Rumiko Takahashi (*Urusei Yatsura, Ranma 1/2, Inuyasha, Madison Ikkoku*), Shigeru Mizuki (*Gegege no Kitaro*) and Mike Mignola. She read comics avidly as a youth: *Weekly Shonen Jump* and *Weekly Shonen Sunday* in particular. Arakawa is a *manga* junkie,[3] as she admits:

'I love to read manga!'
'I love to draw manga so much I don't know what to do!'
'I draw, therefore I am!'
'That's all the proof I need to know that I exist! I'm satisfied with just that!'

---

1 Arakawa agreed to work on the family farm (for seven or eight years, apparently), after which she pursued her ambition of becoming a *mangaka* and going to the capital. While in Hokkaido, she took classes in oil painting.
2 Pseudonym for Yoshinori Nakai and Takashi Shimada.
3 Arakawa says she has a pad by her bed to jot down ideas (but can't understand them the next day).

'The point is I'm a manga idiot'

Arakawa-sensei is a massive fan of *Star Wars*[4] and *Indiana Jones*, but she hasn't read *Harry Potter* or *The Lord of the Rings* (which some might find hard to believe!).

Arakawa-sensei said her family motto was: 'those who don't work, don't deserve to eat'. So work is ingrained in the life-philosophy throughout Arakawa's *manga*. Arakawa is a hard worker: she is known to get back to writing *manga* only a few days after giving birth.

Himoru Arakawa's first name is Himori, but she used Himoru (the male version) as a pseudonym (she also took up the pen name Edward Arakawa). Arakawa said she never intended to give the impression that she was a man. However, it is common in the history of literature for women authors to use male pen names. Even Joanne Rowling was persuaded to use J.K. Rowling because it was thought that boys would be reluctant to read stories by a woman. (*Shonen manga* are aimed at boys).

Himoru Arakawa's first *manga* was *Stray Dog* (1999), published by Square Enix Co., Ltd's *Monthly Shonen Gangen* magazine. Enix set up their *Monthly Shonen Gangen* magazine (in 1991) partly to promote their role-playing games. Square Enix is a games manufacturer (*Dragon Quest, Final Fantasy*) and publisher (they merged in 2003).[5] The *manga* of *Hagane no Renkin-jutsushi* (*Fullmetal Alchemist*, a.k.a. *Alchemists of Steel*) first appeared in *Shonen Gangen* in Japan, published by Square Enix, in July, 2001, when Arakawa was 27 years-old (and collected in volumes from Jan 22, 2002).

The editor of *Fullmetal Alchemist*, one of the most important people in the creation of *manga*, was Yoichi Shimomura at Square Enix. The *omake* of vol. 17 includes a humorous look at editor Shimomura.

The great *manga* artists, Himoru Arakawa reckoned, fulfil the readers' expectations while also confounding them.

Originally intended as a one-off, *Fullmetal Alchemist* ran for 108 installments, until July, 2010 (the number 108 is of course significant in Oriental symbolism – however, as the final chapters are longer, it's more like 110+ chapters, and as each chapter is up to twice a regular *manga* chapter, and sometimes more, in the end it's around 270 regular chapters. There are 27 volumes, which equals about 5,400 pages).

As well as the 108 chapters of *Fullmetal Alchemist*, Square Enix have re-published extra chapters in their magazines, and also published the *manga* in *kanzenban* form. It won the Annual Shogakugan Manga Award in 2003, the Osamu Tezuka Cultural Award, the Eagle Award's 'Favourite Manga' (2010-11), and the Seiun Award in 2011.

In the West, *Fullmetal Alchemist* was published by VIZ[6] Media, LLC

---

4 In one of her *omake* appearances (as a cow, of course), Arakawa splutters, "WHY DID PADME FALL FOR ANAKIN?"

5 Square Enix's magazines *Monthly Shonen Gangen* and *Monthly G-Fantasy* are, like *Melody* (Hakusensha), *Dragon Age* and *Asuka* (Kadokawa Shoten) and *Wings* (Shinshokan), strong on fantasy. Among Square Enix's well-known *manga* are *Sekirei, Soul Eater, Saki, Tokyo Underground, Spiral, Black Butler, Watamote, Inu x Boku SS, Papuwa* and *Space Dandy*.

6 Viz Communications is wholly owned by Japanese company Shogakukan. It began operations in 1987, under the leadership of Seiji Horibuchi in San Francisco.

of San Francisco (English translation by Akira Watanabe, adapted by Egan Loo and Jake Forbes), from 2005 onwards; Viz Media have also published the *manga* in three-volume omnibus books (a new edition appeared to coincide with the live-action movie in 2017, known as *Fullmetal Alchemist: Fullmetal Edition*). Each chapter is 40-50 pages long. The 27 collected volumes of *Fullmetal Alchemist* have had sales in the region of 64 million (up to 2014).

There were Spanish editions of *Fullmetal Alchemist* (from Norma Editorial), German (from Planet Manga), Polish (from Japonica Polonica Fantastica), Swedish (from Bonnier Carlsen), Italian (from Panini Comics), Chinese (from China Children Press & Publication Group) and of course French (from Kurokawa).

There must have been serious discussions about whether to turn *Hagane no Renkin-jutsushi* into a long-running *animé* show of 100s of episodes like the Big Three (*One Piece*, *Naruto* and *Bleach*). The heroes Ed and Al and their chums are perfect for leading an adventure-of-the-week show like the Big Three, or similar animated shows such as *Fairy Tail*.

In December, 2019, Chris Cimi noted (in Otaquest) that

> *Fullmetal Alchemist* continues to stun with every watch and reread. Himoru Arakawa's masterpiece wins over younger fans like it came out yesterday. It's truly dense with content and wide in narrative scope but also a work that's strikingly accessible for a *manga* with so much going on.

Himoru Arakawa may be a mom of three children and a shy artist who prefers not to do interviews and publicity, but make no mistake, her artwork is as violent and vicious as *anyone's* in the whole history of *manga*. Whether they are male, or female, or both, or neither, or alien, or some other gender, or age, or background, whatever, Arakawa can smash up bodies, rip apart heads, slice off limbs, and explode people from the inside just as gleefully and outrageously as the best of 'em. (Arakawa has said that it doesn't matter anymore if an artist is male or female, because some girls love *shonen manga*, and some women love to create it).

Indeed, *mangaka* Himoru Arakawa has made ultra-violence and gore-fests one of her specialities – *The Heroic Legend of Arslan*, *Hero Tales*, *Dæmons of the Shadow Realm* and of course *Fullmetal Alchemist* are simply stuffed with astonishingly savage scenes.[7] It's nothing to Arakawa-sensei, it seems, to depict a sword cutting through someone's skull from top to bottom, their face peeling apart in a mist of blood. (It's beyond 'R' rated or even 'NC-17' rated – many of the scenes would simply never be allowed in commercial cinema or television).

Himoru Arakawa often caricatures herself as a black-and-white-spotted cow (the cartoon image appears in the *Fullmetal Alchemist manga*. Arakawa-sensei portrays herself as a *mangaka* cow, being threatened by

---

7 So it's a surprise to read something like *Silver Spoon*, which's so tame.

Gluttony and Scar, and being hugged by Alex Armstrong).[8] Why? It's to do with Arakawa's origins in rural Hokkaido, where she worked on her parents' farm (in the *Fullmetal Alchemist manga*, the depiction of Resembool, where the trio of heroes hail from – Ed, Al and Winry – recalls Hokkaido (these characters are hicks from the sticks). And Winry can be seen as an idealized version of the younger Arakawa, with Izumi Curtis[9] the tough *sifu* as the older Arakawa, and Seska the librarian as the nerdy Arakawa. Actually, of course it's Edward Elric, and Alphonse Elric, who are the true alter egos of Arakawa in the *manga*). Quite a few *mangaka* produce caricatures of themselves to appear in their comics, instead of photographs of themselves (Arakawa also prefers not to appear much in public).

Himoru Arakawa has been a very lucky *mangaka* in terms of the animated adaptations of her works: three *animé* series are masterpieces (the two *Fullmetal Alchemist* series and *Arslan*), and two are highly enjoyable (*Hero Tales* and *Silver Spoon*).

The hit rate is so high – there must be something about Arakawa's form of storytelling and drawings that filmmakers really respond to.

---

8 One cow cartoon shows Arakawa being shot by Winry, while Ed tries to stop her. She is also menaced by Scar, and yelled at by Roy Mustang (and Edward).

9 Izumi Curtis is more prominent in the *animé* (that she is one of the avatars for author Himoru Arakawa is clear).

Himoru Arakawa

Fullmetal Alchemist on the covers of Monthly Shonen Gangen magazine

02

THE *MANGA* OF HIMORU ARAKAWA

Among Himoru Arakawa's other works in *manga* apart from *Fullmetal Alchemist* are: *Shanghai Yomakikai* (*Demons of Shanghai*, 2000), *Raiden 18* (2005), *Soten no Komori* (*A Bat In Blue Sky*, 2006), *Jushin Enbu* (*Hero Tales,* 2006–2010), *Hyakusho Kizoku* (*Noble Farmer*, 2008), *Gin no Saji* (*Silver Spoon*, 2011-2019) and *Dæmons of the Shadow Realm* (2021-). All of Arakawa's *manga* works feature her distinctive designs – the angular faces with high cheekbones, the glowering expressions, the single line for a down-turned mouth, the crisp, contrasty light and shadows, the plentiful white space and negative space, the geometric precision of the perspectives in the landscapes and architecture, and the wicked sense of humour.

Himoru Arakawa has said:

> Manga are entertainment. They should be fun to read... So I try to remember what I found interesting as a kid when drawing my own manga.

STRAY DOG.
Stray Dog (1999) was a one-shot comic (of three-chapters in length) which was published by Square Enix's *Monthly Shonen Gangen* magazine (establishing a business relationship that did very well for both Arakawa and Square Enix). We're in a mediaeval-style fantasy realm in which humanoid creatures resembling dog-people are developed by nefarious wizards for military purposes (the notion of being a dog of the military was taken up in *Fullmetal Alchemist*, of course).

The two main charas in *Stray Dog* are the *ronin* warrior Fultac (the usual beefy, muscly middle-aged man[1] of Arakawa's art – from the outset of her career, she just loves drawing men with muscles!), and his new sidekick, Kilka, a small foundling military dog that Fultac takes under his wing (reluctantly). Of course li'l Kilka is adorable, and follows Fultac around like, well, a puppy. And Fultac, despite his gruff, he-man exterior, is a sweetie.

---

1 Arakawa likes muscular men: 'men should be buffed and women should be va-voom!'

In the course of a fierce duel between Fultac and a scornful wizard and his military dog, Fultac is wounded (he has his arm ripped off), and Kilka dies saving him. *Stray Dog* closes with Fultac taking on the aged wizard who oversees the military dog operation (in a castle tower), and destroys it.

What's striking about *Stray Dog* is how accomplished Himoru Arakawa's art already was (she was 26), and how she had already developed an approach to drawing *manga* which hasn't changed that much since 1999. The latest chapters of *Arslan Senki* (still in publication) are pretty much in the same style as the early works.

DEMONS OF SHANGHAI.

Demons of Shanghai (*Shanghai Yomakikai*, 2000) is an enjoyable early work from Himoru Arakawa (published in *Monthly Shonen Gangen* just before *Fullmetal Alchemist*). Unfortunately for fans, there is only one volume of *Demons of Shanghai* so far. It is a simple monster hunter format (a favourite form in Japanese *manga*, like *Ogre Slayer*, *Bleach*, *Kekkaishi* and numerous works by Toshio Maeda, including *Legend of the Overfiend*). So you've got a team of demon hunters who're trying to clear Shanghai of monsters (*oni*). Art-wise, there are many links to the *Fullmetal Alchemist manga*, and if you know Arakawa's work, you'll find similar character designs, similar action beats, similar humour, and similar scenarios. Arakawa took up Japanese folk tales again in 2021 with *Dæmjons of the Shadow Realm*.

NOBLE FARMER.

Noble Farmer (*Hyakusho Kizoku*, 2006, pub. in *Wings*) is a short piece (one volume) on farming, with Himoru Arakawa recollecting her years working on a Hokkaido dairy farm, where animals came first, and there was a special bond between beasts and humans. The style is comedy, in the manner of *4-koma*, the four-panel comic strips which Arakawa added to *Fullmetal Alchemist*. Arakawa appears as herself – tho' in her usual cow guise (a cow wearing glasses).

Arakawa-sensei's farming *manga* includes entries on scary bears, on cute horses, on working on a farm, the beauty of milk, and of course on cows. There's no let-up to hard labour throughout the year, and no time for breaks, Arakawa asserts, emphasizing the 'work hard' ethic behind so much of *shonen manga*. (And when she became a *mangaka* in the Big City, it was the same, she said: all work and no play). In *Silver Spoon*, Arakawa expanded on the concept of *Noble Farmer*.

RAIDEN 18.

Raiden 18 (2005-2013) is a delightful riff on the *Frankenstein* novel and legend, with scientist Dr Tachibana's creature becoming an entity with a wayward independence of its/ his own (the *Frankenstein* mythology is a key ingredient in the *Fullmetal Alchemist* series, of course). *Raiden 18* is a comical adventure *manga* (about 100 pages long) with the finest and funniest section being the tournament[2] involving creators and their creatures, whom they've built specially for fighting (a sort of Tim Burtonesque Hallowe'en party in which all sorts of horror movie clichés and monsters are featured). The audience and the monster makers include a Japanese *shinobi*, Chinese demon hunters, a black guy with an Afro, etc. The setting is a cemetery (of course), and the prize is the cemetery (of course) – which means all of the bodies in the ground can be used by the scientists for their experiments. In the event, Tachibana's monster wins the battle royale, taking out all of the rival creatures.

Dr Tachibana herself is an augmented creature, much older than she looks (there's an image of her sitting beside author Mary Shelley, for example). She's been experimenting for centuries, including with a re-animated Joseph Stalin (a scary notion!). Indeed, bodies and body parts, including those of celebrities, are marketed online.

Himoru Arakawa delivers some entertaining, humorous moments in *Raiden 18*, taking recognizable narrative devices and giving them an unusual spin. It's a spoof of the horror genre, and of horror movies in particular (Arakawa, as is obvious from *Fullmetal Alchemist*, is a horror fan). Arakawa delivers an amusing riff on horror and Hallowe'en motifs – the skulls, gravestones, sewn-up bodies, etc.

Raiden 18 also echoes elements of *Fullmetal Alchemist* – the creation of the homunculi, for instance, and of artificial forms of life such as the chimera. As in *Frankenstein* the novel, the relationship between the scientist and his creature forms the core of the piece (or I should say the beating, still-warm heart of it).

The struggle in *Raiden 18* is for freedom – the monster hankers after independence – including from its master/ maker. But Dr Tachibana won't grant that (she has a self-destruct button with which she taunts the monster).

A BAT IN BLUE SKY.

Soten no Komori (*A Bat In Blue Sky*, 2006) was a one-shot story of 64 pages (= three chapters) about a girl *shinobi* (ninja), Henpukumaru. In the preamble, Henpukumaru is taken in by a royal family and befriends the young child, Chiyozuru, the heir. Henpukumaru tries to forget her former life as an assassin so brutally trained she becomes like a beast. But she can't: she is forced back to the *shinobi* life when the mansion is assaulted by assassins intent on wiping out the family, and Chiyozuru.

All of this offers Himoru Arakawa the pretext for staging an intense set-piece of wild ninja action, with swords and chains and spears, in the manner of *Blade of the Immortal* or *Vagabond*. And, like Samura-sensei and Inoue-sensei, the authors of those samurai epics, Arakawa-sensei is just as accomplished at staging bloody battles (this time in the snow).

Henpukumaru is a sister-in-spirit to Lan Fan, the ninja bodyguard to Ling Yao in *Fullmetal Alchemist*; fiercely devoted to her lord, a brilliant warrior, but with oceans of sadness and loneliness surging underneath

---

2 Drawing on *Dragon Ball*, a massive influence on *shonen manga*.

that cool exterior.

DAEMONS OF THE SHADOW REALM.

A much-anticipated new comic from Arakawa-sensei appeared in Dec, 2021 in *Monthly Shonen Gangan* (publ. Square Enix). Entitled *Yomi no Tsugai*,[3] it was a fantasy adventure story built around humans and demons. Structurally, *Dæmons of the Shadow Realm* is founded on pairs and opposites: humans versus demons, past and present, tradition and modernity, city and country, East and West (the usual geo-political rivalry in Japan), light and dark, day and night, twins, brother and sister, two clans, and so on. (Even the chapter titles reflect the emphasis on pairings: 'Asa and Yuru', 'Left and Right', 'Dera and Hana', 'Love and Truth', 'Jin and Yuru' and 'The Tortoise and the Hare').

Dæmons of the Shadow Realm features many familiar Arakawan elements, such as glasses, horses, horse racing, the value of hard work and excessive violence. Glasses-wearing Jin, for instance, is an older version of Sheska in *Fullmetal Alchemist* and Hachiken in *Silver Spoon* (and is thus something of an author surrogate).

The background of *Dæmons of the Shadow Realm* is Japanese folktales featuring *yokai/ ayakashi/ oni* – or, in a Western word, monsters. Himoru Arakawa had already explored Japanese and Asian mythology in *Hero Tales* and *Demons of Shanghai*. So *Dæmons of the Shadow Realm* does come across as a synthesis of Arakawa's previous work, and it draws on many familiar ingredients, such as the political rivalry between the Eastern and Western regions of Nihon, discord between clans (a key element in demon tales), the links between the past (the country) and modernity (the city/ Tokyo), and the old-fashioned house in the middle of Tokyo.

It's common for Japanese comics to be set in the present day but be filled with ancient and traditional elements – old houses with sliding doors, Japanese gardens, strict social (patriarchal) hierarchies, and of course monsters and demons.

Himoru Arakawa relishes creating new forms of demons, and variants on existing ones. The demons also come in two forms – their monstrous form, and a *chibi* form (monstrous form for the action scenes, and *chibi* form for the talky scenes). Arakawa includes a *mangaka* in *Dæmons of the Shadow Realm*. A portly man in his late twenties, he just wants to be left alone so he can write comics in peace.

Dæmons of the Shadow Realm opens with a giant action set-piece, with the invasion of the heroes' village by the forces of Kagemori. When it's over (after several chapters), the warring sides regroup, forge unexpected (and uneasy) alliances, and revelations occur about the characters and their pasts. Altho' Yuru[4] (the young hunter) is at the centre of *Dæmons*, the comic is another team story, with much of the pleasure for the reader deriving from the interactions among the collection of misfits (each one with special powers).

---

3 Forerunners of *Dæmons of the Shadow Realm* might include *Nurarihyon's Grandson, Plunderer, Ninja Scroll, Ayakashi Triangle* and *Ogre Slayer*.
4 He resembles Taito in *Hero Tales*.

Demons of Shanghai (2000).

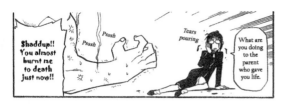

Raiden 18 manga.

03

HERO TALES

JUSHIN ENBU

Hero Tales (*Jushin Enbu*, 2006-10) was much more my cup of tea than my first encounter with *Silver Spoon* (which seemed too tame and too every-day initially for an Arakawa outing – but *Silver Spoon*, especially when helped along by the superb *animé* adaptation, grows on you). *Hero Tales* comprises 21 chapters, collected in five volumes, published in *Gangen Powered* magazine (publ. by Square Enix).

Hero Tales puts the reader right into the realm of mythical, quasi-historical Asia (in the *jiangzhu*, the martial arts world of mythology, to use the Chinese term). A world of Imperial armies and swordsmen and magical swords and samurai duels.

Although Himoru Arakawa takes top billing in *Hero Tales*, it was co-created with Ryou Yashiro, Shinya Oohara and Tetsuya Hayasaka (the *manga* also credits Kusanagi for art setting and Takahiro Yamada with weapons design). The name Huang Jin Zhou on the cover of *Hero Tales* refers to a group that includes Arakawa, Genco, Studio Flag and Zhang Fei Long. (The *manga* had its origins in amateur *manga* and *dojinshi* which Arakawa created with friends back in Hokkaido; it also appeared as an online *manga*).

Hero Tales contains many familiar Arakawan themes, motifs, and of course character designs and action beats. Arakawa-sensei had already brought a significant proportion of Chinese culture and mythology into the *Fullmetal Alchemist manga* with charas such as Prince Ling Yao, Lan Fan, Fuu and Mei Chang (as well as Chinese alchemy). *Hero Tales* is as if we've followed Ling, Mei and Lan back to China (Xing), and stepped back in time, too. Another Arakawa *manga, The Demons of Shanghai,* contained Chinese elements.

Hero Tales reads in part like a grand, Hong Kong action movie (like the *Zu* or *Detective Dee* films of Tsui Hark), or the more recent Mandarin language historical movies from Mainland China, which film in the giant Hengdian World Studios and the Forbidden City (*Hero, House of Flying Daggers, The Banquet, Curse of the Golden Flower*, etc).

The Chinese Imperial setting of *Hero Tales* gives Himoru Arakawa the complex, multi-layered institutions that she enjoys, with their strict social hierarchy, their lavish rituals and costumes, their warring clans and kingdoms, their ancient magic and religion, and their extravagant environments.

Characters in *Hero Tales* include Taito, the angry, naïve youngster who's a wannabe hero and possesses unknown powers (he resembles an older but far less charismatic and enjoyable Edward Elric); his sister, cute, sweet Laila, who thinks her brother is just a dumb brother (crude, stupid, clumsy); Housei, the spirited youth and would-be warrior who's madly in love with Laila (essentially a perennial sidekick for Taito); and Ryuukou Mouten, the priggish, solemn bodyguard assigned to Taito (Ryuukou is not a pretty boy type, like Narsus in *Arslan*, but he's close). There are also assorted patriarchs, warlords, Buddhist monks, fathers, court ministers, ninja, martial arts *sifus* and spies in *Hero Tales*. (There's plenty of exposition in *Hero Tales*, so many of those figures are involved with explaining the background plot).

The group assembled for the adventure in *Hero Tales* (Taito, Laila, Ryuukou, Housei, etc) isn't as compelling or as entertaining as the team in *Fullmetal Alchemist* (and there is far less humour), and thus their adventures aren't as engrossing as Himoru Arakawa's finest work, either. (Arakawa has unashamedly borrowed some of her designs from *Fullmetal Alchemist*, however: the vicious warlord Keiro is based on Führer Bradley, for instance; Arakawa re-used the Führer yet again for *Arslan Senki*. Meanwhile, other character designs from *Fullmetal Alchemist* crop up in *Hero Tales*, such as Mei Chang and Yoki).

But tho' the themes and the story in *Hero Tales* aren't as gripping as *Fullmetal Alchemist* (but how *could* you follow up or top *Fullmetal Alchemist*?!), there are some terrific action scenes, exotic locations, and the artwork has Himoru Arakawa's distinctive, crisp, bright look, which makes her *manga* so easy to read and enjoy.

The quests and goals of the characters in *Hero Tales* are the usual ones in the historical form of the action-adventure genre: Taito wants to get stronger, and to learn to control his powers (there are training sessions); Ryuukou has sworn to protect Taito and also to teach him how to channel his abilities; Housei acts at first as a guide (though Ryuukou immediately distrusts him); and Laila joins the party partly to prevent her brother Taito getting into trouble (the *animé* depicts Laila as the only person who can stop Taito when he loses it). The elders and patriarchs on all sides are fearful of the prophecies and hope to maintain the spiritual equilibrium.

Meanwhile, the antagonists and opponents in *Hero Tales* are the ones really driving the plot, as usual in the action-adventure genre: warlord Keiro hopes to dominate the world, by any means, including spying, coercion, and obtaining magical MacGuffins. Shimei is Keiro's ambiguous fixer, with his own ambitions (he serves Keiro but might betray him for his own ends).

Once the characters begin their journey, *Hero Tales* turns into something of a road movie adventure (as heroic quests often are): the group of heroes encounter new characters and new situations periodically. Some of these are unlikely types: for example, Koyou is a warrior chief who possesses an enormous ship (which the heroes travel on), but he also, improbably, offers a make-up service for women! So Laila partakes of his skills, and is made over so well that the other heroes don't recognize her.

Japanese *manga* (and *manga* from other Asian countries such as Korea with *Yongbi* by Ki Moon Ryu and Junghoo Moon), has explored the legendary era of the *jiangzhu* of mythical China many, many times, with its stories of wandering warriors and magical swords and warlords and palaces and castles. But it always works, doesn't it? – as Hong Kong cinema has shown in 100s of movies. Yes – you've got horses and swords and roving bandits and fearsome tyrants. And some mystical guff about stars and prophecies and gods (the Hokushin-Tenkun – images of the Plough constellation in the night sky are repeated). And secret, all-powerful martial arts techniques.

Hero Tales doesn't hold back on portraying a violent world of Ancient China: guards are smashed in the face (or killed) if they don't do their duty properly, fathers are run through with spears, and when Keiro goes on the war-path, he blasts meteor-size craters in the ground.

HERO TALES – THE *ANIMÉ*

The *animé* adaptation of *Hero Tales* (*Jushin Enbu*, 2007-2008) of 26 episodes was produced by Genco/ Media Factory/ TV Tokyo/ Jyushin Enbu Hero Tales Production Committee, with Studio Flag (animation production). First broadcast: Oct 7, 2007 to Mch 30, 2008. The producers were Fukashi Higashi, Muneyuki Kanbe and Nobusaku Tanaka, chief writer was Mayori Sekijima, directed by Osamu Sekita, music[1] by Tamiya Terashima, animation dir. and character des. by Naoki Sousaka, art dir. by Iho Narita, Youji Shimizu was sound director, and editing by Jun Takuma. In the cast were: Kenichi Suzumura, Akemi Kanda, Banjou Ginga, Yuko Kaida, Yuuki Tai, Atsuko Tanaka, Biichi Satou and Fumiko Orikasa.

Not as lavish nor as compelling as *Fullmetal Alchemist*, and not in the same masterpiece class as samurai *animé* such as *Ninja Scroll*, *Blade of the Immortal* and *Samurai Champloo*, *Hero Tales* was certainly an enjoyable outing: it had the mythical, Chinese settings, the prophecies, the magical

---

1 The theme songs were by Beat Crusaders, High and Mighty Colour and Mai Hoshimura.

powers, the sisterly-brotherly bickering, and of course slambang action.

The *animé* was at its best, perhaps, in its loving evocations of traditional, Chinese culture and society – it portrayed the grand palaces of the Forbidden City, the shadowy, candle-lit, Buddhist temples, the luxurious costumes, and some impressive music cues (from Tamiya Terashima), which offered pleasing pastiches of traditional, Chinese musical forms.[2]

Where *Hero Tales* was let-down was in its script (as often in many television and cinema outings), and its conception (that's not the fault of the writers – it's the production committees, the backers and the producers who decide how long a series will run). There is, simply, not enough material for a 26-show series, and so it's stretched too thin, and there is too much padding and repetition. And even tho' there are many scenes of characterization in *Hero Tales* – often the key strong point in *animé* – the characters don't come alive enough (and they are rather routine). With greater attention spent on the characterizations, and the interactions among the characters, *Hero Tales* might be a much richer series. And work would need to be done on some of the action sequences, which suffered from repetitive staging, particularly when compared to similar scenes in, say, *Naruto* or *One Piece* or *Nobunaga the Fool*. *Hero Tales* had all of the ingredients for a classy series, but it squandered too many of its opportunities.

The budget and schedule of *Hero Tales* is average for the business – this isn't a prestige production with expensive animation like the *Fullmetal Alchemist* adaptations. You can see areas where the animation is struggling to deliver what the script demands.

&.

The typical *Hero Tales animé* episode had Taito getting angry and frustrated with villains and confused over cosmic guff; Laila-chan exasperated over her *baka* brother ('men are hopeless' is a common mantra among the female charas);[3] an older monk chara shedding pearls of wisdom; Keiro stalking about looking ultra-grim; and Housei adding some goofy humour.

In the first two episodes of *Hero Tales*, we are introduced to Taito (Kenichi Suzumura),[4] a troubled hero-type: immature and rebellious, but well-meaning and loyal; his sister Laila (Akemi Kanda), the plucky sister type who's sensitive and endearing; the glum father; the wise, old wizard/ Buddhist monk type (played by the voice of Cornello in *Fullmetal Alchemist* – Kinryuu Arimoto), who delivers a lot of the exposition; the chief antagonist, General Keiro (veteran Banjou Ginga), imposing, muscular, solemn, ambitious; and his henchman, Shimei (Issei Futamata), a wily, dead-but-alive warrior.

Hero Tales opens in fine style just like a Hong Kong martial arts movie, with a giant action sequence that runs for some six minutes, up to

2 *Moribito: Guardian of the Spirit* (2007) features a superb vision of Ancient, Imperial Japan with a similar emphasis on fantasy.
3 They sort of form a 'useless men' group among women.
4 Sound director Youji Shimizu allows voice actor Kenichi Suzumura as Taito to snarl and yell his lines so often it becomes tiresome.

the opening titles. It's a superb duel between Taito and General Keiro, two of the key players and rivals. There's a magical sword that Keiro storms into the temple at Tian Long to steal (in a bid to become Emperor), wasting everybody in sight (except, handily, the heroes). Taito rushes in to defend his home, and is beaten by Keiro repeatedly. Many elements are culled from Chinese action movies: the temple setting (at night), the one-man mission, the Buddhist monks, the magical sword, the blasts of energy, and the visual effects. (Even the action resembles Hong Kong martial arts cinema in the use of props like statues, walls, and floors in the stunts).

The duel ends up unresolved (i.e., 'to be continued' – all the way up to the final show). Keiro possesses the sword (but can't unsheath it); he orders Shimei to test (or kill) Taito, which provides the action climax of the first show (as Shimei uses magic to puppeteer Laila, after he's taken her hostage, in order to force Taito into responding).

In the second episode, Taito learns about his powers, and the young heroes set out on their quest (to Defeat Keiro and Save The World). Old man Sonnei (Kenichi Ogata) adds the explanations about the Seven Stars of the Great Bear, just in case some in the audience weren't paying attention or didn't bring their notes to class (tomorrow's test will include the names of all seven of those all-important stars in the Great Bear constellation, so I hope you have remembered them all:[5] Ryouko Mouten, Hosei Meitoku, Koyo Mougai, Shokaku Choyo, Rinme Shokan, etc).

Further episodes include many additions made to the *Hero Tales* *manga*. In the third episode, for example, our heroes halt on their journey at a town and save it from Imperial officials (as well as a giant rock, the Bear, that crashes onto the town). Helping out a community in a single episode has provided the basis for 100s of TV shows (Arakawa-sensei used the same format in *Fullmetal Alchemist*). A new character, Koyou, is introduced here, with his impossibly large boat (the *Touga*) that sails on handily very wide rivers (Koyou gets the better of a greedy merchant).

In ep. 4, our ragbag team is joined by the mysterious archer, Housei (Yuuki Tai), who falls for Laila instantly (and completely, much to her embarrassment). For Laila, men are fools (especially in matters of lerrrve). And this show is also another helping-a-town scenario (this time, ridding a town of a bullying gang, the familiar *yakuza* plotline of 1,000s of *manga*).

Another bunch of bullies crop up in the next episode of *Hero Tales*, which is also a 'saving-a-community' show – this time a bunch of moppet orphans being looked after by a master thief. The narrative plays out precisely as expected – which is often a bonus; however, *Hero Tales* has already used this format twice, and it is repeating itself even tho' it's only five episodes into its run.

The familiar severe martial arts *sifu* in the *manga* of Himoru Arakawa crops up in episode 9: *Crimson Hero* - Koei (the *sensei* of Housei), who agrees to teach Taito energy manipulation. Built up by

---

5 Including the Japanese versions.

Housei as a horrible hag, Koei of course turns out to be a va-va-voom woman, as Arakawa would say (and a great cook, too!). And she's voiced by mega-star Atsuko Tanaka (Motoko Kusanagi in *Ghost In the Shell*). Indeed, it's a prerequisite of an Arakawa adaptation that it features strong, independent women for the main charas, not weedy women who live in the shadow of men.

Unfortunately (because she's good value), Koei only lasts one and a half episodes of *Hero Tales* – she's nobbled by the villain Keiro's henchman Shimei, forcing the heroes to kill her when Shimei re-animates her from the dead (in the comic, Koei is introduced and dispatched much earlier).

To cheer Housei up about losing his beloved *sifu*, our heroes attempt some comedy. The plot of *Hero Tales* is laid aside for parts of episodes 7: *Sorrowful Phecda* and 8: *What Echoes In the Gorge*. Sad to say, the shows aren't very funny – *One Piece*, this ain't (ah, but very few *animé* shows (well, none!) are as good as *One Piece*). The jokes – hunting animals, getting lost, bad cooking – are laboured.

And so *Hero Tales* continues its merry way through an alternative mythology of Ancient Asia. It's easy to watch, and undemanding (there is plenty of mileage out of evoking the mythical *jianghzu* – Chinese and Hong Kong cinema has dined out on it since the 1920s). Across 26 episodes, tho', it does become a little repetitive: we hear about the warring celestial forces of Tonrou and Hagun many times, and how the seven stars of the Great Bear constellation relate to the characters on Earth. And it's stretched a little thin.

The Big Theme in *Hero Tales* is how to govern a huge nation resembling China (i.e., it's contemporary Japan), and how much influence a figurehead such as the Emperor or leader really has. The big baddie, General Keiro, is gradually humanized, so that he isn't quite the nasty bruiser of the first episodes (we see how things went wrong for him in a late flashback), tho' his ideology of government by force is rightly denounced by Taito. Keiro represents the rightwing ideology of government (or utopia) 'by any means', which our heroes know leads to misery (as history has shown). As soon as a character deploys the notion 'by any means', it instantly damns them.

General Keiro reveals his true colours when he ascends to power (aided by the magical sword MacGuffin), turning some of the populace into zombies. Keiro's corrupt and ultra-violent regime runs riot until the final episodes, when *Hero Tales* climaxes with the expected showdown between the Hagun and the Tonrou (while the rest of the gang of heroes are given something to do – like fight demonic *shinobi* women, or look after Hosei when he's injured).

Hero Tales
by Himoru Arakawa

Chapter 1: Hagun Roars

Hero Tales animé (2007-

04

SILVER SPOON

GIN NO SAJI

SILVER SPOON – THE MANGA

Silver Spoon[1] (*Gin no Saji*, 2011-2019) appeared in *Weekly Shonen Sunday* (publ. by Shogakugan). Each chapter (titled after the seasons) is the customary 19 pages (not twice or more the length, as in the *Fullmetal Alchemist manga*). *Silver Spoon* focusses on Yuugo Hachiken, a 15 year-old youth studying at an agricultural college[2] in Northern Japan (with obvious autobiographical elements – and Himoru Arakawa includes references to her farming background. Altho' it's a farming *manga*, you could call it a food *manga*, or a cooking *manga*, with elements of sports *manga*). The comic was published sporadically later on, as Arakawa dealt with family issues. *Silver Spoon* was animated by A-1 Pictures (2013-14), as a TV series, and a live-action movie (in 2014). The manga won the Tashio Award and the Shogakukan Manga Award (both in 2012).

Sometimes an *animé* version of a *manga* gives you the key to it (and reading the *manga* first can help along the *animé*) – seeing the *animé* of *Silver Spoon* helped me to enjoy *Silver Spoon* as a *manga* further (the comic at first seemed so ordinary).

Silver Spoon is a rather everyday and even 'normal' *manga* seen in comparison to *Fullmetal Alchemist* (if you're looking for something from Arakawa-sensei in the *Fullmetal Alchemist* vein, her later work, *Hero Tales*, is the one to go for). It's in the 'everyday' or 'slice of life' genre, and also draws heavily on cooking/ food *manga*, and sports *manga*.

Silver Spoon is a little preachy in its explorations of farming and agriculture (characters surrounding the hero are continually informing him about this or that agricultural topic). It's an issue that Arakawa-sensei clearly feels strongly about: at times you feel reading the *manga* as if

---

1 The silver spoon refers to the Western custom of giving babies silver spoons – so they'll never go hungry. Food is a major theme in *Silver Spoon*.
2 *Silver Spoon* is a school or college *manga*, yes, but it certainly has a unique setting.

you're listening to a zealous tutor launch into yet another tirade about their favourite subject. (Arakawa acknowledged that *Silver Spoon* is her most directly autobiographical work, and that some of the charas drew on real people – such as the gun-totin', beer drinkin', cap wearin' teacher).

Himoru Arakawa includes several caricatures in *Silver Spoon*: the principal is a tiny man with an egg-shaped head, and Tamako[3] is a huge, egg-shaped[4] woman with a ridiculous face. The horse tutor evokes a wise, solemn Buddha. One teacher resembles Alex Armstrong (with more hair) from *Fullmetal Alchemist*. Fat boy Beppu (and master chef) recalls Gluttony.

The rest of the character designs in *Silver Spoon* include the full range of Arakawan images, tho' some, such as the key female chara, Aki Mikage, are given a softer, rounder appearance (and enormous *manga* eyes). It's striking how often Arakawa draws the faces in permanent expressions of surprise – high-arched eyebrows, and lots of white space above the pupils. No matter how trivial the dialogue is in *Silver Spoon* (and some of it is pedestrian), characters always stop and react as if the speaker has said something utterly thrilling. (Poor Mikagi spends the entire series in a state of spaced bemusement/ surprise/ confusion).

Like many *shonen manga*, *Silver Spoon* is full of 'work hard!' ethics: *gambaru! – do your best… keep moving forward… don't give up!* 'Good work today!' the teens say to each other, echoing the platitudes of the teachers and the authorities at Yezo school. (*Silver Spoon* fits right in with boys *manga* like the Big Three, *Naruto, One Piece* and *Bleach* – where the heroes, no matter much pain they suffer, how much battering they take, they always manage to stand up and stagger onwards. Of course, Monkey D. Luffy, Naruto Uzumaki and Ichigo Kurosaki are extraordinary characters with superhuman abilities, but Hachi-kun is a regular boy).

Silver Spoon focusses on Yuugo Hachiken (who, with his speccy, nerdy appearance resembles a younger, male version of the Himoru Arakawa as she satirizes herself as a cow with glasses.[5] Hachiken's design also draws on Sheska, the geeky librarian in *Fullmetal Alchemist*. Arakawa happily re-uses designs she likes).

Hachiken Yuugo is not an especially compelling character – he's meant to be a sort of everyday kid, somewhat non-descript, to be a reader-identification figure for the audience. He's gone to the Yezo agricultural school in Hokkaido for no apparent reason (well, yes, there *are* reasons), or with no burning goal (unlike the other students, who each have strong personal reasons for attending, such as learning how to run the family farm, which many of them will inherit).

Yuugo Hachiken is the classic outsider figure (Himoru Arakawa uses the popular transfer student motif),[6] our identification figure as we

---

3 Tamako is the most irritating chara in *Silver Spoon*, popping up to frown and berate Hachiken and to lecture him on some aspect of agriculture.
4 'Tamako' means egg in Japanese.
5 There are jokes about glasses, inevitably, including a horse who like riders in glasses.
6 Like many a transfer student in Japanese pop culture, Hachiken is also upper-class, and highly educated (and somewhat different from the other pupils). Tho' he's not a stranger or an outsider – he mucks in.

explore the new world of the far North of Nihon, and the tough worlds of nature and agriculture. Hachiken is the guy who splutters with disgust over the stink of the farms at the college, who is outraged to discover that eggs come out of a chicken's anus, who is frustrated by animals (having no natural empathy with them), and is terrified by bears. Poor Hachiken is overwhelmed by the dedication of the other students (while feeling superior academically to them),[7] who realizes he lacks drive and committment (yet he wants to be number one at the college), and who is exhausted by the harsh regime of farm work[8] (this is a practical establishment, where students're expected to muck in with everyone else in running the place. Hachiken has to rise at four regularly – he has an army of alarm clocks to wake him up).

Yuugo Hachiken is also the geek, the nerd, the over-achieving weakling who's useless at sports and can barely make it round the lap of the college (which, as it's one of the largest agricultural colleges in the nation, has extensive grounds).

All of this is laid out in *Silver Spoon*'s first chapter, where it's no surprise that Yuugo Hachiken's first encounter with an animal is with Himoru Arakawa's totem animal, the cow (tho' it's a cute calf, which Hachiken chases). Cows crop up regularly in the *Silver Spoon manga* (and Arakawa-sensei often links cows to eroticism: the Holstein school club (of guys) drools over the shape of cows, and salivate over cows in a magazine as if they looking at porn; Mikage tells Hachiken she's searching for a big bra – it turns out it's a sort of sling for the cow's udders).

Pizza: it all changes for Yuugo Hachiken when he decides to cook pizza for everyone (including the teachers). Now Hachiken becomes the hero of Yezo College, introducing a Western dish to his chums (that the reversal of fortune pivots around food is typical of *Silver Spoon*).

Being a farming story, the world that *Silver Spoon* depicts is very conservative, traditionalist, hierarchical, and patriarchal, as rural communities tend to be (altho' Himoru Arakawa consciously includes many female charas, to counter the very masculinist bias of the agricultural world).

Life and death, eating and killing are recurring themes in *Silver Spoon*, which doesn't look away from some gruesome sights: butchering deer, beheading chickens, cows giving birth, etc. And every single time that an animal is killed, it's soon eaten, and even Hachiken, disgusted by what goes on in the farming world, has to admit that it's *delicious*!

Parents and children is a recurring theme in *Silver Spoon* – most of the kids at Yezo farm college plan to either (1) work on their parents' farm, or (2) take over their parents' farm, or (3) start up a farm (but using their experience with their parents as a model). Much is made of the Komabas' farm which's too heavily in debt, and goes under; and Mikage's farm, which also owes plenty and has to sell off some of its livestock (including Mikage-chan's beloved horses).

7 Which changes when he receives his results, and everyone else is ahead in farming subjects.
8 The Yezo students have numerous chores to do, have to get up early, are often cleaning out barns, etc.

Like Edward Elric in *Fullmetal Alchemist*, Hachiken has an awkward relationship with his father (and to a lesser extent with his mother). He avoids communicating with his folks, and also resents his drop-out brother Shingo when he turns up at Yezo (repeatedly).

Hachiken's father is one of the very scary middle-aged men that Himoru Arakawa is uncannily brilliant at portraying (everybody thinks he looks like a *yakuza*). In the *animé* of *Silver Spoon*, several charas encounter Hachiken senior and his baleful stare, and think to themselves, *if I look away, I will die!*

There are regular discussions about what Hachiken is going to do after college (he is constantly comparing his lack of ambition with everyone else's clearly-defined ambitions – and feeling inadequate. But then, it doesn't take much for Hachiken to feel inadequate!).

Himoru Arakawa includes some of the harsh realities of the agriculture industry economically – Ichirou Komaba's farm hits hard times, and Mikage's folks have to sell their horses (much to horse-loving Mikage's disappointment).

Like a typical school-based *manga*, *Silver Spoon* follows our hero around the cycle of the year: thus, in Summer, instead of scurrying home (where he doesn't want to be), Hachiken goes to work at a farm. And of course, it's Aki Mikage's farm. (Hachiken is already very fond of Mikage, but she remains coolly oblivious. It's a *long* time before Mikage reciprocates with any feelings towards Hachiken at all (in fact, she's rather dim when it comes to boys, and her dorm chums have to point out obvious things to her, like what happens at Valentine's Day and White Day. And when Hachiken suggests they go to a local shrine together, Mikage doesn't regard it as a date, it's just an afternoon out). Meanwhile, much comedy is mined from Mikage senior exploding with fury every time Hachiken goes anywhere near his precious only daughter. Indeed, this prohibition keeps the would-be lovers apart for most of the *manga*).

As well as a farming, cooking and slice of life *manga*, *Silver Spoon* is also a sports *manga* – there are lengthy scenes depicting one of Japan's favourite games, baseball (played by student Ichirou Komaba), and also the Yezo students watching television of Komaba playing baseball.

One of the great jokes in *Silver Spoon* has the students watching trashy horror movies: one is about killer minotaurs. But if you had a bull's head, the clever students point out pedantically, you wouldn't be able to chew meat! You're a herbivore!

O

Many of the chapters of *Silver Spoon* are built around simple scenarios:[9] like: (A) Hachiken finds a stray puppy;[10] (B) Hachiken frets over Mikage's relationship with Komaba (whom he regards as his love rival – along with any other male who dares to speak to Mikage); (C) Hachiken cooks pizza for everyone; (D) Hachiken joins the horse riding club; (E) Hachiken names a pig and later buys its meat; (F) Hachiken helps

9 Further events in *Silver Spoon* include: Hachiken with the horse-riding club; visiting other farms; the boys cooing over piglets, etc.
10 This was a side-story in *Fullmetal Alchemist*.

out at Mikage's folks' farm in the Summer vacation; (G) Hachiken can't make his horse jump over a hurdle; (H) Hachiken and co. watch Komaba play baseball; (I) Hachie and co. make cheese; (J) Hachiken butchers a roadkill deer, and so on. (And these scenarios are repeated).

Hachiken gets attached to a piglet;[11] names it ('Pork Bowl'); and buys its meat when it's carted off. Everybody else in the *manga* scorns Hachiken for being so emotional over animals which, in the Hokkaido college, are all ultimately destined to become food (later, tho', some of the students admit they got attached to animals on their farms when were kids).

In many chapters of *Silver Spoon*, some new food is introduced, and everybody stops to (1) prepare it, (2) cook it, and (3) eat it. *Silver Spoon* is full of foodie elements, of charas (principally Hachiken) trying new food items: fresh vegetables, for ex, or milk fresh out of a cow,[12] or fresh meat. And it's always *oishii!* (= delicious).

Silver Spoon is so in love with cooking and eating, you'll want to pop down to the store after reading it and buy up all of the sausages, bacon, steaks and noodles they have.

Later, when Mikage decides to try for college, but isn't confident enough for the exams, Hachiken offers to tutor her. More comedy is brought out of this scenario (Hachiken's chums, for instance, are very jealous that Hachiken gets to spend time alone with a girl). And Hachiken uses horses as illustrations to get Mikage interested in Japanese history.

O

As the *manga* approaches the 100th chapter point, it begins to shamelessly repeat itself – so there's a rookie who undergoes some of the same experi-ences that Hachie had, there's a reprise of the making pizza subplot, there's a bit where charas worry about eating cute pigs, there's yet another sporting competition (with, yet again, horses),[13] and yet another repeat of the founding-a-business subplot.

The later chapters of *Silver Spoon* run out of steam a little (an announcement in the *manga* mentions that the schedule of publication will be disrupted while Arakawa-sensei helps to care for a relative. In fact, Arakawa was looking after her husband and son who were ill).

The *Silver Spoon manga* is closed by Arakawa-sensei with several subplots running together: Hachiken's business proposals, and dealing with his father; Mikage passing the entrance exam to an agricultural college; and the romantic subplot. Some of the plot resolutions are rather artificial (like Mikage *père* suddenly appearing just when Hachie has confessed on the phone to Mikage and asked her on a date).

The last chapters include Hachiken visiting Ichirou Komaba in East Russia, where Komaba tries to persuade Hachie to join him on a business venture based in Russia; a brief summary of the plot; and the unresolved romantic subplot. The essence of the ending of *Silver Spoon* is 'to be

---

11 Later in the comic, Hachiken organizes a syndicate to buy some pigs for food among his chums.
12 In one skit, Hachiken tastes milk from a cow, before it's treated, and loves it (but he causes thousands of Yen of spilt milk when the pipe isn't fixed back of the machines properly).
13 Arakawa recreates many of the places and social activities of her home, Hokkaido, such as the Banei sport at Obihiro Racecourse, where horses pull sleds.

continued', or 'life goes on', or 'the best is yet to come' (*Silver Spoon* doesn't end so much as it just stops).

SILVER SPOON – THE *ANIMÉ*

The *animé* of *Silver Spoon* ran from 2013 to 2014 (in two seasons of eleven episodes each). It was produced by A-1 Pictures/ Dentsu Inc./ Fuji TV/ Ezono Production Committee/ Kyoraku Industrial Holdings Co./ Aniplex, produced by Masuo Ueda and Tomonori Ochikoshi, exec. produced by Akitoshi Mori and Shunsuke Saito, written by Taku Kishi-moto, and directed by Tomohiko Ito. Jun Nakai was char. des. and ani. dir.; Takahiro Chiba was also ani. dir. Art dir. by Sawako Takagi, Music by Shusei Murai and Yasuyuki Konno.

In the cast were: Ryohei Kimura (Yuugo Hachiken), Marie Miyake (Aki Mikage), Toru Sakurai (Ichiro Komaba), Nobunaga Shimazaki (Shinnosuke Aikawa), and Ayahi Takagaki (Tamako Inada).

The *animé* of *Silver Spoon* pumps up the humour, exaggerating it greatly from Himoru Arakawa's farming *manga*, so that the antics of Yuugo Hachiken as he reacts to each new scenario at Yezo agricultural college are clownish.

Actor Ryohei Kimura is a great at capturing Hachiken's numerous cries of outrage/ shock/ surprise/ disappointment/ fear, and the *animé* delights in delivering versions of the stunned/ amazed responses that're a key element of Himoru Arakawa's *manga* in its humorous form.

The first episode of *Silver Spoon* follows the *manga* very closely, with only a slight re-jigging of the key events in the first couple of chapters of the comic (two chapters per episode is a typical average for *animé* adapt-ation). The *animé* does add numerous elements, and drops numerous others, and changes the emphasis somewhat, but it sticks to Himoru Arakawa's *manga*.

The first episode charts Yuugo Hachiken's first day at Yezo agri-cultural college, which's absolutely exhausting (images from the day flash thru his mind as he rests – a great touch). And this is only the first day!

Further episodes include a *Great Escape/ X-Files* parody, with the boys planning an elaborate escape bid from their dorm at night, in the manner of WW2 movies, all in order to see... a combine harvester in action in the fields! (The lads drool over this giant machine, but Hachiken can't believe they've been spending so long trying to escape the dorms just for this!).

The *Silver Spoon animé* ends on the same unfinished note as the comic, with plots only partially resolved. Over it all hangs a 'TO BE CONTINUED' feeling. However, the slice of life/ everyday genre in *manga* isn't about grand stories and tumultuous finales. These plots can run and run.

The live-action version of *Silver Spoon* (*Gin no Saji*, 2014) was produced by Tokyo Broadcasting System/ Shogakukan/ Toho/ Dentsu/ Wowow/ Chubu Nippon Boradcasting Company/ Pony Canyon/ T.B.S. Radio & Communications/ Mainichi Broadcasting System/ Hokkaido Broadcasting Company/ R.K.B. Mainichi Broad-casting Corporation/ Gyao/ J.T.B. Corporate Sales/ Wilco Co., distributed by Toho, produced by Hideki Tashiro, Akiko Ikuno, Yoshitaka Takeda and Hideiko Hosino, written by Ryo Takada and Keisuke Yoshida and directed by Keisuke Yoshida. Released Mch 7, 2014. 1h 51m.

The film is a fairly routine interpretation of *Silver Spoon*, delivered in the familiar manner of Japanese live-action films (which come across as average TV movies). The movie is strong on the interactions among the teens, and the cheesy, too-sweet romance between Aki and Hachie is appealing, but it lacks the charm of Arakawa's comic. For those viewers looking for the vision of Arakawa's special sensibility will be disappointed.

Silver Spoon manga by Himoru Arakawa.
(This page and over).

IT TROUBLES ME THAT THIS IS SO DELICIOUS!

I AGREE! IT REALLY IS TROUBLING THAT PIGS TASTE SO GOOD!

YOU WANT ANOTHER?

Silver Spoon SPRINGTIME ⑩

CHAPTER 10 /

I GUESS IT'S TOO MUCH AFTER ALL...

CHAP

CHAP

Silver Spoon (2013-14), this page and over.

05

THE HEROIC LEGEND OF ARSLAN

ARUSURAN SENKI

THE *ARSLAN SENKI MANGA*

The Heroic Legend of Arslan (*Arusuran Senki* = *Arslan War Records*, 2013-, publ. in *Bessatsu Shonen Magazine* from Kodansha, starting in 2013), is an enjoyable *seinen manga* set in an ancient/ mediæval realm reminiscent of the *Arabian Nights* and Arthurian legend. The monthly schedule means, as with *Fullmetal Alchemist*, that the chapters are 30+ pages long (so the whole comic is equivalent to 130-175 chapters). The writer, Yoshiki Tanaka, based the fantasy novels (15 novels to 2016, starting in 1986), on the 19th century *Amir Arsalan-i Namdar* stories by Naqib ul-Mamalik, which were set in Ancient Persia (the country in the comic is called Pars). As well as Ancient Persia,[1] the stories draw on mediæval tales, and bring in historical elements such as the Knights Templar and the Crusades, plus some supernatural ingredients. Lusitania might be Rome, Sindhara India (or perhaps China), and Turan Central Asia. Also, this isn't the first illustration of the texts by Tanaka – there is also a *manga* version by Chisato Nakamura (publ. in *Asuka Fantasy DX*, 1991-96). And of course the inevitable *animé* versions: two *animé* movies (1991 and 1992), and Original Video Animations, which were released in 1993-95. New *animé* adaptations of *Arslan Senki* appeared in 2015 (25 eps.) and 2016 (8 eps.), based on Arakawa and Tanaka's version.

    The Heroic Legend of Arslan focusses on the young Prince Arslan, who isn't great kingly material (at first). Arslan looks up to his father, the king of the land, Andragoras (one of those domineering Shogun/ Emperor figures in historical tales who must be obeyed), but much of the story concerns the adventures of Arslan and a bunch of characters gathered around him, who include: court tactician and swordsman (and would-be painter!) Narsus; dependable ally and master swashbuckler Daryun; crusty, old General Vaphriz; the priestess and archer of Mithra, Farangis;

---

1 The maps make it clear that the region is Persia.

Narsus' enthusiastic and utterly devoted teen assistant; Elam, the feisty, adorable warrior maiden Alfreed; and the womanizer/ drifter/ musician/ con man Gieve. The villains include a mysterioso Man in a Silver Mask,[2] called Hermes or Silvermask; a venal (i.e., psychotic) fire and brimstone Archbishop, Bidon; and the invading Lusitanian army, who are figure-headed by a grotesquely fat, weak and self-absorbed King.[3]

The artwork by Himoru Arakawa is once again in her crisp, clean, linear style, with plenty of white space. (Incredibly, Arakawa yet again uses the character design of Führer Bradley from *Fullmetal Alchemist*, for the warlord Andragoras – to use a recognizable design once more is understandable, but twice more?!). Arakawa also brings in Alex Armstrong from *Fullmetal Alchemist,* in a cameo as a repulsive brute of an officer, who drunkenly brags about killing and frying a baby then forcing its parents to eat it.[4]

As this's primarily a military and action adventure set in the distant past, most of the characters in *Arslan* are guys – from wrinkled veterans to burly, sombre kings and captains – plus the usual retinue of peasants, workers, merchants, knights, soldiers and attendants.

The Heroic Legend of Arslan is also extraordinarily violent. And once again Himoru Arakawa rises to the challenge of portraying excessive aggression with amazing views of decapitations, dismemberments, and of course the mandatory sprays of the red stuff (or black ink, as this is a black-and-white *manga*).

The Heroic Legend of Arslan captures the scale and breadth of mediæval battles and action with an effortless confidence. Himoru Arakawa and writer Yoshiki Tanaka know how to depict a lengthy siege, or a giant battle with smoke, mist, clouds, clashing steel, galloping horses,[5] and hair's-breadth escapes and rescues (there may be some *Berserk* by Kentaro Miura in *Arslan*). Arakawa is an accomplished artist of men in armour on horseback, and discovers novel ways of staging a duel or a cavalry charge. Her animals and humans are completely convincing, and many of the scenes have the grandeur of Renaissance paintings by Paolo Uccello or Albrecht Altdorfer.[6]

As well as cavalry charges and massed battles (challenging for any artist), *Arslan* also includes numerous skirmishes, because the heroes and the villains need to clash regularly in this sort of action-adventure yarn. There are literal cliffhangers, leaps into the abyss, many ambushes by bowmen from above, chases on horseback thru forests and canyons, and many sword duels.

Can women produce battles as epic, as relentless and as vicious as men? Oh yes, they can! – and *The Heroic Legend of Arslan* is proof. As is

---

2 With the annoying name of the 'Man in the Silver Mask'!
3 The design of the tubby king is out of European fairy tales.
4 Soon after this revolting admission, the character is sliced apart.
5 For an artist who loves horses, Arakawa doesn't hold back from filling them with arrows, firing arrows into their eyes, beheading them, and maiming them during the battle scenes.
6 Altdorfer, Uccello and others were studied by the filmmakers of the *Lord of the Rings* movies for the way they depicted mediæval battles.

Fullmetal Alchemist. (In literary fiction, one woman rules supreme over everybody ielse n portraying the most astonishing battles ever – Mary Renault in her Ancient Greek and Alexander the Great novels).

Talking about women – Himoru Arakawa once again provides several va-va-voom designs for the female charas: Farangis and Queen Tahamenay are voluptuous, and Farangis' costume reveals plenty of thigh, hip and breasts. (Farangis may be a priestess, but she dresses like a showgirl. In the ancient world, you could be sexy *and* religious).

Notice that the villains/ rivals in *Arslan Senki* are all male, and many are veteran warriors, but the heroes boast some attractive women in their numbers, such as Alfreed (Alfarid) and Farangis (women who are also formidable fighters, of course).

Magic and wizardy hovers on the margins of *The Heroic Legend of Arslan* – it's not a straight historical adventure piece. There's a magical sword, and Silvermask has sorcerers to aid him who can emerge from walls and the ground, ninja-style. Arakawa and Tanaka have their characters sometimes performing impossible feats of derring-do (such as horses flying through the air).

There is much to enjoy in *Arslan*, from the excitement of the story-telling to the invention and efficiency of the artwork. Let's remember, though, that Himoru Arakawa *didn't* write or create this series – Yoshiki Tanaka did. Thus, Arakawa didn't come up with the characters, the scenarios, the relationships, the themes, etc. Tanaka did. Also, by the time that Arakawa came to *Arslan*, it had already been illustrated in *manga* form, and had been adapted as an *animé*, including a series and movies.

Arslan is old-fashioned storytelling, happy to deliver all of the clichés of the Middle Ages romance and adventure: scheming villains, sly betrayers, disguises, last-minute escapes, and all of the usual settings of the genre (tunnels, sewers, dungeons, palaces, halls, towers, inns, castles, gates, rivers, forests, mountains and battlefields).

The Heroic Legend of Arslan is thoroughly enjoyable – fairly un-demanding (as with many *manga*), but wholly believable and enter-taining. After all, the stories by Naqib ul-Mamalik had already been adapted in *manga* and *animé* by the time that *mangaka* Himoru Arakawa came to illustrate them, so they were tried and tested as entertainments. And this sort of storytelling and material never seems to fail. For the whole history of cinema, for instance, filmmakers have been portraying stories of knights, damsels, horses, battles, castles and palaces. And the action and adventure genre has been a part of literature for at least 3,000 years, since the time of Homer and *The Iliad.*

✦

Arusuran Senki starts out in fine style with two set-pieces: a chase thru the capital Ectabana (a standard ploy in action-adventure tales, amount-ing essentially to a guided tour of the setting), and a stupendous massed battle in the wilderness, in which Andragoras and his army is soundly trounced. The set-pieces set out the breadth and scale of this comic and its epic storytelling style, and also introduce us to the main charas, of course:

Arslan, Andragoras, Vaphriz, etc. And some dastardly villains, like the Man in the Silver Mask (a.k.a. Hermes), who strangles an unarmed woman to death and kills a former friend from the back.

After that, *Arslan* is in full swing, with an outstanding siege sequence, which brings together all of your favourite items in a mediæval-style siege of a stronghold (ladders, catapults, towers, burning oil, sneaking in thru passageways, looting, etc).

The Heroic Legend of Arslan is a comic of endless to-ing and fro-ing: one minute we're in Ecbatana, the next we're in Peshawar, or Sindhara. And up and down the Continental Highway the groups of characters ride or walk – with 10,000 cavalry here, or 20,000 infantry there (the numbers are sized up by Narsus carefully in the cat-and-mouse manœuvring for supremacy. Narsus is so brilliant at strategy and tactics, he never loses, is never wrong, and anybody in power throughout history would be desperate to hire him. The only thing that Narsus is useless at is the one thing that doesn't matter a jot in history or politics – art).

Anyway, no side keeps still for long: holing up in a palace is something that characters such as Prince Guiscard does, but everybody else is on campaigns or one sort of another. That is, *The Heroic Legend of Arslan* portrays a period of constant war. Pars is at war with Lusitania – and Sindhara, and Turan, and, well, everyone. Alliances are brokered from time to time (such as between Pars and Sindhara, though nobody trusts each other completely, and Narsus, Arslan, Daryun and co. definitely don't trust Prince Rajendra of Sindhara). Occasionally, Narsus manipulates the allegiances of opponents against themselves, outwitting leaders such as Prince Rajendra.

With the overthrow of the capital city of Ectabana, the ousting of King Andragoas, and the take-over by the army of Lusitania, our heroes flee into hiding in the mountains. So it's our heroes – Arslan, Narsus, Daryun *et al* – pitted against an invading nation. The struggle to regain the city and the country features all sorts of plot developments, courtly intrigue, poisons, creeping amongst the populace in disguise, duels in back alleys, prising information out of captured victims, etc.

Narratively, much of *Arslan* boils down to a series of cat-and-mouse scenarios, as each side tries to gain the upper hand in the struggle for supremacy in Pars. Inevitably, some of the situations repeat, and some stretch credibility. For ex, as in most action-adventure stories, the heroes and the villains need to interact periodically (usually with a fight or two), only to bounce away back to their lairs again. Some of these action scenes repeat too many times, with Narsus, Daryun or Gieve handily effecting a last-minute rescue, or the Man in the Silvermask (Hermes) managing to encounter Arslan alone on the battlements at night, only to evade capture with the customary dive into the moat. (Arakawa and Tanaka were very reluctant to sacrifice any of their main charas in the heroes' team).

There's a reminder of the lack of true jeopardy in *Arslan Senki* in every chapter: Prince Arslan has the world's finest warrior to guard him (Daryun), the world's finest military politician to advise him (Narsus), the two finest archers (Gieve and Farangis), and a host of devotees.

✦

In the middle chapters of *Arslan*, Arakawa and Tanaka stage a series of cat-and-mouse conflicts between Prince Arslan and his coterie and two Indian Princes who're rivals for the throne. Each Prince has their own army (Gadhevi has a battalion of war elephants). Aided, as ever, by the scarily clever Narsus, Arslan's side gets the better of the Indian Princes several times (including taking one of their supply fortresses – rather a little too easily – and staging an ambush in another seemingly empty stronghold).

Himoru Arakawa delivers many wonderful sequences of convoys of armies and supply trains, of attacks by soldiers on horseback, and of lavish feasts in the aftermath scenes. The mass battle involving war elephants is particualrly fine – Arakawa's skill in drawing animals is superb (and she's not afraid to pin-cushion the beasts with arrows).

The subplot of Arslan's true lineage is kept bubbling in the background (in the figure of Silvermask and the troubled veteran General Bahman). Having learnt that he may not be the true inheritor of the kingdom of Pars, Prince Arslan is beset by doubts (aides such as Daryun try to comfort him. As far as Daryun – and Narsus – are concerned, Arslan is already noble and kind and considerate enough to be a proper leader of the people of Paris, without needing the issue of royal blood).

✦

As with *Fullmetal Alchemist*, one ingredient in *Arusuran Senki* is impossible to miss: religious intolerance. Once again, Arakawa-sensei has evoked a monotheic religious society (Lusitania) where all must bow down before the One God (Yaldabaoth) – or else. Arakawa is mightily critical of such fanaticism, depicting the Lusitanians as using the name of Yaldabaoth to justify/ excuse cruelty – in *Fullmetal Alchemist*, Ed Elric critiques the Leto cult in Liore. (And the bishop Bidon is a caricature of a zealous religious psychopath, the sort of sick soul who enjoys public executions).

Linked to religious intolerance is slavery – all of the societies in the world of *Arslan* are slave-owners. Freeing the slaves is thus one of the goals of the young, idealistic Prince, Arslan. But Narsus, the tactician and another idealist, and a philosophical adviser to Arslan, relates how he freed slaves, only to find that they couldn't integrate satisfactorily into regular society, and they came back to him, begging to be allowed to work.

✦

Some of the later installments of *The Heroic Legend of Arslan* were uneven; this may have been because Himoru Arakawa was occupied with unwell family members. This part of *Arslan* has the look of an editor, a magazine and an artist deciding to wrap things up quickly. Some of the storytelling is sketchy and unsatisfying – there is a Big Battle (of course), several charas expire (as expected), and there's a gladiatorial contest in a Roman-style arena for the fate of the nation.

However, Arakawa-sensei was still producing some marvellous set-pieces. The fight in the stadium to decide which of the rival Indiana Princes will succeed the throne is one of Arakawa's finest works as a *mangaka*. Here, Daryun is pitted against a big, dumb monster (Bahadur), who's insensitive to pain, and who will keep fighting until he kills Daryun.

Arakawa and Tanaka orchestrate a gladiatorial contest with all of the familiar tropes of the Ancient Roman adventure genre. For much of the bout, Daryun is being hurled about and seemingly beaten down. However, he's not the greatest warrior among the heroes for nothing, and he eventually bests the hulk with fire and slits his throat.

Himoru Arakawa doesn't hold back on cooking up a hysterical, pumped-up scene of action – look at the facial expressions she conjures for the onlookers (many of whom are dismayed that even Daryun seems about to lose). It's a scene of high excitement, which's swiftly followed by a series of skirmishes and squabbles, as the spoilt, selfish, arrogant Gadhevi won't accept the defeat of his champion, Bahadur, and kicks up a fuss that leads to the deaths of his Prime Minister and Bahman.

O

Arslan and company continue to wriggle out of every snakepit situation: the Prince is set upon when squads of the two armies, Pars and Lusitania, accidentally stumble into each other in some hunting grounds (a possibility that even the wily Narsus hadn't considered). Skirmishes break out, and the Prince is separated from his Sindharian bodyguard Jaswant and his guards. So he's a 14 year-old boy fighting a group of adults, but he still triumphs (Jaswant eventually hurries to his aid, as does Daryun).

And Prince Arslan and company can even take a fortress without doing anything at all: they'll be near a stronghold, and the commander will sally forth without thinking through the consequences, and the place will fall. In *The Heroic Legend of Arslan*, it seems, you can win simply by doing nothing, or by just being yourself:

You simply exist, and you're a hero.

You simply exist, and you win battles.

It goes so well and too easily for Arslan's contingent that it seems as if the gods have blessed them with ever-lasting good fortune, and have forbidden anything ill happening to them. (Actually, Arslan's mob *don't* partake of gods or belief in gods or in rites to appease gods – and in terms of the ancient world, that is unusual. In *The Heroic Legend of Arslan*, deities are viewed with suspicion or outright disdain – Yaldabaoth is derided as the cruel divinity of a misguided religion. The Prince occasionally talks with a religious believer (such as Etoile), sympathizing with them and their beliefs, but he never entertains such thoughts himself. That the heroes do *not* rely on religion is a key aspect of their make-up in Arakawan ethics. For Arakawa, true, right-thinking heroes don't need the emotional-psychological support of religious belief).

O

Priestess-warrior and all-round super-babe Farangis is given her own adventure when Arslan tasks her with leading 500 men to aid a beleagured fortress. Farangis (with one-eyed Kubard in tow) manages to keep the Turanians at bay until help arrives from the Parsian main force.

Gieve also enjoys an adventure up in the mountains, at Mount Damavant (of a Gothic, fantasy sort), where Silvermask is seeking out the magical sword Rukhnabard that was buried with King Kai Khosrow to appease a Snake God. Silvermask hopes to claim the sword for his own, to aid his rise to power, but the gods are not happy when it's taken from the tomb. Arakawa has fun staging this heroic fantasy scene out of *Indiana Jones* or the *Conan* stories of Robert Howard.

The back-and-forth of the cat-and-mouse conflicts continue in *Arslan*: Silvermask continues to seethe with self-righteous fervour, finding not only Prince Arslan but *everybody* just not good enough, or not obsequious enough. Arslan irks Silvermask no end because he's a natural leader that even wily veterans such as Daryun and Narsus happily follow (even though he's a naïve teenager). For Silvermask, *everyone* should be kowtowing to *him*, and if anybody deserves to be served by the finest strategist in town (Narsus) or the finest warrior in the region (Daryun), it should be him, not the upstart boy. And everyone should be on their knees. All the time.

Silvermask takes the Knights Templars' stronghold (where the zealot Bodin rules over a community of religious devotees). Silvermask's tactics are a little like Narsus's – he lures out the army from the castle (by burning their flag in view of the fortress. The knights, whipped up to fight by the furious Bodin, rush out into an ambush).

The Heroic Legend of Arslan wheels in foes regularly: once one army has been exploited for action potential, another one comes up the Continental Highway: after the Parsians have waged war against the Lusitanians, next are the Sindharians, and then the Turanians.

So the Turanians are the next army in line to be trounced by the impossible-to-beat, blessed-by-the-gods Parsians (maybe because they don't seem to believe in any gods). Another of Narsus's unbelievable strategic tricks has the Turanian main force being fooled by a fake camp at night and lured into tackling members of their own army. With Narsus advising them, it seems that the Parsians can do no wrong. Even when Prince Arslan rushes out to punish the Turanians for killing civilians in plain sight of his fortress, the sly fox Narsus factors it into his schemes.

O

King Andragoras is chained up in jail for much of *The Heroic Legend of Arslan*, following his defeat at the Battle of Atropatene. But he's too strong[7] a character to wither away in a dungeon, and he breaks free. But Tanaka and Arakawa don't have Andragoras instantly ascending to political power and taking control of the whole country – instead, he stages a kind of hostage scenario within the palace, keeping Prince Guiscard as a hostage in the throne room (any guards who try to capture

---

7 Somehow, even though he's been in a dungeon for months, his body is still muscley.

him are cut down). Andragoras is the kind of stubborn, wilful commander who will wait until his subjects bow down before him.

Arslan is not finished yet – chapters continued to be produced.[8] For example, more recent entries have depicted Andragoras now settled into the role of the supreme leader, the Shah who must be obeyed. One of his first acts is to order the Prince to head South and muster an army. On his own. So off Arslan goes, gloomily wishing his *nakama* could join him. Well, they do – Narsus, Daryun and co. orchestrate an escape from the palace and re-join Arslan in the wilderness.

At the port of Gilan, there are further adventues for Prince Arslan and his chums, including with pirates and ships. As usual, Narsus is on hand to orchestrate events and manipulate rivals. Narsus is someone that every government in history would want working for them. During the second battle of Atropane, you'd think that everyone in the region would be wise to Narsus's tricks, but they fall for them again. So again everything goes the heroes' way.

THE *ARSLAN SENKI ANIMÉ*

PRODUCTION.
The *animé* adaptation of Himoru Arakawa's and Yoshiki Tanaka's version of *The Heroic Legend of Arslan* appeared in 2015. The 25 episodes of *Arslan Senki* were shown at 5.00 p.m. on Mainichi Broadcasting System in Nihon between April 5 and September 27, 2015. The second series (of eight eps.), entitled *The Heroic Legend of Arslan: Dust Storm Dance*, ran from July 3 to Aug 21, 2016.

Arslan was produced by Kodansha/ Dentsu/ Mainichi Broadcasting System/ Liden Films/ Arslan Senki Production Committee/ N.B.C. Universal Entertainment, Japan.

Liden Films, Sanzigen Animation Studio and Felix were the animation production companies. It was produced by Fukashi Higashi, Muneyuki Kanbe and Nobusaku Tanaka. It was written by Makoto Uezu (chief writer), along with Koujirou Nakamura and Touko Machida, directed by Noriyuki Abe, music[9] by Taro Iwashiro, char. des. by Kazuo Watanabe and Ushio Tazawa, Shingo Ogiso was chief char. des., art dir. by Tadashi Kudo, sound dir. was Jin Aketagawa, Yukihiro Masumoto was DP, and Mai Hasegawa was editor.

In the cast: Yosuke Kobayashi was Arslan, Daisuke Namikawa was Narsus, Kenn was Gieve, Maaya Sakamoto was Farangis, Natsuki Hanae was Elam, Manami Numakura was Alfreed, Yuuki Kaji was Silvermask and Yoshimasa Hosoya was Daryun.

---

8 Up to 115 chapters by 2023 – equivalent to about 3,500 pages.
9 The opening themes were by Nico Touches the Walls and Uver-world, and the ending themes were by Eir Aoi and Kalafina.

Although directors such as Katsuhiro Otomo, Hayao Miyazaki, Isao Takahata, Mamoru Oshii, and Satoshi Kon are celebrated worldwide as masters of Japanese animation, there are many others who're rarely discussed, but who are up there with the greats: Kenji Kamiyama (*Ghost In the Shell: Stand Alone Complex*), Koji Morimoto (*Memories*), Tetsuro Araki (*Death Note*), Yasuhiro Irie (*Fullmetal Alchemist*) – and I would add Noriyuki Abe. Solely on the basis of his direction of the long-running *Bleach* TV series, plus the spin-off movies, Abe is a genius.

For example, nobody could be better qualified to deliver amazing battle scenes than the team behind the *Bleach* series: in the course of 366 episodes (366!), from 2004.10.05 to 2012.03.27, *Bleach* portrayed every form of combat you can think of. Quite remarkable. Bringing all of that experience to the *Arslan* show results in astonishing action sequences.

Arslan is an outstanding, top-of-the-line, action-adventure TV animated series. Everything works, every department is delivering high quality material, and – even better – it does full justice to the *manga* version of the tales by Arakawa-sensei and Tanaka-sensei.

Have a look at the backgrounds (background art was by Pinewood, Kokoro Trigger and Forest studios), props, designs (conceptual design by Daisuke Niitsuma) and production art – this is amazing work. The colour design (by Aiko Shinohara) bounces off the screen with vibrant reds, oranges, yellows and blues. Art director Tadashi Kudo has done plenty of research into Middle Eastern, Iraqi, Iranian, North African and Ancient Persian culture, and it shows.

The *animé* of *Arslan* shifts the plot about, adds numerous elements, and changes .plenty, but it remains true to the spirit of the *manga*. One change has Lord Vaphriz expiring in a moment of glory, as he attacks Silvermask's soldiers, who've ambushed King Andragoras, as a one-man killing machine. There are flashbacks given to Narsus (to depict his cunning ways – how he set three nations against each other thru the use of rumours and disinformation).

We know how much Himoru Arakawa loves horses – as an *animé* featuring horses, *Arslan* is amazing. Horses, not the easiest animal to draw or to animate (often specialists among animators oversee their animation), are depicted in every conceivable context, including cavalry charges.

We are used now to computer-aided animation delivering massed battles with a cast of thousands, but those in *Arslan* are especially fine. It's months of work and it's very expensive, but it pays off with breathtaking vistas of rival cavalries clashing in vast deserts, the sort of imagery that would take months of preparation to accomplish in live-action (now it's months of slaving away at work stations in Tokyo and Korea).

While none of the charas in *Arslan Senki* are especially deep or multi-faceted, the one who changes the most is the title character. It's Arslan's story and it's a growing up tale, a *Bildungsroman*, with Arslan learning about the complexity and challenges of the adult world. In the Arthurian model, Arslan is Arthur to Narsus' Merlin, the relationship of the teacher and the pupil, the *sifu* and the disciple, found in 1,000s of stories the world over (in this instance, Arslan's tutor is a world-class statesman, swordsman and military philosopher, who's also a terrible painter).

The *animé*, like the *manga*, is very boysy, mansy, malesy – it's men being men amongst men. But there are several prominent female characters – Farangis is a classic, Arakawan woman – a brilliant warrior with a curvaceous body. The *animé* allows the camera to travel slowly over Farangis' breasts or hips before resting upon her face, just to make sure we know that she's va-va-voom. She can fire arrows in rapid succession on horseback – facing backwards! And, another Arakawan trait, she has a higher calling, in being a priestess of Mithra (so she's very spiritual, too). And she's played by a goddess of *animé*, Maaya Sakamoto (the voice of Motoko in the *Ghost In the Shell: Arise* series).

The King's consort, meanwhile, Queen Tahamenay, is another dropdead beauty, with the added glamour of being a literal man-killer (relationships with the Queen end badly for the men). The third prominent female chara is the feisty warrior girl Alfreed (a charming performance by Manami Numakura), who fights with Elam for the attention and affection of *Arslan's* major *bishonen*, Narsus.

One of Himoru Arakawa's favourite forms of comics is the *4-koma*, the four-strip panel format of jokes and comedy. *Arslan* features short (90 second) comic skits featuring the characters from the series. One of the best is Gieve the troubadour thrashing his lute like an electric guitar to a rock song at a pop concert.

The score of *Arslan*, composed by Taro Iwashiro, should also be celebrated – it is written in a traditional, action-adventure form, using a full, Western-style orchestra, and it provides enormous support to the action scenes, perfectly complimenting them with rousing sounds. Also of note are the occasional songs (which Gieve and Farangis sing).

The sound design (by Magic Capsule; Yasumasa Koyama was sound fx editor) in *Arslan* is impressive, with the sound team coming up with some interesting alternatives to the usual sounds of action in mediæval battles. There is a spectacular use of silence at key moments in the drama – such as the heightened scene when a General is put out of his misery by Gieve's arrow.

There is a minor flaw in the screenwriting of *Arslan Senki*: the heroes get out of trouble too easily. Their plans always turn out right, after all. Whatever clever Narsus has schemed up always works. It's just too smug, too pat – and it occurs too often. That, however, is exactly how the comic is played.

✦

THE EPISODES.

Episode one of *Arslan*, 2015-vintage, opens of course with a gigantic battle sequence – which seems to be the default beginning of action *animé* (*Drifters, Berserk, The Rage of Bahamut*, etc, Fight first, talk later). Here we see King Andragoras and his Parsian army triumphing over the enemy. The animation is remarkable, as are the designs and the backgrounds.

Some of the shots are truly outstanding. 'Epic', 'spectacular', 'heroic', 'vast' – *Arslan* delivers all of that before shifting to the victory parade of the conquering forces arriving back in the capital.

The 11 year-old Prince Arslan is introduced in the tried and tested manner of a young King Arthur, a princeling from any of 1,000 action-adventure yarns – sword training with the veteran General Vaphriz. We are introduced his parents – Andragoras and the Queen, Tahamenay (both are haughty, distant parents to the Prince).

The guided tour of the world of *Arslan* takes up most of the second half of ep. 1, as the captured boy Etoile[10] hauls the Prince around the city (in a rather contrived scenario of a chase). The issues of slavery, of rival communities, of the victors and the under-dogs, of the fervent religion of Yaldabaoth, are vividly and economically introduced. The flow of the narrative is smooth and assured – we are in the hands of master storytellers. Even if the tale that the *animé* of *Arslan* spins is one we've seen/ read/ experienced a thousand times before, we are happy to do it all over again when the production is this skilful. (There are some false notes – Etoile is played hysterically shrill (by Yumi Uchiyama), and the lengthy exposition about slavery and religion that s/he delivers is far too eloquent for an 11 year-old).

Part B of ep. 1 introduces us to some of the future heroes who gather around Arslan, such as Kishward, and the number one warrior in the region, Daryan (introduced in a very Arakawan scene, grooming his horse, and quickly revealed to be an expert archer); at the end of the show, Daryan suggests that they contact Narsus. The narrator explains the time-shift, to the Prince aged 14, to prepare for the next episode.

The story of *Arslan* really starts in the 2nd episode: the mass battle that opens the *animé* of *Arslan* is a mere taster of things to come, because in episode two the filmmakers deliver a truly spectacular mediæval battle sequence. This is rousing, exhilarating stuff, brilliantly executed. This is the calamity which sets the story in motion, with King Andragoras' forces suffering a massive defeat, throwing Pars into turmoil.

One of the 100s of additions that the *animé* made to the *manga* by Arakawa and Tanaka was the expansion of the role of the three young boys the same age as Prince Arslan who join the army hoping to protect the Prince. The boys had been seen earlier, picking on the captured slave Etoile. Prior to the battle, they are full of youthful enthusiasm, devoting themselves to protecting the Prince; afterwards, they are slain. Arslan stumbles upon them in the chaos of the battle and is stricken to find them dead.

Arslan is not afraid of depicting the consequences of warfare, and it does so in a moving, convincing manner. When the Prince kills his first soldier, for instance, the *animé* spends some time portraying Arslan's horror afterwards. (The show gets away with the Prince being only 14 but able to kill a full-grown, professional soldier by preparing for the moment. For example, by portraying him improving during his sword

---

10 Brought forward from later in the comic, where he's revealed to be a bratty girl.

training with Lord Vahriz).

Daryun excels himself with a stunning rescue sequence just as Arslan has been beaten to the ground by Kharlan. Daryun is a one-man army – when he's on the warpath (which is often!), he is unstoppable.

Episode two builds up to the big battle in the first part, introducing the traitor Kharlan, the uncertainty of Arslan in his maiden battle, and Daryun, fearing a trap, imploring Andragoras to retreat. Daryun is proven right, and Pars suffers a major defeat.

Once again, we have seen all of this material before, many times – *Arslan* is very traditional filmmaking (despite using every state-of-the-art device available). But it works because it delivers familiar material (clichés, even) with a compassionate and inventive eye.

As every episode of *Arslan Senki* plays, it gets better and better. The filmmakers seem to have boundless ideas when it comes to telling stories, even if the material is traditional, even if the set-pieces are familiar.

Somehow, the 2015 *animé* version of *Arslan* manages to re-invent the wheel, to deliver mass battles once again as something awe-inspiring and terrifying, to stage swordplay and chases as if it's the first time they've ever been put on film.

Budget plays a part, of course – the 2015 television production has a decent amount of Yen to spend. Ironically, if this was live-action, the budget would be 100s of millions of dollars – building those castles, staging battles with thousands of participants, 1,000s of costumes, etc (even if part of the battles were produced with computer-assisted animation).[11]

The characterizations in *The Heroic Legend of Arslan* are thin, admittedly – they have two or three layers, and that's it. This isn't William Shakespeare's *Othello*. In the 2015 *animé*, too, altho' elements were added, the characterizations remain true to the comic, and just as paper-thin. (Actually, though, Shakespeare would thrill to the scenes of mass battles and manly heroism).

But that doesn't matter, because *Arslan Senki* is conceived as an action-adventure yarn, a war in Ancient Persia tale, where super-rich characterizations are not required (or desired).

Also, it's the *mix* of the characters with the story, with the themes, with the action and with the other elements of the piece that makes it work. To make up for the lightweight characters, we have outstanding, rousing battle scenes, feats of derring-do, courtly intrigue, plots and counter-plots, and heavyweight issues such slavery and religious intolerance.

Clever Prince encourages Narsus to come out of retirement and pledge his services in crafty strategy by appealing to Narsus's vanity and his adherence to pursuing painting (he offers him the job of court painter once he assumes power). This occurs in episode 4, when our heroes flee the catastrophe of the Battle of Atropane (and the wrath of King Andragoras)

---

11 The *animé* of *Arslan* happily stages much wilder action than the *manga* – during the remarkable scenes of elephants in a giant battle, for instance, a warrior on a horse leaps onto an elephant to duel with Daryun.

and opt to seek aid from Narsus. Thus begins the formation of the devoted group surrounding Arslan (which continues with Gieve, Alfreed, Farangis *et al*).

A back-story mini-episode occurs in ep. 4, too, which portrays Narsus's brilliant schemes (by playing off three armed forces invading Pars from the East against each other). As the series progresses, Narsus remains triumphant in his military plans (there is a somewhat smug arrogance about Narsus's proposals – whatever he suggests always works).

Gieve receives an impressive introduction when he stands atop the toppermost pinnacle of the battlements of Ectabana and fires an arrow to mercifully free the General from the clutches of the psychotic Archbishop Bidon. This scene is played at the level of super-intense drama, with Bidon berating the General repeatedly for being a heathen and prattling about his god Yaldabaoth. (After this, Gieve wows the Queen and her handmaidens in an audience chamber with his lute playing and singing).

The relationship (or uneasy alliance) between Gieve and Farangis stretches belief a little, and the way that they hook up together, and then pledge their allegiance to Prince Arslan and his cause. Gieve is very taken with Farangis (she has plenty of charms), but how she allows him to accompany her is a tad unconvincing (she's worldly-wise enough to guess that he's a golddigger and womanizer).

The comedy of Narsus being a painter is nicely played in both the *manga* and the *animé* (a recurring gag in many *manga* is that the characters can't draw at all, like Rukia in *Bleach* – or Ed's terrible drawings in *Fullmetal Alchemist*). Of course, we never see what Narsus' pictures look like, but we do see the surprised, dismayed or dumbstruck reactions of the characters who look at it.

❊

The *Arslan Senki animé* builds and builds to a Giant Battle – which is, of course, the *only* way that a battle story and a battle *manga* can finish. It doesn't disappoint: these are some of the finest battles put on screen, whether in live-action, animation, or anything else (again, composer Taro Iwashiro is enhancing the proceedings with stirring, orchestral cues). Of particular note is the slambang duel between Silvermask and Daryun: they meet in a high chamber in the palace of Ectabana: to move them quickly to a setting where they fight each other without others interfering, the filmmakers simply have them falling out of the window into a courtyard below.

The 25 episodes of the first series of *Arslan* close with multiple deaths during the Big Battle – including, very distressingly, women preferring to hurl themselves from a tower instead of allowing themselves to be captured by the victors.

The 2015 *animé* series doesn't resolve all of the plots, however: Arslan is not crowned king, Silvermask (Prince Hermes) is not vanquished, and the story is not brought to a close. But that doesn't mean we don't get plenty of scenes of triumph and victory. (Only marred by the revelation that Etoile is really a young woman not a knight, and she turns out to be an objectionable brat. Etoile is one of those *anime* characters seething with resentment who are just a pain to endure after a while (and Yumi Uchiyama voices her way too annoying). But Arslan is amazingly patient with her).

＊

The sequel series to *Arslan Senki*, *The Heroic Legend of Arslan: Dust Devil Storm Dance* (*Arslan Senki: Fujin Ranbu*, 2016) continued the ancient world saga. The eight episodes ran from July 3 to Aug 21, 2016. It was was produced by Kodansha/ Dentsu/ Mainichi Broadcasting System/ Liden Films/ Arslan Senki Production Committee/ N.B.C. Universal Entertainment, Japan, dir. by Noriyuki Abe, and wr. by Makoto Uezu and Touko Machida. Char. des. and chief ani. dirs: Kazuo Watanabe and Ushio Tazawa. Music: Taro Iwashiro. Art dir.: Tadashi Kudo. With much of the same voice cast as the first season.

Episode one of the *Arslan* sequel introduced all of the existing characters, updating their plotlines, adding some twists (Andragoras escapes from prison), and of course delivering several outstanding scenes.

The filmmaking is once again masterclass, so splendid and grand it's as if you're viewing all of the historical movies from the past 120 years of cinema rolled into one.

The later episodes take our heroes to the coast, to Gilan, with a mandate from Andragoras: to raise an army. Arslan and his entourage become embroiled in the local politics of the port town, which's being exploited by pirates.

The 8 episodes of the *Arslan* sequel series come to an all-too-abrupt close, with the story left hanging in the dusty air of the Middle East, as each group of charas heads for a Grand Battle. Still to be resolved, then, are the fates of Silvermask, Andragoras, and Arslan. (This is from the latter half of the comic, which remains unfinished).

We know how this is going end, of course: there will be a troubled, anxious encounter between Arslan and Andragoras; the old king will expire (not by Arslan's hand, tho'); and there'll be a huge duel between Arslan and Silvermask, possibly with all three would-be kings (with Narsus and Daryun in the mix, too), culminating with Hermes being vanquished (he has been a venal villain), and Arslan crowned king.

The cute subplots – Alfreed and Narsus as 'man and wife', Gieve's longing for Farangis, etc, will likely be left in the air.

The six *Arslan Senki* Original Video Animations (1991-95, a.k.a. *Arslan/ Chronicle of Arslan*), were prod. by Kadokawa Shoten/ K.S.S.,/ M.O.V.I.C./ Shochiku/ Tokyu Agency/ Sony/ Animate Film/ J.C. Staff, produced by Akira Maruta, Kazuhiko Ikeguchi, Keishi Yamazaki, Mitsuhisa Hida, Nagateru Kato, Noriaki Ikeda, Noriko Matsuura, Toshio Suzuki, Yasuhisa Kazama, Yasuhisa Kazama, Kei Sugiyama and Masatoshi Tojo, wr. by Kaori Takada, Megumi Sugihara, Tomoya Miyashita and Megumi Matsuoka, dir. by Mamoru Hamatsu, Tetsuro Amino and Mihiro Yamaguchi, char. des. by Sachiko Kamimura, with music by Norihiro Tsuru.

The voice cast was superb: Kappei Yamaguchi (as Arslan), Akio Ohtsuka, Kazuhiko Inoue, Kazuki Yao, Hiro Yuuki, Jurota Kosugi, Kotono Mitsuishi, Kumiko Watanabe and Akemi Okamura. The 1990s Original Video Animation adaptation of *Arslan Senki* was an impressive animation (which the 2015 series clearly drew on; after all, the 2015 production was a remake).

There seems to have some trouble behind the scenes, suggested by the change in the production houses overseeing the animation (from Animate Film to J.C. Staff). The animation style of *Arslan Senki* was especially outstanding in the delivery of mass battles: it's a huge challenge for animators to keep so many characters and horses in motion. (However, some of the attempts at cinematic devices, like tracking shots, seemed a little clunky).

Elsewhere, some shots tried to emulate live-action camera moves, such as dollying towards then away from a character, but came across as awkward and self-conscious. Also, some of the performance acting, such as the hand gestures, were a little arch and ballerina-like, in the Disneyesque manner (of Disney heroines such as Snow White and Cinders).

However, the 1991-95 *Arslan* features numerous beautiful pieces of animation, including some modest scenes depicting life in the ancient world, the sort of shots and scenes that are often cast aside as an animated series based on action rushes headlong into battle. With art direction by Yuki Ikeda *et al*, colour design by Nouko Mizuta, Shuichi Satou and Yuko Takarada and background art by Yusuke Takeda (Studio Bihou), *Arslan* is a fine looking Original Video Animation series. It presents a convincing vision of Ancient Persia.

The series opened with the giant battle that sees the King beaten, Silvermask in the ascendant, Kharlan as a traitor, and Arslan fleeing with Narsus.

The 1990s version of *Arslan Senki* lacks the humour of the 2015 series, and takes itself rather seriously. Also, it doesn't feature the va-va-voom designs of Himoru Arakawa's women.

Meanwhile, as Prince Arslan, the remarkable Kappei Yamaguchi deilvers a quiet, thoughtful performance (more like his 'L' in *Death Note* than his boisterous, irrepressible Usopp in *One Piece*). Yamaguchi is a superstar actor in Japanese animation – solely on the basis of his turn as Usopp, let alone his numerous other acting roles.

With only six Original Video Animations, the 1990s *Arslan* tells only part of the story. Ep. six, for instance, closes with a big 'to be continued' feeling, as our heroes head South. The plots remain unresolved, which is a pity.

THE HEROIC LEGEND OF ARSLAN

Chapter 30: Shadow of the Snake King

Arslan Senki by Himoru Arakawa (this page and over).

THE HEROIC LEGEND OF ARSLAN

The Heroic Legend of Arslan

ALL TROOPS, YASHASUIIN! THE HEROIC TALE OF THE LIBERATION OF A KINGDOM, BROUGHT ABOUT BY MIRACULOUS TEAMWORK!

MANGA: HIROMU ARAKAWA, ORIGINAL
SCRIPT: YOSHIKI TANAKA
(PUBLISHED BY KOBUNSHA KAPPA NOVELS)

CHAPTER 22: HODIR'S PLOT

The Heroic Legend of Arslan (2015).
(This page and over).

消えない翼

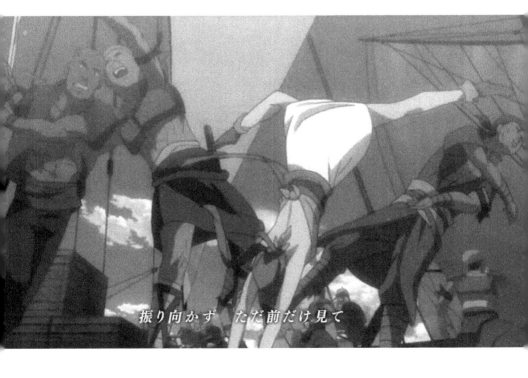

振り向かず ただ前だけ見て

The Heroic Legend
of Arslan, 1990s.

Part Two

Fullmetal Alchemist

Hagane no Renkinjutsushi

鋼の錬金術師

The Manga

0I

FULLMETAL ALCHEMIST

HAGANE NO RENKINSUTSUSHI

THE MANGA

I like B movies. I take a look at this and that, while thinking, 'What the hell is this!? This makes no sense!' till the end. I like that sort of feeling. So an alchemy *manga* was born because I wanted to have that kind of feeling in my *manga*. Thanks to everyone who bought it. While getting into it and thinking, 'What is alchemy supposed to be like this?' Please enjoy it.

Himoru Arakawa, *Fullmetal Alchemist*

FULLMETAL ALCHEMIST MERCHANDIZE.
Fullmetal Alchemist is a massively merchandized franchise. There are:
- 6 light novels,[1] in ten volumes (by Makoto Inoue, 2004-2010);
- soundtrack CDs (plus compilations);[2]
- a trading card game;
- five audio dramas;[3]
- three artbooks (*The Art of Fullmetal Alchemist*);
- three artbooks from the first *animé* (*The Art of Fullmetal Alchemist: The Anime*);
- four guidebooks to the second *animé*;
- three guidebooks to the *manga*;
- five fanbooks (*TV Anime Fullmetal Alchemist Official Fanbooks*);
- video games;
- plush toys; action figures; and key chains…
The novelizations included: *Fullmetal Alchemist and the Broken Angel*

1 Arakawa contributed artwork for the light novels.
2 Four CDs were released for the second *Fullmetal Alchemist* series.
3 There are five audio dramas, including: *The Land of Sand, False Light, Truth's Shadow, Criminals' Scar* and *Ogutare of the Fog*.

(by Makoto Inoue), *Curse of the Crimson Elixir*, *Dream Carnival* and *The Girl Who Succeeds God* (both by Jun Eishima). Also: *Fullmetal Alchemist - Land of Sand*, *Fullmetal Alchemist - The Abducted Alchemist*, *Fullmetal Alchemist - The Valley of White Petals*, *Fullmetal Alchemist - Under the Faraway Sky* and *Fullmetal Alchemist - The Ties That Bind*.

Fullmetal Alchemist was a heavily merchandized and promoted *animé* – the theme song was by L'Arc-en-Ciel, there were video games, CDs, light novels, figurines, trading card games, and all of the usual tie-ins.

Square Enix were a video game company; *Fullmetal Alchemist* was very successful for them. Square Enix has inevitably produced tie-in *Fullmetal Alchemist* games – they include: *Fullmetal Alchemist and the Broken Angel*, *Fullmetal Alchemist 2: Curse of the Crimson Elixir*, *Fullmetal Alchemist 3: God of the Eternal Girl* and *Fullmetal Alchemist: Dream Carnival*; Bandai released R.P.G. games: *Fullmetal Alchemist: Stray Rondo* and *Fullmetal Alchemist: Sonata of Memory* for Gameboy and *Dual Sympathy* for Nintendo D.S. There are other games, for Wii, PlayStation Portable, etc. (Novelizations were also produced of the video games.[4] Yes, novelizations based on video games based on comics – proving that storytelling rules supreme).[5]

The artbooks from Himoru Arakawa (*The Art of Fullmetal Alchemist*) feature the expected high quality images of your favourite characters from the *Fullmetal Alchemist* universe. Most fascinating for fans, perhaps, are the sketches for prototype character designs that Arakawa-sensei has included. So we see early versions of charas such as Zolf Kimbley (with a long, black cloak and wizardly white hair, he resembles Voldemort in *Harry Potter*), Bradley (a pompous oaf with ginger hair and 'tache), Liza Hawkeye (given a blue twin-set and glasses, so she looks like an Office Lady), Winry Rockbell (long, pale hair and red eyes), Alphonse (with armour that looks like a robot), Lust (a striking fetish costume in grey that leaves her midriff and hips bare), and Buccaneer (given a blond, Mohican haircut).

Meanwhile, the artbooks from the *animé* versions of *Fullmetal Alchemist* (*The Art of Fullmetal Alchemist: The Anime*), include many wonderful images used as posters, covers, marketing material, etc. If you compare the *manga* artbooks and the *animé* artbooks, you can see how remarkable the character designers were (Yoshiyuki Ito for the 1st series, Hiroki Kanno for the 2nd series).[6]

THE TIMELINE.

The *Fullmetal Alchemist manga*'s timeline begins with the Elrics arriving in Liore in 1914. That is, it's 1914 in the steam-punk, imaginary world of Amestris (but it does approximate to just b4 the First World War

---

[4] If you find the idea of video games made from *manga* or animation ridiculous (*viz.* Woody Allen deriding novelizations of movies), then a novelization of a computer game seems especially stoopid!

[5] The video games for the PlayStation 2 are: *Fullmetal Alchemist and the Broken Angel*, *Curse of the Crimson Elixir* and *Kami o Tsugu Shojo*.

[6] Mitsuyasu Takekoshi and Naomi Kaneda were guest chara designers.

in our world, and also the 1920s). When the full extent of the history of Amestris is revealed, and just what Father, Hohenheim and the homunculi have been up to, the *Fullmetal Alchemist manga* goes back around 400 years, to 1514 (i.e., to the alchemy of the Renaissance. However, the depiction of the city of Xerxes in the flashback suggests something out of Ancient Greece or Egypt).

There is certainly a genuinely epic scale to the background story of *Fullmetal Alchemist* – because Father, the homunculi and the military government are using an entire country to create an alchemical transmutation circle, and exploiting all of the people in Amestris, in the pursuit of the usual things that villains hunger for: power, immortality, and more power (in the end, Father desires the power of a god).

Fullmetal Alchemist thus depicts the ultimate debasement of the leaders of a nation – sacrificing them all, in order for one individual (Father) to achieve his aims. It's an exaggeration of what governments have done throughout history. Father, after all, started out as a homunculus, a non-human creature (but created by humans – by alchemists): that is, he embodies the Faustian pact with the Devil – he is Satan, he is the trickster, he expresses all of the worst aspects of humanity: to take, to kill, to exploit, without regard for the consequences, and without wanting to pay the price. (Amestris is Japan, of course, making Führer Bradley a stand-in for the Prime Minister and his regime, and also perhaps for the Emperor. In many *animé*, authorities tend to be corrupt and self-serving).

THE WORLD OF *FULLMETAL ALCHEMIST*.

Altho' *Fullmetal Alchemist* is set in an alternative world (Amestris) loosely based on the early 20th century (and in Europe, though it's Europe seen through Japanese culture), it's really about the present day (and the present day in Japan). There are steam trains, old telephones, horses and carts, and Mittel European buildings, the usual paraphernalia of steampunk and quasi-19th century fictions in Japanese animation. But the fashions and costumes in *Fullmetal Alchemist* are often completely 1990s/2000s: Winry has ear piercings and studs, croptops, hoodies, and a mini skirt, Izumi Curtis has dreadlocks, and dresses worn over leggings, Paninya sports army combat pants and a tight Tee shirt, there're tattoos, rectangular (designer) glasses (a *lot* of charas in *Fullmetal Alchemist* wear glasses!), and spikey hair (but what *animé* show or action-adventure *manga doesn't* have spikey hair? Like, none!).

Costume players go for poster boy Ed, tomboy Winry, the military's star couple Mustang and Hawkeye, and *femme fatale* Lust, but not Alphonse so much – full body armour is trickier to make at home (plus you're completely enclosed in material).

It's intriguing, for a British audience of this comic, that author Himoru Arakawa was inspired by the Industrial Revolution (and the era after the Revolution) in Britain. As with Hayao Miyazaki, Isao Takahata and *Laputa: Castle In the Sky* (which drew on the mining communities in

Wales), or *Steam-boy* directed by Katsuhiro Otomo (which was set in Manchester and London), there is a significant influence of 19th century British industrialization in *Fullmetal Alchemist* (you can see it in the mining towns, for instance).

Fullmetal Alchemist is part of the alternative history genre in fantasy literature: one scenario that's popular is imagining what the world would be like if Germany and the Axis Powers had won World War Two. Another sub-genre examines the political and ideological relationship between Japan and Germany in between the two World Wars (comics which visit Germany in this period include *Hellsing*).

Amestris in *Hagane no Renkin Jutsushi* is clearly Japan, but a Europeanized Japan of the late 19th/ early 20th century. The country of Ishbal to the East is obviously and self-consciously modelled on a number of Middle Eastern territories, including Israel, Palestine, Iraq and Iran. Xing, across the desert, has affinities with China, Taiwan and Korea. Creta, to the West, evokes Greece. And Drachma, to the North, is of course Russia (complete with snow and cold and bears and fierce warriors).

China is regarded as a place of the unknown and the exotic in *manga* and *animé*, a completely different country, a place of foreigners: in short, China is just as foreign to Japanese as it is to Westerners (even though plenty of Japanese culture arrived from China). When Japanese go abroad (tho' most don't – they vacation in Japan), they tend to visit Europe or the U.S.A., not other Asian countries (many of which aren't too far away from Japan. (Arakawa and co. used Chinese culture in *Hero Tales*).

So the Middle East, like Europe and the U.S.A., and India and other Asian countries, are subject in *animé* and *manga* to stereotyping and demonization (with the Arabic countries coming off worst – such as in *GoShogun*, *The Crystal Triangle*, *Area 88*, *One Piece*, *Spriggan* and *Fullmetal Alchemist*). As Antonia Levi puts it, the Middle East is a 'place of sand, religious fanaticism, and terrorists' in *animé* (60). And it is too in many North American movies and TV shows (even more so following 9/11).

THE DESIGN AND STYLE OF THE *FULLMETAL ALCHEMIST* COMIC.

The *manga* of *Fullmetal Alchemist* by Hiromu Arakawa was a conventional *manga* production, using all of the usual devices of *manga*: a regular format (typically 3, 4, 5 or 6 panels per page, in horizontal blocks), black outlines on white, plenty of screen tone (a.k.a. 'zip'),[7] floating sound effects (integrated into the artwork), speech bubbles (plus floating bubbles for interior monologues, explanations, etc), speed lines, and cliffhangers at the end of each chapter. Most of the images are medium close-ups or medium shots. There are occasional double-page spreads (or single pages) for stand-out action beats or for scene-setting landscapes (plus the customary splash pages and title pages). Sometimes pages're fragmented into small images. Black backgrounds are used for flashbacks. Slightly different

---

7 Pretty much every page of the *Fullmetal Alchemist manga* includes screen tone.

sizes or shapes of panels indicate a break in the story. Arakawa is fond of using silhouettes, and of losing a face in shadow, with just the eyes white, to emphasize high emotion (such as anger or violence). At highpoints, split frames are employed (placing two close-ups next to each other). Speed lines're just as often used for comical moments as for action (there is a *lot* of comedy in *Fullmetal Alchemist*). Compositions place figures centrally, but also off-centre for effect. Each panel is often different tonally from those adjacent to it: a figure in a black outline against white, for instance (the basic sort of *manga* image), will be placed next to an image with plenty of mid-tone in the backgrounds, with another panel having dark greys or near-blacks.

Each chapter in *Fullmetal Alchemist* is 35-45 pages long, a typical length for a monthly magazine entry, not the usual 19-22 pages of a typical weekly *manga*. Also, the final chapters are more'n twice that, so the 108 chapters of *Fullmetal Alchemist* has the whole *manga* running at more like 120 or more chapters, equivalent to 270 regular *manga* chapters.

For backgrounds and settings, Himoru Arakawa tends to select blocky, rectilinear shapes, with perspectives clearly delineated. She likes to use high-key lighting and strong contrast, as if everything has been lit with Westering but still bright sunlight, so that her backgrounds have the look of the crisp photography of the masters of the early 20th century (Ansel Adams, Edward Weston, Robert Doisneau, etc). (As for atmospheric effects, Arakawa is very fond of rain, and of snow. The whole central section of *Fullmetal Alchemist*, set in Briggs Mountain, is deep in snow and ice. Maybe that's because Arakawa grew up in Northern Japan, where it's colder than the South. But snow and rain also feature in *manga* such as *Vagabond, Blade of the Immortal, Naruto*, etc).

Colour is employed in *Fullmetal Alchemist* only for the cover and sometimes one or two pages, as is standard practice in *manga* (there is more colour in the later issues of *Fullmetal Alchemist*, but the series is still fundamentally b/w, like all *manga*). Occasionally, *mangaka* Hiromu Arakawa employs gouache and watercolour paint (*manga* artists often use watercolours or acrylics for special illustrations like magazine covers, frontispieces, video and DVD covers, etc). Short pieces of extra information (in the *omake* = extras) were occasionally included (at the end), as well as occasional humorous sections at the back, including *chibi/* super-deformed versions of the characters, and also the 4-panel strips, called *4-koma*.[8] (Unfortunately, Viz Media have published *Fullmetal Alchemist* in a small format paperback, which does not do full justice to the intricate art, which demands a larger page size. Some of the translations leave a little to be desired. On the plus side, the art isn't flopped, one of the most irritating tendencies of Western publishers of *manga*. There are very good reasons why artwork is flopped, but also very good reasons why artwork should *not* be flopped!).

The design of the two heroes of *Fullmetal Alchemist* is striking: one of them is a giant suit of mediæval armour (an unusual way of introducing a

8 There's a side-story about Ed and Al as tots, Ed bullying his brother, and having a stern chat with his father.

sort of power suit motif – Japanese *manga* and animation loves its giant robots!). Alphonse is usually depicted with mid-grey screen tone, as with Ed's coat (his pants are black). Later, other suits of armour or hollow bodies are introduced, as commentaries on Alphonse's unusual status. They also develop the metaphysical themes of what constitutes a human being, of the relation between bodies and souls, and the notion of re-animating life (with links to *Frankenstein*, which Arakawa explored in her *Raiden 18 manga*).

The faces in *Fullmetal Alchemist* tend to be drawn with black outlines, with few facial features inside the white spaces of the page beneath. Arakawa-sensei's lines are precise, thin and even – as if she uses a pen with a fine point. If there were rubbings-out of pencil sketches, we don't see them: we only see the clearly-defined outlines for every object.

Ed's eyes (which are very large, in the usual *manga* style), are given very small pupils (and sometimes with/ without irises) – which would, in conventional æsthetics, render him rather unattractive and even mean. And they're gold, like his hair. Again, odd (Ed's design has his head very pale, all done in outlines: because his hair is blond/ gold, it's only defined by the outlines). And the Ishbalians have red eyes,[9] as well as darker skin and, just as odd, white hair (the look of the Ishbalians suggests, above all, *otherness* – these are, for a Japanese audience – which's the main audience for *Fullmetal Alchemist* – foreigners).

For Himoru Arakawa, the race issue in *Fullmetal Alchemist* was partly inspired by the treatment of the Ainu people in Japan. The Ainu are an ancient, aboriginal people that were displaced in the modern era. In contemporary Japan, the Ainu (24,000 of them), now living mainly in Hokkaido (they used to live in Northern Honshu), are the last links to the ancient, Jomon societies; they are sometimes called Caucasian, and are related to the peoples of Siberia.

Eyes – it's one of the memorable inventions of *manga* artist Hiromu Arakawa to include *eyes* as one of the emblems of mystery and power, as well as evil and fate, when the *Fullmetal Alchemist* story reaches the Gate of Truth. You open that ominous door in that white, spaceless space, and behind it is… a giant eye. It's terrific. It's inspired. And Father (and Pride) is comprised at times of nothing but eyes and grinning mouths. Castrating, devouring mouths and castrating, devouring eyes. (No doubt Freudian and post-Freudian theorists would discuss castration and the mother, and the castrating vagina (*vagina denta*) – and *Fullmetal Alchemist* duly includes many vaginal motifs, including bodies, like Gluttony's, which opens up to reveal a monstrous mouth and teeth, or the eye on its side, against black, which also looks like a vulva).

Gates, meanwhile, are a prominent part of Buddhist temples and Shinto temples in Japan, as well as referencing the Gates of Heaven and the Gate sof Hell of Western religion.

Hair is a big deal in the *Fullmetal Alchemist* series (as in many another *manga* and *animé*). Dreadlocks, pony tails, waist-length, blond

9 The red eyes might a joke about *animé*, where red eyes are common, as are eyes of any colour, and also eyes with symbols imprinted on the irises.

hair – and of course – spikey hair! For guys in *Fullmetal Alchemist*, hair tended to be long, often drawn into a pony tail at the back (Ed has plaits). Occasionally men sport dreads (as Izumi Curtis does). Himoru Arakawa has a penchant for depicting a few characters (such as van Hohenheim and Zolf Kimbley, and several in *Arslan Senki*) with a couple of strands of hair falling over the face, from the forehead. If you have long hair, it's irritating. (A common hairstyle in *animé* and *manga* is a thick lock of hair hanging right between the eyes).

The *Hagane no Renkinjutsushi* world is filled with tattoos and jewellery, like *Bleach* and *One Piece,* reflecting the fashions of the 1990s and 2000s (tattoos crop up in many recent movies, for instance, such as *Solomon Kane,* the *Twilight Saga* and *Avengers* – including the tattoos on the chests and backs, usually reserved for villains. And some fans have had tattoos of *Fullmetal Alchemist* symbols; in Japanese culture, it means *yakuza* connections). In *Fullmetal Alchemist,* tattoos have a nefarious element: Scar has a whole arm tattooed (only later is it revealed that it's his brother's arm!). The homunculi have an Ouroboros tattoo on different parts of their body (Gluttony's is on his tongue, of course, and Lust's is on her cleavage, inevitably), which's related to the State Alchemist symbol of the ourosboros (the symbol is a snake eating itself, an ancient image of eternity, cycles, seasons, disintegration and reintegration, self-sufficiency, unity, totality, cyclic time, immortality, 'all is one' (in Greek mythology – which the Elrics boys learn on Yock island), and the wheel of *samsara* (in Hindu and Buddhist religion))).

The military costumes, however, are closely based on real, historical costumes, in particular European (Prussian) ones of the late 19th century and early 20th century. Big, black boots and the distinctive, navy blue greatcoats (with gold seams). No hats, however (unusual, and perhaps chosen because they obscure too much of the face. However, some of the grunts sport hats).

Himoru Arakawa likes her men buff and her women slinky: 'If I draw them too skinny, people will think my poor characters don't eat! Men should be muscular and women should be va-va-voom!'

The *manga* of *Fullmetal Alchemist* uses many of the regular devices of *manga* to create comic moments: smoke or steam rising from a character, girlie flowers ✿ and stars ☆,[10] cartoon sound effects, and of course exaggerated (super-deformed) bodies.

A striking amount of the *manga* and the 2009-10 *animé* series of *Fullmetal Alchemist* takes place amongst snow, in the North of Amestris. Perhaps this reflects artist Himoru Arakawa's childhood in Hokkaido. It means that the filmmakers have, by the end of the long series, drawn every kind of snow, every possible icicle, every snow drift, and every snowy tree imaginable.

---

10 When Alex Armstrong appears, for instance, or Winry, girlie motifs like starry eyes, hearts and flowers are deployed. The *animé* reproduces these devices.

CHARACTERS

EDWARD ELRIC.

Edward Elric is the hero of the *Fullmetal Alchemist* franchise, its poster boy, its key icon. Ed is a volatile mass of contradictions: mercurial, restless, impatient, angry, resentful, determined, self-righteous, stubborn, pig-headed, hungry, cynical, sarcastic, vain, narcissistic, hard-working, lazy, bored, loving, vulnerable, visionary, magical, spiritual, handsome, intelligent, hysterical – and contradictory!

In fact, Edward Elric has pretty much every attribute of every animated star there has ever been. He is a kind of all-purpose *anime* hero, who might fit into 100s of Japanese TV shows. Yet he is also very much the creation of Himoru Arakawa and her *manga Fullmetal Alchemist* (he is *the* Fullmetal Alchemist). In one of the later readers' polls for favourite characters of *Fullmetal Alchemist*, the top 5 were: Ed, Mustang, Hawkeye, Alphonse and Winry.

In *Fullmetal Alchemist*, Edward Elric agrees to become a 'dog of the military', a damning phrase to indicate a lowly employee who has to do whatever the military wants (it comes from Arakawa's early comic *Stray Dog*). Some other alchemists deride the State Alchemists for being 'dogs of the military'[11] (the equivalent might be a 'salaryman', someone who does what they're told, who is a slave to the State machine).

Edward's name was apparently inspired by the 1990 movie *Edward Scissorhands*,[12] and Alphonse from Henri Toulouse-Lautrec (1864-1901).[13] The last name Elric seems to come from *The Elric Saga* by Michael Moorcock, a wonderful cycle of novels in the sword-and-sorcery genre (years before it was colonized by video gamers and Hollywood), but Himoru Arakawa said she hasn't read the *Elric* books by Moorcock (or *Harry Potter* or *The Lord of the Rings*).

J. Clements and H. McCarthy compare Ed to the 'magical girl' genre of *anime*:

> Edward is like a magical girl whose transformation has gotten seriously out of hand; without the help of a guiding angel or animal, he's over-reached himself and now has to try to retrieve normal life. (2006, 209)

Ed is adorable: he acts as both the *shonen* hero and the *shojo* heroine. With Winry relegated to a supporting role, Ed, along with Al, provides plenty of the functions of a heroine in girls' *manga*. When he performs alchemy, for instance, with his coat flapping and hair flying, Edward looks exactly like the tomboy star of *Slayers*, Lina Inverse (they have the same short, skinny bodies, spiky hair, and very similar attitudes and attributes – like being very touchy about their appearance and stature, quick-tempered, and fond of eating).

11 The derision is more prominent in the first *anime* compared to the second *anime* series.
12 Tim Burton is cited as an influence by many *mangaka*, including Kentaro Miura (*Berserk*), Atsushi Ohkubo (*Soul Eater, Fire Force*), and Yana Toboso (*Black Butler*).
13 Toulouse-Lautrec's father was Count Alphonse de Toulouse-Lautrec Monfa.

When Ed performs alchemy, he often includes motifs which personalize his transmutations: his loud-speaker on the train in the fourth chapter of the *manga*, for instance (*Battle On the Train*), has Ed's haircut and looks like a *chibi* Ed; his cars and doors boast funky additions such as a bull's head and horns.

*

ED AND AL.

In the first chapter of *Fullmetal Alchemist manga*, it's Al who first performs alchemy among the Elric brothers[14] – his act is typical for Al, mending a broken radio (i.e., a modest act of helping out and fixing things). So it's Edward who performs the first act of alchemy in the *Fullmetal Alchemist* series in an action/ confrontation context, when he creates a spear to use against the chimera that Father Cornello sends against him.

Thus, that first chapter of *Fullmetal Alchemist* contains plenty of character-based information. How, for instance, Ed Elric stands there quite cool and nonchalant as the chimera monster appears out of the darkness. That tells us that Ed has faced this kind of thing before, that he is very confident in his skills, and that it takes more'n a creature of teeth and claws to get him quaking.

It's Ed E. who is given many of the flashbacks and memories, rather than Al. In the second volume of the *manga*, for instance, Ed remembers transmuting a toy doll, which he gives to his mom. This sweet memory is placed part-way thru the story of Shou Tucker, the madman who transmutes his daughter and dog into a chimera, to add ironic layers to the piece (Tucker admonishes the brothers for wanting to bring their mother back to life using alchemy).

THE HOMUNCULI AND FATHER.

Father, starting out as 'the dwarf in the glass jar', grows into one of those all-powerful villains who can act without shifting their butt: Father can perform alchemy at a distance, sitting on his throne, without trans-mutation circles, without moving, and can stop other people using alchemy.

In the *Fullmetal Alchemist manga*, the sinister figure of Father appears to be orchestrating events behind the scenes, for his own nefarious ends, using his henchmen to carry out his plans. Later, it's revealed that Father is indeed behind everything –· but the Elrics' dad Hohenheim is also implicated, because he was the one who let out the original homunculus in the first place.

The homunculi in *Fullmetal Alchemist* are named (and patterned) after the Seven Deadly Sins[15] or Vices: pride, greed, lust, envy, gluttony, anger and sloth. They are thus aspects of Father's personality (or soul), his spirit familiars or spiritual children (yet the irony is that Father is a

14 They are often referred to as 'Elric *kyoudai*' (= siblings).
15 Japanese *manga* and *animé* enjoys teams based on patterns, numbers and codes. The Seven Deadly Sins of Western religion pop up in *The Seven Deadly Sins* by Nakaba Suzuki (2012-20) and *Sin: The Seven Mortal Sins* (2017).

homunculus – that is, not a human at all, but a creature made by humans. So he or it is ape-ing humans and their religious beliefs). As Hohenheim realizes, what Father was after was a family – so he named himself the Father of a bunch of creatures. But it didn't work. As Hohenheim reminds Father during their fantastic confrontation in the bowels of Central City, homunculi can't achieve that (which drives Father nuts!). Father wants to be human and to give birth and life, but he can't; he is not a god, but he is also not a human. It's the same with Envy: Ed informs Envy that what he really wanted was to be human, was to have friends like the people he despises.

WRATH/ FÜHRER BRADLEY.

There are plenty of villains to loathe in *Fullmetal Alchemist*. One of the most despicable is Führer Bradley,[16] the homunculus Wrath. With his black moustache and eye-patch and the fact that his design recalls both Josef Stalin and Adolf Hitler,[17] Bradley is a truly venal character. I simply can't wait until somebody dispatches this piece of slime. (And it's a *long* time before they do in *Fullmetal Alchemist*!).

The Hitler and Stalin associations make Führer Bradley a very disturbing presence in the *Fullmetal Alchemist* universe. Add to that his revolting attitude towards human life, and his repulsively violent acts, and that he seems to be unkillable, and you have a really nasty piece of •••• (and Hiromu Arakawa keeps Wrath/ Bradley alive right to the very end of the *Fullmetal Alchemist* story – while others, such as Lust and Gluttony are slain earlier. It takes a *huge* amount of effort from the heroes to finally waste Bradley, and they have to cut off his hands at the wrists to do so. This guy simply *won't* die! In the same way that it took years to leave the Reign of Terror in Russia behind).

OTHER CHARACTERS.

Fullmetal Alchemist is a social and sociable *manga* – it is simply stuffed with secondary and minor characters, as well as a large cast of principals. Not for Himoru Arakawa the windswept mountains and lonely roads and dense forests of samurai *manga* and historical dramas – *Fullmetal Alchemist* is firmly entrenched in towns, villages, cities, in communities of all kinds – and new characters are popping up every few pages. (There are some rural and remote spots, tho' – principally Resembool).

ALEX ARMSTRONG. Alex Armstrong is one of the funniest charas in the *Fullmetal Alchemist* universe: a giant, soft-hearted, weepy, feminized guy, with a Germanic, beefcake appearance (with a kiss-curl on his bald pate), who's prone to stripping off his shirt at any opportunity, brandishing his impressive muscles, and performing outrageous acts of muscle-mania. Armstrong is fantastically camp, the sort of character that would

---

16 Pronounced 'Bradrey' by the voice actors of the *animé*.
17 Hitler is invoked several times by Himoru Arakawa in *Fullmetal Alchemist* – she includes characters who look like him (including one, in the Ishbal flashback, who has the staring, robotic eyes of a maniac). Hitler pops up in the flesh in the first *Fullmetal Alchemist* movie.

never appear in a straight action or adventure serial in the Western world (in any media). Because Armstrong is a joke, a caricature, and so out-there his presence disrupts the storytelling, the drama, and anything that's going on – which is precisely why we love him!

When Alex Armstrong first appears, he's surrounded by roses: he embarrasses everyone (nobody really knows how to deal with him), and the Elric brothers find him impossible. But Armstrong is chosen to escort the lads back to Resembool for their first important Return Journey (of all the charas that Himoru Arakawa could've selected for this task of guarding the boys, this is certainly one of the oddest choices![18]).

LING YAO. Ling Yao is an appealing characterization in the second *Fullmetal Alchemist animé* series (as voiced by the wonderful Mamoru Miyano – Raito Yagami in *Death Note*) – an irritatingly cheerful, happy-go-lucky Chinese prince,[19] a cross between a cocky street urchin and a cocky, spoilt aristocratic brat (he infuriates people often – usually Edward. Partly because, if someone's going to get infuriated, it's best if it's Ed, because that's the most entertaining!). Ling's character journey takes on a fascinating turn when the homunculus Greed makes his new home in his body, so the two of them're having an on-going battle for supremacy within Ling's body.

LIZA HAWKEYE. Liza Hawkeye is Roy Mustang's sidekick-cum-helpmeet, a super-cool sniper who's secretly in ♥ with Mustang. She stands by him at all times, and is as devoted as a pet dog (she lives alone with a dog). She puts up with his philandering, his arrogance, his smug self-righteousness, his self-absorption, his stupidity, and his insensitivity… hoping against hope that one day she and he will Be Together. Hawkeye is rightly rewarded for her years of devotion. (Hence, Hawkeye is a fave chara with fans, and with Arakawa. Actually, you can feel how much Arakawa loves her creations).

PRIDE/ SELIM. Pride is a different character in the *Fullmetal Alchemist manga* than in the first *animé*: the comic portrays Pride as a very malicious homunculus (the first homunculus), currently residing in the form of the Führer's 10 year-old son Selim Bradley. In chapter 70: *The First Homunculs*, Liza Hawkeye, recently made the Führer's secretary (much to the irritation of Roy Mustang, who's had his team broken up), rumbles who Selim might be, by putting together a few facts (that the Führer doesn't have any distant relatives, for instance). There's a very creepy moment when Pride encounters Hawkeye from a shadowy doorway: now we see that Pride, with his/ its Cheshire Cat grin and staring eye,[20] is the monstrous force of darkness that's sliced up the reconnaissance crew in the tunnel near Briggs Mountain. This provides one of the finest scenes in the second animated series of *Fullmetal Alchemist*, where a 10 year-old boy threatens a woman in a very creepy

18 Did Arakawa's editor Yoichi Shimomura ask, '*Sensei*, does it have to be *him*?' And of course it did.
19 He *claims* he's a prince – but everyone else sees an irritating youth on the make.
20 The eye and the grin (and the little grasping hands) are an imaginative means of conveying an evil but also playful power. Himoru Arakawa reprised them for the flashback depicting Hohenheim in Xerxes.

manner.

Liza Hawkeye, knowing she is probably going to be killed now she's uncovered Pride's identity, bets everything on telling him what she knows. It seems as foolish as Olivia Armstrong doing the same thing with the Führer in a similar scene, because now Hawkeye is living in fear, looking over her shoulder all the time. And Ms Armstrong, in handing over her advantage to Führer Bradley in exchange for a seat on his inner council, is also making a very difficult bargain. That there are now two powerful women tethered to two homunculi tightens the suspense in the *Fullmetal Alchemist manga*.

ENVY. Envy is a venal villain who despises humanity and relishes causing pain and death. Altho' he has strong competition (from Bradley, Pride, Father, Lust – well, all of the villains), Envy is certainly one of the cruellest. His off-hand, caustic sense of humour ironically enhances his inhumanity. That Envy can impersonate anyone (Father Cornello, Führer Bradley, Hughes' wife Gracia, several soldiers), gives him the opportunity to create all sorts of deadly mischief. In the 2nd *animé*, actor Minami Takayama delivers one of the greatest performances of recent times as Envy.

ASPECTS OF FULLMETAL ALCHEMIST

POLITICS.

The *Fullmetal Alchemist manga* and *animé* is a critique of European fascism and of North American fascism (in addition to Japanese nationalism and racism[21]). It aligns the militarized authorities of fictional Amestris with the governments of Europe and the U.S.A., as well as Japan. *Fullmetal Alchemist* is critical of America's involvement in the Middle East – in the Arab-Israeli War of the 1960s, for instance, or in Libya in the 1980s, in the hostage crises, in the Gulf War of 1991, in the Iraq War, and in the 'war on terror' of the 2000s. The Gulf War and the Iraq War are clearly referred to in the Ishbal rebellion sequence in *Fullmetal Alchemist* (as well as Russia in Afghanistan, and the treatment of the Ainu in Nihon).

World War Two and the defeat of Japan looms large behind many *manga* stories: *Fullmetal Alchemist* offers a war scenario in which the heroes are the victors. Like the simulation and alternative history genre, *Fullmetal Alchemist* portrays Amestris (Japan) as a militarized nation, admittedly, but one which is victorious (in the main – it's Japan after World War One, but definitely not after WW2). However, there is a great deal of sympathy generated for the conquered nation of Ishbal – thus, Hiromu Arakawa is able to re-enact both sides of the victory-defeat coin for modern Japan (Ishbal vividly evokes Japan after 1945, a crushed

---

21 Such as the treatment of the Ainu people.

nation). The Ishbal War is depicted as an 'unjust war', or an 'unjustified war' – raising the question of armed conflict and its 'justifications' by each side.

Anger, Himoru Arakawa says in *Fullmetal Alchemist*, is a natural reaction when senseless things happen, and her *manga* illustrated that:

> it's a natural human reaction to be outraged when senseless things happen. Some things can't be justified or rationalised. I want boys and girls to grow up valuing those feelings.

Throughout *Fullmetal Alchemist,* one is struck by the incredible levels of violence, suffering and death. Not just action, not just stunts and physical gags in all the fights, but real pain, real wounds, and real death. In most fantasy shows, the heroes bounce back relatively unscathed, yes, but in *Fullmetal Alchemist* many secondary characters are killed or wounded. There are pools of blood everywhere. Not only giant amounts of blood, as in OTT horror shows, but blood on the ground spreading out from (what seem to be intended to be) realistic wounds. *Fullmetal Alchemist*'s images of people dying or dead on the soil could be intercut with images from armed conflicts in Bosnia, Iraq, Vietnam, and Somalia, and you couldn't tell the difference.

The *ideological* violence in *Fullmetal Alchemist* is also apparent everywhere, because of the numerous links that the fantasy series makes to the real world, to conflicts such as the Iraq War, the 'war on terror', many Middle Eastern conflicts, and Nazism.

Fullmetal Alchemist is a work where a teacher smashes a 10 year-old child in the face, as she demands respect – she hits him so hard it draws blood and sends him flying out of a boat. If someone did that to us we'd rip their throat out. But in *Fullmetal Alchemist* it's perfectly OK for adults to abuse children time after time after time.[22] (Over the course of the series, pretty much every adult whacks the teen heroes. At least some of them, like Lt. Ross, apologize first![23]).

THEMES AND ISSUES.

The *Fullmetal Alchemist anime* and the *manga* place the human transmutation sequence, the fatal flaw or lack or transgression that the heroes Ed and Al perform, in flashbacks: it has already happened by the time each *Fullmetal Alchemist anime* series and the *manga* have started. But it haunts everything, and colours everything. And then, notice how the story unfolds: very quickly, the Elrics encounter a false religion, with promises of miracles (including bringing a girl's lover back to life). Then they meet a twisted alchemist who's sacrificed his own wife and daughter for his selfish needs. As the *Fullmetal Alchemist* story progresses, Ed and Al confront, again and again, characters and situations which show them the

---

22 A good deal of the problem for Ed and Al Elric in *Fullmetal Alchemist* is that the guiding angels are ambiguous at best and psychotically violent at worst. Genuinely caring helpers or advisers are thin on the ground in Amestris – and the Elrics're reluctant to call on some of them because they know they'll be beaten up! (such as by Izumi Curtis).
23 Which makes the hypocrisy even deeper.

high costs of dealing with life and death issues, and how others have tried and failed to do what they attempted.

There are plenty of moral messages in the *Fullmetal Alchemist* series by Hiromu Arakawa. All of the usual ones are enshrined by the *manga* and the *animés*: work hard, study, try to better yourself, do your bit for your country, don't forget your relatives or your ancestors or where you come from, be loyal, unselfish, kind-hearted, etc etc etc. All of these lessons and codes are built into practically every *manga* and every *animé* you've ever encountered.

But Hiromu Arakawa does add one or two moral statements of her own. The key one is this: *move forward*. It's something that characters in *Fullmetal Alchemist* tell each other (most often Ed and Al): *keep going forward*. It's what Ed tells Rose in the very first adventure of the *Fullmetal Alchemist* series (in both *animés* and in the *manga*): *you've got a lovely pair of legs, Rosie, so get up and start moving*. Or something like that. Ed, being the philosophical mouthpiece of Arakawa-sensei more'n any other chara, embodies that maxim: he is always moving forward. Sometimes impatiently, sometimes awkwardly, and sometimes angrily. Only occasionally is Ed doubting to the point of inertia (Al is more prone to such self-examinations). Sometimes both Ed and Al are thrown into emotional quicksand (such as after the death of the toddler Nina and her dog Alex; Roy Mustang asks them if every set-back is going to stop them from moving forward). Thru Ed, Arakawa is telling the reader and the viewer: *move forward*.

✳

With so many characters dogged by negative traits, and with so many charas that appear at first to be good and true or even 'pure' (or at least, not threatening), but who turn out to be sinister, or even dangerous, who do you root for in *Fullmetal Alchemist*? You root for the Elric brothers, above all, and only one or two other characters (such as Winry, and maybe glasses bookworm Sheska if you're feeling extra specially nerdy. Roy Mustang, Liza Hawkeye and Envy have also been favourites for fans).

Pretty much everybody else in *Fullmetal Alchemist* is either corrupt, devious, manipulative, malicious, insane or psychotically violent to the point of being mass murderers (*Fullmetal Alchemist* contains more mass murderers than almost any comic or fantasy series you can think of).

In *Hagane no Renkinjutsushi*, our heroes are surrounded by villains and jeopardy *on all sides*. There is no purity, no goodness, nothing dependable in the world of *Fullmetal Alchemist* (as to parents – forget it! The Elric lads' mother Trisha is gone, and their father van Hohenheim – well, Ed storms out of the room as soon as he's mentioned! However, Hohenheim is portrayed more sympathetically as the *Fullmetal Alchemist* *manga* and 2nd series wends on). Figures that appear to be kind, parental types (such as Shou Tucker) turn out to be serial killers! And a character who seems to be genuine and kind towards the Elrics, Maes Hughes,[24] is

---

24 Tho' there are subtle hints of Hughes' ambiguity.

killed off halfway thru the series!

HUMOUR.

The *manga* of *Fullmetal Alchemist* contains plenty of cartoony humour, moments when the Elric brothers're reduced to super-deformed charas – squashed, child-like (*chibi*) forms. Himoru Arakawa had a bunch of characters that she enjoyed sending up: Roy Mustang, Alex Armstrong, and of course the Elrics.

The first *animé* series of *Fullmetal Alchemist* has far less humour than the *manga*, and that alters the *manga* considerably: that is, the first animated version made the *Fullmetal Alchemist* series even more serious and gloomy than it was in the *manga* (this is unfortunately a recurring tendency in contemporary *animé* – a good example is the *Ghost In the Shell* franchise: Masamune Shirow's *manga* features plenty of comedy with Motoko Kusanagi, Batou, Togusa, Aramaki, and the gang, but the *Ghost In the Shell: Stand Alone Complex animé*, altho' it's one of the most outstanding TV shows ever made, in any genre or any media, cuts back on the humour, and the two *Ghost In the Shell* movies of 1995 and 2004 cut out comedy almost completely). The second *Fullmetal Alchemist* series remedied this, and included more comedy.

In the background of some of the drawings in *Fullmetal Alchemist*, Himoru Arakawa, like many *mangaka*, includes jokes and portraits of other characters. For instance, Izumi and her hubby Sig are peering at a timetable in the scene where Winry arrives at Central's main rail station.

AUTOMAIL AND ARMS.

Automail. Himoru Arakawa's invention of automail plays a significant part in the *Fullmetal Alchemist* universe. It's everywhere. Ed's arm and leg, of course, but many other charas have it, including dogs. There's even a town dedicated to it (Rush Valley). And automail is integral to the plot (Ed's breaks many times), and it's what links Ed with Winry Rockbell (and to Pinako), professionally, and it gives him legitimate reasons to revisit home. Automail is Awakawa's version of 1. a steampunk motif, and of 2. cyborgization and robotics, and 3. *mecha*, of course – all of which are specialities of Japanese pop culture.

Ed's replacement body parts are also an embodiment of the breaking of the taboo, and Ed's vulnerability: he tends to wear clothes with long-sleeves, so hide his metal arm. Someone who wants to put psychological-moral pressure on Ed can use the automail arm as soon as they see it: Ed's weak points are there for all to see. (But Ed is also proud of it, and is keen to display it, particularly with a grim relish during fights).

As in *Star Wars*,[25] arms are a big deal in *Fullmetal Alchemist* – arms that're cut off, that is. Lan Fan cuts off her arm when she and Ling Yao're being pursued by Führer Bradley (so they can escape); Scar has his

---

25 Arms were oddly a focus for violence in the *Star Wars* films: Ben Kenobi cut off the pest's arm in the space bar, C3PO's arm was torn off, and Han Solo says that Wookie's pull people's arms out their sockets when they lose at space chess. The losing-an-arm motif continued in *The Empire Strikes Back* when Darth Vader cut off Luke Skywalker's arm. The motif has a clear castration element.

brother's tattooed arm sewn on after his brother gives up his life to save him from psycho Zolf Kimbley; and of course Ed has an automail arm (as do plenty of minor characters), and Himoru Arakawa gets an enormous amount of dramatic mileage out of that metal arm (it's used as a pretext to return to Winry Rockbell and the boys' homeland, for instance).

An arm stretching up into the sky is one of the recurring motifs in the *Fullmetal Alchemist manga* (both *animés* also used it). It's a human reaching up to grasp something – glory, fulfilment... or the philosopher's stone. It's often Edward who is raising his metal fist and arm to the heavens, in defiance as well as yearning.

Himoru Arakawa felt she was becoming Edward Elric herself, getting so involved in the writing of the comic: in the *manga* (in 2005), she relates a true story:

> When I went to a get a shiatsu massage after making my last deadline, the masseuse said to me, 'Your right shoulder is really tense'. I almost replied to him, 'That's because it's automail!', because I was sleepy and my head was in a daze as I was thinking about some ideas for the next chapter.

VIOLENCE.

The *manga* of *Fullmetal Alchemist* is without question one of the most *violent* stories of recent times, in any media. Hiromu Arakawa may be a female artist, but that doesn't stop her from delivering an extraordinarily blood-drenched, gore-filled, bone-crunching, skull-splitting, spine-snapping, sword-slashing *manga* epic. Plenty of *manga* are extremely violent, sure, but *Fullmetal Alchemist* goes beyond many of them into an excessive obsession with aggression and suffering. It's way beyond any of the celebrated film directors of movie violence, for example – Sam Peckinpah, Martin Scorsese, 'Beat' Kitano, John Woo, Howard Hawks, or Akira Kurosawa (or, at least, the violence and gore that are allowed in movies by society, censorship organizations, broadcasters, etc).

And the violence in *Fullmetal Alchemist* focusses on *bodies*: while the *Akira manga* by Katsuhiro Otomo (probably the finest of its kind), and the *Ghost In the Shell manga* of Masamune Shirow employ the devastation of *mecha* and buildings (these guys *love* blowing stuff up!), *Fullmetal Alchemist* is all about the body.

In *Fullmetal Alchemist*, characters seem to have unlimited supplies of blood from their livers, because blood is being splurched around the place all the time. Look at the final chapters of *Fullmetal Alchemist* (from around chapter 90 onwards, from the battles in the forest onwards), and you'll find pretty much constant fighting and violence (that is one of the absolute foundations of boys' *manga*, however: it *must* include action followed by action followed by more action).

FULLMETAL ALCHEMIST AND FEMINISM.

Feminism: is *Hagane no Renkinjutsushi* feminist? No. Sure, there are some strong female characters (Winry Rockbell, Izumi Curtis, Olivia

Armstrong, Liza Hawkeye and Lust); yes, the *manga* was written and drawn by a woman (Hiromu Arakawa); and yes, *Fullmetal Alchemist* does explore issues surrounding women (such as: women working – Winry; birth; women bringing up children alone – Trisha and Gracia; and women in military command – Olivia Armstrong). But the Amestris world of *Fullmetal Alchemist* is *entirely* patriarchal, like almost all *manga* and *animé*. And that's as one would expect: *manga* and *animé* is born out of its time and place, like all art, and that time and place – Japan in the 2000s – is still a very patriarchal, very male-oriented society (like most of the West, too). None of the female charas subverts the masculinist society they live in, and few of them even question the prevailing patriarchy. That's partly because a social revolution of that kind is not part of the *manga*.

All of the women in the *Fullmetal Alchemist* series have terrific, idealized, trim figures, and none are overweight. Some could moonlight as super-models (Liza Hawkeye, Izumi Curtis, Olivia Armstrong, Lust and Rose Tomas). Indeed, Ms Armstrong, with her pretty, perpetually pouty pink lips and luxurious blonde locks, might've stepped out of *Charlie's Angels* in the 1970s or *Vogue circa* 1968.

Fullmetal Alchemist, covers for early editions of the manga

2

STORY AND ART BY
HIROMU ARAKAWA

THE SEARCH FOR THE PHILOSOPHER'S STONE.

Hagane no Renkin Jutsushi is full of far more menace and corruption than almost any other comparable *manga* or *animé* series: *Escaflowne, Gundam, Macross Plus, Mushishi, Gunbuster, Moribito, Samurai Champloo* and *Cowboy Bebop,* they all have many violent, difficult and morally ambiguous moments. But for the sense of threat and jeopardy for a couple of teenage boys, *Fullmetal Alchemist* far out-does them.

Maybe that's partly why *Fullmetal Alchemist* has chimed with audiences so deeply: because it reflects a very contemporary world, a hi-tech, capitalist world in which political, social and cultural issues are stuffed with more problems and challenges than any government, any group, any institution, any religion or any individual (or hero) could cope with. (For similar reasons comics like *Death Note, Platinum End, Birdmen* and *Triage-X* chime with audiences).

Fullmetal Alchemist is fascinating for many reasons, but one is definitely the central moral and ethical dilemma: the heroes *cannot* right the wrong that they have experienced. In your typical adventure or fantasy tale (of the Western and North American kind), something wrong is righted, some lack is made good, some corruption or suffering is healed. In *Fullmetal Alchemist,* it is simply not possible for the Elric brothers to turn their misfortune around (no matter how much they dream about it, talk about it, and desire it). Altho' alchemy is a magical occurrence (despite Ed Elric's insistence on it being a 'science'),[1] and despite the inclusion in this marvellous series of fantasy elements such as monsters, chimeras, and superhero-scale stunts, magic (or alchemy) can't fix everything. And it can't solve the heroes' central dilemma.

Thus, altho' Ed and Al Elric have been searching for the philosopher's stone,[2] the supposed cure for all their ills, for years in *Fullmetal Alchemist,* it can't be found. Or they can't find it, and even if they do, every adult has warned them against it (and repeatedly warned them – the warnings and taboos set around the MacGuffin of the *Fullmetal Alchemist* series – the philosopher's stone – are many and formidable. And not just warned them but beaten them senseless in order to get it into their thick skulls). And of course, when they *do* find it, it's not what they expected.

The philosopher's stones in the *Fullmetal Alchemist* series are a MacGuffin or gimmick or motif which can be applied to many aspects of the contemporary world: oil, obviously (countries go to war to create philosopher's stones, and to prolong the lives of the leaders, or one or two people at the top of the political hierarchy). Oil – or money. Or power.

Many characters accuse Edward and Alphonse of committing a taboo, and not being that different from them: Hohenheim, Number 66, Izumi Curtis, Lust, Envy, Shou Tucker, even the demon/ god in the Gateway (in a dream).

By stretching out the Search For the Philosopher's Stone in *Fullmetal*

---

1 If it is a science, and if it is for the common good of the people, as a few charas point out, then why is it shrouded in secrecy?

2 Philosopher's stones have appeared in earlier *animé* – in the *Lupin III* movie *Mystery of Mamo* (1978, a.k.a. *Lupin vs. Clone*).

Alchemist over many years, across this 108-chapter *manga* series, the 51-episode animated TV series of 2003-2004, and the 64 episodes of 2009-2010, the filmmakers at Studio Bones, Square Enix, Mainichi, Aniplex (and the many associated companies) have made it the over-riding goal of the Elric brothers' life. So that the quest dominates their lives. So they can't think of anything else. (Hats off to the screenwriters, headed up by Shou Aikawa (1st series) and Hiroshi Ohnogi (2nd series), for stretching out the premise of the philosopher's stone across the 51-episode series of *animé*! And 64 episodes in the second series!).

Well, one thing's for sure, these are *really determined* kids! Most other kids would've given up by now! And gone to watch TV, play with their cel phones or X-Boxes or tablets, or gone skateboarding. But that is, of course, one of the prerequisites of the action-adventure hero: *never giving up!* (And when other charas seem on the point of giving up, like the two chimeras in the second *Fullmetal Alchemist animé* series, Al is on hand to give them a pep talk). I'm reminded of *manga* magazines such as *Weekly Shonen Jump* which have a moral centre which's summed up in reader surveys by three issues: friendship, perseverance and victory (*Fullmetal Alchemist* certainly has plenty of friendship and perseverance, but the ultimate victory is always deferred until the final episode).

On the other hand, you could also say that *Fullmetal Alchemist*'s Elric lads are stubborn to the point of insanity. Or certainly irritation. Give it up guys! It's not gonna happen! Not only is the pursuit of the philosopher's stone incredibly perilous, not only does it endanger the Elrics numerous times, not only does it pit them against countless foes, including that band of Psychos 'R' Us, the homunculi, it also absorbs years of the Elrics' lives.

But you have to admit that the central premise of kids wanting their bodies back in *Fullmetal Alchemist* is certainly unusual, and it contains plenty of dramatic and thematic juice: it works so well on the thematic, symbolic and mythological levels, and it provides lashings of high drama and vivid interactions. Bodies are central to *Fullmetal Alchemist* – characters hide in bodies (such as Al's armour), get trapped in bodies (inside Gluttony), two souls live in one body (Greed/ Ling Yao), have secret tattoos on their bodies, have bodies augmented with automail, and it's no wonder that there are many doctors dealing with bodies (the Rockbells, the Gold-Toothed Doctor, Dr Knox, Dr Marcoh, and both Father and Hohenheiim act as doctors).

To make it work, *Fullmetal Alchemist*'s characters have to be dead serious where and when it counts, and here the characterizations of Ed and Al Elric, coupled with the truly outstanding voice work of Romi Pak and Rie Kugimiya in both *animés*, drives it all home. Listening to Pak as Ed, you really can believe that he is committed 100% to regaining his limbs, his identity, his wholeness, and to re-instating his brother Al in his real body. Animation may be painted cels and computer-aided elements, but those voices are real (albeit recorded); they have weight, passion, pathos. The designs may be highly stylized (Ed's blond hair with its zigzag bangs! Those huge eyes – which're yellow! That giant, grey suit of pointy, metal armour!), but Ed – and Al – come over as real, living characters.

It's a testament to the talents of the artists at Studio Bones, Square Enix, Mainichi, Aniplex (and all of the many affiliated companies involved in producing *Fullmetal Alchemist*), that the characters come to life, that you buy into their predicament, that you root for them. (The initial premise gives both *Fullmetal Alchemist animés* and the *manga* a hugely powerful narrative engine, which drives the plot along).

The *Fullmetal Alchemist anime* added the notion of incomplete philosopher's stones to the *manga* (called 'red stones'), which the homunculi use to take on human form. In the *manga*, it's Father who creates the homunculi, from philosopher's stones which he produces himself (we witness the bizarre rituals of death and rebirth in Himoru Arakawa's *Fullmetal Alchemist manga*, which inevitably mean Father consuming his offspring).

THE QUEST FOR TRUTH.

The quest for the philosopher's stone is aligned, as it is in the real history of alchemy,[3] with the quest for 'truth'. What is 'truth'? (or the 'truth behind the truth', as *Fullmetal Alchemist* puts it – which, when the Elrics find out what it is, they don't like it at all!). There is no ultimate 'truth' in *Fullmetal Alchemist*, as the Elric boys gradually find out. No Ultimate Anything.

Thus, *Fullmetal Alchemist* has a mature, sophisticated approach to what life is – that there is no Ultimate Truth, no Answer To Everything (echoing the view in postmodern theory that there are no Grand Narratives). That life is complicated, with no easy solutions. *Fullmetal Alchemist* raises important questions about what difference an individual can make, about how the individual has to integrate with society, with his/ her fellow human beings, and about the corruptibility of all humans.

Fullmetal Alchemist is clear: there is no person anywhere who is through and through 'pure' or 'good'. There is nobody who doesn't have flaws. And even the leaders, like the Führer, may be corrupt (in fact, he is a homunculus! As the story in *Fullmetal Alchemist* unfolds, he turns out to be one of the most repulsive villains in all pop culture, East or West). In this respect, and in the others I've just noted, *Fullmetal Alchemist* is the polar opposite of fantasy and adventure stories in the Western world. The moral and ethical complexity of *Fullmetal Alchemist* puts it way beyond most fantasy and adventure series, including the *Harry Potter* series and *The Lord of the Rings* (you stumble across this moral multi-layeredness again and again in Japanese comicbooks and animation).

---

3 Edward insists that alchemy is a *science* (which, for some alchemists in the mediæval and Renaissance era, it was).

Manga creator Arakawa-sensei has not employed every aspect of historical alchemy in *Fullmetal Alchemist*, but she has drawn on many elements from alchemy, including the homunculi, transmutation rituals, some of the symbolism (suns and moons), and the most famous part, the philosopher's stone[4] (which was also, of course, the central conceit of the first *Harry Potter* book;[5] *Fullmetal Alchemist* has been compared to *Harry Potter*.[6] Indeed, the theme (and reality) of the *quest* is actually way more important than *Harry Potter*, for *Fullmetal Alchemist* as a dramatic, on-going story, than the properties of the philosopher's stone itself.) Other *manga* that used alchemy included *Buso Renkin* (2003-06) by Nobuhiro Watsuki and *Enchanter* (2003) by Izumi Kawachi. Meanwhile, characters who can wield magic of all kinds (sometimes using magic circles linked to barriers and portals in the air or on the ground) are everywhere in fantasy stories in Japan.

One element from the history of alchemy that Himoru Arakawa doesn't use much is the dream of an alchemical unity, the royal union of brother and sister, symbolized in alchemy by the conjunction of sun and moon, silver and gold, King and Queen, etc (altho' Ed and Al could be viewed as a brotherly union).[7] Alchemy is a supremely dualistic philo-sophy (in contrast to the animism of Japan's religion, Shintoism), with good set against evil, black against white, etc. *Fullmetal Alchemist* does use the dualism of alchemy, though. (However, there is also a tradition of Chinese alchemy, and alchemy in Taoism – which *Fullmetal Alchemist* embodies in the figures of Mei Chang and Ling Yao. And sometimes the Xingese (Chinese) alchemy (alkahestry) is able to work when the Amestrisian (Japanese) alchemy can't, getting our heroes out of some scrapes). Ed Elric does refer to the union of opposites, however, in the sequence where he and Ling are trapped inside Gluttony's belly.

As to the symbolic colours of alchemy – black, white and gold (or red) – *Fullmetal Alchemist* reserves a dark red or crimson for anything to do with the philosopher's stone. In traditional alchemy, black and white together clearly define the twin poles of life, the eternal dualities of Western religion, from Zoroastrianism/ Manichaeism onwards through Christianity to alchemy and Jungian psychology. In alchemy, of course, black and white refer to particular processes, stages in the transmutation of the elements on the journey towards making the Philosopher's Stone, the Holy Grail of alchemists. Red is colour of blood, passion, anger, sex, danger, and life itself[8] (there are a few references to gold in *Fullmetal*

---

4 Philosopher's stones also appear in Square Enix's computer game *Dragon Quest,* and Hiromu Arakawa made a point of including them in her *manga.*
5 In the U.S.A., the 'philosopher's stone' was changed to the 'sorcerer's stone'.
6 However, Ken Akamatsu's follow-up to *Love Hina*, *Mahou Sensei Negima* (a.k.a. *Magister Negi Magi*, published as *Negima!* in the West), shamelessly steals from *Harry Potter*, as does *Berserk* by Kentaro Miura.
7 However, the union of the opposites is evoked in the story in *manga* and *animé* form by the figure of Father in his Godly guise (Ed and Al also discuss it in brief as kids).
8 Notable is Ed's black suit and red cloak, tho' the colours may have more significance in the look of the clothing than alchemical symbolism.

Alchemist – in the colour of Ed's eyes and hair, for instance, the gold that Ed transmutes to use as a trick, and van Hohenheim is described in legend as the 'golden man' who brought alchemy to Amestris. Both Ed and his father are thus embodiments of alchemy themselves. On a visual level, the filmmakers of the animations of *Fullmetal Alchemist* make extensive use of glowing gold, yellow and oranges. In fact, Ed's visual design does seem to evoke alchemical symbolism, with his red coat, black jacket and pants, and golden hair and eyes).

Fullmetal Alchemist doesn't use the stages of the alchemical process much, either (the black/ white/ red stages in the process of the 'Great Work' of Renaissance alchemy). In sum, Himoru Arakawa has taken only a few aspects of traditional (Western) alchemy (and sometimes just the visual trappings, not the themes or issues alchemy is based on), and then spun her own interpretation of what alchemy is – and within the highly stylized setting of an alternative world (of Amestris).

There are two sequences where Himoru Arakawa does employ several elements from the history of alchemy: one is where our heroes are buried inside the belly of Gluttony, and Ed reconstructs alchemical symbols from the buildings in Xerxes that Gluttony has swallowed. Here, Ed opens the portal (Gateway of Truth) again, becoming very much the familiar alchemist figure of history.

The second sequence is the fascinating flashback to mediæval Xerxes, where we see van Hohenheim encountering the homunculus in the jar. The imagery of crucibles, jars, tubes and liquids is right out of historical alchemy, and the theme of creating life, as well as immortality, is also distinctly alchemical.

The alchemist in history is fundamentally a newer version of shamanism and the archaic shaman: the shaman of ancient times is the ancestor *all* religious types, including the magician, the philosopher, the mystic, the priest, the martyr, the saint, the witch, the angel, the wizard and the pilgrim. (Thus Ed and Al can be regarded as shamen).

Famous Renaissance alchemists and mages in history included Francis Bacon, John Dee,[9] Paracelsus and Cornelius Agrippa. A dip into the internet or any decent textbook on world religion and magic will reveal that real alchemists and real alchemy was *far* stranger than anything in *Fullmetal Alchemist*!

The Renaissance alchemist of Prague, Paracelsus (1493-1541), was apparently the inspiration for van Hohenheim in Hiromu Arakawa's *manga* (Philip von Hohenheim was Paracelsus's real name). Paracelsus said that the second, spiritual birth had to occur in the Mother; one has to die to/ in the Mother first. The same idea occurs in Johann Wolfgang von Goethe's play *Faust*.[10] Paracelsus wrote: 'he who would enter the kingdom of God must first enter with his body into his mother and there die'.[11]

---

9 John Dee was Elizabeth I's court wizard, who communicated with angels.
10 *Fullmetal Alchemist* is an elegant rendition of the Faustian pact, and includes characters, such as the homunculi, right out of the operatic versions of the Faust myth. You could see the homunculi in those street-cool costumes on stage in operas in Verona, Rome, Paris or New York.
11 Paracelsus, quoted in Mircea Eliade: *The Forge and the Crucible*, 154.

Paracelsus and the Renaissance alchemists advocated a 'dying to' the Goddess, much as Catholic mystics speak of 'dying to' Christ. It's about the entry into the 'mother-world'. As Paracelsus says, rebirth is essential, but it requires a sacrifice, and it is in the Mother that it occurs. This is a very ancient belief, this return to the Mother figure, the Goddess of All Things.

Fullmetal Alchemist clearly draws on these notions of sacrifice and femininity, when it's the Elrics' mother Trisha who dies, depriving them of the all-important 'mother-world' (they want their mother back, but also the 'mother-world'. Their bodies, which grew inside their mother, are also linked to the 'mother-world').

In the *Theatricum Chemicum*, Gerhard Dorn says: '[t]ransform yourselves into living philosophical stones!' (quoted by C.G. Jung).[12] And this is precisely what Ed and Al Elric have to do in *Fullmetal Alchemist*, to transform themselves into living philosopher's stones, to become the Holy Grail, the King-and-Queen alchemical unity. (Indeed, Alphonse – the more 'feminine' of the pair, note – becomes a philosopher's stone in himself at the end of the first *animé* series. In the *manga* and the 2nd *animé* series, van Hohenheim says that he is a living philosopher's stone. The homunculi have a philosopher's stone that functions as a heart and power source).

That is, the quest in *Fullmetal Alchemist* (for the Elric boys) is not for the philosopher's stone (that's the outer, dramatic quest), so much as for identity, for self-awareness, for growth from childhood into adulthood. *Fullmetal Alchemist* is essentially the story of growing up: it's a *Bildungsroman*, a rites of passage tale (and it ends with the lads achieving their quest: they have grown into adults, and Ed now has children).

The philosopher's stone of alchemy is also the hermaphrodite or magickal child, the transcendent union of male/ female, black/ white, sun/ moon. For a number of reasons, *Fullmetal Alchemist* discards with the many layers of sexuality in alchemy (alchemy is often couched in erotic terms, of the union of opposites, or male and female energies). One reason is obvious: the heroes of *Fullmetal Alchemist* are kids, which would make bringing the eroticism of alchemy to the forefront problematic.[13]

If you are interested in finding out more about alchemy, I would recommend any book by Mircea Eliade, Joseph Campbell, C.G. Jung and Peter Redgrove.[14]

◆

The transmutation circles or magic circles or symbols in *Fullmetal Alchemist* don't actually mean too much (as also with the words on the Gates of Truth).[15] As in *animé* such as *Bible Black* or *Urotsukidoji*, it's more

12 Quoted in C.G. Jung: *Psychology and Religion: East and West*, 94
13 Altho' if you wanted to you could eroticize the situations and the characters – as fans and *dojnshii* no doubt have! Certainly Al is a more 'feminized' boy, and at the end has a skinny body with long hair that is distinctly feminized.
14 In the 20th century it was C.G. Jung who did more to bring together magic, mysticism, religion, psychology and science than any other individual (one thinks also of J.G. Frazer, Mircea Eliade, Sigmund Freud and Erich Neumann). In Jung's marvellous *Collected Works* one can leap from subjects such as Gnosticism to Chinese alchemy, or from *animus* possession to the *Book of Job.*
15 The tree pattern on the doors of truth resembles the Sephiroth in Qabbalism. Words such as 'Adonai' are written on them.

about how they look (it's the same with Christian[16] iconography in Japanese animation – it's used more for its look, its exoticism, and its vague (usually sinister) associations, than for its actual theological meanings or values). So, no, you probably won't be able to transmute your dead goldfish back to life by copying the magic symbol in one of the chapters! (However, some *really* dedicated *Fullmetal Alchemist* fans have had tattoos on their bodies in the form of the symbols in the series, including the ourosboros).

But, yes, it does look cool in the *animés* when Angry Ed claps his hands and slams them on the ground and the blue lights and the visual effects zap outwards and the transmutation circle glows, and the sound effects team add the mandatory whooshes and crackles (because, of course, no, folks, magic couldn't possibly be silent, and thoughtful, and meditative, and gentle, a matter of deep concentration and slow-moving forces as the magician humbly calls upon the powers of the Earth... No! This is television! This is Show Time! This is animation! So magic has to go BANG! WHOOSH! ZING!).

✳

Why do animation companies in Japan never get Christianity right? They use its symbols all the time – crosses, statues, cathedrals, angels (how they love angels!) – but not one cartoon creator (or *mangaka*) understands the theology, issues or spiritual aspects of Western religion. The Christian religion is clearly utterly foreign to Japanese filmmakers (as Westerners are). All *anime* (and *manga*) use Christianity cosmetically: *Fullmetal Alchemist, Macross Plus, Ghost In the Shell, Hellsing, Cowboy Bebop, The Qwaser of Stigmata, Rage of Bahamut, Samurai Champloo, Fairy Tail, Soul Eater, Death Note, Fire Force, Black Butler, Vampire Knight, Bleach, Drifters, Guin Saga, Seven Deadly Sins, Negima, Trinity Blood, Trinity Seven, Escaflowne*, etc.

A good example of just how free and easy Japanese animators are with Western symbols, and how they use them for their looks and exoticism,[17] disregarding what they mean: Führer Bradley, who's a homunculus, has an evil eye behind his eyepatch. But when he opens it, it has the Star of David on it – and this is the Adolf Hitler-like leader of the very right-wing regime in the fantasy country of Amestris![18] (Sometimes it seems that *manga* and *anime* artists confuse six and five-pointed stars – i.e., the Star of David with the pentacles and pentagrams of occultism and witchcraft. Yes, there *is* a six-pointed star in Tibetan Buddhism which means 'origin of phenomena', but that's not what *Fullmetal Alchemist* refers to).

16 In the vol. 13 *omake*, Himoru Arakawa says that Amestris is not Christian, and festivals like Christmas don't exist.
17 *Anime* will take motifs and symbols from all sorts of places, often just for the look or the feel, disregarding the theological, religious or cultural attributes. As long as it looks exotic and other-worldly, that's cool.
18 Anti-semitism is not a consideration of Japanese animators: they don't seem to realize that they are potentially being offensive. For instance, designer Leiji Masamoto complained that a Star of David was being used to represent the root of evil in a 2002 production of *Space Pirate Captain Harlock* (to be directed by Rintaro), an update of the *Captain Harlock* series. The *anime* production was not broadcast.

If you haven't read Mary Shelley's 1820 novel *Frankenstein*, I highly recommend it. Like *Dracula* by Bram Stoker, it is a novel of incredible emotional and psychological power, a book which consumes the reader, a book with a primal power that hasn't diminished a jot in 200 years.

The *Frankenstein* mythology has numerous links to the *Fullmetal Alchemist* series, including scientific and alchemical quests, the creation of the homunculi (and their ambiguous, troubled relationship with their creator/s), and alchemists acting like gods. Ed and Al Elric can be compared with Viktor Frankenstein (and so can van Hohenheim, Father, Cornello, etc). Himoru Arakawa has produced her own version of *Frankenstein* in the humorous *Raiden 18 manga* (2005).

The novel of *Frankenstein* is comprised of different narratives:[19] the topmost narrative is Mary Shelley's narrator; the next one is Margaret Savile, who appears to collect together the story's documents; Savile's narrative contains the account of Robert Walton, the polar explorer, and Savile's sister; Walton's story takes in that of Victor Frankenstein and his account of creating the monster; the monster has his own story too, contained inside Frankenstein's story. The novel is many-layered, with a number of voices and points-of-view.

As well as *Frankenstein*, Mary Shelley (1797-1851) produced a novella, 5 novels, 2 travelogues, letters, essays, poems, reviews, and many short stories. Shelley's novels included *Valperga* (1823), *The Last Man* (1826), *The Fortunes of Perkin Warbeck* (1830), *Lodore* (1835), and *Falkner* (1837). Her novella, *Matilda*, which dealt with father-daughter incest, was not published until 1959.

Plenty of critics have related the fictional world of *Frankenstein* to Mary Shelley's own life, to issues such as motherhood, childbirth, pregnancy, abortion, illness, etc. To her relationship with the poets Percy Shelley and Lord Byron, with her father William Godwin (who features prominently in Shelley's life), and so on. To early 19th century attitudes towards death, disease, sex, science and marriage. And to Romanticism.

Mary Shelley had four children, but only one survived beyond childhood: a daughter born prematurely in 1815 died after 11 days; William (born in 1816), died aged 3; born in 1817, Clara Everina died one year old; Percy Florence (born in 1819) survived.

Mary Shelley's mother, Mary Wollstonecraft, died 10 days after giving birth to Mary. Shelley used to lie next to her mother's grave in St Pancras Church, reading her father's *Essays On Sepulchres*.

Mary Shelley's great novel and the mythical monster have been the subject of many readings: as class struggle; industrialization's product; a symbol of the French Revolution; as technology; the danger of scientific experimentation; and a 'totalizing monster', in Franco Moretti's term, like

19 A key ingredient in *Frankenstein* is the multiple narrative viewpoints: it is a novel constructed from a variety of elements, like the monster itself: there are letters, journals, and accounts, from a variety of characters. Like *Dracula*, the complexity of *Frankenstein* stems partly from this multi-level approach. There is no trusted, impartial, God-like narrator telling the story in *Frankenstein*.

Dracula, who can never be vanquished.[20] Frankenstein's monster is a multiplitic chameleon, open to a multitude of interpretations.

Frankenstein has also been interpreted as being about the fear of the population explosion; a warning about colonialization (Viktor takes apart the old in order to make the new); about the French Revolution and the Terror; and a protest about classism. Certainly the new debates in science and technology of the early 19th century contributed towards the novel, as pretty much all critics attest: it's known that Mary Shelley and her husband Percy were interested in galvanism, which had been tried on criminals (where the two schools of thought of vitalism and materialism were debated. One recalls that in *Fullmetal Alchemist* prisoners in jail are used as victims in alchemical experiments).

Judith Halberstam, in *Skin Shows: Gothic Horror and the Technology of Monsters*, her excellent feminist interpretation of Gothic fiction past and present, remarked:

> The importance of Mary Shelley's *Frankenstein* (1816) within the Gothic tradition, modern mythology, the history of the novel, and a cultural history of fear and prejudice cannot be emphasized too strongly. (1995, 28)

For Daniel Cottom, 'Frankenstein's monster images the monstrous nature of representation'; it evades definition; it won't be locked down to a single reading.[21] As Halberstam puts it:

> The form of the novel is its monstrosity; its form opens out onto excess because, like the monster of the story, the sum of the novel's parts exceeds the whole. Its structure, the exoskeleton, and not its dignified contents – philosophies of life, meditations on the sublime, senti-mental narratives of family and morality, discussion of æsthetics – makes this novel a monster text. (1995, 31)

Frankenstein locates true horror in the body, in people, not in gods, demons, ghosts or monsters (we note that the body is absolutely central to *Fullmetal Alchemist,* including of course the fates of Ed and Al Elric). For Brian Aldiss, a huge admirer of *Frankenstein*, the novel importantly replaces the priest with the scientist as someone who investigates life's mysteries (in the *Fullmetal Alchemist animé*, it's the alchemist – the young Elrics are very much like young Viktor Frankensteins).

Frankenstein also inaugurates the key element of the 'sense of wonder' in science fiction (the view that sci-fi replaces religious fiction, with its evocations of wonder, mystery, the sublime, the transcendent, aliens and computers as gods or higher powers, cyborgs as angels or desortamons, monsters as Devils, beings from other worlds, shamanic or spiritual journeys to other planets, miraculous events (such as time or space travel), amazing powers, the machines, technology and science replacing the

20 F. Moretti: *Signs Taken For Wonders*, Verso, 1983, 84.
21 J. Halberstam, 31; D. Cottom: "*Frankenstein* and the Monster of Representation", *Substance*, 28, 1980, 60.

occult, the supernatural, the spiritual.

Feminist and cultural critics have pointed out the obvious inter-pretations of the 1931 *Frankenstein* film, and the 1820 novel: the gender role reversals; the feminization of the Viktor Frankenstein character; the homoerotic undertones in the relationship between the scientist and the monster (the monster tells Frankenstein he will be with him on his wedding night); Frankenstein as a latent homosexual; or he's impotent; or it's a Nietzschean sublimation of his sexual desire into his scientific work.

There is no suggestion or hint at all that Edward and Alphonse harbour homoerotic desires for each other – at least, not within the *Fullmetal Alchemist* stories themselves. That some readers/ fans/ viewers discover homosexual/ gay subtexts[22] in their relationship is likely (or inevitable). But they do exhibit passionate feelings for each other – indeed, theirs is the central emotional and psychological connection in the whole series.

Fullmetal Alchemist shares with Katsuhiro Otomo's *Akira* a deep affinity with the Frankenstein myth: for instance, the big themes are very familiar in *Akira*: it's *Frankenstein*, it's science creating monsters, and the monsters rebelling and turning on their masters; it's *Faust* (and the myth of Prometheus), with science (and society) making a pact with the Devil; it's capitalism and the military machine expanding unchecked (including exploiting humans in grotesque experiments); and it's any number of anxieties – about technology, science, militarism, nationalism, youth vs. age, and modern Japan. *Fullmetal Alchemist* mines very much the same sort of social and political territory as *Akira*.

THE LATER CHAPTERS OF *FULLMETAL ALCHEMIST*

The *Fullmetal Alchemist manga* takes the Elrics to the North of Amestris (which the first *animé* series left out completely). Here, guarding Amestris at Briggs Mountain from the country of Drachma (i.e. Russia, one of Japan's ancient rivals), is Alex Armstrong's sister, Olivia. Depicted as a no-nonsense super-bitch with long, white-blonde hair (falling over one eye, of course), pouty, pink lips, a supermodel's body, and a great warrior (even in the extreme cold!) – she's Brunhilde out of the *Ring* cycle – Miss Armstrong is yet another stern, parental figure who comes down hard on the poor Elric brothers. Yes, the community at Briggs Mountain is founded on a tough, Nietzschean survival of the fittest ideology (i.e., it's the roots of fascism). But in this part of the *Fullmetal Alchemist manga*, La Armstrong's role is soon dispensed with (you can only go so far with macho histrionics), and much of the chapter (65: *The Ironclad Rule*) features one of her lieutenants, Miles, delivering a ton of exposition about

22 That Alphonse is feminized, for example; that is, he's given traits often associated with female characters.

the set-up at Briggs Mountain. (Miss Armstrong's distrust of the Elrics is rather over-done in the *Fullmetal Alchemist manga* – after all, the military at Briggs Mountain are part of the government[23] and the military in Amestris – i.e., they're on the same side. I guess it's kind of interesting to have someone who's supposed to be a colleague and supporter turn out to be such a pain in the neck and super-bitch).

However, when the long-delayed entry of the homunculus Sloth occurs (the big guy who's been tunnelling since forever), Olivia Armstrong returns to the fray with a vengeance: now she's captaining a team of tanks as the Briggs Castle community battles against the big, dumb, slow Sloth homunculus. This part of the *Fullmetal Alchemist manga* is a full-on action sequence, with our heroes trying everything to destroy or at least control Sloth.

But the *manga* chapters of *Fullmetal Alchemist* (around the 60th chapter) continue to linger in Briggs Fortress, and it seems as if the *manga* isn't sure of itself, or where it's going. The atmosphere of (Cold War-ish) distrust and suspicion is milked dry (the military at Briggs Mountain are certain that the Elrics are Drachman (= Russian) spies). And thus, our heroes are put in jail – a sure sign that an author doesn't know quite what to do with her characters.)

There's a reconnaissance party exploring the giant tunnel that Sloth carved; there's a shady official visiting Briggs (General Raven); Zolf Kimbley (the Crimson Alchemist) shows up to cause more trouble; and the Elrics yell to be released from prison (all of this was covered in detail in the 2nd *animé* series).

Far more intriguing in the Briggs Mountain section of the *manga* is the sequence of alchemical detective work, where Ed works out that the villains are constructing the whole of the country of Amestris as a potential transmutation circle – presumably to create the mother of all philosopher's stones. Each place where there's been a conflict and bloodshed forms part of the circle. And the tunnel that Sloth's been building connects them all up.

This is the obscenity at the heart of *Fullmetal Alchemist* – that an entire country, and all of its citizens, are part of a giant operation to achieve what appears to be a scientific/ military goal. Later, when it's revealed that the homunculus Father is behind it all, in his bid for immortality and god-like power, the goals shift (but only slightly), while the abhorrence remains the same.

▶

When the Crimson Alchemist Kimbley turns up at Briggs Mountain, the plot thickens – Kimbley is yet another an ambiguous, shadowy figure who clearly has schemes of his own (and also seems to be working for the Führer; or at least, Kimbley uses the authority of the Führer and the military as a cover to achieve his own ends). Tho' he insists to Edward that he's not a pædophile, he does bring along the Elrics' chum Winry (author Himoru Arakawa does stretch credibly from time to time by

---

23 But it's the distrust of the government, which echoes that of Izumi Curtis.

twisting the narrative in order to include characters such as Winry-chan (in the *animé*, Winry insists that she's there to fix up Ed's automail for Winter use). But it's worth having Winry along for the ride).

In the *Fullmetal Alchemist animé* Zolf Kimbley was portrayed as a more out-and-out villain, his role being conflated with that of the *animé-* only character Frank Archer (in the first *animé* series). But at least when Kimbley arrives Ed and Al are let out of prison in order to get moving with a mission. (Kimbley also has an on-going rivalry simmering with Scar – the Kimbley-Scar duel on the railroad speeding thru the snowy night, reminiscent of the Akira Kurosawa-scripted flick *Runaway Train*, is one of the stand-out sequences in the middle of the 2nd *animé* series).

❯

The *Fullmetal Alchemist manga* continues to depict a complicated series of to-ing and fro-ing in and around Briggs Mountain, in chapters 71f. It becomes a little too messy, in terms of plot and action, with the Elrics, Winry, Miles and co. in one group, and Kimbley and his henchmen in another. There is an uneasy alliance with Scar (tho' this is more satisfactorily handled than the version in the first *animé* series, where the Elrics hook up with Scar all too easily, when they should be beating the hell out of him. The second *animé* series followed the *Fullmetal Alchemist manga* closely,[24] and took up nearly a whole episode with the long, talky explanations as to how Ed and Al agree to Winry offering herself up as a hostage for Scar, in order to make their escape. They do so only after being reassured a number of times about Scar's promise, and also because Kimbley & co. are closing in, because a snowstorm's brewing, and because they have to elude the forces from Central City).

❯

Far more interesting, though, are the flashback sequences, which finally reveal the roots of the alchemy in *Fullmetal Alchemist,* and the origins of the shadowy father of the Elric boys, van Hohenheim. The flashback begins in Xerxes: altho' Hohenheim seems to be 400 or so years old[25] (in the first *animé* series), the city of Xerxes is portrayed as an ancient world city (it might be Troy or Carthage or Athens).

Van Hohenheim is introduced in his youth as a lowly slave in a rich household who before long has entered into a Faustian pact with a black blob that floats in an alchemist's glass vessel. When the black amoeba is given a big, Cheshire Cat grin and a staring eye, we can see the link to the darkness in the tunnel at Briggs Castle, and also Pride-as-Selim. At first, the black blob comes over as a trickster demon or god, which's one of the principal personas of the Devil or Satan in world mythology: not evil so much as a force or energy that turns things upside-down, a child-like subversion.

So it's scenario of the Devil and a disciple, Satan and an acolyte, with the first homunculus offering whispered words to van Hohenheim that

24 The first time that Scar is introduced in the *Fullmetal Alchemist manga* is as a serial killer: he kills two guards outside Shou Tucker's place, storms inside and destroys the alchemist and his chimera. That's four people (and the family dog!) in the space of minutes!
25 The homunculi are 100s of years old – if Father created them not too long after the cata-strophe in Xerxes where he was truly born. Thus, they've had plenty of time to study humans.

taunt as well as invite. What is the bait? Immortality, once again (i.e., not dying). Well, it's worked for 1,000s of fantasy, adventure and science fiction stories, why not here? So the homunculus offers immortality – to Hohenheim, and to the King of the country (but of course the homunculus just desires it for itself: this is a homunculus with ambition! Well, it wants to get out of the glass vessel, for a start! There's a limit to what you can do inside a four-inch wide glass jar!).

The Xerxes flashback sequence culminates with a terrifying alchemical ritual, which foreshadows all of the subsequent rituals in *Fullmetal Alchemist*, when the ailing King, on the advice of the homunculus, orders a giant transmutation circle to be created (this section of the *Fullmetal Alchemist* series might usefully have been included as a prologue: it would've set up the origins of alchemy, and van Hohenheim's role in the nefarious deeds).

The lure is immortality – but the cost is human lives. Hohenheim, who's standing inside the circle during the rite, survives, but everyone else in Xerxes dies (Hohenheim wanders out to see the city empty and silent). The only other survivor is the homunculus, of course, now taking on the form of Hohenheim (the one who gave it the blood to thrive in the first place).

The Xerxes flashback sequence explains plenty of information (such as the origins of the Father character, and why Xerxes is now a wasteland, and the Elrics' fathers' role in all this), but the key elements are the motivations (lust for immortality for the King and the homunculus, and for freedom for Hohenheim), and the goals. Now we find out just how and why the homunculus came into being, how Hohenheim was involved, and how the two – Hohenheim and the homunculus – are tied together. We see how Father developed from the blob, and how his relation with the other homunculi works.

We can also appreciate the thematic material that Himoru Arakawa is weaving into the *Fullmetal Alchemist* series: that the homunculus, for example, is called 'Father', and how he/ it takes on the form of the Elric boys' father, Hohenheim. We can see how Hohenheim is depicted as a Viktor Frankenstein or scientist or alchemist figure, a clever explorer of the remote regions of knowledge, who gets more than he bargained for when he makes pacts with the unknown, and with a spirit in a glass jar.

The origins story of *Fullmetal Alchemist* is satisfying dramatically and thematically because it revolves around ancient desires and beliefs – the urge towards immortality (or to not die), for a start, and the desire for power. It also introduces the motifs of alchemical transmutation circles, the alchemical rituals which cost lives, and Faustian pacts with demons.

And with an amoeba-like blob for the chief villain of the whole *Fullmetal Alchemist* series, the homunculus Father, Himoru Arakawa creates a terrific villain, a spirit who is able to wreak havoc from a position of apparent powerlessness (trapped like a genie in a little glass jar), and to grow in stature, all the way up to a god-like entity.

※

In chapter 79: *Bite of the Ant*, there is a giant duel between Envy and the ragbag of misfits that includes Al, Scar, Mei, Marcoh and some chimeras. Finally Envy gets defeated – even in his monstrous state, as a giant, green, dragonish, doggish critter, Marcoh is able to vanquish him. But not entirely: Envy ends up as a tiny, slug-like, snail-like thing (resembling the baby creature in the 1979 *Alien* movie). And altho' he's encased in a glass jar, he's still able to cause trouble (by taunting li'l Mei Chang, who's been sent home to Xing by Scar. Envy may be a snail-like foetus, but if he can talk, he can still wheedle his way into Mei's conscience. Like all the best villains, Envy knows how to exploit his victim's weaknesses).

✳

In later chapters, 70-80, following the too-long Briggs Mountain chapters, the *Fullmetal Alchemist manga* loses its way somewhat (we have to remember that the *manga* was being published in installments over a long period – from 2001 to 2010, and it was consumed by readers in the context of a *manga* magazine that contained many other stories – typical *Monthly Shonen Ganen* stories were: *Soul Eater, Spiral, Watamote, Sekirei, Saki, Tokyo Underground, Inu x Boku SS* and *Papuwa*).

Ed and Al Elric are split up, and join separate groups. Ed winds up with Greed/ Ling, and a couple of chimeras (whom he dubs Donkey Kong and the Lion King). Al is aligned with Pride and Gluttony, and later, Hohenheim. Winry returns to her automail customers (which takes her out of the finale).

Some intriguing elements're introduced, however: for example, Greed takes over the body of Ling Yao, so they become a schizophrenic, Jekyll & Hyde personality (memorably visualized with Greed as a giant, grinning demon, dwarfing the human-scale figure of Ling within Ling's body). Himoru Arakawa squeezes quite a bit of comedy out of the struggles between Greed and Ling inhabiting the same body.

✳

The conversation between Hohenheim and Al is fascinating, as is the later one between Hohenheim and Edward. Here, Hohenheim informs Ed that *he* is the philosopher's stone that they have been searching for. That the philosopher's stone turns out in the end to be a person is a satisfying thematic twist in the tale (the first *Fullmetal Alchemist anime* used that concept, but made Al into a philosopher's stone at the end).

✳

Father emerges into the light in the latter part of the *Fullmetal Alchemist manga*, when Führer Bradley seems to have gone missing (last seen in a railroad train blown up on a bridge by his old rival General Grumman, another officer who has his eye on the top job in Amestris). So Father (accompanied by the homunculus Sloth) steps into the Führer's shoes, and lords it over the officials (and Olivia Armstrong wonders if this could be her moment to seize power). The notion of Father himself materializing in the throne room of Amestris didn't last long: it's better to have Father as a brooding presence underground.

*

The meandering plot in the later part of the *manga* loses sight of what *Fullmetal Alchemist* is about and what the Elrics are fighting for: in this respect, the first *animé* series was more successful in riveting the multiple plots back to the central plot, and the central characters, the Elrics (it's one of the hallmarks of Japanese cinema, that all events are related to the central issue).

However, all is forgiven when the action ramps up to a series of outstanding battles in ch. 86: *Servant of Darkness*, as Ed, Ling/ Greed and the chimeras take on the homunculi Pride and Gluttony in the countryside at night, near the Kanama suburb of Central City. Hiromu Arakawa opts to use watercolours and gouache as well as the usual black lines of *manga*, adding a softer approach to the mid-tones, instead of the harder lines of the screen tone.

Wow! The fighting in the forest intensifies to a wild, untameable level in the *Fullmetal Alchemist manga* in the chapters 84 to 87: clearly the notion of the heroes battling with the homunculi Pride and Gluttony inspired artist Hiromu Arakawa, firing her up to great artistic heights (as it did the filmmakers of the second *animé* series: from this point onwards, the *animé* is pretty much all action). These are among the finest action beats in the *Fullmetal Alchemist manga* – look at the variety in the drawings, all in different sizes, the variety of the drawing styles, and the use of black tone.

The duels are fierce and unrelenting: here's the homunculus Pride – in his two incarnations: as the polite, li'l dutiful son Selim Bradley and as a monster of darkness, all giant eyes and grinning mouths. Pride is a truly daunting opponent – we've seen how viciously those spiky daggers of darkness have sliced up victims (and how a bevy of tough-as-nails soldiers were reduced to quivering wrecks in the tunnel at Briggs Fortress. If you want to show something is scary, have a bunch of tough guys quailing).

Edward Elric comes up with the idea of dousing all the lights in the neighbourhood, so Pride's shadows can't operate in total darkness (would that work? Hmmm…). Unfortunately, that means no one else can see either! (Of course, *mangaka* Hiromu Arakawa has to cheat, and show us where Pride, Gluttony, Ed and the others are – no artist has come up with a satisfying solution to portraying scenes in total blackness!).

The forest battle sequence in *Fullmetal Alchemist* goes on and on, and it's all thrilling stuff. It really is probably the finest sustained sequence of action in the *Fullmetal Alchemist manga*. And at last Alphonse appears, and finally we get to see Hohenheim in an action scenario (apart from the earlier scene where Pride chases him in a tunnel). Hohenheim does something decisive within the story – by (as suggested by Al) imprisoning Pride in a black-out cage (where he can't use his powers. Unfortunately, and to Ed's fury, Al has been caught inside the cage too).

*

There's a minor glitch in the storytelling of *Fullmetal Alchemist* when tiny Selim (Pride) bangs a stick on Al's helmet inside the dirt dome which alerts Father as to his whereabouts,[26] via Morse code! So Kimbley, is sent by Father to Pride, to rescue him. Something a little more convincing than someone hearing Morse code from miles away is required.[27] Unfortunately, the *animé* used the same device – one moment when it should've departed from the *manga*.

✳

One of the memorable set-pieces in the *manga* by Himoru Arakawa was the belly of Gluttony sequence, where Ed, Envy and Ling find themselves swallowed whole by the bloated, simple-minded homunculus. The mythical forerunner is of course Jonah and the whale in the *Bible* (and similar myths), and in stories such as *Pinocchio* (in animation, the interpretation of Gepetto in the whale in the Walt Disney movie of 1940 is one of the stand-outs in the Disney canon).

But in *Fullmetal Alchemist,* it's not sea water that's sloshing around in this Hades, but – what else? – blood! There's something truly repulsive about characters wading knee-deep in blood (it's not something you see often – very difficult to achieve in traditional live-action, for instance. And we know that isn't chicken blood! Or pig blood! It's human). Himoru Arakawa has once again managed to take what seems to be a cliché of Gothic horror and made it anew. We've seen characters falling into garbage compactors (*Star Wars*), and dungeons (any swashbuckler movie), and quicksand (any action-adventure story), but seldom into more blood than poured out of the elevator in *The Shining* (the belly of Gluttony extends into darkness on all sides – it's *huge*). This is authentically creepy.

In the *Fullmetal Alchemist manga*, the scenes where Envy reveals his true self as a monster that's absorbed people is reminiscent of the *Urotsukidoji* series, where demons're composed of corpses.[28] The motif of a monster with skulls or corpses or screaming heads sticking out of it is truly horrific.

●

Following the battles in the forest in chapters 84 to 88, the *Fullmetal Alchemist manga* ramps up to its all-action finale. Whole chapters are given to duels, so it appears as if everybody is fighting everybody else: Ed, Scar & co. vs. chimeras and puppets; Mei Chang vs. Greed; Roy Mustang & co. vs. soldiers; the Armstrongs vs. Sloth; Al vs. Pride and Zolf Kimbley; Mustang vs. Envy, etc.

Some of these fights are long anticipated, and satisfying – Roy Mustang going up against the murderer of his best friend Maes Hughes, for instance: Envy. The Flame Alchemist burns Envy to shreds again and again, working himself up into a frenzy of vengeance (so that only Liza Hawkeye holding a gun to his head – rather preposterously – halts him in his tracks. That is, Hawkeye doesn't want Mustang to become an inhuman murderer). But in the end, the freak Envy, now reduced to his weeny,

26 It's Father who hears the distant tapping, via his endless battery of pipes which seem to connect him with everything in Amestris.
27 That's a feeble piece of storytelling! Where was the *manga* editor when that page got thru?!
28 Victims absorbed into a giant body occur in *Legend of the Overfiend* in the giant demon that is the transformed hero, Nagumo. And also in *Akira*, in the figure of Tetsuo.

shrimp-like status again, opts to kill himself (in a grotesque manner – by ripping the philosopher's stone out of his chest). Mustang is irked – because Envy's suicide robs him of his revenge.

On the down side of these final chapters of the *manga* of *Fullmetal Alchemist,* there are simply too many characters, so that the action scenes're stuffed with people. Despite the numerous villains in *Fullmetal Alchemist,* there ironically aren't enough villains to go round (so new ones have to be created, such as the immortal puppets with souls attached to them, which act as zombies).[29] The action sometimes becomes simply that – just action, and the story, the characters, the relationships, the themes and everything else in *Fullmetal Alchemist* are thrown to one side. So we lose sight of what all of this fighting is actually about. The action also features too many of the secondary characters, so we lose track of our principal charas – Ed and Al Elric. (Here, the 2nd animated series delivered sensational action scenes, and also cut between the groups of charas often, so the dramatic momentum is sustained).

On the plus side, the action sequences in the final chapters of the *Fullmetal Alchemist manga* are stupendous visually. Hiromu Arakawa has delivered her most inspired drawings yet, letting herself spread out across every page with large panels, plenty of speed lines and zipping, crackling alchemical magic, and gouts of blood (always rendered as solid black in the *manga*). Characters are framed in large silhouettes, as fire and smoke and alchemical energy lines zigzag around them.

The narrative and dramatic ingredients may be lacking in the final chapters of the *Fullmetal Alchemist manga,* with action taking over – after all, all of the chief characters are in place, and battle must commence! – but the visual invention and the sheer *energy* blasts across the page. There's a point in an action-adventure *manga* when all of the pieces are in place, and the artists let themselves go. They've done all of the character-based work, all of the set-ups and scenarios, and now they can *fly!* You can see it with Masamune Shirow in his *Appleseed, Dominion: Tank Police* and *Ghost In the Shell manga,* or Katsuhiro Otomo in his *Akira* epic.

The fights go on and on and on and on and on and on... One smashing blow to the skull follows a slash across the chest with a sword... One character spouts a shower of blood from a cut shoulder, while another sustains head injuries that would take down even a special forces professional soldier at their peak in real life... Sloth the giant homunculus is punched in the face repeatedly, and has pointed pillars of stone shoved into his maw and out of the back of his head... And the Flame Alchemist, Roy Mustang, burns to shreds Envy with waves of fire while the critter screams...

There's no end of spectacular imagery in the final chapters of *Fullmetal Alchemist.* It really is *tour-de-force* of *manga* art, with Hiromu Arakawa making every effort to top everything she's done before in the

---

29 As Hiromu Arakawa runs out of villains (as if there weren't enough of them already!), and needing more obstacles for the heroes, she adds henchmen such as the zombie-puppets injected with souls, and the poor dudes who were rejects from the candidates used in the creation of the homunculus Führer Bradley.

nine years of the comic's run.

The finale of *Fullmetal Alchemist* is also, however, fantastically, almost insanely violent (one can imagine a psychologist, looking at *Fullmetal Alchemist*, arguing for Hiromu Arakawa to be taken away and placed in a mental institution). Because the level of aggression is truly disturbing. And it's not only amongst adults – little Mei Chang is also subjected to a lot of violence (and one of the chief villains is a 10 year-old boy, Selim Bradley).

●

In a hostage situation, in TV and movies, the price is never paid: the villain grabs the girl or the child and threatens to kill them, but they never do. The hero always find some way of either (1) dispatching the villain, (2) talking their way out of the situation, or (3) something else happens which alters events.

In *Fullmetal Alchemist*, poor Liza Hawkeye is captured by the Bradley cast-off mutants and has her throat slit: Roy Mustang, Scar and others are nearby and can't stop it. *Whew!* – it's not often that one of the heroines gets slit open so that she's bleeding to death. It's really gruesome. But, this being *Fullmetal Alchemist*, with its life-and-death and beyond-death scenarios, we know there's a possibility that Hawkeye can be resurrected or at least returned from the Gate of Truth. You can't kill the sweet, devoted, determined Hawkeye!

This very extreme scene occurs in the *Fullmetal Alchemist manga* in one of the countless battles in the final fifteen chapters. We've seen Führer Bradley returning from the railroad explosion to fight the guys at the HQ in Central City (there's an extended duel between Buccaneer and Bradley, Greed/ Ling and Bradley, and Lan Fan and Bradley). The fights go on and on, and Bradley proves utterly unkillable, even when he's been run thru with a sword and dropped from the HQ's gateway into the moat.

As the action and battles move closer to the villain's lair under-ground, where the Gold-Toothed Doctor presides over another despicable alchemical ritual, there are multiple duels. The Doctor who keeps a bunch of rejects from the Frankensteinian creation of King Bradley is a partic-ularly venal psychopath, demanding that Roy Mustang open the Gate (by performing human transmutation). It's here that our heroes are defeated by the Bradley cast-offs, and Liza Hawkeye is taken hostage and sliced with a sword.

One thing's for sure in the *Fullmetal Alchemist manga*: Hiromu Arakawa doesn't hold back when it comes to piling on the blood and guts and violence! Yet, despite all of the physical brutality which would finish off any ordinary human within seconds, Arakawa-sensei, like all authors, is very reluctant to sacrifice *any* of her major characters. Thus, altho' the Armstrongs are beaten up badly, they don't die; neither does li'l Mei Chang, or Roy Mustang, or Ed, or Al, or Scar... The big bear from Briggs Mountain, Buccaneer, does eventually die (though only after he's had his arm ripped off by Führer Bradley, and has been stabbed and slashed 147,893 times), and Fuu too expires (also fighting the Führer).

With so many characters to keep track of, to give something to do, and to make all of the comic tie in to the themes and central plots of *Fullmetal Alchemist*, Hiromu Arakawa comes up with an unusual solution to getting rid of some characters: she has Pride/ Selim Bradley eat them! Thus, if it's getting confusing or too difficult maintaining the flow of the events with so many villains, Arakawa has Pride swallow Gluttony! Well, it is of course a fundamental aspect of ancient mythology, and it is also a key motif in fairy tales.

Thus, that ten year-old boy, Selim Bradley, who from the outside seems like a regular Japanese kid, eats Gluttony and also Zolf Kimbley, and then the Gold-Toothed Doctor. And Father bloats up and up, becoming even more of a super-villain, to the point where, in the final chapters of *Fullmetal Alchemist*, his/ its whole body is a black-on-black shape with those grinning Cheshire Cat mouths and staring eyes planted all over it.

●

The finale of *Fullmetal Alchemist* has to pay off a number of storylines, primary among them being the quest of the brothers Ed and Al to attain their bodies (to pay off the scene which opened the whole *manga*). However, the finale's over-arching story is a simple heroes vs. villains battle – it boils down to the heroes (led by Ed, Al, van Hohenheim, Roy Mustang *et al*) fighting the chief baddie, Father, and his henchmen, Pride, Wrath, puppets *et al*.

But *mangaka* Hiromu Arakawa builds in plenty of twists and turns in the climax of *Fullmetal Alchemist*: after quite a bit of finagling to get the chief characters among the heroes into a single, enclosed space (inside Father's body, below Central City), in order to battle the villain, Father, the action comes thick and fast. Everybody is given something to do, and subtextual/ psychological themes are woven into the conflicts. For instance, the victims that Father has chosen for his ultimate transform-ation into a god have all transgressed the laws of alchemy: Ed, Al, Hohenheim and Izumi Curtis (Father includes chess piece versions of them on a drawing of the transmutation circle like a chessboard, as a visual device to summarize his/ its part of the story). In order to include Roy Mustang among the victims, the plot device of forcing him to open the Gate while using his aide Liza Hawkeye as bait is employed. Mustang isn't one of the select few who've crossed the line into death alchemically (he's too strait-laced for that!), but it's fun having him included in the finale.

So Father's ultimate goal is to become even more powerful – to become the hermaphrodite 'perfect being' of alchemy, the 'magickal child', the fusion of opposites, of masculine/ feminine, sun/ moon, black/ white, etc (and later to become (like) a god). To achieve that, Father needs the five 'sacrifices' of the heroes. That's just the beginning, tho' – because pretty soon Father, in his guise as a grinning, glaring demon all in black, has co-opted everybody in Amestris into his evil scheme. The *Fullmetal Alchemist manga* cuts to all of the secondary characters in small panels ranged across the page clutching their chests as the wriggling black hands of Father steal their souls.

We are now into epic, no-holds-barred high fantasy territory in *Fullmetal Alchemist* – Father opens the Gate of the planet itself, transforming himself at the total eclipse into a colossal, black demon, clambering out of a gate the size of Japan and taking on God himself. The impressive, planet-scale imagery is reminiscent of the climax of *Aladdin* (1992), the Disney movie where the evil wizard Jafar aims to become a god, controlling the universe, and of *Princess Mononoke* (1997) and its Shishigami deity (Hayao Miyazaki's influence runs throughout *Fullmetal Alchemist* – the comic, the animated shows, everywhere).

Unfortunately, Father makes a very big mistake when he returns to his lair underneath Central City. Of all the places he could visit, he goes right back to the one place where there's a bunch of people who're desperate to kill him! And those people are some of the few on Earth who *can* kill him! After becoming a god, wouldn't you want retire to a palace in the Tibetan mountains, maybe do a bit of ski-ing, create a few concubines, join the gods' platinum-card club?

No, Father goes right back to Central City in Amestris, to sit on his throne, all regal-like. Nobody can miss the fact that Hiromu Arakawa has designed Father in his god-like guise as reminiscent of Edward Elric (and also van Hohenheim). With his bare chest, blond locks, and chiselled cheekbones, Father's appearance draws on images of rebel angels, including of course Lucifer (in *Paradise Lost* by John Milton), as well as a New Pop band of the early 1980s, and an Ayran fascist.

Father also doesn't look particularly happy, despite attaining a god-level status: he returns to Central City primarily to gloat over the heroes, and to destroy them. Wait – hasn't he got anything better to do?! So *yet another battle* ensues: Father vs. everybody else (Pride appears to be fragmenting slightly – tho' there is a superb duel where the two pint-sized charas – Pride and Edward – go up against each other).

Van Hohenheim gathers everyone around him, and together they combat Father's zipping, zinging, crackling alchemical attacks. Luckily, clever Hohenheim has foreseen what that little, black homunculus in the jar from Xerxes would ultimately try to do, so he's already put in place the means of counter-attacking. There's an amusing moment when Al and Ed're standing behind Hohenheim, helping him to withstand the assaults of the Father-god's magic, and Al says, 'come on, Dad!', while Ed is more to the point: 'don't give up, you old bastard!'

●

And so to the final chapters of the epic *Fullmetal Alchemist manga* saga: I have to admit, I was hoping and expecting the ending to be much more emotional than it was. The *manga* series closes as one would expect, with all of the major and secondary plots tied up. Everybody gets to do their bit in defeating the villains – with Father chief among them. It takes *a lot* to topple this character.

So Alphonse has his body returned to him. What is the price? In true fairy tale style, the cost is Ed's own alchemical powers: it's Ed, in the end, who makes the ultimate sacrifice, offering himself up, Christ-like, to atone for all of his previous sins (primary among them being the desire to bring his mother back to life). Ethically, morally and psychologically (and spiritually), the heroic sacrifice that Ed makes is absolutely correct. It works wonders: but, somehow, it doesn't quite pack the emotional punch that it should do, after 108 long *manga* installments (equivalent to about 270 regular chapters). Somehow, the emotional catharsis isn't quite in place. It's not rushed but not quite long enough or involved enough. Or maybe it's just that we readers hope that this *manga* will run and run forever. (The second *animé* series, however, was much more successful in generating the necessary high emotion and catharsis, to pay off the *long* journey thru this extraordinary story).

But that's a minor quibble, because the ending of the *Fullmetal Alchemist manga* doesn't lack for spectacle, for 'wow' moments, for sheer intensity and action. It is blasting thru the *manga* reader on all levels, a sustained assault on the reader. Of course, nothing less than a stops-all-out ending, in terms of incident and noise, would suffice. *Fullmetal Alchemist* MUST rock in the final pages. And it does.

And there is certainly an immense feeling of relief and rightness when poor, little Alphonse Elric finally has his body returned to him. After all those years of suffering as a hollow suit of mediæval armour! Al has had his moments of doubt, and loneliness, and depression, but his reward is to enter the Gate, to take his (rather emaciated body)[30] back thru the Gate, into the world of Amestris.

The ending of *Fullmetal Alchemist* is beautifully worked out at dramatic, psychological and thematic levels: both Alphonse Elric and Edward Elric sacrifice themselves to save the other; both sacrifices involve alchemy and the transformation of the body; and both pay off everything that's happened previously.

And – koo-koo-ka-choo! – it's sweet romance ♥♥♥ time in the series of *dénouement* scenes as Ed finally plucks up the courage to ask Winry Rockbell out on a date. Well, not quite like that! – but he does confess some of his feelings for her, in his awkward, teenage, roundabout way. And at a railroad station, too! Well, shoot, you might as well use a cliché or two in the final chapters!

One of the curious aspects of the long sequence of *dénouement* scenes in the *Fullmetal Alchemist manga* is that *mangaka* Hiromu Arakawa splits the Elric brothers up: so Al and Ed are going their separate ways, on a mission to research other forms of alchemy. Part of the reason is so that Ed-kun can have his romantic moment with Winry-chan alone, and there's no acknowledgement of Al's feelings for Winry, because he's already far away (there have been hints all thru that it was Ed who was going to Get The Girl). Arakawa also returns the lads to their initial status, as eager, young students, bursting with enthusiasm to study study study[31] (which, of course, is what got them into trouble in the first place,

30 Complete with long toenails, *à la* Howard Hughes, a detail the *animé* also retained.
31 Reflecting the pressure cooker emphasis on education and achievement in modern Japan.

when they raided their father's books for information on alchemy. Alphonse voices his enthusiastic desire to see the world, to see and experience it all. It's part of Arakawa's central philosophy: *you must move forward*).

Speaking of Elric senior, what happens to him? Well, this too is unusual: van Hohenheim traipses off on his own, while the others are busy celebrating their victory, all the way back to the graveside of his wife Trisha in Resembool. To die. Yes, he has some moving final words, droops his head, and expires sitting on the grass in front of her tombstone. (To prepare for this scene, the *Fullmetal Alchemist manga* had already hinted that Hohenheim's time was running out – he is already fragmenting after the battle with the Father-creature, and he tells Edward that he has only one soul left).

WELCOME
BACK.

Winry and the romantic subplot.
The climactic reunion (above).

KYAAAAH!

WAAAAAGH

!?

WEL-
COME
HOME!

AHA
HA!

YEAH
!

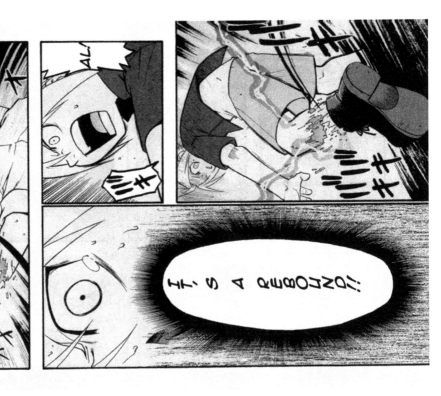

Later pages of the manga, featuring Hohenheim.

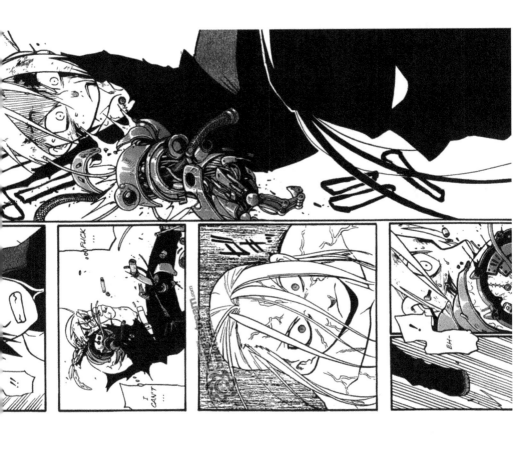

CHAPTER 87 - "AN UNDERGROUND OATH"

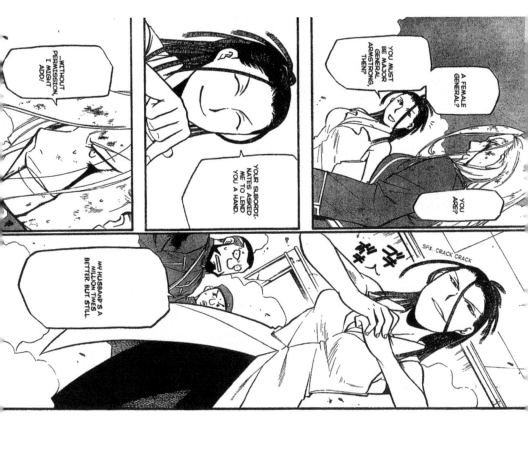

A page from the omake (left).
Arakawa's self-portrait on the
cover of Fullmetal Alchemist (right).

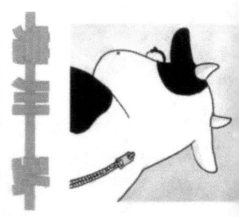

私がこの本のカ
バーなどによく描
いているウシ（3歳）が
「あともう描いてくれよ」
と横目で睨んでくる。
目を描くのがめんどくて
少しバッてつけちゃうから。

02

THE STORY OF THE
FULLMETAL ALCHEMIST MANGA

The following section summarizes the story of the *Fullmetal Alchemist* comicbook by Himoru Arakawa (published in *Monthly Shonen Gangen,* 2001-10) in a concise manner, as the episode guides to the two animated TV series of *Fullmetal Alchemist* also go over the story many times.

There are 108 chapters in the *manga* of *Fullmetal Alchemist* (a magical, symbolic number in the Orient): chapter one: *The Two Alchemists (Futari no Renkin-jutsushi,* published on July 12, 2001), introduces us to Ed and Al Elric, with the amazing scene of the transmutation ritual the lads perform to bring back their mother from death. Comprising only four panels on a single page (over black, the usual indicator of a scene set in the past in *manga*), the transformation scene is absolutely fundamental to the world of *Fullmetal Alchemist,* and the *manga* returns to it several times (and each time proves to be some of the finest moments in the *Fullmetal Alchemist* series, as also in the animated versions). There are many elements that aren't defined, tho' – we don't see Al (Ed calls for him), we don't know what the rite was for or about – the explanations come later. (But we can guess some of it, when we soon see Al as a suit of armour, and when Ed's automail is revealed).

Chapter one: *The Two Alchemists* rapidly introduces the audience to the heroes, El and Al Elric, their arrival in the city of Liore in Amestris, the demonstration of fixing the radio with alchemy, the jokes about Ed's size and people mistaking Al for the Fullmetal Alchemist, to Rose Tomas, to the cult of the Sun God Leto, to Father Cornello, and to issues such as alchemy, religion (and alchemy/ science vs. religion), death, and bringing someone back from the dead (Rose yearns for her dead lover Cain, and makes a bargain with Cornello, which of course mirrors the Elrics' transmutation rite to resurrect their mom).

Notice how Ed derides organized religion as soon as the topic is raised – at the café (by the owner); he has no time for it whatsoever, preferring to trust in the science of alchemy. Ed's scepticism is affirmed many times in *Fullmetal Alchemist* – and forcefully in the conversation with Rose in the church, which contrasts religion with science, spirit with matter, the magical or spiritual realm vs. the real, earthly realm, and hopes and dreams (Rose) vs. hard facts (Ed).

As soon as Father Cornello realizes that a State Alchemist is snooping around Liore, he orders his henchmen to get rid of him (the command automatically damns him – he's just ordered the death of a teenage boy). This swiftly inaugurates the first Big Action Scene in the *Fullmetal Alchemist manga* – the first of literally hundreds! Himoru Arakawa delivers gory, crunching violence and action in the familiar manner for the boys/ young adults audience: bone-crushing punches, people being smashed in the head, and a man pulling a revolver on our teen heroes and firing point blank in their face (Al's helmet goes flying).

The action shows our heroes working as a team, their martial arts moves, and the astonished reactions of people when they see that the suit of armour's hollow. The first action scene also shows how the villains in *Fullmetal Alchemist* have no problem with going from zero to full lethal aggression in moments, and with attacking instantly, and with killing children.

The Elrics want something – the philosopher's stone that Father C. wears set in a ring; the villain, of course, wants to get rid of the pesky kids: chapter one: *The Two Alchemists* climaxes with the expected face-off between the heroes and the villain, and the superb reveal of Ed in his automail as the Fullmetal Alchemist – the sweep of the superhero cloak, the frozen superhero pose, and the superhero frown.

The finale of chapter one: *The Two Alchemists* contains the mandatory smackdowns – Edward versus a chimera – and also the first time that Ed is seen in the present tense using alchemy (to conjure a spear to trounce the monster – a favourite move of Ed's).

The 52 pages of the first chapter of *Fullmetal Alchemist* (*The Two Alchemists*) demonstrates why this *manga* is such a hit, and so fascinating. It's got two wonderful lead characters, it's got an intricate and fully realized fantasy world, it's got a compelling philosophical/ metaphysical background of alchemy, it brings in Big Issues, like death, resurrection, loss, organized religion and political corruption, and of course it delivers terrific action. No wonder, then, that *Fullmetal Alchemist* is a 100% classic, as satisfying, exciting and inventive as *Naruto, Bleach, One Piece* or *Berserk*.

✳

To counter the boysy content of the *Fullmetal Alchemist manga*, Himoru Arakawa has, by page fourteen of volume one, introduced the young, attractive Rose Tomas. A curvaceous late teen with long, flowing hair, she might easily be a possible romantic liaison for Edward (but the romantic potential is not considered at all – it is quite some time before the *manga* acknowledges the teenage desires of the young heroes, Ed and Al).

Chapter two of *Fullmetal Alchemist, The Price of Life* (*Inochi no Daika*), continues directly from the finale of chapter one, with our heroes battling

Father Cornello and his corrupt regime (with Rose Tomas employed as the go-between figure, the conscience, the ordinary person in amongst the battle of wills between religious leaders and alchemists).

This is a key theme in *Fullmetal Alchemist*: the people at the top in *Fullmetal Alchemist* are not to be trusted; they are portrayed as self-serving, vain, sinister, pompous, wicked and dangerous – the government, the cult in Liore, the mining town, etc.

Chapter two: *The Price of Life* dives into a flashback to the transmutation ritual, like chapter one: now we find out plenty more about it (which Ed is explaining to Rose in the present tense). Importantly, we see Al in his human form, the eager younger brother of Edward (and that there is no adult looking after these kids – it's a *long time* before their father is brought into the picture. Hohenheim is talked about for many chapters b4 he enters the frame).

As the conflict with Father Cornello continues, another significant theme is introduced in *Fullmetal Alchemist* – the morality and ethics of the boys wanting to transmute their bodies back to what they were. Cornello is merely the first of many people to point out that the Elrics are dabbling in things that are ethically unsound, and illegal (even tho' Ed insists, with a glower, that they want Cornello's philosopher's stone only to reform their bodies. But when they discover how philosopher's stones're made, they change their minds).

Enough talk! Back with the action! Blam! Rat-at-at-at-at! It's an alchemical fight, the first of many in *Fullmetal Alchemist*: Cornello transmutes his walking stick into a machine gun; the boys respond with a stone wall to protect them from the hail of bullets, a motif reprised numerous times in the comic (and Al acts as a shield for Rose, which he does many times in subsequent chapters for other people). The boys don't always go on the offensive – they are more often defending themselves (usually from adults – yes, this is a story in which our teen heroes are pitted against adults, not against other kids).

After the Elrics escape (beating up more of Cornello's heavies along the way), there are further flashbacks, as Alphonse tells Rose more about what happened years ago in Resembool.

The finale of chapter two: *The Price of Life* and how the boys get the better of Cornello, is ingenious: like an invading army, one of the first things to get control of is the media. So the Elrics set up a scene where Cornello will betray himself via a radio broadcast – using the same broadcasting mechanism that Cornello deploys to sermonize to the populace of Liore.

We know that Father Cornello is going to be no match for our heroes: the face-off between Edward and Cornello is slam-bang action, followed by the kicker that the philosopher's stone that the priest's been using is actually a fake. Ed, isolated in a theatrical spotlight (which Himoru Arakawa uses in her *4-koma*), is furious (and when Ed's eyes turn into black holes, you know he's *really* angry!).

The come-uppance of Father Cornello climaxes with a wonderful flourish – Ed uses the enormous statue of the Sun God Leto to smash down onto the priest.

It's all been for nothing – all of that effort to obtain a philosopher's stone, and it turns out to be a fake. This is a recurring motif in the *Fullmetal Alchemist* series: searching for something that either doesn't exist, or isn't what you thought it was, or that proves dangerous in the end.

Edward's words to Rose Tomas, as she sits dejected on the ground (with the customary giant sun of *manga* in the West), are crucial:

Keep moving forward.

It's one of the mantras of the *Fullmetal Alchemist* series.[1] (And it also expresses the fundamental ethics of *shonen manga*).

The Elric brothers are not killers, and Himoru Arakawa rightly is very reluctant to make them killers (Ed even says that he doesn't want to kill anybody). So it's not the boys who dispatch Father Cornello: that's left up to the homunculi, in the coda of chapter two, *The Price of Life*.

Ah, the homunculi!

They are one of Himoru Arakawa's remarkable inventions. To invent genuinely *new* villains, that we haven't seen before, and who are really threatening, is very difficult (try it!). Each of seven homunculi is given outrageous skills, each one is murderously venomous, and each one is marvellously individualized, with striking and inventive designs. (To confirm how inspiring they are, look at the two *animé* series of *Fullmetal Alchemist*, and how the filmmakers took up Arakawa's concepts and designs and soared with them).

Over a mere five pages in chapter two: *The Price of Life*, Arakawa-sensei brings in the homunculi, and shows them in action. A half-page drawing introduces us to Gluttony and Lust (super-fat Gluttony, a simple-minded oaf, a big ball of hunger, grinning manically, chewing the remains of the chimera he's just eaten (he tries to eat everything he encounters), and slinky Lust, a smouldering and vicious *femme fatale* with her Goth-a-rama outfit, black dress, bouncy cleavage, and long, black, curly tresses – a gift of a look for cosplayers). These two weirdos are the first of a host of monsters that populate *Fullmetal Alchemist*.

Father Cornello turns up, spluttering with angry complaints (the homunculi, it turns out, are behind the religious cult in Liore). Cornello is a mere puppet, then, and once he's out-lived his use, he's topped by the villains.

Edward Elric got his name apparently from the movie *Edward Scissorhands*, and there's an *hommage* to the 1991 movie here, when nasty Lust unleashes her spiky fingers and skewers Cornello in his bald skull. It's the first death of a significant character in the foreground and the present tense of the *Fullmetal Alchemist manga*, and it's perpetrated by the villains on their stooge (and Gluttony eats him, although Lust advises him not to).

✳

---

1 Do you think Arakawa-sensei says it to her kids? Or to her *manga* assistants?!

Chapter three of the *Fullmetal Alchemist manga*, *The Mining Town*, has our heroic duo travelling to a mining community in the countryside (way off to the East of Amestris). They soon discover that the place's down on its luck, and is being run by dodgy authorities (working for the Amestrisian government). This is a self-contained adventure tale, with no homunculi in sight (here, it's the government that's the villain, as with the ruling powers in Liore).

It's here, at the Yousewell mines, in comical scenes, that the Elric boys come face to face with people who don't appreciate what the military government and its State Alchemists are up to, or what they represent. The *Fullmetal Alchemist manga* is keen to show that not everybody thinks highly of alchemy or alchemists – that, in short, the Elrics are not super-heroes who're applauded for protecting the nation.

Kicked out of the Halling family inn (and *very* hungry), Ed Elric seethes with resentment. It's soon revealed that Loki and his administration is dishonest, extorting the poor populace like the Sheriff of Nottingham in a *Robin Hood* scenario. So Ed plays the good Robin Hood, friend of the people, using his status as State Alchemist (complete with the silver watch as a token of political power), to impress Loki and turn the tables.

Chapter three: *The Mining Town* is a classic children's adventure tale, told in a mainly humorous manner, in which child heroes enter a crummy, immoral situation, discover who's exploiting the masses, and render a suitably spectacular come-uppance. Not with action, this time, but with Ed politically out-manœuvring the slimy officer Loki. So the mine is switched ownership from Loki and co. to the innkeeper, Halling.

✳

Chapter four: *Battle On the Train* is a straightforward action-adventure episode, once again portraying the Elric brothers as do-gooders, scuppering the nefarious, kidnapping plans of some Eastern extremists, the 'Blue Squad' (headed up by their brutish, eye-patched commander, Bald).

Every action beat you can think of using railroads and rival outfits battling for control of the train, within an action-adventure context that draws heavily on the American cowboy genre, is included in chapter four: *Battle On the Train* (in the *animé*, the filmmakers added plenty more). It's enjoyable fun with no one getting seriously hurt (well, General Hakuro does have part of his ear shot off by the heavies), and, at the end, Bald slices up two Amestrian guards (and in turn is fried by Roy Mustang).

Which brings us to some of the important new charas introduced in chapter four: *Battle On the Train* of *Fullmetal Alchemist*: toppermost is Colonel Roy Mustang, Ed's boss in the Amestrisian military. Suave, handsome, smug, self-confident, a ladies' man, the 'Flame Alchemist' irritates Edward automatically, just by his mere existence (so it's the familiar antsy relationship between the hero and his boss).

Liza (Riza)[2] Hawkeye is the second recurring chara introduced in

2 Some translations use 'Riza' instead of 'Liza' (it's the Japanese 'R' and 'L' issue again). I quite like 'Riza', even tho' it's obviously meant to be 'Liza', because Hawkeye's full name is 'Elizabeth' (Roy Mustang uses it as a code name). So 'Liza' it is in this study.

chapter four, *Battle On the Train*: pretty, quiet, modest, hard-working, dignified, a dutiful soldier, a crack shot, and ever-loyal to her crush, Roy Mustang, it's easy to see why Hawkeye is a fan favourite (she's placed third behind Ed and Mustang in some readers' polls of fave charas in *Fullmetal Alchemist*).

❀

Volume one of *Fullmetal Alchemist* closes with some 4-*koma*, some humorous self-portraits of Himoru Arakawa (as a cow being menaced by Scar), and Roy Mustang joking that volume two will feature him as the hero, in a re-titled *manga, Flame Alchemist*.

Himoru Arakawa has stated that she enjoys producing the *omake*, the bits added onto the *manga* chapters published in the magazines. Actually, many *mangaka* are the same – it's an opportunity to cut loose, and not take everything so seriously, including to send themselves up. (Actually, Arakawa includes many humorous moments within the *Fullmetal Alchemist* chapters, with *chibi* charas, and self-referential jokes).

✳

Chapter five: *The Alchemist's Suffering* (= *Renkin-jutsushi no Kuno*, pub. May 22, 2002) introduces and develops several important issues, and returns the *Fullmetal Alchemist* enterprise to much more sober territory (as in the first two chapters). One is that the Elric boys are engaged on a programme of research into alchemy, introduced in the Liore chapters (hoping to find a way of getting their bodies back). The second is that they are working under the jurisdiction of the military, and of Roy Mustang's outfit in particular. Third is the character Shou Tucker, the 'Sewing Life Alchemist', a guy who's apparently transmuted a chimera, a living, talking creature.

In both animated versions of *Fullmetal Alchemist*, and in the *manga*, chapter five: *The Alchemist's Suffering* is where things taken a downbeat turn in the present tense, after the traumatic prologue in the past.

Shou Tucker is a middle-aged, glasses-wearing,[3] unshaven loser, a deadbeat dad (as they say in *The Simpsons*), someone who's on his last ounce of luck, and desperately needs a victory in his alchemical research in order to pass the annual exam (to receive funding for more research).

While the Elrics are impressed by the library of books at Shou Tucker's place (Edward is immediately engrossed in a book when he visits), much creepier is the sight of jars and cages containing botched biological experiments (introducing a Frankensteinian, ye olde alchemie theme).

There are many scenes in chapter five: *The Alchemist's Suffering* featuring the *kawaii* daughter Nina of Tucker, and the giant dog Alexander, which are sweet and gentle. Why so many drawings of fooling around outside with the dawg and the girl? Because Tucker-san soon transmutes them into a chimera (thereby damning them to a miserable existence which ends soon with their death at hands of Scar).

When Edward Elric hurls Shou Tucker against a wall and punches

---

3 All you see are the blank circles of his glasses.

him repeatedly, it's a much more serious kind of violence and action in *Hagane no Renkinjutsushi*: the chapter takes *Fullmetal Alchemist* into very cruel territory, where a father will sacrifice his daughter in order to succeed in his job.

This is another moment in the animated TV series of *Fullmetal Alchemist*, following the opening scenes, where the hero loses his leg, when you go, *whoa!*, this is *not* going to be an action-adventure show where no one really gets hurt ('cept the odd villain). This show is going to go *there* – to those nasty, shadowy zones where d-e-a-t-h rules.

Afterwards, of course it's raining, as the Elrics sit on the steps of their military HQ, dejected, angry, feeling miserable that they weren't able to save Nina. Roy Mustang's unsympathetic response is the tough love twist on Himoru Arakawa's mantra: *you must move forward*: 'how long do you plan on staying depressed?... Can you afford to be held back by some-thing so small?'

Well, if *one* serial killer isn't enough for you, chapter five: *The Alchemist's Suffering* introduces *two*! Please welcome, ladies and gentle-men, one of Himoru Arakawa's most vicious characters, a mass murderer and religious zealot: Scar. White hair, red eyes, shades, chunky jacket and a white scar on his noggin – Scar is on a one-man-mission to rid the world of heathens, blasphemers, heretics and anyone who opposes the God Ishbala, or the monotheistic, Ishbalian way of life.

And that includes alchemists: Scar cuts his way thru two guards to enter Shou Tucker's home, where he swiftly dispatches the hapless Tucker, intoning, 'Alchemists who have strayed from the path of God must die!' And Tucker explodes from the inside in a shower of blood, while the chimera Nina watches... And then Scar slays Nina. Talk about grim!

Chapter six: *The Right Hand of Destruction* continues the story of the Elrics in East City, with Scar now on the loose and killing State Alchemists.

The Right Hand of Destruction opens with a *kawaii* flashback of Edward (aged about six) running to his mom in the garden and present-ing her with an alchemically-created toy dog. This turns out to be a dream of Ed's, as he wakes up in bed, with the ghostly figure of his mom Trisha now accusing him that he couldn't put her back together.

So Edward Elric is not in a good place emotionally when he reports in with Alphonse at Roy Mustang's office that morning. The Big News in the military corridors is that Shou Tucker has been killed (both *animé* version altered the sequence of events in this part of *Fullmetal Alchemist*). And the killer is still on the loose.

The homunculi make an appearance here in chapter six: *The Right Hand of Destruction*, after disappearing for quite some time (since the end of chapter two: *The Price of Life*). Once again, Lust looks down scornfully on humanity from on high (we see street gangs beating each other up with steel pipes, as if they've wandered in from *Akira* by Katsuhiro Otomo).

Impersonating Father Cornello, a new homunculi is introduced, the fan favourite Envy: he's great value in the *manga*, but oh boy!, it's the filmmakers of the two *animé* versions of *Fullmetal Alchemist* that *really* go to town with Envy, turning him into a major diva. Spiky hair, black, cut-away top, black shorts, black wristbands, and wielding more attitude than a whole classroom full of neurotic, antsy schoolkids, Envy is a marvellous creation by Himoru Arakawa of the spirit of wicked, naughty play and downright murderous intent. (Envy's skill? Chameleon qualities – he prefers to impersonate people and create havoc and confusion with lies and deception. He doesn't like to fight – only later do we get to see the colossal monster that seethes within Envy).

So the Elric boys are sitting below the town clock in the middle of East City while there's a killer on the loose (when they're supposed to be holed up in their hotel). A very dumb guard calls to them out loud, when Scar happens to sauntering nearby, and overhears. Rapidly the expected confrontation occurs, the guard is attacked, the boys run, Scar pursues, and this time it's a proper, life-and-death battle.

While Bald's gang might've assaulted our heroes, that occurred within the lighter, more playful context of the adventure on the railroad train in chapter 4: *Battle On the Train*. But on the streets of East City, there is no doubt that Scar is determined to kill them (or Edward, at least). Himoru Arakawa delivers marvellous imagery of smashing, punching, slashing action, as the Elrics try their darnedest to avoid being splurched into bloody goo by Scar.

A full-grown psycho versus a 12 year-old boy? The *Hagane no Renkinjutsushi* series is full of such smackdowns. Once again, the device of attackers being foxed by Al being hollow and Ed having automail is used (Scar thinks he's trounced them, but no).

Ed is quick, but Scar is quicker this time: the climactic fight in the sixth chapter of *Fullmetal Alchemist* ends with Scar grabbing Ed's auto-mail arm and destroying it: this forms the last image in the chapter, a full-page drawing of Ed looking astonished, the pieces of the mechanical arm pinging apart,[4] with speed lines as the background. (The arm-destruction occurs again – most significantly in the battle with the Father-creature in the climax of *Fullmetal Alchemist*).

❋

Chapter seven: *After the Rain* plays out the cliffhanger and climax of the previous chapter. It opens with Edward in agony, his arm burst into pieces, with Scar towering above him, preparing to kill him. Alphonse screams out, 'EDWARD!', and the rain tumbles down. But Ed won't run, won't leave his injured brother behind.

Just in time, Roy Mustang's team arrive (by car): Mustang fires off a warning shot. It's revealed that Scar's behind the killing of alchemists, including Shou Tucker & co. Scar brags, Mustang yells, and then, as the action begins, the speed lines pop out (behind eight out of nine panels on two pages, for example). As Liza Hawkeye knows well, Mustang's fiery

---

4 This may be an *hommage* to Tetsuo in *Akira*.

alchemy doesn't work in rain, so, using guns in both hands *à la* the gangster films of Hong Kong cinema (popularized tho' not invented by John Woo), she fires at Scar. Unfortunately, tho' Hawkeye is a sniper and a great shot, she can't nail Scar at close range. So it's up to Alex Armstrong to strut his stuff, in the first big action sequence featuring the 'Strong Arm Alchemist' himself.

Both *animé* versions of *Fullmetal Alchemist* greatly enjoyed depicting Alex Armstrong going into battle, and it's easy in the *manga* to see why: with his pompous pontifications, his comical, he-man design, his ridiculously optimistic, zealous attitude to life, his proud boasts about his family, and his camp/ feminized affectations (like ripping off his shirt), Armstrong is always good value ('why did he take his shirt off?', Liza Hawkeye wonders, as Armstrong steps into an overhead spotlight). You can see that Armstrong is a favourite character with Arakawa-sensei: big, muscley guys are her kinda man! ('Men should be buffed and women should be va-voom!').

Scar has met his match in Alex Armstrong: they smash into each other repeatedly, until Liza Hawkeye takes aim and fires at Scar. When his glasses ping off, it's revealed that Scar is an Ishbalian, which means plenty to military men like Roy Mustang and Alex Armstrong (and Liza Hawkeye, too).

After Scar escapes into the sewers (the first of numerous escapes by Scar, even when surrounded by armed soldiers and being shot at), the *dénouement* after the bust-up involves Ed and Al: '*baka!*' Alphonse punches his baka-brother for not running when he had a chance. They argue. The soldiers nearby watch them. At least we're still alive, Alphonse insists. Yes: that is something: it's better than the alternative, as Jackie Collins puts it!

✳

Chapter 7: *After the Rain* of *Fullmetal Alchemist* then switches to the first of several explanations of what Ishbal is: a nation to the East whose religious differences with Amestris put them into conflict with the government. In the civil war with Ishbal, alchemists were sent into battle.

The conflab in Roy Mustang's office, involving many of the key players – Hawkeye, Armstrong, Hughes, Falman, etc – is crucial in outlining one of Himoru Arakawa's chief themes in the *Fullmetal Alchemist* series: intolerance in the political, social and religious arenas (and linked to issues such as race, immigration, refugees, etc).

On a more practical note, chapter 7: *After the Rain* closes with a beat that pushes the narrative towards the next chapter: Edward needs a new arm (so he can use alchemy, for one thing). So he has to make a trip to go see Winry and Pinako, his mechanics. There's a nice joke at the end of chapter seven: Liza Hawkeye sets it up: 'If Edward can't use alchemy, then he's just...' And the other characters fill in the blank: he's just: 'a little brat who swears a lot', 'an arrogant pip-squeak', 'useless, just useless'...

✳

Chapter 8: *The Road of Hope* opens with more humour, as nobody can

spare the time to babysit the Elric brothers back to Resembool, except...
Alex Armstrong. Talk about travelling with a very embarrassing
companion! Armstrong is like an annoying dad who, whatever he does, is
just *annoying*. And everybody stares at him. And the Elrics wish they were
travelling with someone infinitely less conspicuous. (Why did Arakawa
select Armstrong as the bodyguard for the boys? He's good value,
entertaining, humorous, and not an ordinary soldier (or character); also,
Armstrong acts as a sympathetic sounding-board for the Elrics. Later, we
discover that Armstrong has his own unusual family set-up).

So the Elrics journey Back Home (*tadaima*), to Resembool, with
Alphonse, who's been broken up by Scar, travelling inside a wooden crate
in the carriage with the sheep (!).[5] There's a touching goodbye from Maes
Hughes (soon to die), and some characterization scenes. Here having Alex
Armstrong as a bodyguard has advantages – he recognizes Doctor Tim
Marcoh on the station platform. Soon the Elrics and Armstrong are in
pursuit (Lust the homunculus is also on the train, travelling incognito –
she's tailing the Elrics, and she also has business with Marcoh).

Dr Marcoh flees shiftily ('shifty' is one of his key attributes), and it
takes A. Armstrong and the Elrics a while to track down where he's
living. Marcoh embodies the guilt and shame of working for the military
in the Ishbal War, and also the troubled issue of philosopher's stones
(these are what the Elrics are seeking). Marcoh is a nervous, shaken soul,
taken to running away from his problems (he literally runs away many
times in *Fullmetal Alchemist*).

Here, however, *Fullmetal Alchemist* wheels in the real philosopher's
stones into the foreground of the story (the one that Cornello used in Liore
was an impure compound). Edward is thrilled, imagining he's closer to
discovering the secrets of alchemy. Tim Marcoh, tho', refuses to tell them
more, or to hand over his research data.

At the railroad station, as the party is about to leave, Dr Marcoh
hurries up, having changed his mind. He won't give them the philosopher's stone (which's used to heal people), but he offers the Elrics hints
at how to find his research (which turns to be hugely difficult!).

So, there isn't much action in chapter 8: *The Road of Hope* – until, that
is, Lust also pays a visit to Dr Marcoh's place. Lust is much more
persuasive and aggressive than the Elrics – she pins Marcoh to the wall
with her Edward Scissorhands claws. Here we find out that the
homunculi are partially unkillable – Marcoh attacks Lust with a spike of
stone through the chest, but she/ it doesn't die (but she doesn't say that
she's been 'killed once', so maybe repeated attempts will do the job).

What does Lust want from Tim Marcoh? The research data on the
philosopher's stone, the same as the Elric lads. She also mentions that
Marcoh is going to be a 'human sacrifice' (what this means is revealed
much later in *Fullmetal Alchemist*, and Marcoh isn't one of the five
sacrifices in Father's plans). Thus ends volume two of *Fullmetal Alchemist*,
with dual quests for the philosopher's stone and Marcoh's research.

---

5 Couldn't they have brought his head at least to travel with them in the carriage?!

❀

A Home With a Family Waiting, chapter nine of the *Fullmetal Alchemist manga*, is one of the sweeter installments, as the Elric brothers reach their homeland, Resembool. It's a 'coming home' episode, a back-to-roots chapter.

A Home With a Family Waiting re-introduces two important charas not seen for a long time: Winry and Pinako Rockbell, the girl-next-door and possible girlfriend character, and the grandmother/ adviser figure. Both Winry and Pinako are good value, and any scene set in Resembool in *Fullmetal Alchemist* is beautifully realized (in both of the *animés*, too) – Arakawa has certainly nailed the concept of 'home' and 'homeland' perfectly.

There isn't any action in chapter 9: *A Home With a Family Waiting* (unless you count Ed and Al sparring, to exercise their rejuvenated bodies). Instead, it's chiefly characterization and back-story – as you'd expect from a 'coming home' episode. So we have Pinako and Ed yelling at each other (jokily) about their height, you have Winry chucking a spanner at Ed (mandatory in every Ed-Winry encounter), because he's wrecked her carefully-made-with-love automail again, you have Pinako and Winry fixing and re-fitting Ed's automail, etc.

The most important scene in 9: *A Home With a Family Waiting* is where Edward Elric visits the grave of his mother – set on (of course) a windswept hillside (a recurring scene in *manga* and *animé*, where ancestors are never forgotten). And, as often in *animé* and *manga*, this scene leads in to some back-story – to, you guessed it, the transmutation ritual of the very first page of *Fullmetal Alchemist* (where Alphonse carried the unconscious, wounded Ed to the Rockbells' place. The Rockbells are, understandably, absolutely shocked and upset at the sight of the maimed Ed and Al transformed into a suit of armour appearing on their doorstep. (Arakawa can't keep depicting scenes of people freaking out at Al's appearance – it would become wearisome[6] – but she includes reactions where it counts).

Several parcels of minor but significant back-story/ characterization in the fully metallic alchemy series are also included here: Pinako tells Armstrong that the Ishbal War took Winry's parents (including Pinako's son), for instance (so Winry is an orphan, like the Elrics, with their dead mother and absent father). And it's ironic that the war gives them so many customers for their automail, prosthetic business.

Death, war, dead parents, maimed children – the themes and issues that *Fullmetal Alchemist* grapples with are the bleakest in human history. Yet the drawings, in delicate, black outlines, suggest that this is a light-hearted *shojo manga*.

But once Edward regains his artificial limbs, his first job is to restore Alphonse. That done, the boys are soon sparring in the garden. More talk – this time to re-state the goals of the characters, in particular of Ed and Al. Next day, Ed is up and ready to go, not even bothering to wake Winry

6 That's why it's dropped, and the notion of someone walking around in full battle armour is simply ignored.

(she stumbles out of bed for a sleepy *sayonara*).

✻

Chapter 10, *Kenja no Ishi* (*The Philosopher's Stone*), takes the boys back to Central City, where they're immediately put into the care of two military guards, 2nd Lieutenant Maria Ross and Sargeant Denny Brosh (the next batch of parental surrogates for the Elrics. Alas, they are by-the-book grunts, nowhere near as entertaining as Major Armstrong). The kids head straight for the research library – only to find it in charred ruins (courtesy of Lust, who got there first. As she confesses to Gluttony, she didn't have time to go thru all of the books, so she torched the lot! Ah, that's the homunculi for you! Not big book readers!).

How Himoru Arakawa gets around this particular set-back for the Elric brothers is really over-the-top (or just plain hopeless): she introduces the speccy Sheska, the shy, humble Chief Nerd of Central City, who can – get this! – memorize everything she's ever read! So she simply writes out Doctor Marcoh's handwritten book (until she's hauled away by Maes Hughes to work for him). The boys get down to decoding *1,000 Meals For Daily Living*, the recipe book where Marcoh has hidden his alchemical findings (a cookery book is not a mistake – there are many thematic links between cooking and alchemy). Decoding arcane alchemical texts is a recurring motif in *Fullmetal Alchemist* – Scar's brother's work, Marcoh's research, or Father's plans, etc.

Meanwhile in chapter 10: *The Philosopher's Stone*, Scar is still at large (in East City): Gluttony,[7] who can smell an Ishbalian miles off, has a go at nobbling him (in the sewers), and fails.

Chapter 10: *The Philosopher's Stone* ends on an Ominous Note: Ed 'n' Al eventually decipher Tim Marcoh's cookbook, and are stunned: the chief ingredient for making the philosopher's stone is 'A LIVING HUMAN BEING!!'

Well, we could sort of guess where the alchemical researches were heading. But Himoru Arakawa develops this concept beyond the obvious and the sensational: she gives the use of human beings in alchemy a powerful spiritual and thematic edge.

✻

Chapter 11: *The Two Guardians* continues directly from chapter 10, with the brothers suddenly stopped dead in their tracks by their new, grim discovery.

The question that's debated at length by the boys and their minders Ross and Brosh now is: who else knows about this? Does anybody in the military government know? Who can they tell? Alex Armstrong is brought into the loop, advising that they keep it quiet until he finds out more.

Along with this plotline – the Elrics seeking the philosopher's stone – Himoru Arakawa includes Scar creating mayhem, and also the homun-

---

7 Arakawa places Lust and Gluttony in the same space as Mustang and co., as it enhances the storytelling – by sitting on the roof, while he's seen in an office below. Now this is just silly – two characters like Lust and Gluttony stand out a mile, and they are shown in a military compound in full daylight (and during a man-hunt for a serial killer when security would be tighter'n ever!).

culi with *their* quest (which includes both items – tackling Scar, and searching for the philosopher's stone). At this point, we still haven't met all of the homunculi, don't know really what their overall objective is, how many there are, what their operation or resources comprise of, or who's controlling them (if anyone).

There are many scenes of the brothers sitting about and talking in chapter 11: *The Two Guardians,* as they decide what to do next, and whether they're going to remain in their damaged states for the rest of their lives.

Once again, it's Edward Elric who realizes that there must be more to Dr Marcoh's research. He remembers Marcoh talking about 'the truth that lies within the truth'. Edward takes up a map of Central City; Armstrong points out the locations of the alchemical laboratories; Ed reckons it must be the one next to the prison (where fresh corpses can be obtained with nobody asking any questions).

Ordered to say put while Alex Armstrong does some investigating of his own, of course the first thing the brothers do is to climb out of the window at night and sneak off to visit the mysterious fifth laboratory on their own. The nighttime escapade rapidly accelerates into parallel action scenes, with two formidable (and dead) adversaries: Number 48 and Number 66 (two former criminals, now hollow suits of armour, just like Alphonse, and tasked with guarding Lab 5. It's typical that Arakawa should add not one but two hollow men to offer a mirror to Al's fate. Well, two are needed, of course, because there are two brother heroes to fight).

Number 66 attacks Alphonse outside the laboratory, while Ed is set upon by Number 48 (who's actually two brothers), after discovering a giant, alchemical circle drawn on the floor of the main hall. Out come the speed lines as Himoru Arakawa delivers a terrific double duel for the Elrics, intercutting talk with sudden, brutal motion. Alphonse is going to be OK, as he's already a hollow suit of armour, but Ed has to work hard to defeat the two criminals transformed inside Number 48 (he is cut up in the process)

❋

Chapter 12: *The Definition of Human* continues the two duels of chapter 11 at laboratory 5. Number 66 can't beat Alphonse, so he tries psychological tactics – by sewing seeds of doubt in the young boy that he might not really be Alphonse Elric, but something his brother conjured up using alchemy. This induces a crisis of identity for Al (which continues into the following chapters). It is a little silly that Al should believe anything an enemy who's trying to kill him should say – but then, he is a fourteen year-old kid, not a veteran warrior (where the best method is: kill first, talk later).

Meanwhile, it takes all of Edward's cunning and strength to defeat the suit of armour that is Number 48. He uses tricks to confuse Number 48, and thinks he's won; but Number 48 is two souls joined together, and revives to attack Ed.

But Edward doesn't get to find out all he wants from Number 48, after defeating him, because this is the moment where Himoru Arakawa has chosen to reveal the homunculi to our heroes: Lust and Envy loom out of the darkness. Their first act is to kill Number 48. The last page of chapter 12: *The Definition of Human* depicts the two homunculi grinning at Ed, who realizes that these guys are at a whole other level of weirdness and menace.

❊

Chapter 13 of *Fullmetal Alchemist* (*Steel Body*) continues directly again from the end of the previous chapter: Envy grabs a sword and stabs the blood-seal of the body of Number 48. He dies. Edward watches in horror – it's as neat a demonstration of the threat the homunculi offer our heroes as you could imagine, because Ed's brother Al just happens to be a hollow suit of armour with a seal of blood, too.

Edward is attacked by Envy, but the homunculi tell him they've got to let him live. Meanwhile, outside, reinforcements arrive, to help Alphonse. The laboratory is detonated by the homunculi (a reprise of the torching of the research library). Envy carries out an out-cold Ed on his shoulder. Our heroes flee. Nearby, a new chara, Zolf Kimbley, rejoices in jail at the sound of the explosions (a reminder of the Ishbal rebellion that he participated in). Ed recovers in hospital: here Lt. Ross literally slaps some sense into Ed. Winry promises by phone to travel to Central to fix Ed's automail (in another of their comically prickly conversations). And Al, poor Al, sinks into a depression over having his identity and origins questioned.

✳

Chapter 14: *The Feelings of an Only Child* brings one of the main female charas of Himoru Arakawa's *Fullmetal Alchemist manga* into the foreground again: Winry Rockbell. She arrives in Central, and meets Alex Armstrong. Winry fixes Ed's automail. They talk. Al slopes off to sulk. Roy Mustang argues with his opposite number, Maes Hughes (item: marriage, item: his cute daughter, item: Edward being in hospital). Hughes visits the Elric, and drags Winry off to see his family for his daughter Elicia's birthday party (a reprise of hauling Seska away to work for him).

Not a homunculus in sight, no duels to the death, and no grand action sequences. Instead, chapter 14: *The Feelings of an Only Child* is all about characterization, telling us more about the Elrics, Winry, Hughes and Mustang (principally); Winry bonds with Elicia-chan; Hughes tells her that the Elrics are typical boys, who don't want to worry anybody about their problems; Ed tells Winry that Al's been acting odd recently. The title of chapter 14 – *The Feelings of an Only Child* – refers to Winry, and Winry is the central character here. The chapter climaxes with an argument between Alphonse and Ed, with Winry stuck in the middle: 'I DIDN'T WANT TO GET THIS BODY!' Al yells.

✳

Chapter 15: *Steel Heart* exploits the rift between the two teenage brothers. Al seethes, sulks, bottles it up, and then explodes. Both Winry and Ed're shocked – they've never seen Alphonse like this. Winry performs one of her recurring functions in Himoru Arakawa's *Fullmetal Alchemist manga* – to act as an intermediary btn the Elrics brothers, and also to be our muggle stand-in (Winry-chan is extra-cute, but she isn't an alchemist, chimera or homunculus). In this chapter, Winry plays mother, hammering some sense into Al with a spanner (Winry points out to Al that it's ridiculous that someone would transmute a fake brother in a hollow suit of armour). Winry orders Al to go and talk to Ed, and yells at the boys to stop being boys. (Several charas yell at the Elrics from time to time – here, it's Ross, Winry, and later, Armstrong).

How do the brothers resolve their disagreements? – by sparring, of course. And after the rush of physical activity, they get to say what they really wanted to say (in the customary *Fullmetal Alchemist* pose: lying back in a cruciform pose, looking up at the heavens). (Winry-chan and Maes Hughes watch this reconciliation from the doorway at the top of the stairs. In the *animé*, of course Winry weeps, crying the tears the lads refuse to shed).

*

The second half of chapter 15: *Steel Heart* returns us to the villains' central plot of *Fullmetal Alchemist*: the homunculi, what they're after, what happened at the 5th laboratory, and what the homunculi said (Edward draws a rubbish sketch of Envy to show the alchemists).

Who should turn up here, but Führer Bradley, the leader of the nation of Amestris, no less. We still don't know that Bradley is a homunculus, but the fact that he's sticking his nose in here is suspect (the officers around Ed's hospital are stunned – Ed does seem to attract some high-power visitors. It's as if you're having a secret conflab and Adolf Hitler walks in). The Führer commands everyone to keep the homunculi secret.

Ed and Al decide to go to Dublith (to meet their *sensei*, Izumi Curtis), and Winry-chan begs them to take her along, and to stop at Rush Valley (Automail Heaven), along the way. With the teenagers out of the way, the *Fullmetal Alchemist* shifts into much more solemn territory, with a sequence leading to the death of a significant chara, Maes Hughes.

Altho' the Führer has warned them to maintain secrecy, and not to trust anybody in the military, Maes Hughes continues his investigations. Very soon, he encounters the deadly homunculus Lust. She's quick with her extendible talons, but Hughes is also as nifty as a ninja with his throwing knife (however, a non-alchemist human is no match for a homunculus).

At this point, Maes Hughes does something that seems foolish: he doesn't call upon aides, or guards, or anyone to assist him, but tries to make a phone call to Roy Mustang. He's alone, he's wounded, and he goes outside at night to a call-box (for some reason, it's a British-style phone box), to keep the call secret.

The very nasty Envy is the homunculus who kills Hughes-san – by impersonating Lt. Ross, then Hughes' wife Gracia. As Hughes momentarily hesitates, he's shot. Mustang yells on the other end of the line, but the phone's dead. Now we see why Himoru Arakawa built up Hughes as an important secondary character, and also emphasized his home life, with a loving wife and an adorable daughter (that he enthuses over to everyone in sight). Notice, too, that Hughes has interacted with the two main charas many times, and also Winry-chan and Mustang-san – and Armstrong, Bradley, Ross and Brosh, etc. So his loss is felt by many characters.

*

Chapter 16: *Separate Ways* (which features a photograph of Mustang and Hughes from the past on its splash page), opens with the heroes re-setting their goals and their motives. As they journey (by train, yet again) to the South, they re-affirm their objectives: to ask their *sensei* about human transmutation, to pursue their quest of retrieving their bodies (and to get strong again).

While they eat a pie cooked by Maes Hughes' wife Gracia, in an ironic parallel scene, Hughes-san is receiving the full dramatic send-off, with a funeral with military honours. Everyone weeps, including Mustang. He resolves to uncover the people behind Hughes' murder. Armstrong goes against the Führer's orders, and tells Mustang a little about what Hughes was investigating (it's enough to give Mustang and Hawkeye some clues).

The *Fullmetal Alchemist manga* now switches pace and location, moving to the dreams of Scar, recovering in the Ishbal refugee camp: he remembers being attacked by the homunculi (really, after being set upon by Gluttony *and* Lust, Scar should be ash now). Scar wakes, discovers he's in an Ishbalian slum, and converses with the village elders.

*

Chapter 17: *The Boomtown of the Broken Down* is a side-story, as the Elric brothers stop off in Rush Valley (largely to please the automail fanatic Winry Rockbell). This is a lengthy side-story, and a departure from the gloomy main plots of *Fullmetal Alchemist*. It's an opportunity for some fun and games for the Elrics (Edward joins an arm-wrestling competition in the street, for instance – using alchemy to cheat). Ed's silver pocket watch is snaffled by a thief, Bunny (Paninya in the *anime*). A young, black woman in a black Tee shirt and combat pants (with a particularly Tezukan design), Bunny is a little too smug and too good. The chase that ensues is provides light entertainment, with broad, cartoony alchemical action and Bunny always one step ahead of the lads. (And it consumes most of the chapter).

*

The side-story continues in chapter 18: *The Value of Sincerity,* with the brothers allowing Winry to talk them into visiting the automail manufacturer way up in the mountains who made the automail legs that Bunny wears (she was rendered a cripple by an accident). Among the multiple plots in chapter 18: *The Value of Sincerity* are: Winry begging the stern, old automailer Tommy to take her on as an apprentice; the back-story of Bunny; Winry discovering what Ed wrote inside his watch; and the set-piece: Lear's wife Sadila is about to give birth.

✳

The birth sequence continues in chapter 19: *I'll Do It For You Guys!* In the adventure genre, when someone gives birth, it has to be nighttime, and raining, and miles to the nearest doctor, and the rope bridge is broken, etc (births can't occur in pleasant, daytime settings, in a fully-resourced hospital). So Winry, Bunny and Lear deliver the baby, in some of Himoru Arakawa's funniest scenes of mass panic (very entertaining in the *animé*, where it was Hughes' wife Gracia who had the baby). The subtext is clear: you alchemists can perform magic, but *real magic* is giving birth! Yes, *you* try making a living, breathing human being with science or magic!

Ed and Al're humbled – and delighted. 'That's wonderful! The baby's born!... this is the birth of a new life!' In the aftermath scenes, Ed and Winry have one of their sweetest exchanges in Himoru Arakawa's *manga*, as Winry tells Ed that she saw what he'd written in his pocket watch. Grumpy automail engineer Tommy is stunned to discover that Winry is Pinako Rockbell's granddaughter (he has scary memories of her), but grudgingly agrees to teach her some automailing secrets. Which leaves Ed and Al free to continue their trip South, to Dublith.[8]

Chapter 19: *I'll Do It For You Guys!* closes with the brothers reaching Dublith, and walking to the butcher's store run by their former teacher, Izumi Curtis. The meeting is built up in the boys' minds as something to be feared, and the storytelling emphasizes that their *sensei* is a formidable person. The chapter ends with the towering figure of Sig, Curtis's hubby, brandishing a bloody butcher's knife (Sig is a big, silent softie, but it's par for the course in the action-adventure to introduce each new chara as a potential threat. Certainly, Sig *looks* threatening!).

✳

Chapter 20: *The Terror of the Teacher* (*Sensei no Kyofu*) introduces the intimidating character of Izumi Curtis (a favourite chara for Himoru Arakawa). Scarily violent, imperious, stern and loudly proud to call herself a housewife, Curtis is also motherly and kind (when she chooses to be! But don't get on her wrong side!). She sports her hair in dreads and braids, wears a housecoat over black leggings, and has the body of a supermodel (another Arakawan 'va-va-voom' woman). She has also, like the Elrics, performed the illegal and dangerous alchemical ritual of human transmutation. It backfired, leaving Curtis with damaged internal organs (presumably including her womb – implied but not mentioned). So that Curtis is the perfect person for the Elrics to see to ask about human transmutation. She is also an authority figure who transgressed just like the Elrics did, offering further ironic commentary on their plight.

But not until Izumi Curtis has smashed the kids around aggressively (and repeatedly) for becoming dogs of the military, and for performing illegal alchemical rituals. The first time we see the Elrics' *sensei*, she's in bed; but she has enough energy to kick the lads flying in a double-page image (afterwards, she coughs up blood, which she does regularly, after each expenditure of energy).

---

8 There's no discussion about leaving a teenage girl with some people they've only just met.

A vital plot point is introduced here in *Fullmetal Alchemist*: in Central City, the Curtises met a guy they think was called Hohenheim – the Elrics' father (Ed goes into an immediate and deep sulk). There's talk around the kitchen table. The boys demonstrate their alchemical skills outside: when Curtis sees that Edward doesn't need to draw a transmutation circle, she is immediately suspicious. So, Ed has also seen 'that thing' (we don't know exactly what yet – the Gate of Truth).

This is the central theme of the *Fullmetal Alchemist manga* – interrupted by a demonstration of the theme from a bunch of kids from the neighbourhood: they have brought their toy train, which's broken. Izumi Curtis agrees to fix it, but not by using alchemy (introducing a key tenet of people who use magic – not every problem requires spells). A little girl, Manny, brings a dead kitten: 'Chiko's not moving'. Can the *sensei* fix that, too? Nope: it's dead. D-e-a-d. 'Living things are different from toys. I'm not God', Curtis admits. (This is, admittedly, highly artificial and on-the-nail story construction).

Next – we're at the kitten's new grave on a hillside, where Curtis-sensei and Edward Elric discuss the burning issue consuming the Elric brothers: human transmutation. The boys are shame-faced throughout this sequence, confronting their *sensei* with the awful truth that they attempted human transmutation, and were grievously injured in the process. What happened? Curtis wants to know. So Edward launches into the tale of that fateful day: this is one of the finest sequences in Himoru Arakawa's *manga*.

✻

Chapter 21: *The Brothers' Secret* (*Futari dake no Himitsu*) tells the story of the lengthy flashback to the ritual the Elrics performed as pre-teens. This is a magnificent section of the *Fullmetal Alchemist manga* – and it's a textbook example of how to orchestrate back-story and flashbacks, and to make them pay off in the present tense.

Home life is evoked – Himoru Arakawa-style: the Elric brothers are seen examining books in their father's study, and drawing alchemical circles on the floor. And they demonstrate to their mom Trisha how much they've learnt about alchemy just from books. 'To make our Mom praise us – this simple wish started our interest in alchemy'.

The back-story is covered montage-style, with short vignettes to illustrate events running over several years. Until that fateful moment – when the boys discover their mom dead on the floor (note the tropes, typical of Himoru Arakawa, of food and cooking (both the Elrics and their mom carry vegetables and fruit) – which perfectly express the maternal realm of symbolic – and real – plenitude).

The scene where the kids sit and sit at their mother's graveside, when it's getting late, and cold, and Al's complaining, is where It All Starts: this is where Edward suggests: 'maybe we could revive mom!'

Panels of the kids at school are included here (not in either of the animations): Edward expresses the feelings of millions of school kids every day all around the world: 'It's boring!' (We know that Ed, a smart-ass kid if ever there was one, would be a troublesome tyke to teach! But

Ed is right: *school is boring!*).

Winry R. is kept out of the loop, and the boys go home from school to continue their secret studies at night: 'if we could revive a dead person, everyone would be happy too!' Ed's seething resentment of van Hohenheim is introduced several times: that bastard didn't even come home for mom's funeral! Edward gripes.

❊

Moving the back-story along now, Himoru Arakawa introduces one of her favourite characters: Izumi Curtis, a housewife who's proud to called herself a housewife! (As Arakawa recalled, the scene of 'Who the hell are you!?' 'I'm a housewife!' was 'a scene that I wanted to do for a long time'). When you introduce an important character, it enhances the piece if you can have them Doing Something Significant: here, it's saving the community from flooding, using alchemy.

In a panicky scene of heavy rain and people rushing about with sandbags trying to stop a river breaking its banks, Izumi Curtis happens by, along with her silent giant hubby, Sig. The Elrics are watching the efforts of the men to hold back the river. Curtis uses alchemy to build instant embankments. Everybody's amazed. But when Curtis hacks up blood, the price of alchemical power, the Faustian bargain (equivalent exchange), is vividly represented.

It's here that the brothers beg, plead and demand to be taught alchemy (because they've got only so far with their studies from books). Yes, folks, school may be boring, but good teachers are still valuable in *Fullmetal Alchemist*. The scenes are comically; the Elrics call Curtis old woman (which Curtis hates); they hang onto her legs and arms while she tries to shake them off; eventually, big sis Curtis (with the help of Pinako), is persuaded (the expression of solemn determination on the boys' faces is marvellously done (it's one of the iconic scenes in *Fullmetal Alchemist*, and is reprised later).)

The method, though, for the training of Izumi Curtis, is a tad unusual for an initiation trial: if they survive a month on an island in a lake without food or water (and come back with a good answer to the riddle, 'one is all, all is one'), she will train them in alchemy.

Curtis-sensei embodies the phrase 'tough love': the Elrics are furious to discover that their alchemical training involves a hellish month on a food-less, shelter-less deserted island. Well, not quite deserted – a dude in a grinning animal mask and wielding a club plays havoc, chasing the boys about and fighting them.

❊

Chapter 22: *The Masked Man* continues the trials and tribulations of the 11 and 10 year-old Elric brothers on Jack Island. Fleeing from the maniac terrorizing them (he wants them off 'his' island), or finding animals to eat, takes all of the boys' efforts. How do you kill a rabbit looking up at you with big, sad, Disney eyes? You can't – so a fox steals it. And when the kids finally catch a fish, it's nabbed by the madman in the mask.

The insane routine goes on and on – the creepy, abusive nature of a grown man beating up two young, unarmed kids (for no apparent reason), is avoided (the guy simply yells at them to leave his island). Eventually, too exhausted to even move, and starving, the boys collapse. The man cooks some fish for them.

Edward Elric works out the answer to the 'one is all, all is one' riddle by applying it to the food chain: it's the 'circle of life' routine from *The Lion King*. Everything is connected to everything else. You die, you become food for other living things or systems.

So when Izumi Curtis turns up in the rowing boat, ready to collect the Elric lads, after the month is up, they have their answer ready: "'One' is me, 'All' is the world'. Big sister Curtis laughs (at the solemn intensity of the boys), then agrees to teach them. They are over-joyed. And in the boat they meet the guy in the mask – he's Mason,[9] sent by Curtis to look after them. 'Then why did you make him attack us!!' Edward yells. 'Fool! This way you can learn more in a month!' is Curtis's answer.

❋

Chapter 23: *Knocking On Heaven's Door* continues this extended flashback to the childhood of the Elrics. They return to Resembool, fix a wrecked sheep cottage using alchemy, return for more training with Curtis-sensei,[10] and plan their grandest scheme: to bring their mom back to life (without telling their teacher).

So we approach the Great Mistake once again in the Elrics' past, this time after following their months of training in alchemy (notice that Curtis-sensei hasn't told them about being able to transmute without using a circle, which she calls 'true knowledge').

The boys gather the ingredients of a human being: 35 litres of water, 20 kilos of carbon, 4 litres of ammonia, 1.5 kilos of lime, etc (it's a rare story which boils down humans to simply a list of ingredients, like a recipe). Put them in a tin bath. Draw the alchemical circle on the floor. Prick their fingers for drops of blood. And begin the ritual.

This time round, Himoru Arakawa reveals different views of that calamitous event – such as the little, black grabbing hands and arms, the disintegration of Alphonse and Ed's leg, Ed stretching out to Al to grasp his hand, and Ed ending up at the giant Gates of Truth.

This is the first time we visit the limbo of the Gates of Truth (not heaven, not hell, not purgatory, not anywhere familiar), and encounter the brilliant device of the grinning demon/ god/ self/ universe/ all/ one that sits nearby. Himoru Arakawa's artwork becomes truly inspired, as she evokes abstract, cosmic events, using lots of white space, the demon/ god being defined negatively (inside, it's a white space, with a hazy, black outline[11]), the doors opening, the enormous eye in the blackness, and the twisting, grabbing hands.

Yanked inside the Gates of Truth, Ed Elric undergoes a cosmic trip, with flashes of history zipping past (dinosaurs, wars, foetuses, eyes,

---

9 Left out of the 2nd series.
10 She duels with both of them while reading a book, and lecturing about alchemy.
11 That might be made with an ink diffuser.

skeletons). A D.N.A. spiral.[12] Ed upside-down. His leg disintegrating. Emerging from the Gates of Truth, the demon/ god tells Ed that he's just experienced 'true knowledge' (i.e., everything, all at once).

In his Viktor Frankenstein mode, as a scientist or explorer who wants to go further, do more, have more, Edward E. asks the demon/ god if he can see it again: 'there was true knowledge regarding human transmutation. What I needed to know is just ahead!' Himoru Arakawa introduces the Faustian bargain right here: the demon/ god, with that scary, cheesy grin, takes the 'passage fee' to get here: Edward's leg.

Now we return to Resembool again, with Ed clutching his leg, screaming (another upside-down image). He sees the botched creature in the middle of the alchemical circle. 'It wasn't supposed to be like this... This is not what we wanted.'

In a state of fury and hysteria, Edward Elric, at his most exposed, vulnerable, desperate and terrified, begs and pleads for the powers to return Alphonse to him. 'Return him to me! He's my only brother!' he cries. Here's where Ed writes the bloodseal inside the suit of armour, and bonds Alphonse's soul to it. The price is his arm (we see the demon/ god in the Gates of Truth limbo absorbing Ed's arm. 'That fool. He's back for more').

This is a magnificent example of storytelling, with Himoru Arakawa balancing spiritual/ cosmic spectacle with intense emotions and yearning. Arakawa develops some unusual symbols and images to portray the extreme metaphysical experiences: an eye, a grinning demon, grabbing hands, giant gates, disintegrating limbs. There really isn't another *manga* quite like this.

✳

12 The D.N.A. spiral, plus the cosmic trip, might be an *hommage* to the end of *Akira*.

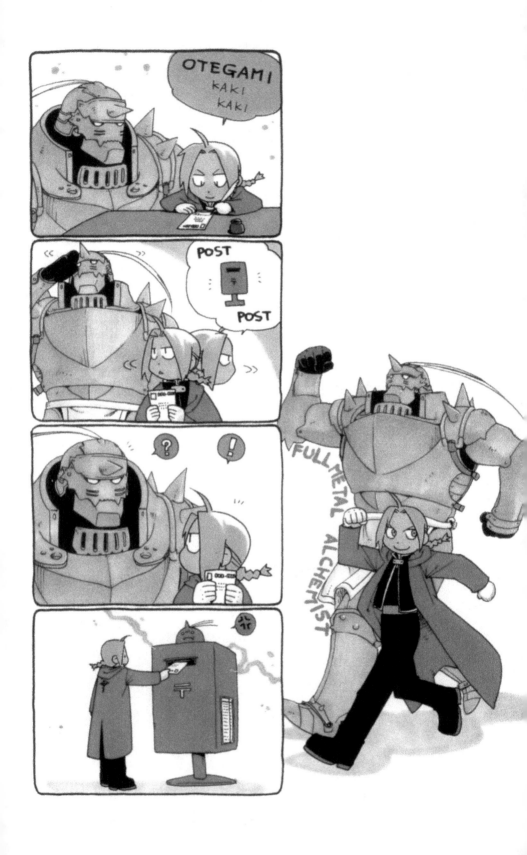

Chapter 24: *Fullmetal Alchemist* shifts the flashback sequence a few days or perhaps weeks onward. The chapter contains plenty of story-telling – an invitation to join the military; Ed's automail operations; a trip to East City; the alchemy exam; and Ed becoming a State Alchemist.

Now Roy Mustang re-enters the story (accompanied, as ever, by his shadow, Liza Hawkeye). He's travelled to Resembool to enlist the Elrics in the military (which's under-staffed following the Ishbal Rebellion). Here, Mustang has paperwork which says that Edward is 31. No, he's 11, the soldier guiding the visitors to East City tells him. So it's a mistake that Mustang goes to Resembool at all.

Roy Mustang's first response, on seeing the blood and the alchemical circle in the Elrics' home, is anger: when he reaches the Rockbells' place, he demands to know what happened. Ed is in a wheelchair, and Al is, well, he's a suit of armour. Both boys are chastened, ashamed, hanging their heads (Ed's eyes are in shadow).

But Roy Mustang is determined to have them enlist – he entices them by saying they would have access research material that might enable them to find out how to regain their bodies. For Mustang, the choice is simple: between living in hopelessness with a suit of armour for a brother, or selling yourself to the military with the possibility of finding a way to recover. (The irony is that, at the end of *Fullmetal Alchemist*, tho' the lads have learnt loads and have plenty of alchemical experience, they didn't need to enlist in the military at all. They could've achieved the final result in *Fullmetal Alchemist* without that).

Pinako Rockbell remains sceptical throughout the meeting (she has a low opinion of State Alchemists, and the military, as does Izumi Curtis, another of Himoru Arakawa's key female charas). Meanwhile, an important but modest conversation takes place outside the kitchen btn Winry Rockbell and Liza Hawkeye. Winry, who doesn't like the military either, asks Hawkeye if she's ever shot anybody. Hawkeye answers, yes. The combustible nugget of back-story about the death of Winry's parents is held back for later.

Edward opts to have automail fitted, a very painful operation. A year passes: the procedure is successful (Ed and Al're depicted sparring in the garden). The boys go to East City, meet Roy Mustang, travel onward to Central City, and Ed takes the alchemy exam (attempting an attack on the Führer, too). Ed's given a new name – 'Fullmetal Alchemist' – his pocket State Alchemist watch, and a uniform. (A flashback reveals that the Elrics have burnt their home, so there is nowhere to come back to. I bet that was Edward's idea! It's extreme, eh? How about selling it, to raise some cash? No? OK, how about donating it to some worthy causes – local, homeless folk, for example?).

✳

Chapter 25 of *Fullmetal Alchemist* – *Master and Apprentice* (*Shitei no Kejime*), resolves some of the issues between Izumi Curtis and her alchemy pupils. There always a price, right? Curtis-sensei informs the Elrics that some of her internal organs were removed when she tried to transmute her dead baby. After some understanding discussion, and a motherly hug, Curtis decides to end their apprenticeship: 'YOU GUYS ARE OUT'. The Shrimp realizes why: Curtis says, 'I didn't teach you alchemy so you could turn your bodies into that'. So they leave. And go to the rail station, where Sig informs them that tho' they're not Curtis-sensei's students, they can still talk to her. Immediately, in typical Edward Elric-style (and typical Himoru Arakawa-style), they do an about-turn, and head back to the butcher's store. Kneeling in humility, they beg their *sensei* for information about how they might recover their bodies.

The second half of chapter 25: *Master and Apprentice* shifts the focus to Roy Mustang, gathering his troops for a move to Central City (with the aid of General Grumman, a wily, old fox who also has an eye, like Mustang, on the top job, of Führer, which he attains at the end). Himoru Arakawa depicts a 'getting the band' together sequence, in a montage-style, moving to each member in vignettes (Hawkeye's gun training, Huey's fixing a phone, Breda's playing *Shogi* (a Japanese game), etc).

A new character is introduced now, a spy for the homunculus Greed, operating out of the Devil's Nest bar. Bido is a chimera with a long, reptilian tail – a weasly guy who sneaks about, and easily eludes the alchemical barriers put up by the Elric brothers when they run into him on the streets. (Yes, it is yet another alchemical battle in a back alley. But they do land some hefty punches on the guy).

The second new figure to be introduced in ch. 25: *Master and Apprentice* is Greed. He's portrayed as a Japanese *yakuza*, a handsome, cool guy in round glasses and spiky hair, with a girl on each arm on the couch, lording it over his gang in the basement of the Devil's Nest bar. (The girls don't last long – after this, Greed is surrounded by grizzled chimera types).

Greed proves to be a very entertaining character in the *Fullmetal Alchemist* universe: vain, arrogant, cool and deadly. A snappy dresser, with a sly grin, Greed seems to have everything – but of course, he wants *more* (as all mob bosses do! Especially when they're called Greed!).

❋

Chapter 26: *To Meet the Master* employs a rather artificial means of separating the Elric brothers (so that Alphonse can be captured by Greed's crew): Edward leaves for the Southern HQ for the annual assessment of State Alchemists (he suddenly remembers what he had to do). Off Ed goes, by train, while Al is kept behind by Izumi Curtis.

Meanwhile, the *manga* switches focus to Scar, recovering in the Ishbal refugee camp. After talk with the village elders (where Scar affirms he'll continue his programme of killing alchemists), Scar departs. But not after demonstrating just how mean he is (by wasting some guys who've come to collect the bounty on Scar's head). The elder tells Scar he'll have to break this cycle of vengeance. Instead, 'you have to endure it'. (A minor chara, Loki, the lieutenant lording it over the mining community in chapter 3: *The Mining Town*, is brought back by Arakawa-sensei, and becomes an unwilling and rather hopeless, cowardly and devious sidekick to Scar. Even though Loki has just sold out Scar to the bounty hunters).

✳

The second half of chapter 26: *To Meet the Master* stars Alphonse Elric – he's allowed to shine in his own major action sequence without his big brother stealing the limelight (as Ed, diva that he is, tends to do!).

Alphonse-kun is lured to the Devil's Nest bar by Bido (again, this is rather artificially achieved). The reason given is that Al is keen to know what happened to him at the Gates of Truth (this was discussed between Curtis and the brothers earlier. If they could find out, they might have some clues to regaining their bodies).

The bozos hanging about outside at the Devil's Nest are no match for Alphonse, even tho' several of them are chimeras. Their orders are to bring Al before Greed, but that's not easy when he's a suit of armour who never feels tired or pain, and can run for miles.

This action sequence is extended too long, really, for the narrative requirements (that's true of many *shonen manga!*), but it does serve to demonstrate the attributes of this new bunch of charas, the chimeras that Greed has in his employ (in fact, the Devil's Nest sequence features numerous duels, involving Ed, Greed, Al, Curtis, Armstrong, Bradley and all of the chimeras, as if Arakawa's editor Yoichi Shimomura asked for a ton of action).

There's an icky moment for Al, when the lovely Martel[1] dives inside his body and operates him from inside (it's not everyday, after all, that a beautiful and dangerous magical being leaps inside your body! Even in the world of *Fullmetal Alchemist*). In the event, it takes both Martel and Roa to subdue Alphonse (the heavyweight Roa jumps on top of him).

✳

Chapter 27: *The Beasts of Dublith* has Al captured by Greed's mob of misfits, henchmen and chimeras. These are charas combined with the body of a snake, a dog, a crocodile, etc. Most of them are actually not evil (they were in the military, and were used in experiments in laboratories).

Now we're introduced to Greed, the new homunculus. His goal? To find out more about alchemy and immortality. After all, he *is* called Greed:

> I'm very greedy! I want everything in this world! Fame also! Land too! I want money! I want women!

Don't we all! – Hearing this, Alphonse E., in his naïve, sweet way, decides that Greed's crew are not so nice after all. He attacks Greed, but it doesn't have much effect. Now we are shown some of Greed's powers: first up is regeneration. Having his head smashed off by Roa with a mallet is a rather extreme (and messy) demonstration (it grows back swiftly).

Greed's interesting, however, because he is the rebel among the

---

1 Martel is given a design that takes Himoru Arakawa's penchant for charas with slips of hair hanging loose from their foreheads to extremes. So she has a long, floppy strand of hair floating in front of her face all the time.

homunculi, an outcast, with his own plans, independent of the rest of the homuny folk, who work for Father. (And it's Greed who survives to the very last, among all of the homunculi, until the Father-creature tops him in the finale).

After a brief visit to the South HQ, to see what Ed Elric's up to (encountering Führer Bradley and Alex Armstrong, among others), the story moves to the Curtises' butcher's shop. Izumi Curtis is worried about Al, who's been missing for some time. The following sequence is one of the most enjoyable in the *Fullmetal Alchemist* series – it's where Curtis becomes Jet Li or Jackie Chan, a one-woman army, walking into Devil's Nest and calmly and effortlessly beating up every henchman who stands in her way (Arakawa's love of Hong Kong action cinema manifests itself many times in her comics).

What could be more fun than a self-confessed housewife who's also a brilliant martial artist and alchemist? And seeing her trounce weirdo after weirdo? Housewives aren't usually superheroes, but Himoru Arakawa seems to be enjoying herself with the characterization of Curtis.

When she's angry, she's *very* angry! *Sensei* is, as the Elrics know well, a formidable personality, and not someone you want as your enemy! The way that Izumi Curtis stalks into the Devil's Nest bar, tossing heavies aside like toys, is terrific – and even Alphonse is quaking (Curtis bawls him out, as expected, calling him a *baka* – 'why the hell did you get kidnapped?!'). Everybody in the bar is stunned – they've never met an opponent like this. One of them asks, 'Who the hell are you?', and Curtis replies, in a 3/4-page image, 'I'M A HOUSEWIFE!!' (this provides the climax of chapter 27: *The Beasts of Dublith*).

✳

Chapter 28: *A Fool's Courage* continues with the fun and games at the Devil's Nest bar involving Izumi and Sig Curtis versus Greed and his mob. When Curtis punches Greed, and he doesn't hit the deck, she realizes that he isn't wholly human (everybody else has been floored by the housewife). Greed, meanwhile, is gentlemanly, and prefers not to fight women.

Alphonse tells Curtis that Greed is a homunculus, and Greed tells Curtis that all he wants is information on how to transmute a soul. An exchange of info, then. Curtis doesn't like it, but she agrees that Edward might be able to provide that.

The *manga* of *Fullmetal Alchemist* duly switches focus to Ed, arriving back from Southern HQ in Dublith. At the railroad station he meets, of all people, the Führer, in a Hawaiian shirt, on vacation (and accompanied by Alex Armstrong. These are two people Ed really doesn't want to see). Bradley visits the butcher's, and wants to see Curtis (Sig stalls him). That Bradley acts so oddly so often, popping up in unusual places, should worry observers. Armstrong and Sig compare muscley bodies in a testosterone-fest (this scene, which recurs in *Fullmetal Alchemist*, might be a *hommage* to the scene in the movie *Laputa: Castle In the Sky*, 1986).

Well, yes, the ruler of the country who just happens to show up in a butcher's shop in a small town while pretending to be on vacation is an artificial situation, a way for *mangaka* Himoru Arakawa to bring her vast ensemble of characters together. It convinces only at the level that Bradley is a homunculus, and he's going to take care of Greed and company (under orders from Father, no doubt). But we don't know that yet, we just see the Stalin/ Hitler figure of Bradley who enjoys hanging out with working class butchers, or prefers to conflab with underlings in the suburbs rather than fellow politicos in the city.

Anyhoo, we know that Edward Elric is going to march into Devil's Nest to rescue his brother. And he does. Like Izumi Curtis, Ed has a *very* short temper – he will fly off the handle at the slightest provocation – and a bunch of guys who've kidnapped his beloved brother give him plenty of provocation! Edward's reply to Greed:

'DON'T TALK SHIT WITH ME!!! YOU KIDNAPPED MY
BROTHER! YOU INJURED MY MASTER!! AND YOU STILL HAVE
THE GUTS TO DEMAND EQUAL TRADE?!'

Himoru Arakawa draws our Ed in fury in large panels, including a double-pager: 'VILLAINS WILL GET NO EQUAL TRADE!' he cries, pointing his finger (like Naruto when he's at his most bullish in *Naruto*). Greed claps weakly, sarcastically. Dorchette is soon mincemeat at Ed's hands. And so the expected Edward vs. Greed smackdown begins. Ed is good, transmuting the stone floor into pointy missiles, but Greed smashes every attack.

Ed learns that Greed is at a whole other level from any opponent he's faced, including Scar and Curtis. He can grow a protective carapace that makes him like a N. American superhero of the 1950s or 1960s. And while Ed faces off against the Super-Greed, Al is hauled away by Roa and the other chimeras: the chapter closes with the appearance of Führer Bradley and his team. The chimeras stands no chance, as the Führer soon demonstrates (Hitler and Stalin might've been psychopathic megalomaniacs, but they weren't unkillable geniuses with swords like the homunculus Bradley[2]).

✻

Chapter 29: *Eye of the King* (*O no Me*) depicts the invasion of the Devil's Nest outfit by the Amestrisian military. They have orders to slay everybody except choice items like Edward and Alphonse. Meanwhile, Greed is smashing our hero Ed about savagely (the teen heroes of *Fullmetal Alchemist* receive *a lot* of beatings). Once again, it takes Edward a while to remember his alchemical training and knowledge, to find a way of breaking thru Greed's superhero shield (he attacks the carbon it's constructed from).

In a corridor underground, Roa is duelling with Armstrong (which swiftly becomes another of Himoru Arakawa's vicious boxing matches. For a shy, retiring, female artist, who doesn't like appearing in public,

---

2 But they didn't need to be – there was an endless supply of flunkeys to carry out their mass murders.

Arakawa-sensei sure does enjoy drawing burly he-men bashing the bejesus out of each other!).

Führer Bradley displays his mean fighting abilities, slicing up Dorchette and other opponents, including Roa. Greed has opted to flee, but he runs into the Führer (and Ed's been restrained by the military guards – he's desperate to go after Al). The action of chapter 29: *Eye of the King* climaxes with the meeting btn Greed and the Führer (it's something we haven't seen before – two homunculi fighting).

✳

Chapter 30: *The Truth Inside the Armor* has the chimeras Roa and Dorchette reviving, rushing to their master Greed's aid, only to be dispatched by the truly horrible Führer Bradley (Greed also seems down for the count, after being slain 15 times by Bradley).

Martel can't bear to see her comrades being defeated by Führer Bradley, but Alphonse won't let her out of his hollow suit of armour. Using Al's arm, she attacks Bradley, but the Führer stabs her. It's a disgusting sequence, where Martel dies inside Alphonse's hollow body.

The trauma is intense enough for Alphonse Elric to pass out and relive some of his experiences in the Gate of Truth years ago, seen in two double-page drawings that flash back to numerous moments in Al's life, in small, irregularly-sized panels (his father holding him as a baby, his smiling mother, Ed reaching for him, the grinning demon, and his body disintegrating...). In the second double-pager, Al is being literally torn apart by cosmic forces, clutching his brother's arm as he disappears.

Chapter 30: *The Truth Inside the Armor* reveals even more of Führer Bradley's nastiness: it's the aftermath of the Devil's Nest raid, and even Ed is questioning why the leader of Amestris has everyone at the bar killed. Poor Martel is a corpse covered with a blanket, and Al's body had to be cut open to pull her out (a grotesque birth image).

The Führer coldly informs the Elrics that if they have made deals with the homunculi and Devil's Nest crew, they might be executed by the military as traitors. There is no love lost btn the brothers and the Führer, and they're glad when he finally departs. They reaffirm their desire to stay in the military if they can find something more about the philo-sopher's stone. (Ed rubs off Martel's blood from Al's suit of armour – not a job anyone would relish doing. Later, Winry cleans Al's armour).

Chapter 30: *The Truth Inside the Armor* shifts time and place now, with a visit to a secondary but much-loved character in the world of *Fullmetal Alchemist*: Liza Hawkeye. She's a woman walking home alone at night, and is disturbed by someone (or something) lurking in a shadowy alley (the scenario is reprised later, with Selim).

It's Barry the Chopper (a.k.a. Number 66), the manic suit of armour from way back in chapter 11: *The Two Guardians*, and the fifth laboratory scenes. Number 66 does his usual knife-waving, scary spectre routine, expecting the victim to quake and wail, but he's picked the wrong person this time: Liza Hawkeye has a couple of pistols with her, and let's loose instantly. Hawkeye telephones Mustang and takes Number 66 into custody.

Chapter 31: *Onore no O o Kamu Hebi* (*The Snake That Eats Its Own Tail*) is one of the most important chapters in the *Fullmetal Alchemist* franchise. Himoru Arakawa and her editor Yoichi Shimomura have decided that it's time, a third of the way thru this incredible comic series, to reveal the Chief Villain, and what the homunculi are up to.

Chapter 31: *The Snake That Eats Its Own Tail* is split into two halves, and both focus on the threat to Amestris posed by the homunculi and the corruption in the military government. In the first half, Number 66 (Barry the Chopper) is hauled before Roy Mustang and his team.

Number 66 is a slippery customer, but during the investigation, Mustang is able to extract some unsettling information. Such as, the military have been conducting experiments involving criminals and corpses, and trying to create philosopher's stones. It's enough to set Mustang on a course to discover the 'truth behind the truth'. (Number 66 is put into the care of Vato Falman; Falman asserts his determination to follow Mustang).

Now Himoru Arakawa's *manga* switches to one of her grandest sequences in *Fullmetal Alchemist*: the introduction of the Super-Villain, his lair, his minions (the homunculi), and his power. The sequence begins with a narrative movement down and down – right below the HQ of the government, no less, the villain has his base (the downward motion is reprised many times for the Father scenes). The signature image in the chapter, across a double page, introduces Father, the Big Baddie of *Fullmetal Alchemist*: he sits on a throne on a circular platform. Pipes from all directions snake towards him, entering the chair (and presumably his body, a familiar sci-fi motif). Beside him there's a table with wine, a glass, a skull, a candle, books, a mortar and pestle (for grinding up alchemical materials), and some alchemical apparatus (we will soon see this gear being used).

Seen in three-quarter profile, Himoru Arakawa teases the reader at first, declining to offer the full view of Father's face. So we have shadowy glimpses, but we do see a grim, solemn patriarch with a beard, who might've stepped out of the *Old Testament*. He is reading a book of alchemy.

It's an image of immense power: this guy doesn't have to move from his throne to get everything he wants done.

We are swiftly introduced to the homunculi we have already met: Führer Bradley (who's come to report to Father), Lust, Gluttony, Envy, and a new homunculus, Sloth (seen in two drawings – an ogre standing in a tunnel). What Sloth is doing we don't quite know yet (Lust says he's lazy, but he's working).

And then there's Greed: keeping up the Biblical/ Judæo-Christian imagery, Greed is held captive hanging from the ceiling on a stone cross (Japanese artists are fond of using crucifixion as a motif, just they like they

♥ angels, churches, and other paraphernalia of Western religion). Greed is chained to the cross, and still has Bradley's four swords pinning him down at energy points.

Yet Greed remains surprisingly chipper (maybe he's not sure at this point what's going to happen to him, and if you can die many times, and yet not die, maybe he thinks he'll be OK). So Greed's making sarcastic swipes at Envy's weird dress sense, Gluttony's obesity, and telling Lust, 'you're as hot as ever, 'Ultimate Lance''. Greed, who's been absent as a rebel from the team of homunculi for a century, wonders who Bradley is: Lust tells him that he's Wrath (Anger), a recent (60 year-old) addition, a homunculus who can age (so he'll fit in with humans).

Thus, we have now met Lust, Gluttony, Envy, Sloth, Wrath and Greed: that's six of the Seven Deadly Sins: the seventh and final homunculus (Selim = Pride) is introduced at the close of the chapter. Father stops their bickering with a word. He speaks with Greed, revealing that part of Father is in Greed, and he calls him his son (demonstrating that it was Father who created the homunculi). Father asks Greed if he'll work for him again. Of course, Greed, ever the rebel with his own agenda, answers: 'No!'

What does Father do? Ah, well, this is the reveal-of-the-Super-Villain scene, right? And what do nasty villains do when we first meet them? They do something callous, of course! Thus, instantly, a circular pit opens below Greed, who's hanging above it. It's hot, it's bubbling with alchemical goo, and Greed is lowered into it. Screaming, he expires, yelling at his homunculi comrades about Hell.

Father watches impassively as Greed is burnt and dissolved in the enormous, alchemical vat, with flames and bolts of energy boiling in the air above. Thru the pipes around the vat the essence of the melted Greed plops, until it's just a drip from a glass flask into a wine glass. And Father knocks back the liquid, re-absorbing his son.

This is a superb slice of Gothic monstrosity from Himoru Arakawa, evoking Father's god-like powers, his vampirism/ cannibalism, his pose as the Arch Alchemist (performing an alchemist experiment), his brutality, and his mystery (because we still don't know exactly what Father is after. But we know it can't be good for our heroes!).

The seventh homunculus in Father's set based on the Seven Sins of Judæo-Christianity is introduced next: what could be cuter, sweeter and more endearing than a ten year-old child? Who is so devoted to his father, and worships him? Who has a smiley, eager disposition?

Meet Selim Bradley, who runs down a colonnade[3] to greet his father returning home from work (after just witnessing Greed's demise). We see Selim, his mom, his father the Führer, and it seems like a happy family. But it's later that Selim shows his true colours, as the fiercely destructive homunculus Pride.

❀

Chapter 32: *Envoy of the East* continues the amazing run of chapters in

---

3 Note the pattern of shadows in the colonnade – Pride manifests as deadly shadows.

Fullmetal Alchemist by introducing two of Himoru Arakawa's most appealing characters: the tiny Mei Chang (and her *kawaii*, 10-inch tall, pet panda, Xiao Mei), and Prince Ling Yao (and his ninja bodyguards Lan Fan and Fu). Both are from Xing (i.e., China), both have trekked across the desert to Amestris, both are searching for the secrets of immortality and/ or alchemy, and both are totally delightful, exaggerated charas, that lift any scene they're a part of.

The design and culture of Mei Chang, Lan Fan and Ling Yao are olde worlde, from the China of the *jiangzhu*, the mythical time of martial arts and wandering heroes, of Oriental princes and their clans. (They might've stepped in from *Hero Tales*, which Himoru Arakawa illustrated in 2006-2010).

We meet Mei Chang first: do you remember the mines of Yousewell, back in chapter 3: *The Mining Town*? We return there for the introduction of Mei: she's lying face-down on the ground, arms out-stretched, exhausted after crossing the desert. The boy Kayal (from the inn) meets Mei first, stepping on her head as he runs to the mine to deliver lunch to his pa (the inn-keeper).

Mei Chang sports long, black, braided hair, big, round eyes, and traditional, Chinese clothes (she could've stepped out of any of 100s of Hong Kong action movies). Right away she bonds with Kayal (he gives her some much-needed food), and very soon she's demonstrating her impressive alchemical skills: a mine's collapsed, containing Kayal's dad, and Mei comes to the rescue. She has *shinobi* throwing stars, which she uses to conjure a safe exit (including a neat door) among the fallen rocks. (Her kind act types Mei as a do-gooder, a helper).

Mei Chang is absolutely adorable when she goes into action (with her panda Xiao copying her every gesture). The miners're overjoyed at their escape, and Mei's treated to a celebratory feast back at the pub. (On hearing about the Fullmetal Alchemist, Mei builds him up in her mind as a *bishonen* hero out of *shojo manga*, and decides to travel to find Ed Elric. This becomes a recurring gag – Mei with stars in her eyes, full of lerrve. The object of her affections, tho', changes to Alphonse after she's met the Elric brothers).

❖

The scene shifts to Rush Valley, and a character we haven't seen for some time: Winry Rockbell. And what's Winry-chan doing when we first see her? Only hard at work (she works for Garfiel, a burly but very camp guy, who gives Alex Armstrong some competition for gay, camp associations).

Yes, the Elrics're back in Rush Valley, for Elric to have his automail fixed, yet again (following his extremely rigorous bout with Greed). We meet the other Rush Valley charas – Bunny/ Paninya, Tommy, etc (from chapter 15). Once the automail's fixed, the Elrics're heading back to Central City (Winry begs to come along too).[4]

In the street, the boys encounter a youth lying face-down, apparently

---

4 Himoru Arakawa likes to include Winry-chan, but she doesn't always find convincing reasons for Winry to keep tagging along.

dead or unconscious: this is Ling Yao (the scenario repeats the scene with Kayal and Mei Chang, down to Ling eating food at the finder's expense. But Ling can devour lots more'n Mei! And Ed doesn't want to pay the bill in the restaurant!). There's an instant dislike between the two (they are the same age – 15).

Ling Yao talks about his homeland, and draws a makeshift map on the ground: this is first time we've really seen Amestris put into geographical context: there's Xing (China) to the East, Drachma (Russia) to the North, and Creta (Greece/ Turkey) to the West.

Both Mei Chang and Ling Yao enlarge the story of *Fullmetal Alchemist* considerably: they are the first foreign characters introduced for some time (Scar and the Ishbalians being the others); and they bring foreign alchemy/ magic. Ling also mentions Xerxes (which features in the Hohenheim flashback), and Drachma to the North, protected by Briggs Mountain (where the *Fullmetal Alchemist manga* spends a *lot* of time later on).

And when Ling Yao confesses that he's searching for info on alchemy, and on the philosopher's stone, that gets the Elrics' attention right away. But when Ed declines telling Ling anything about the philosopher's stone, instantly his ninja bodyguards appear, Lan Fan and Fuu. With their black ninja outfits and theatrical masks, they are fearsome sidekicks for Ling (and they are completely devoted to him. To them, he's the prince of their clan, and everybody should bow down to him).

With chapters 31 and 32, Himoru Arakawa and her editor Yoichi Shimomura have introduced many vital elements in the *Fullmetal Alchemist* franchise: (1) enlarging the scope of the series by bringing in Xingese charas (and another form of alchemy), (2) by finally wheeling the super-villain into the foreground; and (3) introducing other countries, such as Drachma and Xing, and the important setting of Briggs Mountain. The only major character not yet introduced fully is the Elrics' father, van Hohenheim.

❁

Chapter 33: *Showdown In Rush Valley:* now, well, if you introduce two *shinobi*, the first thing that's got to happen is some fighting, right? Oh yes – Ed's pitted against Lan Fan, and Al against Fuu. It's Edward who starts the fight, however: he doesn't like the way that Ling Yao goes about his business. The duels spread out rapidly across Rush Valley, onto the roofs, the walls, the warehouses, the alleys, etc. Ed discovers that he's fighting a girl (when he smashes her mask), and Al's duelling an old man.

The action culminates with explosives, and both Al and Ed manage to get the better of the Xingese ninjas, stringing them up (using skills they learnt on Jack Island). Ling Yao turns up (when the fighting's over, of course! – he's quite a laidback/ lazy character. He'll fight, but he'd prefer to let his guards do that). He's impressed that the Elrics have trounced and captured his bodyguards, and offers them a job: 'Become my underlings and let's take over a nation?' And when the townspeople of Rush Valley gather, demanding recompense for the damage caused by the fighting, Ling and guards sneakily vanish.

Back at Garfiel's automail store, the characters assemble: Winry-chan's furious that Ed's busted his automail arm yet again (in a humorous drawing, Winry's wielding a chainsaw and chasing Ed), Ling Yao turns up, having decided to follow Ed, and Ed resents Ling on every level (everyone teases him about finding a new friend).

Chapter 33: *Showdown In Rush Valley* closes with a six-page reminder that Scar the Ishbalian assassin is still in the mix. Now he's travelling by horse and cart, along with the ever-hapless Loki. Nothing happens except that Scar looms as grim as #•! and Loki quakes in fear, and Scar mutters, 'Shut up and keep moving' (reminders that Scar or the homunculi are still in the loop often close chapters in the*Fullmetal Alchemist manga*).

❀

Chapter 34: *The Footsteps of a War Comrade* pushes our heroes into motion again: and, yes, once again, they're back on the railroad (a much classier way of travelling than a boring motor car). After more talk between Ling Yao and the Elrics, the scene shifts to Vato Falman and Jean Havoc – Falman has the very unenviable task of looking after Number 66 in a safe house. He's the insane and murderous hollow suit of armour, and Falman's job is to ensure that Number 66 doesn't rush off and start slicing people up (would you want to be stuck in a shabby hovel with an insane serial killer?!).

Another narrative shift: to the military records office, where Envy, in the disguise of Captain Focker, spies on Colonel Mustang (asleep in the office), and questions Sheska the bookworm about Mustang's research (so when the real Focker turns up, Sheska is very confused). A flashback to the Ishbal War depicts Alex Armstrong weeping hysterically over the pointless deaths of innocent people. The flashback occurs during a chat in a restroom btn Mustang and Armstrong.

The death of Maes Hughes (seen in the Ishbal flashback, where he worked alongside Roy Mustang), looms large in this chapter (Mustang is determined to hunt down the killer), culminating in a lengthy capture-trial-and-escape sequence (of Lieutenant Maria Ross). At this point, the Elrics still don't know that Hughes has been slain (their superiors in the military are trying to keep it from them).

Envy reports back to Lust and the homunculi: Lust speaks ominously about Roy Mustang being 'a leading candidate' as their 'human sacrifice' (this is a tease – we don't what this means yet, but it doesn't sound good!). Lust also suggests that she is manipulating the military (by having Mustang transferred to Central City. That the homunculi are orchestrating the placements of characters like Mustang is disturbing. Especially when Mustang is trying to out-manœuvre sections of the military at this same time).

In the military HQ's canteen, Lt. Ross is arrested by Henry Douglas from the military police (he's a mean, grey-haired puppet of the government) on suspicion of Hughes' death. This is Franz Kafka time, or Philip K. Dick time, or paranoia thriller time, when someone is arrested and imprisoned to act as a fall guy for the powers that be. That it's Maria Ross, a dutiful, hard-working soldier, with no motive, enhances the absurdity (no motive is offered by either side).

Jean Havoc is the hapless inside man – it turns out that the new girlfriend he was bragging about to Vato Falman is none other than Lust herself (well, she *is* a looker!). The *animé* adaptations ran with this, and had Lust appearing as Scar's brother's lover, as well as Lujon's lover.

❀

Chapter 35: *The Sacrifical Lamb* continues the Maes Hughes-Maria Ross plot: our heroes return to Central City, still unaware that Hughes is dead (they talk about going to visit him). Roy Mustang makes a critical error of judgement here, in not telling the Elrics and Winry about Hughes' death when they ask about him (he wants them to have as few obstacles as possible, he says. Liza Hawkeye doesn't approve).

Lt. Ross is interrogated by the army cops. Instead of getting right down to key questions like *why*, the talk is about accounting for bullets fired and alibis. So it's as if the military has already agreed that Ross is guilty, and alibis like Ross being at her parents' house can't be used.

Himoru Arakawa withholds a vital piece of information here, and instead depicts the apparent murder of Lt. Ross at the hands of Colonel Mustang from the point-of-view of our heroes, Ed and Al Elric. Number 66 seems to be involved – he asks to speak to Mustang.

Alphonse rushes in to the hotel room where they are staying (Ed's pondering over his alchemy notebook). In the newspaper, Edward discovers the terrible news that Lt. Ross has been arrested for the murder of Maes Hughes. They hurry into action (to find out what happened, and probably to confront Mustang, who lied to them). Later, Winry Rockbell wanders into their room, and finds the newspaper.

Number 66 storms the military prison in a terrific action sequence: being already dead, Number 66 is kind of unstoppable (so the guards have no chance of topping him). Number 66 springs Lt. Ross from her cell, and also Ling Yao (who was discovered by the authorities at the railroad station, as a foreigner).

In an improbable coincidence, who should Number 66 and Ling Yao run into on the dark streets but Edward and Alphonse? So it's a case of, 'You!', and 'You?!', and, 'Hey, it's you!!' While Number 66 acts as belligerent as ever (waving his swords, always up for for a bout of slicin' an' dicin'), Ross legs it... only for her to encounter, in yet another back alley, the superhero figure of Colonel Mustang, with the mandatory cloak flying in the breeze, and the superhero scowl. 'FOOM!' – an almighty bang and fire and smoke (we don't see the actual murder), and Edward dashes over to discover that Ross has seemingly been incinerated to charred nothingness by Mustang. It's a suitably high drama finale to chapter 35: *The Sacrifical Lamb* (it is some time (weeks, at least) before we discover exactly what happened that night).

❀

Chapter 36: *Alchemist In Distress* continues directly from the end of chapter 35, with Edward grabbing Roy Mustang's lapels and demanding to know what's going on. It's all a show – Mustang's unrepentant, somewhat superior attitude, is for the sake of the military, who soon arrive on the scene. If Ed and Al thought about it, they'd realize that this was going too far even for Mustang. Henry Douglas and the military cops're furious, because they can't even identify the body from the charred remains (Mustang insists that the orders were to shoot to kill if she resisted, and he says she did).

A hospital scene with a doctor confirms that Lt. Ross was the victim: once again, we don't yet know that this doctor (Knox) is in cahoots (reluctantly) with Col. Mustang over the cover-up of Ross. Alex Armstrong once again displays his emotions, weeping (Mustang suggests some time off). Falman tears his hair out having to deal with Number 66 and now another hanger-on, Ling Yao (and soon his ninja bodyguards arrive). Ed and Al wonder how they're going to tell Winry about Maes Hughes, only to find that she's left.

Winry Rockbell has gone to visit Maes Hughes' family. This sequence has nothing to do with alchemists battling superheroes, or homunculi attacking our heroes, but is about coming to terms with death. Ed and Al speak to Gracia, who asks them to come pick up Winry. They do: here, Gracia tells them that her husband will've died in vain if the Elrics give up their research. This is the dramatic pay-off of the death of Hughes: to harden the resolve of the heroes, to encourage them to Move Forward when they seem to have stalled again.

Edward Elric is appealing when he's depressed, when he doesn't know what to do, when he loses his Edwardness. Here, he sits in the restaurant of the hotel with a fork in his mouth, feeling forlorn and confused: 'I don't know *what* to believe in anymore'. Lt. Ross's 'death', plus Hughes' death, has really thrown the Elrics off-track (Al says that if people are going to die, then he doesn't want his body back).

Chapter 36: *Alchemist In Distress* closes with three pages of the homunculi discussing their nefarious plans, a reminder that the villains are never far away in *Fullmetal Alchemist*. They decide to send out one of their caged victims, Barry the Chopper (a maniac in a mask).

❀

Chapter 37: *The Body of a Criminal* continues the Roy Mustang-Number 66-Falman-Ross storyline: Mustang is pulling strings behind the scenes (pretending to be on the phone to several girlfriends, for instance, when he's really talking in code to his team out in the field).

The Elrics have hit another dead-end, and they're not sure what to do now that both Hughes and Ross are dead (they think). Ed has taken to lazing about on the couch or the bed: to show how desperate they are, Ed asks Winry-chan for her advice (which he's never done before!). In one of Himoru Arakawa's occasional lapses in storytelling and structure, Alex Armstrong turns up and drags Edward away (on the pretext that he needs some automail repairs – and Armstrong has just punched his automail arm! And despite Winry, his regular automail mechanic, being right there!). So Edward is absent from the following chapters, where the action is busy and intense. (Ed has his own adventures – in Resembool and then in the Eastern desert, and then meeting Hohenheim and digging up a grave).

Vato Falman and Number 66 at the safe house receive a 'visitor' – in the form of a maadman in a mask intent on killing them. This is Barry the Chopper, released by the homunculi to create hell among the heroes. Havoc, Falman and Lan Fan fight against Barry the Chopper, who seems unkillable (because the body he possesses is already dead; hence the awful smell!). Hawkeye helps out by sniping from a nearby church tower. (Fuu has gone on the trek in the desert with Ed).

The action is depicted in Himoru Arakawa's familiar intense style. Col. Mustang follows it all via radio back at the military HQ, relayed by Cain Furey. Part-way thru the heroes vs. Barry the Chopper fight, Arakawa introduces a marvellous twist: Number 66 yells, 'THAT'S MY BODY!' Jean Havoc is like, 'what?', and Number 66 explains: 'My body came to get its soul back'.

And what does Number 66 want to do with his body? Slice it up, of course! – 'How many people get the chance to slice and dice their own bodies?! I can cut up my own body with my own two hands!' So the homunculi (or maybe the military) have transmuted some schlub into Barry the Chopper's dead body, and re-animated it.

Meanwhile, another homunculus, Envy, is embarking on yet another duel, this time with Lan Fan. And up in the church tower, Liza Hawkeye is put into the scariest situation for her thus far in the *Fullmetal Alchemist manga*: the arrival of the homunculus Gluttony. The enormous monster isn't bothered by bullets (no matter how many she fires at it/ him). Roy Mustang yells down the radio as Hawkeye tries to escape the creature.

The Liza Hawkeye vs. Gluttony cliffhanger provides the climax for chapter 37 (and for the ninth *tankobon* of *Fullmetal Alchemist*). Arakawa puts her sniper in peril repeatedly – she's threatened by the monster-boy Selim later, for example. There are some fun *omake* strips at the back of the volume, including a page from a guest artist, Moritaishi-sensei.

▶

Chapter 38: *Signal To Strike* re-introduces the super-villain of *Fullmetal Alchemist*, Father, who's not been seen for some time (tho' he's working away in the shadows). Lust reports in briefly. Envy is being killed repeatedly by Lan Fan, tho' unfortunately he doesn't die. The Xingese (Chinese) charas in *Fullmetal Alchemist* can sense when a homunculus is nearby, and can see thru Envy's disguises. They are also sensitive to geomancy (earth magic), and they know that something isn't right in the country of Amestris (Mei Chang also senses this). Alphonse decides to go with Ling Yao to see what's going on.

Forget all of that, though – what's happening to Liza Hawkeye up in the bell tower with the homunculus Gluttony? He's got her in his grasp, she firing rounds into his fat skull, and it seems to be the end for Liza-chan. That old favourite of action-adventure yarns, the faithful dog, is wheeled in by Himoru Arakawa, yapping and growling at Gluttony, and leaping onto his back (which momentarily distracts him). Then Cain Furey rushes to the rescue, and they both fire at Gluttony. But, again, the oaf won't die. 'Time to eat!' he slathers, looming over our heroes. The Last Minute Rescue comes this time in the form of Col. Mustang, demonstrating his flamey alchemical powers, and sending Gluttony flying out the window.

There's another dog – Envy transmutes into a dog, but Lan Fan still senses who he is, and throws a *shuriken* into his eye. (What *manga* artist can resist dogs? Especially a farm girl from the countryside like Himoru Arakawa?! She loves dogs, she says in the *omake* of *Fullmetal Alchemist*, even tho' she's been bitten thrice).

It's at this point – with a dog being stabbed in the eye and transforming back into Envy, on all fours, that Alphonse and Ling Yao turn up. When Colonel Mustang marches into the situation, he immediately takes charge (as he always does – being the future President/ Führer-in-the-making).

❧

We are now building up to one of the outstanding sequences in the *Fullmetal Alchemist manga*, and one of Roy Mustang's most perilous experiences, when he and Jean Havoc face off against the homunculus Lust.

There are a lot of charas for Himoru Arakawa-sensei to juggle at this point: Mustang, Hawkeye, Havoc and Falman; Number 66 and Barry the Chopper; Alphonse; Ling Yao and his guards; and the homunculi Lust, Gluttony and Envy. (Finding something worthwhile for each of them to do takes some thought).

So it's Number 66 who pursues his body Barry the Chopper to an abandoned alchemy laboratory (number three), which just happens to be the homunculi's current crib. To investigate it, the team of Havoc, Alphonse, Hawkeye and Mustang split up (as in a horror story in a haunted castle, this is a fatal error!).

In one of the disused labs, strewn with trash, the incredible confrontation between Colonel Mustang and Jean Havoc with Lust takes place. Himoru Arakawa is really getting into her stride in depicting exaggerated and extreme action sequences: this is one of her best. The psychological subtext just happens to be girlfriends – and of course both Mustang and Havoc are known for their womanizing. Havoc has been dating Lust (he just can't resist boobs, he confesses, and Lust has a fine pair. Arakawa was happy that her editor Yoichi Shimomura allowed her to keep in Lust's breasts). Lust is the first character that Mustang kills for some time (he hasn't slain Lt. Ross); that Mustang attacks two women plays into his persona as a ladies' man.

On seeing the ourosboros tattoo, Col. Mustang doesn't need to hear any more from Lust before opening fire. Battered a little, Lust doesn't die. Now she does something very silly: she shows the soldiers the philosopher's stone in her chest that's her ♥ (pulling apart the skin). It's sort of excusable because she's a gloating villain who's intending to kill both guys, and fully confident that she can, but of course she also gives them a clue as to how to beat her.

So the fight begins – with Lust bursting open the overhead pipes in the lab, to drown Col. Mustang's fire gloves; the soldiers counter by fleeing, and filling the room with hydrogen, which Havoc ignites with his Zippo. Boom! The explosion is fierce, and most opponents would be fried. But not unkillable homunculi! Havoc is the first victim of Lust's Edward Scissorhands claws, rising from the rubble to pierce Havoc in the torso. Mustang shoots his gun. 'It'll take more than that to kill me!' shrieks Lust (we knew that!). So Mustang stamps on her, thrusts his hands into her chest, and yanks out her philosopher's stone (depicting in a gory drawing, with speed lines behind the figures, Lust screaming, and Mustang at his meanest).

Now Himoru Arakawa ups the ante, introducing Gothic horror imagery out of Edgar Allan Poe or Mary Shelley, with Lust disintegrating (to bones and muscles and a grinning skeleton), while also re-animating. Just as Mustang was preparing to heal Havoc using the philosopher's stone, Lust has recovered enough to stab him in the side (this forms the climax of chapter 38: *Signal To Strike*. (This scene is a gift to animators – because it's got everything. And the animated version doesn't disappoint).

❯

Chapter 39: *Complications At Central* is an important chapter in *Fullmetal Alchemist* because it portrays the death of a homunculus at the hands of a human, albeit an alchemist (Father had destroyed Greed in his bunker earlier, but that was a homunculus killing (or melting down) another homunculus).

But before Roy Mustang is able to achieve that, he is tortured by Lust, now seemingly resurrected to her former power. After stabbing Mustang, and gloating over him groaning on the floor next to Havoc, Lust makes another mistake (a classic villain's mistake): she doesn't finish off the Colonel completely; instead, she leaves the laboratory.

The other pair exploring the abandoned third lab, Alphonse Elric and Liza Hawkeye, discover Number 66 and the seemingly dead body of Barry the Chopper in a huge chamber (which has a large, alchemical symbol on the some out-size doors, which evoke, of course, the Gates of Truth. This setting appears later).

Meanwhile, the Xingese charas, Lan Fan and Ling Yao, are battling two homunculi, no less – Gluttony and Envy. And they're fast discovering that homunculi are darned difficult to destroy. Ling quips, 'can we just skip to the part where you guys surrender?'

Despite their talents for slicing and dicing and numerous martial arts, Lan Fan and Ling Yao wouldn't be able to best Gluttony and Envy on their own; they clash again, much later in the comic. But luckily the creatures are called away by the Führer, who's chosen to visit the lab (which's why Himoru Arakawa included images of Bradley at the start of the chapter).

So Lust slinks into the chamber in the lab, angry but confident that on her own she can take on Alphonse, Hawkeye and Number 66. She starts with Number 66, smashing apart his armour.

When she turns to Liza Hawkeye, Lust cruelly taunts her with news of Roy Mustang's death (which types Lust as an especially vindictive villain). The usually composed and calm Hawkeye explodes at this news, the worst thing she could hear (even tho' she, as a professional soldier, should know better than believing the enemy – and Mustang tells her so afterwards, as well as not giving in to despair).

This is the first time that we really see Hawkeye-chan losing it in the *Fullmetal Alchemist manga*. She blasts away with her guns, again and again. The bullets hit, Lust judders under their impact, but she remains standing. And then Hawkeye is beaten, and falls to her knees in defeat, weeping (this is very disturbing).

Now it's Alphonse's turn to be the hero: this is a great moment for the younger Elric, when Al moves defensively in between Lust and Hawkeye, tells her to get up and flee, transforms a spear from the floor, and creates a protective wall around Hawkeye (and, handily, Al, being a suit of armour, is able to withstand being pierced by Lust's lances several times).

It's here that Colonel Mustang staggers into the chamber, blasting into Lust with his flame alchemy (he's temporarily (and painfully) patched himself up with alchemy). Mustang launches balls of flame at Lust seven or eight times (an astonishing sequence in the 2nd *Fullmetal Alchemist animé*). Each time, Lust is fried, becoming a screaming, demonic silhouette, deteriorating yet somehow clinging onto life (because life is precious, right?).

It's a high voltage sequence:[5] at the end of it, there's a Mexican stand-off image, seen in profile: Lust reaches out one last time with her claws, ending up inches from Mustang's forehead, and Mustang holds out his arm, preparing for the final explosion.

Lust dies. *Dies!*

Her form crumbles into tiny, rectilinear pieces (we saw this effect back in the first pages of the *Fullmetal Alchemist manga*). And then her dis-integrating skeleton collapses. As does Col. Mustang, from the pain. (And the Führer, watching from a shadowed doorway, exits. Why does he leave? Maybe he thinks that Mustang's flame alchemy might be his match? But would Mustang attack the leader of the country? Maybe Bradley thinks it would complicate matters too much if he got involved. The Führer explains this to an angry Envy later, in Father's bunker; he reckoned that Mustang might be useful if he is kept alive; Mustang becomes one of the 'human sacrifices').

Chapter 39: *Complications At Central* closes with a couple of minor scenes: an emotional Winry-chan welcomes Alphonse back; the Führer orders ambulances; and the body that was Barry the Chopper picks up Number 66's bloodseal and seems to break it.

▶

Chapter 40: *Philosopher From the West*: so what's been happening

---

5 The sequence is reprised in part when Mustang and Hawkeye take on Envy later.

with Edward Elric? Last seen being dragged off by the impossible-to-avoid Alex Armstrong, we meet Ed (in appealing pastel colours) arriving at Resembool. Ed's been kept in the dark, but when he meets 2nd Lt. Breda at the station in Resembool, he knows that something's up.

In a café, they meet Mr Han, a Xingese guide. Edward, as expected, angrily demands what's going on. Answer? – they're going East. And East means... the desert. The very hot desert. Himoru Arakawa takes *Fullmetal Alchemist* into old-fashioned, action-adventure territory, putting our heroes onto horses, trekking across sand dunes.

The destination? – Xerxes, a new location in the *Fullmetal Alchemist manga*, and an important one (it's the setting for the superb Hohenheim origins flashback). Xerxes is a ruined city evoking ancient world cities such as Persepolis, Troy, Thebes, etc. It's pillars, walls, broken stones everywhere.

The signature image of chapter 40: *Philosopher From the West* is a full page drawing of Edward in a ruined church.[6] Across one wall is an enormous, alchemical wheel (in the same place as a stained glass, West window would be in a Cathedral). Himoru Arakawa has adapted famous mediæval images of alchemy – the suns and the texts written in concentric circles is familiar, but Arakawa has added the lion-serpent at the centre. (Ed will remember this image later, where it pays off with Ed working out what the enemy's up to, and when he discovers part of it inside Gluttony).

Fuu leads the party to the second surprise element in chapter 40: *Philosopher From the West*: Lt. Maria Ross, very much alive and smiling. Ed's amazed, and Armstrong strips off, as usual, for another gush of tears and a manly hug (which Ross comically tries to avoid). Heyman Breda explains how the scheme to spring Ross worked.

The Xerxes trip also provides some back-story for a major character soon to be introduced: the 'Philosopher From the West'. Fuu explains that in Xing they have legends about this guy, who brought alchemy to Xing; Ed relates a similar children's tale.

The 'Philosopher From the West' of the title of the chapter is van Hohenheim, one of the most intriguing charas in *Fullmetal Alchemist*; certainly he's the most mysterious. I think Hohenheim is a terrific creation by Himoru Arakawa – a powerful wizard, the guy who was instrumental in the whole problem of the homunculi, who's actually a bungling and rather ineffectual dad (and he's the butt of jokes, too).

Van Hohenheim is introduced at the end of chapter 40: *Philosopher From the West*. It's a very late appearance for a key member of the Elrics' family, but Hohenheim has been glimpsed several times in the corners of *Fullmetal Alchemist* (in flashbacks), and we've heard Edward complain about him, too.

Like Edward earlier, van Hohenheim is depicted arriving at Resembool rail station (where the station master and the ticket lady seem to recognize him). Hohenheim, who hasn't been in Resembool for years,

---

6 The church also echoes a mosque.

goes straight to his home. There's nothing there except charred remains.

Himoru Arakawa teases the reader, as with Father, withholding the full reveal of Hohenheim's face (actually, we haven't seen Father fully yet, either). So we see his beard, parts of his face, etc (noting that the beard is trimmed exactly the same as Father's). Hohenheim's design also includes glasses, long hair in a pony tail, a suit and tie, and a briefcase.

Cut to Pinako in her home: what she's doing? Only going thru some photo albums, perusing the past (we see images of the younger Elrics, inc. a young Pinako). Den the dog growls: who's at the door? In two panels, Himoru Arakawa depicts our first look at Hohenheim, at the door, and Pinako's astonishment: 'Hohenheim!!'

A lovely touch, typical of *manga* and *animé*, has a gust of wind blowing in thru the doorway, and ruffling the pages of the photo album on the table. Two panels, which close the chapter, portray a C.U. of Hohenheim, and a snapshot of Hohenheim and the young Pinako, grinning at the camera (and the date, 'Sep '66' – presumably meant to be 1866).

Chapter 40: *Philosopher From the West* isn't only about Edward and his pa, tho': with the previous chapter being such a biggie in terms of action and story (and the death of a major chara, Lust), there are the inevitable Aftermath Scenes. Down in the bunker, Envy and Gluttony weep and moan about Lust dying; Father moves – for the first time – shifting from his throne to approach the Führer. Father wants to know if Roy Mustang can open the portal for them. Father seems satisfied (it's the first time we see him smile).

▶

Meanwhile, Havoc and Mustang are recovering in hospital. There is lots of talk about What Happened and What To Do Next. A map is produced, and Mustang's team discovers that within a short radius of lab three is central HQ, and the Führer's residence.

Chapter 41: *On the Palm of an Arrogant Human Being* goes into flashback mode, to explain exactly what Col. Mustang was doing behind the scenes to save Lt. Ross (Number 66's idea was to spring her from jail, however). In the present day, in Xerxes, Heyman Breda finishes up his story, and the team decide what to do next (Breda has more influence in the *manga* than the *animé*, with his own sequence in the next chapter). They pool their information, discussing the homunculi (including drawing sketches of them). Edward resets his motives by stating, in a full-page image (with a giant cross in the background!), 'I have no choice but to move forward!'

So it's time for goodbyes, as the charas get into motion once more: farewell to Lt. Ross, who departs with Fuu for Xing (she makes a striking return in the finale of *Fullmetal Alchemist*). Edward dashes back to the alchemical hall, to check on that mural once more, in the era b4 you take a snap with a cel phone. (There are five suns, he notes – which relates to the five 'sacrifices' later – tho' part of the circle is broken off).

An important encounter occurs now, between Ed Elric and some surviving Ishbalians. As well as keeping the Ishbalian political issue alive, this scene also reminds us of Scar, and also the doctors who helped them in the war, the Rockbells (this will pay off in the scene where Winry confronts Scar).

From Xerxes, it's back to Resembool (Himoru Arakawa cuts out the return trek). Edward leaves Breda and Armstrong, and heads over to the Pinako's home, to have his automail fixed.

Here the meeting between Hohenheim and Edward takes place – their first encounter in the foreground and present tense of the *manga* of *Fullmetal Alchemist*. Who is the guy standing by his mother's grave? Ed wonders. He rushes over, with images from his childhood flashing before him (peeping into his father's study as a five year-old). Ed stares (no, *glares*) at Hohenheim, and Hohenheim turns to look at him – this provides the finale of chapter 41: *On the Palm of an Arrogant Human Being*.

❧

Chapter 42: *The Father Standing Before a Grave* deepens and thickens the *Fullmetal Alchemist* narrative with a long-awaited encounter between Hohenheim and Edward Elric: father and son, two powerful alchemists. It's a superb scene, as they stand in front of Trisha's grave – their wife and mother.

Edward is accusing, angry, stubborn, confused: Hohenheim is bewildered by Ed's sudden outburst, playing humble and nonchalant. But Hohenheim also tells his son that he reckoned he burnt down his house because he didn't want to be reminded of the mistake he and Al had made.

Whatever van Hohenheim says or does, it winds Edward up! Father and son simply can't get along. When Hohenheim follows Ed to the Rockbells' home, and when he says they even wear their hair the same, Ed fumes (he quickly braids his hair, to be different. Who wants to be told they have the same hairstyle as their father?! *Euww!*).

While Edward E. lies awake in bed, he overhears a crucial conversation between his father and Pinako. Was the person or thing transmuted by the Elrics really their mother? Hohenheim muses. Pinako is astonished: that they went thru all of that agony, and it wasn't even their mother? That's sick. Himoru Arakawa cuts to a drawing of Ed standing in the bedroom, stricken by this new knowledge (Hohenheim seems to know that Ed might be listening. Certainly, his suggestion has a major impact on the story).

Pinako Rockbell is one of the few people who stands up to Hohenheim, and tells him that he's been a bad father (when something's gone wrong, she blames Hohenheim). If he'd been there for the boys when they grew up, they never would've tried to transmute Trisha. She's right.

Hohenheim tries to be a good father, but he just can't do it. He reaches out to Ed, but can't make that final connection.

Hohenheim leaves the following morning, as enigmatic as ever. His parting shot is to tell Pinako that terrible things are going to happen in Amestris. Pinako won't run, tho': 'terrible things happen in this country every year, all the time'. Picking up a photo of the family, Hohenheim departs.

This is grand storytelling – the bright, clear drawings by Arakawa-sensei seem suitable for a fluffy *shojo* comic about after-school clubs. But no, it's life, and death, and families, and the unbreakable bonds between parents and children.

And Ed, in particular, as the hero of *Fullmetal Alchemist*, is set onto a new course of action, calling into doubt everything that he and Al have done. (There is a positive outcome, however – Ed now has clues that Alphonse's body may still be in the Gateway).

Shifting to the hotel where Alphonse and Winry are staying (and they're running out of dough for the room – especially with Ling Yao and Lan Fan spongeing off them!), they discuss – what else? – but Al's father, Hohenheim. Ling and Lan are fascinated – because Al, in that suit of armour, seems immortal. But Al knows that what's tying his soul to his new body is tenuous. We also hear about Ling's story – he's a prince (Al and Winry can't believe it, and laugh), the emperor's 12th child.

The talk of souls and bodies and immortality links up with the themes in the Ed and Hohenheim scenes in Resembool.

❯

In the hospital, Dr Knox, the weary, cynical doctor, castigates Col. Mustang for his cavalier ways. Knox tells Mustang that Jean Havoc won't walk again. Heyman Breda has the idea of asking for help from Dr Marcoh, who might be able to perform some alchemically-charged healing, using a philosopher's stone. (This is reprised in the finale of *Fullmetal Alchemist*, when Marcoh offers Mustang to heal his blindness with a philosopher's stone).

So Heyman Breda gets to have his own mission and moment to shine, when he travels to Dr Marcoh. Unfortunately, Envy, in Breda's form, gets there first, and drags Marcoh away.

❖

Chapter 43: *River of Mud* features a lovely splash page depicting our heroes enjoying a band of musicians playing raucously in a restaurant. The action continues the discussion about Alphonse, childhood, transmutation, etc, btn Winry Rockbell, Al Elric, Ling Yao and Lan Fan.

In this section of *Fullmetal Alchemist*, now halfway thru, Himoru Arakawa is really getting into the theology, metaphysics and philosophy of what it would mean to transmute a person, what it would mean to travel to the Gate of Truth limbo, and how Ed and Al can regain their bodies. Ed, Pinako and Hohenheim are also musing on the same issues.

Alphonse-kun complains to Winry-chan about not being able to sleep, or eat, or feel. Al is caught in a a desensitized no-man's-land, an in-between zone. Both Winry and Al find this upsetting and dispiriting (especially when Ed isn't there to talk about it).

But the Fullmetal Alchemist *is* dreaming about it: Himoru Arakawa gives Edward another dream: he's imagining being in the Gate of Truth limbo, and demanding that Truth/ God gives him Al back. The grinning demon insists that, no, it was Edward's fault in the first place. And Ed is compared to Shou Tucker, who transmuted his daughter, Nina.

The following morning, van Hohenheim leaves (b4 Ed is up). Ed moves into action: he is determined to move ahead with his alchemical investigations, which now means making sure that what the boys transmuted wasn't their mother.

Under the burnt, gaunt tree near the remains of their home on the hill, Ed and Pinako set to work with shovels: to dig up what Pinako buried years before. The undertaking sickens Ed – literally (he retches). But he continues to dig, in the rain (graves always mean rain in Japanese pop culture, it seems).

As the grave-digging scene progresses, it becomes full-on, Gothic horror, with Ed descending into a frantic, sickened state, while Pinako looks on in sympathy. Himoru Arakawa gives this scene the Big Treatment because it's a turning point in the fortunes of the Elrics. (Ed is portrayed with many agonized expressions, slumping down on all-fours).

Eventually, they discover hair in the dirt, then bones. The hair is the wrong colour, the body isn't the right size: in short, this skeleton is *not* Trisha, the brothers' mom. From despair to insane laughter – it seems like Ed has lost it. But he realizes, in a big C.U. run over two pages: 'Al can be returned to normal!!'

We don't know exactly *how* yet (but Ed is now convinced that part of Al exists in the Gateway; in which case, by paying the right toll, his body can be brought back). And this becomes the finale of the entire *Fullmetal Alchemist* comic (along with the demise of Father).

Now, Himoru Arakawa cuts away from this slice of Victorian, Brontëan gloom to a light-hearted scene of Mei Chang meeting Loki and Scar. Mei is revived (from collapsing from hunger, again), and thanks Loki on her knees. When she asks after Edward Elric, Loki is comically furious (it was Edward who tricked Loki into losing ownership of Yousewell mine, inaugurating his downfall to his current sorry state).

It's such a pity that the delightful and endearing and *kawaii* Mei Chang should be teamed up with Loki (a cowardly loser) and Scar (a zealous serial killer), rather than the Elrics (who have Ling Yao and Lan Fan with them).

We meet Scar next, going head-to-head with Giolo Comanchi, an alchemist determined to bring Scar in. With his wooden leg, top hat, handlebar moustache and olde worlde speech, Comanchi, the 'Silver Alchemist', displays an unusual, spinning top form of alchemy. Unfortunately, it's not powerful enough to nobble Scar. Comanchi is last seen glugging underwater in a nearby river.

❖

Chapter 44: *The Unnamed Grave*, as the title suggests, continues the grave-digging sequence involving Pinako and Edward. The skeleton that Ed re-buries is definitely not Trisha, and it means that Ed transmuted someone else. A number of pieces of a metaphysical jigsaw are falling into place, made up of souls, spirits and bodies.

Ed Elric is now in alchemical-philosophical detective mode: first, he calls up his *sensei*, Izumi Curtis, on the phone. Talk about re-opening old wounds! What does Ed ask Curtis, but this: 'was the life that you transmuted really your child?'

Understandably, Curtis slams down the phone in anger. Ed checks with Pinako that he and Al are really Trisha's children. Pinako assures him that they are (she helped to deliver them).[7] She also tells Ed Trisha's final message to Hohenheim (which she wants Ed to relay): that she hasn't kept her promise, that she will be dying first.

With a simple cut across a slightly wider gutter (the space between panels), Edward is back in Central City, at the hotel with Winry and Alphonse. Ed's first task is to kick out the hangers-on leeching off him, Ling Yao and Lan Fan (a funny moment), then get down to fixing his brother's broken armour. But the most burning issue is to tell Alphonse all he's learnt so far.

---

7 Presumably, even in rural Resembool, in this world there would be birth records.

Pages from the finale of Fullmetal Alchemist (this page and over).

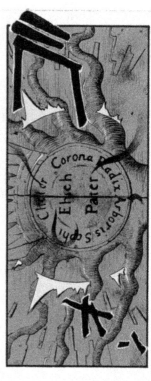

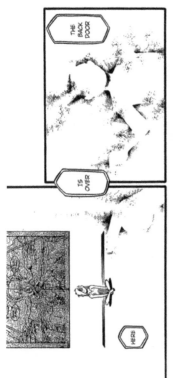

THAT AIN'T HUMAN...

YEAH...

I CAN'T BELIEVE IT...

Chapter 5
An Alchemist's Anguish

Chapter 34:
Footsteps of a Comrade.

I'LL BE RIGHT BACK...

A HUMAN TRANSMUTATION CIRCLE?!

HERE COMES THE FULLMETAL ALCHEMIST'S FINAL TRANSMUTATION!

The finale of Fullmetal Alchemist

There's a brief allusion to a romantic sub-plot (when Winry remembers that she rejected both Al and Ed as possible suitors in their youth), then the kids get down to serious discussions about Alphonse's soul, and how to regain their bodies.

Most enjoyable of all here are the flashbacks that Himoru Arakawa provides to the fateful day of the transmutation, to the demon-god in the Gateway of Truth, to Al slipping away to the other side, and to the giant eye. This is all critical material which will pay off in the finale of the *Fullmetal Alchemist manga*.

When Curtis calls Edward, this time she thanks him. Why? Because after thinking about it, he has put her mind to rest that the child that she transmuted was not her baby. Curtis weeps, but she's relieved. (This is indeed a peculiar story for boys when the heroes are relieved because a major, life-and-death spell they performed *wasn't* successful. It links to a notion in fairy tales: at the end of a fairy tale, the hero often doesn't *gain* something – treasure, a princess, marriage – but *recognizes* something that they always had – beauty, truth, goodness, pizza, etc).

An emotional and important conversation occurs now, between the Elrics brothers on the stairs of their hotel (it's overheard by Ling and Lan Fan and Winry, who're nearby). The boys re-set their goals and their motives (once again): 'I'm going to get my body back and I'm not going to lose anyone else in the process!'

❖

A scene at the hospital is next, where Havoc and Mustang argue – the paralyzed Jean Havoc wants to give up, and leave the military, and Colonel Mustang insists that he'll get better. Because stubborn, immovable Mustang will never let down his men, or allow them to fail.

And then Scar returns: the man with a scar on his forehead and an intricate tattoo on his arm. Li'l Mei Chang is introduced by Loki to Scar.

❖

Chapter 45: *Scar's Return* – yes, gloomy bruiser Scar is back. But he doesn't enter the fray until the end of the chapter. First, there is more discussion between Ed and Al about what happened on that fateful night, and how they can get their bodies back (Winry listens, fretting).

Edward introduces the notion that people are linked spiritually to the limbo of the Gateway of Truth. Thus, Ed may sleep a lot because he's sleeping for the Alphonse that's trapped in the other realm (more is made of the spiritual connection later, and it becomes critical in the finale).

The upshot of the lengthy discussion in the hotel is that they need to speak to a homunculus to clarify certain issues. To do so, they will endeavour to draw out the secretive homunculi with some outrageous and high profile acts. (Meanwhile, Winry decides that she can now return to Garfiel's automail workshop).

As usual, Ling Yao and Lan Fan are lurking in the background (outside the hotel window), and they've heard everything (Himoru Arakawa finds comical ways of keeping the Xingese charas in the loop). They want to team up with the Elrics in taking on the homunculi. They remind the lads that they can be useful – they can sense when the homunculi are nearby.

The 'come and get it!' sequence, where Edward and Alphonse rush about the city fixing things for anyone who asks (buildings, broken vases, children's buggies, walking sticks), are delightful. This is where Himoru Arakawa depicts the Elrics in comical poses, wielding fans, thumbs up, grinning cheesily, winking at the viewer (both animated shows are especially adept at portraying the Elrics when they go to town).

Eventually, they grab the attention of Col. Mustang: they meet, and exchange intel. And at that moment, who should appear but the Ishbalian maniac Scar. Which's just what the Elric lads want: they are going 'fishing', as Ed puts it.

Chapter 45: *Scar's Return* climaxes with a series of duels between the Elrics and Scar. (Once again, Scar proves impossible to nobble). These wild fights continue into the following chapter, as Ling Yao, Lan Fan, the Führer and Gluttony get involved.

Mustang and Hawkeye commandeer Cain Furey's radio set to broadcast false reports about sightings of Scar, in order to lure out the military. Führer Bradley takes the bait (accompanied by Gluttony). So now we have the Xingese guys versus Bradley, and the Elrics versus Scar and Gluttony.

Chapter 46: *The Distant Image of Their Backs* opens with a change of pace, setting and character: we are now with van Hohenheim for an 8-page side-story. He's travelling in a horse-drawn coach and happily contemplating the photo he took from Pinako's house of his family. After a brief (and odd) chat about the photo (Hohenheim mentions that he and Edward had an argument, and he might not be seeing him for some time), the coach is attacked by bandits.

The ruffians grab the horses, halt the coach, and turn on the passengers. Hohenheim places himself in front of them, to defend them. Here is the first reveal of Hohenheim not being all that he seems, when one of the bandits, brandishing a gun, stupidly fires. But Hohenheim doesn't fall; he stands in the coach, apparently unaffected. The other bandits shoot at the Elrics' father, but still he doesn't expire.

The bandits flee; the cops show up (the coachman cleverly let loose a warning flare); and the passengers are amazed by Hohenheim, who's riddled with bullet holes. But all Hohenheim is concerned about is his precious photograph.

Back to the chases: Gluttony and the Führer are steaming into the pursuit of our heroes: Ling Yao, carrying an injured Lan Fan, has to use all of his cunning (and his strength) to counter the attentions of two murderous homunculi. Ling goes sword-to-scimitar with the Führer, and cuts off Gluttony's head (which soon grows back). The fight continues inside an abandoned building (Ling still has Lan Fan on his back). Clever Ling tosses in a flash bomb, which blinds Gluttony and Bradley. But not, unfortunately, the homunculus's infernal eye underneath his eye-patch.

Himoru Arakawa is now cutting away from one duel to other scenes then back to another duel. So there's a brief cemetery scene, with Winry Rockbell visiting Maes Hughes' grave with his wife Gracia and child. This sad, thematic scene evokes Winry's parents and Winry as a child (seen in flashbacks). It's dramatic preparation for the encounter with the murderer of Winry's folks – Scar.

And who should pop up in the next scene? – Scar, of course. He's still duelling the Elric lads. They are deploying all of their alchemical skills to combat Scar (by now, surely, Scar should be so injured he wouldn't offer much opposition? Alas, no: Scar is still able to fight as if he's just arrived on the latest camel from Ishbal. And he continues to fight right up to the end).

The Elrics yell at Scar about Shou Tucker and his daughter chimera, accusing him of killing her. At this point, as the Elrics and Scar stand in a wrecked back street, Winry Rockbell hurries into the scene (having overhead someone talking about the brothers).

Edward Elric is off on one of his rants, this time accusing Scar of killing two doctors in the Ishbal War. Alphonse has seen Winry turn up in a side alley, but Ed hasn't. However, it's too late – Winry has heard Ed's accusations. (Yes, dramatically it is rather artificially constructed – one character just happening to overhear another character is usually a contrived scene, it's invented by the author here to force a confrontation).

Himoru Arakawa stages a full-on ethical and moral encounter between Winry Rockbell and Scar: the question is, what would you do if you came face to face with the murderer of both of your parents? And you had a gun right there?

Yes – the gun. Himoru Arakawa has rightly steered clear of arming her teen heroes with guns. Why? Partly because it's been done millions of times before, partly because of the moral issues, and partly because guns are not needed for the heroes – because they have alchemical powers.

But placing a gun in Winry Rockbell's hands is something else. If Himoru Arakawa is reluctant to make the Elrics killers, she is even more reluctant with Winry. Edward is shocked to see Winry holding the revolver, and begs her to put it down (as Al does). Scar acknowledges that the girl has every right to shoot him.

This is where we see Winry Rockbell really lose it for the first time in the *Fullmetal Alchemist manga*, screaming in agony: 'GIVE THEM BACK!! GIVE ME BACK MY MOM AND DAD!!' She points the weapon at Scar, which forms our final scene in chapter 46: *The Distant Image of Their Backs*.

Chapter 47: *A Girl In the Grip of Battles Past and Present* continues the dual action scenes: Ed, Al and now Winry vs. Scar, and Gluttony and Bradley vs. Ling Yao and Lan Fan. (To counter the bleak mood, tho', the splash page of chapter 47 is an appealing colour image of Winry, Mei Chang and Liza Hawkeye, three of the comic's key female characters, thus far).

The face-off btn Winry and Scar is kept simmering for several pages by Arakawa-sensei (well, you have to milk a confrontation like this! It's taken, after all, some finagling to manœuvre the lovely Winry into position so she can be holding her parents' killer at gun-point).

In the end, of course Winry Rockbell doesn't shoot, and the smackdown between Scar and the Elrics continues. In one memorable beat, Edward hurls himself in front of Winry to protect her, while Scar bears down upon them from above, raising his arm to perform that scary destructive alchemy. At that moment, as Ed glares up at him (glaring as only Edward Elric can glare!), Scar flashes back to the moment in the Ishbal War when his brother stood in between him and Zolf Kimbley). The hesitation is long enough for Alphonse to land a crushing blow to Scar's tattooed arm (which, come on, would break anybody's arm! This is tough, mediæval armour we're talking about! Al must weigh a ton, and he's hitting Scar full force!).

Alphonse now has Scar on the run, harrying him alchemically with those rows of stone blocks which erupt from the ground. He yells at Ed to protect Winry.

There's a touching aftermath scene now, btn Ed-kun and Winry-chan. Letting go of the gun (finally!), she breaks down into tears. *You were meant to save lives, not take them,* Edward tells her gently (yes, Ed is being kind and considerate here! – not ploughing in heavy-handed, as usual!). Leaving Winry in the protection of the military police, Ed rushes off to help his brother fight Scar.

❖

Meanwhile, Ling Yao and Lan Fan manage to escape Eye-Patch and Glut-Bag for the moment. They flee thru the city streets. Unfortunately, they're being herded (by Gluttony) to a dead end. Lan Fan is anguished because she is slowing her beloved Prince down. She begs him to leave her and escape on his own (which Ling will never do, of course).

They are running out of possibilities, until Lan Fan comes up with an extraordinary and daring solution: Gluttony is tracking them by their scent, so they need to throw him/ it off their trail. To achieve this, she cuts off her injured arm! Owww!

Yes, that is how deep Lan Fan's devotion is to her Prince. Would you cut off your arm for your boss?! Admittedly, the context does play a part – because Ling and Lan are being chased by two creatures that will without doubt destroy them. In a typical piece of grotesque, Arakawan eccentricity, Lan bandages her severed arm to a dog, so that the Führer is led the wrong way by the mutt (meanwhile, the Xingese heroes take shelter in the sewers, where they hope the water and the stench will cover their tracks).

Alphonse Elric takes centre stage now, pursuing Scar to a favourite setting in *Fullmetal Alchemist* for fights (and for many an action-adventure yarn) – an industrial/ railroad zone (where there are water towers to alchemize). Ed zooms into the fray with a flying kick at Scar (one of Himoru Arakawa's favourite martial arts moves – she is clearly a fan of martial arts).

In another pause in the action (Arakawa-sensei always builds in lots of pauses, when the characters glower at each other, and sometimes talk), the fat boy homunculus Gluttony enters the arena. He and Scar began to fight (again, when he's smashed against a wooden warehouse by Gluttony, Scar should really be severely injured).

And now Ling Yao makes a surprise and welcome appearance, leaping out of a manhole (he's been in the sewers, taking care of Lan Fan). Ling lands on top of Gluttony and jams a grenade down the monster's maw. It explodes, sending fragments of his body all over the place. Before Gluts has time to rejuvenate himself, clever Ling is on the case: asking Edward to alchemize a metal cable (from nearby rails), he binds up the homunculus. Bingo – one captured homunculus.

○

Chapter 48: *A Promise Made By Those Who Wait* finishes off the lengthy dual action sequences with two more surprise appearances: from Liza Hawkeye (who shoots at Scar and injures him in the leg. No, Liza, no – the head, the head! Please, somebody, shoot this guy in the skull!).

Liza Hawkeye, however, handily arrives in a car (and in civvie disguise – because now Col. Mustang's team are assuming that higher-ups in the military might be corrupt), and Ling humps the bound Gluttony (who must weigh several tons) into the car. Ed lands a final punch on Scar's mug; but just as Ed and Al prepare to deal with Scar, who should fly out of nowhere (with another martial arts shadowless kick) but Mei Chang.

That someone as endearing as Mei Chang should be defending Scar from the Elric brothers is a bitterly ironic twist (of course, li'l Mei doesn't know that it is the Elric boys, whom she idolizes, that she is attacking). Everybody is stunned by the arrival of this new, 3' 6" tall warrior, and her pet panda,[1] and by the impressive demonstration of her Xingese alchemy/ alkahestry (which uses a water tower to create clouds of steam or fog, under cover of which, she and Scar vanish).

In the aftermath of the duels, Mei Chang heals Scar's leg wound; Scar, Loki and Mei discuss what they're going to do next. But Mei's pet, Xiao Mei, is missing – Alphonse has picked her up (we know he is partial to pets like cats).

When the Elrics're re-united with Winry Rockbell (who's been waiting for them, as she always does), who should be there, but the leader of Amestris, the Führer. Having Bradley pop up all over the place, where he's not expected (or wanted), is over-done in the *Fullmetal Alchemist manga*. But then, he *is* a homunculus, and one of the enemy. So having him create obstacles makes sense. Seeing the Führer take tea with Winry-chan is disturbing, though – like walking in to see your sister chatting politely with Adolf Hitler.

Winry R. receives a phone call, and hears that many customers are asking after her at Garfiel's automail store (she has already decided to

---

1 They call it a cat, a dog, a raccoon.

travel there). A parallel scene has Jean Havoc's mom visiting him in hospital (a reminder of the costs of the enterprise of battling the homunculi, because Havoc is paralyzed).

When Winry-chan departs Himoru Arakawa spends some time on the farewell (at the railroad station, yet again). Why? Because it will be some time before the Elric brothers see Winry Rockbell again, and because Winry acts as the moral conscience for the Elrics. Also, Winry is partly what is at stake, what they are fighting for (and she embodies the link to Resembool, their childhood home).

Summoning up his courage, Edward Elric yells something at Winry which she doesn't hear. So he repeats it:

THE NEXT TIME I MAKE YOU CRY, THEY'LL BE TEARS OF JOY!! AL AND I WILL GET OUR ORIGINAL BODIES BACK NO MATTER WHAT, AND WE'LL MAKE YOU SO HAPPY THAT YOU'LL CRY!

And there are reminders in the drawings of the Elrics burning their home, and leaving Resembool. As Winry watches them leave the platform, she muses, 'Maybe I've been in love with him from a long time ago...'

○

A new location's introduced now, as our heroes gather at an abandoned house in the countryside (in the suburbs of Central City). Col. Mustang is over-seeing operations, with Doctor Knox and Liza Hawkeye looking after Lan Fan. Everyone exchanges information and recuperates (Ling Yao, the Elrics, etc). Ling tells them that he reckons that King Bradley is a homunculus (everyone's stunned. But it does explain plenty).

Unfortunately, they choose to talk right outside the room where they've got Gluttony tied up. When the fat boy hears the name of Col. Mustang, he /it instantly seethes with fury – because Mustang killed his beloved chum Lust (yes, I know, it probably isn't a good idea to discuss vital matters within earshot of a murderous psychopath). 'YOU KILLED LUST', Gluttony hisses, expanding and exploding, forming our finale to chapter 48.

○

Chapter 49: *A Monster Among Men* – enough with the talk, it's time for some action! But that's in 11 pages – because first, we have the teasing introduction of the final homunculus, Pride. We don't see him/ it yet – instead, we hear Pride speaking from behind a closed door to the Führer. As Bradley and Pride talk (Bradley muses on his life), Himoru Arakawa includes a classic image of entrapment: a moth flying close to a lamp and being caught in a spider's web (the *animé* series paid tribute to this moment). The motif of Pride as a lurker in the shadows recurs many times – including when Liza Hawkeye first encounters it/ him.

Next, Envy brings some food to the imprisoned Dr Marcoh in the bunker below Central City. Envy, as usual, gloats (his default position and his favourite pastime), while Marcoh ruminates angrily: he has worked out that the homunculi are going to create an enormous transmutation circle involving the whole of Amestris. (Edward comes to the same conclusion not long after this).

Now back to the action, at the house at night near a forest: Gluttony has broken free. To the amazement of Hawkeye, Mustang, the Elrics *et al*, Gluttony's torso has ripped open to reveal a void inside, with a giant eye, on its side, peering out. Glut's ribs are pulled back, looking like teeth round a huge maw (another toothed vagina image). As Ling tells Lan: 'the monster has another monster inside its stomach'.

Gluttony attacks Colonel Mustang – the ribs extend (like Lust's fingers), shredding all in its path. Our heroes flee. Pulling on his special gloves, the Flame Alchemist goes into battle – but the new Gluttony simply swallows the alchemical fire, like Natsu Dragneel in *Fairy Tail*. Whatever they try, they can't seem to do much against this new Glutters. Wisely, some of them bolt – the doctor, Hawkeye, Lan Fan and the Colonel, leaving the three lads – Ling Yao and the Elrics – to take on Glut-boy. (Hawkeye gives Ed a gun – 'a tool for killing people', Al calls it. Look at Ed's face – he so doesn't want to pick up that gun! He flashes back in his memory to when Winry held the pistol).

So now our heroes're crouched down in the bushes in a forest where a monster rages, wondering how the #### they're going kill it. Out of the night trots a ghostly horse, with glowing eyes (like something out of Henry Fuseli's Gothic art): it's Envy, in one of his more unusual impersonations. As the horse transforms (slowly) into the usual grinning, spikey-haired Envy, we come to the end of chapter 49.

O

Chapter 50: *In the Belly of the Beast* climaxes with the beginning of one of the outstanding sequences in Himoru Arakawa's *Fullmetal Alchemist manga* – our heroes get trapped inside the infinite stomach and sea of blood of a monster. First, the chapter continues the smackdown in the forest between the heroes and the homunculi. As soon as Envy materializes, Edward attacks him. In a pause in the fight, Envy informs Glut-head that he cannot eat the Elrics or Col. Mustang, but Ling Yao is on the menu.

So the Chinese Prince goes up against Envy, while the Elric lads take on the Gluster. Arakawa-sensei includes her favourite sword duelling moves, but Envy is no ordinary opponent: he (or it) can regenerate, and he/ it can turn his arms into hissing serpents (Ling chops off Envy's arm and leg, but they grow back). Meanwhile, Ed and Al find it difficult to keep Glutsie imprisoned.

When Envy cleverly transforms into Lan Fan, Ling Yao hesitates, standing above him. And he's right in the firing line for Gluttony's next attack; Edward throws himself towards Ling, to help him. Just then, Glut-man's maw and ribs-as-teeth-or-claws scythe through the area, cleaning up both Ed and Ling, and Al's arm, and (the upper) half of Envy, and a scooped-out hollow of earth.

Oops! Gluttony has eaten them. Al launches himself at Gluttony, screaming hysterically, 'Big brother! My big brother! Bring him back!'

○

Modest scenes follow – of Dr Knox and Lan Fan (she mourns her missing arm, as you might do); of Col. Mustang and Hawkeye; and of Mustang encountering a colleague, General Raven. This leads to Mustang confiding in Raven, that the Führer of Amestris might be a homunculus (he's been encouraged to search out some allies by Maes Hughes). Only Mustang has entrusted himself to the wrong man, because Raven leads Mustang straight into a den of vipers – a high level meeting of Amestrisian politicos, headed up by the Führer himself[2] (the sudden switch of scenes is artificial, but this is *manga*, after all). Bradley glowers at Mustang: 'so what if I am a homunculus? Is there a problem?'

Edward Elric wakes up in a total nightmare – he is lying in a sea of blood in a place of infinite darkness. This is one of Arakawa-sensei's most imaginative sections of *Fullmetal Alchemist* – the limbo of death and ruination inside Gluttony (this homunculus is a botched attempt by Father to fashion a portal to the Gate of Truth). It's a perfect visualization of the Kristevan abject, a zone where everything winds up that's been rejected from the body, from society, from culture.

Broken pillars, skeletons, part of a car, and the last flickers of the flames that Roy Mustang hurled at Gluttony lie about, half-sunk in the red slime: Ed is very confused. He works out that they must have been swallowed, and the liquid swirling around his feet is blood. He looks around, sees nothing but shadows, and cries out, in a full page drawing that closes chapter 50: 'WHERE AM I!?'

○

Chapter 51: *A Portal In the Darkness* is a *tour-de-force* of *manga* storytelling, taking our heroes into a surreal non-place, Himoru Arakawa's version of Purgatory or Hell. It looks as if Edward E. is on his own, with no way out. He wanders about, shouting, until he meets Ling Yao (handily, they can make flaming torches from the remains of Mustang's alchemy). They explore, discovering the car, bits of the house, and Al's hand (which Ed picks up. So he knows that Al is probably all right, tho' no doubt worried about him. Later, he forgets to keep the hand, when they manage to escape).

Edward is determined to get out, no matter what. He alchemizes a hole in a piece of soil. They drop the torch into it and of course it never reaches the bottom, just falls and falls (as they always do in adventure yarns). Ed takes out Hawkeye's gun, and shoots it in different directions. Nothing. No impact, and no echo.

By now, Ed and Ling are faltering, with no food or water and no sign of any way out. Ling collapses first. Ed threatens to leave him (only half-serious), but ends up carrying him. In a moment of mad desperation, Ed takes off his boots and suggests they do a Charlie Chaplin – and eat his boots ('I saw it in a movie when I was a kid, there was a scene of a shoe being boiled and eaten'). Ling's not convinced, even tho' he's at death's door. But, yes, they do eat the boots.

---

2 This is reprised with Olivia Armstrong later.

Just then, Himoru Arakawa introduces a third character: trudging thru the blood ocean is someone they so don't want to see – Envy. After trading the expected insults (mandatory any time that Envy enters a scene – especially one that includes Ed!), Envy wearily informs them that there's no way out. Really. Seriously. Definitely. Because Gluttony 'is an artificial Portal of Truth created by Father' (but the experiment failed).

Ling and Edward are incensed by Envy's fatalistic attitude, how he keeps on insisting that there's no way out, and that they're going to die here. 'It can't be true, if I die, what's going to happen to Al?' Ed mutters (Ed's thoughts go straight to Alphonse any time something threatening occurs).

Ed Elric moves into detective mode: if the Führer is a homunculus, then the issue of corruption runs deep: lab number five, the homunculi, the philosopher's stones, and the Ishbal War – they're all connected. Ah, Ishbal – Envy can't help gloating once more, bragging about how he was the soldier who shot the child which set off the civil war.

Edward can't believe what he's hearing – because the Ishbal War killed thousands, including Winry Rockbell's folks, left the region in ruins (and affected his homeland), turned people into refugees, and led to a damaged, murderous ghoul like Scar.

So after plenty of talk, it's time for action; Edward hurls himself at Envy. But his punch has no effect. Even tho' he hates fighting, Envy, reckoning that they're going to die in Gluttony's belly anyway, decides to transform into his real guise: a colossal dog-lizard-monster (massive, scaly body, 8 legs (including his own legs, enlarged), a grotesque head filled with teeth, and, erupting from his sides, the screaming heads of transmuted people). Spread across two pages, the picture of the Envy-monster ups the ante considerably in the *Fullmetal Alchemist* comic. There's a lavish and exciting smackdown now, with our heroes being thrown about all over the place.

○

Elsewhere in chapter 51: *A Portal In the Darkness*, Loki, Mei Chang and Scar talk; we hear some of Mei's back-story (and how she found the tiny panda, Xiao Mei, in a distinctly Miyazakian flashback).

Meanwhile, a dejected Alphonse Elric sits on the ground in the forest, with Gluttony hovering uncomfortably nearby (he remembers, at least, that he's not allowed to eat Al, and that he shouldn't've swallowed Ling, Envy and Edward).

Himoru Arakawa's storytelling makes an interesting twist now: it's unusual, but it's convincing: when he hears about Gluttony's 'Father', Alphonse asks the homunculus to take him to his 'Father' (so maybe he can find out out how to rescue Ed). This works far more successfully than the similar uneasy alliance between the Elrics and Scar in the first *Fullmetal Alchemist* TV series – partly because it portrays Alphonse cleverly exploiting Gluttony's simple-minded, child-like personality (Glutsie is a personality who needs to be told what to do, all the time). So when Gluttony asks Al, 'if I take you there, will Father be happy?', Al of course answers, 'He'll be happy'. (Narratively, Arakawa wants to re-unite Ed and Al, naturally, and also to have them meet Father at the same time).

○

Chapter 52: *Lord of the Demon's Lair* opens with a defeated Col. Mustang talking to the Führer of Amestris over a nice cup of tea. Mustang wonders why he's been kept alive, now he knows so much (he doesn't know yet that the homunculi are going to be using him as a human sacrifice). Unbeknownst to Mustang, the Führer has already made his move to disperse Mustang's loyal team to the far corners of Amestris, in a divide-and-conquer tactic (with Liza Hawkeye to be kept close at hand, as the Führer's aide).

Meanwhile, Mei Chang is desperately seeking her pet panda Xiao Mei. In a rather too-obvious coincidence she (and Scar) witness Alphonse and Gluttony heading down an alley just as they're passing by), and into tunnels that lead to Fathers lair. We don't need Mei to tell us that the energy down there is scary and forbidding.

○

Now back to Envy, Ling Yao and Ed Elric in the belly of the beast (it's ironic that as Alphonse teams up uneasily with Gluttony, his brother is trapped inside Glutsie's body). Furious action scenes follow, with Ling and Edward using all of their (considerable) skills to smash Envy about (even tho' we can guess that Himoru Arakawa won't sacrifice a character as powerful as Envy just yet. Indeed, Envy requires multiple attacks to nobble him, and he receives about the finest death scene in the *Fullmetal Alchemist* franchise).

Confronted with a pathetic skull springing out of the Envy-monster's body that whimpers, 'kill me!', is enough to make Ed hesitate from attacking Envy (the motif is used 100s of times in the action-adventure genre, and Arakawa has already employed it for the moment when Envy bewildered Maes Hughes by impersonating his wife). The souls trapped inside Envy are lost and agonized: they utter tormented cries like, 'mother', 'big brother', 'sis', 'let's play', 'kill me', 'anybody', 'give me back my child' and 'don't look at me'.

It's too much for Edward Elric: he collapses, and is absorbed inside Envy body, as the lost souls grab hold of him, and pull him up inside Envy's maw. In Envy's body, Ed is surrounded by pleading, forlorn spirits: 'I don't want to die', 'join us', 'die with us'. (This scene is reminiscent of the moment in *Princess Mononoke* (1997) when Ashitaka and San are absorbed inside the boar-god).

But Edward Elric isn't the hero of *Fullmetal Alchemist* for nothing: he might be exhausted, famished, thirsty, has a broken arm and has little hope of escaping the hell of Gluttony's belly (and now Envy's body), but his mind never stops working. Flashing thru his consciousness are the fragments of the wall of Xerxes with the alchemical symbol on it which he saw back in the desert, and Envy's 'heart', the philosopher's stone. Now he knows how they can escape. He kicks his way out of Envy's gullet.

Mei Chang and Scar're battling batches of chimeras in the tunnels below Central City, as they head towards Father's bunker. Chapter 52: *Lord of the Demon's Lair* climaxes with the re-appearance of Father (sitting in his customary position on his throne). He is intrigued, because his guardians (the chimeras) are stirring, and someone is coming.

○

Chapter 53: *Signpost of the Soul* is one of the finest chapters in Himoru Arakawa's *œuvre*. The first part depicts the origins story of King Bradley (related by the Führer to Mustang): it is one of those despicable scientific experiments on humans conducted by Nazis (the Doctor With the Gold Tooth presiding over the operation here is very much in the cartoon Nazi manner). Father the super-villain of *Fullmetal Alchemist* has ordered the creation of an artificial homunculus, using a human specimen. There are heartless scenes of training and education, followed by gruesome medical tests, where a philosopher's stone is injected into the subject. Of course, most of the guys die from the injection of energy and dead souls, but Bradley manages to survive (the effects of the philosopher's stone create intense agony. Of course – when was the creation of a super-human creature portrayed as a calm, quiet, relaxing event?!).

Back to Alphonse E. and Gluttony now: they have reached the inner sanctum of Father. One can see Alphonse's complete amazement when he confronts the tall, bearded, imposing figure of Father, who is the splitting image of his own father: 'Dad?' And Father looks bemused: 'who are you?'

In Gluttony's belly, Edward Elric is piecing together the mystery of the alchemical mural from Xerxes (Envy has gathered the pieces of the broken building). In this part of *Fullmetal Alchemist*, Himoru Arakawa draws on historical alchemy, with references to alchemical symbols such as the sun (= the soul), the moon (= the spirit), and the lion swallowing the sun (= the philosopher's stone). There is a good deal of talk to set up the idea that Ed is going to use the lost souls trapped in Envy's body to open the false portal in Gluttony's body, in order to reach the real Gateway of Truth (using himself as the toll).

It's a talky preamble, but this is fascinating stuff, when Arakawa-sensei draws heavily on real alchemical metaphysics. After Ed has sketched a transmutation circle on the ground (following the one in the Xerxes mural), he asks Envy if the whole of Xerxes was used in a transmutation ritual. Envy (still gloating and superior), isn't saying; Ed also guesses that what's happening now in Amestris is the same thing. Except, this time, the whole nation will be employed, rather than the city-state of Xerxes.

Listening, Ling Yao wonders who it was who wanted to surpass even God (soon we will meet that figure). The characters prepare to dive into the portal once Edward opens it. He apologizes to the lost souls that he's going to use to transmute. (Ed is in a heightened, near-hysterical state – understandable, because this is a very dangerous operation which Edward hasn't done before. There are many things that can go wrong, and in spells of this kind, when things go wrong, they go *very* wrong).

Thus begins one of the stand-out sequences in the *Fullmetal Alchemist manga* – with Edward Elric performing the life-and-death alchemical ritual to escape from the endless limbo of Gluttony's stomach (if they don't do it soon, they will die of starvation).

It's a stunningly realized sequence, climaxing chapter 53: *Signpost of the Soul:* out comes the iconography of the Gateway of Truth: the giant eye, the black, grabbing arms, the disintegrating bodies, the zigzagging energy bolts, and the grinning demon-god.

In a moment of genius, Himoru Arakawa introduces *two* Gateways, allowing Edward to turn round see the body of his brother Alphonse: sitting on the ground, nude and bone-thin, with ragged hair, Al is waiting for his soul to reappear (from his own portal). This is the first time that Ed has seen his brother in his proper form (tho' wasting away) since the fateful night when they tried to transmute their dead mother back in Resembool.

Across a double page, we see Edward in close-up, and Alphonse behind him. It's a marvellous, magical moment – and it's highly emotional. And as soon as Ed realizes that the boy over there is his beloved brother, he rushes towards him. And of course that is the instant when the grasping hands wrest him backwards, through his own portal.

'AL!!' Edward screams, struggling against the little, grabbing hands that're wrenching him backwards thru the Gateway of Truth. Himoru Arakawa orchestrates some superbly judged angles and points-of-view imagery in this sequence, as Ed reaches out to Alphonse, hoping to take him back through the portal, to rejoin his soul.

But he can't – 'You're not my soul', Alphonse's body says.[3] Al's expression of sadness and bemused acceptance as he watches his brother struggling in the doorway with the elemental forces of life and death is priceless: Edward screams at Al: 'One day soon, I'm coming to get you, no matter what!'

This is genius storytelling.

And the pay-off of this thrilling sequence is two magnificent moments to round off chapter 53: *Signpost of the Soul*: the first has our heroes emerging from Gluttony's belly, with Edward being re-united with Alphonse. This is a spectacle of birth-like imagery, as the characters erupt from the stomach of Gluttony (with blood and energy and speed lines). Indeed, Alphonse even picks up Edward like a baby at birth, upside-down (with placenta-like coils around his legs).

The reunion of the brothers is played for high emotion plus comedy. After all, these two characters are what *Fullmetal Alchemist* is all about, and the *manga* generates its deepest emotions when they are in the foreground. This is a truly, properly dramatic reunion for the brothers.

The second magical beat is when Edward sees Father: here we have the full reveal of the super-villain, Father. And, yes, he looks exactly like the boys' pa, van Hohenheim. Notice, too, that we see Father for the first time when Edward first sees him (not Alphonse), because the full

---

3 Ed realizes that they are connected through their souls.

revelation has been saved to form the climax of chapter 53 (and Himoru Arakawa often privileges Ed's point-of-view).

We are halfway thru the 108 chapters of *Fullmetal Alchemist*, and Himoru Arakawa has pulled out all the stops to deliver some very fine artwork and some truly inspired storytelling. This is a *manga* that goes to some very unusual places, and is very fantastical, but it completely convinces, partly because the emotional structure is so solid.

○

Chapter 54: *The Fool's Struggle* opens with the all-important confront-ation between the Elric brothers and the arch-villain of Himoru Arakawa's *Fullmetal Alchemist*, Father. Intriguingly, Arakawa gives Father some eccentric quirks – like looming in suddenly towards the lads, or grabbing Edward's head. And, incredibly, Father *smiles*! Yes, he *grins* – tho' this is about the only time in the *manga* that he does (yet Father, when he was the homunculus in the jar, often smirked – but like the Cheshire Cat in *Alice's Adventures In Wonderland*).

Father is amused to think that van Hohenheim had children. But the fact that Hohenheim is still alive is more worrying for Father – because Hohenheim is about the only person on the planet who can offer a serious threat to Father (after all, it was Hohenheim, as the flashbacks to Xerxes later on illustrate, who released the homunculus from the glass jar).

Anyhoo, apart from appearing creepy and strange (mandatory for any villain in Japanese pop culture), Father also performs some very significant acts: he fixes Alphonse's lost hand and Edward's broken arm and ribs. Thus, he acts like a parent, healing the kids. But he does this, of course, for his own ends (to keep the boys intact, as they are going to be sacrifices in Father's bid for Godhood).

It doesn't take long for Edward E. to turn against Father, when he realizes that he is the progenitor of the homunculi, and the super-villain behind much of the evil in Amestris. So Ed attacks Father. Which we know will be completely ineffectual. After all, if Ed can't best Scar, or one of the homunculi on their own, he has no hope against Father. Also, two homunculi are right there, too: Gluttony and Envy (still in his monster-dog form, and Ed and Ling together couldn't defeat Envy). But, after bringing together some of the main charas, Arakawa-sensei of course has to have them fight (it would be crazy to lose this opportunity!).

Father sighs, unaffected by any of the attacks of Edward or Ling Yao. He turns to leave, unleashing a blast wave of alchemical energy at the same time. This deactivates the Elrics' ability to alchemize. The energy moves out from Central City, right up into the mountains, so that even van Hohenheim is aware of it, as he walks with a guide (he's researching into Father's plans).

Once the lads can't transmute, it doesn't take long for the Envy-beast to have Al and Ed pinned down on the ground, with his claws (while Gluttony sits on top of Ling – *ouch*! that has got to hurt!).

Now Father, who is the dominant figure in this group (despite the best efforts of our heroes), makes a fascinating decision: to rebirth Greed using the body of Ling Yao. From his forehead, out pops a third eye, dripping with philosopher's stone liquid. The Elrics are incensed, but unable to do much – they can't perform alchemy, and they're trapped by the Envy-monster. In desperation, Ed pulls out the gun that Hawkeye gave him, but he hesitates again (when confronted by the forlorn, weeping heads bulging out of the Envy-creature).

But then there's a superb narrative twist from Himoru Arakawa – Ling Yao *wants* to be implanted with the philosopher's stone! Yes, Ling has plenty of avarice – for immortality, for power (and to return to Xing with something substantial).

So Father lets the philosopher's stone drip onto Ling Yao's face. The alchemical transformation is intensely painful. Ling screams, clenching his fist, crawling on the floor. 'I'm the future Emperor of Xing!' he cries, before screaming again.

A terrific artistic choice by Himoru Arakawa occurs now, taking us *inside* Ling Yao's soul: against a background of elongated, Hallowe'en masks, and using a black border around the drawings (to differentiate them from regular narration), we see Ling's body floating, and the huge, scary demon-mask appearance of Greed. Arakawa portrays a conversation in a spiritual zone between Greed and Ling (the filmmakers in the 2nd *animé* series of *Fullmetal Alchemist* did full justice to this concept, using reds and blacks, and a zooming movement).

Ling Yao is happy to give up his body to Greed, much to Greed's surprise: 'it's like a dream come true!!' So Greed takes possession of it (tho' Himoru Arakawa plays with the notion that Ling is still somewhere inside, and Edward can't help but address Greed-Ling as Ling. After all, Edward was partly responsible for Greed's injuries. The Greed-and-Ling double-act in one body plays out many times in the subsequent chapters. Often charas aren't sure at first which one is dominant).

◯

Chapter 55: *The Avarice of Two* continues the amazing duologue inside Ling Yao's body between the souls of Ling and Greed. Well, Greed might've met his match here with Ling, in the greedy, hungry stakes. There's no way that Ling will lose face by going back to Xing empty-handed, so having his body possessed by an insanely avaricious homunculus works for him.

With this startling twist in the plot of *Fullmetal Alchemist* dealt with, Himoru Arakawa wheels in Scar and Mei Chang, for a demonstration of several types of alchemy – Ed and Al's Amestrisian alchemy, Father's mysterious powers, Scar's destructive, Ishbalian talents, and Mei's Xingese, dragonish alkrahestry.

Before the inevitable fights (Himoru Arakawa never forgets – or her editors never allow her to forget – that this is a *shonen manga*, being published in a boys' magazine, where fighting is everywhere), there's time for a little comedy. Mei Chang has been idolizing Edward Elric as a pop idol-type, a *bishonen* hunk that she enshrines in her over-heated, romantic imagination in he♥rts-and-flowers, *shojo manga* style. So when Mei is confronted with the *chibi* fullmetal alchemist, she can't believe it. Such a let-down! All of her lovey-dovey illusions are shattered. 'You took advantage of the naïvety of a maiden, you little rice grain man!!' she yells. They've never met, of course, but Ed is right back at her: 'what did you say, you little rice grain girl!?'

Then the fights begin – Gluttony versus Scar, Mei Chang versus Ed, Scar versus the Envy-monster, Gluttony versus Mei, Ling/ Greed versus Edward, and Scar versus Father. As the Elrics're unable to use alchemy, clever Edward tells Scar a snippet of info he knows'll wind up the Ishbalian no end (Scar teeters on the verge of hysteria all the time), and turn the scarred man against the homunculi: that it was these guys, the homunculi, who started the Ishbalian War.

So Scar goes to work (not even bothering to corroborate Edward's story), attempting to attack Envy, Gluttony and even Father. Doesn't work, of course. The super-villain is intrigued: he thought he knew everything about alchemy, but how is it that both Scar and the tiny Xingese girl can use alchemy, when he has just disabled it?

The Gluttony versus Mei Chang fight is very nasty – nobody wants to see li'l Mei being beaten to shreds by the psychopathic tub of lard that is Gluttony. Luckily, Alphonse Elric hurries over to the rescue, and spirits Mei-chan away. Aided (for now) by Scar, they battle their way past the chimeras in the corridor.

Meanwhile, Ling-Greed is duking it out with Ed Elric . They're both punching and kicking, but, without the ability to alchemize, Ed relies on his martial arts skills and his automail limbs. The scene ends in a stalemate, with Himoru Arakawa running out of time to give the chapter a satisfying close. Father orders Greed/ Ling to take them to Wrath (the Führer).

✱

Chapter 56: *The Lion of the Round Table* continues the high fantasy events in Father's bunker below Central City. Father yanks out Gluttony's heart (his philosopher's stone), promising to recreate him.

Ed and Al're recuperating back in neutral territory; they discuss what happened with Father & co.; Edward takes a shower (leading to the inevitable jokes about nudity, when Ed emerges from the shower – because Alphonse is harbouring the injured Mei Chang inside his armour). Envy, in the guise of an Amestrisian guard, is watching over the lads, and takes them to meet the Führer, who's still talking to Col. Mustang. Here, all three of our heroes wonder whether they could nobble the homunculus Wrath, because they're alone in a room with him.

Belligerent as ever, Edward Elric wants to resign from military service, and gives up his silver pocket watch (the equivalent of handing in your badge for a cop). The Führer, however, insists that he *will* serve the military, and threatens Ed with the possibility of harming Winry Rockbell (you can imagine how Ed reacts to that!). This time, however, the homunculi have gotten the better of our heroes, and they have to submit.

As they leave, Himoru Arakawa replays the moment when Führer

Bradley thrusts his sword into Al's armour (he heard Mei Chang sneeze earlier). Luckily, li'l Mei has slid into one of Al's legs, to miss the sword.

Several short conversations scenes follow: Mustang is re-united with Hawkeye and Armstrong; Ed and Al talk with Ling Yao (he gives them a message to relay to Lan Fan); Ed calls up Winry at Garfiel's place, to check she's OK (and that the Führer hasn't made any moves yet); Al goes to see Dr Knox and Lan Fan; and the Führer talks to Greed-Ling.

And as he wanders around the city performing alchemical works of repair, Edward E. ponders on the issue of Father, and how he was able to nullify their form of alchemy.

✳

Chapter 57: *Scars of Ishbal* features several small groups of characters (Al + Lan Fan, Armstrong + Hawkeye + Mustang, Knox + Al, etc), discussing the implications of recent events – that the Führer is a homunculus, what the homunculi are up to, and how this relates to the Ishbalian War. We are re-setting goals and ambitions and motives (once again).

More amusing is the encounter between Mei Chang and Lan Fan, two fiercely proud, Xingese women. Yes, of *course* they tussle as soon as they meet! – Mei's throwing her *shuriken*, and Lan Fan is climbing out of bed to do battle. There is plenty of glaring and aggressive badinage, with Alphonse trying to keep the peace between them (and not really understanding intense, Xingese rivalries between clans). Until Dr Knox walks in, sees his patients misbehaving in horror, and angrily orders them to rest.

The theme of the Ishbal War looms large in this chapter – it takes up the whole of the next volume of *Fullmetal Alchemist*. For ex, Dr Knox talks about being haunted by what he experienced there, and Scar encounters Dr Marcoh, one of the alchemists involved in the war.

In this meeting, Dr Marcoh at first pretends to be Mauro, a doctor captured by the homunculi. But Marcoh embodies the guilt and shame of the Ishbal War, and soon he confesses to being Tim Marcoh.

Meanwhile, Edward Elric decides to pay Liza Hawkeye a visit (ostensibly to return her pistol). But the real point of dropping by is to inaugurate the lengthy flashback of the Ishbal War. That this long tale comes from the viewpoint of Hawkeye (whom author Himoru Arakawa seems to identify with), is significant – but more significant, of course, is that the story is told to the main character of *Fullmetal Alchemist*, Ed Elric. (The 'fan service' moment of Hawkeye taking a shower when Ed calls is shameless – it reveals Hawkeye's alchemical tattoo on her back, of course, but it also depicts the character naked. Well, this *is* a *shonen manga*!).[4] This volume ends with more *omake* (including a short story depicting the young Elric family, when the boys were toddlers).

✳

Chapter 58: *The Footsteps of Ruin* begins the lengthy flashback to the

---

4 In her Q & A entries, Arakawa said her assistants argued with her about Hawkeye's body shape (they thought it was too skinny). Arakawa insisted that Hawkeye's shoulders would be broad from her military training, but her hips would be 'bada-boom!'

Ishbal War (it takes up the four chapters of volume 15 of *Fullmetal Alchemist*). This is a crucial chapter in Himoru Arakawa's *Fullmetal Alchemist* saga. Arakawa-sensei said she looked at movies, documentaries, and interviewed veterans of WW2. Altho' *Fullmetal Alchemist* is a fantasy adventure series for boys, it is also Arakawa-sensei's alternative history of the 20th century, and her alternative history of two World Wars. Apart from the alchemical elements, the images and scenarios are very much taken from history.

And moral questions are raised throughout this volume: what is war for? why are civilians being deliberately killed? and why are alchemists, who should work for the good of humankind, being used as weapons?

The characters spearheading the Ishbal flashback include Roy Mustang, Liza Hawkeye, Alex Armstrong, Maes Hughes, Zolf Kimbley, and of course Scar and his brother. Before we get to Ishbal seven years earlier, there is another flashback, where we meet a young Mustang (several years before the Ishbal War). He is apprenticed to Hawkeye's father, who teaches him alchemy. Master Hawkeye is the familiar stern, eccentric teacher, who (like Izumi Curtis with the Elrics), despises the military, and scorns Mustang for wanting to be a 'dog of the military'. Hawkeye has passed on the secrets of his flame alchemy to his daughter Liza. He is ill, and expires soon.

This glimpse into the back-story of both Liza H. and Roy M. doesn't last long, but it establishes the power relation btn them, the unspoken erotic desire, and the call of duty (Mustang's resolve to work for the military, and to rise to the top, and Hawkeye's determination to protect him).

Which leads us into the present tense, and Ed Elric visiting Liza Hawkeye in her modest *aparto*. They talk at the table (Hawkeye cleans her gun), and the conversation leads towards the topic of Ishbal. This fascinates Himoru Arakawa – the issue of a nation invaded by a larger, better-equipped force (which evokes Japan, but many other scenarios, principally the Middle East).

Himoru Arakawa begins the four Ishbal flashback chapters with the victims – the Ishbalians. Scenes include: Scar, his brother, and arguments about alchemy (Scar would prefer it if his brother forgot all about blasphemous alchemy); a narrative shift to Winry's parents, the Rockbell doctors (they're told to leave Ishbal, but opt to stay and continue to heal people); scenes of the Amestrisian government locking up Ishbalian officers; and the 'Presidential Decree Number 306' (this evokes the many orders of the Nazi regime leading up to and during WWII).

This is the moment when the military sends in its secret weapons to end the Ishbalian War – State Alchemists (including charas such as Mustang and Kimbley).

✳

Chapter 59: *The Immoral Alchemist* continues the Descent Into Hell that Himoru Arakawa portrays in her *Fullmetal Alchemist manga*. The 'immoral alchemist' of the title of this chapter is Dr Marcoh: he is presiding over revolting alchemical experiments in the secret fifth laboratory in Central City, which use living humans as fodder (in this case, Ishbalians).

This is *very* grim material, which draws on the grotesque medical experiments that the Nazis performed during WW2 (*Fullmetal Alchemist* is certainly as bitter and bleak as any comic in Japan, including all of the examples trotted out as 'dark'). When Dr Marcoh performs the transmutation, five victims expire (very painfully) – all to produce one tiny philosopher's stone (which is subsequently used to kill Ishbalians).

The following scenes of Amestrisian soldiers, aided by State Alchemists, killing women, children and old folk as well as able-bodied Ishbalian men are like a documentary of 20th century horrors (where, according to some estimates, 260 million people were killed by their own governments). This is Amestris as a 'genocidal state' (as a critic described Nazi Germany in the 1930s).

Alex Armstrong, haunted by what the military is doing, lets some Ishbalians go free (by forging a hole in a wall), only for the old couple to then be slaughtered by the Crimson Alchemist[5] (who informs Armstrong that he would be court-martialed if anyone saw what he did). We also see Roy Mustang employing his flame alchemy (learnt from Hawkeye senior) to slay more Ishbalians (one victim berates Mustang as he dies that alchemy should be used for the good of mankind. Mustang has this issue pushed in his face repeatedly).

When Mustang meets his old buddy Maes Hughes, the tone lightens a teensy bit (tho' the topic of conversation is the war). Liza Hawkeye is introduced too, with the shamelessly over-the-top gimmick of saving Mustang and Hughes from a murderous Ishbalian wielding a knife by sniping him from a church tower. (When Hawkeye encounters Mustang a little later, it seems to be the first time they've seen each other since the flashback at the Hawkeyes' home in ch. 58).

Further scenes in chapter 59 depict the military brass examining the philosopher's stone fashioned by Dr Marcoh, and a meeting btn Marcoh and Dr Knox (where they discuss the moral question of why doctors, who should be healing people, are being used to kill people).

✳

Chapter 60: *In the Absence of God* continues the Ishbal War sequence (God is *very* absent in these chapters of *Fullmetal Alchemist*). The chapter opens with another flashback to the earlier lives of Mustang and Hawkeye: they bond at her father's graveside. Here we discover that Old Hawkeye passed on the secrets of his flame alchemy in a bizarre and creepy manner – by tattooing them on his daughter's back! Ouch! Thanks, Dad! How about using a notebook, like everybody else! Even a Death Note would be preferrable to this! (This is one of the more out-there concepts in *Fullmetal Alchemist* – somehow, it works with a violent anti-hero like Scar to have alchemical tattoos, but not the lovely Liza-chan!).

Anyway, Liza Hawkeye turns away from Roy Mustang slightly, to

5 A.k.a. the Red Lotus.

expose her back, and suggests that Mustang might be able to decipher her Daddy's coded secrets.

To do good, to use alchemy well, is the hope here. But not to use alchemy as an instrument of war. 'How could we have fallen so low?' asks Hawkeye, as the *Fullmetal Alchemist manga* returns to the present tense. Himoru Arakawa employs a striking and rare use of reversed tones in a double-pager, so the drawings are white outlines over black, to express the horrors of war – images of burnt bodies, weeping children, rows of corpses, and the main charas in action.

During a break in hostilities, some of the key charas offer differing points-of-view on the Ishbal conflict: Zolf Kimbley voices the stance of the professional soldier's pride in his job, and derides peaceniks. Col. Mustang and Liza Hawkeye are ashamed at how far they've slipped morally. Maes Hughes's reasons are practical: 'it's simple: I don't want to die. That's all'. And poor Armstrong is crying, holding a dead child, and asking, 'Why?' (Armstrong is depicted as a big softie in the military, breaking down and weeping several times – to the disgust of his colleagues).

The carnage in Ishbal continues: Basque Grand[6] turns up and wields some of his steam-punk iron and blood alchemy. Ishbalians die. Commodore Fesler orders more men into battle (from the safety of a hut, behind the lines); when they hesitate, Basque shoots Fesler and assumes command.

The Ishbalains' Supreme Cleric, Logue Lowe, offers himself up to the Führer in exchange for a cease-fire. No dice. Bradley is unsympathetic: for him, there is no bargaining, and one life is only worth one life. Scenes follow of refugee camps, of the Rockbell doctors trying to save lives, and of an Adolf Hitler lookalike ordering Kimbley to get rid of the Rockbells.

＊

Chapter 61: *The Hero of Ishbal* depicts the invasion of Ishbal by the Amestrisian military. Zolf Kimbley, powered by philosopher's stones, wreaks havoc by blowing up whole town blocks. Kimbley is a psychopath who gets off on the sound of 'rapturous destruction' (he's one of the scariest charas in *Fullmetal Alchemist*, a mass murderer utterly without remorse).

This is the moment when the Crimson Alchemist attacks an Ishbalian town, wounding Scar and his brother (the brother leaps in front of Scar to protect him). To save Scar, his brother cuts off his arm and joins it onto Scar (using alchemy).

When Scar wakens, he's in hospital, being tended by the Rockbells. In his rage against Amestrisians, he kills them, then flees. And he vows – as if we needed telling – 'VENGEANCE!'

In one of the final acts of hostility, Roy Mustang kills a wounded, cornered Ishbalian, whose last words are:

'I WILL NEVER FORGIVE YOU'.

---

6 Basque Grand is named after Bismarck.

In the following scenes, the military are getting ready to go home. They drink, but there is no joy for Mustang, Hughes, Hawkeye and others who reckon they've just been through Hell. At an army parade, Mustang looks up at the Führer, presiding over the gathering, and asserts his ambition to become the leader of Amestris. Kimbley slays a group of officers (to hide the fact that he's stolen philosopher's stones).

Mustang and Hawkeye have another of their serious, sad conversations (over a grave the lieutenant's just dug for an Ishbalian child). Hawkeye begs Mustang to burn off the tattoo from her back, so that there'll be no more flame alchemists. The formation of Mustang's unit occurs next (with Hawkeye signing up).

✳

Chapter 62: *Beyond the Dream* brings us to the end of the Liza Hawkeye-narrated flashback, with Hawkeye and Edward Elric sitting in her kitchen. It's vital that Ed knows everything about Ishbal, because it gives him clues how to defeat the villain (Father) at the end of *Fullmetal Alchemist*.

Now we switch to Dr Knox, Mei Chang, and Alphonse Elric (at Dr Knox's house), and Edward being re-united with his brother (on the streets nearby). They talk: their goals and dreams are re-set here (again). Scar discusses similar issues with Dr Marcoh, also stating his aims.

Himoru Arakawa now gets her characters in motion: Dr Marcoh is smuggled out of Father's clutches (and is painfully disfigured by Scar using alchemy, so he can't be recognized⁷), and Mei Chang leaves Dr Knox, to join up with Scar, Loki and Marcoh. Oh, what a pity that Mei opts to re-join those losers (as Knox puts it: 'you're travelling with a serial killer?! Don't do it!!'). Mei insists that Scar is a good person. (We'd much prefer to see Mei team up with the Elrics. I wouldn't go anywhere near Scar if I was in Amestris – he wrecks Dr Marcoh's face without even asking first! There *are* less agonized forms of travelling in disguise! Can't Marcoh rustle up one of Lupin III's masks?!).

Spy thriller shenanigans follow among Colonel Mustang and his troop – there are coded conversations, meetings in bars, assignations with 'Madame Christmas', fake dates with girls, messages hidden in chess pieces, etc.

So where is the new destination of the characters in *Fullmetal Alchemist*? The North – this is where much of the action in the following chapters is set.

The Elrics are hunting for Mei Chang, because she might be able to tell them more about Xingese alchemy. Instead, they run into Roy Mustang: this is a significant meeting, because they won't see anybody from Central City for some time when they travel North to Briggs Mountain.

✳

Chapter 63: *The Promise Made For 520 Cents* – the title comes from some money that Mustang lends Edward Elric. It becomes a running joke between them (with a promise from Mustang to become President of

Amestris, and turn the nation into a democracy). Instead of finding Mei Chang, they run into Fuu, the old bodyguard of Ling Yao's, who's back from the Xingese desert. The lads take Fuu to see his granddaughter Lan Fan, still recovering at Dr Knox's place. Once again, there are declarations of goals, this time from the Xingese charas Fuu and Lan Fan (that's after Fuu has slapped his granddaughter hard in the face for being so stupid for losing her arm!).

Much of chapter 63: *The Promise Made For 520 Cents* comprises Himoru Arakawa organizing her characters into new or re-established groups, re-setting their intentions and destinations, and manœurving them into place (exactly like chess pieces), as she sets up the following plotlines.

So further movements of groups of characters are charted in ch. 63: Mei Chang at the railroad station (bumping into General Grumman in drag); Dr Knox's estranged children paying an unexpected (and awkward) visit; Grumman meeting Col. Mustang at a cemetery (at the grave of Maes Hughes, of course), where they exchange info; and Zolf Kimbley is sprung from prison by the homunculi. Some foreshadowing is revealed in the graveyard scene, when Grumman tells Mustang that the military has been developing 'immortal soldiers'.

Finally, in a library, where the Elric brothers are still searching for alchemical clues, they are given their best hint yet: Mei Chang has been spotted heading North (Grumman saw her at the station). At last, the boys can move (Ed muses that they might have to cross the desert to Xing, if they want to find out about Xingese alchemy. But surely there might be a way of discovering alchemical info from other people in Amestris – especially in the capital city. But no, I guess it's more exciting if the lads chase after a teenage girl heading North!).

It's Alex Armstrong who gives Ed Elric the good news about the sighting of Mei Chang; why? because it's Armstrong sister Olivia Maria who presides over the North/ Briggs chapters of *Fullmetal Alchemist* (Armstrong hands Ed a letter of introduction for his sister). Himoru Arakawa teases us with a low angle, shadowy, 3/4-page image of Olivia A., our first view of her, flanked by her flunkies Buccaneer and Miles.

✳

Chapter 64: *The Northern Wall of Briggs* opens with yet another library scene (yes, the Elric lads certainly do spend a lot of time in libraries!). This time it's a light-hearted scene where Selim Bradley admires Alphonse: ten year-old Selim is depicted in *shojo manga*-style, with too-big eyes and a starry background (at this point, we don't know that li'l Selim is actually a psychopathic homunculus). This's why Himoru Arakawa includes a seemingly minor scene with Selim – because he is the last homunculus to be revealed, and because the Elrics are moving North very soon, so it's a last chance for them to meet him in his *kawaii* boy guise.

Indeed, Edward hurries into the library to drag Alphonse away, as they're off again (after the customary jokes about Ed's height: 'Wow!! You really are a tiny alchemist, just like everyone says!!' Selim gushes. Just the kind of comment that Ed loves to hear!).

So everybody's heading North in *Fullmetal Alchemist* – the cold, tough, icy world of thousands of adventure tales (Arakawa-sensei, hailing from Hokkaido in the Far North of Japan's archipelago, has a particular fondness for snowy, mountainous realms, which she portrayed in the follow-up *manga Silver Spoon*). Zolf Kimbley is at a railroad yard (tipped off by his men), as is Scar. Here comes Part One of the inevitable Kimbley vs. Scar smackdown. (Marcoh and Chang are making their way North separately, trudging thru snow to another abandoned cottage; and there's a single page devoted to Winry, to remind us of a chara not seen for many pages, phoning the Elrics from Garfiel's store. Winry also turns up in the North, later).

Meanwhile, we cut to the Elric siblings now already in the North, in the foothills below Briggs Mountain. Icy blasts of wind, deep snow, and biting cold – welcome to Briggs! Where survival is all. We encounter the soldier Buccaneer first – introduced as a scary, Russian Bear looming out of a blizzard. When your heroes trek to a major, new setting, you can expect action and duels in the adventure genre, rather than smiles and cups of coffee in the soap opera genre. So, the first order of business is to feature a fight in snow, Ed's automail freezing up, and Buccaneer and his guards treating the Elrics as spies from Drachma (Russia).

After all, what with the previous chapter (63: *The Promise Made For 520 Cents*), plus the many Ishbal War flashback chapters, it's been a long time since we saw Ed and Al fighting. And as the fog clears, we have our first look at Major General Olivia Maria Armstrong, the hard-as-nails commander of Briggs Mountain (tall, blonde,[8] steely, imperious, stubborn, proud, professional, and someone you don't want to cross – she's the ice princess, the snow warrior, Brunhilde), followed, a few pages later, by a double-page spread depicting the Briggs Fortress – a vast concrete and stone wall or dam constructed across a valley.

✲

Chapter 65: *The Ironclad Rule* introduces us to the tough regime at Briggs Fortress. After the boys have been fixed up by the automail techies (they even charge for their coffee! It's 100 cents! Ed is not amused!), Olivia Armstrong pays them a visit. Like the lengthy scene with Miles that follows, these are exposition scenes, which set out the hierarchy and rules of Briggs Fort (because we will be spending quite some time up in the snowy, Northern regions of Amestris). The Elrics don't tell Armstrong everything, but she doesn't give up (she waits until she has the right setting for a full interrogation). One reason that Armstrong is patient is because she wants their knowledge of new alchemical arts – in Briggs, on Drachma's doorstep, any new military techniques are welcome.

Miles takes the brothers on the Welcome To Briggs Tour (he's an Ishbalian (on his grandfather's side), one of Himoru Arakawa's ways of keeping the Ishbal War issue alive). Thus, there is more discussion of the Ishbal conflict, a topic that fascinates Arakawa-sensei. Miles also delivers

---

8 The colour pages that begin the next chapter depict Olivia with yellow-blonde hair, blue eyes, and pink lips.

some characterization and back-story for Major Armstrong (evoking just how scary she is).

For one of several times in the *Fullmetal Alchemist manga*, the Elric boys are given an actual job to do. (Remember, Briggs Mountain is Himoru Arakawa's version of Hokkaido, the tough North of Japan where she grew up, and where, she tells us, everybody has to work). So the lads are told to knock off the icicles hanging from the ceilings with a stick, which can be dangerous when they're large. (This idea's not wasted, either – icicles are used in the scene where the homunculus Sloth is bested).

＊

We now return to the Zolf Kimbley vs. Scar Smackdown – this is Part Two: in the unlikely but certainly spectacular setting of a train rushing through snow-laden forests (like a scene from the movie *Runaway Train*, 1985, or the *Lone Ranger* remake of 2013), the two opponents continue their battle (it's also another resumption of the War of Ishbal).

Scar manages to stab the State Alchemist with a piece of pipe, but Kimbley, severely wounded, is somehow able to uncouple the carriages, allowing him to flee into the night – thus putting off the resolution of the smackdown yet again. (These are two despicable charas we would be happy to see rip each other to shreds).

Back at Briggs Fortress, the tour comes to an end in the lower levels. Himoru Arakawa has vividly evoked a macho, harsh world of tunnels, pipes, walkways, gruff men, weaponry and extreme cold – something like a Russian submarine crossed with a dam and a military station of the Cold War era near the North Pole (with obvious echoes of the uneasy relationship between Russia and Japan in the disputed Northern islands of the archipelago).

Now the penultimate homunculus in *Fullmetal Alchemist* is intro-duced – Sloth. As in a horror story, it's/ he's first heard as a digging sound inside a metal pipe. A double page spread (seen from the perspective of the Elrics), reveals Sloth in close-up: an ugly giant with a black skull cap, topless, wearing braces, he/ it is shown literally clawing his/ its way through the bedrock with his/ its fists. To Sloth, as with the very laidback Shikamaru in *Naruto*, making an effort is a pain.

＊

Chapter 66: *The Snow Queen* (the title of course refers to Major General Olivia Maria Armstrong, the ruler of Briggs Fortress with a blade of iron), is partly a Monster of the Week outing, with the giant Sloth causing havoc when it erupts from the tunnel below the fort. Now it's battle stations, as everybody tries to kill the thing. Luckily, Sloth is slow and very stupid, but also unkillable and extremely strong.

Unfortunately for the Elrics, they just happen to be nearest the homunculus when it emerges, and they know what it is, which seems to confirm to onlookers that they really are Drachman spies.

The weaponry deployed against Sloth rapidly escalates from handguns to a bazooka (wielded by Major Armstrong, of course), all the way up to a tank. Himoru Arakawa may be a mom with two kids, but that doesn't mean she can't be an artist who gets down and dirty with the boys, and can deliver a tanks vs. monster scenario, in the manner of Katsuhiro Otomo (*Akira*), Masamune Shirow (*Appleseed*), or Hayao Miyazaki (*Nausicaä*).

Yes, Japanese *mangaka* are seldom happier than when they're drawing tanks battling monsters! Boom! Bang! But even tank shells don't have much effect; and the Sloth creature can regenerate, too.

The E. boys help (protecting some soldiers from falling debris with an alchemized stone wall), but stopping a homunculus will take more than Elrician alchemy. Some rough-and-ready, Briggs Fortress know-how is required: it's Major General Armstrong who comes up with the solution: it's the Ice Queen's moment to shine.

In keeping with Himoru Arakawa's emphasis on the severe cold of the Far North, it's the low temperature that nobbles Sloth. The sequence is great fun – Sloth is bashed and banged by several tanks into a big service elevator, and taken to a higher level, which has a gate with a walkway. Ed and Buccaneer douse the monster with vehicle fuel, and everybody does their bit to help to shove it off the walkway, to the snow below, where it rapidly freezes (Buccaneer throws it, Armstrong pushes it with a tank, Falman shoots down an icicle which confuses it, and the Elrics launch themselves at it with martial arts kicks).

Chapter 66: *The Snow Queen* ends with the mystery of the attack and the tunnel still to be solved, and the Elric brothers tied up as spies again.

✷

Chapter 67: *Burgeoning Borders* delivers the full reveal of the Super-Villain's Plans – at last! 67: *Burgeoning Borders* starts with the lads back in jail, and Miles visiting Zolf Kimbley in hospital (recovering following his duel with Scar); there's no love lost btn them (Kimbley is an arrogant •••• as usual).

A new chara, General Raven, is introduced (50s, grey beard), visiting Kimbley, accompanied by a shady guy we've seen lurking about during the fifth laboratory rites in chapter 53: *Signpost of the Soul* – the Doctor With the Gold Tooth (i.e., a version of a Nazi scientist); this hateful man turns up during the finale of *Fullmetal Alchemist*.

Meanwhile, the scouting party has returned from the tunnel below Briggs, and found nothing except that the tunnel is very, very long. So Major General Armstrong becomes the Strong Leader again, and leads a group into the hole, accompanied by the Elrics. Down the tunnel, far from eavesdroppers, Armstrong demands to know everything the boys can tell her. So Edward launches into the spiel of their story (leaving out certain facts). Ellipsing the telling of the tale (which we know very well), we cut to the after-discussion, as Armstrong & co. absorb what they've heard (the Führer's a homunculus... the philosopher's stone... widespread corrupt-ion... etc).

Now comes the reveal of the whole plot in *Fullmetal Alchemist* – well, most of it: notice that it's Edward Elric who's leading this scene: after all, he is the main character. Using a map to illustrate his argument, Ed shows us that the enemy is planning to create a giant transmutation circle using the whole of Amestris.

This is a smart piece of writing from Himoru Arakawa – how she begins with Edward marking on the map the sites of major calamities with massive causalities in Amestris, going back to 1558 ('the Riviere Incident'), when Amestris was founded. The sick truth is that the Powers That Be have been orchestrating catastrophes all over Amestris specifically to engineer bloodshed and the creation of philosopher's stones. So the whole country is nothing but a machine or vessel for carrying out the villains' schemes. Ed's drawing on the map forms an alchemical circle, with Briggs Mountain as the next victim. (And the tunnel? That's for the flow of blood, altho' this isn't stated yet).

This is Himoru Arakawa's version of what world governments have been doing to their countries throughout the modern era: exploitation and corruption is everywhere in military-industrial complexes and governments. Some 260 million people were killed by their governments in the 20th century.

Edward Elric leads the next beat of *Fullmetal Alchemist* too, when he suggests to Major Armstrong that they trick General Raven into telling them about the villains' plans. This is a version of the episode in chapter two, *The Price of Life,* in Liore, when Father Cornello unwittingly betrayed himself on radio. Here, Armstrong chats with Raven in an office, while our heroes listen in nearby via a hidden microphone. Raven comes across as a wily, old politico who's also a lecher (fondling Armstrong's shoulder). We know that Briggs' super-bitch is aching to slash this degenerate, old twit.

It's here that we find out that Amestris's military is developing an immortal army (the first hints of an important component in the finale of *Fullmetal Alchemist,* with a band of difficult-to-kill henchmen).

These scenes are intercut with Dr Marcoh and Mei Chang in the abandoned house in the snowy wilds discussing the scientific issues of Amestrisian alchemy versus Xingese alchemy (a.k.a. alkhahestry or purification arts), which are linked thematically to the Briggs Fortress scenes.

Finally in chapter 67: *Burgeoning Borders* we catch up with van Hohenheim, the mysterious alchemist who's not been seen for some time (but will crop up soon in the Xerxes flashback).

Working alone (as ever), van Hohenheim is also doing his bit to combat the corruption in Amestris. He's standing on a hillside under a starry sky (like many a wizard), and he calls upon the spirits living inside him – naming them: Meiyo, Coran, Gianni, Willard, etc. Clawing at his bare chest, Hohenheim releases the sprites (we don't know what their mission is just yet, because ch. 67 ends now).

✳

Chapter 68: *Portrait of a Family* contains two memorable sequences: the reveal of the final homunculus, Pride, as a fearsome monster, and another dip into the back-story of van Hohenheim and the Elrics.

The flashback to van Hohenheim's past, when he was a regular father with a family, emphasizes once again his estrangement from his children. His wife Trisha tries to encourage him to be affectionate, but he's wary of his bad influence. Hohenheim tells us, while talking to his wife, that he's lived a long time, and seen lots of death. (This is the first time that Hohenheim ruminates on his unnaturally long life. Just how much his wife knows about it isn't clarified. Instead, Trisha remains optimistic and cheerful, and tries to keep Hohenheim away from the demons troubling him).

This is the flashback when the Elric family has their photograph taken (Trisha seems to be aware than her husband might disappear at any moment, so she wants a pic of the family together). While Trisha encourages him to smile for the camera, Hohenheim is weeping.

Exactly why Hohenheim is wracked with guilt, how he became sort of immortal, and what he's done with his 100s of years of life, isn't explained yet.

The Hohenheim flashbacks also include images of the Elric brothers as ultra-cute moppets. Ed spies on his father at work in his study – where he is drawing the transmutation on a map of Amestris, because Hohenheim knew what the homunculi were up to before anyone else (including Maes Hughes, who discovered it independently, later). After all, it was Hohenheim who let the cat out of the bag, the first homunculus out of the glass jar (who became Father).

Before he leaves (early in the morning), van Hohenheim fixes up a swing on a tree outside the house for the boys to play with, his final fatherly act. And then he's gone out the front door, and we switch to the present day, with Hohenheim once again contemplating the family photograph (sitting beside an open fire at night – the 2nd *animé* series used this chapter for episode 36: *Family Portrait*).

☆

The narrative of the *Fullmetal Alchemist manga* switches back to Briggs Fortress, and the expedition party in the tunnel (the one that went on ahead, not Armstrong, Buccaneer and the Elrics). Now Himoru Arakawa introduces the last homunculus, a masterpiece of invention and visualization – Pride, a monster of shadows, eyes, rows of grinning teeth, and sharp claws and arms. An impressive double-page drawing portrays the Pride-monster in full effect, a curving, grinning, shadowy malevolence (Hohenheim later points out that Pride's form, being the first homunculus made by Father, is based on the dwarf in the flask).

The search party is sliced to pieces, horses, men, equipment and all. And back at the tunnel, the guards on watch hear sounds in the distance: it's a riderless horse (a cliché of the action-adventure genre, but it works!), mad with fear.

The alarm is raised, and it interrupts the conflab between General Raven and Major General Armstrong (and not a moment too soon for Armstrong, who's been trying her hardest to dampen down her murderous seething!).

Following their eavesdropping session, the Elrics are tied up with rope (for appearance's sake), and they run into one of the nastiest characters in *Fullmetal Alchemist* in the corridors at Briggs, Zolf Kimbley (it's their first face-to-face encounter – the first of several).

Everybody convenes in the basement, with its still-unsolved mystery tunnel, and ponders on what could've happened to the scouting party (when only someone's arm made it back, tied to the horse). General Raven exerts his authority, recommending that the tunnel be sealed up (only he knows, at this point, what the tunnel is for, altho' Edward is likely piecing things together).

Chapter 68: *Portrait of a Family* closes with a couple of pages featuring Winry Rockbell at Garfiel's store (she's depicted doing – what else? – automail repair, which's all Winry seems to do. Well, it *is* her job, but doesn't she get any down-time? Doesn't she hang out with friends?). There's a phone call for her – only later do we find out that Zolf Kimbley is going to bring Winry up to Briggs (to use her as a bargaining chip with the Elrics).

This is an artificial move in the *Fullmetal Alchemist* story, but it does bring Winry-chan back into the centre of the action for a while (and places her beside the Elric brothers). Because, apart from tiger-fierce Major Armstrong and occasional appearances by the ever-reliable Lt. Hawkeye, this part of *Fullmetal Alchemist* boasts few female charas.

☆

Chapter 69: *The Foundation of Briggs* opens with General Raven questioning the Elric boys in jail (they instinctively don't trust him, and are reluctant to co-operate).

Armstrong and Raven oversee the construction to seal up the tunnel. Nobody at the fortress is happy that Armstrong, Briggs' mother bear, seems to have capitulated to Raven (and by extension, to Central Command), and is doing what he's ordered. While Miles stalls Kimbley elsewhere (to keep him out of the way), the homunculus Sloth is brought up from the ground outside, still frozen and unconscious. As Sloth awakens in the warm, Raven is able to control it, commanding it to leap into the hole and continue its work. Raven tells the assembled military at Briggs that the homunculus is a chimera who's working for the government.

Major General Armstrong has had just enough of General Raven by now, and here comes the retaliation we expected ages ago: she attacks the officer with her sword, slashing him so he falls into some wet concrete at the construction site. Goodbye one corrupt general (a minor detail has Armstrong wiping her sword of blood with her white gloves, and Buccaneer, knowing what his commander likes, handing her a new pair).

Clever Armstrong has also ordered a separate entrance to the tunnel to be built (courtesy of Edward Elric). Thus, with General Raven out of the way, operations at Briggs Mountain might get back to normal. Unfortunately, there is an unwelcome side effect of nobbling Raven: the Crimson Alchemist asserts himself, stating that with Raven gone 'missing', he is now the direct representative of the Führer's authority in the North. (And subsequently Armstrong is ordered to go to Central City).

Indeed, Zolf Kimbley is not only difficult to circumvent or fool, he has also done something that enrages the Elric brothers no end: he has invited their childhood friend Winry Rockbell to come to Briggs Mountain. 'BAKA!' they yell when they glimpse Winry-chan from their prison cell. Winry might be glad to see them, but they sure aren't happy to see her. This provides the finale to chapter 69: *The Foundation of Briggs* (and volume 17 of *Fullmetal Alchemist*).

Meanwhile, at the house in the forest in the mountains, Tim Marcoh and Mei Chang continue to debate the problems of different forms of alchemy; Scar eventually turns up, with news that they've been discovered, and have to move out; and in Central, Roy Mustang is still gathering information, meeting women messengers and buying lots of flowers from informants who poses as sellers.

Himoru Arakawa is fond of General Armstrong, so when the action has to leave Briggs (we couldn't stay in the mountains for the rest of the comic), Arakawa has Armstrong moving to Central City. There are reasons offered within the plot (such as Armstrong's ambitions in her career), but it's really so that Arakawa can continue to use Armstrong in the story.

☆

Chapter 70: *The First Homunculus* opens with a chat between Winry and Edward as she services his automail (in the infirmary, which doesn't have any privacy, as people wander in and out; Zolf Kimbley seems reluctant to let anyone out of his sight). Ed warns Winry not to trust Kimbley (a brief flashback depicts Kimbley picking up Winry from the railroad station, acting on his best behaviour). There is the usual mild banter between the two, as their feelings for each other are of course unspoken, erupting in embarrassed misunderstandings.

Once Winry Rockbell's lightened the atmosphere for a mo', she's swiftly swept away (to study Northern automail construction with one of the techies at Briggs – engineering heaven for our girlie geek – Winry remains a passionate devotee of automail throughout *Fullmetal Alchemist*). Meanwhile,[9] Zolf Kimbley rounds on Edward, to reveal the real reason he's brought Winry to Briggs (as a bargaining chip/ insurance). Kimbley sets out Ed's three jobs (by command of the Führer): to search for Scar; to find Dr Marcoh; and to 'carve a crest of blood' at Briggs (referring to the bloodshed which Father and the homunculi need to create their philosopher's stone). Well, we can guess that Edward isn't going to fulfil this last task! This is a blunt order from the military to kill.

☆

In the action sequence in chapter 70: *The First Honunculus,* Buccaneer heads up another scouting party in the tunnel: this is a terrific horror genre sequence, with a suspenseful build-up b4 the homunculus Pride is encountered. For ex, the party finds human remains, then two survivors, sitting in the darkness. But they're in a weak and frightened state, having

---

9 Another 'meanwhile': back in Central, Roy Mustang continues to gather information.

already met the fearsome monster that is Pride (Himoru Arakawa draws the trembling, terrified surviving soldiers in a very exaggerated style). 'Turn out the lights... it's coming... the shadow is coming!!' the soldier whimpers.

Now we find out that the monster uses light and dark as a means to move around – it needs light to cast shadows, as it's a shadow-beast, and it must move over floors, walls, ceilings (later, the claws and arms move about in space). And it does come: sliding around the walls of the tunnel, we see the giant eyes and shadow arms of the Pride-monster, reaching out towards Buccaneer's group.

At this moment, Himoru Arakawa makes a wonderful switch in the narrative, to Liza Hawkeye, who's delivering a package of papers to the Führer's household late at night in Central City. Just why *Fullmetal Alchemist* cuts to Hawkeye at this point emerges shortly: as Hawkeye talks to the Führer's wife (Bradley is not there), a shadow looms on the carpet behind Hawkeye: she turns: it's Selim, the King's son (revealed on the next page). Hawkeye's fearful expression suggests that someone or something more threatening than a small boy in pyjamas is standing behind her.

This is but the first of several hints that Selim Bradley is not all that he seems, because the Führer's wife tells Lt. Hawkeye that Selim is a distant relative of Bradley's; but we know that Bradley is a homunculus, kept in isolation, so he won't have any relations, distant or otherwise.

Liza Hawkeye pieces this together as she leaves the Führer's residence: walking along a dark colonnade, she suddenly stops, experiencing the maleficent presence she felt before.[10] This is one of Himoru Arakawa's most successful evocations of evil in action, a truly creepy scene: Selim Bradley lurks in an alcove, and speaks with Hawkeye. She doesn't turn around. He realizes she has found him out.

The Big Reveal of the first homunculus, Pride, comes in a full page drawing of Selim in the alcove, eyes glowing, with the eyes of the Pride-monster looming out of shadows behind him.

Great storytelling, great pacing and surprises, great art – this scene is one reason why the *Fullmetal Alchemist manga* is so impressive.

☆

Chapter 71: *In the Grip of the Red Lotus* continues the sinister confrontation between Selim-Pride and Liza Hawkeye. The chapter opens with a visual device that Himoru Arakawa employs from time to time: a page divided into four slim, vertical panels. When Selim-Pride sends his/ its black arms and hands towards Hawkeye (across the ground), transfixed to the spot, it is a genuinely frightening moment: Hawkeye knows that this monster could kill her instantly. Instead, Pride-Selim toys with the woman, the arms and hands sliding over her body, choking her neck, and cutting her cheek. In this sadomasochistic scenario, Pride decides to leave Hawkeye alive, knowing that she can't tell anyone else. (A mistake, of course, because Hawkeye informs Mustang soon, in code).

---

10 In the 4-*koma* at the back of vol. 18, Hawkeye's dog Bayate pisses on the shadow-monster Pride. 'Agh, my eyes!!'

We return now to Edward Elric and the Crimson Alchemist: Ed refuses to having anything to do with Zolf Kimbley's insane, murderous plan. When he asks Kimbley why he's siding with the homunculi, the man replies that he's curious to see who will win, the humans or the homunculi. Himoru Arakawa portrays Kimbley as a grinning, arrogant, evil presence. He plays his trump card: the philosopher's stone, placing it b4 Edward, knowing that this is something the Elrics have been desperate to get their hands on. (A replay of the scene with Dr Marcoh in the early chapters – both times Ed refuses to take the philosopher's stone, including by force).

Now that Edward Elric is being pushed into a corner by Zolf Kimbley, he asks to speak with Al and Winry (back in the jail, but with Kimbley listening nearby). So now the lads have to do some underhand manœuvring of their own – pretending to work for Kimbley, but secretly trying to out-wit him.

More scenes of strategies and plans follow – Kimbley and Armstrong; Al and Winry; Armstrong and Miles. Each side is trying to secure the best angle on events: Kimbley is using the Führer's power to get Scar; Ed wants Mei Chang's information (as does Armstrong, for use at Briggs – and she has to deal with the problem of reporting General Raven 'missing').

So, off goes the group to the town where Scar was spotted (a huge, abandoned, iced-over former mining town – it's a snowy version of the Yousewell mining town in chapter 3: *The Mining Town*). Winry Rockbell squeezes into the car (using the pretext of researching cold weather automail; not a great excuse – Winry also pretends to cry. Exasperated, Kimbley reluctantly agrees to her coming along).

Giving their minders the slip, the Elric brothers soon run into Mei Chang and Dr Marcoh, which allows Himoru Arakawa to include some of her OTT *shojo* skits (really, Arakawa should give Mei a *manga* of her own! Or maybe all of the *Fullmetal Alchemist* women – Curtis, Armstrong, Winry, Pinako, etc). Mei's adoration of Al, portrayed with girlie he♥rts and flowers, is very amusing (of course Al, being a 15 year-old boy, is clueless about her gushy affection). But when Winry emerges from Al's armour, where she's been hiding, Mei's jealous streak emerges.

Scar is discovered in an empty building by two of Zolf Kimbley's men – who turn out to be chimeras (both transform into man-beasts with special powers, which provides the climax to chapter 71: *In the Grip of the Red Lotus*).

✰

Chapter 72: *A Chain of Negativity, a Pebble of Goodness* opens with Liza Hawkeye yet again. Hawkeye is fast becoming a favourite chara for Himoru Arakawa. Well, let's sum up why: she's a young, attractive woman ('va-va-voom!' as Arakawa says women should be), she's a crack-shot, she's a loyal worker (and workaholic, like her creator), she's independent and lives alone with a dog (Arakawa is very fond of dogs), and she has an unspoken attachment with one of the best catches among the guys in the *Fullmetal Alchemist manga*, Roy Mustang.

In (the curiously-titled) chapter 72: *A Chain of Negativity, a Pebble of Goodness*, we follow Liza Hawkeye coming home. Then she gets a phone call.

That's all there is, story-wise, but the scene is played like a horror movie (all you need is a Girl and a Monster, as storytellers of horror know well), with shadows, and eyes gleaming in the darkness of Hawkeye's apartment (it's her dog). Thus, Hawkeye continues to be haunted by her very unsettling encounter with the Pride-monster.

And just then, who should call on the phone? Only Roy Mustang! Oh, Roy, honey, how do you always know just when to call?! Mustang senses that something's up, but they're still communicating in code (with exchanging flowers as the code), so neither side can say (soon, tho', Hawkeye finds a way to tell Mustang that Selim Bradley is a homunculus).

So here comes some out-size action in *Fullmetal Alchemist*, as Scar defends the attacks from the two chimeras. Ed and Al Elric hurry over (after talking with Dr Marcoh, Mei Chang & co.). By rights, Scar should be long dead, with the number (and ferocity) of fights his creator has had him under-take. But no, here is the Ishbalian warrior battling two hulking man-beasts.

Now Himoru Arakawa introduces an unusual switch in the motives and means for our heroes: they want to exploit Scar for their own ends. Thus, they launch themselves against the chimeras (who are Zolf Kimbley's lackeys); there are 8 pages of the Elrics fighting the chimeras: fast, broad action, and plenty of humour. Then they manage to get the better of Scar, pinning him to a block of concrete rubble via some cables.

At this point, Scar should be tied up, put in a strait jacket, blindfolded, gagged, beaten senseless, injected with sedatives, bound with explosive chains that incinerate the victim should they try to move an inch, and taken to a maximum security prison on Mars. Failing that, he should be shot through the head. Repeatedly. Then decapitated. Then his body burnt.

Instead, Scar is once again allowed to live on, but this time the twist is that Miles from Briggs Fortress is overseeing the secret deal – and Miles is part-Ishbalian (keeping the Ishbalain issue in play). The aim here of the heroes is to out-wit the Führer's lapdog, Zolf Kimbley, and to secure Dr Marcoh and Mei Chang.

The wild card in the proceedings is Winry Rockbell; Edward expresses the voice of reason: *what are you doing here?!* Winry is here to contribute a feminine, alternative, independent take on events (Winry's goals, for example, aren't the same as any of the other main groups of characters, including the Elrics; Winry is also not tied to or representing any institution. She's also not a superhero or warrior, like most of the other characters).

Thus, Winry Rockbell's first act is to tend to Scar's wounds (to the astonishment and dismay of all present!), and to offer up the morality of moving on (but maybe not forgiveness yet). Scar, ashamed, knows that Winry has the right to kill him (which's what he would do, and what he wants to do to Zolf Kimbley).

Himoru Arakawa now shifts the narrative mechanism of *Fullmetal Alchemist* slightly, and has the heroes being ahead of us, the audience. We don't know it yet, but the heroes have made a deal with Scar, to put on a show of kidnapping for Zolf Kimbley's sake, so they can escape. Bumping up Winry's role once more, Arakawa gives the idea for this piece of flim-flam to La Rockbell (as expected, the Elrics protest loudly! The concept of Scar pretending to take Winry captive is not one they would've come up with!).

But this ruse climaxes chapter 72: *A Chain of Negativity, a Pebble of Goodness*, with an explosion, Ed yelling at Kimbley, and Scar material-izing on top of the building (clutching an unconscious Winry), in a reprise of the scene where Kimbley stood on a building in Ishbal above Scar and his brother.

☆

Chapter 73: *A Daydream* back-tracks an hour or so, before Zolf Kimbley arrived, to depict the convoluted discussion scene between the Elrics, Winry Rockbell, Miles, the chimeras, Loki, Dr Marcoh and Mei Chang. Here, they decide on the play-acted kidnapping plan, while the others exit via the mine tunnels, to make their way back to Briggs Mountain.

Alphonse E. is given a minor but significant role here, when the chimeras, who're tied up, say it would be better if they were killed (because that's what Zolf Kimbley will do to them when he finds that they failed). No, no: Alphonse in particular is firmly opposed to any suggestion of suicide or of giving up (he is a soul in a suit of armour, remember!). *He's* not abandoning the idea of getting back his body, so nobody else is allowed to give up on whatever *their* dream is.

> I don't believe in never. *Hope* keeps me going, and, finally, hope has given us a lead on how we might get our bodies back... No matter how many years it takes, *I* won't give up.

Once the (rather over-written and unnecessarily complicated) discussions have taken place, the cheat begins. Edward screams at Kimbley, grabbing his lapels, Kimbley is outraged by this, and by Scar being one step ahead, and causing the building to crumble, before fleeing, and there's a snowstorm brewing.

☆

Further elements in chapter 73: *A Daydream* include scenes of the heroes travelling thru the mine tunnels (Loki proves useful here, one of the few times he affects the plot); the snowstorm slows everybody down; Mei Chang has a crisis of conscience (she's still no nearer to odiscovering the secrets of immortality); Winry feels guilty about abandoning her automail customers; and Miles finds out that Major Armstrong has left Briggs

Fortress, and some honchos from Central HQ are wandering about, trying to discover what happened to General Raven.

So the heroes need to get a message to the fortress, to warn everyone. Alphonse Elric offers to go, because he can withstand the cold and the storm. Chapter 73: *A Daydream* closes with the daydream of the title: Alphonse has an adventure on his own, wading thru deep snow, howling winds, and the white-out of the snowstorm. In this unreal setting, Al has an out-of-body experienc, which takes him, or his spirit, or his soul, to the Gateway of Truth. And what does he find there, standing in front of those imposing doors? Only his own body – now a gaunt, long-haired, under-nourished form. Al in his armour and his body reach out for each other. The soul and the body yearn for each other. But it's not time for them to be re-united yet: this is an important piece of foreshadowing (as well as a reminder of that metaphysical realm, the Gateway).

And then, in a bit of after-thought, Himoru Arakawa adds a brief (two-page) scene featuring Father, the super-villain of *Fullmetal Alchemist* who hasn't been seen for a while. He's sitting on his throne, as usual, playing the God-as-chess-player, moving pieces around the board. He has drawn the five-pointed alchemical circle which will be ignited in the finale of *Fullmetal Alchemist*, and he's placing Goth-*chibi* chess pieces on it, which represent the human 'sacrifices': Ed, Al, Hohenheim, and perhaps Izumi Curtis, and finally one more person...

☆

Fullmetal Alchemist Artbook (this page and over).

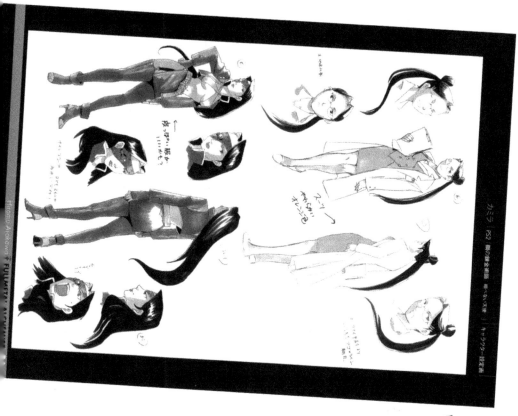

↑ Riza Hawkeye

Chapter 74: *The Dwarf In the Flask* (*Furasuku no Naka no Kobito*, published March, 2008) is an important section of *Fullmetal Alchemist*. It opens with Olivia Armstrong arriving in Central HQ, and bumping into Roy Mustang, on her way to meet the Führer (there's no love lost between these two). It's the meeting of the two sword-wielders in the *Fullmetal Alchemist manga*; Armstrong knows that she is walking into the lion's den. But that is the Briggs way! (The Tiger meets the Bear, as Buccaneer puts it). The Führer leads Armstrong into a high-level political meeting, to take General Raven's place.

Over lunch in the cafeteria, Col. Mustang and Lt. Hawkeye talk in code, so that she can tell him that the Führer's son is a homunculus (hidden within idle banter). Meanwhile, at the Curtises' butcher's store, flunkies from Central City are searching for Mr and Mrs Curtis (presumably because Curtis is going to be one of Father's 'sacrifices'). Bido overhears the soldiers, and pursues them.[1]

Now Himoru Arakawa's *manga* switches to Father, in the underground bunker and the start of the one of the most fascinating sections of *Fullmetal Alchemist*. In fact, it is the Beginning of Everything: Father is dreaming back to the time when... he was nothing but a sooty-black sprite in a glass jar in an alchemist's laboratory in Renaissance-era Xerxes, the now-ruined city (and the birthplace of alchemy).

So, finally – and three-quarters of the way thru the 108 chapter-run of *Fullmetal Alchemist* – Himoru Arakawa reveals the full story of How It All Started. It began with curiosity, and ignorance, and a craving for power and immortality.

Back then, four hundred years ago, van Hohenheim was a lowly slave in Xerxes, so lowly he didn't even have a name. His job? To mop the floor of the lab when his alchemist master was away. The Faustian bargain begins in *Fullmetal Alchemist* with an intriguing conflab between 'the dwarf in the flask' and a slave. Unfortunately for Hohenheim – and for all of Amestris – the homunculus is way ahead of him; he's a crafty, smart operator. He knows how to manipulate the slave.

The homunculus begins by giving Hohenheim a name (instead of '23'), persuading him that the life of a servant can be transcended, and that it possesses special knowledge which will thrill his superiors. (We also discover that the homunculus was created using some of Hohenheim's blood, which makes them brothers/ twins/ doubles, and Hohenheim is kind of the father of the homunculus. Thus Hohenheim's feelings of guilt over the whole homunculi and Father and Amestris issue).

The conception of the first homunculus – as a puff of black soot with a crescent moon grin of teeth and a gleaming eye, is marvellous. Chapter 74: *The Dwarf In the Flask* closes with the dwarf in the flask announcing his name: 'Homunculus'.

☆

Chapter 75: *The Last Days of Xerxes* continues the fascinating flashback set in Renaissance Xerxes. Some years have now past, and the

---

[1] With the *Cape Fear* gag of hiding underneath their vehicle.

homunculus has been teaching slave number 23 to read and write – and to become an alchemist. (A great touch has Hohenheim indulging the homunculus, taking him out onto a balcony, to enjoy the view of the city, but Hohenheim's master, the court alchemist, is much sterner, treating the homunculus (rightly) as merely a test subject).

Now comes the moment that the homunculus has been working towards for years: he is brought before the King of Xerxes. The Faustian pact here is of course immortality – which's what all aged, bearded rulers seem to want in fantasy adventure stories. The homunculus tells the King he knows how to achieve it, but the details are left out. Instead, the flashback cuts to scenes of the populace of Xerxes digging an enormous ditch – around the whole nation (which they think, thanking their masters, is for irrigation. They imagine their rulers are looking after them).

Following the bloodshed carried out by soldiers at key points around the country, the transmutation circle is nearly ready. The ailing King is anxious for the rite to begin. In the reception hall of the palace everyone is assembled: the King, the alchemists, and of course the homunculus. At first the ritual seems to be working, but soon the grasping, black hands from the other side of the Gateway erupt from the magic circle, and the populace is collapsing (even the livestock). Over four pages, Himoru Arakawa delivers spectacular, *Akira*-style scenes of cosmic mayhem: the rite creates a giant eye which emerges from the epicenter of the transmutation circle, right over the city (so instead of the familiar hemisphere of energy from an atomic blast, it's a colossal eye); bolts of alchemical energy zigzag thru the night sky; and the black arms zoom everywhere, taking lives.

Now Himoru Arakawa employs a science fiction trope: a single survivor waking up after a massive catastrophe with nobody left alive. It's Hohenheim who's survived – he wanders thru palace corridors piled with corpses, and out onto a balcony. He doesn't know what's going on – until a figure behind him addresses him. A page split into 2 panels depicts Hohenheim looking in horror at… himself – that is, at the homunculus who's taken on the form of his 'father', Hohenheim. The homunculus tells Hohenheim what he's done: half of the citizens of Xerxes are inside him, and the other half are inside the homunculus. (Thus, the homunculus reckons that both he and Hohenheim are immortal).

The flashback closes with a switch to Hohenheim in the present day (so the homunculus and Hohenheim book-end the flashback to Xerxes, one of the finest sections of Himoru Arakawa's *Fullmetal Alchemist manga*). Waking from a dream (we know that Hohenheim has been going back over his life, looking for ways of defeating Father the homunculus), he encounters the Curtises (who are returning from their travels). After a brief chat, Izumi has another of her fainting spells. Hohenheim recognizes that Izumi has also attempted human transmutation: to her husband's Sig's horror, Hohenheim performs some alchemical healing, which involves thrusting his hand inside Izumi's stomach magically. With the organs re-arranged, Izumi is already feeling better. The chapter ends with

Hohenheim telling the astonished Curtises: 'I am the philosopher's stone'.

☆

Chapter 76: *Shape of a Person, Shape of a Stone* continues the discussion of the philosopher's stone – parallelling Ed Elric in the Northern mining town explaining about the philosopher's stone to Miles and co., and Hohenheim and the Curtises (a case of 'like father, like son'). Miles also mentions that Ed is too soft-hearted, in his refusal to kill. This soon manifests itself in the face-off btn Ed and Zolf Kimbley.

Meanwhile, Winry Rockbell, Scar, Mei Chang and party meet up with Alphonse, and Ed and Miles and company join them. The plan to foil Kimbley is put to the test when they encounter the Crimson Alchemist. Miles' plan is to lure Kimbley out into the open, so his men can kill him using sniper rifles from nearby buildings. But Kimbley is too smart (he can sense the killing intent nearby), and he opens hostilities with an alchemical explosion, during which he flees (his signature move – he only attacks when he knows he has the advantage). Kimbley's henchmen, the chimera, lay into Edward (they can smell him in the snowstorm). The fight shifts into that favourite location of storytellers for action scenes – a factory (where there are props like boxes of gunpowder, girders, and tons of machinery to play with). Edward gets the better of the chimeras (blinding them with ammonia), but of course he can't bring himself to kill Kimbley. The Crimson Alchemist taunts Ed by waving a philosopher's stone in front of his face. During their duel, Kimbley sets off an explosion which shatters an enormous mine engine, and Ed and everyone else go umbling into the darkness.

Chapter 76: *Shape of a Person, Shape of a Stone* closes with one of the scariest experiences for Edward Elric in the *Fullmetal Alchemist manga*: his body has been pierced thru his side by a steel girder. Losing blood, and in excruciating pain, Ed collapses – and, in a marvellous touch, so does Alphonse (who's elsewhere), confirming that they are linked spiritually (via the Gateway of Truth). The last page of ch. 76 features three large drawings: of Winry Rockbell, staring down, concerned, and of Ed and Al, both head-first on the ground, passed out.

★

Chapter 77: *The Tables Are Turned: A New Transmutation Circle* continues with Ed Elric's life-and-death predicament, pinioned to the ground with a steel bar through his torso. Ed manages to cut off part of the girder, but he needs the help of the chimeras nearby to pull it out, while he seals up the wound with alchemy (using his own life as the source of energy). So, altho' they've been ordered by Kimbley to capture Edward, he rescues the two chimeras from the rubble, and hopes they'll help him. They do, of course.

Out in the snow, Winry Rockbell, Scar, Dr Marcoh and co. are struggling towards Briggs Mountain, carrying Alphonse Elric (who's been taken to pieces, to make him easier to carry). When they stop, Mei Chang contributes an important piece of information to the *Fullmetal Alchemist* enterprise: she suggests a way of deciphering the book: by taking the pages where certain phrases occur (such as 'golden man'), and arrange the pages on the floor.

This is a mirror scene of the one in chapter 67: *Burgeoning Borders,* when Edward demonstrated the extent of the enemy's plans. Mei Chang draws over the pages, to create the familiar transmutation circle which will soon cover all of Amestris.

Alphonse Elric (now getting back to normal) has the bright idea of literally reversing the pages. When the pages are turned over, and the points are joined up, it forms a counter-circle – a circle of alchemy (combining Xingese and Amestrisian alchemy), which will negate the plans of the homunculi (this is what Hohenheim is working towards). It is a literal expression of looking at things from a different angle.

But what happened to Zolf Kimbley? Did he expire in the giant explosion and collapse of 100s of tons of mining machinery? No chance! Villains like the Crimson Alchemist don't die like that in fantasy adventures like this! No, Kimbley is wandering about in the mine tunnels, hoping to find some clues to the whereabouts of Scar & co.

Zolf Kimbley encounters the homunculus Pride, in his monstrous form, as shadows in the tunnel. There's no hope that Pride will slay Kimbley, because he's still useful.[2] Pride delivers a command from Father: create a 'blood-soaked crest' at Briggs. Because Father's plans are coming to fruition: we see images of Sloth, of the tunnel, of Pride, and of Father.

✱

Chapter 78: *The Seven Deadly Sins* depicts the venal strategies of Father and the homunculi accelerating – producing carnage around Amestris (Cain Furey, for instance, is portrayed in a WW1 trench scenario, desperately trying to elude enemy fire). Sloth completes the tunnel. In Liore (one of the centres of chaos, instigated by the homunculi), Hohenheim turns up at Rose Tomas's café, where she's doing her bit for the noble cause by doling out food (a rather unnecessarily silly drawing shows Hohenheim crawling on the floor, begging for grub). Hohenheim investigates the tunnel beneath Liore's Cathedral, to see how far along the villains are with their plans. Hohenheim reveals some more of his alchemical powers (building a bridge of stone to traverse a noxious, flooded tunnel, and battling Pride).

The Hohenheim versus Pride face-off is an enjoyable action sequence – Pride reveals how powerful it/ he is, and Hohenheim displays more alchemy (in defence). Hohenheim notes how Pride resembles the original homunculus in the jar (eyes and a mouth in black); Pride offers the explanation of the seven sins and the creation of the homunculi. Hohenheim declares war: 'tell Father that slave number 23 is on his way'. We cut to Father, looking grim: 'I'll be waiting for you'.

Fullmetal Alchemist now shifts time and place to Briggs Mountain, and an unexpected development: Zolf Kimbley has changed sides, and aligned himself with the Drachman (Russian) military, to stage an attack on the fortress. But Kimbley knows, having recently toured Briggs, that it

---

2 In the finale, however, Pride eats Kimbley whole.

will take more than this force marching in the snow to take it.

✶

Chapter 79: *Bite of the Ant* - Himoru Arakawa doesn't show the carnage of the battle between Briggs and Drachma: she cuts to the aftermath, when Zolf Kimbley and the Drachman general (plus some guards) seem to be the only survivors in a sea of corpses. Kimbley has succeeded in creating 'a crest of blood', as ordered by Father via Pride. Maintaining his reputation as a revolting sub-human, he exhibits no remorse when the general and his aides are killed.

The *Fullmetal Alchemist* makes an entertaining shift now, with a narrative twist that ups the stakes and turns the tables somewhat: the capture of the homunculus Envy. Posing an Ishbalian who wants to see Doctor Marcoh (and aided by the chimeras), Envy turns up in the snowbound region near Briggs. Envy seems confident that he'll be able to snag Marcoh, not realizing that he's walked into a trap, and that our heroes have lured him there. Stepping on mines under the snow (in reality, alchemical circles ignited by Mei Chang from a distance), Envy is blown about repeatedly (and getting more furious by the minute - Envy is highly amusing when he's angry!).

But when Envy transforms into his monster guise, he goes on the offensive. Even with Scar, the chimeras and others tackling the Envy-monster, they are no match for him. With a long, snaky tongue comprised of dead souls, Envy captures Dr Marcoh. Gloating, Envy once again thinks he has the upper hand; but then Marcoh performs one of his most significant acts in *Fullmetal Alchemist* - he destroys the Envy-monster. In a series of brilliantly designed drawings, the Envy-creature is disintegrated in stages (as the philosopher's stone inside Envy is crushed): a screaming monster... the souls flopping out of the monster's mouth like ectoplasm... Envy reduced to humanoid form, crawling in the snow from the wreckage of his monster-body... Envy dying, collapsed in the snow... a snail-like critter pops out of his third eye... This is all that's left of Envy – an eye, a tail, a mouth, a tiny, pathetic thing that whimpers, 'don't look at me' (the *animé* did full justice to this scene, which is a gift to animators, who love bodily transformations more than almost anything).

This is one of Himoru Arakawa's more inventive turns in the *Fullmetal Alchemist manga,* and where the Japanese fascination with transformation, with people containing multiple selves, takes it into a metaphoric zone of its own. There's a poetic truth in Envy's final form being an ugly, squirming thing – that the heroes flick, kick, hold by its tail, and treat as dirt.

✶

Chapter 80: *The Prodigal Father Returns* opens with one of the funnier beats in the *Fullmetal Alchemist manga* – where Envy, in his snail-critter guise, latches onto Loki's neck, hoping to control him like a puppet. Trying to use Loki as a hostage, Envy is gutted when nobody moves a muscle, because no one cares much about the loser Loki. Envy is summarily jammed into a glass jar to keep him out of mischief. The sequence humorously conveys Envy's much-reduced powers – now he's a feeble figure of amusement, and, like the homunculus in the Renaissance flashback in Xerxes, he now lives in a glass jar. But sly Envy still manages to create trouble – by using his powers of persuasion.

Scar comes up with an unexpected suggestion: that Mei Chang return to Xing, taking Envy with her. The reasoning is that Mei can use Envy as an example of an immortal being, and that she'd be better off not getting involved in Amestris's politics any more. Doesn't wholly make sense, but it does offer the chance for Mei to have an adventure of her own – because for much of the time, she is simply tagging along with everybody else.

So Mei Chang departs across the snow for Yousewell (after some tearful *sayonaras* – to Alphonse-sama most of all, of course – she leaps to hug him and weeps). The mining community (including the boy Kyle) welcomes Mei back, offering her food and lodging (their generosity humbles her). Now Envy starts his scheming – manipulating Mei's conscience, like a demon talking in her ear, so she turns back, and heads for Central City, which's what Envy wants, of course – so he can regain his body (did no one think that asking a young girl to carry a homunculus – a known mass murderer – was a dodgy enterprise?).

Next is a short scene where the Führer tells Liza Hawkeye that he knows she knows – but, as with Olivia Armstrong, he is not going to do anything about it. And speaking of the blonde boss of Briggs, here comes Major Armstrong, storming thru the corridors of Central's military HQ, as scary and unforgiving as ever. After a brief spat with her brother (whom she continues to scorn as too weak), Himoru Arakawa uses Armstrong as the audience stand-in for the introduction of a new threat in the *Fullmetal Alchemist* saga: the 'immortal army'.

Arakawa-sensei has decided that a bunch of deadly, zombie-like puppets would be handy as opponents in the upcoming battles of the finale of *Fullmetal Alchemist* (there are 27 chapters to run of *Fullmetal Alchemist* from here, and loads of them feature blistering action). In the basement of the HQ (thru several locked doors), the army of dolls lies in readiness – hanging upside-down, in rows, robotic, with a single eye and a large mouth. (They are artificial, with souls inserted from victims of Amestris's military conquests).

That revelation would serve as a suitable climax to chapter 80, but instead Himoru Arakawa employs the reunion of Alphonse Elric with his father, van Hohenheim (at Rose Tomas's café in Liore), for the last pages. It's another of Hohenheim's goofy appearances – holding a pot he's just cleaned, and wearing a headscarf and an apron (Himoru Arakawa enjoys putting the heroes' biggest brain and magical powerhouse in silly situations – as if Gandalf were reduced to washing dishes at the *Prancing Pony* in Bree in *The Lord of the Rings*).

✸

Chapter 81: *A Full Recovery* continues with the meeting btn father, son and childhood friend (Winry) in Liore. Much pointing, and many cries of, 'You!', and 'My vintage armour!', and 'You're...' Well, after all, it is apparently ten years since father and offspring have seen each other. And it's an awkward meeting, with neither side knowing quite what to say (both are undemonstrative Japanese males – hugging is not an option!). Hohenheim is called away, and Al decides he'll follow on, and try to talk to his pa.

And now *Fullmetal Alchemist* needs to decide what to do with this group of charas: the solution is one that Himoru Arakawa is very fond of: *work* (it's the key activity in her follow-up manga, *Silver Spoon*). In *Fullmetal Alchemist*, everybody has to work: so Hohenheim, the most powerful alchemist in Amestris, is helping out with chores at a humble cafe (and some builders nearby); so Al goes to help him; so the chimeras drag off Loki to work; and so Rose also hauls Winry away.

Now comes a 'fan service' moment in this amazing boys' comic: Winry Rockbell, the main female star of *Fullmetal Alchemist*, is depicted nude, bathing. In fact, this is a rare scene of Girlie Time – two girls being together – as Rose Tomas and Winry chat, drink tea, choose what clothes to wear, but what do they discuss?... boys! (Edward and Alphonse, of course).

Bido (the slimy Devil's Nest chimera) has his own adventure creeping around the bowels of the military HQ – encountering the mannequin soldiers, and the chimera creatures guarding Father's lair.

Hohenheim and Alphonse Elric bond further, after ten years apart. Hohenheim decides to tell his son the whole story (his story, which's the story of the founding of Amestris, the Story of Everything). Somewhere up North, Hohenheim's other son, Edward, is being patched up by a couple of old doctors running a backstreet practice. Unfortunately, the authorities are able to track down Ed and the two chimeras from a withdrawal of dough from Ed's State Alchemist's bank account. A spy genre scenario ensues, with the military heavies threatening the doctors and the chimeras (who're pretending to be patients), until Ed returns from a shopping spree (for food, of course – Ed is depicted eating more than any other chara in *Fullmetal Alchemist*. Here, he's stuffing his face, as usual – got to build up his strength after nearly dying). The chapter closes with a full page picture of Edward, fist (and teeth) clenched, frowning, looking like he means business: this is the 'full recovery' of the chapter's title: the Fullmetal Alchemist is back!

★

Chapter 82: *Family By Spirit* continues the pursuit of Edward Elric and his chimera buddies by the authorities: this is the chapter where Ed alchemically transforms a car (during a car chase) into what he regards as something very cool: a 1970s, North American, customized paint job (flames), bull's horns, pointy mudflaps, etc (it looks even better in colour in the *animé*!).

Back to Al Elric and his dad: Alphonse processes the extraordinary story that Hohenheim has just told him. Himoru Arakawa plants some seeds which will pay off later: for instance, the concept of the special day (a.k.a. 'Promised Day') that Father is waiting for (involving astronomical alignments). Father and son re-assert their goals: to stop Father and the homunculi.

Near Father's bunker, Bido runs into Greed – or, rather, the new Greed in Ling Yao's body. It's confusing – especially when the new Greed kills Bido, supposedly his friend.3 The new Greed and the old Greed battle for supremacy inside Ling Yao's body, while Ling's soul looks on.

Greed's torment as the Jeckyll and Hyde parts of him collide leads him to attack the Führer, in Bradley's home, while his wife and 'son', Selim, watch in horror. The Führer wields those vicious blades, but tho' the duel is fierce, its outcome is postponed when Greed flees. (There's an artificial aspect to this part of the narrative of *Fullmetal Alchemist*, as if the action sequence has been tagged on, due to the demands of making a *shonen manga*).

Himoru Arakawa is moving her chess pieces around the board of *Fullmetal Alchemist* rapidly now, just like Father in the bunker with his chess board in the shape of the Amestrisian alchemical circle. So Arakawa has shifted Ed and co. to the abandoned house outside Central City (where Edward hopes to rendezvous with Alphonse), and who should turn up moments later, but Greed (tho' when Greed collapses on the floor, it seems as if Ling Yao is now uppermost inside Ling, in Ling's familiar pose of fainting from hunger).

✳

Chapter 83: *The Promised Day* announces that the finale of *Fullmetal Alchemist* is about to start, as the *manga* flits around many of the main characters. The chapter opens with lots of talk. Greed-Ling tells Ed Elric, Heinkel and Darius about the 'Promised Day' of Father's; Ed offers Greed-Ling the chance to work on their side; Greed, of course, declines – he wants to do things *his* way. In the event, they team up anyway, with Ed and co. agreeing to work for Greed (on the surface at least; Greed is flattered, while Ed just wants to get things moving).

A humorous scene at the Armstrong mansion follows: in a frivolous bit of business, all of the Armstrong family depart, leaving Olivia A. and Alex A. to fight over the ownership of the country house. Maria wins (later, Armstrong uses her former home to house troops – hence her uneasy alliance with Roy Mustang).

News of the upcoming 'Promised Day' spreads – to Sig Curtis, to the commanders at Briggs Fortress, to General Grumman, to Liza Hawkeye, etc. Izumi C. is up in the North, delivering a message (with a reprise of the 'I'm a housewife!' gag). Hawkeye meets her friend Becky (who conveys a message from Grumman, who in turn passes it on to Jean Havoc, who hands the msg to Colonel Mustang (in a cigarette pack).) Anyway, all of this rather routine spy genre stuff means that Mustang, Grumman and co. are gathering allies who're going to fight the homunculi and the homunculi-controlled military when the conflict erupts.

✳

Chapter 84: *Shadow of the Pursuer* begins with an unnecessary but

---

3 Greed's been given the job of policing the perimeters of Father's domain.

colourful scene that's probably close to Himoru Arakawa's heart: the Spring Sheep Festival in Resembool (Arakawa, hailing from a family of farmers, will no doubt have visited these staples of the seasonal cycle of the rural year). The reason for including the scene is that Winry Rockbell is travelling in secret (in a milk churn!) to her home.

The reunion of several characters, including Ed and Winry, is dealt with in a comical scene that once again features 'fan service' images of Winry undressing. Edward (eating as usual) happens to be in her room. Cue screams from Winry, Ed being whacked with a spanner, and the guys who've rushed over to see what the ruckus is about are thrown out by Winry-chan: 'GET THE HELL OUT OF MY ROOM, NOW!'

When Ed Elric has his automail fixed (yet again!), there are the inevitable scenes where Winry and Ed discuss what's going on (Ed recommends that Winry and grandma Pinako leave the country),[4] and scenes where the motives and the goals of the heroes are re-stated.

Scar, Dr Marcoh and the chimeras're re-united in Liore in the following scene, with Scar taking the group to meet some Ishbalians, who're also going to do their bit in the build-up to the 'Promised Day' (Ishbalian refugees are gathering around Central City).

Meanwhile, the Führer is being detained in the North by General Grumman and his military team who're putting on a display of exercises in a parade ground. The aim of Grumman is to delay Bradley (and also to prepare for his demise in an assassination – Grumman has his eye on the top job in Amestris, like Mustang).

Chapter 84: *Shadow of the Pursuer* closes with an action sequence involving Alphonse Elric encountering the homunculi Pride and Gluttony (set in one of Himoru Arakawa's favourite spots, railroad sidings). This is the moment when Al is brought down by Pride, and taken over (Al fights back, but almost no one can best two homunculi working together – even Hohenheim finds Pride a handful).

✳

Chapter 85: *The Empty Box* (pub. Dec, 2008) opens with an unusual scene: Olivia Armstrong surveying her empty mansion (won in the duel with her brother Alex), and Roy Mustang paying a visit. Once again, the bickering btn the two is foregrounded (altho' Armstrong and Mustang might be a strong pairing romantically in the *Fullmetal Alchemist* world, Armstrong doesn't express any interest in men or romance, and certainly not in Mustang! The Flame Alchemist, tho', is the chief womanizer in the series). So when Mustang presents Armstrong with some flowers, she chucks them away: 'I don't need your stinking flowers!' (but not before she's read the secret message that Mustang slipped in the wrapping: that Selim is a homunculus).

Now comes the assassination plot, which's straight out of a World War Two movie (we know that Himoru Arakawa watched plenty for research for *Fullmetal Alchemist*). This sequence, where the train is blown up on a railroad bridge over a river, is a piece of *The Bridge On the River*

---

4 Ironically, this is also what Hohenheim suggested to Pinako. Winry explodes.

Kwai (or many a cowboy movie).

Unfortunately, altho' the carriages have been hurled into the air, we can guess that Führer Bradley will survive. But with the Führer out of the way, Colonel Mustang's team can start to makes their move into the military infrastructure (and so can General Grumman).

Back in the military HQ in Central City, the crusty, old generals who run the country are in uproar with the disappearance of the Führer. Major General Olivia Armstrong sits at her place at the big, conference table, pondering on the empty throne where the Führer sits. This could be her chance, she thinks, to seize power in amongst the squabbling.

No such luck: a brilliant revelation occurs now – the giant homunculus Sloth looms high over Major Armstrong in her chair, acting as the bodyguard to no less than Father: calm yourselves, he tells the committee, 'I am still in Central'. This's the first time we've seen Father stir from his underground bunker (so presumably Father thinks that the Führer ist kaput).

✻

Edward Elric is re-united with his father von Hohenheim in the usual manner: he punches his dad in the face. After Ed's had his moment to express his feelings (every diva needs that moment!), they get down to talking. And now Daddy Hohenheim relates the whole story of the homunculi, the dwarf in the glass jar, and his own role in the nefarious doings. Like his brother, Edward is gobsmacked by the long and nasty tale of Father in Xerxes.

'I'm the philosopher's stone you've been searching for,' Hohenheim tells his stunned son. Of course not. When Ed delivers Trisha's message to Hohenheim (from Pinako), Hohenheim weeps[5] (she says she couldn't keep her promise and went on ahead of him – into the realm of the dead).

After Edward's fixed up his beloved red cloak ('it's a bad-ass, tough-guy colour! Gets the blood boiling!'), the finale of chapter 85: *The Empty Box* (and the announcement of the next action sequence), arrives in the form of Alphonse Elric, looming out of the shadows. Shadows being the clue – poor Al is being controlled by the shadow-monster Pride. Out shoot the black claws and arms, and in a creepy drawing Pride's eyes peep from inside Al's armoured helmet (three slit eyes in one eye-hole).

✻

Chapter 86: *Servant of Darkness* launches into one of the major action sequences in Himoru Arakawa's *Fullmetal Alchemist manga:* with all of the characters in place, it's time to begin: it's Gluttony and Pride versus Ed, Greed/ Ling and the chimera. The setting: a forest at night, near Kanama. (And it's one of the longest sequences, too).

Following the customary macho taunts hurled from each side, the bust-up starts. Pride attacks, and the heroes defend; clever Edward works out that the homunculus Pride is scuppered in total darkness, so he frazzles the nearby electricity poles, which causes a black-out in the neighbourhood.

---

5 Edward finds it embarrassing when his pa cries.

Unfortunately, Pride has brought along Gluttony, who possesses a magical sense of smell, so he can pinpoint the heroes in the dark; our heroes in turn have the chimera, who also have heightened senses. So the chimera (Heinkel), that Ed dubs 'Lion King', can attack Selim-Pride in the moonless, starless night (no matter how odd it feels to be slamming into an eleven year-old boy).

Meanwhile, Gluttony is rampaging – and Greed/ Ling, Edward and 'Donkey Kong' battle the monster. Gluttony unleashes his belly-maw, hoping to swallow Ed and co., only to be attacked by Lan Fan (Himoru Arakawa's favourite *shinobi* in *Fullmetal Alchemist*), who's now recovered, and dives into the fray with a surprise entrance.

Chapter 86: *Servant of Darkness* is wall-to-wall action, with Himoru Arakawa in her element: she's got monsters, magic, ninjas, and out-size bedlam.

✸

Chapter 87: *An Oath Made In the Underground* returns the story to the war genre and the spy thriller genre, with Roy Mustang and his devoted crew preparing their political move. First, Mustang investigates the mystery of Selim Bradley, aided by Madame Christmas (Mustang's foster mom) – an 11 year-old kid who doesn't seem to age in photographs going back 20, 35 and 50 years ago (the homunculi are probably 100s of years old).

Colonel Mustang meets his team in the sewers (always with the sewers!), after blowing up Christmas's bar (to elude the authorities gathering outside). Mustang's chief directive to his troops is: 'DO NOT DIE!'

Meanwhile, Father presides over a meeting of the generals at HQ, bored out of his mind by what he sees as humans' pointless activities (such as Mustang & co. kidnapping the Führer's wife).

In the forest, the multiple battles continue – Lan Fan fights Gluttony, the chimera Heinkel tries to dispatch Pride, and Edward meets Fuu. When Ed takes on Pride, we are in pure *shonen manga* territory – rapid, over-the-top action, yelled insults, and teenage charas battling it out. It's fast, it's fantastical, and it's very enjoyable (even tho' the multi-bladed and much larger Pride should win out against Ed with his single automail arm, even if it is tipped with carbon fibre, a lesson he's learnt from Greed).

The issue of light and dark is deployed again, with Fuu using a flash-bang to best Pride (he can't operate in the brilliance of the flash-bang). Locating an opponent in the darkness is crucial in this conflict, and Pride opts to do something that sickens the human observers: he devours Gluttony, in order to use Glut-boy's powers of smell. Yes, even humans don't stoop to eating their own kind (usually!), but the homunculi are that much more desperate.

✸

Chapter 88: *The Understanding Between Father and Son* continues the debacle in the forest in the night that never seems to end, with Pride now able to sense the position of every foe. Ling Yao/ Greed and Lan Fan leap about, trying to avoid the slashing, chomping attacks of Pride.

The flash-bang dissolves Pride's grip on Alphonse Elric's armour, so he's able to inhabit it again. Hohenheim shows up here, and father and son hatch a plot to beat Pride: Hohenheim buys them some time, by chatting with Pride so that Alphonse can move into position, trapping the homunculus is a dome fashioned from soil. In the total darkness inside the sphere, Pride isn't able to use his monsterish talents. Al and Pride discuss the differences between homunculi and humans as they while away the hours in the earth tomb (and Pride starts to tap on Alphonse's head, which would be annoying if Al were human. It's this sound which alerts Father to Pride's whereabouts).

✳

In chapter 89: *Soldier's Return* our heroes re-group during the day after the long, long night (Scar, Dr Marcoh, Loki & co. turn up). In this aftermath section, the usual explanations, reasons, motives and goals are offered.

Now Roy Mustang and his team are making their presence known in Central City: they're wounding soldiers but refusing to kill them, they're creating confusion among the authorities, and they've captured Mrs Bradley. Himoru Arakawa takes her time in depicting the seeds of Mustang's rebellion, with numerous brief scenes of short conversations intercut with sudden bursts of gunfire. Central's officers can't capture Mustang's mob (they even have aid that arrives in the unlikely form of an ice cream van packed with ammunition and weaponry, driven by Rebecca, Liza Hawkeye's chum. Maria Ross is back from Xing, to help out. We also see Denny Brosh waking to find the city in panic).

✳

Chapter 90: *Army of Immortals* continues to build and build the suspense of the *Fullmetal Alchemist* manga, working up to the climactic chapters. In ch. 90, the storytelling shifts between talk-based characterization scenes (such as Ed Elric talking with his father, Hohenheim), and action sequences (such as Olivia Armstrong taking control of two generals).

Major Armstrong is under arrest in the war room at Central City HQ: unfortunately, the bozos who're keeping guard forgot to divest her of her sword. So she's able to stab and slash and hold one guy at bay with her sword and another with a swiped gun. Armstrong gloats – confident that her Briggs bears will tear up the badly-trained Central soldiers.

Below Central, Father continues to wait for his Big Moment: the *chi* under the city is rising: old Fuu is aware of it, as are the dogs on the streets. As he sits on his throne, connected to everything via miles of pipes, Father hears Pride tapping Morse code on Al's armour, far away (Father dispatches Zolf Kimbley to release him).

Thus, the goal of our heroes is to nobble Father and his nefarious plans. That's one goal: the other key aim is for the heroes to regain their bodies. Other sub-plots include: Col. Mustang's bid for Presidency, the expiation of the Ishbal rebellion, the Winry-Edward romance, the Xingese charas' quest for immortality, and Hohenheim making good his mistake of letting the dwarf out of the flask.

The heroes move from the outskirts of Central City towards the military HQ. With the city in uproar, and soldiers everywhere, they need a secret way in to Father's lair: of course, once again, it's tunnels (this time thru one of the research laboratories).

The heroes split up to look for Father (Hohenheim and Lan Fan, Ed and Scar, etc). At this point, the authorities in desperation let loose the immortal army they've developed, providing the *manga* with ravenous henchmen who offer a serious obstacle, yet who can also be killed without remorse (they are essentially dummies fitted with philosopher's stones).

Back at the mound trapping Pride with Alphonse, Zolf Kimbley shows up, sets Selim free, and attacks Heinkel and Al.

✳

Chapter 91: *A Reunion of Alchemists* continues the conflict at the earth mound: Alphonse Elric rescues the injured Heinkel then goes up against Kimbley and Pride (using the power-up of a philosopher's stone that Heinkel picked up).

Below HQ, Mei Chang defends herself against the army of immortals using her martial arts, and balancing Envy in the glass jar (like a gag from a Hong Kong action movie, as she tries to keep the glass from toppling and breaking). But Envy manages to fly free, sink his canines into one of the puppets, and swiftly regain his dog-monster form. Nearby, Ed Elric, Scar and the chimeras're also battling the zombie army.

In the upper corridors of HQ, Major Armstrong works out how to gain control of the command structure, in order to ensure the safety of her Briggs troops. At this point, the giant homunculus Sloth makes his grand entrance (squashing one of Olivia's opponents flat). When Sloth enters the frame it inaugurates a very lengthy action sequence in which Armstrong, her brother Alex and others try to trounce the monster. (Note that Sloth was at Briggs Fortress, where Armstrong encountered him).

Chapter 91: *A Reunion of Alchemists* climaxes with van Hohenheim coming face to face with Father in his bunker: these are the two most powerful alchemists in the *Fullmetal Alchemist* series: to evoke that power, both are depicted in casual poses: Father is sitting down and reading a book, and Hohenheim wanders in with his hands in his pockets as if he's just stopped by on a whim.

○

Chapter 92: *With Everyone's Strength* switches to Alphonse taking on Pride and Zolf Kimbley in the suburbs outside Central City. The issue of a philosopher's stone being made with human lives is addressed, but as Heinkel and Al are in a desperate situation, they decide to use it. It takes all of Alphonse's ingenuity to out-manœuvre Pride and Kimbley (especially as Kimbley also has a philosopher's stone). This is one of Alphonse's finest action scenes in the *manga*. The face-off closes the chapter, with Al, Marcoh and the chimeras managing to get the better of Pride and Kimbley – and the chimeras sink their teeth into the Crimson

Alchemist, delivering the death blow.

Now Himoru Arakawa has several battles set in motion, and she shifts between them: Armstrong & co. vs. Sloth, Al vs. Kimbley and Pride, Ed & co. vs. the immortals, Mei vs. Envy, and Hohenheim vs. Father.

Olivia A. soon discovers that guns and swords are useless against the homunculus Sloth. When she's trapped in the ogre's fists, her brother Alex saves her (much to her irritation – she's the older sister, and being helped by her younger brother in any capacity is not something she relishes).

Now Himoru Arakawa introduces an amusing concept to the Armstrongs versus Sloth fight: the dim-witted behemoth can also dash at high speed. But he moves so fast he can't control himself, and crashes into walls.

❊

Chapter 93: *Arch-enemy* ties up the lengthy confrontations in the Kanama suburb with an enjoyable (if unbelievable) *deus ex machina* rescue: it's Loki, driving a car, who races in to save our heroes from Pride's slashing claws (Loki complains about the others hogging the limelight).

Now Zolf Kimbley's bleeding to death on the ground after being bitten in the throat by a chimera. Reprising the scene of Pride consuming Gluttony, *Fullmetal Alchemist* has Pride cannibalizing Kimbley too (which partly proves his undoing, in the face-off with Edward Elric in the finale).

While a ten year-old boy eats a middle-aged psychopath for dinner, the *Fullmetal Alchemist manga* switches (again) to the Sloth vs. Armstrongs smackdown (the comic returns several times later). Himoru Arakawa adds a couple of complications to the mix: (1) Central City soldiers arrive to corner Olivia Armstrong, with orders to kill her on sight; and (2) the immortal puppets break in. (Alex A. has temporarily stalled Sloth by jamming a stone bolt in its maw. Unfortunately, the homunculus won't die yet).

Indeed, Himoru Arakawa exploits the zombies to the full – she has Ed, Scar and co. continuing to fight them, as well as Mei Chang; soon, they're joined by Roy Mustang, whose flame alchemy is handy in frying the critters.

So there isn't a lot of storytelling going on here – we are into one fight after another, in true *shonen manga* style, where Action Reigns Supreme, where Action Is All. *Fullmetal Alchemist* is a battle *manga*, after all, and this is the climactic ending of a long-running story, so once the charas are in place, with suitably formidable opponents blocking their path, Arakawa-sensei isn't going to let the opportunity pass for major action sequences. (Notice that Envy enters the story just when the last of the zombies has been dispatched by Mustang, switching one opponent for another in the standard *shonen manga* manner).

The blam-blam-blammy-blam action, however, is finally put aside (for a moment, at least), when the groups of characters meet: Envy, Mei Chang, Ed Elric, Scar, Col. Mustang, Lt. Hawkeye, the chimeras *et al.*

Mustang wants to know one thing: does the homunculus Envy know who killed Maes Hughes? (This subplot has been simmering in the background for many chapters). Chapter 93: *Arch-enemy* closes with Envy's gloating admission that he was the one (in a great touch, Envy also changes into Hughes' wife Gracia – demonstrating his ability to shape-shift to our heroes, and to flashback to that moment).

❋

Chapter 94: *The Flames of Vengeance* delays the brutal duel between the Flame Alchemist and Envy the homunculus with a change of pace and tone: *Fullmetal Alchemist* switches to Heyman Breda, Lt. Ross, Kain Furey and co. who've kidnapped the Führer's wife. They've taken her to a radio station so she can be interviewed on air and tell the populace of Amestris the truth (it's a piece of media propaganda, reprising what the Elrics did in Liore in the first chapters of *Fullmetal Alchemist*).

Now Col. Mustang puts on his Fierce Face, his 'I Mean Business' persona, telling Ed Elric and Scar and the others to leave Envy to him. They go; Liza Hawkeye stays (of course! – try separating Hawkeye from Mustang!). Envy transforms into his dog-dragon guise, but it doesn't help: he's still attacked by Mustang's flame alchemy.

So Colonel Mustang assaults Envy repeatedly – no matter how much the homunculus dodges and leaps, or how he tries his disguises (Maes Hughes, even Mustang), he can't best the alchemist (tho' Envy's desperate attempt to wrong-foot Liza Hawkeye nearly works, when he changes into Mustang and gets uncomfortably close).

Himoru Arakawa depicts Envy being frazzled in twisted silhouettes, until at last the homunculus is reduced to a tiny, snail-like creature (which, in an inspired sequence, pops out of Envy's third eye). The 2009-10 *Fullmetal Alchemist 2* series rendered this sequence brilliantly.

❋

Chapter 95: *Beyond the Inferno.* At this point, however, just as the Flame Alchemist is about to put Envy out of his/ its misery, squashing the critter under his boot, Liza Hawkeye pulls a gun on him (ridiculous and unconvincing, but wildly melodramatic!). The issue of being consumed by vengeance so it sickens the soul is rather preachily delivered here: both Liza-chan and Edward-kun don't want to see Mustang-san descending to the level of bestial (non-human) hatred. In the end, of course, Mustang realizes the error of his ways, and backs down.

Now Envy shows what he's made of: in spite of being a feeble creature four inches long, he can still manipulate humans. He has enough information about the people in this scene – Mustang, Hawkeye, Scar and Elric – to know how to play them off against each other.

Oh, it drives Envy *nuts* to see how smug and self-satisfied humans are, how they keep fighting back when they appear to be beaten, and how, worst of all, they patronize him with their self-righteousness ('DAMN YOU ALL!'). Envy is called 'Envy' after all, and it wounds him deeply to have the pint-sized Fullmetal Alchemist telling him that he's secretly jealous of humans.

For Envy, it's the 'ultimate insult' having Edward Elric under-standing him best of all in the end. So what does the homunculus do? Only commits suicide! – just so the humans who mock him can't have the pleasure of ending his life. Envy bites Ed's finger, escapes, falls to the floor, and yanks out his heart – the philosopher's stone – and expires.

Certainly it's grotesque, and operatic, and it does include that Japanese issue of honour and suicide, but it's also great storytelling. To portray Envy reduced to this ignoble demise throws the grand themes of *Fullmetal Alchemist* into relief again.

Meanwhile, the battle to bring down the giant Sloth continues in Central HQ: the Armstrongs deploy chains to bind the homunculus. And the boys from Briggs Mountain arrive to take control of the HQ, led by Buccaneer.

Chapter 95: *Beyond the Inferno* climaxes with one of Himoru Arakawa's favourite moments: Izumi Curtis turning up to announce, 'I'm a housewife!' Except here, for once, she decides to show off, and declares, 'I'M AN ALCHEMIST!'

✳

Chapter 96: *The Two Heroines* continues the parallel action sequences: the fight with Sloth continues, as does the struggle for control of Central HQ; at the end of the chapter, the narrative turns to the meeting of the two most powerful magicians in *Fullmetal Alchemist*, Father and van Hohenheim.

The arrival of housewife Izumi Curtis means that it's a woman who helps to triumph over the seemingly unstoppable homunculus Sloth (there is an inevitable sisterly exchange between Curtis and Olivia Armstrong). Yes, Curtis may be a willowy woman, but she can wrestle a giant and hurl him over her shoulder across the room (so her husband, Sig, can pound him more). The two Armstrongs gawp in disbelief.

Finally, after much effort, Sloth is defeated, dissolving into dust (even dying is 'such a bother' to poor Sloth).

★

So van Hohenheim and Father come face to face at last: Hohenheim acts as nonchalant as if he's out for an evening stroll, while Father glowers. He states his aim: to become a perfect being (he has a perpetual chip on his shoulder about being a homunculus). After the customary exchange of belligerent words, the action begins: Father attacks van Hohenheim repeatedly, and Hohenheim deflects his attacks (complaining that he's not that much good at fighting, but somehow managing to wriggle free of Father's alchemical barrage).

Following the duel between the two sorcerers, Arakawa-sensei opts for that favourite gesture of Japanese fantasy: the arm used as a sword to thrust thru the torso. Father gloats, thinking he can grab Hohenheim's philosopher's stone and defeat him (forgetting for the moment that Hohenheim is a philosopher's stone in himself, and he has half a million souls inside him – 536,329 people, to be precise).

✳

Chapter 97: *The Two Philosophers* develops the confrontation between the two wizards further: van Hohenheim reminds Father that he can best him using the souls that he has got to know individually in the 100s of years since the catastrophe in Xerxes engineered by the homunculus in the glass jar (we see a brief flashbacks of the young Hohenheim, lost in the Xingese desert, having survived Xerxes. This is where the myth of the golden man emerging from the desert began). Father has never bothered to converse with the souls trapped inside him – it illustrates another fundamental difference between humans and homunculi (and those Xerxesians help to bring down Father in the end).

Placing the two most powerful beings in her epic saga together, Arakawa-sensei enjoys herself in coming up with suitably spectacular and weird ways in which the battle for supremacy can be dramatized. Hohenheim wants to destroy Father's container, his body, his form, to send him back to being a homunculus trapped in a flask. But Father is one of those Japanese villains who can continually rejuvenate himself, no matter how much he's bombarded. So he sloughs off his skin like a snake, emerging as black goop from his mouth, becoming a grinning, black demon with eyes and mouths sliding across his body like Pride (and he eats his former body, continuing the theme of the villains in *Fullmetal Alchemist* as cannibals).

We switch to the aftermath of the Central HQ running battle, with Olivia Armstrong and her Briggs soldiers apparently victorious (they have the headquarters commanders tied to chairs). Unfortunately, who should return at this moment, but the unkillable psychopath, the Führer, which inaugurates yet another bout of bashin', slicin', yellin', grimacin' and killin'.

Himoru Arakawa is thoroughly in her element here – this seemingly shy female artist from rural Hokkaido is capable of delivering slamming, grinding action as fierce and bloody as any writer or filmmaker you can name. For ex, Arakawa-sensei orchestrates a marvellous re-introduction for Führer Bradley: a one-man assault on the military headquarters – racing up the grand, exterior staircase below the main gate, which's being guarded by a tank. Then, having demolished the tank and its operators (plus the guards on either side), Bradley also takes down the Bear of Briggs Mountain, Buccaneer.

❋

Chapter 98: *Infinite Greed:* Greed joins the battle against the one-man army that is Führer Bradley. So now, somehow, old man Bradley is fighting the furious Greed, plus the wounded but dogged Buccaneer, plus assorted guards (whom he slashes to pieces), and soon Ling Yao's bodyguards. Yet still nobody is able to take the Führer down! There are three fearsome warriors against the Führer (Greed, Fuu and Buccaneer), but Bradley out-matches them all.

Elsewhere in Central Command, Izumi Curtis and Olivia Armstrong are interrogating a brigadier general (Edison), using unusual methods of extracting info about the corrupt regime in the military (they kick him on the ground – rather indelicate for key female charas in *Fullmetal Alchemist*). The returned Maria Ross is re-united with Denny Brosh (he bursts into tears – he thought she'd been killed). And our heroes (Ed, Mustang, Scar, Hawkeye *et al*) are getting closer to Father in his bunker: they've found the secret staircase that leads from the Führer's office underground).

❀

Chapter 99: *Eternal Rest* adds even more incidents to the Führer versus everybody fight: Fuu and Greed/ Ling Yao are leaping about all over the place as they try to get behind the Führer's defence of slashing swords. All three guys work together to trounce the Führer (for ex, Buccaneer stabs *through* Fuu's torso to reach Bradley, hitting him in the chest. The Buckster only does this after Fuu has hurled himself against the Führer with bombs strapped to his chest, and the Führer slashes him, so he's near death). But even such desperate measures aren't enough to nail the Führer, tho' both Fuu and Buccaneer expire during this brawl. (It's Scar who nobbles Wrath/ Bradley in the end).

Meanwhile, down below the military HQ, our heroes can't simply waltz into the super-villain's compound like they're calling round for tea and cakes. No. They have to encounter obstacle after obstacle. This time, it's the turn of the degenerate scientist with the golden tooth, a sly, vicious Doctor modelled on Nazis in pop culture. Gold-Tooth Man's goal is to obtain the 'sacrifices' for Father (Mustang, Ed, Al, Izumi and others). To help him, he is flanked by the rejects from the scientific experiment to create the super-human King Bradley (each one is a grim, blank-faced automaton wielding a sword like the Führer. They follow the Doctor's orders completely, including throwing themselves in front of Liza Hawkeye's bullets).

At the end of ch. 99: *Eternal Rest*, a narrative turning-point occurs when the Doctor activates a five-pointed transmutation circle, which opens up a giant eye beneath the human sacrifices: Ed, Al and Curtis. Each of them vanish, pulled away by the little, black hands from the Gateway.

❀

Chapter 100: *The Forbidden Door* (celebrated on the cover of *Monthly Shonen Gangen* as the 100th installment of *Fullmetal Alchemist*), switches back to the fight between the Führer, Greed, Fuu and the others outside the main entrance of Central HQ. The old stalwart of the action-adventure genre, the literal cliffhanger, has the Führer bested by Greed, and hanging off the side of the staircase, above the moat. Bradley falls, seemingly to his death, but he lands in deep water (which never kills an unkillable villain) – and, anyway, he spots a sewer port handily nearby. So we know that the Führer is going to be back to create more havoc.

Greed transforms into his 1960s superhero carapace and creates mayhem; Buccaneer dies (loyal to Briggs to the end); and the fateful eclipse creeps closer.

Now the *Fullmetal Alchemist* comic brings our heroes to meet the super-villain finally, for the climactic battle. Izumi Curtis, Ed and Al Elric topple into Father's bunker (tho' Al's soul's with his body for the moment), where the homunculus now takes on the guise of a man-shaped shadow filled with eyes and mouths, like Pride. But he has tried to absorb van Hohenheim (and the philosopher's stones inside him), and ended up with Hohenheim only partially integrated (his head sticks out, so he's able to converse with his sons – a rather ugly image).

Upstairs, the battle rages between Col. Mustang, Lt. Hawkeye, Scar *et al* and the Doctor With the Gold Tooth and the Führer-reject henchmen. After some furious action, our heroes are all pinned down, and the Doctor orders the Flame Alchemist to open the Gate. To persuade him, the Doctor uses an outrageous ploy: not to threaten the heroine (Liza H.), or even to rough her up a bit, but to slit her throat!

❄

This forms the climax of chapter 100: *The Forbidden Door*; in chapter 101: *The Fifth Human Sacrifice*, the narrative first switches to Armstrong and co. discussing the developments of the take-over of Central HQ, only returning to Liza Hawkeye bleeding to death on the floor on page ten.

The Doctor With the Gold Tooth continues to run the show, commanding Col. Mustang to open the Gate, using the dying Hawkeye as the sacrifice (he already has a transmutation circle drawn on the floor). Before the blackmail pays off, however, the tables're turned when the Doctor is captured by the chimera Zanpano with the goopy saliva, and hauled up into the roof. Mei Chang, and the chimeras Heinkel and 'Donkey Kong' join our heroes, set them free, and nobble the Bradley clones. Mei stops the worst of the bleeding for Hawkeye.

But just when it seems as if our heroes can take a breather, and they're out of danger, who should reappear, but everybody's favourite psycho-path and leader of the nation, the Führer. They face off, glower and exchange macho taunts (Bradley picks up the phial of the philosopher's stone which Mei Chang has her beady, Xingese eyes on). And then Pride also made a grand entrance (from above, slicing thru the Doctor and Zanpano).

The Führer grabs two swords and pins Roy Mustang to the floor, through his palms. Pride is working for Father still, as is the Doctor With the Gold Tooth, but Pride now does something which seems a little strange: he uses the Doctor as the sacrifice to open the Gate, not one of the people nearby (Liza Hawkeye would be an obvious choice). So it's the Nazi Doctor who's stabbed through the middle by Pride's arms, and used to provide the fifth sacrifice for Father down below.

❄

In chapter 102: *Before the Door* the transmutation is performed, and Roy Mustang disappears, taken to Father's bunker (leaving behind the lump of flesh that was the Doctor). We follow Mustang to the Gateway of Truth (the first time for him), where he encounters the grinning demon. For Mustang, the price of the journey thru the Gate is his sight (thus, blinded, he is unable to use his flame alchemy, which has been troublesome from the enemy's point-of-view).

Father presides over the scene where the sacrifices are assembled: the Elrics, Izumi, Mustang and (inside Father), van Hohenheim (Mei Chang joins them – she's able to enter Father's magical domain using Xingese alkahestry).

Alphonse, however, is still with his body in the Gateway of Truth. This is a marvellous scene, where the soul and the body of Alphonse Elric are re-united. This might be the end-point of one of the main plot strands of *Fullmetal Alchemist*, but Al realizes that his body has wasted away, become too thin and weak, and he can't fight in his body as it is. So Al decides *not* to re-unite with his body just yet, but to put it off until he has fought with his friends to save Amestris (putting the nation, and his friends, before his own desires). Al promises his body that he will return to claim it (a reprise of Ed promising the same to Alphonse). When Al comes back to his armour form, Father is delighted: the fifth sacrifice is here, and the ritual can begin

Back up top, it's left to the nameless Scar to battle the nameless Führer: it's apt that it's Scar who deals the final blow to Bradley/ Wrath, as the emissary of Ishbal, the nation devastated by the Führer's military regime.

❊

Chapter 103: *For Whose Sake* continues the climax of *Fullmetal Alchemist* with scenes of our heroes gathered in Father's bunker (which, he asserts, is 'inside' him, and not part of the ordinary world). They assess their predicament: they have two homunculi to beat. On their side, however, they have several alchemists (even tho' Colonel Mustang is blind), and the Elrics are able to use alchemy (which was nixed before, by Father). So Al and Ed attack Pride (who's already wounded), smashing blocks of stone into him.

Meanwhile Mei Chang boldly announces that she'll be taking on Father (because he appears to be immortal, and Mei never forgets her goal of attaining the secrets of immortality). But it'll take more'n a ninja dagger to affect a homunculus who's already close to possessing god-like powers. Father repels Mei's knife (hurling it back, greatly enlarged), and Mei's soundly beaten.

Himoru Arakawa cuts away to the multiple storylines erupting around Central City, such as the Ishbalians taking on the military, the capture of Bradley's wife, and Scar and Bradley having their fight to the death (these are two characters who really should've expired months ago).

❊

Chapter 104: *The Center of the World* – the alchemical duels in Father's bunker provide many opportunities for mayhem, and Himoru Arakawa keeps returning to them. This is, after all, the climactic sequence in *Fullmetal Alchemist*, when all the stops are pulled out, and it's all systems go.

So Edward orders his brother to look after Mei Chang (injured after trying to attack Father), while he tackles Pride the homunculus: it's two *chibis* slugging away at each other (Ed fights rough, headbutting Pride, who wasn't expecting that).

Enjoyable as the duels are – Izumi Curtis creates an enormous crossbow from stone, Father transmutes a handgun and fires it at Mei Chang, but Alphonse E. leaps in between them and shields her – Father realizes it's time for the alchemical ceremony to begin. So he grasps each of the 'sacrifices' in his black arms (a version of the familiar tentacles of Nipponese fantasy).

Outside the bunker, spectators are getting ready to view the total eclipse (wearing sunglasses); but on the next page, there's a jolt, a shudder, and the people who know what the eclipse will really portend are stopped in their tracks (some think it's an earthquake). Himoru Arakawa employs a doube-page spread to encompass many of her secondary characters, all across Amestris, in small panels. Yes, when Something Momentous is going to happen in *manga*, some long-foreseen event, a *mangaka* might cut to many characters, or show them all in one double page drawing, as here.

Now Father announces his intention open the Gate of the Planet itself: in this part of *Fullmetal Alchemist*, Himoru Arakawa draws Father as an insane monster with a body composed of eyes sliding over a black, shapeless shape, and a head that's nothing but a giant eye and a giant mouth. As if Father is all greed and desire at this point – and Greed the homunculus duly appears to attempt to scupper Father's plans one more time. Doesn't work – Father is too far gone now to be stopped.

Arakawa-sensei is certainly accomplished at portraying hysteria and insanity – here, she gives Father preposterously flamboyant gestures and expressions, so that he's a cackling demon who thinks he can challenge God himself. And he does!

When Father activates the Gate (by slamming one of its/ his arms onto the chessboard, 'the true center'), holes and eyes appear in the torsos of the five sacrifices, each of whom is imprisoned by Father's black, Mr Tickle arms. The eruption of energy is enormous – it expands outwards from Father in the customary hemisphere of *animé* and *manga*, used for atomic bombs, supernatural events, and cataclysms (a marvellous touch has the sphere of energy visualized as a dark ball which swallows Scar and the Führer).

Finally, there's a planetary view, depicting the whole of Amestris from space turned into an alchemical transmutation circle. Zigzags of energy zip everywhere, and the black arms of death creep from the ground like whips, stealing the souls of everyone. They clutch their chests and throats and collapse – Miles, Grumman, Gracia and Elicia, the Führer's wife, even – *noooo!* – Winry-chan and old Pinako.

And now Himoru Arakawa delivers her most spectacular imagery in all of *Fullmetal Alchemist* – at least in terms of the concept, and the scale: a magical gateway opens in the country of Amestris, a gate 100s of miles wide. And climbing out of it is the figure of Father the homunculus – only now he's the size of a small country. The views are colossal – we are up in space here, with the curve of the Earth below, and the Father-demon clambers out of the gateway like he's climbing out of a coffin the size of Texas.

The Father-demon stretches up its arm (one of the signature motifs in *Fullmetal Alchemist*) – reaching for the heavens – literally, this time. Reaching for God. Cleverly, Arakawa-sensei uses the eclipsed sun as an image of God (the sun has been an image of divinity for eons. Of course, without that beautiful star we wouldn't be here, and there'd be no Earth).

What does the Father-demon want? Only to eat God – yes, it's going to reach up and grab God and drag him/ it back to Earth. An eye opens up in black space – with, in a clever touch, the eclipsed sun as its pupil.

Is it successful? Did the Father-demon-soul get what it wanted? Before the revelation of the new creature that Father becomes, at the end of the chapter, *Fullmetal Alchemist* moves to views of the population of Amestris collapsed, seemingly dead: soldiers, Alex Armstrong, Gracia and her daughter Elicia, and many others.

Back in the bunker below Central City, the five sacrifices come round, gasping and injured. Our hero, Edward Elric, is the first to collect himself and ask the dreaded question: 'did you turn all those people into a philosopher's stone?!'

Wreathed in smoke, a figure steps forward: there are big close-ups of Edward and Hohenheim, until, on the last page of chapter 104: *The Center of the World*, the new creature is revealed: a youth with long hair, glaring eyes, and wearing a robe around its waist (revealing a muscley, naked torso). The Father-youth has a distinctly angelic and ancient look, Greek perhaps (a call-back to the Xerxes sequence, echoing the homunculus in the flask's origins in Xerxes). A rebel angel, then, who also resembles both the younger Hohenheim and his son, Edward. (This guy or creature will be the chief opponent in the subsequent spectacular action scenes).

❊

Chapter 105: *The Throne of God* continues the extraordinary finale of Himoru Arakawa's *Fullmetal Alchemist manga* with the first of several sequences where our heroes battle the Father-youth. Because what is the first thing that the Father-super-being does? Kills! Or, rather, *attempts* to kill – to dispatch our heroes.

Well, once a villain, always a villain – that's the rule here. So altho' he/ it has the powers of a god (or has become God, having suppressed God), what doe it or he choose to do? Kill someone!

Not celebrate? Not break open the champers and party? If you'd just become a god, and achieved your wildest dreams, wouldn't you want to party a little? Or try out your new, god-like powers? But no – the Father-youth remains the resentful, vain, jealous tyke he/ it always was.

Oh, we know he/ it has to get rid of Hohenheim, Ed and co. soon, because they won't stand back and watch him/ it take over the world. So it/ he attacks them – but luckily Hohenheim is onto him/ it already, and gathers everyone to his side, where he's able withstand the Father-youth's assault of energy.

6 There's a colour-page flashback, to the Elrics in their father's study, contemplating a book on alchemy which talks of the perfect, immortal being – in short, godhood.

The Father-youth, looking bored on his stone throne, recalls Tetsuo in Katsuhiro Otomo's *Akira*. There's a joke on not even having to lift a finger, as the creature taps his finger on the arm of the throne and all hell breaks loose (the Father-youth is now a super-alchemist, who can perform colossal magical acts without moving a muscle).

The battle of wits and god-given power between van Hohenheim and the Father-creature is wonderful to behold: it's one of those climactic sequences that reward the journey thru an epic narrative. How the dwarf-in-the-flask is so haughty and arrogant with its new-found powers, and how crafty Hohenheim has already been putting things in place to counter-attack.

For instance, the Father-monster alchemically materializes a tiny sun in his hand (i.e., a nuclear bomb), and is about to use it, when he experiences the first inklings of a flaw in his new godhood: the souls that van Hohen-heim absorbed, back in Xerxes, are making their presence felt, under-mining the Father-monster's powers. (Meanwhile, Hohenheim explains that the people of Amestris are not dead, that their souls remain tied to their bodies via their spirits).

Himoru Arakawa's artwork in this part of *Fullmetal Alchemist* is enormously imaginative – how she has the souls inside Hohenheim from Xerxes speaking in speech bubbles against black (of their determination to help the Amestrisians), how the counter-attack is nation-wide, seen from space, how the souls return to the bodies of the people of Amestris as a surging vortex of energy (rising out of the Father-youth, into the sky), re-entering their bodies collapsed on the ground.

Gradually, painfully, the fallen characters come back to life (Winry Rockbell gets pride of place among them), as they wonder what just happened. This is great storytelling – outrageous and grand, decidedly abstract (and metaphysical, really), yet completely convincing.

His/ its power may have been reduced by the re-animation of the populace of Amestris and the loss of their souls, but the Father-creature is still as aggressive and antsy as ever, attacking our heroes with waves of energy. Van Hohenheim is put to the test in defending everyone, and Himoru Arakawa includes a touching moment when his two sons stand behind him and encourage him (it's one of the few times that Edward acknowledges his father, and calls him 'Dad').

❀

Meanwhile, back up top, Scar and the Führer are still going at it, with swords swinging, alchemical transmutations, and spears of stone. It's apt that it should be Scar who duels Bradley finally – after all, it was the Führer's regime that perpetrated the Ishbalian War, where Scar and his countrymen lost nearly everything.

The Führer's taunts Scar that there is no God – and just as he is distracted by the beginning of the end of the eclipse (the image of the sun as an image of God), Scar manages to slice off his hands. For your average warrior, that would be enough to end a swordfight. But in Japanese *manga*, characters like the Führer never give up – and he holds his sword between his teeth (like Zoro in *One Piece*), cutting Scar in the torso.

Lan Fan arrives on the scene, to avenge her grandfather Fuu: Führer Bradley, lying on the ground, seemingly beaten at last, is utterly unrepentant. And he expires (or seems to), without Lan Fan delivering the final blow (he taunts her for missing her chance for revenge).

With the last of his energy, Scar sets in motion the anti-transmutation circle that's been built throughout Amestris: Lan Fan finds a philosopher's stone (on Bradley), and Scar uses it to ignite the circle. Thus, Scar receives a kind of redemption, doing his bit to defeat the homunculi and Father (and to make good his brother's death at the hands of the Amestrisian regime).

And back down in the bunker, this is the moment, Hohenheim yells, when they can all blitz the Father-monster as one: so all of the alchemists still standing (Ed, Al, Mei, Izumi *et al*), hurl the best they've got at the Father-thing. With some militant words from Edward (about kicking ass), the chapter ends.

The last chapters of *Fullmetal Alchemist* are much longer – some are over twice or three times the usual length (so the magical number of 108 is cheated. And, anyway, the chapters in *Fullmetal Alchemist* are already twice the length of regular *manga* chapters. So the whole series is about 270 regular-length chapters).

❀

Chapter 106: *The Abyss of Pride* (*Puraido no Shinen*) opens with a brief explanation of alchemy from Scar (who suggests that Father and his experiments with philosopher's stones have unbalanced how alchemy operates). But then we're back with our heroes battling the sullen God-youth that was once Father: stone fists, stone projectiles on chains, stone spikes and stone cannons – the Elric boys are throwing all they can alchemize at the frowny God-man who just stands there, with his arms folded (Izumi Curtis adds a stone column, and Greed has an iron girder). Hohenheim encourages them to continue, maintaining that every little bit helps, and that the freak is using all of his power to defend himself.

To add a new/ old element to the all-action finale, Himoru Arakawa reprises the vat of molten lava that was used to transmute the old Greed into a philosopher's stone (way back in chapter 31: *The Snake That Eats Its Own Tail*). Greed hopes to thrust the Father-creature into the tub, but Edward tips it over, where the liquid swamps the target. Most folk would be destroyed, but the Father-youth simply alchemizes the material into missiles to hurl at our heroes.

And then the Father-being rises to the surface, to ground level, as Arakawa-sensei decides to take the fight outside – for a change of scene, to include new ingredients in the battle, and to have a more spectacular setting for the ending (the Father-youth's move is explained by Hohenheim as their enemy searching for new victims to transmute into philosopher's stones).

Edward opts to stay behind to deal with Pride, the only remaining homunculus, apart from the dwarf in the flask. The others – Izumi,

Mustang, Alphonse – alchemize themselves up and out of the bunker on moving pillars of stone. There's a tearful reunion of Izumi and her hubby, Sig. Greed contemplates the corpse of King Bradley.

The Edward versus Pride smackdown unravels in the expected manner: plenty of hurled insults followed by two short bodies smashing into each other. Pride is still a homunculus, however, and those black arms are still very powerful: Pride, realizing his body is fragmenting, captures Ed and hopes to use him as his new container.

As Pride appears to be gaining the upper hand – he has Edward pinned by his wrists – Himoru Arakawa makes an unusual turn, bringing back Zolf Kimbley, who's spirit still resides inside Pride. This is a reprise of the unusual Greed and Ling Yao relationship, with one character existing in spirit-form inside the other. And Kimbley isn't under Pride's thumb (or soul) yet: he revolts, which gives Edward enough time to wrench himself free from Pride's clutches, and attack him.

Even stranger, and way more abstract, is the beat where Edward invades Pride in the form of a philosopher's stone. Errr, it's not wholly clear how this works, but anyway, it's played out as Edward in spirit-form smashing into Pride in spirit-form (visualized as a young, naked boy), with Edward gripping the kids' skull. We cut abruptly from the chaotic (spiritual) interior of Pride to a double-page drawing of Ed punching the homunculus's head with full force (wisely using his automail arm), disintegrating it into a spray of small pieces.

Pride dies – his body becoming trails of black dust and splinters. And in a reprise of Envy's 'true' form, Pride is visualized as a tiny baby, an inch or two long, which Edward examines in his palm. Ed leaves the child lying safely on his red coat.

❊

This duel and death might be the climax of this chapter, 106: *The Abyss of Pride*, but these finale chapters are longer (as Arakawa-sensei packs in so much narrative), so we continue (with fourteen more pages): now the *Fullmetal Alchemist manga* switches back to the super-villain, the only homunculus left to defeat: we are up top, in a courtyard of the military HQ, where the Father-creature is hoping to act like an alchemical vampire (sucking out the energy of people to use as philosopher's stones to replenish himself).

The Father-freak is attacking Briggs guards (not physically – this is a super-being who just stands, glowering, and let its/ his magic do the dirty work of sucking out someone's soul). Luckily, van Hohenheim is back in the fray, launching alchemical missiles at the Father-youth. Hohey is soon flanked by Mei Chang, Alphonse Elric and Izumi Curtis.

Van Hohenheim derides the homunculus for despising humans yet wanting to be like them. You homunculi, Hohenheim asserts, cannot give birth. Oh, but we can, the Father-critter replies, and proceeds to allow some of the dead souls trapped inside him to emerge, splurging out of his torso in a travesty of birth. The first soul to stumble towards Hohenheim is, suitably, the King of Xerxes (the national leader from 100s of years ago who commanded Hohenheim's master to aid the homunculus in granting him immortal life, which's where this whole mess of houmculi started).

Continuing the theme of mocking birth, a baby crawls up to Izumi Curtis's foot, and children gather around Alphonse Elric. Just as Edward appears in the courtyard (after dispatching Pride), the Father-being lets loose an almighty blast of energy, which demolishes the dead souls staggering in front of him, busts Ed's automail arm, and sends everyone else flying.

◯
Chapter 107: *The Finale Battle* (*Saigo no Tatakai*) was published Nov 22, 2010 (with the last chapter) ...What just happened? Nobody's sure yet, but Greed sums it up neatly: the chief homunculus is going nuts. Greed also reminds everyone that the Father-creature has zillions of human souls inside him, which makes him very dangerous.

Before the battle with the last remaining homunculus continues, however, there is an intense discussion among the heroes about who is going to fight. The scene is partly played for humour: Greed advises leaving the women and the non-alchemists behind. That includes Olivia Armstrong – but she is never one to stand down from a fight, even tho' she's injured. On the radio telephone, her Briggs Mountain men remind her that they can still operate without their commander, and urge her to rest.

So Major Armstrong falls back, handing over command to Greed, Mustang, her brother Alex, Lt. Hawkeye and the others who still want to fight. There's a moving interlude where Olivia Armstrong passes the Führer's corpse, and tells him that her Briggs troops were strong (with Scar injured nearby).

❊
Only now do we return to the courtyard and the scene of devastation from the Father-being's explosion. Himoru Arakawa creates a wonderfully emotional scenario now, with Alphonse Elric and his father protecting the rest of the group: Al sits in front of Mei Chang and Xiao Mei, and Hohenheim kneels to defend Edward and Izumi Curtis. They have their arms outstretched, in the gesture of protection seen in many *manga* and *animé* (and not only in the fantasy genre), and both suffer tremendously: Alphonse's armour is battered and broken, and he collapses; Hohenheim's clothes are in rags, and his arms are smoking. (This moment cleverly clears the way for Edward to be the hero who finally trounces Father).

Of all the things you could do when you are a god – just think! So many things! Sadly, the Father-creature has a feeble imagination, because once he's become a god, all he/ it can think of to do is to fight the heroes and try to kill them. Eh? Why doesn't he/ it simply rejuvenate himself fully first? Then he/ it can take on Hohenheim, the Elrics and the others: he/ it could fly off somewhere without alchemists and start to fashion philosopher's stones, returning once he's/ it's invincible.

Thus, the Father-youth picks up Hohenheim and hurls him aside: as he/ it stands over Izumi Curtis and Edward Elric, he/ it begins to attack them with energy bolts. Luckily, the Briggs men have got their act together, and fire at him/ it, which gives them a chance to snatch Curtis and Ed and hurry away with them.

Col. Mustang, still blind, joins the attacks on the Father-thing now, with the ever-faithful Liza Hawkeye standing beside him and helping him to aim his flames at the target. Now it's a free-for-all, as everybody has a go at nobbling the Father-being: Lan Fan, Mustang, Alex Armstrong, Izumi Curtis, the Briggs soldiers and the chimeras – they're all trying to make the target use up his/ its power. Yet nothing seems to be working: when he/ it is encased in a dome of stone and incinerated by Flame Alchemy, he/ it manages to emerge apparently unscathed.

This is partly because no matter what those characters try, wonderful as they are, they are all secondary characters, and the only three charas who will finally nail the Father-homunculus are the three Elrics, father and two sons.

Greed, still arguing with the body he resides inside of – Ling Yao, launches himself at the Father-figure, punching him in the eye. It's a grotesque image when Greed's arm sinks into the enemy's face, and he/ it begins to suck out Greed's philosopher's stone. The Father-god gloats at Greed, but this was apparently a decoy, because now Edward Elric lunges at the god-like mirror image of himself. The Father-entity is still strong, however, and is able to deflect Ed's attack from the rear – but with his hand, van Hohenheim notes well, not with his alchemical energy (it destroys Ed's automail arm, though, in another drawing which features the parts of Ed's arm falling to pieces).

Thus, van Hohenheim realizes that the dwarf in the jar is getting weaker, if he's blocking attacks physically, and he can't contain the god-power he's absorbed. This proves to be a turning-point in the all-out battle with the Father-creature.

Waves of energy sweep outwards from the Father-creature again, blasting into our heroes (who're already exhausted and injured). The monster, now acting like a zombie, staggers upright, searching for someone or something to turn into a philosopher's stone. Its/ his gaze turns to three people nearby: it's the heroic trio of *Fullmetal Alchemist*: Ed and Al Elric, and their pa, Hohenheim. All three are on the ground – and Edward has been pinned to a concrete block by a wire screw (the sort used to hold concrete together). It is, again, a crucifixion image, with Ed's outstretched arm pierced near the shoulder.

With the Father-being lurching over towards Ed Elric, like a mindless zombie towards its prey, and everyone in a weakened state (and Hohenheim urging Ed to run), Alphonse makes a critical decision, which leads towards the resolution of the ending of *Fullmetal Alchemist*: he enlists Mei Chang's (reluctant) help in using alchemy to transmute Ed's arm back, in a reverse exchange. This is a marvellous, heroic moment for Alphonse, where one of the primary aspects of the hero – sacrifice – pays off big time.

Edward Elric realizes what his younger brother is about to do, and yells at him to stop. Too late – Al claps his hands together and performs the transmutation (whispering, 'brother... win'). Himoru Arakawa's artwork is suitably stark and vivid, using full blacks and silhouettes.

Alphonse Elric is taken to that place you never want to go – the limbo of the Gateway of Truth, where his body is waiting for him. Al's body reunites with his soul, visualizied as the clasping of hands. The point is that once Al's body (in armour) is there, he can't get back unless someone rescues him (Al is counting on his brother to do that). The grinning demon is there, too, as always, wondering what Edward will sacrifice to travel to the Gate when he comes for his brother. (Once again, we are so impressed by the imagery and motifs that Himoru Arakawa has developed to portray very abstract/ metaphysical occurrences like souls and bodies being re-united, or surrogate/ stand-in bodies disappearing, or charas ending up somewhere between life and death. *This is genius storytelling*).

Edward regaining his arm is depicted, rightly, in a double-page drawing (against the same white of the limbo): it's an important moment. Tho' it's typical that after his shock and surprise have registered, Ed immediately yells at his *baka* brother (who's nearby, lying lifeless on the ground).

But Edward immediately puts his re-gained arm to use, transmuting the earth below into a column that smashes into the Father-creature, and pulling the metal spike out of his other arm. And then it's a battle of alchemists – Ed versus his lookalike, shadow self: Edward is letting loose alchemical transmutations all over the place. Out come some of his favourite moves: the spear, the pointed column, and of course the simple but effective punch to the face (these are some of the last times that Ed ever uses alchemy).

It's working! The Father-critter is being slammed about. It's moving that the people observing begin to cheer Edward on – they're yelling 'Edward!' and 'Get him, kid!'

❍

Chapter 108: *The Journey's End* (*Tabiji no Hate*) ...And so to the final chapter of this masterwork. The cover of the magazine *Shonen Gangen* for this chapter features the *Fullmetal Alchemist* team, of course, plus the customary message to the readers: 'thank you all!'

The last chapter (actually the length of five regular *manga* chapters) continues the Big Finale Fight, with the hero beating up the super-villain using his fists. The colour pages depict the Father-creature toppling – with the grotesque motif of the staring eye lodged in his gaping mouth.

Now the Father-thing is very unstable: on the ground, on all fours, he suddenly bloats up, releasing more energy. And then he staggers towards Greed, thrusting his arm into Greed's torso, to absorb him. Yes – because the subplot of Greed-and-Ling Yao needs to be resolved (and Greed is the last remaining homunculus, apart from the Father-monster).

Thus, we have the last of the arguments raging within Ling Yao's body in *Fullmetal Alchemist*, between the Greed-spirit and Ling's soul. The motif of 'a boy and his demon' is marvellously evoked in Himoru Arakawa's artwork, with Ling grabbing hold of the tail-end of the Hallowe'en-like ghost-shape of the Greed-sprite (this was one of countless highlights in the finale of the 2nd *Fullmetal Alchemist animé*).

The Father-creature lunges towards Greed, to extract his power, but Greed enters the Father-being, leaving Ling Yao behind, and promising to weaken his creator from within. Until, that is, the Father-thing destroys Greed with a rapid snap of his jaws (Greed, tho', is given a moving send-off, like the other homunculi, as he dissolves into dust and nothingness).

Now Edward Elric performs his customary move: a punch – this time through the torso of the Father-monster: the people of Xerxes are able to clamber out of the hole in the Father-monster that Ed's made. Visualized as an army of grasping, black arms, the Xerxes souls attack the Father-creature, reducing it to ziiip…

…So that the homunculus who dreamed of being a god finds itself once more a tiny, spherical puff of soot with one eye – but this time floating in the white limbo of the Gateway of Truth. There follows one of Himoru Arakawa's marvellous metaphysical interchanges – between the dwarf in the flask and its spiritual counterpart in the Gateway – the grinning demon who, in a great touch, is the mirror image of the Father-homunculus (and calls itself the World, Space, the Truth, the All, and the One).

Poor dwarf-homunculus, angry, indignant – and terrified – to be reduced to this after so nearly achieving godhood. The grinning demon announces itself as the homunculus's despair – and the Gate opens, and the black arms fly out, pulling the Father-dwarf into limbo, which is the last we see of him.

O

Now we switch to the other grand plot of *Fullmetal Alchemist* – the fate of the Elric brothers. We all want to know if they're going to regain their bodies fully and forever. Ed kneels beside Alphonse's lifeless armour (along with Mei Chang).[7] There must be a way to bring Al back from the Gateway of Truth – but without using the philosopher's stone which Ling Yao offers him, or using Hohenheim's life, which he proposes.

This is a moving scene in *Fullmetal Alchemist*, with the principal characters standing or sitting around Edward and Alphonse, looking on sadly. The moment between Ed and Hohenheim, where the Elrics' father offers up his soul to use in exchange for Al, is wonderful, hitting just the right note of pathos and humour (and finally affirming their relationship).

Then comes Himoru Arakawa's final dramatic gesture in the *Fullmetal Alchemist* epic comic – one brother rescuing another through a heroic sacrifice. It plays into multiple themes in the *Fullmetal Alchemist* series, and seems to be a perfectly judged ending. Not Ed giving up his life, or his limbs, but his alchemy.

---

7 Not, as we might expect, Hohenheim – this is his son here!

It works: Edward draws his last ever transmutation circle in the dirt, stands in the middle of it, claps his hands, and performs his final alchemical act. Hohenheim, Izumi Curtis, Alex Armstrong and co. look on in shock, but they can't stop Ed, who disappears to the Gateway of Truth…

…So there is a second metaphysical conversation with the grinning demon, the other/ all/ one/ god/ world, in the limbo of the Gateway. Edward, fully confident of his decision to revoke his powers[8] (smiling quietly to himself), tells the grinning demon that he is ready to sacrifice his alchemy and become an ordinary human being. Because that's all he ever was. And he won't need alchemy anyway if he has friends. It's a great moment of affirmation by Edward – which the demon, the All, the One, the World, the God acknowledges by replying: 'that's the right answer, alchemist'.

So Edward Elric gives up his alchemy by clapping his hands to the doors, and there is Alphonse waiting for him. A full-page drawing depicts the brothers walking through doors like a heavenly gateway, back to the world.

Once Alphonse and Edward Elric materialize in the courtyard of the Central's HQ, there are a series of hugs and tearful reunions – Mei Chang, Hohenheim, Izumi Curtis, Sig, Alex Armstrong, etc.

Once the embraces and the sobbings are over, the story of *Fullmetal Alchemist* is essentially finished: the super-villain has been defeated; Amestris has been saved; the people's souls have been returned; Alphonse is back from Neverland; and the Elrics have their bodies renewed.

I think that Himoru Arakawa could've indulged herself with deepening the emotional charis at the end of *Fullmetal Alchemist* (as the *animé* did). It seems over too swiftly.

O

The fully alchemical comic shifts into a series of *dénouement* scenes, which tie up several of the subplots (including: the Armstrongs; Ed Elric delivering the doll-size Selim to a weepy Mrs Bradley; Colonel Mustang's ambitions (and eyesight); Lin Yao and co. returning to Xing (with Mei Chang); the death of Hohenheim; and Liza Hawkeye meeting Rebecca).

An important *dénouement* scene in ch. 108 of *Fullmetal Alchemist* occurs between Dr Knox, Dr Marcoh and Roy Mustang: Marcoh offers to use a philosopher's stone he has to heal Mustang's sight – only now that he's going to step into the Führer's shoes, Marcoh makes Mustang promise to create a new Ishbal, and to have the refugees moved there. Mustang agrees. (Scar is saved by Olivia Armstrong in order to work under Miles in restoring the land of Ishbal; Armstrong returns to Briggs Mountain).

Similar vows of reconciliation and peace occur in another significant scene, which resolves the subplots surrounding the Xingese folk: Ling Yao offers to acknowledge and protect Mei Chang's clan when he becomes

---

8 You could argue that Edward E. giving up his alchemical powers is not enough of a 'payment' or a sacrifice, but, in the world of *Fullmetal Alchemist*, and in Ed's life, alchemy is fundamental (it's his art, his profession). It echoes characters such as Ged in the *Earthsea* books of Ursula Le Guin, who uses all of his powers up in order to save Earthsea in *The Farthest Shore*.

emperor. The Xingese characters depart for their homeland.

In amongst the emotional farewells in *Fullmetal Alchemist* is the demise of van Hohenheim: Himoru Arakawa elides a *sayonara* with his children (which seems a little heartless),[9] and cuts straight to Hohenheim already expired at his wife Trisha's graveside. He's discovered by Pinako Rockbell, who's come to put some flowers on the grave (presumably it's several days later).

Finally, after many of the secondary charas have enjoyed their final appearances in this epic *manga*, we return to our stars, Edward and Alphonse Elric. It is days or weeks later,[10] and we have the Big Homecoming Sequence. *Tadaima...* 'Home' is of course Resembool... and one house in particular: the Rockbells' place. (Of course it's a sunny, blue-sky day).

The reunion with Winry Rockbell is played for laughter and tears, and a Big Hug, spread across two pages. It's the Fairy Tale Ending, yes, and the 2001-2010 comic could finish right there, but Himoru Arakawa opted to continue for another 24 pages, to take her characters into the future.

O

First: we leap forward two years... Edward Elric attempts alchemy (he's fixing the Rockbells' roof), and of course... nothing happens. He calls Alphonse up to enjoy the view – of the perfect, sunny, gentle, hills-and-fields landscape. This is a reminder of what has been won in the story (or regained, because it was always there) – the beautiful world... life itself. Both brothers are getting restless – for travel, for knowledge, for adventure.

A curious scene depicts the rehabilitation of the homunculi – Mrs Bradley has taken in the baby Selim, and raised it (he's grown rapidly in two years, from a two-inch foetus to a six year-old boy). General Grumman (now the Führer) visits her, and wonders if humans and homunculi can live together.

Alphonse visits Maes Hughes' widow Gracia and Elicia, announcing his ambition to pursue his alchemical research further – by travelling to Xing, to study alchemy with Mei Chang. His aim? To help the two chimeras regain their original forms (he meets them in a café; they all affirm their goals for travelling and studying). So Al is in motion, tho' journeying without his brother (he's going East, and Ed is heading West).

Pride of place in the *Fullmetal Alchemist manga* is accorded to Edward Elric, the wilful, stubborn, vain, irksome, smart, talented, mercurial, workaholic, energetic, charismatic, unstoppable and handsome hero of the 2001-10 Japanese comic.

There are two chief elements of the 8 pages of the Edward Elric scenes that close *Fullmetal Alchemist*: the romantic subplot with Winry Rockbell and Ed's new life. So, to the romance first: yes, it hasn't been a major ingredient of *Fullmetal Alchemist*, which has remained a *shonen manga* to

---

9 In the *animé*, the send-off is between Hohenheim and Alex Armstrong, with the men politely thanking each other.
10 Alphonse is back in new clothes with his long hair trimmed.

the last, but it's a delight to see the two teens finally embracing. Of course, their encounter – at the clichéd setting of a railroad station – is awkward and embarrassed. No kiss, but a big hug – and then, with a toot from the steam engine, Ed is gone.

◯

The final two pages of *Fullmetal Alchemist* comprise a series of snapshots – photographs spread on a table, throwing the story into the far future: Edward Elric and Winry Rockbell grin broadly, holding two children; behind them stand Mei Chang and Edward (so presumably Al is back from Xing, and has brought the Xingese warrior with him); Jean Havoc is training to walk, watched over by Heyman Breda and Lt. Ross;[11] Col. Mustang and Liza Hawkeye are at some outdoor, military ceremony; Ling Yao is crowned Emperor; Miles and Scar are travelling; the Curtises show off their muscles; Vato Falman is in the North; Olivia and her brother Alex Armstrong pose; the chimeras are with Loki; and Pinako Rockbell tends the twin graves of Trisha and van Hohenheim.

Thus is this extraordinary and one-of-a-kind epic *manga* brought to a close.

EXTRAS AND SIDE STORIES (*OMAKE* AND *GAIDEN*)

From the first volume onwards, Himoru Arakawa began to produce 4-*koma* for *Fullmetal Alchemist*. Among the many jokes were Alphonse complaining about being put into a suit of armour, and couldn't his brother find something smaller?; Al worrying about getting a girlfriend if he looks like a suit of armour; Al wondering what to do about the loincloth he wears; Al finding kittens; Ed being teased about his height; Mustang bragging about being the star attraction of *Fullmetal Alchemist*; Mustang announcing that women in military will wear mini-skirts (or that the military will be all women); cheesy, camp pictures of Alex Armstrong; the charas dressed as *yakuza* gangs (a regular motif in *manga*, along with visiting the beach and a hot spring); Pinako's pointy hair; Al trying out different hairstyles; and Lust cracking walnuts between her boobs.

Several of the extras (= *omake*) and side stories (= *gaiden*) in *Fullmetal Alchemist* focus on the third 'family' that Ed and Al Elric are part of – the military personnel centred around Colonel Mustang's office (the first family being their own, and the second being the Rockbells).

Most of the extras/ *omake* are lighthearted (as all of the 4-*koma* strips are), apart from stories such as *His Battlefield Once More* and *The Elric Family*.

Many of the 4-*koma* ideas appeared in the 4-*Koma Theatre* section of

11 In the *animé*, Havoc is going to receive alchemical healing using the philosopher's stone given by Dr Marcoh, before he uses it on Mustang's vision.

the *Fullmetal Alchemist* Original Video Animations for the second TV series.

In some of the *omake*, Himoru Arakawa answers readers' letters (like, when are the characters' birthdays? Arakawa-sensei won't say, but Ed's is in Winter). She's in her cow-with-glasses guise: 'The Cow Tells All!!' Names come from a European names dictionary; and military names from fighters and planes.

The *gaiden* (side stories) of *Fullmetal Alchemist* include:

❀ *The Military Festival*[12] is an 8-page side-story (used in the 1st *anime* series), where Roy Mustang and Edward have a duel, in answer to their colleagues wondering who would be the strongest.

❀ *Dog of the Military* – where Sergeant Furey finds a stray dog and tries to find a home for it (in the end, it's Liza Hawkeye who takes the dog in); the title, 'dog of the military', is often used derisorily in *Fullmetal Alchemist* to describe military men who become mere cogs in the military machine.

❀ *Fight On, 2nd Lieutenant* is about Jean Havoc's romantic adventures at the Armstrong household (he's invited there when Col. Mustang asks Armstrong to help out with Havoc's love life). The Armstrongs are a bunch of caricature aristos who dwell in a lavish mansion out of a *shojo manga* set in 18th century Europe (such as *The Rose of Versailles*).

After meeting the scary father, mother and others, Jean Havoc reckons that the daughter, Kathleen, will be grotesque: the joke is, she's a *kawaii* blonde, but her hobby is lifting pianos, and a 'normal' man like Havoc is not muscly enough for her. *Fight On, 2nd Lieutenant* was used in the *anime* series.

❀ *His Battlefield Once More* is a serious short story comprising an intense conversation between Roy Mustang and his best friend, Maes Hughes. The topic? War – killing – death… what are we fighting for? Why do we have to kill?

The scene is the past, during the Ishbal War: Roy Mustang sits dejected, while Maes Hughes tries to cheer him up. When the scene switches to the present day, Mustang finds he's been dreaming: his team surrounds him, in his office, giving him work to do. (So what was it all for? So that life could carry on, perhaps). The *anime* used all of *His Battlefield Once More* (and the Original Video Animations also drew on this story).

❀ *Simple People* is about the sisterly-brotherly-possibly-romantic relations between the Elrics and Winry Rockbell. The MacGuffins here are some earrings that Edward buys his automail mechanic when he keeps turning up with his automail wrecked. As it's an Edward-and-Winry story, there are misunderstandings, yelling scenes, and of course beats where Winry-chan smashes Ed's head.

There's a teensy bit of women's solidarity in *Simple People*: Winry starts wearing earrings because of Liza Hawkeye's example, and Hawkeye in turn wears her hair long, following Winry. (The earrings

12 The *manga* side-story, where Edward Elric and Roy Mustang have a friendly challenge, was used in the first *Fullmetal Alchemist* series: it appeared in *Gangan Powered* in Spring, 2002.

motif was taken up in the *animé* – Winry gives them to Ed for safekeeping, and one of the Original Video Animations told this story; and earrings are a motif in *The Sacred Star of Milos* movie).

✽ *The Elric Family* is a story of Ed and Al when they were tots: Edward whacks Alphonse, gets told off by his mom, grumbles, is given fatherly advice from Hohenheim, and sort of makes it up with Al at the end.

✽ *Tales of a Master* is one of the longer extras in *Fullmetal Alchemist* (18 pages): it concerns one of Himoru Arakawa's favourite characters, Izumi Curtis, and the legend of how she survived her month in the wilds of the North, near Briggs Fortress. Like the Elrics begging Curtis to teach them, Curtis as an 18 year-old girl visited a famous alchemist, Silver Steiner:[13] he challenged her to survive for a month in the North. Curtis cheats – nobbling soldiers from nearby Briggs Mountain, and stealing their supplies (Curtis also becomes the top predator in the snowy forest – kicking wolves, duelling with deer, and even wrestling bears). *Tales of a Master* ends with the discovery that Silver Steiner died years ago, and it's his brother, Gold, the martial artist, who's hard of hearing (and set her challenge, thinking she wanted to learn fighting techniques). The whole side-story was animated in the Original Video Animations.

✽ *Akatsuki no Ouji* (*Prologue*) concerns the imminent arrival of the Prince of Aerugo, a country South of Amestris, which has got the capital buzzing. The story isn't really a story, it's more a mood or character piece, where we pay single-panel visits to characters such as Armstrong, Hawkeye, Bradley, Scar, Mustang, Winry, etc. Issues such as the Ishbal War are evoked (which Aerugo was involved in), and the Elrics are searching the streets for the panda/ cat pet of the *chibi* Xingese girl, Mei Chang.

---

13 Stein means *stone*, appropriately for a story about philosopher's stones.

チェス駒一覧

白チームと黒チームそれぞれ18体ずつあり、キング、クイーン、ルーク、ナイト、ビショップ、ポーンの6種類に分けられる。駒の背中に刻印されている文字（白：K・Q・R・N・B・P／黒：K・Q・R・N・B・P）で確認できるぞ。

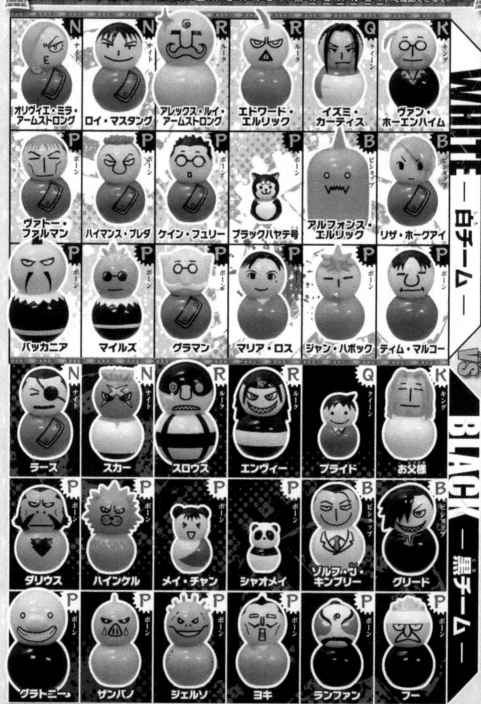

WHITE —白チーム—

N ナイト	**N** ナイト	**R** ルーク	**R** ルーク	**Q** クイーン	**K** キング
オリヴィエ・ミラ・アームストロング	ロイ・マスタング	アレックス・ルイ・アームストロング	エドワード・エルリック	イズミ・カーティス	ヴァン・ホーエンハイム
P ポーン	**P** ポーン	**P** ポーン		**B** ビショップ	**B** ビショップ
ヴァトー・ファルマン	ハイマンス・ブレダ	ケイン・フュリー	ブラックハヤテ号	アルフォンス・エルリック	リザ・ホークアイ
P ポーン	**P** ポーン	**P** ポーン	**P** ポーン	**P** ポーン	**P** ポーン
バッカニア	マイルズ	グラマン	マリア・ロス	ジャン・ハボック	ティム・マルコー

VS

BLACK —黒チーム—

N ナイト	**N** ナイト	**R** ルーク	**R** ルーク	**Q** クイーン	**K** キング
ラース	スカー	スロウス	エンヴィー	プライド	お父様
P ポーン	**P** ポーン	**P** ポーン	**P** ポーン	**B** ビショップ	**B** ビショップ
ダリウス	ハインケル	メイ・チャン	シャオメイ	ゾルフ・J・キンブリー	グリード
P ポーン	**P** ポーン	**P** ポーン	**P** ポーン	**P** ポーン	**P** ポーン
グラトニー	ザンパノ	ジェルソ	ヨキ	ランファン	フー

※写真は試作品です。実際の商品とは多少異なる場合がございます。

Part Three

Fullmetal Alchemist

Hagane no Renkinjutsushi

鋼の錬金術師

The Anime

01

FULLMETAL ALCHEMIST AND THE JAPANESE ANIMATION INDUSTRY

The world of Japanese animation is instantly recognizable: characters with spiky hair, red hair, purple hair, long hair • hair blowing in the breeze • giant eyes • tiny mouths • snub, pointy noses • women with pneumatic bodies and big breasts • guys with muscle-bound bodies • superheroes • grimaces showing lots of teeth • elfin ears • cat-girls (*nyah!*) • angels, crosses, churches • feathers • grizzled, old guys who smoke • child-like *shojo* figures • tall, skinny villains • high schools • people who can fly • grotesque transformations • excessive violence • technofetishism • robots • *mecha* • more robots • more *mecha* • mobile power suits • explosions • spaceships • jets • helicopters • motorbikes • guns, guns and more guns • characters holding guns at every opportunity • samurai swords • swordplay • swords vs. guns • cloaks • teams, gangs, clans, harems, after-school clubs • lightning storms • the ocean • expressions of awe and joy: *sugoi! subarashi!* • noisy disbelief (*eeeeeeeh?!*) • hysterical reactions to *everything* • girls in swimwear • flashes of underwear • the colours green and silver and red • headbands • silly hats • comic sidekicks like dogs or cute critters • stuffed toys • evil villains • nerds (*otaku*) • festivals • kimonos • cherry blossom pillow moments • *saké* • Tokyo • futuristic cities, gloomy cities • always skyscrapers and mean streets (always with the skyscrapers!) • theme parks • giant moons • neon signs • tentacles • monsters • demons • blood and guts • masochism • suicide• and last but not least: the atomic bombs dropped on Japan by the United States of North America.

Japan has the biggest animation industry in the world,[1] and many would agree with me that it's also the finest. That Japan is one of the richest nations on Earth plays a part (at the height of the Bubble Economy in the 1980s, Japan had 16% of the global economic power, and 60% of real estate wealth). The famous TV shows, Original Video Animations, TV specials, videos, and movies in *animé* include: *Digimon, Pokémon, Dr Slump, Star Blazers, Akira, Legend of the Overfiend, One Piece, Macross, Naruto, Evangelion, Gunbuster, Gundam, Lupin III, Patlabor, Cowboy Bebop, Astro Boy, Ghost In the Shell*, and Studio Ghibli's output. According to Helen McCarthy, animation in Japan accounted for 6% of films released in late 1998, 25-30% of videos, and 3-6% of television shows made in Japan.

In 2013, a 13-episode TV *animé* (= one season) cost about $2 million, with a 26-episode series costing up to $4 million (with around $100,000-300,000 spent per episode).

In 2005 (a year after the first *animé* of *Fullmetal Alchemist*), there were 430 *animé* production studios in Japan, and most of them were in Tokyo. (And that's one of the reasons why so many *animé* shows are set in Tokyo). The *animé* market was worth about ¥20 billion ($200m) in 2004.

Animation studios themselves become the centre of attention for *animé* fans, and fans will follow particular animation houses and their work. The famous ones include Production I.G., Sunrise/ Bandai, Studio 4°C, Pierrot, Gainax, Madhouse, Pioneer, Tezuka, Gonzo, Clamp, Bones, Toei, and Studio Ghibli. *Fullmetal Alchemist* was produced by Studio Bones, Aniplex, Square Enix, Mainichi Broadcasting System, and a host of other companies (for big productions like this, dozens of companies produce in-between animation, key animation, 2nd key animation, ink and paint, backgrounds and other material. For ex, for the second series, 34 companies provided 2nd key animation and 84 (!) companies produced in-between animation, including many famous *animé* houses such as Studio Ghibli, Production I.G., Tatsunoko, Satelight, Studio 4 C, J.C. Staff, P.A. Works and Studio Deen).

There are many links to the Japanese *animé* tradition in *Fullmetal Alchemist*. For instance, young heroes, youth vs. old age, *mecha* (the automail and steam-punk culture), the ambiguous view of institutions like religion and governments, Japanese mythology, war, the military machine, and fantasy. The motifs that crop up in thousands of *animé* products are also found in *Fullmetal Alchemist*.

An important thing to remember about Japanese *animé* is that it is an industry that can sustain itself by producing movies and TV shows for a *domestic* audience: it doesn't need television syndication or releases overseas (but it will always take them up if available). In other words, one of the reasons that the Japanese animation industry is the biggest in the world is because there is such a large market in Japan itself for animation. (*Fullmetal Alchemist* was duly released Western territories, in dubbed

---

1 The U.S.A. is next, then Korea.

versions – France, Germany, Spain and Italy, for example, have strong markets for *animé*).

That also means that Japanese *animé* filmmakers can make their films and TV shows for a *homegrown* market, and don't need to pander to an international (or an American) audience. *Fullmetal Alchemist* is very much a *Japanese* product, and was made primarily for the *Japanese* market. So the animated Original Video Animations and TV series can reflect and explore local or national culture, and don't need to build in elements that will appeal to a global audience (no need to shift the action to, say, New York or Chicago, and turn their characters into Americans).

European filmmakers can similarly make movies only for their own national audience, as *Fullmetal Alchemist* was made for the Japanese market, but they tend to be much smaller (or cheaper) movies and TV shows (which's why much of *animé* comprises lower budget Original Video Animations). A country such as France can sustain a huge production of movies per year because it has the largest film industry in Europe (that's one of the reasons why French movies travel outside France). And it means that France can make much bigger movies (it has more government investment than many other countries)[2]

Although the prestige *animé* movies and Original Video Animations receive much of the media's attention (especially outside Japan), most of animation in Japan is produced, like both *Fullmetal Alchemist* series, for television (as well as commercials and corporate work). A movie is 80, 90 (rarely over 100 minutes) of animation, but a big *animé* series on television runs to large numbers of 22 minute episodes. Look at the numbers of shows: *Doraemon* (over 2,000 episodes by 2004), *Astro Boy* (193 episodes x 30m – first series), *Dragon Ball* (153 episodes), *Dragon Ball Z* (291 episodes), *Galaxy Express* (114 episodes), *Mazinger Z* (92 episodes), *Gatchomon* (105 episodes), *Legend of Galactic Heroes* (110 episodes), *Maison Ikkoku* (96 episodes), *Naruto* (720 episodes), *Digimon* (205 episodes), *One Piece* (1,000+), *Pokemon* (550 episodes and counting), and *Sailor Moon* (200 episodes). The two *Fullmetal Alchemist* series add up to 115 shows (plus the Original Video Animations and movies).

Lonely Planet's travel guide to Japan makes some useful points about contemporary Japan:

> First, Japan is an island nation. Second, until WWII, Japan was never conquered by an outside power, nor was it heavily influenced by Christian missionaries. Third, until the beginning of last century, the majority of Japanese lived in close-knit rural farming communities. Fourth, most of Japan is covered in steep mountains, so the few flat areas of the country are quite crowded – people literally live on top of each other. Finally, for almost all of its history, Japan has been a strictly hierarchical place, with something approximating a caste system during the Edo period. (C. Rowthorn, 2007)

WWII and the Occupation had enormous effects on the Japanese

---

2 And the French love animated movies, as they love comicbooks and fantasy art.

movie industry, which still resonate today. In *A History of Narrative Film*, still the finest single book on cinema (if you need to have one book on cinema, this is the one), David Cook set the scene:

> When World War II ended on August 14, 1945, much of Japan lay in ruins. The massive fire-bombing of its sixty cities from March through June 1945 and the dropping of atomic bombs on Hiroshima and Nagasaki had resulted in some 900,000 casualties and the nearly total paralysis of civilian life. On the morning of August 15, when Emperor Hirohito broadcast to his subjects the news that the war had ended and that Japan had lost, there was widespread disbelief. Never in their history had the Japanese people been defeated or the nation occupied, and so the circumstances of the American Occupation, 1945-52, were utterly unique. (783)

Following WWII American military bases remained in Japan (as in many parts of the world, including Europe), and the Americans stationed in Japan had an influence on Japanese culture. Certainly *Fullmetal Alchemist* deals with the issues of an occupying force (with the uneasy relation between Ishbal and Amestris).

One of the first animated TV series in Japan, *Astro Boy* (1963), had a science fiction and *Pinocchio* theme.[3] *Astro Boy*, from Osamu Tezuka's *manga Ambassador Atom* (*Atom Taishi*, 1951-68), introduced themes which would resonate in *animé* ever since: the son of a scientist dies in a car crash and is recreated as a robot; and the robot wants to become real. It's the 'doll with a soul' theme (in Japanese folklore, 'dolls loved and cared for could develop an actual soul', noted Gilles Poitras [2001, 19]). The homunculi in *Fullmetal Alchemist* are linked to this theme.

Gilles Poitras defined *animé* in his excellent *Anime Companion:*

> anime is not to be confused with cartoons. Anime uses animation to tell stories and entertain, but it does so in ways that have barely been touched on in Western animation. While the U.S. continues to pump out cartoons with gag stories, musicals with cute animals, animated sitcoms, and testosterone-laced TV fare, the Japanese have been using anime to cover every literary and cinematic genre imaginable in a highly competitive market that encourages new story ideas and the creative reworking of older ideas and themes. (vii)

The genres of Japanese animation include pretty much all of those in live-action, as well as some genres particular to *animé*: comedy; romance; crime; action-adventure; horror; historical drama; science fiction[4] (including *mecha*, cyberpunk, war, epics); fantasy (including comics; supernatural tales; myths and legends; and superheroes); animal stories; martial arts; children's stories; epics; erotica; porn; and sports stories.[5]

---

3 Actually, *Manga Calendar*, from the Otagi company, was the first series, running from 1962 to 1964, but *Astro Boy* is usually taken as the breakthrough *animé* series.
4 More people consume science fiction in Japan than anywhere else.
5 Although it is regarded as popular culture, Japanese *animé* draws on high culture, including woodblock prints, *ukiyo-e*, *Kabuki* theatre, painting, and classical music.

Gilles Poitras noted in *The Anime Companion* that *animé* has more genres than exist in Western cinema (43).

In live-action, genres are divided into *jidai-geki* = period movies (typically in the feudal age), and *gendai-geki* = set in the contemporary era.[6] There are further categories within the two genres. Fantasy and science fiction are two key genres in *animé*.

The Japanese film industry has been one of the most prolific historically, producing over 400 movies a year. The Japanese movie business has been dominated by studio conglomerates, just like the North American system, since the 1920s (the big guns are Nikkatsu, Shochiku, Toho,[7] Toei, Shintoho and Daiei). Although the independent film sector has grown since the 1980s, the major studios continue to take up most of film production. And most Japanese film directors work for the major studios in some form or another, or for television.

Like the films of Yasujiro Ozu or Kenji Mizoguchi or Akira Kurosawa, *Fullmetal Alchemist* in *manga* or *animé* form is very Japanese. But *Fullmetal Alchemist* is also – like the movies of Yasujiro Ozu, Kenji Mizoguchi and Akira Kurosawa – a show which can and does travel around the world. (Most TV shows don't. Most TV shows don't get released or shown outside their country of origin. Or put it this way: even if you are adventurous and have gone out of your way to see movies and TV shows from many other countries, you will not actually be able to see most of the movies or TV shows made within any country, unless you live there).

Other notable filmmakers in Japanese cinema, apart from the *sensei* himself (Akira Kurosawa) include: Yasujiro Ozu, Kenji Mizoguchi, and Ichikawa Kon, and Japanese New Wave directors, such as Nagisa Oshima, Hiroshi Teshigahara, Masashiro Shinoda, Takeshi Kitano and Yoshishige Yoshida.

Among the classic films of Japanese cinema are: *Tokyo Story*, *The Flavour of Green Tea Over Rice*, *The Life of Oharu*, *Ohayu*, *Sansho Dayu*, *Kwaidan*, *Early Summer*, *Woman of the Dunes*, *Ugetsu Monogatari*, and *Ai No Corrida* (*In the Realm of the Senses*). And of course, anything by Akira Kurosawa (even one of Kurosawa's minor films is finer than many filmmakers' best efforts). (The filmmakers of *Fullmetal Alchemist* are steeped in the Japanese film and *animé* tradition – you can see it throughout both *Fullmetal Alchemist* series).

In Japan, the director is king of the movie-making industry, rather than the star or producer; the director will often appear above the title, and is often used in marketing more than stars. The director is 'the paternalistic head of his own production "family"', as Gerald Mast and Bruce Kawin explain in *A Short History of the Movies*, a social structure which echoes Japanese society (1992b, 409). Needless to say, Himoru Arakawa's name is used most in the marketing of the *Fullmetal Alchemist* shows.

---

6 See G. Mast, 1992b, 410.
7 Toho, founded in the 1930s from a number of smaller companies, is best known as the studio of *Godzilla*, Hayao Miyazaki and Akira Kurosawa.

In Japanese animation, terms like 'director' and 'designer' don't have the same meaning as in the Western film industry. 'Director' might refer to a 'wide range' of different jobs (H. McCarthy, 1996, 9). It's customary, for instance, for designers to have a speciality, and to be brought onto a production to exploit that gift.

Japan is one of the major film markets in the world – for North American movies, yes, but also for movies from everywhere. And when it comes to animation, there is a huge appetite for it in Japan. That helps to sustain *anime*. Without that large, national market, and that enthusiastic response to animated movies and television, it would be more difficult for animatioin to flourish. x

You can see this operating in blockbuster, North American movies, which consciously target a range of audiences (casting actors from different countries, for instance). Those ultra-high budget American movies have to generate half their money back from international sales (since the Nineties), so the films have to be able to play in Italy or Israel or Argentina as well as in North America.

Japanese *anime* sells in the Western world via Original Video Animations,[8] streaming, videos and DVDs, TV shows, and related *manga* comics. Animated series and movies are prepared for the Western market[9] with English language dubs (nearly always using North American actors and American-style English), and also subtitles (there is also a subculture of fans subtitling shows).

In Japanese animation, there are many differences between the English subtitles – which presumably translate the Japanese dialogue (though not all of it) – and the English dubbed versions. There are lines in the English subtitles which don't appear in the English dubbed versions – and vice versa. Background sounds and additional lines of dialogue are also added. This means that *Fullmetal Alchemist* has a slightly different impact in its Japanese subtitled and English dubbed versions.

ANIMÉ AND MANGA

Manga are certainly huge in Japan, and more so than in any other country (though they are on the increase in some places). North America doesn't have a comicbook tradition anything like *manga* culture in Japan: in Japan, a *manga* like *Shonen Jump* has sold 6 million copies a week, enormous numbers.[10] (And even when sales of *manga* have declined, the numbers

8 O.V.A. means Original Video Animation (a.k.a. O.A.V. = Original Animé/ Animation Video) – referring to sell-through videos, which may be linked to TV shows or movies, and, of course, *manga*.
9 In the West, the markets for *anime* and *manga* are mainly male.
10 In a 1994 speech, Hayao Miyazaki compared that 6 million with the video sales of *Beauty and the Beast* in the U.S.A.: 20 million, for a nation with twice the population of Japan. Selling 20 million in America would be like selling 10 million in Japan, Miyazaki suggested, and *Shonen Jump* sells 6 million *manga* a week!

involved are still colossal).

Japan has the most sophisticated, the most varied, the funniest, the most entertaining, and by far the most imaginative comicbook culture in the world. Yes, we know that France, Germany, Spain, Italy, China, Korea, Britain and the U.S.A. (among others) have thriving comicbook industries, but none of them come anywhere near Japan.

In Japan, the audience for *manga* is pretty much everybody: the stigma in the West attached to comics simply doesn't exist: *everyone* reads *manga*. The Japanese *manga* market is bigger than the *animé* market. *Manga* also requires far fewer personnel to create, and is cheaper to disseminate.

In 2000 in Japan there were 15 monthly magazines, 10 twice-weekly magazines, and 12 weeklies. Some have print runs of over a million copies. *Manga* accounted for about a quarter of all publishing sales (about 550 billion Yen/ $5.5 billion). *Manga* absorbed around 40% of Japan's printed matter. The average spend on *manga* was 4,500 Yen ($45) for everybody living in Japan. According to VIZ Media, the *manga* market in Japan in 2006 was worth $4.28 billion (and $250m in the U.S.A.).

Manga and *animé* are closely aligned commercially as well as culturally. Many *animé* shows are based on *manga* (and some of the big shows have their own *manga* spin-offs). *Manga* can be a cheaper means of testing out if a story will work with an audience. There are many more *manga* stories than *animé* stories. Thus, *animé* has a huge source of stories to draw on, alongside novels, plays, TV shows, video games[11] and all the other products that can be adapted.

The crossover between *manga* and *animé* is well-known (many animations are *manga* first, and *manga* are in turn produced from movies). There is also a crossover into computer games, board games, card games, pop music and online gaming. *Fullmetal Alchemist* was published by Square Enix, known for their computer games (Himoru Arakawa was conscious of this when she started writing *Fullmetal Alchemist*).

Manga magazines and books read right to left; some translations in the West (such as from Dark Horse and Viz in North America), have tried to maintain the right-to-left format, without flopping the artwork. The *Fullmetal Alchemist manga* is published in right-to-left form in the West (but unfortunately not in a large size).

Manga in translation are often published as *tankobon*, collected *manga* stories (partly because, as in Japan, there is more money in *tankobon* than in *manga* magazines).[12] Famous *manga* works such as *Ghost In the Shell, Nausicaä of the Valley of the Wind* and *Fullmetal Alchemist* are republished as *tankobon*. *Tankobon* have a longer shelf life than throwaway magazines, and usually stay in print much longer than magazines.

Certainly *manga* and *animé* have been important in depicting Japanese culture overseas – and it will be for many their first encounter with Japanese culture.[13] *Manga* and *animé* are popular in many Western

---

11 Among the well-known *manga* and *animé* that were based on computer games were *Final Fantasy, Pokémon,* and *Sakura Wars.*
12 G. Poitras, 2001, 66.
13 See G. Poitras, 2001, 8.

markets, including France, Britain, Italy, Spain, Germany, and into Hong Kong, South America, and South-East Asia.14 The U.S.A. is the primary market outside Japan. In Europe, *animé* is most popular in France (and France has a substantial animation industry). Sci-fi, cyber-punk and steam-punk are also much-loved in France, as are comicbooks and graphic novels.

Manga has become more popular in North America and Europe in the 2000s, with new *manga* magazines being launched by the big Japanese publishers (such as *Daisuki, Banzai* and *Manga Power* in Germany, *Shonen* in France, and *Shonen Jump* in the U.S.A.). In the mid-2000s, the *manga* market in the U.S.A, was $40-50 million, and the *animé* market was $400-500 million.

ANIMATION IN PRODUCTION

> Those who join in the work of animation are people who dream more than others and who wish to convey those dreams to others. After a while they realize how incredibly difficult it is to entertain others.

Hayao Miyazaki (2009, 25)

Animation is a long, hard slog – *very* labour intensive, with projects like feature films sometimes taking up to three or four years complete. It requires a particular kind of individual, then, to maintain a high level of enthusiasm and interest, to stay focussed on the project and not be distracted into other things. Stanley Kubrick spoke of keeping hold of his initial inspiration for making a movie all the way through the long process of development, pre-production, shooting, post-production and distribution. You have to hang on to whatever it was that really excited you about doing the project in the first place (a production that doesn't have that initial spark of excitement and fascination can all too easily lose its momentum and energy).

I haven't visited an animation studio in Tokyo, but in every 'making of' *animé* documentary, in every photo, and in every account, every animation house is a shabby building of messy desks and work stations in which animators, ink-and-paint women, in-betweeners, *mecha* designers, character designers, C.G. technicians and the rest of the staff, slave away at all hours. There are no plush, front office buildings, as at the Disney Studios in Burbank or Pixar in Northern California. The new Studio Ghibli building among Tokyo animation houses is about the only one with an upmarket, front office feel (and on the main floors of Ghibli, it's animators and their desks and shelves crammed into small spaces again – look at the 'making of' documentary about *Spirited Away*).

14 H. McCarthy, 1996, 7.

It is commonplace for animators and staff to sleep under their desks in animation houses in Tokyo. Visitors from the West to companies such as Production I.G. have been surprised by that, and by the tiny working spaces that even high-ranking animators have: just a desk and a few shelves. Cables run over the floor, DVDs, posters, toys and photocopied timing sheets are packed in everywhere, and there's not much space btn the workers and their chairs. Staff eat their *bento* boxes at their desks (taking less than an hour for lunch). They often have multiple jobs, not just one. Look at a photo of any animation house in Tokyo, and you'll see every nook is crammed with stuff (the offices of the *Fullmetal Alchemist* teams would be full of research material on every aspect of recent European history and culture, in order to recreate the look of the quasi-European country of Amestris and the literally thousands of backgrounds and layouts that the two *Fullmetal Alchemist* series demanded). And it's not unknown for staff to have nervous breakdowns due to the heavy workload (as with director Hideaki Anno on *The End of Evangelion*, and Tomomi Mochizuki after working on Ghibli's *Ocean Waves*).

If you dream of flying to Tokyo and working at Studio Ghibli, Sunrise or Toei or one of the other 450 *animé* houses, be prepared to work very hard, and for long hours (12-14 hours a day, plus every other Saturday), to eat your lunch at your desk (and sometimes sleep there), to enjoy few perks and benefits, to do many tasks (photocopying, say, or website design), and make barely enough to live.[15]

Animation is hard work for little pay.

The typical 30 minute (= 22 mins) *animé* TV show costs ¥10 million. (There are about 100 Yen to the US dollar, so 10 million Yen is about $100,000).

In 1987, Hayao Miyazaki described the typical animator as young, good-natured, and poor. They made less than ¥100,000 a month (= $1,000). They were paid ¥400 ($4) a page for theatrical movies and ¥150 ($1.50) a page for TV animation. Miyazaki reckoned there were about 2,500 in animators Japan (2009, 135). There were around 3,000 *manga* artists working in Japan in 2000 (not including assistants or contributors to anthologies). In 2001 a typical salary in *animé* was estimated at $15,000-20,000; many workers still lived with their parents, or supplemented their income elsewhere. In 2015, the average pay was $27,700.

Everybody who works in animation knows about the sheer struggle of production. It is an industry for workaholics ('without workaholics, Japan's animation could never be sustained', Hayao Miyazaki remarked [ib., 187]). It is hard work all the way, and there is no way of creating it without months of labour. 'Works of art are created by those who are prepared to go to the limit,' asserted Miyazaki (1991).

For the *auteurs* of Japanese animation, pursuing animation means pursing perfection – or something as good as one can produce. Sometimes animators sleep on the floor in the studio: this was more common in

---

15 You'll have to speak Japanese, too.

Japanese animation in the 1970s and 1980s than one would think: it wasn't unknown for animators to stay at work all day, and sleep there too, getting up to carry on. I would imagine that today the intensive, workaholic nature of animation in Tokyo is still prevalent, despite unions, labour laws and all the rest (yes, and animators still sleep under their desks). You can see from any of the 115 episodes of *Fullmetal Alchemist* that it took a *huge* amount of work to create that *Anime* Bliss.

Japanese animation is still a lot cheaper than the North American equivalent: in 1985, the Mouse House's *Black Cauldron* cost $25 million (it was a troubled production, and a very disappointing movie for everybody concerned). The animated Disney and Pixar movies of recent times have included the following budgets: *Tarzan* $115m (or $142m or $150m, depending on sources); *Treasure Planet* $140m; *Ratatouille* $150m; and *Home On the Range* $110m.

These figures aren't really helpful, because movie budgets are notoriously difficult to check accurately: no one wants to admit how much money something *really* cost, or *exactly* how much they're earning (and Hollywood studios routinely exaggerate figures like budgets and grosses). But you know that if the budgets are one hundred million dollars or more, then *somebody somewhere* is making a lot of money.[16]

It's hard to believe that movies like *Home On the Range* or *Tarzan* from the Mouse House could have cost over $110 million or $115 million (or *The Black Cauldron* costing $25m in 1985), but there are all sorts of economic factors to consider. The piece-work labour of Japanese *anime* is going to be cheaper than hiring staff on a permanent basis that occurs more in North American animation.[17] Living costs, unions and working conditions in Japan and America are further factors. The much longer production schedules of American animated movies must contribute to the higher costs too: Disney and Pixar movies can take 3 or more years. However, the large crews of hundreds of workers aren't hired for all of those years, but it's safe to say that the production teams in American (and Western) feature animation can be larger than those in the Japanese animation industry, and that they are hired for longer periods. All of which drives costs up (at the same time, Western animation companies farm out work to outfits in countries such as Korea, China, Thailand and India, just as the Japanese animation industry does. And they are paid less).

In recent years, the accounts of people who work in the Japanese animation industry paint a depressing picture of the pressures and stresses:

• overtime is common (beyond an average 9-hour work-day), and often not paid;[18]

16 As William Goldman noted, there's a lot of money to be had in simply *making* a film, regardless of whether it's released or seen or not. And some people make a living out of producing movies, including existing on development deals and other deals, and many of those films aren't shot, and some that *are* filmed aren't released.
17 Hayao Miyazaki often complained about the piecework system of producing animation in Japan, which turned out work like an assembly line, instead of the hand-crafted and personal, artistic approach that Miyazaki favoured.
18 Companies find loopholes to avoid paying.

• production assistants who travel or drive around Tokyo have to pay for part or all of their own travel expenses;

• harassment or abuse (often psychological) is not uncommon;

• companies exploit their workers' dedication to their jobs (they need the work, and if they leave, will someone else hire them?);

• taking vacations is discouraged - workers are expected to be available all the time in case they're needed.

THE ANIMATION PROCESS.

In the Japanese animation industry, the script comes first. Storyboards and image boards are drawn when the script is completed (but sometimes before then). The storyboards are called *e-conte* (a combination of *ei*, picture, and continuity). On *Fullmetal Alchemist*, there were whole teams drawing the storyboards (directors like to do that – if they have time) – drawing the storyboards is very labour intensive, there's no easy way of doing them).

The chief storyboard artists of the first *Fullmetal Alchemist* series were: Kenji Yasuda, Masahiro Ando, Shinsaku Sasaki, Soichi Masui, Tamaki Nakatsu, Tarou Iwasaki, Norimitsu Suzuki, and director Seiji Mizushima (each contributing more'n 4 episodes). The chief storyboard artists of the second *Fullmetal Alchemist* series were: Iwao Teraoka, Minoru Ohara, Shinji Ishihira and director Yasuhiro Irie (each drawing more'n 5 episodes). The two *Fullmetal Alchemist* series would require thousands and thousands of drawings.

Once the film is complete as far as the storyboard stage, plus indications of dialogue. frames and sound effects, it goes to the key animators: they put the show together as key animation (the animation at the beginning and the end of an action).[19] In-between work means animating the movements between the key frames which the key animators have drawn, using time sheets. At the same time, the drawings are cleaned up (one single outline will be chosen, for example, from a mass of pencil lines). Throughout this and all stages of animation, drawings and artwork are being tweaked and adjusted (each stage is reviewed, and directors often oversee each process). (Sometimes storyboards are collated with dialogue, music and sound fx, as animatics ('line tests'),[20] and sometimes pencil tests of animation are produced).

Once the drawings have been completed, they are transferred to cels (celluloid), and inked and painted. In computer-aided animation, some stages of the process today are achieved with the help of computers or tablets,[21] such as colour, photography, 3-D simulations, etc. (however, Studio Bones is known for its emphasis on hand-drawn animation on paper) Software can streamline the in-between animation process, for example, though key animators still have to oversee the work. Colour is one obvious area of difference between computer-assisted animation and

19 Keyframes or main poses are drawn by the animators or animation directors; assistant animators will usually draw the halfway poses between the keyframes; in-betweeners are animators (often trainees) who draw the frames in between the keyframes.
20 Sometimes using the Quick Action Recorder.
21 Tablets are often used for drawing.

ink and paint animation. There are millions of colours available in the digital realm, existing only in the computer.

Finally, the cels are photographed (a whole complex process in itself). Photographic and special effects may be added at this stage. (However, animation doesn't always use 24 frames per second, called 'ones' or 'singles': it often goes to 'twos' or 'doubles' (12 frames a second) or 'threes' (8 frames per second).[22] Even the most sophisticated and expensive movies use those frame rates).

CELS VERSUS COMPUTERS

Most Japanese animation is still fundamentally 2-D/ cel animation in its approach, but computers and computer-aided effects and devices are increasingly employed (especially since the mid-1990s). Cel animation in movies is already as supremely *technological* and *industrial* as computers or digital technology. *Everything* in movies is *technological*, everything is fake, everything is a highly sophisticated cultural form created by humans for mass entertainment, to be screened with sophisticated machines in very particular cultural environments. So whether it's done with machines and tools like cameras or pencils or paintbrushes or computers isn't really the point. (And audiences don't care: they want a good story, they want to be entertained).

A common gripe is that computer-aided additions to scenes don't really mesh with traditional, flat 2-D animation. For instance, Disney's *Treasure Planet, Atlantis, The Rescuers Down Under* and Warner Bros' *The Iron Man* have used computer-assisted (so-called 3-D) elements placed into hand-drawn (but probably computer-inked) 2-D animation. The digital elements often look floaty and disconnected to the rest of the scenes. With its fantasy elements, its alternative world, its steam-punk cultures, *Fullmetal Alchemist* inevitably opted to use plenty of computer-aided animation. But the overall look of the 115 shows is still traditional cel animation.

However, using computers is just another tool out of many that animation employs: a common view, still being voiced by critics who should know better, is that: *cel animation = good, computer animation = bad*. No – because all animation is *already* highly technological.[23]

If you visited an animation house in Tokyo, London, or Hollywood (or the many out-sourced centres in, say, India or Korea), you'd find tons

22 Bones' C.E.O. Masahiko Minami said that one of the problems with Japanese animation was to produce animation using 'threes': 'There is an industrial history of not wanting to spend money on the full 24 frames per second that Disney always did'.
23 Film critics really should visit film studios from time to time, to dispel the falsehoods that they perpetuate. For instance, that some movie sets look made out of cardboard: actually, *all* movie sets are constructed from bits of wood or foam or cardboard and painted, then they're torn down as soon as shooting stops on them.

of technology and machines, with computers being just one among multitudes. For instance, the cameras employed to photograph the cels are very sophisticated. And they always have been: have a look at the famous multiplane camera designed by William Garity at the Walt Disney Studio in Burbank in the 1930s, which required a group of technicians to operate. The cel vs. C.G.I. argument merely trots out the ancient oppositions between old and new, or tradition and modernism.

02

FULLMETAL ALCHEMIST

HAGANE NO RENKINSUTSUSHI

THE FIRST ANIME SERIES

THE PRODUCTION OF THE *FULLMETAL ALCHEMIST* TV SERIES.
Fullmetal Alchemist (*Hagane no Renkinjutsushi* a.k.a. *Hagaren*, 2003-2004) is a big fantasy franchise based on the *manga* by Hiromu Arakawa (the writer and the artist), a best-selling, very popular comic (50 million or more units sold by the 2000s).

The *Fullmetal Alchemist* franchise includes, like all the high profile (and expensive) *animé* franchises, TV shows, movies, spin-off Original Video Animations, soundtracks, computer games, toys, and tie-in books. If *Fullmetal Alchemist* were made in live-action, the actors would be Japanese (Himoru Arakawa said she has discussed this with her assistants many times). And they were, when the live-action film appeared in 2017. And Stephen Chow, Chinese mega-star (*Kung Fu Hustle, Shaolin Soccer*), would direct it. It was not directed by Chow; it was aimed mainly at the Japanese market. An exhibition was mounted in 2017 to tie-in with the live-action movie. Arakawa drew some additional comics for this.

The 51-part TV *animé* show (2003-04) of *Fullmetal Alchemist* was a co-production between Aniplex/ Studio Bones/ Mainichi Broadcasting System/ Square Enix. The executive producers were: Hideo Katsu-mata, Kouji Taguchi and Seiji Takeda, and the producers were: Hiro Maruyama, Masahiko Minami and Ryo Oyama. The TV show was directed by Atsushi Ootsuki, Johei Matsuura, Jun Fukuda and Kazuki Kakuda, with Seiji Mizushima[24] as the overall director.[25] The chief writer

---

24 Seiji Mizushima's credits include *Shaman King* and *Slayers Next*.
25 In Japanese animation, terms like 'director' and 'designer' don't have the same meaning as in the Western film industry. 'Director' might refer to a 'wide range' of different jobs (H. McCarthy, 1996, 9). It's customary, for instance, for designers to have a speciality, and to be brought onto a production to exploit that gift.

was Shou Aikawa. It was broadcast from October 4, 2003 to October 2, 2004 on the Tokyo Broadcasting System, at six p.m. on Saturdays.[26]

Studio Bones, involved in all *animé* incarnations of *Fullmetal Alchemist*, was founded in 1998 by a group of filmmakers from Sunrise (including director Shinichiro Watanabe (*Cowboy Bebop, Samurai Champloo, Animatrix*), Masahiko Minami, producer, Hiroshi Osaka, and Toshihiro Kawamoto, animator). Studio Bones began with producing the *Cowboy Bebop* movie and the *Escaflowne* movie. Bones' work included *Cowboy Bebop* (1998), *Darker Than Black, Berserk* (2012), *Eureka 7, Soul Eater, Sword of the Stranger*, the *Pokémon* films, *Gundam, Ghost Slayers Ayashi, Space Dandy* (2012), *Wolf's Rain* (2003), the *Escaflowne* movie (2000) and *RahXephon* (2002).

The Bones studio is divided into several sub-studios, each of which operates independently, led by a producer. There were five sub-studios in 2018 (with four based at Bones' headquarters). Yoshihiro Oyabu, who joined Bones in 2003 for the first *Fullmetal Alchemist* series ran Studio C in the 2010s (when it was solely dedicated to producing *My Hero Academia*).

According to head honcho Masahiko Minami (in 2018), *Fullmetal Alchemist* was an important title for Studio Bones:

> a big turning point was *Fullmetal Alchemist*. Not only was it a grand undertaking, but it also aired nationally at 6 p.m. on Saturdays, a huge timeslot. It became incredibly popular overseas, too.

According to Masahiko Minami, it was animator Yoshiyuki Ito who first read the *Fullmetal Alchemist* comic and showed it to his boss, Minami: 'I thought Bones should make the animation, and contacted the publisher at once, and that's how we got to produce the work'.[27]

It was agreed from the outset that the *animé* adaptation would contain original material,[28] Minami asserted:

> When we started the first series, the *manga* was still in the early stages and the pacing was not yet determined. So we made the animation with the premise that original elements would be included from the beginning. The reason why we threw in the original story in the first half was so we could depict the story in the latter half. (2020)

Producer Taguichi Koji said that Square Enix's investment in *Fullmetal Alchemist*, the 1st series, was USD $5.5 million (500 million Yen). Each episode of *Fullmetal Alchemist* cost between $110,000 and $220,000. The sales of the *manga* increased dramatically following the airing of the *animé* (one of the reasons why Square Enix produced it): rising from 150,00 before to 1,500,000 afterwards (per volume).

---

26 And in the U.S.A. by Cartoon Network's Adult Swim from November 6, 2004.
27 A. Osmond, Manga Entertainment.
28 The second series took the *manga* as its *Bible,* as the production crew said, but it didn't adapt the whole of the comic. Entire stories were left out – such as the mining town and the railroad adventure.

The two adaptations of *Fullmetal Alchemist* share numerous elements. But the first series had one huge advantage: it went first. Thus, the first adaptation got to define the look, the sound, the voices, the character designs, the artwork and backgrounds, the music and everything else. A subsequent adaptation of *Fullmetal Alchemist* could've ignored all of that, but it wisely chose to build on the first series.

The *Fullmetal Alchemist* TV series was written by Akatsuki Yamatoya, Aiya Yoshinaga, Jun Ishikawa, Katsuhijo Takayama, Natsuko Takahashi, Shou Aikawa and Toshiki Inoue[29] (chief writer Aikawa wrote by far the most number of episodes in the first series – 30 in all. Aikawa is thus one of the most important collaborators on the whole *Fullmetal Alchemist* series).

One of the chief reasons that both series of *Fullmetal Alchemist* were so spectacular was due to the great team of writers assembled by the production. The two head writers – Shou Aikawa and Hiroshi Ohnogi – were were veterans of the *animé* business.

Music was by Michiru Oshima[30] (b. 1961), and played by the Moscow International Orchestra (many Japanese animations like to use Russian or Eastern European orchestras). Oshima has extensive credits (including composing symphonies and classical pieces). Her credits include *Godzilla* movies, PlayStation games, *Arc the Lad*, *Like Asura*, *The Sun Also Rises*, *125 Years Memory*, *Year One In the North*, *Project Blue Earth SOS*, *Sound of the Sky*, *Buddha* (**Osamu Tezuka**), *Snow White With the Red Hair*, and *Kimi to, Nami ni Noretara*.

Art director was Kazuyuki Hashimoto; character designer was Yoshiyuki Ito;[31] Hideo Narita did the art design; Takefumi Anzai created additional production design; Junya Ishigaki designed the chimera; the DPs were Susumu Fukushi and Toru Fukushi; sound director was Masafumi Mima (for both series); sound effects by Soundbox; sound production by Techno Sound; and the editor was Hiroaki Itabe (at Japanese Film). 20 storyboard artists are credited.

There were four opening themes and four end titles themes composed for the series, by Porno Graffiti ('Melissa'), L'Arc-en-Ciel ('Ready Steady Go'), Cool Joke ('Undo'), and Asian Kung-Fu Generation ('Rewrite') for the opening songs; the end credits songs were: Nana Kitade ('Indelible Sin'), Yellow Generation ('Beyond the Door'), Crystal Kay ('Motherland') and Sowelu ('I Will').

Huge TV shows like *Fullmetal Alchemist* demand many animators, too many to list, but some of them included Eiko Saito, Hideki Ito, Hiroki Kanno, Hiroko Oguri, Junichiro Taniguchi, Kanami Sekiguchi, Kazumi

---

29 Toshiki Inoue has numerous credits in animation, including some of celebrated works: *Ninja Scroll*, *Death Note*, *Kamen Rider*, *Ranma 1/2*, *Urusei Yatsura*, *Dark Cat*, *Dirty Pair*, *Iron Man*, *Galaxy Angel*, *Yu-Gi-Oh!*, *Witch Blade*, *Dr Slump*, *Dragon Ball* and *Fist of the North Star*.
30 Website: michiru-oshima.net
31 Jeremy Crocker: 'We also witness some of anime's best character designs. You'll never confuse characters in *Fullmetal Alchemist*, as each character has a distinct appearance. Some very calculated care was taken to make sure that no two characters looked even remotely alike. It's especially important because most characters are part of the military and, thus, will be seen mainly in their uniforms. The one exception is Ed, who almost always wears variations on his familiar black suit and red coat.'

Inadome, Akitoshi Maeda, Koji Sugiura, Kumiko Takahashi, and Makoto Koga. As with most of the really expensive shows, most of those animators were veterans who've worked on many, many shows. (You need several really experienced veterans to oversee the animation teams, who can tackle the numerous challenges that crop up).

The team that worked on *Fullmetal Alchemist* included many stars of the *animé* world. For instance, Shinji Aramaki was production designer on *Fullmetal Alchemist*. A famous *mecha* designer, Aramaki's credits include *Gundam, Megazone 23, Bubblegum Crisis, Wolf's Rain,* the *Appleseed* remakes (which he directed), *Ultraman, Ghost In the Shell:" Stand Alone Complex: 2045, Blade Runner: Black Lotus,* and *Astro Boy* (the remake). He also helmed the best of the segments of the *Halo: Legends animé* compendium (2010), a shoot-em-up, men-on-a-mission tale.

A huge number of companies[32] were involved in the making of *Fullmetal Alchemist*. For instance, for the 2-D animation, apart from Studio Bones, animation houses included: Brains Base, Earl Anime, M.S.C., Noside, Picture Magic, Studio Liberty, Studio Wombat, SynergySP, Tokyo Animation Center and Wao World. Background art was by Green and Kusanagi.

Other animation houses involved in the animation of *Fullmetal Alchemist* included many famous names from Japanese animation, such as Mushi Productions, Sakura Create, Studio Cockpit, Oh! Production, Studio 4°C, Artland, and the most famous animation studio in Japan, Studio Ghibli. (So when a big *animé* series is being produced in Tokyo, everybody in town will know about it, and it seems as if everyone is working on it).

The second *Fullmetal Alchemist* series was released in 2009-10 (it was titled *Fullmetal Alchemist: Brotherhood* in the West. Each of the two *Fullmetal Alchemist* series had a movie released at the end of each run, which tied up parts of the plots (released in cinemas in Japan, on video and DVD in the Western world). There were also side stories of *Fullmetal Alchemist* developed in a series of Original Video Animations (also collected on DVD), a common ploy in *animé* production (it's called capitalism – milking a vein until it runs dry).

The DVD and video releases of *Fullmetal Alchemist* have few extras. By far the most useful piece is the 'making of' documentary that comes with the second *Fullmetal Alchemist* movie, *The Sacred Star of Milos*. It details the production of the 2011 movie, and many of the issues that surround the production of animation. (The Western DVD releases contain some audio commentaries – alas, not by the Japanese voice cast,

32 This is a fuller list of the many companies contributing to the production of the first *Fullmetal Alchemist* series: Civilization, Code, Daume, Digital Network Animation, Diomedia, Dogakobo, FAI International, Fanout, Frontline, J.C. Staff, M.S.C., MSJ Musashino Production Office, P.A. Works, Picture Magic, Production I.G, Production Reed, Studio Boomerang, Studio Comet, Studio Deen, Studio Elle, Studio Fantasia, Studio Ghibli, Studio Gimlet, Studio Live, Studio Wombat, Sunny Side Up, Tamazawa Company, Tatsunoko Production, Telecome, T.Y.O. Animations, Ufotable, Wao World, Yumeta Company, Z.E.X.C.S., Nomad, D-Colors, Triple A, Wish, B.T.O., Brains Base, Earl Anime, Noside, Studio Liberty, SynergySP, Tokyo Animation Center, Wao World, A.C.G.T., A.I., A.I.C. Spirits, A.I.C. Takarazuka, Anime Spot, A.P.P.P., Asahi Production, Azeta Pictures, Beat Frog, and C.2.C.

but by the North American actors, who are dreadfully dull. Unfortunately, many English language releases of *anime* shows include only commentaries by the North American casts, which are of minor interest at best).

Once again, for full details of *anime* credits, the best place to start looking online is the Anime News Network (which has cross-references to all of the major *anime* productions).

○

When they run across 13 or 26 or 52 episodes, an *anime* series, at its best, can become completely gripping. *Anime* producers are able to squeeze into 22 minutes a ton of story, a ton of characters and characterization, a ton of themes and issues, and a ton of outstanding animation.

I've found myself becoming totally enthralled by *anime* TV series such as *Moribito: Guardian of the Spirit, Mushishi, Escaflowne, Macross Plus, Bleach, Rage of Bahamut, Naruto, Aquarioin, Aquarioin Evol,* and of course *Cowboy Bebop, One Piece* and *Ghost In the Shell: Stand Alone Complex.*

Both *Fullmetal Alchemist* series boast the most fully realized worlds in recent *anime*, even including all of the obvious contenders – and the master himself, Hayao Miyazaki. The level of research and imagination on display is staggering: the art direction and background art is second to none. It's a fantastical mix of 20th century Europe (and Japan) that completely convinces in literally thousands and thousands of new settings and spaces. Solely in terms of its design and art direction, *Fullmetal Alchemist* is in a class of its own.

It's difficult to think of an *anime* series which portrays a wider range of people or a more extraordinary series of scenes. *Fullmetal Alchemist* really is one of the most remarkable works of filmmaking ever.

THE VOICE CAST.
The voice cast of the first *Fullmetal Alchemist* series included:

Rie Kugimiya – Alphonse Elric
Romi Pak – Edward Elric
Masashi Ebara – Hohenheim
Megumi Toyoguchi – Winry Rockbell
Houko Kuwashima – Rose Tomas
Michiko Neya – Riza Hawkeye
Miyoko Asou – Pinako Rockbell
Toru Ohkawa – Roy Mustang
Keiji Fujiwara – Maes Hughes
Kenji Utsumi – Alex Louis Armstrong
Hidekatsu Shibata – Fuhrer Bradley and Pride
Junichi Suwabe – Greed
Nana Mizuki – Wrath
Mayumi Yamaguchi – Envy
Yuuko Satou – Lust
Yumi Kakazu – Lyra

Makoto Nagai – Shou Tucker
Ryotaro Okiayu – Scar
Shoko Tsuda – Izumi Curtis
Kinryuu Arimoto – Priest Cornello
Rumi Kasahara – Martel

It's notable that this *animé*, which seems so boysy, so masculine, this action-packed story of two magical brothers, with its wars, battles, duels, monsters, military establishment, and the like, was written by a woman – Arakawa-sensei. It was Arakawa and her *manga* that created the characters, the situations, the relationships, the conflicts, the goals and the themes of *Fullmetal Alchemist*.

Also worth noting: the two leads in *Fullmetal Alchemist* are played by women:[33] Romi Pak (b. 1972) plays Edward Elric (Pak, a veteran of a *huge* number of *animés*, is well-known for voicing many young, often teen characters): so it's a 32 year-old woman playing a teenage boy. Pak's credits include: *Beyblade, Batman, Pokemon, Toriko, Yes! Precure 5 GoGo!, Black Butler, Bleach* (as fan favourite Hitsugaya Toshiro, a brother to Ed Elric), *Blood +, Digimon, Hellsing, Hunter x Hunter, Gundam, Lupin III, Naruto* (she's Temari), *Ninja Scroll* (as Tsubute), *Persona 4, One Piece, Sengoku Basara* and *Shaman King*.

Rie Kugimiya[34] voices Alphonse Elric. Kugimiya (b. 1979) has credits including: *Nodame Cantabile, Pokémon, Queen's Blade, Rosario + Vampire* (playing the delightful and very kooky Mizore), *Aria the Scarlet Ammo, Bleach* (playing Karin Kurosaki, Ichigo's sister), *Eden's Zero, DD Fist of the North Star, Fairy Tail* (as Happy the flying cat – aye, sir!), *Familiar of Zero, Gintama, Guardian Hearts, Hayate the Combat Butler* (as Nagi Sanzenin), *Hidamari Sketch* (as Chika), *Shakugan no Shana* (as Shana), *Mobile Suit Gundam 00, Magical Girl Lyrical Nanoha* (as Alisa Bannings), *Hetalia – Axis Powers, Inazuma Eleven, Kingdom, Utawarerumono* and *Battle Spirits* (and she has sung numerous theme songs).

You hear Rie Kugimiya saying the single word *nii-san* ('brother') a million different ways over the course of the *Fullmetal Alchemist* series (and into the second series and the movies): in terror, in hysteria, angry, sad, indifferent, pleading, cajoling, yelling, whispering, and – most often – affectionately (this is a textbook example of how an actor can say one word – *nii-san* – in ten million different ways). The voice actors always say 'Eduardo' (the French version of Edward), and also 'Edo'.

Both Romi Pak and Rie Kugimiya are *absolutely sensational* as Ed and Al in both *Fullmetal Alchemist* TV series and both *Fullmetal Alchemist* movies – two of the finest performances in all *animé*, without question. If this was live-action, Pak and Kugimiya would be showered with every acting award going. The amount of emotion[35] and drama that Pak and Kugimiya put into their performances is utterly remarkable. *Fullmetal Alchemist* is unthinkable without Pak and Kugimiya, just as *Cowboy Bebop*

---

33 As are some of the other male charas – a common practice in *animé*.
34 Kugimiya has her own blog online. Alas, it's only in Japanese.
35 Ed Elric is portrayed as little too weepy and anguished in the first *Fullmetal Alchemist* series, I think – particularly in the episodes involving Shou Tucker and Barry the Chopper.

is unimaginable without Kôichi Yamadera, Unsho Ishizuka,[36] Megumi Hayashibara and Aoi Tada, or *Ghost In the Shell* without Atsuko Tanaka, Akio Otsuka and Kôichi Yamadera (again), or *Naruto* without Junko Takeuchi. These *seiyu* are some of the true superstars of *animé* (and thus of any cinema anywhere); their voice work is simply astounding. If you're a fan of *Fullmetal Alchemist*, you will want to watch the show in the original language (there is no way a dub can match these outstanding performances). Sound director[37] Masafumi Mima should also be applauded for encouraging these vocal performances.

ADAPTING THE *FULLMETAL ALCHEMIST MANGA*: COMPARING THE *MANGA* AND THE *ANIMÉ*.

The 2003-2004 *animé* series follows the first half of the *Fullmetal Alchemist manga* series sort of closely, but diverges from the middle section onwards.

All of the changes in the TV shows are typical of any translation from *manga* to *animé*. But with Himoru Arakawa a living author (she was thirty when the first *animé* was produced), the filmmakers had an author who was still around (Arakawa-sensei sat in on meetings for the production of the *animé*, but she did not write any of the episodes. Anyway, she already had written the whole thing once! And drawn it! Indeed, that's one reason why *mangaka* often don't get involved in the animated versions of their comics, because they've already Been There, Done That (Katsuhiro Otomo (*Akira*) is well-known for not wanting to repeat himself). They are also *very* busy people).

In 2017, Arakawa said that she read the scripts of the *animé* adaptations, but left the filmmakers alone to get on with it – they were the specialists, after all: 'please do whatever you want', she told the production team.

Animé is *animé* and *manga* is *manga*, Himoru Arakawa asserted: that is, Arakawa recognized that they are different artforms. An adaptation is a new work. Consequently, Arakawa didn't regard the *animé* series as 'betraying' her comic, or not adapting it fully, chapter-by-chapter.

Typically, publishers accept proposals from *animé* companies for adapting their publications; the publisher then shows the proposals to their authors. At that point, a *mangaka* might have ideas about the proposal, or ask for it to be changed, and so on. So Arakawa could've advised her publisher Square Enix that she would prefer a different approach to the one that Bones, Aniplex, Mainichi *et al* had suggested.

It's likely that *mangaka* Himoru Arakawa was influenced by the TV adaptation of her *Fullmetal Alchemist* series when she was writing the later installments of the *manga* (that's happened with Tite Kubo and *Bleach*, for instance). After all, the first *Fullmetal Alchemist animé* series was a major undertaking, produced by a vast team of skilled veterans of the animation business (including artists, designers, writers, composers

---

36 He's the voice of Hohenheim in the second *Fullmetal Alchemist* series.
37 In *animé*, it's the sound director who works with the actors in the studio, relaying the direction of the director.

and producers every bit as talented as Arakawa-sensei). When Arakawa saw what the filmmakers did with her characters and her story, it's probable that she was inspired in all sorts of ways.

The *animé* version of *Fullmetal Alchemist* followed the *manga* by Hiromu Arakawa very closely at times. Perhaps too closely – that is, sometimes *Fullmetal Alchemist* might've benefitted from a looser, freer approach to the *manga*. And I don't only mean that the first series departed from the main storyline of the *Fullmetal Alchemist manga* halfway thru, or that the second series adhered to the plots of the *manga* even more closely (there are aspects to the storytelling in the *manga* that animation filmmakers would probably have changed if they were making a free adaptation).

There's no doubt that sometimes the screenwriting wanders off the main track in the first series of *Fullmetal Alchemist*. It's understandable over the course of a 50-something episode series, and sometimes you will see the writers being pulled back by the producers to the main storyline (often those 'resetting' or 'rebooting' scenes will involve Ed and Al discussing their primary quest on their own. And they don't always agree: part of the point of splitting the hero into two, into two brothers, is to express different viewpoints and different ways of doing things. Thus, Edward-kun is all for diving in wholesale without second thoughts (like Kaneda in *Akira*, Ed embodies the word 'impulsive'!), while Alphonse-kun is much more circumspect and cautious. However, in the *manga* and in the *animé*, it's very much Ed who is the leader of the two, who drives most of the drama and the action).

That the Elric children didn't resurrect their mother, but the thing that was created was a homunculus (whom they later encounter), is fascinating and ugly. That they went thru that pain and were maimed, but it wasn't their mother after all, is blackly ironic. (The *Fullmetal Alchemist manga* makes more of this than the *animé*, when it has Ed – and grandma Pinako – digging up the remains of the creature that Pinako buried. The *animé* alters this sub-plot: it depicts Ed at his mother's grave. The 2nd series of *Fullmetal Alchemist* follows the *manga* closer).

The first *animé* series adaptation of *Fullmetal Alchemist* invented a whole batch of characters that weren't in the *manga* by Himoru Arakawa.[38] Some were created to replace characters that had been dropped from the *animé* – Dante replaces Father, most obviously (but Frank Archer replaces Maes Hughes). Some of the characters were switched around (now it's Pride not Wrath who becomes Führer Bradley). Some were invented for just one episode (such as super-thief Psiren in 10: *The Phantom Thief*).

The characters cooked up for the *Fullmetal Alchemist animé* included Dante, now the super-villain behind the scenes; Lyra, her protegé; Juliet Douglas, the Führer's secretary (and another homunculus), who looks like the Elrics' mom (both the mom and Douglas are voiced by Yoshino Takamori); Belsio, Nash's friend; Nash Tringham; Fletcher and Russell

[38] Meanwhile some characters were dropped from the *manga*, including Ling, Lan Fan and Mei (the Chinese/ Xingese characters).

Tringham; Elisa, Lamac's daughter; tomboy Clause (in Linta); the thief by night (and nurse by day) Clara a.k.a. Psiren; Frank Archer; Majahal and Karin, Majahal's lover; Leo and Rick in Ishbal; Lujon and Lydia/ Libia.

While both *animé* series of *Hagane no Renkinjutsushi* followed Himoru Arakawa's *manga* closely at many points (the second series was much closer than the first), they also dived into particular episodes in the *manga* and expanded them greatly, or altered them dramatically. For example, the serial killer Barry the Chopper appears in a flashback sequence in the *Fullmetal Alchemist manga*, but the first *animé* TV show fleshed out the character, and brought him into the foreground of the piece (so that he is now interacting directly with Ed and Al. In the second *Fullmetal Alchemist* series, Tucker appears in a stylized, storybook flashback). The girl thief, Paninya, whom Ed chases across the roofs, was given a different characterization and context in the (first) *animé* (much of this section of the *manga* was rewritten). Some parts of the *manga* were dropped entirely (there's an episode where Number 66, the former Barry the Chopper, is questioned, which was left out). Parts of the *manga* were rearranged. Some sections that were flashbacks were put into the present tense (and vice versa). Altho' the second series was a much closer interpretation of the *Fullmetal Alchemist manga*, it still changed plenty of elements.

A significant departure in the first *animé* series from the *Fullmetal Alchemist manga* was the excision of the sub-plot which has Roy Mustang apparently killing Lt. Ross for the murder of (his friend) Maes Hughes. In the *manga*, the revelation that Hughes-san has been killed (and murdered) comes out much earlier (to the Elric brothers, at least). Lt. Ross, so clearly a diligent and committed soldier, is framed for the murder, and a call goes out (from Führer Bradley) to kill her when she escapes (altho' we know later that it was probably Bradley who ordered Hughes' execution). Mustang seems to burn her to death in an alley (also putting Mustang into an even bleaker place – he has also killed Winry's parents, again on orders from the military, as the 1st *animé* has it). But it turns out later that it was a ruse to trick the military.

Ed and Al find this out just after it's happened, and understandably they go ballistic (the hollow suit of armour, Number 66, the ghost of Barry the serial killer, is also involved). But all of this was dropped from the 2003-2004 *animé* of *Fullmetal Alchemist*.

Another significant departure from the *manga* version comes in the middle section of the first series of *Fullmetal Alchemist* not long after this episode: Roy Mustang faces off against Lust, and kills her. The *animé* opted to keep Lust alive as a major villain (her 1950s, American TV vamp persona was too good to waste. And Lust is the only female among the villains – until the *animé* also introduced charas such as Dante and Lyra, both not in the *manga*). In the *Fullmetal Alchemist manga*, the sequence where Mustang (and Havoc) go up against Lust is a big action sequence, with Lust appearing to have bested Mustang for a time (she pierces his side with her Wolverine/ Edward Scissorhands claws). But Mustang, ever the hero, uses his fiery alchemy to seal his wounds (ouch!) and staggers up to trounce Lust (what a hero!). The second *Fullmetal Alchemist* series followed this plotting closely.

The second *Fullmetal Alchemist* TV series, and the full *Fullmetal Alchemist manga*, have many additions and advantages over the first *Fullmetal Alchemist* series: one is the character of Father, and the much bigger, and grander scheme of the top homunculus – to become a god, no less. Another are energetic, super-dynamic characters such as, among the villains, Envy, the later Greed, and Selim-Pride, and, among the heroes, Ling Yao, little Mei Xiao (and the other Xingese charas). Another are outstanding set-pieces such as Edward and Ling in the belly of Gluttony, with Envy in his monster guise. Another is the whole Northern/ Briggs Mountain sequence, with Maria Armstrong and her fierce cohorts.

The character of Ling Yao (from Xing – i.e., China) is an important (tho' still minor) character in the middle section of the *Fullmetal Alchemist manga* series, but not in the 1st *animé* series (his ninja-like henchmen, including Lan Fan – he's a Prince – were also absent). Happily, Ling Yao, Lan Fan and little Mei Chang appeared in the 2nd series, where they were enormous entertainment value.

In the *Fullmetal Alchemist manga*, the alchemy of Xing (China) – dubbed Rentan Jutsu (but called alkahestry in the 2nd *animé* series) – is a significant subplot, mirroring the (European/ Japanese) alchemy of Amestris. The search for an elixir which will grant immortality is a key ingredient in Chinese alchemy (they're always searching for immortality in Chinese *wuxia pian* and historical movies, usually for the Emperor), and in *Fullmetal Alchemist* characters such as Ling Yao and Mei Chang are looking for the secret, to help their clans and families back home (it also crops up in *animé* such as *Princess Mononoke*). Indeed, Xing is the only significant nation in *Fullmetal Alchemist* apart from Ishbal, that's explored outside of Amestris (tho' forces from Drachma (Russia) attempt – and fail – to assault Briggs Mountain, and Xerxes features in a flashback).

The whole middle section of the *Fullmetal Alchemist manga*, where Ed and Al enter the belly of Gluttony to discover a fetid underworld and encounter more obstacles and monsters, was not in the first *animé* series (but became one of the stand-out sequences in the second *animé*). Another significant excision was the mastermind character of Father, another of the many shadowy, ambiguous but very powerful figures in fantasy *animé*, who bears more'n a passing resemblance to the Elrics' father Hohenheim (while the super-being that Father becomes in the finale resembles Ed).

Both the *animés* and the *manga* depict the homunculi as both quasi-immortal (or fairly indestructible), with regenerative capabilities, and also vulnerable to attacks. Kill them enough times, and they might just stay dead (but don't count on it!). Battering homunculi around isn't enough: it's best to rip out their philosopher's stones (if you can get close enough). In other words, Himoru Arakawa wants the homunculi to be formidable opponents, but flawed. The trick is working out where the flaws lie.

❯

The characterizations in the *Fullmetal Alchemist manga* by Hiromu Arakawa were followed closely by the *animé* team, tho' they also departed from the *manga* many times, too (as always in going from *manga* to *animé* – and in both *Fullmetal Alchemist* series, too). For instance, Arakawa (and her assistants) might've got sick and tired of drawing Al's hollow suit of armour 100s of times, but the animation would require thousands of drawings. So elements of the *manga*, such as that all-important armour suit, would be simplified and streamlined.

Adapting *manga* usually means only part of a series can be put into a movie, and with long-running *manga*, that means only a small proportion (and adapting your own *manga*, as Hayao Miyazaki knew, could be extra difficult, because it is your own work). However, as with many of the finest movies, the *story* is merely *one ingredient* in a vast display of spectacular elements. Yes, decent stories and characters are essential to the success of most movies, but with an *animé* series like *Fullmetal Alchemist*, story and character aren't everything. It's the same with movies such as *Intolerance, Star Wars, Citizen Kane, Sunrise, Pierrot le Fou*, Hong Kong martial arts movies, and, in *animé*, *Akira, Legend of the Overfiend, Cowboy Bebop, Aquariion, Escaflowne* and *Ghost In the Shell*.

As with a Hollywood musical, you don't need to know the story, or to be able to follow the story, or to know which character is which, to get so much out of the finest *animé* productions, including *Fullmetal Alchemist*. You go along for the ride, you submerge yourself in the experience. With *animé* like *Escaflowne, Samurai Champloo, Fairy Tail* or *Moribito* – or movies such as *An American In Paris, Once Upon a Time In China*, a Jan Svankmajer animation (*Alice*), a Walerian Borowczyk flick (*Immoral Tales*) – you submit to the experience, to the feeling, to the adrenalin rush. (But in *Fullmetal Alchemist*, yes, it is actually the characters and their relationships that you remember most).

THE CHARACTERS.

Fullmetal Alchemist was the story of two brothers, Edward and Alphonse Elric. Edward Elric is the hero, the fullmetal alchemist of the title. He is a troubled figure, partially a cyborg with his artificial limbs (how Japanese animation loves its heroes to be constructed from a collage of materials – no nation adores robots and augmented humans like Japan!).

Ed Elric is cocky, self-confident, handsome, charismatic, a born leader, but he's also stubborn, insensitive, selfish, opinionated, hotly-tempered, and neurotic. His much-taller brother Al, meanwhile, becomes a soul that lives in a suit of hollow armour[39] (robots with real souls are another staple of Japanese *animé* and *manga*, the *Ghost In the Shell* series and *Mighty Atom* being among the most famous. It's linked to the doll with a heart and the *Pinocchio* theme). Al is the sweeter of the two brothers

---

39 Ed ties his brother's soul to a nearby suit of armour in the opening sequence.

(he has lost more, perhaps), the one quicker to make up, quicker to forgive and forget (but he also often defers to his older but shorter brother). Al is the conscience of the pair, slower to act, more thoughtful, yet also more trusting – and more naïve. (He also has far less dialogue than Edward – in some episodes, Al often barely speaks).

The two brothers mean that the hero of *Fullmetal Alchemist* is split into two – for all of the obvious reasons. It means that *Fullmetal Alchemist* is a buddy format, which employs all of the expected joshing, the reversals, the misunderstandings, the falling-outs and the making-ups between two friends/ co-workers/ brothers.

The *Fullmetal Alchemist manga* presents the homunculi as the off-spring of Father, created to carry out his nefarious goals (power, immortality, more power). The 2003-04 *animé* adaptation of *Fullmetal Alchemist* gives the homunculi their independence, as they band together (but also rebel), with some of them (such as Lust), hoping to become human. In the *animé*, the homunculi're created when humans attempt trans-mutation.

The *Fullmetal Alchemist manga* introduced the shadowy, powerful figure of Father as one of the super-minds behind the whole homunculi and philosopher's stone plots. A tall, imposing character with a striking resemblance to the Elric's daddy, Hohenheim, Father was dropped entirely from the first *animé* series of *Fullmetal Alchemist* – to be replaced by the character of Dante (and in part by the character of Juliet Douglas), partly because Himoru Arakawa's *manga* wasn't finished when the *animé* was created, and the *animé* created its own story. But Father makes a satisfyingly creepy and very threatening appearance in the second *Fullmetal Alchemist* series (it's interesting that the writers opted to have two women as the chief villains in the first *Fullmetal Alchemist* series – Dante and Juliet Douglas).

Ed Elric's commanding officer in East City is Roy Mustang (Toru Ohkawa), 'the hero of Ishbal', a youngish, darkly handsome man whose confident, sarcastic attitude ticks off Ed mightily. Mustang is what Ed might grow up to be – respected amongst his colleagues, adored by female colleagues (and even secretly loved by his female sidekick Liza Hawkeye – Michiko Neya), but ultimately just too self-righteous and arrogant for his own good. Mustang also functions as that narrative staple, the hero's boss, with whom heroes everywhere have problematic relationships. Mustang bosses Ed about, and he hates it. Ed has a real issue with authority! (Mustang is the 'Flame Alchemist', who uses gloves made from pyrotex to ignite waves of flames. And all it takes – how cool is this?! – is a simple click of the fingers! Mustang simply stands there, with his superhero cloak flapping in slo-mo, and, like a jazz hep cat, snaps his fingers!).

Roy Mustang has a bunch of characters working for him, who act as the familiar team in *manga* and *animé* – Denny Brosh, Cain Furey, Jean Havoc, Vato Falman and Liza Hawkeye. As the *Fullmetal Alchemist manga* and *animé* progress, their characters become fleshed out (tho' only

Hawkeye is given decisive acts; they have more to do in the second animated series).

In the *animé*, it's Roy Mustang who kills Winry's doctor parents; in the *Fullmetal Alchemist manga*, it's Scar (the switch plays against Mustang's character, and makes him a much more ambiguous personality in the first *animé* series.)

STYLE.

The format of each episode of the first *Fullmetal Alchemist* series is a standard one for animated series in Japan: there is an opening prologue of a minute or so which typically ends on a teaser or cliffhanger. Then come the opening credits, with Alphonse (not Edward) narrating the explanation about alchemy's exchange (over a shot of the family photo of the Elric family). The opening credits feature a pop song (by Porno Graffiti, L'Arc-en-Ciel, Cool Joke and Asian Kung-Fu Generation) playing under images of characters from the series in iconic poses. Each episode has a halfway commercial break. The bumpers or 'eye-catches' in and out of the commercial breaks feature one or two characters in an iconic pose. The shows usually end with a momentous piece of business. The closing credits have similar iconic beats as the opening credits (but they also change several times during the series' run, and have different theme music with each alteration. Again, standard practice for a long-running show. The songs were byNana Kitade, Yellow Generation, Crystal Kay, and Sowelu.

The design of the characters in both of the *Fullmetal Alchemist animé* series, one of the toughest gigs, partly because there are 100s of characters, is hugely impressive: characters pop out of the screen with instantly recognizable silhouettes (critics have acclaimed the designers for differentiating such a vast cast of characters). The designers (Yoshiyuki Ito for the 1st series, Hiroki Kanno for the 2nd series) have also captured the look of *mangaka* Hiromu Arakawa's designs (including her penchant for sleek figures, for characters that look like fashion models with chiselled features, for characters that combine the look of the 1920s with the 1990s, and for characters in motion in battle leaning forward in frozen martial arts poses, like something out of an Osamu Tezuka *manga* from the 1960s).

Character design is one area that many *mangaka* are *very* precious about when their work is translated into animation – after all, they have spent months and years living with these characters (and going thru a range of variations at the design stage).

The character designer of *Fullmetal Alchemist*, Yoshiyuki Ito, is a veteran of numerous shows, include many *animé* classics, such as *Cowboy Bebop* and *Soul Eater* (Ito also did some of the storyboards and directed some episodes). Indeed, if you look at the wonderful Anime News Network website, you will see that most of the team behind *Fullmetal Alchemist* have also worked on many of your favourite shows. *Animé* creators rarely stay with one show or one type of *animé* throughout their careers – they'll work on all sorts of things. Some designers are specialist who work on one element of a show – monsters or *mecvha*, say.

One of the reasons that *Fullmetal Alchemist* is so strong in animated form in its two series is that Himoru Arakawa gives animators some amazing characters to work with, the sort of characters that animators love to put on screen: divas such as Ed Elric, Greed and Envy, cute moppets such as Mei and her panda, and vicious villains such as Lust and Selim/ Pride.

Fullmetal Alchemist employs a lot of static imagery, despite being animation. Often the camera pans over artwork to create the illusiion of movement, or uses images as freeze frames, or employs crowd scenes where nobody moves. All standard procedures in animation, to keep costs down. (But the way that Japanese animation uses static scenes is different from Western animation, and is related to the stylization and abstractions of the 'floating world' of woodblock prints).

The background art in both *Fullmetal Alchemist* series is remarkable. Not only for its reproductions of exotic locales like deserts, snowy mountains and capital cities, but its intricate evocations of small towns, street corners, hotels, stores, and modest houses. And for a (heightened) portrayal of Middle Europe in the early-to-mid-20th century, *Fullmetal Alchemist* is only matched by the cinema of Hayao Miyazaki. Look at those beautifully crafted streets, or the apartments furnished with modernist couches and framed photographs, and everything with a lived-in feel. For art direction, production design, props, *mecha* design cinematography and lighting, *Fullmetal Alchemist* is in a class of its own.

The colours are vivid in the *Fullmetal Alchemist animé* series. Sometimes the filmmakers taken advantage of new digital technology which can create glows and flares on top of images, simulating late afternoon light (which Hiromu Arakawa is fond of). I have mentioned visual effects a lot – as visual effects animations, the two *animé* series of *Fullmetal Alchemist* are exceptioinal. Not only do they do pretty much *everything* that has been achieved in visual effects animation since its inception in the late 1890s/ early 1900s, they add their own spin, their own rhythm, their own language.

When the boys perform alchemy in the *Fullmetal Alchemist manga*, there are wind effects blowing their clothes and hair, whooshing sound effects, plenty of bright light, speed lines to emphasize the action, and zigzag zips of magical energy.

The sound design team (at Soundbox and Techno Sound) have also enhanced the quality of the visual effects animation no end, accurately and imaginatively interpreting what the animators and techies were trying to achieve, and making it work in the world of sound. A visual effect without the right sound accompanying it can fall flat all too easily. The sound in *Fullmetal Alchemist* really punches home the vfx animation. (Aniplex oversaw music production; the soundtrack was released by

Aniplex's parent company, Sony Music Entertainment Japan).[40]

It's intriguing coming back to the first *Hagane no Renkinjutsusi* series after watching all of the second series: the animation is lighter, airier (and less money has been spent on it). In some ways, the first *Fullmetal Alchemist* series is more satisfying, from a script and filmmaking point-of-view, even tho' the animation is slicker in the second series.

The humour in *Fullmetal Alchemist* is a vital ingredient – it balances the heavyweight themes and issues, and some of the intense action (sometimes humour's inserted right in the midst of seemingly serious or action scenes). Arakawa-sensei has emphasized that humour was an essential element of *Fullmetal Alchemist*. The comedy is played very broadly at times (especially with Edward, with his wild facial expressions and OTT cartoony effects). A good deal of mileage is squeezed out of people mistaking Alphonse for the Fullmetal Alchemist, or for being Edward's senior; Edward always reacts with apoplectic anger (only in the later *Fullmetal Alchemist* episodes are the size gags dropped). The bickering of the brothers is another recurring comical motif (pretty much mandatory if you're going to split your hero into two people).

One of the episodes – 13: *Fullmetal vs. Flame* – becomes very silly, and even the usually sedate (and smug) Roy Mustang goofs around (meanwhile, one of the other officers, Hughes-san, shows everybody pictures of his beloved daughter, whether they want to see them or not. That gag of the over-proud father is exploited rather too often).

Characters freaking out when they discover that Alphonse is a hollow suit of armour is employed many times in *Fullmetal Alchemist* – and often Himoru Arakawa uses Al as the first victim in an attack. So, in the *manga*, one of Father Cornello's henchmen thrusts a pistol in Al's face and shoots him (everybody is stunned to find out that Al's helmet flies off and there's nothing inside). When the Elric boys encounter Scar for the time, the psycho thinks he's ripped Al to pieces, only to see that Al is hollow.

Similarly, Himoru Arakawa employs the automail trope many times with Edward Elric – first up in the *Fullmetal Alchemist manga* is the chimera conjured by Father Cornello, who chomps on Ed's arm, thinking it's got him. With a flourish of his cloak, a double-page drawing (56-57) reveals the Fullmetal Alchemist in all his glory – with a metal arm. This ruse is replayed many times (next is, again, when Scar attacks the brothers in the street).

There's a deliberate attempt in the first *Fullmetal Alchemist anime* series to increase the input of the female characters: Izumi Curtis, for example, appears far more than she does in the *manga*. The chief villain, Dante, was a woman (it's Father in the *manga*). Other female villains were created: Juliet Douglas and Lyra. Lust was given an episode of her own (episode 35: *Reunion of the Fallen*). 'Winry is the hero of own story', according to Caitlin Donovan (in the Mary Sue).

---

40 Aniplex was owned by the Sony corporation in Japan; Aniplex backed many *anime* shows, and was also involved with music production, merchandizing, toys, etc. Aniplex produced the music for *Fullmetal Alchemist*, for example, and also staged a festival to publicize the first *Fullmetal Alchemist* series (publicity was another speciality of Aniplex).

One reason 'there are so many wonderful women in 'Fullmetal'', according to Himoru Arakawa, is because the work ethic was instilled into her, growing up on a farm in Hokkaido.

CONTEMPORARY POLITICS.

Manga artist Hiromu Arakawa consciously built in plenty of social and political themes and issues into *Fullmetal Alchemist*. Many are blatantly obvious – such as the oppressed and dispossessed people of Ishbal (a.k.a. Ishval; evoking not only Arabic and Islamic societies, and Jewish societies, but also refugees of many kinds), or the exploration of 20th century fascism (the State Alchemists as well as other elements of the *Fullmetal Alchemist* world evoke National Socialism of the 1920s and 1930s, and fascism across Europe, not only in Germany, and nationalism in Japan in the early 20th century).

But there are also more subtle evocations of political and social issues in *Fullmetal Alchemist* – for instance, the emphasis on immigrants and outsiders[41] (a staple of Japanese animation), on displaced people and refugees, on the corruption inside the military-industrial machine, and on the inter-connectedness of social and political issues (*Fullmetal Alchemist* explores the knock-on effects of doing something in one social arena, how it reverberates in other areas).

Fullmetal Alchemist was created as a *manga* and as an *animé* series in the early 2000s of 9/11 and post-9/11, of the 'war on terror', the Iraq War, the Afghanistan War, the hunt for Osama bin Laden, the strikes against the Taliban, the continuing tension in North Korea, and other conflicts. *Animé* outings that reflected this dangerous, paranoid era included *Howl's Moving Castle*, *Ghost In the Shell: Stand Alone Complex*, *Eden of the East* and *Paranoia Agent*.

Arakawa has also suggested that the Ainu in Japan were inspirations for the Ishbalians (the presence of the Ainu is strong in Arakawa's roots in Hokkaido). An Ainu character appears in *Silver Spoon*.

THEMES.

Fullmetal Alchemist enshrines many of the usual attributes of Japanese animation and *manga* – such as the importance of hard work, studying and staying in school, the value of loyalty, respect and honour, the necessity of working in groups and getting along with other people, deference to elders and people in authority, and determination and not giving up (but also knowing when to quit!). You'll see these values all over Japanese animation, and not only in the shows based, like *Fullmetal Alchemist*, *Naruto*, *Dominion: Tank Police*, *Darling In the Franxx*, *Aquarioin* and *One Piece*, around groups.

In this respect, *Fullmetal Alchemist* is wholly about contemporary Japan, like most *animé*. That is, it is a profoundly *Japanese* show, altho' it appeals to an international audience, and it is very much about the 2000s, about a post-9/11, post-Bubble Economy political climate (nobody can

41 *Ghost In the Shell: Stand Alone Complex* also explored the issue of immigrants and foreigners in depth.

miss that many of the communities in *Fullmetal Alchemist* are struggling to survive economically, and some episodes depict industries, such as mining, that are in jeopardy. All of that relates to contemporary Japan in the years following the bursting of the Bubble Economy in 1989-90).

Fullmetal Alchemist is astonishingly violent. Not only are people regularly murdered, there are close-ups of corpses and pools of blood. Children are killed. Soldiers fire upon innocent bystanders. And so much of the story concerns war-torn communities: it's like the histories of Europe/ Japan/ Middle East in the 19th and 20th centuries compressed into the span of a decade.

In the midst of this, our heroes, Ed and Al Elric, find themselves situated anxiously somewhere between the State Alchemists, who are tied to the military (indeed, are an adjunct of the military), and the 'ordinary people' of each community they encounter.

Meanwhile, the State Alchemists themselves in *Fullmetal Alchemist* are not 'pure' or 'innocent': they are in fact agents of the State, and as such are no different from the armed forces or the police. That is, a right-wing organization paid for by the people and run by the government. As the 2003-2004 *Fullmetal Alchemist* TV series unfolds, we find out that the State Alchemists have been involved in some very dubious incidents. The sarcastic, smug Roy Mustang, for example, killed two doctors in cold blood (this was altered from the *manga*, where it was Scar who dispatched Winry Rockbell's parents).

The leader in the Amestris world of *Fullmetal Alchemist* has the politically loaded title of Führer (a tall, grim man with an eye-patch! How did *he* get elected?! He is also called the King and the President). Indeed, the Germanic/ Bavarian aspects of the State Alchemists (as well as the settings of the world of *Fullmetal Alchemist*, which look like Mittel Europe), are obvious: with their blue uniforms, their moustaches and monocles, their pompous, self-righteous attitudes, their insistence on military codes, and their devotion to the Führer, they might represent Germany up to and just after the First World War. Indeed, the first *Fullmetal Alchemist* movie explored the rise of Nazism in post-WW1 Germany, making explicit the themes of the TV series.[42]

The writers of the adaptations of *Fullmetal Alchemist* lose no opportunity in putting the Elric brothers up against numerous authority figures, parental figures, surrogate mothers, surrogate fathers, aunts, uncles, priests, officers, you name it. *Fullmetal Alchemist* is very much about young people negotiating the complicated and corrupt world of adults.[43] And, quite often, the brother heroes're whacked physically when they transgress boundaries or break laws or disappoint their elders.

I got to say, after so many episodes of similar treatment from authority figures and parental surrogates, it does become a little wearisome in its repetition and its patronizing attitudes and its incredible violence against children. Are the Elric brothers still children, when they're

42 The animators also give the soldiers of Amestris the bright blue eyes of Ayran invaders.
43 As Jason Yadao puts it in *The Rough Guide To Manga*, 'everyone, it seems, has something to hide, some tragedy for which they are trying to atone' (125).

teenagers? Maybe not, but they still get treated like children, and still get physically beaten like children (they are teenagers throughout all of the *Fullmetal Alchemist* series, apart from the epilogue).

RELIGION.

That *Hagane no Renkinj Jutsushi* is taking on Big Themes is announced from the opening episode, which depicts a community being hoodwinked by false religion. The Arch Villain, Father Cornello, a big, burly official with a perpetual patronizing smile,[44] is using alchemy to fool the populace into thinking he's performing miracles by the grace of God. God? Yes – *that* God. Well, *a* God. That is, it's clearly a Western deity (the Sun God Leto) in the manner of Yahweh/ Jehovah/ Allah/ Zeus/ God (who appears as a colossal statue in the church,[45] and who is summoned as a literal *deus ex machina* by Edward in the final confrontation between him and Cornello in episode two).

Piping his pompous sermons out to the city by radio, Father Cornello is using a philosopher's stone (worn in a ring, but it turns out to be a fake, like Cornello's cult), to tame the inhabitants to do what he wants. Meanwhile, there's a sweet young thing called Rose Tomas who just wants her boyfriend Cain to come back from the dead (as you do), which Cornello has promised (Cornello has a creepy relationship with Rose that hints at father-daughter incest).

The attack of Cornello's leonine chimera on Edward offers the first reveal in the *manga* of Ed's 'fullmetal' status – the creature can't bite thru his arm or his leg. (Cornello instantly assumes that the boys have tried human transmutation, even tho' artificial limbs are commonplace in this fantasy world).

'When anime uses religion as a story element, it is usually because of its ability to generate conflict,' note J. Clements and H. McCarthy (2006, 533), and this's certainly true of *Fullmetal Alchemist*.

You can see just from a brief description that *Fullmetal Alchemist* is far more sophisticated and multi-layered than similar stories in TV and cinema in the Western world. And the filmmakers at Bones, Aniplex, Mainichi *et al* do all of this in 22-minute episodes.[46]

THE CRITICS.

The 2003-2004 *Fullmetal Alchemist* animated series has everything: great characters, strong action scenes, excellent animation, stunning background art, fabulous settings, complex themes and issues, and plenty of humour.[47]

The first *Fullmetal Alchemist* series was voted the number one *anime* in history in two TV Asahi polls online. 'A deeply involving series with

44 He's reminiscent of Cæsar in the *Urotsukidoji* series.
45 The design of Leto, an imposing patriarch with a long beard, resembles images of Zeus.
46 Tho' the first two episodes do form a continuous story, with a climactic moment offering the cliffhanger of the first episode.
47 The inclusion of the other world – which is something like our world – is one of the genius touches in the first *Fullmetal Alchemist* series. One of the chief reasons for introducing it is to give us the multi-layered ending, with the brothers alive but separated.

humour, action, adventure, conflict, scares and genuine pathos, *Fullmetal Alchemist* is a hugely rewarding experience', according to Colin Odell and Michelle Le Blanc (2013, 147).

Jeremy Crocker in Anime News Network (2004) wrote:

> Be warned, though: Don't trust anybody in the show. One of the greatest things about this series is the ability to mislead the viewers into a false sense of security. Motives and intents change rapidly; the nicest character can quickly become the vilest. And of course, it goes both ways.

For Giona Nazzaro, 'although less chaotic than [Eichiro] Oda's designs [in *One Piece*] – there is the same formal and cultural syncretism and use of graphic violence, which is extreme but seems reduced in a context fed by references to steampunk literature and traditional alchemy'.[48]

'Even among the highest ranks of anime series, *Fullmetal Alchemist* stands out for the tightness and elegance of its carefully constructed plot', Julie Davis noted in *Zettai! Anime Classics* (122).

---

48 In C. Chatrian, 267.

Fullmetal Alchemist Animé Artbook (this page and over).

03

FULLMETAL ALCHEMIST

HAGANE NO RENKINSUTSUSHI

THE FIRST ANIME SERIES: EPISODE GUIDE

Episode 1. *Those Who Challenge the Sun*

Episode 2. *Body of the Sanctioned*

The *animé* of *Fullmetal Alchemist* opens (in episode one: *Those Who Challenge the Sun* = *Taiyo ni Odumu Mono*, broadcast on October 4, 2003), the same way as the long-running *Fullmetal Alchemist manga* by Himoru Arakawa did: with the inciting incident which launches the emotional and psychological core of the *Fullmetal Alchemist* franchise: indeed, so important is this two-and-a-half-minute prologue, it powers along the central quest of the *Fullmetal Alchemist* franchise, and is behind everything that Edward and Alphonse Elric do: Ed and Al, as children, are experimenting with alchemical magic. They are trying to bring their dead mother Trisha back to life. They draw a 'transformation circle' on the floor (one of the key devices or MacGuffins in the *Fullmetal Alchemist* franchise),[1] clap their hands, and begin the magic (in Japan, part of prayer is done by clapping the hands twice). Unfortunately, it goes horribly wrong, and the *Fullmetal Alchemist* series opens with the image of two maimed children: Edward loses his leg and arm (and dripping blood), while Alphonse seems to have been killed (there is small, empty crater and his clothes're left behind). The short, two-and-a-half-minute prologue closes with emotive close-ups of Edward's traumatized face, as he gasps, 'it wasn't supposed to be like this!'

---

1 You can bet that plenty of kids have doodled transmutation circles on their school books.

Thus, from that thrilling and cataclysmic prologue in episode 1: *Those Who Challenge the Sun*, the first *Fullmetal Alchemist* TV show expands outwards. The inciting incident gives Edward and Alphonse Elric plenty of goals and motives: one being to find a way of becoming whole again (Edward has a metal arm and leg, while Alphonse is forced to inhabit a suit of armour – a hollow robot (Ed gives up his arm to achieve this transmutation of the soul for Al).) Hence their quest for the philosopher's stone, a real, historical slice of the mythology of mediæval alchemy.

The drive to enchant their maimed bodies back to what they were propels the Elric kids in the early episodes of *Fullmetal Alchemist:* thus, they both travel to the capital (Central City) to try to become State Alchemists (in the event, only Ed is able to take the tough exam, because Al is, well, not all there, so to speak! Poor Al – he does have the rough end of the deal – a suit of armour without the fun bits of the human body can't be great (Al takes out a notepad and writes down things he want to eat when he regains his body. It's cute!). However, Al can still perform alchemy – you see Al rapidly sketching a transmutation circle out of chalk on the ground, sometimes in 1/15th of a second, in between flying punches in the middle of a fight.

The two-and-a-half-minute prologue of 1.1: *Those Who Challenge the Sun* also announces to the audience that this is going to be a somewhat bloody enterprise – it is going to maim its heroes in the first couple of minutes! (There's a C.U. of Ed's bloody limb). The prologue closes with a creepy shot of the botched creature's upside-down head as it glares at Edward. And it includes many of the motifs of the *Fullmetal Alchemist* series: the transformation circle, the magic, the visual effects, short bursts of intense drama, kids who can perform spells, a searing, orchestral soundtrack, etc. (Additional filmic devices in the prologue include smoke and energy waves, subjective camera, and images going in and out of focus. Notice the colour in the magical rite – waves of yellow, which picks up Ed's colour scheme (his hair, his eyes), to underscore that it's Ed's fervour that's driving the urge to pursue alchemy and resurrect their mother).

The *Fullmetal Alchemist manga* by Himoru Arakawa also opened with the same catastrophic scene of the Elrics' failed transmutation – but it has only one page in the comic (of four drawings). It's only later on in the *manga* – at the start of chapter two, *The Price of Life* – that we discover more of the boys' alchemical ritual. (For instance, in the *manga*, Alphonse isn't shown, only the aftermath of the transmutation ritual).

✳

When the 2003-04 *animé* shifts to the present day, we are somewhere outside Liore: it's a desert landscape (that's not in the *manga*); there are captions with info about the boys' ages (15 and 14). A comedic scene introduces us to the Elrics – it's a change of tone that the *Fullmetal Alchemist* series often uses, going from high drama to comedy (as does the *manga*).

The core of *Fullmetal Alchemist* is the two brothers, Ed and Al Elric, and their relationship. It's how they work together that forms the heart of the 2003-2004 and 2009-2010 series. Voice actors Romi Pak and Rie Kugimiya must be cited here, for delivering wonderful and convincing performances. But it's Edward who is the Fullmetal Alchemist of the title, who drives most of the plots. Ed is the rebel, the idealist, the artist, the scientist, the one who yearns and moves and pushes the story along. And, with his boots, spiky, blond hair in a plait, and skinny frame in black pants and black jacket, and red overcoat, he's a very contemporary kid (he might be in a J-pop band. Ed also resembles Lina Inverse from *Slayers* in many respects).

The first two episodes of *Fullmetal Alchemist* – 1: *Those Who Challenge the Sun* (= *Taiyo ni Odumu Mono*) and 2: *Body of the Sanctioned* (= *Kini no Karada*) – explore a community (Liore) corrupted by the ruling powers, led by Father Cornello (Kinryuu Arimoto – he played Dr Knox in the second series. Liore will be revisited towards the end of the first *Fullmetal Alchemist* series, and again in the second series). The episodes, which follow Himoru Arakawa's *manga* closely (the *manga* also opens with the same plots), depict a false religion, a cult of the sun (the Sun God Leto), in which religious leaders are exploiting the gullibility of the citiens (by pretending to perform 'miracles' – actually acts of alchemy). There is also a (fake) philosopher's stone wielded by the arch villain of the episodes, Father Cornello. And a young woman (Rose Tomas – Houko Kuwashima) who's caught in a moral muddle in the middle (*Fullmetal Alchemist* often brings in a young woman to offer a female counter-point to the boysy Elric boys. Usually it's their childhood friend Winry Rockbell (Megumi Toyoguchi).)

Much of the information is delivered in a simple exposition scene (a typical 'watering-hole' scene) at a roadside café (as in the *manga*), which includes info about the Elrics, about Liore, about the Sun God cult, and shows the boys performing alchemy to fix a broken radio (the radio is foreshadowing for the finale of the first two shows).

In the first two episodes of the animated *Fullmetal Alchemist*, Rose Tomas is a romantic soul who pines after her dead lover Cain – the priest Cornello has promised to bring him back to life. This minor sub-plot thus mirrors the central quest of the *Hagane no Renkinjutsushi* series (the Elrics encounter situations like this all the time). Rose turns up later in the *Fullmetal Alchemist* series in a Virgin Mary guise, as the 'Holy Mother'.

In pitting the young Elric brothers against the corruption and exploitation of Father Cornello[2] and his followers in the town of Liore, the writers and the filmmakers of *Fullmetal Alchemist* are making a very strong statement about the scope and ambition of the 2003-04 TV series. Because these are distinctly 'grown-up' issues, and also very social and political issues. Exposing a poisonous religion (which's clearly drawn on Christianity and Western religion), goes way beyond the arena of your usual *animé* series (or any TV series). That the corruption and lies are

2 Cornello recalls the corrupt priest Mozgus in the *Berserk manga* (1989-2021) by Kentaro Miura.

exposed by a couple of kids makes it all the more poignant and revealing (it's worth noting that depictions of Christianity, Judaism and Western religion in Japanese animation are often as corrupt regimes – institutions that're distinctly 'foreign', exotic and non-Japanese).

Notice too how much the *Fullmetal Alchemist* *animé* focusses on Edward Elric's objective/ realist/ cynical attitude to religion (his disbelief is chiefly directed at Rose and Cornello). This is a fairly scornful teenager when it comes to institutions like the military (Ed doesn't trust them at all!) and religion.

The first two episodes of *Fullmetal Alchemist* also focus a good deal on Rose Tomas and her reactions to Ed and Al and their views. Rose is desperate to believe, even when the evidence contradicts her desires. She is caught in between the science/ alchemy of the Elrics and Cornello's false religion of Leto. She doubts the brothers for a long time, and by the end of episode two, she is defeated by the collapse of her faith (and she accuses the Elrics of ruining the hopes and dreams of the townsfolk by introducing an unwanted dose of 'reality'. They prefer the dream, she thinks).

✳

On top of that, the first two episodes of *Fullmetal Alchemist* introduce us to so many ingredients that turn up in the series, such as: (1) to the main characters, (2) to the world of Amestris, where alchemy is real and the historical eras run from late 19th century steam-punk to very contemporary fashions[3] and imagery, (3) to the mix of high drama and broad humour, (4) to the arch villains of the series, the homunculi, and of course (5) to slam-bang action.

Action – oh yes, when *Fullmetal Alchemist* gets going, it ramps up to full-on action sequences which exploit animation to the full. No need for giant robots and spaceships and lasers, because with alchemy and transformations *Fullmetal Alchemist* has plenty of gimmicks and tricks for wowing the audience. In the first episodes of *Fullmetal Alchemist*, the Elric brothers go up against Father Cornello and his cohorts – including a chimera (a monster created by alchemists – the filmmakers also added a giant, green bird to the *manga*, picking up the bird motif), and multiple transformations (we also find out one of the limitations of alchemy – because every magical gift in folk tales and fairy tales has to have boundaries – it can only transmute material that's immediately, physically to hand (and mass-for-mass, Al explains, tho' the filmmakers forget the rules when it suits them!). Thus, the boys often transmute stone and bricks into shapes, because that's what they can lay their hands on in the immediate area – literally, in the walls or floors of wherever they happen to be. Those limitations force the animators to come up with all sorts of unusual weaponry and defensive systems for the Elric brothers to use in fights).

The action scene with Father Cornello in episode one: *Those Who*

---

3 The costumes developed by *manga* artist Hiromu Arakawa and enhanced to the max by the character designer (Yoshiyuki Ito) of the *animé* are thoroughly contemporary: earrings, tattoos, croptops, combat pants, chunky boots, fake fur-lined jackets, etc. (The *animé* designers have one significant advantage over the *manga*: they can create their fashion in full colour throughout).

Challenge the Sun also introduces us to Edward Elric as the Fullmetal Alchemist of the title: when his signature red cloak is torn by the chimera, Edward pulls it off his metal arm (an image used in the TV trailers): in an iconic, superhero pose, the automail arm and leg're revealed – here's our Fullmetal Alchemist, one of the most spectacular characters in recent Japanese pop culture – with the customary sweep of the superhero cloak.

*

Like many *animé* series, *Fullmetal Alchemist* has villains that re-appear throughout the series – the vicious and despicable homunculi – Gluttony (Yasuhiro Takato) and Lust (Yuuko Satou) – are introduced in the first two episodes,[4] as well as Envy[5] (Mayumi Yamaguchi). They are named after – what a surprise! – the Seven Sins of Judæo-Christianity[6] – Occidental religion is employed throughout *Fullmetal Alchemist*, which helps it to resonate so deeply with Western audiences.

Fullmetal Alchemist's homunculi are authentically fearsome and formidable (in contrast to so many villains in many action or adventure franchises). Yet they are also kept mysterious for a *long* time – their motivations and their goals are not revealed for many, many episodes of *Fullmetal Alchemist*, in both *animé* series (and even then they don't agree amongst themselves – they are only a loose collective of individuals (there are rebels, too, such as Greed). Occasionally, they refer to a mysterious, unnamed character who appears to be their boss. The first *Fullmetal Alchemist* series, we remember, was produced (in 2003-04) b4 the *manga* was complete (in 2010), so some aspects of the villains were created for the TV show).

But for now all we need to know is: these guys are *baaad*! The *Fullmetal Alchemist* series also has, like most *animé* series, villains that appear in single episodes, in the usual 'Monster of the Week' format. In the first two shows, it's the fat, pompous, grinning bully Father Cornello (he has eyes that disappear into slits, very common in *animé*). How Cornello is dispatched is inventive: the Elric boys trick him into announcing his nefarious schemes to the populace via a radio broadcast (using a church bell as a loudspeaker – another satire on organized religion).[7] True, it takes some tricksy finagling by the screenwriter Shou Aikawa (following the *manga* by Himoru Arakawa, with alterations) to make this work. But it has a poetic justice to it (and is more convincing than the boys telling the populace that their leader is a crazy fake. For a start, how do you tell thousands of people something, without resorting to mass media? In the time allotted to a TV show, that is! Besides, nobody seems to want to listen to the boys – they don't want to hear what Edward tells them, as seen in the fountain scene).

The cult of Leto might be a critique of the Sublime Truth (Aum

---

4 Lust is introduced much earlier than in the *manga*: she is sitting at the bar of the café in the opening scene in Liore.
5 Tho' in his guise as Cornello.
6 The Seven Sins also appear in shows such as *Trinity Seven, The Seven Deadly Sins* and *Seven Mortal Sins*.
7 Radio becomes an important dramatic device later on in the *Fullmetal Alchemist* series: it's used to lure out Scar, and the Führer's wife appears in a crucial interview in the finale.

Shinrikyo) sect, the Hindu-Buddhist cult led by Shoko Asahhara, which was thought to be behind the nerve gas attacks in Tokyo's subways of 1995 (as well as killing opponents and plotting to overthrow society. Aum's leader was in prison). In animation, *Cowboy Bebop*, *Ghost In the Shell: Stand Alone Complex* and *Death Note* have also parodied this cult.

It's striking that the first *Fullmetal Alchemist* series leaves aside the tremendous villains of the homunculi for a long time. Here you have readymade psychos and weirdos, which the second series of *Fullmetal Alchemist* exploited to the full. But the first *Fullmetal Alchemist* series placed them on the sidelines, instead continuing to present dubious alchemists, untrustworthy father figures, and out-and-out unbelievable (though slinky) antagonists such as the catwoman burglar Psiren (however, Barry the Chopper and Shou Tucker are certainly memorable villains from episodes 1.6 and 1.8).

*

What's striking is not only that Himoru Arakawa begins the *Hagane no Renkinjutsushi* series with the evocation of a fake religious cult, she contrasts that with the 'science' of alchemy (certainly it's a bold step – it's no simple, humble task for the Elric brothers, like rescuing a cat from a tree: no, *Fullmetal Alchemist* opens very ambitiously from the get-go).

Notice that the first act of alchemy that takes place in the present tense of *Fullmetal Alchemist* is Alphonse Elric fixing the radio he accidentally breaks, a modest but impressive piece of magic.[8] That is, a scene depicting alchemy as a positive force, which can mend what's broken (and it offers a telling contrast with the brothers' desire to mend the ultimate break in life – death. But you can't fix death or illness as easily as a machine like a radio. In fact, the *Fullmetal Alchemist* series is firm on this point: you *cannot* 'fix' death... You *cannot* bring someone back to life). Meanwhile, the first time we see Ed performing alchemy is also characteristic: he fashions a flashy weapon from the floor!

The flashback in the *Fullmetal Alchemist manga* – and in the *animé* – also contrasts two groups of people who want to bring back someone who's dead, and the ways they're going about it: Rose Tomas hopes her boyfriend Cain can be returned from the dead, and she turns to religion and faith in God. The Elrics want their mother returned to them (and their maimed bodies), but by using alchemy. Both the Judæo-Christian-like cult of the Sun God Leto and the 'science' of alchemy are forms of belief, ways of looking at the world and life, and both have their flaws as well as their bonuses (the scene in the church, where the Elrics discuss the issue of death and resurrection with Rose, defines the central topic of the *Fullmetal Alchemist* series clearly).

As Himoru Arakawa said of *Fullmetal Alchemist*: 'The philosophical question, 'what does it mean to be living?', became the central pillar that filled the pages of the story'.

▲

The filmmakers of the first *Hagane no Renkinjutsushi* series have

---

8 That is foreshadowing, too, because the radio is the way in which the Elrics scupper Father Cornello.

followed the *manga* by Himoru Arakawa closely, but they have also added 100s of elements, and altered the story, too. They have introduced the villains earlier (such as Lust in the café scene), added monsters (the green bird), exaggerated the miracles that Father Cornello performs, added scenes of the faithful of Liore listening to their radios at a set time, changed the way that Cray attempts to dispatch the brothers (now it's in the church), changed the timeline, and also added scenes.

For example, the Elrics're first introduced in their older personas (with their ages changed to 14 and 15) in the desert, on their way to Liore (in the world of the *Fullmetal Alchemist manga*, the desert is far to the East, on the way to Xerxes and Xing. The scene recalls a later scene in the second *Fullmetal Alchemist* series, when van Hohenheim is depicted wandering lost in the desert). The scene is there to establish the personalities of the brothers (this's the first time we see them after their failed transmutation). There is some comic repartee which fills in some characterization for Ed and Al: we soon find out that altho' he's much smaller, Ed is very much the leader of the duo (Ed is regularly called '*chibi*-san' or something similar, which drives him nuts).

Introducing comedy right after a super-intense dramatic scene is one of the primary structural motifs of Arakawa-sensei's comic. It re-sets the story, relaxes the audience, and offers a breather. Comedy in *animé* of this kind isn't 'added on', isn't an artificial element, it's *absolutely fundamental*.

Other added scenes in *Fullmetal Alchemist* include one where Rose Tomas encounters her 'resurrected' lover, Cain (he turns out to be a chimera in the form of a giant bird). In a sinister image, like a sick nuptial scene, 'Cain' appears on a four poster bed, uttering 'Ro-se' behind drapes (it's a variation on the chimera created by Shou Tucker). In a subsequent scene, Cornello shows Rose the chimera, then promptly exits the room, locking her in, hoping it'll devour her, because he wants to get rid of all the people who know about the philosopher's stone. (What a cad! But, as it's the feeble kind of chimera, it expires on the floor, much to Rose's horror, after Al's leapt to her rescue – the *animé* elides Al nobbling the creature, and focusses on Rose's reaction). The statues of Leto come to life and attack our heroes *en masse* (this was used twice). Ed is imprisoned in a basement, and Alphonse tunnels in and places a mic in the wall. (This addition of the Cornello-Edward conflict fleshes out the running time of the second *Fullmetal Alchemist* episode, because in the *manga* the resolution is much quicker). Cornello's philosopher's stone rebounds (which gives Edward a chance to gain the upper hand); there's an *hommage* to the bio-mechanical arm of Tetsuo from *Akira* here.

Another alteration/ addition has Envy impersonating Cornello (who was killed by Gluttony, not Lust, as in the *manga*). This brings forward the concept of the homunculi politically destabilizing towns around Amestris (also, Lust mentions that the homunculi have used Liore to draw alchemists to it, which isn't in the *manga*. In the *animé*, the homunculi want to use alchemists for their own ends – to become human. This is a departure from Himoru Arakawa's *manga*, where the homunculi are all ultimately slaves of Father and his grand plan of becoming a god).

The first two episodes of *Fullmetal Alchemist* 'cover an amazing amount of material', as Julie Davies noted in *Zettai! Anime Classics* (122). And the themes of the series are set out, too, and Liore also features prominently later on: 'It's an impressive feat of continuity,' Davis remarked, 'and the story builds smoothly and believably to a fantastic final confrontation' (ibid).

Episodes 3. *Mother*

Episode 3 (*Mother* = *Okasan*) of *Fullmetal Alchemist* is a masterpiece of animation, and one of the great installments of *Fullmetal Alchemist* – of both series and any of the movies and Original Video Animations. Just look at how much writer Shou Aikawa squeezes into this episode!

Mother is entirely a flashback sequence, which explores the childhoods of Edward and Alphonse Elric: there are Hayao Miyazakian evocations of the mother-world, a happy childhood vision of blue skies, green grass, moorland, lakes, mountains and a young mother (Trisha – Yoshino Takamori – she plays the Elrics' mom in both series), who encourages the kids in the pursuit of alchemy (even at this young age, Edward is out-doing Alphonse, and we can see that Ed is more ambitious, more driven – as well as more impatient, and much, much angrier!).

However, there is a black cloud in their lives: the usual œdipal conflict, as their father (van Hohenheim – Masashi Ebara), also an alchemist, is absent. Edward in particular resents his absence, and its effect on his mom (notice that, in the title sequence, shown at the top of each *Fullmetal Alchemist* show, in the photograph of the happy family, there is a blur right over the father's face, so his identity remains something of a mystery (a common motif in *animé*). And *Mother* also retains that enigma about Hohenheim).

Himoru Arakawa's *manga* of *Fullmetal Alchemist* introduces the father van Hohenheim visually in a flashback sequence during the visit to the *sensei*, Izumi Curtis[9] (Shoko Tsuda – she played Curtis in both series): we see the father with his nose in his alchemical books, and a young Ed Elric at the door looking in.

Ah, the absent or distant father – how fantasy literature has mined that particular seam to the max! In *Fullmetal Alchemist*, it's mainly Ed who carries the intense, œdipal tensions, the bottled-up resentment (Ed of course blames his father's absence for his mother's illness – but it was a contagious disease). But the father doesn't appear in the present tense of the first *animé* series for a long time – you have to wait and wait for it.

As the childhood episodes progress in *Fullmetal Alchemist* – set in the Elrics' homeland of Resembool – a rural, farming community (an idealized version of Himoru Arakawa's roots in Hokkaido, perhaps,

9 Izumi Curtis is more prominent in the *animé* (that she is one of the avatars for author Himoru Arakawa is clear).

which she further explored in *Silver Spoon*) – the idyll comes to an end in a melodramatic manner, with the wasting away of the mother Trisha (Edward partly blames his father for his mother's illness – for being absent for too long). Thus the prologue which opens the 51-episode TV series of *Fullmetal Alchemist* is given more emotional and psychological weight. We go back to the alchemical experiment in the prologue,[10] and see how the children have studied their father's books and are putting their discoveries into practice (we have to suspend plenty of disbelief that two pre-teens could resurrect the dead just by learning how to do it in books! But that's what you can do if you *really* learn from books, folks! So keep a-studyin', kids!).[11]

Now we see the transmutation ritual (from the prologue of episode one) in full: the Elrics drawing the transformation circle on the floor at home, in their father's study, with the constituent elements of the human body at the centre of the magic circle in a tin bath (there is a litany of the body's physical ingredients: so many ounces (or grams) of iron, of lime, of carbon, of salt, and litres of water, etc).[12] And now we see exactly how the lads' resurrection experiment went horribly wrong (subsequent flash-backs to this scene will reveal slightly more, or slightly different images, each time, reflecting the parcelling-out of the flashbacks in Himoru Arakawa's *manga*).

The raising-the-dead ritual in 1.3: *Mother* is a masterpiece of staging and animation, with of course plenty of visual effects animation (since when did you see a Big Magical Spell in TV or cinema which *didn't* involve at least bright light, and ingredients like loud sound effects, and a powerful music cue? Like, never! Since the German silent movie era, spells/ magic/ wizardry is always accompanied by light).

The agony of the boys is brilliantly, strongly portrayed in ep. 3: *Mother*, with voice actresses Romi Pak and Rie Kugimiya delivering incredible performances as the wannabe Harry Potters. The filmmakers don't hold back on the consequences of the botched rite: we see plenty of blood, and the stumps of Edward Elric's limbs – and the remarkable footage of Al being sucked into the Black Hole of Nowhere, beyond the Gates of Truth, and Edward reaching out but unable to grasp his hand. (The first *Fullmetal Alchemist* series also includes more of the aftermath of the ceremony, with Al holding Ed in his arms, and taking him to Pinako and Winry).

The Elric boys do acknowledge that they were wrong, and that the fault was with them. They admit their mistakes – that's one attribute that distinguishes them from the villains. Because *Fullmetal Alchemist* uses one of the fundamental taboos of fairy tales and fantasy: that you can't bring someone back to life. You can't, you can't, you can't!

Fullmetal Alchemist also employs a simple morality of exchange (calling it 'equivalent exchange'): alchemy in this TV animated series

10 Which handily enables the producers to re-use the same footage.
11 And also that nobody seems to be looking after the kids, either.
12 As if this is all a person is in the end – just a bunch of chemicals and substances. As the Elric boys learn to their dismay, there is more to a human being than physical attributes.

means exchanging one thing for another (dubbed the 'Law of Equivalent Exchange' and the 'Law of Conservation of Energy'). You can't get something for nothing here. For alchemy to work, it has to be exchanged for something else. There has to be a sacrifice (it's another way of depicting the Faustian pact of Western literature. It also reminds me of the *Earthsea* books by Ursula Le Guin, which speak of the cosmic balance of power in the world, and how magic mustn't upset that balance).[13]

What makes the morality of *Fullmetal Alchemist* work is the bare physical facts of the exchange (that is, the universe has physical laws which can't be altered, so you've just got to live with them), coupled with the earnestness of the Elric boys. Wanting to bring your mother back to life is completely understandable. The boys might be misguided (the grandmother figure Pinako (Miyoko Asou – she was Pinako in both series) tells them it is wrong, and should not be done), but you can understand where they are coming from.

When their mother Trisha dies, the Elric kids're helped by their neighbours: one is the severe grandmother Pinako who acts as an authority figure (enforcing the expected limits and prohibitions), and the other is a childhood friend, a girl, Pinako's granddaughter, Winry Rockbell (Megumi Toyoguchi[14]) (the filmmakers often put a girl into the mix, for all of the obvious reasons, of audience, appeal, theme, drama, romance – in the 2005 *Fullmetal Alchemist* movie, it's Noah (Miyu Sawai), in the first two episodes of *Fullmetal Alchemist*, it's Rose Tomas; in the 3rd and 4th episodes, it's Winry; later on, it's Martel, etc).

Winry Rockbell is shown weeping following the news of the death of her parents, a scene which appears (in flashback) much later in the *Fullmetal Alchemist manga*. Here, it dramatically foreshadows the Elrics' mother death, and is also linked narratively to the brothers' ideas that people can be brought back to life (this is really superb screenwriting!). Ed suggests that they could do it; Pinako's response is instant and firm: *no*; meanwhile, Winry, distraught, insists that no one can come back. (Winry's parents' demise also foreshadows a theme that will preoccupy the *anime* series: war. The Rockbells were doctors who went to help in the Ishbal conflict).

And then the death scene – in most children's or teenagers' stories of this fantasy/ adventure kind, the parents are usually already out of the picture. It's not often done to go back and show the death of a parent in

---

13 In the first *Earthsea* book, the wizard Gensher talks about 'the balance of light and dark, life and death, good and evil'. In the *Earthsea* cycle, what the hero Ged has to learn is not to fight situations, but to 'go with the flow' (a Taoist notion). Ged has to align himself with 'the Way', with the Tao. Ogion and other wizards speak of the balance of magic in the world, but Ged has to learn the hard way about that balance. As a youngster, it doesn't seem real to him, doesn't have any substance. He can't see the (effects of the) 'balance' or 'the Way' in operation, in the real world. It's too much in the abstract still. It takes real events, like summoning up the dead and loosing the shadow, for Ged to realize there are far greater forces at work in the world, and they can directly, adversely affect him. *Fullmetal Alchemist* has a similar breach of the balance of magic without its scene of the two heroes trying to raise their mother from the dead.
14 Toyoguchi (b. Jan 2, 1978) is another veteran of *anime* who's been in everything: she is the sexy gunslinger Revy in *Black Lagoon*, Haruka in *Senran Kagura*, Hikari in *Pokemon*, Yukari in *Persona 3*, Klan Klang in *Macross Frontier*, Sei in *Maria Watches Over Us*, Chifuyu in *Infinite Stratos*, Meg in *Burst Angel*, Kiyoko in *Initial D*, Tsukasa in *Ichigo 100%*, Mimiru in *Hack/ Sign*, and Mihiro in *Gundam*.

full, as here, and in the foreground of the piece. But – wow! – it sure gives the *Fullmetal Alchemist* series a huge injection of emotion!

On her deathbed, Trisha's last words are encouragements for her children. They both hold her hand, which falls. It's beautifully achieved – as is the subsequent cemetery scene, played out in long shot and successive lap dissolves, as everybody leaves except for Ed and Al, standing before the grave (sort of following the *Fullmetal Alchemist manga*). It's here (against the beloved molten orange sunset sky of *animé*), that Edward utters the fateful words of a four-foot six Viktor Frankenstein: let's bring mom back to life.

This is really tremendous filmmaking!

Indeed, the filmmakers rarely put a foot wrong in the early episodes of the first *Fullmetal Alchemist* series; the animation, the staging, the visuals, the themes, the characters, the action and above all the storytelling are just marvellous to behold (and Michiru Oshima's music performs outstanding accompaniments – in particular the lovely choral cue that fades up in the last part of the *Mother* episode, a song of wistful yearning).

These filmmakers know storytelling inside-out. Only once or twice do they slip up: having Edward and Alphonse burn their childhood house down when they decide to leave to become State Alchemists is way too extreme an act (but it is in the *Fullmetal Alchemist manga*). You just don't do that to your beloved childhood home! It's the invading knights/ soldiers/ aliens/ baddies who do that! It's the nasty men on horseback who ride into the village to rape and pillage and torch the place! You don't have the heroes burning their *own* house down! Come on, whose idea at the writing table was that?

✳

In episode 3: *Mother*, the filmmakers depart from the *manga* by Himoru Arakawa at many points – this is, after all, mainly an anime-only episode, but with a dead true emotional structure. A big departure is that the alchemically metallic *manga* goes straight from the events in Liore to another adventure, in the mining town (seen in a following *animé* episode). The filmmakers also introduce Major (sometimes called Colonel)[15] Roy Mustang (Toru Ohkawa) who appears out of the rainstorm on the night of the ritual (yes, of course, it's raining hard that night! Never miss a chance for some Gothic atmospherics). Mustang (a fan favourite chara), announces the government's interest in the Elrics (perhaps even more'n their father).

Episode 3: *Mother* also adds short vignettes from the Elrics' early life: we see them at several ages, often performing or studying alchemy. They make a doll for Winry Rockbell (which scares her), for instance, and toys for their mother (the dog – which comes from the *manga*). They write letters to their pa, following their mom's death (which's a legitimate reason for Roy Mustang paying a visit – tho' a rainy evening is not a civil time to call! Pinako rightly tells Mustang to leave immediately).

Training with an alchemy teacher is noted in the voiceover, but not

15 Notice how the filmmakers *always* have the characters using the official names of the military characters: Titles are very important in Japanese society.

shown much – yet. We come back to it later (instead, 3: *Mother* glosses over that, but does include some images from York Island, couched in a flickbook style).

You can see, from the above paragraphs, just how much the filmmakers have shoe-horned into episode 3: *Mother*! – and we haven't yet mentioned items such as the medical operation performed by Pinako and Winry to attach Ed's automail, or the important scenes at the lakeside when Ed and Al spar with each other (seen in silhouette), and decide to become alchemists for the government, so they can work out how to become whole again.

This is a vital scene, and it also expresses the differences btn the brothers – how Edward is always pushing harder than Alphonse, how Al follows his brother's example, and also how much they are devoted to each other.

Episode 4. *A Forger's Love*

This episode is the first of the major inventions by the writers and producers of the 2003-04 *Fullmetal Alchemist* series, to bulk up the series to a 51-episode run (the previous episode, 3: *Mother*, was also largely invention, tho' it expanded upon material already in the *Fullmetal Alchemist manga*. Episode four, tho', is chiefly invention).

It plays rather like an episode of *Scooby Doo* or a kids' TV show or a *Harry Potter* outing, where pesky, nosy kids meet dodgy, older characters and uncover dubious goings-on in a neighbourhood (another 'Sins of the Fathers' trope, with the younger generation in Japan showing the oldsters just what they think of them and their corrupt ways. *Animé* dines out on conflicts between the younger generation and the older generation all the time). Episode 4: *A Forger's Love* takes up many elements from elsewhere in the *Fullmetal Alchemist manga*, and re-arranges them: stopping on a train journey; encountering a questionable alchemist (this looks forward to Shou Tucker); a young girl character (who crossdresses); and explorations of the resurrection of the dead theme (which reflects the Elrics' transmutation).

A Forger's Love includes a high drama scenario featuring the sinister alchemist Majhal (Takaya Hashi) who's exploring the murkier sides of alchemy (he's trying to resurrect his dead lover Karin using the souls of girls from the village which're fused to mannequins that he's fashioned to look like Karin. But Karin didn't die (in a spectacular mountain road accident) – she aged and lost her memory, and has recently remembered all, and made her way back to Majhal). Majhal is another of the many ambiguous authority and father figures in the *Fullmetal Alchemist* series (that he is highly regarded by the local community is also part of the mystery).

The Elric brothers meet a girl, Clause (Akiko Yajima), who's dressed as a boy: her sister died some time ago, and Clause is keen to discover the secrets of her demise (suspecting the murderer may be the mysterious zombie that haunts the area, as local legend has it). The alchemist Majhal, who corresponds by letter with the Elrics' father Hohenheim, invites the lads to his place for a cup of tea and a chat. Ed, ever restless and impatient, gets right to the point: they want to know anything that'll help them pursue the possibility of restoring their bodies. (The new charas here, Karin, Clause and Majhal, don't appear in the *Fullmetal Alchemist manga*).

As episode 4: *A Forger's Love* progresses, it's entertaining and swiftly-paced, tho' it lacks the passion and fire of the finer *Fullmetal Alchemist* shows, and the mystery that the pint-sized sleuths solve is a little too pat and unengaging (it's Ed Elric who takes the lead, once again). However, episode 4: *A Forger's Love* does depict the two Elrics in full flight, working together, and revealing more of their personalities. (For instance, the boys discuss their plans on the train. We also see them catching a purse-snatcher using alchemy at a rail station. Like the *Scooby Doo* or *Harry Potter* teams, they are rather irritating do-gooders at this point).

Show 4: *A Forger's Love* works thematically: it mirrors once again the Elrics' desire to bring back their mother from the dead. This time, it's adult, romantic love, between Majhal and Karin, that drives Majhal to try to resurrect Karin. So Majhal's goal is understandable – but killing young girls is not the way to go about achieving it! (Majhal is the first of a whole coven of serial killers introduced rapidly in this series – they include the religious zealot from Hell, Scar; Barry the Chopper, the blade-wielding slasher from Hell; and Tucker, the Bad Father from Hell).

❀

Episode 4: *A Forger's Love* moves to an action finale with our heroes imprisoned by Majhal, while he kidnaps little Clause in order to conduct another alchemical bonding of spirits to mannequins (having rejected the aged Karin when she is revealed by Edward Elric. Majhal is so fixated on his obsession with the young Karin and her blue roses, he can't see or won't acknowledge the real person who stands in front of him).

I have noted that Himoru Arakawa, like most authors with teen heroes, doesn't want either of the Elric brothers to be a killer, but Majhal does fight with the Elrics, and he is killed in the struggle. The boys rush in to save the princess – Clause is tied to a chair in the middle of an alchemical transmutation circle drawn on the floor. Majhal responds by magically fashioning a sword: during the struggle, it spins in the air, and impales Majhal (so it's really an accident; and the filmmakers are careful to show that Majhal attacked them first, and that he is also about to kill Clause, and has also slain others). This is the first death in the present tense of the *Fullmetal Alchemist* series (the first of many!). Majhal had it coming to him, by the morality of this show (and adventure and fantasy shows of this type): he has kidnapped and killed several girls from the village over the years.

Episode 5. *The Man With the Mechanical Arm (Dash! Automail)*

On the way to the capital (Central) in episode 5: *The Man With the Mechanical Arm (Dash! Automail)*, before the Elrics had become State Alchemists (so this episode takes place *before* the first two episodes), there's a classic kids-versus-bad-guys adventure, as Elrics Ed and Al scupper a bunch of criminals (led by bad guy Bald) taking over a railroad train (in order to take a General hostage and force the release of one of their number). It might have come from an Enid Blyton story, a cowboy movie from the 1930s-1970s, a TV serial from the 1960s-1970s, or any of 100s of *manga*. It was dropped from the 2nd series, but appeared in the live-action movies.

The Man With the Mechanical Arm is a fun episode in the first *Fullmetal Alchemist* run in which there is no life-or-death threat (tho' death is of course on offer from the kidnapping gang[16]), and the emphasis is on broad humour and out-size action (plus, the episode, scripted by Aya Yoshinaga, has time for slower, softer scenes, which could be taken as padding. It's some 7.5 minutes, for instance, before the thugs start their take-over of the train).

The filmmakers include every stunt and gag you've ever seen set on a railroad train. And of course our brave heroes win the day, and trump the villains with some alchemical bravado. Edward Elric transmutes the sides of a carriage into a cannon which fires at a heavy on the roof, and uses the water supply for the locomotive to stage a flood which scuppers the bad guys.[17] Meanwhile, Alphonse gets to beat up some villains (repeatedly), and have them fire rounds at him which bounce back and injure them (a gag used once in the *manga*, and twice here).

Episode 5: *The Man With the Mechanical Arm (Dash! Automail)* is a knockabout, boysy adventure, with our heroes coming over as plucky kids who have the intelligence and means to run rings around the dim-witted bad guys. The theme of the military is important, however: the show introduces many of the characters in the Army of Amestris who become key secondary characters as the series unfolds: Mustang, Hughes, Falman, and Hawkeye.

The Elric brothers're on their way to Central City in order to become State Alchemists, and to work for the military (so this show follows on from the end of 4: *A Forger's Love*): the chief bad guy, Bald, is a resentful, former soldier who now despises the military (the villains' aim is to hold an officer, General Hakuro, and his family hostage).

Episode 5: *The Man With the Mechanical Arm (Dash! Automail)* follows Himoru Arakawa's *manga* for most of the time, but it does add elements of its own. For instance, Maes Hughes is introduced here: he's on the train[18] (our heroes team up with him, so they don't defeat the heavies wholly on their own; Falman is also there). Bringing Hughes-san in here is a ploy to introduce the audience to him earlier, because his death is a

---

16 There is plenty of aggression on display, however, and characters are punched many times.
17 Would that work? Maybe not, but it's a fun variation on the railroad adventure scenario.
18 Frank Archer is also introduced on a train – in episode 29: *The Untainted Child.*

major catalyst in *Fullmetal Alchemist*'s over-arching story (this is why there are several scenes where Hughes is enthusing over his wife and baby-to-be, much to the irritation of Roy Mustang – to make his death all the more tragic later on).

Also, *Fullmetal Alchemist* is full of useless or negligent or even murderous fathers – Hohenheim is the first one cited in the series, and Tucker is soon introduced (in ep. 6) – a man who kills his wife and daughter. Hughes thus offers a positive, cheerful contrast to these bad eggs.

Other additions to episode 5: *The Man With the Mechanical Arm* include yet another moppet for the Elrics to bond with (Marin, played by Emi Motoi), and several minor charas (among the train passengers).

Running over only four pages in the *Fullmetal Alchemist manga*, the face-off btn Bald and Ed Elric is much bigger than that in the *animé*. Much *longer*, for a start: as they grapple hands and automail arms, Bald explains plenty, over several pages of monologue (while Maes Hughes listens, injured after being shot).

There is also the suggestion in *The Man With the Mechanical Arm* that Colonel Roy Mustang, the 'Flame Alchemist', is manipulating events, as well as the Elric brothers themselves (the ambiguity of Mustang is a running gag in the *Fullmetal Alchemist* series, tho' not made explicit – in the second *animé* series of *Fullmetal Alchemist*, he's played straighter). At the end of episode 5: *The Man With the Mechanical Arm*, Mustang, as in the *manga*, is waiting at Central's railroad station for the train: Bald makes one last bid to escape, and Mustang demonstrates why he is called the 'Flame Alchemist' (frazzling Bald, but not killing him). Mustang informs the Elrics that they are able to take the exam to become State Alchemists.

It becomes a minor sub-plot of *Fullmetal Alchemist* that the military's officers exploit the Elrics, so they become (derided as) 'dogs of the military'. This recurring put-down is one of the political critiques of the *Fullmetal Alchemist* series – that soldiers and officers are simply 'dogs of the military', or the puppets of politicians. *Join the Army and become a slave*, to put it another way. Yet in *Fullmetal Alchemist*, the State Alchemists also work 'for the people', and characters such as Ed Elric remind other characters of that when they are stepping away from working for the common good (in this episode, 1.5: *The Man With the Mechanical Arm (Dash! Automail)*, the Elrics are working for the good guys – they automatically side with the hostages (despite the fact that the kidnappers, the 'Blue Squad', have their own agenda (Bald explains that was he was also in the military). We have already seen the brothers stopping and imprisoning a street thief, and bringing a wayward alchemist (Majhal) to justice, and uncovering a fake religion).

Episode 6. *The Alchemy Exam*

In episode 6: *The Alchemy Exam* of *Fullmetal Alchemist*, the Elric boys are deep into studying for the State Alchemist examination (we are still in the flashback structure, where Ed is 12 and Al is 11).[19] *Fullmetal Alchemist* is no different from thousands of *manga* and *anime* in emphasizing the value of working hard, of studying, of achieving your full potential (if you consume a lot of Japanese pop culture, you can't help noticing that the Japanese portray themselves as a nation of workaholics and over-achievers. *Gambaru*! (do your best) is a recurring phrase exchanged in this sort of show. Throwing your *all* into every pursuit is absolutely essential). *Fullmetal Alchemist* is not really a franchise about magical kids *à la Harry Potter* (tho' it is that, too), it's really about growing up, about finding your way in the complicated adult world, about discovering your true identity, about being a teenager, about being cast adrift in the world after your parents die or disappear.

There is also a family theme in episode 1.6: *The Alchemy Exam* – the Elrics are present when Maes Hughes' wife Gracia goes into labour, a scene largely played for very broad, hysterical comedy (everybody's rushing around panicking. The voice actresses let themselves rip with some wild and funny screaming). There's a nice comment in this episode, when Ed and co. are confronted with Gracia about to give birth, while hubby Maes Hughes dashes away to fetch the doctor in a snowstorm, and Ed realizes that altho' alchemy is amazing, it isn't a patch on a mother having a baby! *Manga* author Hiromu Arakawa is stating the obvious to men, in the manner of Mel Brooks: you guys might have alchemy and magic, but, *oh!*, can you make a baby?!

The score for episode 6: *The Alchemy Exam* is a traditional, Western, orchestral score, unashamedly sweet, in keeping with the emphasis on families and babies. Composer Michiru Oshima delivers some lovely cues which seem to evoke early Gustav Mahler or Dimitri Shostakovitch (opting for many Western, classical musical forms fits the world of Amestris, with its Central European flavour, even tho' Amestris is, of course, really Japan).

Meanwhile, it's Al Elric who is narrating the events of episode 6: *The Alchemy Exam*, from some point in the future, a big departure from the *manga* (which doesn't go in much for those novelistic devices). This show was written by Natsuko Takahashi.

The Elrics are staying with Shou Tucker (Makoto Nagai), his daughter Nina and their dog Alex. Tucker is a hapless alchemist who turns out to be a very nasty guy, exploiting his wife and his daughter and even his pet pooch in the pursuit of alchemical fame (which we see very soon. But not in this episode, which's generally a sweet show. So, enjoy the scenes of the kids playing in the snow, or the family chatting at the dinner table, or Ed and Al deep into their book studies in the library, because they won't last forever).

The first *Fullmetal Alchemist* series alters the *Fullmetal Alchemist manga* at this point, including:

(1) adding an entry exam for State Alchemists;

---

19 Al is persuaded (by Roy Mustang) not to take the exam. Ed receives a silver pocket watch (which's exploited by the screenwriters later, when it's thought to amplify alchemy, which isn't in the *manga*).

(2) shifting the birth from another part of the *manga*;

(3) having the Elrics stay with Tucker-san & co. much longer (it might be weeks);

(4) adding a birthday party for Ed (at Hughes' place – this is a variation on Winry being invited by Hughes to his child's birthday party);

(5) adding scenes where the Elrics're hanging out with Nina and the family dog Alex;

(6) adding (recurring) scenes where the boys ruminate on events in their bedroom at night;

and (7) adding a narration for Alphonse Elric.

The alchemy exam itself is broken down into sections – a written paper; an interview with the high-ranking officials (including the first introduction of Führer Bradley); and a practical session, where would-be State Alchemists are tested in the parade grounds (Führer Bradley presides over the exams, in his jolly persona, b4 he becomes the Psycho From Hell).

In both *animé* series Hidekatsu Shibata, a famous voice in *animé*, played the Führer (he's the Third Hokage in *Naruto*, Igneel/ narrator in *Fairy Tail*, and Dragon senior in *One Piece*). Shibata can be the kindly grandfather type (as in *Naruto*), but he's also very commanding (and scary at times), the voice of a Shogun. Shibata is completely convincing as a military ruler.

Edward Elric watches the grown-up alchemists before him conjure impressive transmutations. But when they go wrong (a balloon of gas crashes into a tall pillar), Ed rushes in to save the day by performing alchemy without using a transmutation circle (and hence passing the alchemy exam with flying colours).

In the final scene (again with the beloved molten-golden-sunset *mise-en-scène*), as the boys walk back to Shou Tucker's home, Edward insists that he is going to grant Al's wish, and get his body back. Which gives us our sweet ending. (Alphonse's disappointment that he can't take the State Alchemist's Exam is touched on, but not as much as if it was *Ed* who had been denied entrance![20]).

Episode 7. *Night of the Chimera's Cry*

Bang!

In episode 7 of *Fullmetal Alchemist* – *Night of the Chimera's Cry* (broadcast on November 15, 2003) – serious themes return to *Fullmetal Alchemist* following two much lighter shows, and the issues are dramatized to an operatic level (we're back to that incredibly intense opening prologue in the opening episode, and the death of the mother in ep. 3), in one of the most hard-hitting *Fullmetal Alchemist* episodes (beautifully scripted by head writer Shou Aikawa).

And as this is very much an Edward Elric show, and as it's so highly

---

20 Mustang's manipulations behind the scenes are touched on, too: he tells Hawkeye that he wasn't expecting Alphonse to pass the written exam. Thus, in an alley, Mustang informs Al that can't take the exam; Al is very disheartened.

melodramatic, voice actress Romi Pak must be celebrated here. Actors love this kind of role, where they can go all-out in pursuing deep emotions and expressing them. At times, even when every other cinematic element is sensational, it's the voice acting that really cuts through.

In *Night of the Chimera's Cry*, the down-on-his-luck State Alchemist Shou Tucker, who's taken in the Elric boys while they study for the alchemy exam in Central City, turns out to be *very* twisted. As the *Night of the Chimera's Cry* episode unfolds, you're not quite sure how it's going to play out: *animé* shows often do this – they have the ability (actually difficult to achieve), to surprise you again and again. (The themes had already been explored in episode 4: *A Forger's Love*, where the alchemist Majhal had kidnapped local girls and killed them. However, the tone of that episode was a little lighter, played more like a children's mystery story or a TV adventure serial, and the girls weren't killed on screen).

So when Shou Tucker transmutes his own daughter (the *kawaii* cutie Nina – Satomi Koorogi)[21] and the family dog Alexander into a chimera (a magical beast that can talk and understand words), *Fullmetal Alchemist* becomes pretty creepy and very cruel. Edward Elric is on Tucker's case: he realizes that two years ago Tucker transmuted his own wife into a chimera (but the creature didn't survive, according to Tucker).

To build up the characters of Nina and her dog, there are *kawaii* scenes early on in episode 7: *Night of the Chimera's Cry* (such as Nina writing a letter to her mom – which mirrors Edward Elric writing to Winry (in English) about becoming a State Alchemist – we see Ed brandishing his pocket watch at the top of the episode, which picks up from the finale of the previous episode, of the Alchemists' Exam).

For a TV show to introduce a cute girl like Nina and then to kill her is fairly unusual and *very* extreme. And the family dog! (You're kidding? – *not* the dog?! Yes, even the dawg!). And it's not done as a joke: this part of *Fullmetal Alchemist* isn't *The Simpsons* (like one of the *Simpsons'* marvellous Hallowe'en episodes), it's played straight.

And the filmmakers of *Fullmetal Alchemist* don't stop there: they depict Ed and Al Elric sneaking in to Shou Tucker's home and uncovering the truth; they have Ed confronting Tucker with his diabolical schemes, and Ed launching himself at Tucker, punching him repeatedly and very hard (and as if he knows he deserves it, the pathetic Tucker doesn't defend himself). Again, it's pretty rare to have a young character (twelve years-old) seriously attacking an adult like this. Then the filmmakers go even further: they introduce a sinister, spiky-haired bruiser with a nefarious tattoo on his arm (who isn't explained yet, but we know he's got to be a villain; earlier, the military have alerted us to a serial killer on the loose). And this guy – later identified as Scar (Ryotaro Okiayu) – kills the Nina-and-dog chimera in an alley! (While spouting out about the work of God). Wow!

And there's a moral issue at stake here, which the chief *Fullmetal Alchemist* writer Shou Aikawa foregrounds: Shou Tucker, on the floor

21 Cute characters – *kawaii* – are a staple of Japanese animation: Pikachu in *Pokémon,* for example, or young women in *manga* and *animé.*

after Ed Elric's smashed his face with his fist again and again, says he's not that much different from Ed and Al, who've also played around with human life in their pursuit of alchemy. So Ed might not be successful when he tries to transmute Nina and the dog back into their former selves. There is thus a genuine ethical complexity and ambiguity to *Fullmetal Alchemist* – this is not just a crazy cartoon about magical kids, it has a real heart, a real thoughtfulness.

Thus, by episode 7: *Night of the Chimera's Cry*, the filmmakers have depicted two instances where alchemy is not used for the good of all, but for the selfish pursuits of very dubious ends by two middle-aged men. And they have pitted two young and idealistic characters against these corrupt, mis-led and vicious guys. (An added moral complexity is introduced for our heroes: joining the Army means becoming 'a dog of the military', according to Edward – State Alchemists are used as weapons).

▼

The finale of this vivid, classy episode shifts into Gothic horror territory: at night, the Elrics hurry back to the Tucker home, finding the alchemist in the basement, surrounded by his botched experiments (angry animals in cages), with transmutation circles drawn everywhere, including on the ceiling. The filmmaking includes German Expressionist shadows and low-level, glowing lighting.

Edward Elric is leading the drama throughout this episode (with Alphonse able to do little but hang onto his coattails): the show cuts back to Ed's close-up many times as he questions Shou Tucker, examines the chimera, and has his suspicions confirmed, that Tucker has transmuted his daughter Nina and dog Alex into a chimera. While Ed has punched Tucker, Ed himself gets whacked on the head – by Basque Grand, outside Tucker's home, when the alchemist is taken away by the authorities. (There is a slight flub in the adaptation from the *Fullmetal Alchemist manga* here: when Edward performs alchemy to prevent the Army van taking away Tucker and the chimera, the chimera escapes into the night. That the Elrics take too long to race after it is silly; that the Nina-dog chimera doesn't come over to them but wanders off is also unconvincing. But it's necessary, so that the chimera can encounter Scar in the alley. Oh dear, of all the alleys in all of Amestris, the chimera has to enter this one! The *Fullmetal Alchemist* series contains plenty of dark alleys!).

The night of Gothic horror culminates in episode 7: *Night of the Chimera's Cry* with the truly awful scene of Scar killing the chimera, and Ed and Al Elric discovering the splattered remains of the chimera on the wall of the alley soon afterwards. It's very nasty stuff: however you look at it, a five year-old girl has been killed in order for her father to pass an exam which will give him research funding.

▼

Ed Elric does some detective spadework in episode 7: *Night of the Chimera's Cry*, visiting the State library to uncover information on Shou Tucker, but he's denied access (we first meet Sheska here); resourceful Ed goes to see Maes Hughes, and finds out that Tucker's wife died.

Of the many additions and alterations to the chapter in the *manga* (*The Alchemist's Suffering*), Basque Grand is introduced to act an obstacle to Ed's investigations; Grand's an officer who's backing Tucker-san's alchemical experiments. When the 'Iron Blood Alchemist' finds out that Ed has been investigating Tucker, he has the Elrics taken out of Tucker's home (at gunpoint! And they're kids!). The second *Fullmetal Alchemist* series barely used Grand.

▼

Scar is introduced in episode 7: *Night of the Chimera's Cry* as a powerful but haunted and hunted man: he is soon revealed as the serial killer who's nobbling State Alchemists in his one-man Mission From God (but also, yes, he *is* walking around Central City in daylight with a very distinctive look, despite being a Wanted Man! Well, this is before he starts his killing spree).

However, when we first meet Scar, he's on the steps of the library, and Edward Elric bumps into him and accidentally rips his jacket, uncovering the arm of alchemical tattoos which Scar inherited from his brother (along with the actual arm itself!). Scar flees like a guilty child, to lurk in yet another dark alley, which's where the very unfortunate chimera Nina ends up. (Earlier, there was a scene in another alley where the military are investigating a corpse, another victim of the killer. This beat (and its consequence), added to the *manga*, leads Edward to pass out as he flashes back to the transmutation ritual of years ago. (In a gruesome touch, the woman's corpse is posed similarly to the botched creature of the Elrics' mom).

Many of the additions to Himoru Arakawa's *manga* push Edward Elric into the foreground, making the inquiries into Shou Tucker even more emotional for him. So there are scenes added to the *manga* – such as where Ed faints, where he sees a murder victim, where he talks about what happened with Tucker (afterwards), where Ed visits the library (and meets Scar), where he encounters Basque Grand and his squad blocking his investigation, etc.

A big departure from the *manga* has Shou Tucker surviving: in the *manga*, he is dispatched by Scar (who then turns on the Nina-chimera and kills it, too). In the morality of *manga* aimed at teens, Tucker should die for killing his wife and his daughter. But the filmmakers opted to bring back Tucker later on (as a chimera!).

Episode 8. *The Philosopher's Stone*

And in the next episode, 8: *The Philosopher's Stone*, the chief writer on *Fullmetal Alchemist*, Shou Aikawa, screws up the moral complexity even tighter, when it's revealed that the mass murderer and chief suspect Barry the Chopper (shame about the name!) wasn't the serial killer who slew Nina and the dog Alex transmuted into the chimera – there is *another* psycho on the loose! Two serial killers in one show! Talk about about *heavy* and *sinister*! No, *chotto* – by episode 8 of this series we have seen four serial killers, no less: Majihal in ep. 4, Tucker, Scar and now Barry the Chopper.

So when cute, blonde, girlie, tomboy Winry Rockbell treks from the Resembool homeland to see her childhood friends the Elric brothers in the capital (to congratulate Edward on becoming a State Alchemist), she is captured by this new murderer (who dresses as a woman – a touch of crossdressing and *Psycho*. Yes, it is a cliché of genre fiction that murderers have to be sexually mixed up, or perverse, or enact some gender confusion). Winry's brought into the narrative of *The Philosopher's Stone* largely to be a victim for Edward Elric[22] to rescue – because Ed is also captured (and taken to a meat factory, where the carcasses of pigs and cows are hung up – a total cliché as a setting for a serial killer outing or any thriller, but it works. It looks forward to Arakawa's *Silver Spoon* comic).

The new mass murderer, Barry the Chopper (terrific OTT voice work by Kentarou Itou),[23] is one of those manic, giggling freaks who laugh as they slice 'n' dice (he's killed 23 people! For kicks! He admits it was all for kicks!). And so poor Edward Elric is once again pitted against a crazed adult, tied to a chair while Barry makes ready to chop him up with a meat cleaver *à la Sweeney Todd*. Winry is chained up like a piece of meat. The filmmakers push the jeopardy to the max, with Ed being repeatedly threatened, cut with the blade, struggling to free Winry, and barely escaping Barry's attacks, until Alphonse intercedes, to stop his brother killing the murderer, as he did with Ed and Shou Tucker.

Don't let the bright colours, the goofy comedy and the charming character designs fool you that this isn't 'dark' or bitter: this series has already depicted multiple deaths, child murder, plenty of violence, resurrection from the dead, and insane psychos flailing meat cleavers and cutting our hero.

❋

Meanwhile in episode 8: *The Philosopher's Stone*, Alphonse Elric introduces the theme of the philosopher's stone, a key motif which will loom large in the rest of the *Fullmetal Alchemist animé* series. Edward is instantly dismissive (his instinct proves him right), but Al reckons it might be some help in their quest to regain their bodies (Ed is still deeply affected by Nina's death, and spends quite a bit of episodes 7 and 8 raging about it – to anybody who'll listen). We also see Al encountering Führer Bradley, as well as Liza Hawkeye (added from the *manga*). The Führer encourages Al in his search for the philosopher's stone – we don't know why yet (because it's part of the homunculi's plans). Here, the leader of Amestris is depicted as an indulgent, kindly uncle, not the psychopath he becomes. (Hidekatsu Shibata can do polite, gentle, reassuring voices as well as stern Emperors).

Nobody can miss just how much Edward Elric is portrayed in a

---

22 Ed is much more to the fore in this episode. Ed is usually at the front of the action in *Fullmetal Alchemist*, and the series is nearly always at its finest when Ed (and Al) are at the forefront.
23 The depiction of Barry the serial killer is ridiculously over-cooked (it includes grotesque wide angle close-ups, for instance).

hysterical, tearful state in episodes 7 and 8 of the first series of *Fullmetal Alchemist*. It's probably too much with the weeping and the sulking, tho' it usually is Edward who carries the emotional catharsis in *Fullmetal Alchemist*. Ed is by far the most passionate character in the series – and one of the most fiery in all *animé* (again, the way that voice actress Romi Pak delivers the role, and the way that she has been directed by sound director Masafumi Mima, enhances Ed's highly emotional states no end).

❀

Elsewhere in episode 8: *The Philosopher's Stone*, Edward Elric has several arguments with Roy Mustang – he hands in his State Alchemist pocket watch, disillusioned by being a 'dog of the military' (Ed deeply resents being ordered to investigate Shou Tucker's alchemical research. For him, Tucker is a callous murderer, and the chore of going thru the guy's research and having to feed the botched creature experiments in Tucker's laboratory probably irks both Elrics). By the end of the show, he takes up the job again, now he knows that being a State Alchemist gives him special privileges for research into philosopher's stones and other arcane alchemical matters. And Scar is kept in the loop, with some rather contrived encounters with our heroes (like bumping into Edward in the street, a reprise of the library encounter, which is seen in a brief flashback montage). At the end of the episode, Scar spots that Ed has his pocket watch back again – so now he is a potential victim for Scar.

❀

The filmmakers have departed from the *manga* by Himoru Arakawa at numerous points in episode 8 of *Fullmetal Alchemist* – having Winry Rockbell being kidnapped (which the *manga* doesn't do, or have her come to Central City like this); the whole Barry the Chopper section[24] (with Ed captured, and the subsequent fight); Al meeting Führer Bradley and Liza Hawkeye; and Shou Tucker facing a firing squad, described to Ed by Hughes and glimpsed in flashback (in the *manga*, Scar kills both Tucker and his chimera).

THE SINS OF THE FATHERS.

The twistedness of the father figures in *Fullmetal Alchemist* is instantly apparent – this is a TV series that's all about the Sins of the Fathers, about how the Sins of the Fathers are visited upon their offspring (it's about the uneasy relationship between the older and the younger generation in Japan, a recurring motif in *animé* and *manga*), about how ambiguous and corrupt the adult world looks to children, and about how there are so few really genuinely decent guys in the world anymore.

Who can Ed and Al Elric in *Fullmetal Alchemist* look up to? Answer: almost nobody.

Who can they rely on? Answer: almost nobody.

Who can Ed and Al trust? Answer: almost nobody.

In *Fullmetal Alchemist*, kids are thrown back on their own resources. And when adults do take them into their homes, supposedly to feed them

---

24 The filmmakers have taken the back-story of Barry the Chopper from a later installment of the *manga*, and expanded it and brought it into the present tense of the series.

and look after them, they turn out to be murderers, who transmute their own wives, children and dogs in the pursuit of alchemical perfection!

Thus, *Fullmetal Alchemist* is also all about the search for the lost mother-world, those comforting arms that go around you with no weirdness attached, no subterfuge, no conditions, and nothing expected in return. Unconditional love – how Ed and Al crave it, to the point where they want to find the famed philosopher's stone of alchemy in order to transmute their bodies (and perhaps even bring back their mother). The loss of the mother haunts all of *Fullmetal Alchemist,* and the father substitutes that are introduced are *all* disappointing to the Elric boys: the men are portrayed as weak, violent, over-ambitious, dictatorial, unforgiving, manipulative, over-bearing, and insensitive. By Ishtar, is there *one single decent man* in the world of *Fullmetal Alchemist*? Not really! Even characters such as Roy Mustang, the alchemist officer who was early on introduced as an important father figure to Ed and Al, and apparently on the side of 'good' and "right', is also ambiguous: he takes the 'tough love' approach to Ed. For Mustang, Ed may be a twelve year-old State Alchemist (and given the monicker 'Fullmetal Alchemist' in this episode), but he is also a kid that needs to be told what to do. (And some of the mother surrogates are dubious, too: Izumi Curtis, for example, their former teacher, seems to have the Elric boys' best interests at heart, and she gives them that Big, Motherly Hug, but she is also psychotically violent towards them, and repressively aggressive. And Lt. Ross, an officer assigned to look over them, smacks Ed full in the face!).

Episode 9. *Be Thou For the People (The Dog of the Military's Silver Watch)*

The following two episodes of *Fullmetal Alchemist* are not filled with the same heavyweight issues – or at least, not issues loaded down with death. In episode 9: *Be Thou For the People (The Dog of the Military's Silver Watch)*, Ed and Al Elric travel by train to help a mining community at Youswell (yes, it's rough, working class, and grimy, as all mining communities are in every movie or TV show you've seen),[25] which's being exploited by the fat cats (the villains have distinct Nazi attributes – yes, the capitalists who run mines (or any industry) are always cigar-chomping pig-men).

Thru a not wholly convincing act of subversion (involving conjuring up fake gold bars using alchemy),[26] Ed and Al manage to trick the bad guys (led by oily, sly, cowardly, effete Lieutenant Yoki – a terrific performance of a low-down weasel by Kazuki Yao – he's also wonderful

---

25 The mining town evokes the one in *Laputa: Castle In the Sky*: Hayao Miyazaki and Isao Takahata and the Ghibli team visited Wales in 1985 for research on *Laputa: Castle In the Sky*: 'I was in Wales just after the miners' strike [Miyazaki recalled in 1999]. I really admired the way the miners' unions fought to the very end for their jobs and communities, and I wanted to reflect the strength of those communities in my film. I saw so many places with abandoned machinery, abandoned mines – the fabric of the industry was there, but no people. It made a strong impression on me. A whole industry with no work.'

26 No one in the target audience of *Fullmetal Alchemist* of young males is going to buy this. It's as silly in the *manga*.

as Franky and Mr 2 in *One Piece*),[27] out of ownership of the mine (this's handily accomplished without solicitors or lawyers[28]), and in the process also re-build the inn the villains destroyed, thus becoming the heroes of the mining town (and their fame spreads as Heroes Of The People – which foreshadows the appearance of their impostors in *The Other Brothers Elric*, coming up in one episode's time).

In amongst the action-adventure shenanigans in 1.9: *Be Thou For the People (The Dog of the Military's Silver Watch)*, there is a strong undercurrent of a political message – to help the workers rebel against their oppressors, in true Communist/ Marxist style, and also that Ed is a revolutionary in the making, a future Che Guevara (altho' he resists from helping at first, using the 'reluctant hero' model, and sarcastically muses on the fate of the State Alchemist working 'for the people'. By this time in *Fullmetal Alchemist*, Edward is already very disillusioned with working for the military machine).

The political oppression of the People's Republic of China might also be an affinity here, as well as the former Soviet Union (and both China and Russia in relation to Japan, which has an uncertain relationship with them).[29] After all, episode 1.9: *Be Thou For the People* has evoked the familiar leftist issues of workers and bosses, citizens and taxes, work as exploitation (for little pay), the violent oppression by the bosses, and the wish-fulfilment of the workers getting to own the mine.[30]

The new charas – Halling (owner of the inn) and his son Kyle – are the most prominent here (character designer Yoshiyuki Ito does a terrific job in matching the designs of Himoru Arakawa and making them work in animation. All of Arakawa's comics feature burly guys prominently).

Meanwhile, Roy Mustang lurks behind-the-scenes (he hands Edward Elric his mission at the top of the show, just like the police chief in thousands of cop shows), and the heroes get to act like heroes – Alphonse rescues Kyle from the rubble of the wrecked inn, and Edward steps in to save Kyle (again) from the wrath of Lt. Yoki (when in an over-the-top moment, Yoki orders his henchmen to punish the boy – with a sword! Well, this *is* a Japanese show).

Alas, Winry Rockbell, who's (usually) good value, and brings a feminine presence into the boysy *Fullmetal Alchemist anime*, is still playing the Girlfriend Of The Hero role, and vanishes from the episode *Be Thou for the People* after a brief shopping spree – in which she goes goo-goo and ga-ga over the amazing tools on sale in Central City (Winry is the *mecha*-nut who fixes Ed's automail – she gives him a little can of oil as a keepsake).[31] Only in *anime* does a girl clutch a new screwdriver she's found at a stall to her cheek and coo over its wooden handle!

---

27 Yao is also in *Bastard, Mobile Suit Gundam ZZ, Aquarion, Death Note* and *Jankenmann*, among many others.
28 No lawyer would endorse that! – lawyers don't seem to have been invented in this fantasy world... yay!
29 Himoru Arakawa references both China and Russia in her *manga*.
30 And at a more modest level, it reflects the lot of animators in Nihon – over-worked, under-paid, and definitely exploited by their bosses.
31 Which he uses, griping that Winry might've done better to look after his body not his automail.

Adaption-wise, episode 9: *Be Thou For the People* follows Himoru Arakawa's *Fullmetal Alchemist manga* closely, but adds many elements. Chief among these is a new female character called Lyra[32] (Yumi Kakazu), who works for Lt. Yoki. Lyra is a wannabe alchemist (and later she is one of the villains). She has a black costume (including a short skirt), and a solemn look (she'd be the mean girl in class in a *shojo manga* set in a high school).

Lyra is included to balance up the masculine bias of the *Fullmetal Alchemist* show, to add an alchemical threat to the Elrics, to offer a thematic commentary on alchemy, and also to provide some action for the finale (when, inevitably, Ed and Lyra duel).

❋

One thing's striking about the first ten or so episodes of the first *Fullmetal Alchemist* series – an over-arching storyline has not really emerged. We know that the Elric brothers are keen to rejuvenate their bodies, but that is balanced with the villains' evil schemes in *Fullmetal Alchemist*. Thus far, the villains have been served up as a 'Threat Of The Week', to be disposed of at the end of each episode. The recurring figures, meaning, principally, the homunculi, are still somewhat vague presences.

Episode 10. *The Phantom Thief*

The next episode, 10: *The Phantom Thief,* is *Fullmetal Alchemist*'s version of (and *hommage* to) *Lupin III* by Monkey Punch, an enormous franchise in Japan (there are other links between *Fullmetal Alchemist* and *Lupin III* – not least the 100s of filmmakers who produced *Fullmetal Alchemist*, many of whom, like everyone else in Tokyo's industry it seems, worked on the *Lupin III* franchise at some point or other).

Episode 10: *The Phantom Thief Psiren* is essentially an indulgent (but fun) side-story (that's not in the *Fullmetal Alchemist manga* by Himoru Arakawa), that takes numerous elements from the *Lupin III* series: a slinky, cat-suited burglar in black (Psiren, voiced by Miho Shiraishi), a version of Fujiko Mine in *Lupin III,* is one step ahead of Ed and Al Elric, and the authorities, led by the chief policeman who evokes Inspector Zenigata of Interpol, Lupin's rival, from the *Lupin* series (voiced by Fumihiko Tachiki – he was Sloth in the second series).

Sidenote: *Lupin III* is a big franchise based on a *manga* series by Monkey Punch (a.k.a. Kazuhiko Kato, 1937-2019); the first series ran from 1967 to 1972, by the T.M.S Studio, with further series from 1977-80 and 1997 (and more recent series – 2012, 2015, 2018, etc).[33] As well as *manga*, there were 200 TV shows, a live-action film in 1974 (a 1969 movie had

---

32 Possibly named after Lyra Silvertongue in the *His Dark Materials* (1995-2000) series by Philip Pullman.
33 Copyright issues arose when the *Lupin* franchise was sold in the West, because French author Maurice LeBlanc had created Arsène Lupin, and Monkey Punch had used LeBlanc's character as an influence. So for video and other releases in the West, Lupin is called Rupan III or Wolf or Vidoq the Fourth. When the show was aired by Nippon TV, it was renamed *Cliffhanger.*

been made but not released), an animated picture in 1978 (*Lupin vs. the Clone*, a.k.a. *Lupin III: The Secret of Mamo*), *The Castle of Cagliostro* (1979), Hayao Miyazaki's first feature as director, which was the follow-up to *Lupin vs. the Clone*, and more *Lupin III* films (17 features on TV and 6 movies released in cinemas).[34] Plus video games, a musical, music, Original Video Animations, TV specials, and loads of spin-off *manga* (such as Lupin in the 22nd century). And plenty of merchandizing.

❖

As in many a *Lupin III* TV show, Psiren in *Fullmetal Alchemist* isn't an all-out villain, more of a Robin Hood figure who's supporting the Venice-like city of Aquroya by helping to save its buildings (and she's a nurse called Clara by day – what a heroine!).

Later, always racing ahead of our heroes, Psiren/ Clara becomes a nun, then a teacher, as each building (a hospital, a convent, a school) is demolished. While the Elrics can't quite grasp all of this, Psiren becomes a hero of the people of Aquroya because, like Venice, it's sinking into the lake, and the Aquroyans need all the help they can get in drawing attention to their doomed but beloved city. (The format of episode 1.10 is essentially a riff on the Yousewell episode, where the Elrics help a mining town, and the Majhal episode, where the heroes meet a dubious alchemist, Lyra).

The writer of *The Phantom Thief* (Toshiki Inoue) exploits the budding erotic longings of our mid-teen[35] heroes: both Elric boys are placed beside Psiren (in one moment, apprehending Psiren after an alchemical duel, Ed accidentally grabs Psiren's breasts as he sits on top of her (like hapless goofs in 100s of *animé* comedies, such as Keitaro with Naru in *Love Hina*), then recoils in horror, as he realizes: 'you're a woman!). And of course, when Psiren wants to use her powers of alchemy, she unzips her shirt to reveal a transmutation circle written on her cleavage (which links her to the character of the homunculus Lust, who has a tattoo in the same spot).

The flirtatious relationship of Psiren/ Clara and Edward Elric is among the most intimate and overtly erotic in both *Fullmetal Alchemist* TV series: Psiren/ Clara isn't a fellow, innocent teen like Winry Rockbell, but a young woman with one of those classic, super-babe bodies that abound in Japanese animation. It's the first, full appearance in the series of Himoru Arakawa's 'va-va-voom' woman. (Even Psiren's cat-suit is cut away to reveal more skin – character designers in *animé* enjoy concocting ridiculous costumes for their sexy heroines. And she sports bunny ears, another staple of *animé*. Here Yoshiyuki Ito was the character designer and, as Psiren isn't in Himoru Arakawa's *manga*, he had more leeway).

Alphonse Elric, meanwhile, is not quite at the same stage of Freudian, psychosexual development as his brother Edward: instead of seeing Psiren's body as *Playboy* material, he sees his momma! Al goes kookoo over Psiren/ Clara's motherly attributes, and worships her as a reminder

---

34 Including: *Lupin III: Legend of the Gold of Babylon*, 1985, *Lupin III: The Fuma Conspiracy*, 1988, *Lupin III: Voyage To Danger*, 1993, *Lupin III: Pursuit of Harimao's Treasure*, 1995, *Lupin III: Dead Or Alive*, 1996, *Lupin III: Island of Assassins*, 1997, *Lupin III: Crisis In Tokyo*, 1998, and *Lupin III: Missed By a Dollar*, 2000.
35 The captions at the top of the show indicate that Ed and Al are 15 and 14.

of his dead mom. *Kawaii* – and he refuses to believe that Clara could be a crook.

❁

As to the central themes of the *Fullmetal Alchemist* franchise, episode 10: *The Phantom Thief* does refer to them: the Elric boys're on the look-out for info on philosopher's stones (which's why they stopped on the train at Aquroya in the first place – they're *en route* reporting in to Ed's feared boss Roy Mustang). Edward, in particular, asks any adult if they know anything about philosopher's stones, if they show any hint of knowledge of them. Psiren/ Clara doesn't know much, but she does give the brothers the idea of going to Xenotime. It's not much, but it's about only significant contribution to the over-arching plot of *Fullmetal Alchemist*. (Thus, the show begins and ends with the brothers on the train, as they often are in *Fullmetal Alchemist*, and the Aquroya visit was just another adventure on their journey).

There are one or two dramatic motifs woven into the mix of episode 10: *The Phantom Thief*, to demonstrate that someone in the production team was tracking the content when they made this show: Ed's voracious appetite,[36] for example (he eats in several scenes, until he gets sick, precipitating a visit to the hospital. Which's where we meet Psiren in her guise as a kindly nurse). And Ed's cheating at cards on the train (which links up with Psiren's use of cards as weapons, a device not uncommon in *manga* and *animé*, as is gambling).

Episodes 11 and 12. *The Other Brothers Elric*

This is the first episode (of a two-parter, *The Other Brothers Elric* (episodes 11 and 12 of the first *Fullmetal Alchemist* series), where the quality of scriptwriting (by Natsuko Takahashi) in this show is notably inferior to the previous episodes. *The Other Brothers Elric* is an anime-original story (not in the *manga*), which uses the themes and motifs of *Fullmetal Alchemist* and applies them to a new scenario (it was based on the first *Fullmetal Alchemist* light novel, *Fullmetal Alchemist: The Land of Sand*, by Makoto Inoue). Unfortunately, although this is only episode 11 of the series, there are already repetitions of earlier episodes (such as dodgy, middle-aged alchemists, another town down on its luck, etc). But repetitions are also found in the comic, of course (several charas in the Army, for ex, repeat others, and there isn't really a pressing thematic need to split the heavies into seven homunculi).

So, in *The Other Brothers Elric*, the Edward and Alphonse Elric arrive at yet another beleaguered, industrial community (Xenotime) using early 20th century technology (recalling Yousewell in episode 9), and endeavour to help the situation. Once again there is a mystery to solve, sinister father figures/ bosses to battle, and weak, father figures to aid, understand or forgive. Once again our heroes're thrown out of an inn

---

36 A minor motif in the show is eating – like 100s of characters in *animé*, Ed loves his food. He's eating in many scenes, and the inspector bribes him with a whole table laden with food. And altho' this is a kind of European world, Ed eats Japanese food, with chopsticks.

when it's found out that they're State Alchemists (as in episode 9), and once again our heroes struggle to prove their good name.

In *The Other Brothers Elric*, our boys're up against two brothers (the Tringhams) who're impostors, right down to the blond hair and teen appeal, and the bossy, older one and the sweeter, younger one (*Fullmetal Alchemist* exploits clones, doubles and copycats of the Elric brothers a few times (the first *Fullmetal Alchemist* movie did, too). These charas, and the events in the episodes, were invented for the first *animé* series).

The larger, background story of *The Other Brothers Elric* involves disease (again) and the medicine for it (which's inevitably linked to the quest for the philosopher's stone – the crimson water which's been developed here is part of the potential cure). And, once again, the pursuit of alchemical secrets has serious side-effects, creating a disease that spreads thru the community (altho' these scenes were added to the comicbook, *manga* writer Hiromu Arakawa makes many statements about the consequences of scientific and medical research. For Arakawa, the pursuit of science and knowledge is not a 'pure' nor 'noble' activity, but one fraught with moral and ethical ambiguity).

There are also shady or absent father figures in *The Other Brothers Elric* who've discovered or developed the alchemical cures (such as Mugiar, Tim Marcoh and Nash Tringham). The Elrics are pursuing these dubious figures (white, middle-aged men, yet again), for news of the philosopher's stone, as well as performing the usual goals of teenage adventures (such as solving mysteries and righting wrongs).

Among the new charas in episodes 11-12: *The Other Brothers Elric* are: Mugiar (a.k.a. Mugwar/ Magwall – Takayuki Godai), a dodgy alchemist (a variation on Dr Marcoh) who's working for the homunculus Lust (she's in disguise – but we know who she is!). Belshio (Toshihiko Seki) is also a mystifying figure (one of his functions is to provide the Elrics with a place to stay – the *Fullmetal Alchemist animé* likes to explain that often, even tho' it's part of the fantasy/ adventure that such info is completely unnecessary). And the Tringham brothers – Fletcher (Minako Arakawa) and Russell (Kousuke Okano). And Elisia (Motoko Kumai) whom the Elrics save in a mining accident (Elisia hangs around with Belshio and his bowl of lemons).[37]

In the scenario involving alchemy and philosopher's stones invented for the animated TV series of *Fullmetal Alchemist*, it isn't human lives that're part of the recipe (not revealed fully yet), but deadly, red water (which of course looks like blood). The depiction of the alchemical experiments in *The Other Brothers Elric* recalls mining operations, where exploiting natural resources is achieved on an industrial scale (far from the hand-crafted approach of a laboratory in mediæval alchemy. We recall Himoru Arakawa's fascination with the Industrial Revolution in Britain). The toxic, red liquid evokes industrial waste, substances (associated with traditional alchemy) such as mercury or lead, and nuclear technology (there are links to the use of water in the production of

---

37 In every scene, Belshio carries a bowl or basket of lemons!

nuclear power).

So in this new down-on-its-luck community of Xenotime (a former gold mine), there's a Big House up on the hill[38] where the impostor alchemists are desperately trying to brew up a philosopher's stone (they are in competition with Mugiar and his operation, which's also poisoning the town). Ed and Al Elric sneak in, and pretty soon Ed and Russell are duelling each other (providing the mandatory action beats, tho' this is really teenage boys scrapping).

Unfortunately, the Tringham brothers are rather boring and predictable, and thus their goals (and the fights) don't carry much dramatic weight. Too much of *The Other Brothers Elric* is obvious and also repeats earlier adventures. (And the comparisons btn the two sets of brothers are too pat – how the Tringhams are continuing their father's alchemical research, for instance, and how the Elrics have an alchemist father who's the epitome of ambiguity and absence).

❊

In episode 12, the second half of the two-parter *The Other Brothers Elric*, the two sets of brothers work together against Mugiar, who turns out to be a fiendish villain. There's a lengthy flashback, narrated by Belshio, involving the Tringham boys' father, Nash Tringham, the alchemist who developed the toxic red water. He is another failed father and husband (clearly evoking van Hohenheim, tho' not as dashing or handsome – he's unshaven, clad in a dirt-coloured raincoat and looks forlorn all the time), who seems resigned to the fact that he is a wash-out. While characters berate him for his uselessness (such as Belshio and Mugiar), Tringham continues to be a loser (this no doubt endears the Tringham sons to Edward Elric, who has a resentful, ambivalent relationship with his own father, Hohenheim). Tim Marcoh, the alchemist doctor, crops up in ep. 12 (healing a girl with a philosopher's stone), as does Lust (both Tringham and Mugiar are in part variations of Marcoh).

Action-wise, *The Other Brothers Elric* is disappointing in its repetitions of better action scenes in better episodes of *Fullmetal Alchemist*. Once again it's the familiar kids' show format of a bunch of children and teens going up against a villainous, middle-aged man (he's not an alchemist, but he has a sort of red-water-concentrating invention which acts as a gun. This is an expansion of the *mecha* enhanced by the philosopher's stone wielded by Cornello in episode one. It also looks forward to the uranium ball in the first *Fullmetal Alchemist* movie). Each of the alchemical brothers gets to do their bit in defeating the villain Mugiar (his demise is the classic adventure serial one of being crushed by his own invention, the red water spring and mine, which collapses around him).

How our teen heroes save the town from immolation by the toxic crimson water is part-Hayao Miyazaki and part-junk Now Edward is able to alchemize earthwork defences as impressive as the Great Wall of China to keep the water at bay (bigger than anything he's built so far), while plant expert Fletcher transmutes the forest into a means of

---

38 Echoing Loki's plush digs in Yousewell overlooking the town.

vanquishing the stuff. The sequence is too quick, too neat, and too easy, with the transformation of the ecology seen in *Nausicaä of the Valley of the Wind* occurring in seconds.

What, so now our teenage heroes have god-like powers? With a chalk circle scrawled on a tree and a clap of the hands, they can turn an ecological disaster around just like that? Darn, why didn't they do it months ago, and stop the townsfolk suffering? To persuade us to buy this claptrap, composer Michiru Oshima delivers a huge action-adventure movie cue.

The *dénouement* of *The Other Brothers Elric* is irksome in its triteness and emotional syrup – with the Tringham sons now vowing to pursue a better way of life, to move forward, and to abandon their former work (Russell, in a letter to Edward Elric, states that he has been impressed by Ed, and will mend his ways. It's a gallon of too much syrup here, which the *Fullmetal Alchemist* series doesn't need).

But in amongst the kiddy adventures in episode 1.12: *The Other Brothers Elric* (which don't particularly convince), there is a gruesome plot: the townsfolk are becoming ill from the red water. A sinister twist is hinted at in the background: Mugiar suggests that pregnant women be made to drink the red water, so that their foetuses will be juicy with the stuff to create philosopher's stones. This is grotesque, putting *Fullmetal Alchemist* in a very malignant place (and retaining the theme in Himoru Arakawa's *Fullmetal Alchemist manga* of using human lives to create philosopher's stones). This show is the climax of the the first season of 12 episodes.

Episode 13. *Fullmetal vs. Flame*

Episode 13: *Fullmetal vs. Flame* is mostly a humorous show, with plenty of light-hearted material (the opening scenes involve cute animals, for instance – Alphonse Elric finding a stray cat, and Roy Mustang's team cooing over a pooch). So that it's some five or so minutes b4 the central issues of *Fullmetal Alchemist* are addressed (in *animé* terms, that's a long time to meander from the main plots). But it's welcome, and it's a staple of longer series so take breaks from the railroad engine of the main plot.

Episode 13: *Fullmetal vs. Flame* focusses on the tempestuous Edward Elric-Roy Mustang relationship. How do alchemists settle arguments? With duels, of course (boys will be boys, after all). So Ed and Mustang fight it out in the parade grounds of the military compound (Ed is pursuing information on Dr Marcoh and the philosopher's stone, and if he wins, he'll be given the info).[39]

Again, this was expanded from the *manga* – the first *Fullmetal Alchemist* series emphasizes the antsy relationship between Ed and Mustang from the *manga* – and it's a version of the Mustang—Elric duel in the *omake* (the extras), the humorous, 8-page side-story called *The*

---

39 In the *manga*, it's the workers in Mustang's office who wonder who's the strongest; in the cartoon, the impetus comes from Ed.

Military Festival.[40] And competitions and sports events are a *huge* ingredient in *manga* and *animé* in Japan: you find them everywhere, with some *manga*, such as *Naruto, Fairy Tail* and *Mahou Sensei Negima*, taking up chapter after chapter with every detail of competitors battling it out in an arena.

Edward Elric sustains the serious central theme of *Fullmetal Alchemist* by referring to the philosopher's stone and Doctor Marcoh (which is his hidden reason for staging the alchemists' duel). Alphonse is tagging along, and following his brother's initiative, as so often in *Fullmetal Alchemist*.

The animated version of the duel in the parade grounds takes elements from the *omake* side-story *The Military Festival* in the *manga*, and adds numerous ingredients of its own. It ends in a kind of draw, the sort of John Woo-inspired stand-off that crops up a lot in *animé*: the participants freeze in an iconic pose – Edward Elric with his automail blade arm at Roy Mustang's throat, and Mustang just about to click his fingers for the last time (i.e., it's a cheat, a way of having both sides sort of victorious).

Towards the end of episode 13: *Fullmetal vs. Flame*, however, the weightier themes in Himoru Arakawa's *Fullmetal Alchemist* franchise is introduced in three short scenes: 1. the Ishbal War (here dubbed the 'Eastern Rebellion' or the 'Ishbal Rebellion'). The show takes a rapid turn towards tragedy and conflict when it has Roy Mustang experiencing a flashback to the Ishbal War, as he came face-to-face with a trembling, female opponent holding a rifle and quivering in fear on the floor in a room (this is narrated to Edward Elric, as they clear up after the alchemists' duel (the setting is yet another molten-gold sunset). Composer Michiru Oshima adds an echoey, distinctly Western harmonica theme, an unusual choice, for this particular reminiscence). And Mustang kills the woman, just as she's about to pull the trigger (she is plainly not a professional soldier, but a civilian who's taken up a gun).

So the jokey mood of episode 13: *Fullmetal vs. Flame* is instantly swept aside, in favour of civil war, and depictions of extreme scenes which haunt the participants. (Several military officers, such as Führer Bradley, are also hovering on the edges of this episode – most of which is set in the military HQ).

2. The unrest in the city of Liore is introduced as Hughes and Mustang relax with a drink, reminding us that the homunculi continue to stir up trouble.

3. And at the very end of ep. 13: *Fullmetal vs. Flame*, there's the return of the serial killer on the loose, the thoroughly despicable Scar, seen wasting a State Alchemist in a back alley at night after obtaining some intel (this time with a sinister choral cue added by Michiru Oshima). Thus, lighthearted this show might be, but it ends with an on-screen death.

---

40 The *manga* side-story, where Edward Elric and Roy Mustang have a friendly challenge, appeared in *Gangan Powered* in Spring, 2002 (and is included in the collected volumes of *Fullmetal Alchemist*).

Episode 14. *Destruction's Right Hand*

This is an extremely bitter show for something airing at six o'clock on Saturday evenings. Now we can see why episode 13: *Fullmetal vs. Flame* was mainly a humorous show, because the following show is very grim, and is stuffed with disturbing and serious imagery and themes, including a civil war, rioting, the Army firing on civilians, pools of blood, huge numbers of bloody corpses, plus gory on-screen deaths (including one right in front of the Elric brothers).

In episode 14: *Destruction's Right Hand* (and episode 15: *The Ishbal Massacre*), the volatile, complex issue of Ishbal and the conflict there is explored, while Scar (who's from Ishbal) is also creating merry hell for the State Alchemists. (The Ishbal War is dubbed an 'uprising' or a 'rebellion' by the Amestrisian authorities, whereas Dr Marcoh assures us it was a massacre).

Scar is a lunatic intent on destroying State Alchemists because they are an offence to God (for Scar, only the deity can create, and humans must remain humble humans. It's OK, tho', for him to destroy, using alchemy! Because in the mediæval and Renaissance eras (of our world), alchemy, as it's used in *Fullmetal Alchemist*, would be regarded by many as heathen and witchcraft). From the time that Scar was linked to the death of the chimera creature made up of Shou Tucker's daughter Nina and the family pooch Alexander in episode 7: *Night of the Chimera's Cry*, the audience is aching for someone to tear out Scar's throat.

But Scar is allowed to go on and on killing and killing and killing. And nobody, not nobody nohow, anyhow, whynow, can stop him! Including some of the biggest, burliest State Alchemists (such as Alex Armstrong, the 'Strong Arm Alchemist', whose arms are very strong). And Scar is allowed to live on and on as a villain way past his sell-by date (and other villains, such as Shou Tucker and even Barry the Chopper, are resurrected. This is where the second *Fullmetal Alchemist* series works so much better, because by then Himoru Arakawa had created the full retinue of homunculi and villains).

Edward Elric also runs into Scar a few times, but manages to escape death (using all of the usual action-adventure genre get-out clauses). And no one can catch Scar, even tho' the dimwit hangs about in broad daylight on the streets, easily recognizable with his very contemporary, spikey hair-do and oblong-rimmed glasses (he looks like a personal trainer for Arnold Schwarzenegger, or a bodyguard, maybe, for Madonna).

❃

We also see the town of Liore descending into civil war in episode 14: *Destruction's Right Hand* – thus, it is an Ishbal War happening in the present tense (this was added to the *manga*). The images are distressing – many corpses, blood-stained pavements, soldiers shooting at civilians, and people fleeing or cowering in fear (Rose Tomas in prominent in these scenes, protecting a clutch of small children. Continuing the theme of martial oppression, she is smacked in the face by a grunt hoping for intel).

We see a little more of the homunculi having their way in Liore (Lust, Gluttony and Envy), where the cult of Father Cornello and the sun-god Leto continues (despite Ed and Al Elric uncovering Cornello and his Leto cult as a sham). Lust finally voices some of the goals of the homunculi – not stating exactly what they are, but at least she/ it insists that they have goals, and they need Edward Elric to fulfil them.

This is also the first significant reveal of Envy, in his guise as an arrogant, vain youth with very long, spiky hair, shorts, and a croptop. The reveal follows the *manga* closely, including Cornello's aide Cray stumbling upon the three homunculi and being chomped by Gluttony for his trouble.

✤

Meanwhile in episode 14: *Destruction's Right Hand*, the Elric boys are still hunting down information on Dr Tim Marcoh (Kouji Totani) and the philosopher's stone, in their quest to recover their bodies (the issues are inter-related, because Marcoh was involved with the war in Ishabl, leading to many deaths (Marcoh's disfigured but not killed by the military in Himoru Arakawa's *manga*).)

The Elrics visit Dr Marcoh, who tells them about Ishbal: he is haunted by his experiences there, and the things he did (or was made to do). Ed, tho', is keen to pursue the philosopher's stone, and discovers one, or something like it – the red water.

Basque Grand, virtually ignored in the second *Fullmetal Alchemist* series,[41] makes another appearance. He is in charge of the research on the philosopher's stone, and the Elrics recognize that they won't be able to sweet talk a guy like Grand into letting them pursue their research (Grand is a military man thru and thru).

So Dr Marcoh is hauled away by Basque Grand and the military, complaining loudly to anybody who can hear. But out of nowhere, Scar is right there, in the street, stopping the car, and dispatching the Iron Alchemist within moments. It's a scene where someone is killed right in front of the teenage brothers, with them being unable to do anything about it (and in a grotesque manner, blown up from the inside, with blood gushing from multiple wounds. There is a *lot* of blood and carnage in this episode of *Fullmetal Alchemist* – and a lot more than many an 'R' rated or 'NC-17' rated Western movie or TV show. And the victim isn't a feeble, oldster, but a powerful and burly alchemist and commander).

Then follows a duel between Edward and Alphonse Elric and Scar – which we know because we are only a quarter way into the *Fullmetal Alchemist* series that they haven't got a chance of winning. Both Ed and Al get their moment to shine, attacking Scar (Ed), or defending Ed from Scar (Al),[42] or simply hurrying away from Scar with Dr Marcoh in tow. As in the *manga*, there are reveals of Ed's automail, and Al's hollow armour.

The fight with Scar continues in a side tunnel (always with the tunnels in *Fullmetal Alchemist*!), and tho' the brothers seal it up, Scar keeps advancing. Like the Terminator, like countless horror movie villains with

41 He's killed by Scar early on.
42 Alphonse Elric often plays a defensive, protective role.

supernatural powers of regeneration and persistence, Scar is unstoppable. The arrival of Alex Armstrong is an entertaining beat, providing the much-needed rescue (reversed from the *manga*, where Armstrong is tasked with guarding the Elrics on their travels, and is already with them).

Episode 15. *The Ishbal Massacre.*

Scripted by head writer Shou Aikawa (who also wrote the group of episodes at this point in the series), this is one of the finest episodes in the first *Fullmetal Alchemist* TV show, with plenty of drama, cliffhangers, and emotive action, plus the Elrics sustain major damage from the biggest threat yet – Scar. Jean-Luc Godard's advice to young filmmakers is: *have something to say*. Now, we know plenty of TV shows and movies which *don't* have much to say! But in episode 15: *The Ishbal Massacre*, the *Fullmetal Alchemist* series has plenty to say. Partly because it picks one of the most explosive subjects in human history – war. And not just any war, but the fiercest, the cruellest and most desperate kind of war: civil war.

So episode 15: *The Ishbal Massacre* continues the horrific scenes of the previous episode: the central section comprises a series of flashbacks to the Ishbal War. Doctor Marcoh[43] narrates this lengthy sequence to the two Elric brothers, as they flee from the villain Scar (watching some kids playing innocently in the back streets of East City (a great touch) brings to mind the Ishbal War for Marcoh – but then, the slightest thing does: he is a man so haunted by his former deeds, he is perpetually on edge, and apt to flee at any moment, which he does here).

Make no mistake, though *Fullmetal Alchemist* is an animated TV cartoon, it has imagery and themes as potent and tragic as any war movie in the history of cinema. Including, yes, all of the masterpieces of the combat film genre. This is gruesome, gruelling stuff. We see civilians and soldiers dying *en masse* as the Amestrian government sends in the State Alchemists. We see Roy Mustang executing two doctors at point blank range with a pistol (and later we see Mustang, drunk, desperate, holding a gun to his head at the scene of the crime); we see riots escalating into armed conflict; and we see State Alchemists invading Ishbal and causing colossal devastation (with their alchemical powers enhanced by the incomplete but still powerful philosopher's stones – which Dr Marcoh supplies)…

The sub-plot in *Hagane no Renkinjutsushi* about Ishbal is a clear evocation of contemporary, Middle Eastern politics, including the Arab-Israeli War of the late 1960s, the Gulf War and the Iraq War (Ishbal is depicted in the flashback as a devout and monotheistic, religious nation where alchemy is seen as heretical. The visuals in this episode emphasize the links between the religion of Ishbal and Islam). Unfortunately, the notion of humanizing the serial killer Scar, when we've already seen him ruthlessly killing so many people (Maes Hughes says it's dozens), and

---

43 In the comic, it's Liza Hawkeye.

linking him to the Ishbal political issue, compromises feelings of compassion for Ishbal's fate.

✳

One of the many murky events in episode 15: *The Ishbal Massacre* has Roy Mustang being ordered to kill two doctors, the Rockbells – these are Winry-chan's parents. This will play out later – when Winry Rockbell finds out that the military government were involved in her parents' demise; in the *Fullmetal Alchemist manga*, it was Scar, which makes much more sense). Mustang is about to commit suicide when Dr Marcoh intervenes at the last moment (these scenes were added to the *manga*). Presumably the switch was made to give more depth to Mustang's character – and it also lays more personal blame at the military rulers of Amestris (Edward collapses when he hears what Marcoh tells him).

Doctor Marcoh represents guilt, guilt guilt about the Ishbal War. Guilt—shame—war crime. He is a man wracked with remorse over what he saw and did in Ishbal (his philosopher's stones aid the alchemists in creating mass destruction). In the first *Fullmetal Alchemist* series, we discover that the war became a massacre which went on for seven years.

❀

Episode 15: *The Ishbal Massacre* shifts from the past to the present day – Alex Armstrong tackles Scar, as does Roy Mustang, but the Ishbalian escapes; the flashbacks depict Armstrong in Ishbal, as well as alchemists such as Basque Grand (who becomes a multi-barrel gun using the magic of the philosopher's stone), Mustang burning up whole streets, and Zolf Kimbley (who stands on top of a building yelling with insane joy at the devastation he can unleash when aided by a philosopher's stone).

In these episodes of *Fullmetal Alchemist*, Scar is a one-man army and no amount of soldiers and alchemists can defeat him (or even find him, even tho' he stands out a mile!).[44] Scar has everybody on the run, including our heroes, with Tim Marcoh tagging along. There is plenty of action, plenty of to-ing and fro-ing, but nothing is resolved narratively (we are only a third of the way thru the first *Fullmetal Alchemist* TV series): so Scar escapes, Alex Armstrong rescues our heroes, and Dr Marcoh is whisked away.[45]

Episode 15: *The Ishbal Massacre* culminates with an exciting scene where Scar has the Elric brothers and Dr Marcoh at his mercy in yet another side street of Eastern City. The Elrics are still not a match for Scar: Alphonse has his armour wrecked, and Edward has his automail arm shattered, in two, slow motion close-ups (as Ed stares in horror).

This is the scene where Ed Elric accepts his doom, waiting for Scar to deliver the killing blow, while Alphonse yells at him to run. In the *Fullmetal Alchemist manga* and in each *animé*, it's one of the most dramatic sequences. Well, yes, we know that Ed and Al won't die right here, in episode 15 of a 51-episode run, but it's still a thrilling moment. (Here the

---

44 In one scene, Scar's simply lounging against a wall on a back street. But he's seen, shot at, and flees.

45 Dr Marcoh refuses to travel to Resembool, because that's where the Rockbells' daughter lives – and he feels partly responsible for their deaths.

boys're saved by Dr Marcoh, who wields a philosopher's stone as a weapon, and hurls it at Scar. The red blob activates the alchemical tattoos on Scar's arm, and is absorbed, and he flees. This was added to the *manga* – tho' the next action beat, where Scar runs into Mustang, Hawkeye *et al*, is from the comic).

Yet just as crucial is the *dénouement*, where Alphonse Elric yells at his brother for being a *baka* and not bolting when he had a chance. With their bodies falling apart, the boys are in a sorry state, as they admit, but they are still alive, as Alphonse insists. They have to move forward.

At the end of this action-packed and very impressive episode of Japanese animation, Dr Marcoh is taken away by the authorities. The producers have added the character of Führer's secretary, Juliet Douglas, to Himoru Arakawa's *manga* – and cleverly given her the same appearance (and the same voice – by actress Yoshino Takamori) as the Elrics' dead mom Trisha. Thus is the longed-for mother, the person the Elric kids would love to see more than any other, brought into the present tense of the *Fullmetal Alchemist* series. (Al is taken by the sight of the secretary standing next to the limo – he thinks he's seen (and heard) his mom).

Fullmetal Alchemist, the first series (this page and over).

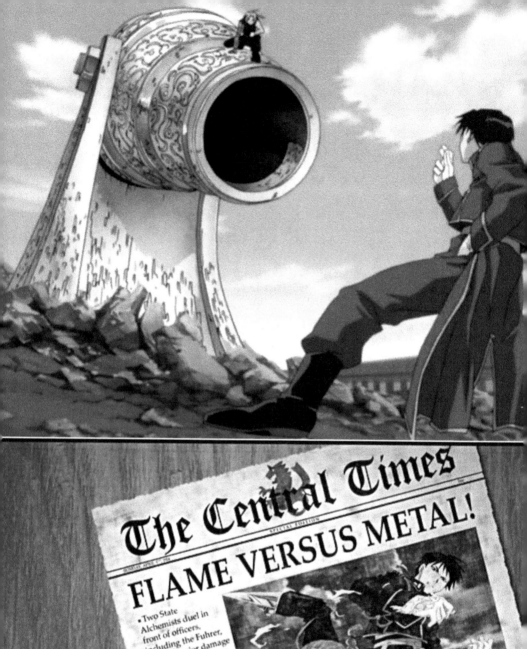

The Central Times
SPECIAL EDITION

FLAME VERSUS METAL!

• Two State Alchemists duel in front of officers, including the Fuhrer, causing major damage to East City's military headquarters.

By Tamane Cole
Staff Writer

Episode 16. *That Which Is Lost.*

In episode 16 of *Fullmetal Alchemist* – *That Which Is Lost* – the Elric boys travel back to their Resembool homeland (accompanied by the beefcake alchemist Alex Louis Armstrong (a marvellous vocal performance by Kenji Utsumi),[1] who might have stepped out of Seventies camp pop act Village People; Armstrong loses no opportunity in stripping off his top to brandish his muscles Charles Atlas-style, striking ridiculous he-man poses, bragging about his family and his alchemical prowess, while surrounded by floating pink stars, orange twinkles, flowers and ultra-girlie accoutrements. Gay? Camp? Sure! Funny, too. There is no equivalent in mainstream, Western entertainment of characters like this in the context of an action-adventure tale).[2] Characters stand there and gawp at Armstrong, asking, but why does he have to undress?! Why is he so eager to rip off his shirt at the slightest provocation?! If you have to ask that, well, you're watching the wrong show!

With his moustache and bald pate, Alex Armstrong[3] also has a distinctly Germanic, WW1-era look (he'd be right at home in Berlin's Love Parade). (Ed and Al Elric aren't keen on being accompanied and mummied by camp Armstrong: they know he means well, but what a pain having a guy who weeps at the drop of a hat, or strips off his shirt to reveal a buff body that's spent hours in the gym (teens of any gender would cringe at the thought of being chaperoned by Armstrong).[4] God knows what the *shonen* audience, young males, make of Armstrong: he's one of those characters in *manga* and *animé* that probably befuddle first-timers in the Western world. Their reaction is likely the same as Ed and Al's: embarrassed and uncomfortable. They probably much prefer Roy Mustang, the super-cool Flame Alchemist who has women adoring him. Or maybe not Mustang, seeing as he's been revealed now as the executor of Winry's folks)

◆

Along the way there are, inevitably, some adventures in the first *Fullmetal Alchemist* series which amount to side-stories, some of them acting as comic relief after the more seriously dramatic events of the previous episodes. So, stopping because Al's been misplaced from the train, Ed has his leg stolen, and Al goes missing (he's taken by a kid of about his age (Miwa Matsumoto) who mistakes him for a suit of armour. It's a silly gag, a variation on the time when Martel dives inside Al's

1 The wonderful Kenji Utsumi (1937-2013) played Appledelhi in *Cowboy Bebop*, the scary demon Nosferatu Zodd in *Berserk*, Mino in *Basilisk*, and appeared in everything from *Dragon Ball* to *Dr Slump*.
2 Whether Armstrong is homosexual or not isn't addressed by the *manga* or the *animés*, but there are plenty of other characters who exhibit aspects of homosexuality as portrayed by cultural stereotypes. For instance, Garfiel, who runs the automail store in Rush Valley where Winry works, is depicted as an out-there camp personality.
3 Unfortunately, in the later episodes the series doesn't know what to do with Armstrong, and uses him as a gloomy presence, on the margins.
4 Another gag carried by Armstrong is that he's a terrific artist: usually, when characters are asked to draw something to make a point, their sketches are horrible (like Rukia in *Bleach*). Arakawa uses the same gag in *Arslan Senki* for Narsus, but reversed: now, when people see what Narsus has been painting, they're horrified.

armour. Al and the youth talk as the boy cycles home, crashing repeatedly). And it's completely unbelievable how the sister (Miyu Matsuki) trounces Ed, runs up a ladder and hurls a wooden crate on top of him (we've already seen Ed going up against several formidable opponents), and how she's able to snaffle his automail while he's unconscious (it would take Winry longer than that to take off the leg! And it would hurt, too!).

Yet weighty issues, principally the Ishbal War, are woven into the episode. For example, the grandfather (Takayuki Sugo) of the girl who whipped away Ed's steel limb, lost his leg in the Ishbal rebellion, and doesn't want an automail replacement, because the lost limb reminds him of that fatal conflict (so the girl stealing the automail is actually a set-up for the sombre kitchen table talk between the guy and Ed about Ishbal).

Much of episode 16: *That Which Is Lost* was anime-only and not in the *Fullmetal Alchemist* manga, but the show retains the same balance between comedy and serious issues, and keeps the Elric brothers in the centre of the frame.

◆

Meanwhile, Doctor Marcoh runs into Lust and Gluttony in a hotel room, and is severely injured. Following the action in the *manga*, Marcoh manages to maim Lust. (Marcoh survives much longer in the second *Fullmetal Alchemist* series. Dr Marcoh's function in the world of *Fullmetal Alchemist* is to embody guilt and shame over the Ishbal War, and conflicting political allegiances: Marcoh is the war criminal who is haunted and tormented by being entrapped into using his scientific research for evil deeds in the Ishbalian War).

Episode 16: *That Which Is Lost* is one of the first shows in the 2004 *Fullmetal Alchemist* series to depict the homunculi really doing what they do best: being nasty sons-of-guns. A vamp from 1950s Americana in a clinging dress that provides more than enough bouncy cleavage for the whole *Fullmetal Alchemist* series, Lust is a terrific screen villain (and the filmmakers know it, and maximize Lust's every appearance; indeed, they include her in other roles, such as Scar's brother's lover. Himoru Arakawa also clearly enjoyed writing for Lust). And to make sure the audience can't take their eyes off those springy breasts, there's a sinister tattoo nestling between them.

Here we see Lust pinning down Dr Marcoh in his hotel[5] with her extendible, Edward Scissorhands claws. And when Marcoh retaliates with some alchemy of his own, and spears Lust thru the torso, we see the first indication that the homunculi are very difficult to kill (Lust says she's already died before).

Episode 17. *The House of the Waiting Family*

Episode 17: *House of the Waiting Family* is one of the sweetest, gentlest episodes of the first *Fullmetal Alchemist* series – and one of the best (it was

5 How did the homunculi find Marcoh so quickly? Because the Führer and his secretary are homunculi!

written by Natsuko Takahashi). It's the Coming Home episode of *Fullmetal Alchemist*, with all of the usual Going Home narrative beats: discussions of the past, revelations of back-story and characterization, getting in touch with family, visiting gravesides, and re-establishing goals and motives.

Back in Resembool, their homeland, the Elric guys have cute, blonde, tomboy Winry Rockbell waiting for them, who happens to be a genius at fixing machines, along with granny Pinako (i.e., Winry is the ideal girlfriend for *otakus* – she even has ear piercings, a croptop, overalls pulled down to expose her midriff, and long, blonde hair. Her usual costume comprises a short mini skirt that only just covers her panties). Great at repairing anything, a total gearhead, but also tough, and sweet, and caring – *aaah*, Winry-chan has it all! Both Elric boys have crushes on her (without knowing it). But now Ed is older – 15, and hormones're kicking in. As usual, the romance isn't fulfilled (it's barely even suggested here), and doesn't go beyond unspoken desires.

The trip home in episode 1.17: *House of the Waiting Family* includes the inevitable reminiscences about the Elric boys' childhood (they visit their mom's grave, and their childhood home), the re-statements of the central quest, and more explorations of the background to the central characters. We see the Elrics remembering their mom (no mention of dad Hohenheim yet), pondering on their burnt home, thinking back to the moment when they wanted to bring their mother back to life, and contemplating just what 'home' means. (There are also vital evocations of rural landscapes, clearly significant for *mangaka* Himoru Arakawa, of farmland and hills and sunsets – and even starry, starry skies. In one shot there's a black-and-white cow,[6] added to the *animé* – which's a nod to how Arakawa presents herself in her comics).

Both animated series of *Fullmetal Alchemist* were especially fine with rendering the homeland of the Elric brothers, but I think this episode trumps the similar one in the second *Fullmetal Alchemist* series (episode 6: *Road of Hope*). It keeps the characterizations foregrounded, stopping storytelling completely for character studies and insights into the back-stories of the heroes. There is also a delicacy to the humour which keeps the scenes light yet still emotional.[7] (And Alex Armstrong has more dramatic impact in this episode than in the equivalent episode in the 2nd series (2:6) – particularly in reminding the Elrics of what 'home' and 'family' means. The comical over-reactions of Armstrong are also delightfully played. And Megumi Toyoguchi has more input than usual, too, as Winry Rockbell. This is the show where Winry discovers what Edward had written inside his State Alchemist's pocket watch, reminding her of the emotional core of the *Fullmetal Alchemist* series).

In sum, episode 17: *House of the Waiting Family* is a very satisfying show, dramatically, because it re-sets the characters (but in a much more

6 Being led by a girl – a potential girlfriend for Alphonse, perhaps? But he can't remember her – this is the first hint of Al pondering on his origins. Upstairs, he admits to Ed that he can't remember his friends.

7 Going home is also about going back into the past, and about memory – and in episode 17: *House of the Waiting Family*, Alphonse Elric wonders if he is losing his memory.

complete manner than a summary episode or a clip show, that simply re-shuffles existing animation into a sort of story). In a typical adventure tale, the heroes will leave the homeland and only return at the end (usually triumphant): *Fullmetal Alchemist* indulges itself by returning to 'home' at intervals (using the pretext of Ed needing his automail repaired – which's a good dramatic reason, after all, because not only is automail complicated, it ties into the theme of the boys searching for ways of re-establishing their bodies). And Winry, grandma and the hound are always there, waiting for them.

There's a clever use of a flashlight as a dramatic device to close ep. 17 on a sweet-sweet note – how the boys' mother would flash a lamp when it was time to come home from playing outside. And when the Elrics return from their sunset walks, there's Winry holding a light to guide them home. This is a good example of how filmmakers can enhance the original work.

Episode 18. *Marcoh's Notes*

In episode 18: *Marcoh's Notes,* two young guards (Denny Brosh (Masao Harada) and Lieutenant Maria Ross (Mitsuki Saiga)) are assigned to look after Elrics Ed and Al while serial killer Scar is still on the loose in Central City (partly to offer a change to having Alex Armstrong around – also, Brosh and Ross aren't alchemists, which puts the Elrics in greater danger with an opponent like Scar). Unfortunately, one of them – Lt. Ross – is an irritating snoop and auntie figure. True, Ross's there to keep an eye on the boys, and dramatically to offer some resistance and obstacles to their alchemical quest (and to be an authority figure), but she is also annoyingly self-righteous (as Roy Mustang is, too).

Luckily, the alchemist boys rebel against being housebound, and they are still hunting down any information on how to make a philosopher's stone (yes, we're still hanging onto that narrative chestnut. Because the lads, bless them, just want their mom back, right? No, I mean their *bodies* back. *Right*).

So it's off to the library, only to discover it's burnt down (courtesy of the freakish villains of the *Fullmetal Alchemist* series, the homunculi). By now, Lust (Yuuko Satou) and Gluttony (Yasuhiro Takato), a truly bizarre duo of villains, are one step ahead of the game (as villains tend to be). But the motives and goals of homunculi also change a little as the fully alchemical series progresses. At first, they act as simple but psychotic bad guys, as obstacles and hunters for our heroes. But later it's revealed that the homunculi are also searching for the philosopher's stone – which was, of course, one of the primary quests of mediæval alchemy (we find out later why – they want their humanity back, or to achieve something like humanity – this was altered from the *Fullmetal Alchemist manga,* where the homunculi are all servants of arch-baddie Father). So they want to keep Ed and Al alive, because they need the Elrics to find the philo-sopher's stone for them (in which case, burning down the library, which might've given Ed and Al some clues, is dumb).[8]

Manga author Hiromu Arakawa now comes up with a preposterous solution to the problem of the ruined library, a narrative device which would be laughed out of any meeting of screenwriters or producers: she introduces a character (Sheska – Naomi Wakabayashi – we saw her first in ep. 7) who has memorized, word for word, all of the missing books!

Oh *come on!*

Hmm, a young bookworm (a stand-in for *otaku* and nerds everywhere) has consigned every word of Tim Marcoh's journals to memory! Even the worst Hollywood hokum about spiritual quests in an action-adventure format (*Indiana Jones, National Treasure, X-Men* and *Harry Potter*) doesn't stoop that low![9]

So up steps Glasses Girl Sheska, and she writes out (by hand!) all of Tim Marcoh's jottings (in three days! What a worker! She's the ultimate assistant for an author or filmmaker). Turns out that Dr Marcoh hid his findings within a cookbook. Seems like a mistake? Not to Ed – Ed and Al dive in to decipher the code.

The finale of episode 18: *Marcoh's Notes* combines the Elrics discovering the magical ingredient in creating philosopher's stones (human lives) with Scar encountering Lust and Gluttony (the filmmakers add a girl-friend for Scar's brother – and who plays that lover? Why, Lust, of course. Yes, Scar would recognize that sly grin anywhere. The literal human cost of producing a philosopher's stone adds a powerful thematic layer to the *Fullmetal Alchemist* series (the mythology of the philosopher's stones, like the homunculi, is one of *mangaka* Himoru Arakawa's wonderful inventions).

The showdown in the library where Lust and Gluttony fight with Scar is the first time we've really seen the homunculi in action – and it doesn't disappoint. The action is furious and wild, and stuffed with energetic visual effects and frantic sound effects editing (and one human, Scar, is able to duel two homunculi, and escape with his life).

The scene is shifted to the end of episode 18: *Marcoh's Notes*, after being introduced in the opening sequence, presumably so the duel can form the action element of the finale of the show (because there isn't much action elsewhere, as the Elric brothers are at the moment embarked upon a quest for knowledge, which involves visits to libraries and lots of pondering over documents – not the most visually gripping of scenarios).

The dramatic structure shifts around the material from the comic, and gives Scar a dream or memory – about his brother, and a second memory, of the fight with the homunculi. This sort of narrative composition elevates Scar to almost the third main character in *Fullmetal Alchemist*, after Ed and Al (only major characters are allocated dream or memory sequences).

---

8 To be fair, the fire starting is a sort of accident when the homunculi are battling Scar.
9 Well, some North American movies do.

Episode 19. *The Truth Behind the Truth*

In episode 19: *The Truth Behind the Truth* (a.k.a. *The Truth Behind Truths*) of the first *Fullmetal Alchemist* series, Edward and Alphonse uncover the truth behind Tim Marcoh's alchemical research: that the construction of a philosopher's stone requires a human sacrifice (actually, several, says Ed). Of course: the costs of anything worthwhile or significant in the world of *Fullmetal Alchemist* are always going to be high. 'No pain no gain', to use a dumb Americanism. Or, in the case of *Fullmetal Alchemist,* 'no death no life'. Stuff's got to die for other stuff to live, right? *Right.* ('All is one', as the boys learnt at great cost on Jack Island from their harsh *sensei,* Izumi Curtis).

The uncovering of the truth behind the philosopher's stone sends the Elric brothers into a tailspin. They collapse in on themselves, sitting listlessly in their bedroom, watching the ceiling fan turning. Edward doesn't want to know anymore: he's had enough. It takes a lengthy (and on the nail) pep talk from the irritating Lt. Ross to galvanize the Elrics back into action. You kind of wish that characters such as Ross weren't part of the mix, but they are useful from a structural point-of-view, giving the heroes something to kick against thematically (and in a different manner from the homunculi. She takes over part of Col. Mustang's role in the comic). We have to remember, too, that the Elrics still haven't encountered the homunculi, tho' there's been no shortage of formidable opponents for the teen heroes.

By now we are into multiple treasure hunts in *Fullmetal Alchemist* – Ed and Al for the philosopher's stone, the homunculi for their own nefarious goals (but also the philosopher's stone), the military has its own agenda, and Scar is hot on the tail of pretty much everybody (he has it in for the homunculi, for the military, for the State Alchemists, for all Amestrisians, and for the Elrics. So what is Scar *for*, seeing as how he seems to be *against* everything? Well, he's 'for' Ishbal, of course, and his idea of righteousness and justice. There is also the issue of his brother and achieving vengeance).

The Elric brothers in episode 19: *The Truth Behind the Truth* discover the whereabouts of a secret (5th) laboratory, sited next to a prison (thus proving fresh meat for the alchemical experiments – convicted criminals, who are dragged in from next door). Naturally the boys head over there (at night), and the rest of the cast of *Fullmetal Alchemist* soon follow (as usual, Ed is leading these scenes – when Edward's enthusiasm and energy is high, he becomes the natural leader of everything in the *Fullmetal Alchemist* show; and it's Ed who works out where the experiments were conducted).

How many times have fantasy and adventure filmmakers *hommaged* the prologue of *Raiders of the Lost Ark?* With the fearsome boobytraps in underground tunnels, and of course the giant, rolling ball,[10] as Indiana Jones raids another tomb and escapes by the skin of his teeth. Here it's

---

10 Used before in *Journey to the Centre of the Earth* (1959).

Edward Elric dodging the spears and swords that flick out of the walls (in a sequence added to the *Fullmetal Alchemist manga*, to pep up the threat in the approach to the fifth laboratory). Arakawa is a big fan of *Indiana Jones*.

The Elrics fight two bad guys (Number 48 ('Slicer') and Number 66), who're hollow suits of armour, just like Alphonse Elric (one of them is the resurrected serial killer Barry the Chopper – another case of the screen-writers preferring to bring back a villain instead of creating a new one. And 'Slicer' is formed from two brothers joined together, another comment on the Elrics themselves).

Tho' the fights are fun and well-staged, they do go on and on, way beyond any of the previous duels in the *Fullmetal Alchemist* series, and way beyond, needless to say, the necessities of the drama (but complaining about that is also way off the point!). After all, this is *shonen animé* from a *shonen manga*, where the golden rule, the absolute rule, the foundational rule is: action followed by more action followed by more action. And on and on. All the time.

Yet the first *Fullmetal Alchemist* series can survive such self-indulgence and padding, because of the characters, the characterizations, the wit, the gripping themes, the stellar filmmaking, and the intensity with which Ed and Al pursue their dream of finding the philosopher's stone to restore their damaged bodies. The discovery that creating a philosopher's stone requires human beings (as basic fodder) is kind of inevitable, but also fits the story and the themes of *Fullmetal Alchemist* (which is: the price of being alive is high. It's literally blood and guts). In *Fullmetal Alchemist*, nothing is free, nobody gets something for nothing. You must *work work work* (hence all the scenes, in all of the episodes at this stage in the *Fullmetal Alchemist* series, set in libraries, or in the boys' rooms in Central City, where they're surrounded by books and papers and are studying studying studying. You can use *Fullmetal Alchemist* as a study aid for students at school: it gets across the necessity of hard work and hard studying very well! That is, altho' *Fullmetal Alchemist* isn't a high school or university story, like so many in *manga* and *animé*, it has plenty of the aspects of school stories, including tough teachers, difficult assignments, exams, and plenty of studying. Indeed, you could argue that the primary theme of *Fullmetal Alchemist* is not the price of life, or growing up, or the importance of family and siblings, but education).

◆

Also part of the mix in episode 19: *The Truth Behind the Truth* are items such as: (1) Scar, hot on the trail of the Elric brothers. There's a fire fight in a library, and Scar enters the Elrics' room, discovering the map on the table (and using a magical means of copying all of Doctor Marcoh's papers). Much of this was added to the *Fullmetal Alchemist manga*. (2) A short scene with Maes Hughes, and Sheska, frantically copying court cases from her incredible photographic memory (Sheska should never have owned up to having a perfect memory – she could guess she'd be exploited and over-worked!) (3) Brief scenes of the homunculi discussing events (to keep them in the loop), and a little glimpse of Envy's talent for shape-changing (he turns into a surly, sarky Edward).

Episode 20. *Soul of the Guardian*

In episode 20: *Soul of the Guardian* (broadcast Feb 21, 2004) the duels between each Elric brother and the hollow suits of armour continue (indeed, the filmmakers happily replay footage from the previous episode, tho' edited, to form their prologue before the credits – a standard recap format in *animé*). It takes a *long* time for the fights to play out, with Edward Elric being put to the test repeatedly by the endlessly energetic Slicer. Meanwhile, outside the 5th laboratory, Alphonse is smashing Number 66 about, until the former serial killer discovers that Al has a brother inside the building, and uses that against him, playing mind games with the teenager. (Once again, Kentarou Itou provides hilariously hysterical voice work, and the animators under-score it with some great frozen poses).

You keep waiting for Edward Elric to use alchemy against Slicer, rather than his automail arm (which's falling apart anyway, because of a single bolt that Winry-chan forgot to put in – we cut to an embarrassed Winry back in Resembool in the previous episode; in this episode, we hear her disembodied voice). Eventually, and ironically, Ed remembers the villain Scar's use of destruction (one of the stages of alchemy), and that finally defeats the two brothers welded into one suit of armour.

In terms of storytelling, episode 20: *Soul of the Guardian* slows right down in order to include a *lot* of fighting (editor Tetsuro Fujita cuts from one fight to another, as Himoru Arakawa's *manga* does, tho' much more'n the *manga*). Nevertheless, thematic points are being made (about brothers, and about the philosopher's stones, and alchemy), and there is teensy bit of narrative information included with the fifth laboratory scenes. (And secondary charas, such as Scar, Lt. Ross and Armstrong, make fleeting appearances – partly to remind us that they are on their way to help the Elrics).

You can see the difference in the pacing of the two *Fullmetal Alchemist* series here: the second series (of 2009 and 2010), of 64 episodes, dealt with fifth laboratory duels in episode 8 (*The Fifth Laboratory*), while this first *Fullmetal Alchemist* series, of 51 episodes, is still in the fifth laboratory in episode 20. Partly because the second *Fullmetal Alchemist* series had so much more story to get through, of course. But this is also why the first series seems more satisfying in adapting the early chapters of the *manga*, because it's taking more time with them.

Episode 21. *The Red Glow*

Now we see why the lighter, sunnier shows in *Fullmetal Alchemist* are essential structurally, because in these episodes we are in either a prison or an oppressive laboratory, serious threats come from everywhere (the homunculi, Scar, Numbers 66 and 48, a botched attempt at resurrection, a resurrected child-killer (Tucker), the released psychopath Kimbley, plus a new homunculus, Greed), and a man kills himself in front of Edward as the boy tries to stop him.

In episodes 19: *The Truth Behind the Truth*, 20: *Soul of the Guardian* and 21: *The Red Glow*, *Fullmetal Alchemist* shifts into some very odd, creepy territory. Ed and Al's pursuit of the philosopher's stone is taking them into some unusual and sinister areas. Episode 21: *The Red Glow* is a grim, sober show, with few humorous touches (most come from Number 66). Following the (too-long) duels with the hollow suits of armour (who are resurrected, executed criminals) in the secret fifth laboratory, several new villains/ threats are introduced.

One of the disturbing sequences in this crammed show has Ed witnessing a suicide from a few feet away and being unable to prevent it. The scene is played at the hysterical pitch that Japanese television revels in – any chance for loud melodramatics is exploited on Japanese TV. The torso and two arms of Number 48 decides he can't go on in his present form, so he breaks the blood seal on his body. Edward literally grapples with the brother in the torso (as if he's fighting someone with a knife or a gun, holding onto the arm). The way the scene's staged is both macabre and comical. It's a heightened combination of humour and pathos.

Again, the issue of suicide is very alarming in Japanese fiction (in the *manga*, it's Lust and Envy who appear now and dispatch Number 66). The scene was added to the *animé*, but it is perfectly in sync with the moral debate in this part of Himoru Arakawa's comic. It's a variation on the dialogue we've just heard – that Edward is ethically obliged to regard the two brothers of Number 66 as human, and that he won't kill them. This is classy screenwriting (by chief writer Shou Aikawa).

◆

Ed Elric encounters strange creatures in the form of chimera in a corridor (with the head of Number 66 guiding him). The failed alchemist Shou Tucker, the very creepy guy who transmuted his wife, child and dog into chimeras, is their leader/ creator. Now Tucker is a chimera himself (commanding a gang of chimeras – the unusual character design of Tucker (by Yoshiyuki Ito) has part of his head, shoulders and torso sewn into the chimera's bulky, bear-like body up over its back, so his head's upside-down.[11] It sounds simple, but it's genuinely unsettling, which is enhanced by the whispered delivery of voice actor Makoto Nagai). Ed is very alarmed to see Tucker in this form – but that isn't the end of the surprises that Tucker springs on him.

The 'Crimson Alchemist', Zolf J. Kimbley (Yuji Ueda),[12] is led out of the nearby jail (we can guess that soon he'll overcome the guards, as evil prisoners tend to do). Basque Grand (Shin Aomori, who's being impersonated by the homunculus Envy) is also stalking the corridors.

The biggest introduction, though, is given to Greed (*animé* star Junichi Suwabe – *Highschool of the Dead, Bakuman, Space Dandy, Black Butler*, etc).

11 The image links to the 'mother' in the Elrics' transmutation spell.
12 Another veterna of 100s of *animé*, he was Bido and Jean Havoc in the 2nd series.

In a prison cell with alchemical circles on the floor, walls and ceiling, Greed is released from captivity by Number 66 (when he flees from Scar).

Meanwhile in ep. 21: *The Red Glow*, Scar is humanized a little in a flashback to Ishbal, and given a brother. So Scar and his *nii-san*, who also gets into alchemy, mirror the Elric brothers again (as does Scar's arm and Ed's lost arm). We see Scar's brother delving deep into alchemy, covering his naked body in magical symbols, so he becomes an alchemical vessel in his own body (a recurring motif in *Fullmetal Alchemist*). While the war in Ishbal rages, and the younger Scar tries to reason with his sibling, his brother simply wanders off in an apparently crazed state.

Further resonances between the Scar siblings and the Elric brothers is that Scar's brother was trying to resurrect a dead lover. We see successive flashbacks, and each time there are hints of a bungled alchemical experiment, similar to the one the Elrics performed. (In other flashbacks, she is given the features of Lust. However, when Scar confronts Lust about this, she says she doesn't know what he's talking about).

Alphonse, outside the laboratory (following the protracted duel with hollow suit of armour Number 66), teams up with Scar, which is problematic, seeing as Scar is a mass murderer (including of State Alchemists!), and a truly nasty villain – and he also is determined to kill Al's brother Edward! That Al joins forces with Scar is very disturbing (remember that Al is really a fourteen year-old kid). Yet Al instinctively protects Scar from the flying debris when Number 66 activated the explosives at the lab.

So with scenes featuring Al and Scar, and Scar and his brother in the past, and Ed and Shou Tucker, *Fullmetal Alchemist* is exploring very murky territory morally, with both brothers associating with known serial killers.

The homunculi – Lust, Envy and Greed, etc (named after the Seven Sins of Western religion) – are good value as villainous characters. Resembling outcasts of the U.S. TV's *Addams Family* or *Dark Shadows*, they add violence and menace, as well as another bunch of charas who're looking for the philosopher's stone.[13] (In the very talky subsequent episode, 22: *Created Human*, we find out that the homunculi are artificial creatures, who desire to be human: they can't perform alchemy, so that's why they need the *chibi* State Alchemist Edward Elric to find the philosopher's stone.)

The level of *threat* and *coercion* and *sheer nastiness* is very, very strong in *Fullmetal Alchemist*. Far, far stronger and creepier than your average action-adventure movie or even your average horror movie. In the middle episodes, when Ed and Al reach Central City, and are exploring the 5th laboratory, and all of the malignantghj secrets it contains, the corruption and threat is very powerfully portrayed (and it comes from numerous sources, each of which is corrupt, damaged and venal).

---

13 Lust's inevitably portrayed as a shadowy, sinister *femme fatale* (she sprouts Edward Scissorhands' or *X-Men's* Wolverine's blades when she goes into action). Envy is depicted as an androgynous youth who's a twisted reflection of Edward.

▼

The homunculi come face-to-face with Scar and Alphonse Elric (so it's Al, not Edward, who sees the homunculi up close first). Al is soon duelling with Gluttony, and Scar with Lust. Greed enters a locked zone of the penitentiary to enlist some of the jailbirds in his gang (some of which are in cages and are not human). Zolf Kimbley is taken out of his cell in another building by guards. And Edward, in the climactic sequence of 21: *The Red Glow*, after battling lion-like chimeras in a corridor (slicing them up with his bladed arm), is led by Tucker-san into a chamber set up for alchemical transmutations (it's the equivalent of the Big, Expensive Set or the Villain's Lair in an action-adventure flick). The chamber has the red water of near-philosopher's stones on tap (in vessels placed at six points). There's a large transmutation circle drawn on the floor, the walls are shimmering (and it's lit by the lurid pink-purple light that signifies something strange and sinister in *animé*).

To emphasize how menacing these scenes are, the filmmakers give Ed a particularly haggard appearance, with black rings around his eyes (after all, he has just struggled thru a savage duel, and is wounded in several places, and lost a lot of blood. But Ed is also a very determined boy, a pint-sized alchemical visionary pursuing the secrets of creation).14

Episode 22. *Created Human*

Episode 22: *Created Human* is the climax of the first part of the 2004-2005 *Fullmetal Alchemist* series, bringing together most of the major characters, the villains, and the secondary characters for a showdown in the fifth laboratory (this important episode was scripted by the head writer, Shou Aikawa).

It's one of the finest episodes in either *Fullmetal Alchemist* series – great script, great situations, great action, and great filmmaking. It's shows like this which are one of the reasons that Japanese animation is among the greatest storytelling artforms in the world. When it comes to producing that immense *whoosh* of dramatic energy and pleasure for the viewer, where you're rooting for the heroes, where you're on the edge of your seat, Japanese *animé* is truly remarkable.

Indeed, you could argue that this climactic sequence (episodes 19 to 21) offer a more dramatically satisfying finale than the last episodes of the 1st *Fullmetal Alchemist* series. What's at stake, the goals, the motives and so on are much the same (tho' the finale plays out with the addition of the Elrics' pa, Hohenheim, and Dante, the chief homunculus). Ep 22: *Created Human* is also a pricey episode, where a lot more Yen is spent on the visual effects budget.

The setting for the finale of the first half of *Fullmetal Alchemist*? Why, a transmutation ritual of alchemy, of course – that is, a massive alchemical ceremony in which Edward Elric is forced by the homunculi to

14 Many of these elements were added to Himoru Arakawa's *manga* (for instance, in the *Fullmetal Alchemist manga*, Lust and Envy appear at the end of Ed's duel with Number 48, killing the guard).

perform alchemy. Episode 22: *Created Human* is very verbose – it's where we find out about the homunculi, about the military's involvement in alchemy, and more about the philosopher's stone. Where Ed comes face-to-face with the homunculi in their undisguised forms (he attacks Basque Grand, for instance, knowing that he is being impersonated). And where we meet more new charas – such as Martel and Greed's gang.

Episode 22: *Created Human* is also very hazardous, with the intimidation and coercion suffered by the Elric brothers reaching very violent levels. Remember, these are *teenagers*, but they are being beaten in graphic detail by a bunch of adults, and imprisoned and manipulated in a very forbidding manner. And being forced to kill 20 or so men in a magical ritual.

Ed Elric is pummelled and kicked repeatedly by the sarcastic and thoroughly despicable Envy, so he's beaten down to the floor (his automail arm chooses this moment to completely break – it was weakened in the preceding duel with Number 48), and poor Al is pinned to the wall and then to the floor by Lust (and Al has a piece of his armour bitten off by Gluttony). To see your heroes being smashed about by psychopaths is alarming – the *manga* doesn't held back, and the two *animé* series don't, either.

'So this is the truth behind the truth', Edward Elric mutters, as he is pushed into a corner of aggressive coercion. Ed finds himself in the midst of a moral dilemma, being forced to do something (use alchemy which will transmute living humans beings, albeit prisoners) against his will, in order to save his brother (and the situation). Lust breaks the blood-seal on Number 48's helmet, which kills the guard. This is used as an example of what will happen to Alphonse in the next beat (this is terrific screen-writing – saving that moment of Number 48's death, to make it pay off here).

The scene is high drama, hysterical and operatic: Alphonse screams at Edward not to do it: a bunch of prisoners cower in fear inside the transmutation circle (Gluttony lurks beyond the circle, giggling with insane hunger): the homunculi stand to one side, watching in anticipation (the Tucker-chimera has also joined the homunculi – up to this point, Ed thought that he would be transmuting the red water to make a philosopher's stone, but not using real people). Lust holds Al's armour in her pincers, one of her claws poised over the blood-seal inside Alphonse (the equivalent in *Fullmetal Alchemist* of holding someone at gunpoint).

The filmmakers milk these moments – rightly: they've got the audience on the edge of their seats, with an inventive and perilous cliffhanger. But Ed Elric crumples, unable to continue. At this point, before the homunculi can put even more pressure on the Elrics to perform alchemy for them, Scar (who's been observing the rite from above thru a secret opening), smashes apart the ceiling (altho' Scar has his own agenda, that he turns out to be the Elrics' rescuer is morally problematic – the military arrive minutes later).

Meanwhile, the military, led by the Führer himself (and Hughes-san[15]), is also outside, preparing to run in and rescue the boys. We still don't know yet that the Führer is in fact a homunculus – and we're halfway thru the *Fullmetal Alchemist* series! We also haven't met arch-homunculus Dante,[16] or her aide, Julia Douglas. (Much of this episode is invented from the *Fullmetal Alchemist manga* by Himoru Arakawa, but the anime-only sections which are firmly fitted to the narrative scheme of the *manga*. After all, this is an episode that the producers will have thought long and hard about).

Episode 22: *Created Human* also departs from the *Fullmetal Alchemist manga* in having Edward Elric being overcome by the spilled red water on the floor, so that he appears possessed, out of control, his alchemical powers enhanced too much (it's a familiar image in Japanese animation of a youth who's lost control, who's swamped by supernatural powers). This is a marvellous narrative twist that comes out of the spirit of the comic, taking the drama to another level.

At this point, the irritating auntie figure of Lt. Ross performs her major act in the first *Fullmetal Alchemist* series: she approaches Ed thru swirling clouds of energy, and gives him a hug: *okasan* ('mother'), Ed whispers, closing his eyes. The vortex dissipates. This is great filmmaking!

What is the 'truth behind the truth'? It is this: that the adult world is corrupt and complicated, that it is full of pain, that nothing is simple, or morally black and white, and that Ed and Al Elric cannot hang onto being children anymore. They have to grow up. Or they have to lose something of themselves in order to be able to deal with nasty pieces of work like Lust and her fellow psychopathic homunculi. (Lust explains to Edward that being grown-up means making sacrifices).

Fullmetal Alchemist is thus very bleak stuff, because it depicts a twisted, infected world, where very few of the adults that surround our teenage heroes seem to have any moral backbone, or seem to be working for good or for right. No adult plays fair, no adult is reliable, no adult is without major faults. Even the smugly self-righteous Roy Mustang has been involved in nefarious deeds (including the cold-blooded execution of innocents).

So the Elric lads hang onto the image of their mother, as the one thing in the whole world that is pure and good. Once again, it's the *seriousness* which the drama is played by the principal characters (and their amazing voice talents – Romi Pak and Rie Kugimiya are incredible in this episode), coupled with outstanding animation, music, sound effects, visual effects *et al*, that makes it all work in *Fullmetal Alchemist* (incidentally, and tellingly, there are *no* comical moments in episode 22: *Created Human*, and even when the psycho Envy taunts Ed about being a pipsqueak (a super-chibi), it's the first time it isn't played for laughs).

---

15 In a piece of visual comedy, both Hughes and the Führer are seen in cute patterned pyjamas.
16 Edward points us in that direction, when he says that someone must've created the homunculi in the first place.
17 The way that the quarrel was developed was unusual – it had Alphonse being thrown into

There are also a lot of newer characters in this batch of *Fullmetal Alchemist* episodes, including the 'Crimson Alchemist', Zolf J. Kimbley, and Basque Grand (who's being impersonated by the homunculus Envy), plus Envy, and assorted prisoners and bad guys, including Greed, and Martel, who break out of the prison in the chaos (we see much more of them later). Altho' writer Shou Aikawa and the filmmakers invented much of this show, the script was certainly in the spirit of *Fullmetal Alchemist*, as well as employing its chief motifs and themes.

Episode 23. *Heart of Steel*

Thankfully, the first *Fullmetal Alchemist* series lightens up considerably in the next episode – 23: *Heart of Steel*, which contains plenty of humour, and also the arrival in Central City of Winry Rockbell, the cute, blonde, tomboy automail (cyborgization) mechanic, who acts as the conscience of the Elric brothers (if *they're* not going cry, *she* will; if *they're* not going to talky-talk, *she* will! She's a girl, right? She's good at crying and emoting!).

The topic of milk comes up: Ed won't drink it, but for Winry, as a partial author avatar for Himoru Arakawa, who grew up on a dairy farm in Hokkaido, milk is a Big Deal! So Winry insists that Ed drink his milk (he wants to grow, doesn't he?). As the teens argue, multiple versions of Arakawa's caricature drawing – a black-and-white cow with glasses – float in the background (it's an appropriate cameo for the *mangaka*).

It's an aftermath episode, a catch-up episode, comprising long talky scenes around Edward Elric's hospital bed coupled with flashbacks to the traumas of the 5th laboratory scenes. (In the *manga*, it's chapter 15: *Steel Heart*).

There's also the first major rift between the alchemist *kyoudai* – they fall out over, inevitably, their central quest, of rejuvenating their former selves. Alphonse has been corrupted by Barry the serial killer's ramblings and mind games about whether Ed really did transmute him into a suit of armour. It doesn't convince at all, but it does lead to yet another fall-out between the brothers (we always have to remember that the eight-foot tall suit of armour contains the soul of a 14 year-old boy, who looks up to his brother).

The *Hagane no Renkinjutsushi* series contains plenty of teenage huffing and sulking: in 1.23: *Heart of Steel*, Winry Rockbell also huffs off (when the boys won't tell her all they know. The strongest relationship in *Fullmetal Alchemist*, by far, is between the brothers). Of course the sulks and piques don't last long: Winry is intercepted by family man and all-round good guy Maes Hughes (Keiji Fujiwara – he was Hughes in both *Fullmetal Alchemist* series), and is taken to his home for his beloved daughter's birthday party (these smaller-scale, domestic scenes prepare the ground for one of the key deaths in the *Fullmetal Alchemist* series, of Hughes). However, the boys, who make up when they talk, are kept apart for longer, over into the next episode (they wander away from each other, with Al acting like a manic depressive, sitting alone and not communicating with anybody). Al's mope is extended far longer in the first *Fullmetal Alchemist* series – too long, really.

Indeed, Alphonse Elric's dialogue consists entirely of muted *hmmms* until he finally explodes. To Ed's and Winry's astonishment and dismay, Al hysterically asserts that maybe he isn't real, and is a fake concocted by his brother (he is the 'heart of steel' of the episode's title). That Ed could create fake memories Al should realize is pretty far-fetched (how would you do that? – it's god-like. But then, bonding a soul to a suit of armour is also fairly godly).

Splitting your hero into two people enables you to have intense scenes of conflict like this – Al's outburst swiftly and powerfully brings out the passions bubbling underneath the central relationship of *Fullmetal Alchemist* (similarly, Edward's breezy, casual dismissal of the events in the 5th laboratory incenses Lt. Ross so much she slaps him in the face (apologizing before and after, of course). Yes, Edward gets beaten around plenty in this part of *Fullmetal Alchemist* – by suits of armour, by Envy, by alchemical rituals, even by his bodyguards, etc).

Sweet moments, silly moments, weepy moments, touchy-feely moments – ep. 23 is not about action and story at all, but about characters. It is, in short, one of the chief reasons that *Fullmetal Alchemist* has a high dramatic impact as a TV show – because it *stops* the headlong rush of story-story-story, and takes *time* to explore the characters. (So many shows and movies don't this essential dramatic work, because it is *work*, it does take time to conceive and write), so that, when the characters reach the climactic scenes, the audience's connection to them is so much weaker.

What makes *Fullmetal Alchemist* fly, in other words, is that we have spent so much time with Edward and Alphonse Elric, we get to know them quite well.

Episode 24. *Bonding Memories*

The following episode, 24: *Bonding (of) Memories*, heals the mis-understanding between the Elric brothers.[17] Ed Elric dives in to save his brother from Barry the Chopper in the suit of hollow armour (altho' it's Scar who finally stomps on Number 66's helmet. Having already brought him back once, it's possible the *Fullmetal Alchemist* writers might do so again, however. The point of reviving villains is that it means using a villain who has some emotional or dramatic connection to the heroes, instead of having to establish that all over again with a new chara).

In episode 24: *Bonding Memories* it is Alphonse Elric who's the centre of attention, rather than Edward (as usual). Al goes A.W.O.L., storming

---

17 The way that the quarrel was developed was unusual – it had Alphonse being thrown into

off in a huge sulk into the streets, and getting involved with a bunch of Ishbalians (and Scar). And the *Fullmetal Alchemist* series itself goes A.W.O.L. here, too: this is where the 2004-05 series really departs from the *manga*. Among the inventions from Himoru Arakawa's *manga* are a group of hired guns being given orders (by Juliet Douglas) to set upon the Ishbalians in Central City: there are distressing scenes of widespread mayhem. The authorities are not shown doing anything about the quasi-military mercenaries. Douglas reveals her true colours when the mercenaries' leader meets her and is dispatched. (This is Douglas's first decisive act in *Fullmetal Alchemist* – to commission the mercenaries to attack the Ishbalians, and then to rub out their leader).

In episodes 24 and 25 of *Fullmetal Alchemist* (*Bonding Memories* and *Words of Farewell*), the issue of Ishbal arises again, with yet another assault on its people (who've now come to Central City, and're hiding – in the sewers!). The Western world's deeply troubled relationship with the Middle East is once again foregrounded in this very contemporary piece of filmmaking. There's no doubt that this is racial extermination – a bunch of fascist bullies armed to the teeth go up against unarmed civilians.

Also very troubling is the humanizing of the serial killer Scar: this guy has been depicted as a despicable mass murderer (with repeated attempts at killing our heroes), yet in the middle episodes of the first *Fullmetal Alchemist* series he hooks up with Alphonse Elric, and is humanized by the filmmakers. It's another example of the pop culture of Japan portraying very ambiguous villains, tho' Scar has been so odious, how can he now be the buddy of our heroes?

In the action finale of episode 1.24: *Bonding Memories*, the two brothers're re-united (improbably, Winry-chan is present too, to enhance the sweetness of the brotherly reunion, of course, but in the *Fullmetal Alchemist manga* Winry is usually far away from danger and action. Putting Winry right next to the battle with the mercenaries is problematic). Turns out that what Edward was trying to say to Alphonse was to ask him if he blamed him for attaching his soul to a suit of armour. (The 'let's make-up' scenes are a little smug and self-satisfied, which jars with the killings that have been depicted just moments earlier. Some of the action here is a little too unconvincing[18]).

The script of 1:24: *Bonding Memories*, by Toshiki Inoue, is one of the shakier installments in *Fullmetal Alchemist* – partly because it makes too many leaps in the storytelling that defy belief, and because it stretches the characterizations too far.

When Scar departs with the Ishbalians (on a boat on a river), the series says *sayonara* to one segment of the series (we are halfway through the run now). It seems as if one plot strand is ending – but others are emerging from the shadows (such as Crichton, the Führer's flunkey).

---

18 And we get tired of the depiction of Edward Elric as an overly-weepy, angst-ridden teenager.

Episode 25. *Words of Farewell*

There is a death of a secondary character, Maes Hughes, in the next episode – 25: *Words of Farewell* (the second *animé* series of *Fullmetal Alchemist* also made much of Hughes' demise). He's the second-in-command to Roy Mustang, is *crazy* about his new baby (he shows *everyone* his family snapshots), and is another of numerous father figures to the Elric brothers (Hughes is a much better surrogate father than Tucker – he also plays a brief fatherly role to Winry Rockbell).

Hughes-san follows up the leads about the 5th laboratory, and uncovers a connection to the military, and to Captain Juliet Douglas in particular, a sinister, middle-aged woman (invented for the *Fullmetal Alchemist animé*) who works right in the heart of the military machine, in the Führer's office (a post taken up by Liza Hawkeye in the *manga*).

Unfortunately, although Maes Hughes is a canny operator within the State Alchemist and military hierarchy, he is finally trapped and topped by the homunculi: Lust and Envy are hot on his tail. Hughes manages to elude them for a while, but they catch up with him soon and kill him (in a vicious scene in a (British) telephone booth, with Envy tauntingly taking on the form of Hughes' wife Gracia – Kotono Mitsuishi).

Maes Hughes receives a major send-off in *Fullmetal Alchemist,* with a big cemetery scene (offering yet another opportunity for the filmmakers to wheel on all of the ensemble cast, so they can have their poignant moments. Composer Michiru Oshima creates a lovely orchestral cue for this scene, and also employs piano cues with elaborate flourishes which're deployed several times in these middle episodes of *Fullmetal Alchemist.* The filmmakers rightly let the music do the emotional work here, and dispense with dialogue for a while).

Hughes-san wasn't a main character, but his death reverberates throughout the rest of the fully, metally alchemical series, with its hints of corruption within the military (and the government). Thus the characterization of Maes Hughes was developed to make his death even more piquant: he was given a young family, a charming personality, and a new child, whom he doted on (the heroes even witness the birth of the baby).

But episode 1.25: *Words of Farewell* closes on a more upbeat note, with the Elric brothers on their way to Ishbal, or the Southern reaches of Amestris, which have a high concentration of Ishbalians (it takes them a *long* time to get there!), to pursue further their quest for the philosopher's stone (and this time they have Winry Rockbell with them, which lightens things up – though we can guess that Winry is going to be put at risk by the bad guys, with the Elric brothers probably having to save her. After all, she does play the role of the princess somewhat in *Fullmetal Alchemist,* albeit a tomboy princess great at fixing things. Winry is keen to visit Rush Valley, an automail heaven).

In the 2009-10 *Fullmetal Alchemist: Brotherhood* series, the *effect* of Maes Hughes's death on the Elric brothers (and Winry Rockbell) is given a *huge* amount of screen time. There is scene after scene of Ed, Al and

Winry looking glum, morose, sombre, tearful, angry, and glum again, and teary again, and furious again. Well, it's laudable when an action-adventure/ fantasy/ comedy *animé* pauses to mourn the death of a character; but the impact of Hughes' death on our heroes is *really* milked to the max. Also, Hughes is not a major character. But I guess he represents what is at stake, and the losses that the quest of the Elrics might help to create along the way (that Hughes was a family man of course enhances the abomination of his demise, and he is the good, doting father that the Elrics didn't have as kids). Other writers might've opted to up the stakes by having Winry, say, or Izumi Curtis, or Pinako, die (or be injured), which would've had more emotional impact on the Elrics, because their link to Winry goes back to their childhoods.

✳

Episode 25: *Words of Farewell* has other elements, too: for a start, it is not a straightforward, A-to-B-to-C progression of events: there are several flashbacks. In this episode, for instance, we see the usually prim, proper and smug Roy Mustang dishevelled and unkempt, haunted by what he did in the war (and going about his own research into the deeper secrets of alchemy in his rooms. We see buckets of blood scattered around the room – not a good sign!). In this flashback, which takes place soon after the Ishbal War is over, Mustang is near-suicidal (a gun is displayed prominently on the table when Hughes-san talks to Mustang about his depression, and about finding ways to end it all). To complicate matters, the episode returns to this flashback again. (One of the sources for this sequence is the *gaiden* (extra) story, *His Battlefield Once More*).

Meanwhile, Scar is kept in the loop of *Fullmetal Alchemist* series one: last seen floating off into the sunset with a bunch of Isbalians on a boat (a scene that didn't really fit in with the tone of Himoru Arakawa's *manga*),[19] we see Scar thinking back (again) to the Ishbal War, in an attack on a caravan of Ishbalians in the desert at night from Zolf Kimbley and other alchemists. The theme of revenge is introduced again, when Scar's Master returns (in the present tense): vengeance will eat away your soul. But Scar won't let it lie. So when a motorcycle gang turns up at the Ishbals' encampment at night, with the sole aim of terrorizing the refugees with some roughneck bullying, Scar exits a tent to take on the thugs, attacking a couple of them with some alchemical magic; one has his arm ripped off, another is killed; the rest wisely flee. (And yet, when episode 25: *Words of Farewell* cuts to the Elrics on the train in the present tense, Alphonse insists that Scar 'isn't really a bad man'! Edward, meanwhile, rightly says that Scar shouldn't be allowed to get away with murdering State Alchemists. Darn right: Scar should've been destroyed twenty episodes ago!).

Episode 26. *Her Reason*

Episode 26: *Her Reason*, set in Rush Valley, is a largely light-hearted outing, concentrating on the Elric brothers and their relationship with

---

19 Similar scenes occur in *Hero Tales*.

Winry Rockbell (one girl and two boys – that's going to cause problems of romantic rivalry, surely?!).[20]

There's also another young woman in ep. 1.26: Paninya (Kyoko Hikami), who uses a lot of automail (she was wounded in a railroad accident as a child, revealed in a flashback montage. A five year-old girl with stumps for two legs and an arm is a pitiful sight[21]). Paninya is portrayed as a female counterpart of Edward Elric (and, with her combat-patterened pants and tight croptop, she might be appearing in a J-pop band in her spare time[22]). Paninya goes up against Ed in a long chase played mainly for laughs (in the *Fullmetal Alchemist manga*, the chase is dull and goes on forever) – which's part of Winry's plan to get her own back on Ed, and also to persuade him to recognize the value of her own automail, in which she takes great pride (and for Ed to appreciate that Paninya's automail is very fine, too).

Episode 1.26: *Her Reason* also allows for the brothers' childhood buddy Winry Rockbell to exert her influence over the Elric boys – this is one of her Big Episodes in *Fullmetal Alchemist*. She's gone to Rush Valley partly because it's the Automail Capital of this world of Amestris (and Winry is a major tech-head, fetishizing automail with the passion of an *anime* or pop idol *otaku*). The scenes of Winry drooling excessively over the *mecha* on display in the stores' windows are amusing (while a girl nearby slobbers over a new ring). And so miffed is Winry that Elric cheated in an automail arm wrestling competition (which was itself run by cheats, who used alchemy – a circle's drawn on the underside of the table), she whacks him – twice (and Al – *and* the cowardly shysters), before storming off (girls beating up boys is a staple of *manga*, and Himoru Arakawa never lets an opportunity slip by to depict a strong woman!).

Some of narrative material in episode 26: *Her Reason* was altered for the *anime*, because the *Fullmetal Alchemist manga* had a different story. In Himoru Arakawa's *manga*, characters from Xing or Shin (i.e., presumably China, but also perhaps Korea) are introduced. A cocky con-man, Prince Ling Yao, is the principal chara, with his henchmen that the Elrics fight (these charas recur in the *manga*, but're dropped from the *anime*. Their characterizations in the first *Fullmetal Alchemist* series are also different. In the *manga* and in the second *anime*, Ling Yao plays much bigger role which, ultimately, is more satisfying). For the *anime*, the story was altered.

Meanwhile, back in East City, episode 26: *Her Reason* keeps the over-arching plot ticking over with scenes of Roy Mustang and Liza Hawkeye contemplating the aftermath of the murder of Maes Hughes. The key plot point here is that Major Armstrong confirms that someone higher up in the military organization might be involved. In another departure from the *Fullmetal Alchemist manga*, Izumi Curtis, the brothers' alchemy *sensei*, and

---

20 The *manga* makes more of the potential love triangle than the *anime*. Indeed, the *manga* is more explicit in some respects than the *anime*.
21 But the show doesn't dwell on it for too long.
22 As the drummer, of course.

her husband Sig, are hunting the boys down (storming into Mustang's office – amusingly, though rather unbelievably).

Episode 27. *Teacher*.

Episodes 27: *Teacher*, 28: *All Is One, One Is All* and 29: *The Untainted Child* (co-written by Akatsuki Yamatoya, Katsuhiko Takayama, and Shou Aikawa) form a group of shows in *Fullmetal Alchemist* which delve into the early childhood of Ed and Al Elric, including discussions of their plans to resurrect their mother Trisha. These are extended flashback sequences, in which the screenwriters once again mine the early years of the heroes, but here they go back and stage full-length scenes, rather than brief montages.

Including long flashbacks like this may be due to the way that *animé* series are broadcast in seasons of 13, 26, 39 or 52 episode runs. *Fullmetal Alchemist* runs to 51 episodes (it was broadcast over a year, from October 4, 2003 to October 2, 2004, so a break at episode 26 makes sense. In which case, the flashbacks in these episodes *Teacher, All Is One, One Is All* and *The Untainted Child*, act as reminders for newer viewers of the key moment in the past of the Elric brothers, when they decided to break the taboo in alchemy of bringing back the dead. (Another device is a clip or recap show, which the 2nd *Fullmetal Alchemist* series did). Also, long-running *animé* series usually summarize key plots, sometimes just in one or two lines of dialogue, sometimes by recycling a shot or two, sometimes with longer montages, and sometimes with a pre-titles prologue which sets out the world of the *animé* (as in *One Piece*). Viewers are dipping in and out of TV shows which run over months, and not watching them every week, so summaries are essential.

✳

In episode 27: *Teacher* there's yet another authority figure that's introduced – this time the brothers' early *sensei*, the teacher who taught them the rudiments of alchemy, Izumi Curtis (Shoko Tsuda – she was also Curtis in the 2nd series). She's a young woman (maybe late twenties) with dreadlocks, and a sombre attitude to life and learning. Curtis has a fabulous figure with a prominent cleavage (another 'va-va voom' women from Himoru Arakawa), and a tailored white dress over black leggings. (Curtis is accompanied by a gigantic, taciturn boulder of a man, a hulk of a husband, Segu (Sig) Curtis (Seiji Sasaki – he was also Sig in the second series), who says barely a word. Sig just has to stand there to get his message across, or to glower). At the height of one dramatic scene, as she storms a den of bad guys and wastes them all, she defines herself with a yell: 'A HOUSEWIFE!' (This is one of the things that *manga* author Himoru Arakawa had wanted Curtis to say: it gets a prominent position in the *manga*, too.)

The flashbacks in episodes *Teacher, All Is One, One Is All* and *The Untainted Child* include scenes where the Elric brothers (in their pre-cursed condition) beg Izumi Curtis to teach them alchemy (in the scene where Curtis prevents a river from flooding during heavy rain, which closely follows the *Fullmetal Alchemist manga*. The Elrics try to help, and fail, and witness Curtis using alchemy. Afterwards, they plead to be taught alchemy). Like Ed, Curtis flies off the handle when she's treated or viewed in the wrong (or disrespectful) manner (when the kids call her old woman, for instance, or when they mention State Alchemists on the train, whom Curtis derides (like Pinako) as the 'dogs of the military', she goes as nuts as Ed does when someone mentions his height).

In fact, characters who act as prima donnas and divas, blowing up at the slightest slight, are found throughout the *Fullmetal Alchemist* series – and throughout *animé* (think of Tetsuo in *Akira* or the demons in *Urotsukidoji* (*Fullmetal Alchemist* writer Shou Aikawa worked on the *Overfiend* series).[23] The cries of loneliness, of the inability to express oneself, of the angst of being young and misunderstood, is passionately and brilliantly expressed in *Fullmetal Alchemist*, *Akira* and the *Urotsukidoji* series (you can also find those feelings in *Gunbuster*, *Ghost In the Shell*, *Paranoia Agent*, *Evangelion* and *Escaflowne*).)

For some time, it seems as if episode 27: *Teacher* is going to be a light-hearted show in *Fullmetal Alchemist*: there are evocations of cats giving birth, jokey encounters between pupils and teachers, and depictions of rural life in Dublith. However, the writer (Katsuhiko Takayama) is slipping in references to the key themes of *Fullmetal Alchemist*: for instance, the cat dies giving birth, and Izumi Curtis explains to a weeping child that once something dies, it is gone for good (Curtis delivers quite a lot of Arakawan life-philosophy here, about the flow of energy and the cycle of the natural world and how death is part of that flow). There are foreshadowing hints about Curtis's lost child.[24]

And training scenes, too, as Izumi Curtis puts the lads thru their paces in the garden (using the wonderful motif in series such as *Naruto* of a teacher (Kakashi-sensei) calmly reading a book while fighting off opponents).

▼

When, in the finale of episode 1.27: *Sensei* (in another graveside, molten sunset setting), Ed and Al Elric admit that they tried to bring their mother Trisha back to life, what does Izumi Curtis do? She beats them very hard and for a long time – it's a really vicious beating. An adult hitting children. Afterwards, she hugs them. Tough love, eh, folks? Whacking the hell out of children, then hugging them! (And they don't dare to hit back, of course). Yes – *Fullmetal Alchemist* is full of so many scenes of incredible violence and abuse by adults against children, as in *One Piece*. (In the second *animé* of 2009-10, the first thing Curtis does when

23 The demons in the *Legend of the Overfiend* series are similarly diva-like, such pouters and poseurs, such cry babies and sulkers. They are highly neurotic and vulnerable, sensitive to the slightest slight against their dignity or manhood – and they over-react to the teensiest insult with expressions of colossal violence (just as Edward blows up at any slight – especially over his height!). And that's Tetsuo in *Akira* – a neurotic over-reacting to everything; Tetsuo speeds from zero to fury in 3 seconds.
24 It's very artificial and on the nail that Arakawa wheels in a cute girl and her dead pet as soon as the Elrics meet Curtis.

she meets the Elrics is to hit them).

The full depiction of Izumi Curtis's back-story is delayed: there are hints of it, but it's not until later that we find out out that Curtis also tried human transmutation (which makes her violent abuse of the Elric brothers both more understandable and a little bit forgivable, but also very hypocritical).

Episode 28. *All Is One, One Is All.*

There's a long excursion to an island in the middle of a lake in *Fullmetal Alchemist,* where Izumi Curtis-*sensei* leaves her charges in order for them to *think* about what they've done (it's a shorter sequence in the second *Fullmetal* series, but was still included because it's thematically important). We enter another lengthy flashback sequence, to Jack (a.k.a. Yock) Island and the same predicament, when Curtis dropped off the boys on the island in order for them to survive for a month (in Himoru Arakawa's *manga,* the structure of the flashback is handled slightly differently, but the impact remains pretty much the same). In the first *Fullmetal Alchemist* series, episode 28: *All Is One, One Is All* cuts back and forth between the past and the present, with the brothers remembering their earlier time on the island. (There is far more interaction between the present and the past in the adaptation, including many inventive links between the two).

So it's *Lord of the Flies* time, it's *Robinson Crusoe* time. True, it's an artificial narrative construct, artistically, but it does mean we're spending more time with Ed and Al Elric rather than some of the far less interesting secondary characters (no matter how hard the filmmaking team try, some of the characters placed around the boys aren't as compelling or as entertaining). Indeed, there are no cuts away to Roy Mustang, the homunculi or other members of the cast in episode 28: *All Is One, One Is All.*

The 2004 *animé* show includes scenes of the boys as tweens surviving with nothing but a hunting knife on an island (the kind of game that children play, but the Elrics endure it for real). Played for comedy, but with a serious point to make: that you have to kill to live, that animals have to be sliced up if you're going to eat meat (this is one of *mangaka* Himoru Arakawa's recurring themes – she grew up on a farm in Hokkaido, remember. It permeates *Silver Spoon,* for instance, and *animé* such as *Earth Maiden Arjuna*).

So we see the lads struggling with one of the primary goals of being human: finding food (finding shelter is easier, it seems – altho' exposure to cold kills much quicker than lack of nosh or water). Foxes, rabbits, birds, fish, bugs and mushrooms are part of the cycle of life here: a snared rabbit looks up at the Elrics with Big Disney Eyes, and the brothers can't kill it. Mushrooms make them sick, and fish take a *long* time to catch. Meanwhile, Izumi Curtis's assistant from the butcher's shop turns up to terrorize the kids wearing a mask and wielding a wooden club (his first appearance is at night, as Edward wakes, to make it extra-creepy).

Much of episode 28: *All Is One, One Is All* comes straight out of the *Fullmetal Alchemist manga,* but there are departures. Winry Rockbell, for instance, comes along for the ride (but she doesn't get why Izumi Curtis is doing this at all). The writers have invented a new character here, too: a sort-of-son of Curtis, who's running wild on the island (later, he's revealed to be a homunculus). His introduction is the climax of this show.

Meanwhile, it's worth noting that we're over halfway thru the first *Fullmetal Alchemist* series, and we have seen only brief glimpses of the homunculi, and have no real idea of what they're after or who created them. We don't know who the mastermind is behind it all, and we haven't seen the Gateway of Truth, or the spiritual limbo, or any of the many elements which the later *Fullmetal Alchemist manga* installments and the second series depicted (the second adaptation covered this material in episode 12 out of a 64-episode run).

Episode 29. *The Untainted Child*

In episode 29: *The Untainted Child* the Elric brothers are still under the thrall of *sensei* Izumi Curtis. Oh dear, she becomes a tiresomely grim and immovable personality (with the perpetual down-turned mouth of so many charas in *Fullmetal Alchemist:* artist Hiromu Arakawa spends ages drawing each character, then she adds a single line to the face, a short ellipse, like a cel phone icon, the down-turned bracket: ( ).

Despite that slinky figure (with the mandatory *animé* cleavage), and the cool dreadlocks, Izumi Curtis is actually a stuck-up, solemn auntie-type, yet another of countless stern, firm teachers and parental substitutes in Japanese animation (altho' she's motherly, Curtis's gender is totally secondary to her status as the teacher and authority figure to the Elric boys). We know there's likely to be a troubled past to Curtis-sensei (what adult chara *doesn't* have a nefarious history in *Fullmetal Alchemist*?!), and she does cough up blood a lot (one of the surest signs a character's going to die real soon in TV/ cinema. Indeed, after a couple of coughs, Curtis should be dead already! But this being an *animé* where everything is s-t-r-e-t-c-h-e-d o-u-t for a l-o-n-g time, Curtis doesn't pop her clogs for many episodes).

The filmmakers depart even further from the *Fullmetal Alchemist manga* by Himoru Arakawa with this episode: the child discovered on the island turns out to have Edward Elric's arm and leg (thus linking Ed to Izumi Curtis, and making the child something like a brother, and Curtis something like a mother). Creating Wrath with Ed's arm and leg makes sense at a thematic and psychological level, if not quite at a dramatic level; but it does develop the theme in the *Fullmetal Alchemist* universe of arms in particular being grafted onto other bodies (principally with Scar and his brother).

There are scenes of the boy Wrath being taken into care by Izumi

Curtis, and fed, and of the Elrics questioning him about his origins. (Winry Rockbell is still around, another alteration from the *manga* of *Fullmetal Alchemist*. Himoru Arakawa knew there wasn't much that Winry could do here, and wisely left her behind in Resembool).

Among the secondary charas, other changes from the *Fullmetal Alchemist manga* include Sheska remonstrating Roy Mustang about the investigation of the murder of her former boss Maes Hughes (something she would never do in the Himoru Arakawa's *manga* – where she's far too conscious of her status, and also way too shy). And another new chara is introduced: Frank Archer (Sho Hayami – best-known as the super-villlain Sosuke Aizen in *Bleach*): a thin, pale, supercilious guy who is going to act as an obstacle/ rival within the military.

▼

On the plus side, episode 1.29: *The Untainted Child* does offer even more explorations of that fateful day when Elrics Edward and Alphonse decided to try to bring their mom back to life using magic. It's a spectacular sequence (narrated by Ed at the Curtises' kitchen table) employing the full arsenal of visual effects filmmaking, using many imaginative images to evoke an other-world and spiritual experiences. *Fullmetal Alchemist* is especially effective when it tackles abstract and metaphysical concepts and philosophies – it's something that Japanese animation seems better suited at exploring than any other filmmakers. It's a swirling kaleidoscope of colours, movements, patterns, sounds and music, culminating with washes to white (white, in *Fullmetal Alchemist* and Japanese animation, seems a much better image for ultimate origins than black – the white of the *manga* page, of the Oriental void).

You got to give the screenwriters of *Fullmetal Alchemist* (chief writer Sho Aikawa, and Akatsuki Yamatoya, Aiya Yoshinaga, Jun Ishikawa, Katsuhijo Takayama, Natsuko Takahashi, and Toshiki Inoue), every credit for exploiting that two-minute opening prologue and concept, which started off volume one of Himoru Arakawa's comic, for everything it's got. When I said earlier that the opening prologue reverberates throughout the *Fullmetal Alchemist* series, I wasn't kidding! It lurks behind pretty much every episode, and in the run of episodes here,*Teacher*, *All Is One, One Is All* and *The Untainted Child*, it's pushed into the foreground yet again.

Now we see the authors of the *Fullmetal Alchemist* show going back to the alchemical experiment and wondering just *how* it would've worked, and exactly *what* happened – in addition to Ed Elric losing his limbs, and Al seeming to die. Now we see a journey to another world, an under-world, a Hell; there's a giant gateway (very reminiscent of the famous sculpture by Auguste Rodin, *Gates of Hell*, and also the Baptistery door in Florence by Lorenzo Ghiberti (1401, which're known as *The Gate of Paradise*))[25] they're terrifying images of Alphonse as a corpse (and also the boys' mother); there're little, black sprites[26] that hover around and tease Ed.

---

25 A phrase coined by Michelangelo Buonarroti.
26 Here they're given little eyes.

So the flashback goes on – but it all amounts to unsolved mystery, with Ed and Al Elric only getting further slices of enigma and the unknown, but no closer, it seems, to the 'truth', or to finding out how to manufacture a philosopher's stone, or to regaining the bodies they long for. At the end of episode 1.29: *The Untainted Child* Izumi Curtis travels back to Jack Island to confirm what she suspects about the foundling.

Of course – you're not going to satisfy the heroes' primary desire halfway thru a 51-episode TV series, right? No! What's remarkable is just how much dramatic juice the screenwriters (led by Shou Aikawa) manage to extract from the initial premise (indeed, that is one of the marks of a great screenwriter – someone who can take a concept and s-q-u-e-e-z-e every ounce, every smidgen, every tiny dot of dramatic essence out of it. And we've all seen shows and movies where the initial idea has been flogged to death, right? Yes. But in *Fullmetal Alchemist*, we buy it, because of the way it's handled, the way it's played, the way it's parcelled out in small amounts, and also because the concept is definitely fascinating: can you bring someone you♥ back to life?).

The *manga* of *Fullmetal Alchemist* at this point offers extra information about the fateful day when the Elric brothers crossed the threshold into a beyond-life realm. It also includes more scenes involving the mysterious figure that haunts (and taunts) Ed in the other world. Himoru Arakawa's *manga* includes elements that were dropped for the *animé*, such as the shadowy figure defining what Ed was encountering as the ultimate truth, or God, or you, or the universe. There were also closer looks at the botched creature that the brothers' alchemical spell conjured up (Ed recoils in horror against the wall when he contemplates the black, twisted mess of the creature in the centre of the transmutation circle). Much of this material in the *manga* was included in the second *Fullmetal Alchemist* series.

The introduction of a simple-minded foundling in the Jack Island sequence is an intriguing new character[27] – especially when he appears to be the shadow of Edward Elric[28] (right down to the chara design of long, dark hair, to complement Ed's blond locks), and he may even have Ed's arm and leg! That Wrath (Nana Mizuki)[29] is also great at alchemy, has mysterious origins, but is also a charming boy in a way, enhances the impact (and it's nice to see the Elric brothers being put beside people their own age, instead of the endless procession of stern or dangerous adults). Of course, the personality of Wrath does change pretty rapidly! – and he becomes yet another of the homunculi bent on savaging the brothers.

The talkiness of some of the flashbacks and montages in the middle episodes of the first *Fullmetal Alchemist* series are forgiven and swept

---

27 Wrath's a new character – in the *Fullmetal Alchemist manga* and in the second *animé*, Izumi Curtis's child is very dead, and cannot be brought back to life.

28 Seen from a distance, Alphonse mistakes Wrath for his brother.

29 Nana Mizuki (b. 1980) is the voice of Wrath in the first series and Lan Fan in the second series. Mizuki is a big music star in Nippon, selling out a week of concerts at the Budokan (she sings theme songs). Mizuki has huge credits in *animé*, including the voice of Hinata in *Naruto*, Moka in *Rosario and Vampire*, Cure Blossom in *Heartcatch Precure!*, Tsubasa Kazanari in *Symphogear*, Namo in *Love Hina*, Fate Testarossa in *Magical Girl Lyrical Nanoha*, and Oboro in *Basilisk*. Mizuki specializes in cute, sweet, innocent and timidly-voiced characters.

away by the terrific action scenes in episode 29: *The Untainted Child*. We're back on Jack Island again, and Ed Elric wants his arm and leg back from Wrath. Now we see Wrath revealing his true colours, as a homunculus with magical powers, in battles with Al and Ed.

❀

In amongst these episodes of *Fullmetal Alchemist* series one, the homunculi are hovering in the background as truly despicable villains. There are some *very* nasty bad guys in the *Hagane no Renkin Jutsushi* series, and the homunculi are some of the worst. They might dress and have hair like a Japanese pop band, but they are really vicious pieces of work. The homunculi are characters you'd love to see torn to pieces, as so many other charas are. But of course, they won't be – the more formidable the opponents in drama, the greater the heroes' triumph when they finally beat them (so it's going to be put off to the end).

Disguise is another motif that's trotted out in these middle episodes of *Fullmetal Alchemist* (probably a few too many times – and the film-makers don't remind the audience enough times as to whether that is the Führer in a scene or an impostor). The homunculi are experts at becoming anyone they like, so they impersonate the Führer (and of course, nobody bothers to check if that *is* the real Führer, that he's not where the Führer should be, that some of his orders're odd, or raises an eyebrow that he's travelling virtually alone).

Episode 30. *Assault On South Headquarters*

The next episodes of *Fullmetal Alchemist* – 30: *Assault On South Headquarters*, 31: *Sin* and 32: *Dante of the Deep Forest* – comprise a series of brutal fight scenes in which characters battle it out. By now, we've seen so many of these sorts of scenes, they do tend to become not only repetitive but also ineffectual and inconclusive. We see Al and Ed Elric and Izumi Curtis fighting the homunculi and assorted Bad Guys, but nothing is resolved, and the Bad Guys haul off Al at the end of the episode (when Winry's not around, Alphonse is often the character selected to be the Princess Who Needs Rescuing). So there's yet another *to be continued...* closing each episode.

Episode 30: *Assault On South Headquarters* is a busy, story-stuffed show, involving many characters and many locations. Izumi Curtis is at heart of this episode, and the South Headquarters are the setting for some of the battles: Curtis wants her li'l 'son' Wrath back, but the military (including Archer and Armstrong) manage to secure him, only for the other homunculi (including Envy impersonating Führer Bradley) to capture him (in a subsequent episode). Zolf Kimbley, Greed and the chimera Bido are also involved.

Episode 30: *Assault On South Headquarters* departs from the *Fullmetal Alchemist manga* all over the place. Now the Elrics are chatting to Wrath up on a roof; now Frank Archer and Alex Armstrong capture Wrath; now the Elrics encounter the cheeky, sly, lizard chimera Bido, who gets the better of them; now Izumi Curtis is storming a military hospital to fetch her 'child' back; now the homunculi and Devil's Nest chimera are also desperate to obtain Wrath; now when Armstrong faces Sig in the butcher's shop, demanding to know where the Elric brothers are, they indulge in a very camp (and funny) display of muscles and torsos (bonding thru the expression of masculine strength and the body beautiful. It's a *very* homosocial sequence).

We find out the hidden secret that Izumi Curtis has been hiding: she transformed her dead baby, just born, into a living thing. But it wasn't a human being: it was a homunculus, a freak that she hid away on the island. The reasons for Curtis breaking the taboo against re-animating life are understandable, as with Ed and Al Elric trying to bring back their dead mother. She's the mom who can't bear the thought of having a dead baby (in the chaos of the botched ritual, Curtis loses some of her internal organs, which's why she coughs up blood. One of them was presumably her womb, tho' that isn't stated in either *manga* or *animé* – even tho' a doctor points to a human cutaway model).

But there's a difference: the Elric lads were kids, ten or so. But Izumi Curtis was an adult when she broke the taboo – an adult who knew what she was doing, and who knew the consequences. This makes Curtis a hypocrite – she'll beat the Elric brothers really harshly (and continue to do so a number of times afterwards), for a crime or transgression she has committed herself, and as a knowing adult.

The first *Fullmetal Alchemist animé* series also bumps up Izumi Curtis's role considerably from the *manga*, by including so much material with Curtis and Wrath (I would imagine that Himoru Arakawa was happy with this, as Curtis is a chara she seems to have affection for. Curtis is also a character type that crops up many times in Arakawa's work). The 2009-10 TV adaption of *Fullmetal Alchemist* corrected the imbalance. (The sombreness of these middle episodes of the first *Fullmetal Alchemist* series also mean far less humour – isn't it time for another shopping spree for Winry Rockbell, or for someone else to draw attention to Ed Elric's height?! The team at Studio Bones/ Mainichi/ Aniplex/ Square Enix and the numerous associated companies do lose themselves in the high drama and weighty seriousness of the life-and-death story at times, and forget that humour is one of the essential ingredients in Japanese animation, even in the midst of the most desperate, solemn outings. Again, that's where the second *Fullmetal Alchemist* series improves upon the first one).

Izumi Curtis performing her one-woman-army assault on the hospital where her 'son' Wrath is being held (strapped to a bed) is a terrific sequence (it's a variation on Curtis's solo invasion of the Devil's Nest bar in the *manga*). It's Curtis's finest moment, as she makes mince-meat of anyone who tries to stand in her way. She is the mother-wolf, ferocious in the protection of her offspring. The sequence culminates with a multiple stand-off in the hospital corridors, as the homunculi, Frank Archer and Alex Armstrong, the Elrics, the Führer/ Envy and Kimbley and Bido converge.

The filmmakers have dragged poor Winry Rockbell along for the ride throughout these middle episodes of *Fullmetal Alchemist*. Unfortunately, she has absolutely nothing to do too often, except to stand on the sidelines and fret and complain that nobody tells her anything. So the silent giant Sig, husband of Izumi Curtis, is the unlikely character chosen to narrate the back-story of Curtis and her desperate ache to be a mother of a living, breathing child (Sig, voiced by Seiji Sasaki in both series, has an amazingly deep voice which suits the hulk that is Sig). And Sig relates the story to Winry, standing next to her as they watch the hospital shake and grow bizarre outcrops like rock-made bruises, as Curtis-sensei makes her way to the ward where Wrath is being held.

❁

Meanwhile (there are lot of 'meanwhiles' at this point in the *Fullmetal Alchemist* series), the Scar sub-plot is kept bubbling along (Loki[30] sees Scar in a refugee camp, which the group of Ishbalians visit, and where Loki has ended up). He telephones the central military command, and speaks to Juliet Douglas. Roy Mustang and his team are mobilized to deal with Scar.

We are also introduced to the homunculus Greed and his entourage at the Devil's Nest bar, which includes the mandatory heavies, the babe Martel (a.k.a. Marta), Zolf Kimbley and a couple of groupies draped over Greed (who assumes the pose of a *yakuza* big shot in a hostess club).

The homunculus Greed is an appealing character in all of the forms of the *Fullmetal Alchemist* story – an outsize prima donna, cocky, arrogant, vain, and cruel (Junichi Suwabe plays Greed as a casual, cool dude, not given to hysterical outbursts like the second series' Greed, voiced by Yuichi Nakamura). With his dark glasses and snazzy, black jacket with white, fake fur trimming, Greed's one of the better-dressed of the villains, with a charisma that makes being a Bad Guy cool. He and the homunculi and the chimeras are also after Wrath – so that Wrath becomes the central MacGuffin of this part of the *Fullmetal Alchemist* series.

Episode 31. *Sin*

Episode 31: *Sin* is another episode of much to-ing and fro-ing, plenty of twists and turns in the storytelling, as we follow a host of groups of characters. The screenwriting (by Shou Aikawa) isn't wholly on top of everything here (pretty much all of the storylines have now departed from the *Fullmetal Alchemist manga* and are going their own, sweet way).

The homunculi are in full force now – Greed, Envy, Wrath and Sloth (Juliet Douglas) are all entering the fray (plus charas such as Bido, Zolf Kimbley and Izumi Curtis, who're linked to them).

Most appealing in episode 31: *Sin* is the focus on the life-and-death issues at the heart of the *Fullmetal Alchemist* saga: Edward and Alphonse

---

30 In the *manga* and the 2nd series, Loki is a weasly, weedy, cowardly sidekick who hangs around the main characters (such as Scar, Marcoh and Mei Chang). If *Fullmetal Alchemist* was live-action, Loki would be played by a crusty, old character actor, and would probably steal every scene he was in.

Elric track Izumi Curtis and her 'son' Wrath to Jack Island: during the confrontation, much is revealed now of the other-world of the Gateway of Truth: the filmmakers depict the ritual that Curtis undertook to resurrect her dead baby (at night, in pouring rain, of course). We see Curtis handing over her mutated, alive child to the grasping, black hands behind the Doorway (in the section related by Curtis). We see (in the section narrated by Wrath), how he bided his time in the Gateway, waiting for the moment when Edward appeared at the Doorway, demanding Al's life, seen in the prologue of episode one (and Wrath took Ed's arm and leg).

It is at moments like this when the *Fullmetal Alchemist* series really deepens and thickens its dramatic power. Now we can see how the characters of Izumi Curtis, the two Elrics and Wrath are intimately inter-linked. *Mangaka* Himoru Arakawa created a marvellous series of motifs (gateways, grasping, black creatures, giant eyes, a white limbo realm), and dramatic devices (the equivalent exchange of alchemy, human transmutation in magic circles), to portray issues of life and death.

✳

As for action, episode 31: *Sin* has plenty: Izumi Curtis and Alex Armstrong duking it out in the hospital corridors (Armstrong seems to be beaten by a woman!);[31] Bido attacking Ed; Al (and Kimbley) grabbing Bido; Kimbley attacking Al; and Edward launching himself at Curtis and Wrath (twice! – the image of Ed lunging towards the camera in fury, alchemically transmuting his automail arm into a sword, is one of the icons of the *Fullmetal Alchemist* series).

In the many departures from the *Fullmetal Alchemist manga*, the homunculi are also converging on Jack Island, to get their hands on Wrath, as well as our heroes; Bido and Zolf Kimbley are hovering on the sidelines; Envy corrupts Wrath with some philosopher's stones, which he gobbles like candy; Curtis's back-story of dead babies is different; Frank Archer offers Zolf Kimbley a place in the military; Scar and co. are holing up in a refugee camp; and the military, led by Roy Mustang, are heading their way to capture Scar.

One aspect of episode 31: *Sin* is just how grimly it is played throughout: there are only one or two attempts at humour (and they are brief). Instead, everybody plays their scenes with their smiles on upside-down. Even characters we can rely on for some lighthearted banter are restrained.

Episode 32. *Dante of the Deep Forest*

By the time of episode 32: *Dante of the Deep Forest*, the first *Fullmetal Alchemist* series has departed from the *manga* by Himoru Arakawa in many respects, tho' it still retains many of the story elements, but trans-posed to new contexts and scenarios. At the heart of the conflict is still the homunculus Wrath and his uneasy relationship with his 'mother' Izumi Curtis and rivals Al and Ed Elric.

31 In the *manga* and the 2nd series, Armstrong has a scary sister, more powerful than he is – Maria.

On Jack Island, the Elrics continue to battle with Wrath, with Alphonse leading the way, hurling himself at Wrath. And here's why Himoru Arakawa left Winry Rockbell behind in Resembool – because she simply doesn't understand about homunculi! So Winry-chan (included in this *animé* version) bleats like a lamb when Alphonse attacks Wrath; Al tries to explain: he's a homunculus, he isn't human, and he's got Ed's arm and leg!

Yet nothing is resolved in episode 32: *Dante of the Deep Forest*: Ed and Al Elric fail to nail Wrath; they meet Juliet Douglas and Envy posing as Führer Bradley on the sand (Douglas and Envy have been watching events from afar); they return to the Curtises' butcher's store. The *animé* follows the *Fullmetal Alchemist manga* in having Curtis-sensei expelling the boys, which they take to mean they have to leave. At the railroad station, Sig patiently explains that now they can approach Curtis as equals. So Ed immediately decides to head back (this's a classic piece of Ed-ism!). In Curtis-sensei's bedroom, the lads demand any piece of information that their former teacher can share with them about the philosopher's stone, or how to get their bodies back. (Everybody else is listening in outside the window. They expect the Elrics to be beaten up by Curtis-sensei. She does throw a *lot* of meat knives at them!).

So Izumi Curtis sends the Elrics to learn from her own teacher, Dante, in her mansion retreat in a forest (on the pretext of fetching some medicine). Dante (Kazuko Sugiyama) is the major villain invented for the first *Fullmetal Alchemist* series, taking the place of Father in Arakawa-sensei's *manga*. Dante[32] is introduced first as a kindly, old, grandmother figure, chatting politely to the visiting brothers in her sunny garden while picking plants for healing. Her home is a neat and tidy realm of dried flowers, lamps, and late 19th century chintz. Compared to the scenes with Father in the *Fullmetal Alchemist manga* and the second *Fullmetal Alchemist* series, as a super-villain brooding in a subterranean bunker, this is a dramatic turn-about! It's a mis-lead, of course (one of the hints is that Lyra is working for Dante as a maid – and Lyra's undertaken a personality change, too. But her first appearance, as a ditzy maid, is another false front).

✳

Meanwhile – the military party led by Colonel Mustang has reached the Southern refugee town, where a confrontation's staged between the military and the Ishbalians. Securing Scar is the goal here, but when the soldiers cross the gap between the two sides to check the identity of the crowd on the other side, two of the homunculi, Lust and Gluttony, create a ruckus by killing Loki and several other Ishbalians. Some of the soldiers open fire on the Ishbalaians until they're stopped. The scene's a version of the moment in the *Fullmetal Alchemist manga* when Envy killed a child, which set off a riot. (With its references to real conflicts in recent history, this is very grim stuff – it includes soldiers firing on unarmed civilians).

Another meanwhile – Greed and his Devil's Nest crew are also head-

---

32 Here we have a mention of Hohenheim of Light, the boys' father, after a very long gap.

ing for Dante's woodland home: their goal, as with the homunculi, is to secure the Elric brothers. Greed cases the joint from up in a tree, ninja-style. Rather too easily, Greed knocks Ed unconscious, and Alphonse's surrounded in the kitchen.

Episode 33. *Al, Captured*

By now, the first *Fullmetal Alchemist* series is juggling a huge cast of characters, but not quite as successfully as in some of the other episodes. For a start, the goals and motives of each group, plus their characteristics, are somewhat samey – but at least the homunculus Wrath is out of the way for the time being (the filmmakers had gone as far as they could with him, and he was rather tiresome after a while, and the Izumi-Wrath plot seemed a little over-long), and in steps Greed and his mob at the Devil's Nest bar to be the next set of opponents to create trouble for our heroes.

In episode 33: *Al, Captured*, poor Alphonse is nabbed by the Bad Guys (but not after a brutal fight), and spends quite a bit of time being hauled around by them (the small but fierce chimera snake-woman Martel controls Al by jumping inside the hollow suit of armour, an icky moment for Alphonse!). Splitting the hero into two characters, Ed and Al Elric, means that one of them can be captured by the villains while the other can search for him and rescue him.

In all forms of *Fullmetal Alchemist*, the over-riding passion is of the brothers for each other. If one of them's in trouble, the other thinks of nothing but rescuing him.

The scene at the Devil's Nest bar follows the *Fullmetal Alchemist manga* in most of its key narrative areas, but also departs from it. There's a lengthy exploration of Greed and what he's after – the secrets of trans-mutation from Alphonse Elric (which's why his mob've captured him). In between a *lot* of talk, there are outbursts of action: Al attacks Greed with an alchemically-transmuted stone, but discovers that Greed can survive (stones and rocks rearing up out of the ground are never enough to stop any villain for long in *Fullmetal Alchemist*).

When Izumi Curtis and her husband Sig arrive at the commercial break, to announce, 'A HOUSEWIFE!', in response to Greed's question, 'who are you?', the action becomes even more intense. Curtis deals with Greed's crew pretty quickly, tho' soon finds out that Greed isn't a push-over. Greed, who prefers not to fight women, defends himself with his amazing shield carapace. (Even the usually restrained Sig joins the fray).

✳

Meanwhile, the military're preparing to storm Devil's Nest, led by Frank Archer (with Alex Armstrong in tow – poor, camp he-man Armstrong has to spend most of the first *Fullmetal Alchemist* series dragging along behind the pale, utterly humourless Archer, with far too few moments to assert himself). Zolf Kimbley is also hovering on the borders of the action, stealing something (it might be philosopher's stones) from a safe (in the *manga*, Kimbley has a drug addict's lust for gobbling philosopher's stones). But from Greed's blenching reaction, we can guess that it might be Greed's human remains. There's a brief but telling encounter between Izumi Curtis and her *sensei*, Dante, in which the first cracks in the persona of the kindly grandma.

And what about Edward Elric? Since being smashed in the face by Greed in the previous episode, he stands up (slowly and painfully), and tries to attack the homunculus, but gets nowhere. Edward can't save Al from being kidnapped, and for much of episode 33: *Al, Captured* he's racing around town asking everybody he meets for a clue as to Al's where-abouts (in a musical montage which uses a pop song). Eventually, he discovers (from Alex Armstrong), that his *onii-san* is at the Devil's Nest lair.

So Edward Elric hurries over there, to find Izumi Curtis and Greed deep in battle. Ed has met his match here, in more ways than one. Greed taunts Ed with an important point – that he doesn't have the heart/ guts to kill. But that doesn't stop Ed protecting Al and Izumi, and fighting Greed with everything he's got. It's a fierce and impressive action sequence, tho' we know that Ed hasn't got a hope of winning just by using his trans-formed sword arm. We also know that Greed is right – Edward will not become a killer, and will not be allowed to kill by the filmmakers (or by us!).

Thus, episode 33: *Al, Captured* ends with no change in the circum-stances of the chief protagonists: Alphonse Elric is still being held by Greed and his crew, and Edward is hauled off at gunpoint by the military police to see Frank Archer.

✳

The filmmakers at Bones, Mainichi, Aniplex *et al* introduce yet another female sidekick for our teenage heroes around this point in the series: Martel (a.k.a. Marta, played by Rumi Kasahara). She is a chimera with an agenda (don't all the characters have issues and agendas in *Fullmetal Alchemist*? Yes!). But forget about her magical creature status, because she is a young, attractive woman (clad in a tight top, with a striking tattoo). She is also fierce, independent, and a formidable opponent (as if a female chara created by Himoru Arakawa could be anything else!).

The filmmakers invent an amusing and yucky way of having the slinky, young Martel interact with the Elric brothers – she dives inside Al's suit of armour! How would a teenage boy feel about having a girl jumping inside his body?! Yes – *exactly*!

Of course, Martel has a different goal from our heroes, but they do tag along together (Martel drives the brothers across the desert to Ishbal on a motorcycle with a trailer). In the 2nd adaption of *Fullmetal Alchemist*, poor Martel is dispatched as quickly as she is in Himoru Arakawa's *manga*, in the midst of the Devil's Nest raid.

Fullmetal Alchemist, animation production art (this page and over).

The voice cast of Fullmetal Alchemist: Romi Pak (Ed, top) and Rie Kugimiya (Al, above).

Episode 34. *Theory of Avarice*

Whew, 51 episodes is a l-o-n-g haul, eh? Will *Fullmetal Alchemist* ever end? Will the writers bring the 2003-2004 show to a conclusion? Will the Elric siblings discover the philosopher's stone and make their bodies whole again? In all likelihood: *no*. (But in the end, *yes*).

In the next episode of *Fullmetal Alchemist*, 1.34: *Theory of Avarice*, the on-going battle between the heroes and the homunculi continues. In these episodes – 33: *Al, Captured* and 34: *Theory of Avarice* – there is a lengthy assault by the military and the good guys (led by Izumi Curtis and Edward) on the HQ of the villains (the Devil's Nest bar). This is one of many departures that the *animé* makes from the *Fullmetal Alchemist manga*. It plays out differently in the *manga*, which features Führer Bradley (Hidekatsu Shibata) as a one-man army, wielding swords and leaping about like a samurai on speed, slaughtering many victims.

Thus, the moment when Führer Bradley kills Martel is also staged differently in the Japanese *animé*, where Bradley simply walks up to Al, who seems apparently frozen to the spot, and stabs Martel inside the suit of armour. In the *Fullmetal Alchemist manga*, there is a much more convincing struggle in the midst of a battle.

Also, the sequence where Izumi Curtis walks into the Bad Guys' lair on her own, taking on every single member of the gang, is much more satisfying in the *Fullmetal Alchemist manga* than it is in the first *animé* (altho' there are impressive, vivid scenes of Curtis-*sensei* wielding her alchemy and martial arts).

At this point in the *animé* and in the *manga* of *Fullmetal Alchemist*, the characterization of some of the villains does tend to merge into one: Greed[1] and Zolf Kimbley look similar (grim, youngish middle-aged men with spikey hair), and so does Frank Archer (tho' his behaviour is noticeably buttoned-down and prim, and he's so pale he's inhuman). The obstacles for the Elric brothers also become somewhat interchangeable. To differentiate Greed as a villain, *manga* artist Himoru Arakawa had him transform into something resembling a superhero baddie from the golden age of comicbooks in the U.S.A. – the kind of grinning demon that Spider-man or Superman might have gone up against on the crime-stained streets of Gotham.

In episode 34: *Theory of Avarice*, Edward duels the villain Greed in a lengthy smackdown at Dante's palatial country home (Dante now appears to be dead, but isn't).[2] The creepy Lyra[3] (Yumi Kakazu) disables Greed by luring him close to the bones of the human he was, and by placing him inside a transmutation circle (he vomits up the philosopher's stones that were helping to keep him alive (or alive-but-dead, whatever he was), which weakens him). This's the scene from the *Fullmetal Alchemist*

---

1 Greed of course wants *everything*! Women, money, gold, power, you name it, he *wants* it. 'There is no such thing as no such thing', is one of his mantras. He has a superhero carapace which turns him into a near-indestructible villain (he is the 'Ultimate Shield').
2 Greed in the *animé* is based on one of Dante's lovers. But she isn't able to control him.
3 You're correct if you think that Lyra is creepy – she's later revealed to be Dante in disguise. But the design of Lyra signals that to *animé* fans anyway.

manga where Greed is punished by Father for his misdemeanours.

Earlier, Greed taunted Edward Elric that he hasn't got the guts to kill someone. It's one of the dilemmas that writers of fiction featuring young people have to tackle: do you want your teenage heroes to become killers? Jo Rowling struggled with that in the *Harry Potter* series, and Philip Pullman did in the *His Dark Materials* trilogy and in the *Sally Lockhart* series.

If possible, no. No, you don't want Harry Potter (*Harry Potter and the Sorcerer's Stone*) or Lyra Silvertongue (*The Golden Compass*) – or Edward Elric – to become a murderer. For lots of reasons. But in episode 1.34: *Theory of Avarice*, the filmmakers at Aniplex, Bones, Mainichi Broadcasting System and Square Enix engineer a scenario where Ed does seem to kill Greed – but in special circumstances: Greed has been weakened by Lyra/ Dante, and by the fact that his bodily remains are nearby (this is a snippet of special knowledge – to destroy a homunculi, you kill them near their bones). The detail of the flaw in Greed's shield is also introduced – Ed works out how to weaken it by deduction (like a good schoolboy who knows his chemistry).

Edward Elric would (probably) stop attacking Greed if he offered up his brother Alphonse. He would leave with Al if he could – this's what he wants most of all. But we are now two-thirds into the 51-episode series of *Fullmetal Alchemist,* so it's perhaps time for the hero to kill someone (after all, he's been trying to numerous times!). So Ed slices Greed thru the heart after weakening his shield (at the climax of a stunningly choreographed fight sequence). Importantly, Ed feels instant remorse (and the *animé* explores that in the scene; it doesn't cut to more action someplace else).

❋

A grim episode, then: episode 34: *Theory of Avarice* contains the death of a major character, and plenty of scenes of action: Alex Armstrong and some soldiers battle the chimeras Roa and Dolcetto; Lust and Gluttony destroy the chimera; Frank Archer does a deal with Zolf Kimbley and Shou Tucker (revealing, in voiceover, his goal of creating more chimeras); Ed, Izumi Curtis and Sig sneak away from being under guard by Archer's crew; Al tries to prevent Martel from leaving his armour; and at the end of the show, our heroes've buried Greed and what was Dante.

And what does one do with Winry Rockbell, in amongst this life-and-death action? The filmmakers have kept her around, but they shunt her to one side, here: episode 34: *Theory of Avarice* opens with Winry minding the Curtises' butcher's store (with a shot that *hommages* Kiki in the bakery in *Kiki's Delivery Service*, 1989), and bring her in at the end, when the Elrics decide they're going to Ishbal.

❋

The overarching story of *Fullmetal Alchemist* remains clear as a bell, but the multiplicity of villains does become wearying in these middle section episodes of the first animated series. Just how many adversaries are our teenage heroes going to face? Well, pretty much *everybody*! Thus, as soon as one villain is dispatched (or flees), another one or two is wheeled into place (because obstacles are a fundamental ingredient of all drama, and in an action-adventure format, obstacles usually take the form of more villains).

In all of this spectacle and action, the first *Fullmetal Alchemist* series does become a little murky and indistinct. And you can see the filmmakers at Studio Bones, Aniplex, Mainichi Broadcasting System and Square Enix *et al* grasping around for some new way of staging an alchemical duel, a new way of introducing a Bad Guy, a new way of dispatching a victim. Repetition is a fundamental element of all long-running *animé* and *manga*, of course (and all long-form storytelling). The trick is to slip it past the reader or audience without them recognizing it.

No one has yet come up with a 51-episode *animé* action-adventure-based series without repeating themselves occasionally. (If you can, get on the next jumbo jet to Tokyo and show them how to do it! You won't be paid much, you will work *incredibly* hard (with long hours and unpaid over-time), but you will have the satisfaction of trumping the finest storytellers and filmmakers in the world!).

Episode 35: *Reunion of the Fallen*

The next episode, 35: *Reunion of the Fallen*, is probably the oddest mix of dramatic ingredients in the *Fullmetal Alchemist* franchise. It sidelines our heroes for an invented side-story featuring, of all people, Lust, the *femme fatale* homunculus with her slinky *Addams Family*, dominatrix demeanour, her clingy, black dress that emphasizes her giant breasts bouncing in from 1950s Americana, and her mean and moody glare. Don't mess with Lust; she is b*aaad* news! She has extendible fingers that become daggers. Guys don't stand a chance – one look at that purple lipstick and those red eyes and those cascading black tresses, and they are smitten.

So a guy does fall for Lust – the hapless alchemist Lujon (Takehito Koyasu). Well, you know *that* relationship can't fly – especially as Lujon is already betrothed to a young, local woman, Lydia (Fumiko Orikasa[4] – she's Rukia in *Bleach* – called 'Libia', curiously, in the subtitles). Lydia/ Libia and Lujon aren't in Himoru Arakawa's *Fullmetal Alchemist manga*, and neither is any part of this story.

Those homunculi are truly revolting villains. Even in *animé*, which features some of the nastiest bad guys in all contemporary culture, East or West, the homunculi in *Fullmetal Alchemist* are absolutely vicious. In 35: *Reunion of the Fallen*, they develop a fatal disease that ravages a community with the sole purpose of forcing the inhabitants (including Lujon) to search for the philosopher's stone (the illness is a kind of literal fossilization (dubbed 'fossilitis'), transmuting humans into stone, so they

4 The credits of Fumiko Orikasa (born in Taito, Tokyo in 1972) include: Kyubei in *Gintama*, Rumiko in *Higurashi no Naku Koro ni Rei*, Aki in *Inazuma Eleven*, Rinko in *Kinnikuman Nisei*, Satsuki in *Kuroko's Basketball*, Lotte in *Little Witch Academia*, Miss Valentine in *One Piece*, Kim in *Rahxephon*, Reiko in *Sket Dance*, Karin in *Stratos 4*, Kaaya in *The Tower of Druaga: the Sword of Uruk*, Shizuka in *Vampire Knight*, Meia in *Vandread*, and the wonderful Victoria Seras in both *Hellsing* series.

expire (quickly) with screaming grimaces and hands the size of footballs, covered in layers of white brick. *Not* a nice way to go!).

The story of episode 35: *Reunion of the Fallen* is fully, shamelessly melodramatic, like a Harlequin or Mills and Boon paperback or a classic, romantic 19th century novel squeezed into 22 minutes. The show contains numerous tropes from the romantic melodrama genre: the jilted bride, the other woman portrayed as a *femme fatale*, the erotic triangle, the rural, European settings, the trysts in sunlit woodland, the endless rides in carriages pulled by horses down long, leafy lanes – it's *Fullmetal Alchemist*'s version of a Thomas Hardy or a Jane Austen novel.

In episode 1.35: *Reunion of the Fallen*, the writer (Toshiki Inoue) orchestrates a dual-track narrative, with the story flitting between two years in the past and the present day (plus flashbacks-within-flashbacks, as Lust has memories of another man she was involved with – Scar's brother, no less). The show tracks the Lujon-Lust romance, flitting back and forth between the present and the past, *and* Lust's affair with another guy, *and* the history of the fossilitis disease, *and* the romantic triangle with Lust-Lujon-Lydia.

Thus, several tons of story are packed into 22 minutes, with Lujon falling for Lust while being engaged to Lydia; Lujon trying to save people from the mineralization disease (but his philosopher's stone is fake (or weak), and needs to be topped up periodically by Lust);[5] Lujon helping a boy injured in a car crash; Envy, Lust and Gluttony musing on the death of Greed; and Ed, Al and Winry travelling South to Ishbal and encountering some of the characters from the story (such as Lydia) in the present day (it's a classic means of joining together two plot strands, from the past, in the present. But our heroes don't have much to do except to listen to the story, so it's also rather artificial).

Thus, about the only significant thing that our trio of heroic teens (Ed, Al an' Winry) do in *Reunion of the Fallen* is to save a young woman (Lydia) from being terrorized by a group of local thugs (a not uncommon scene in *manga* and *animé*). It's likely that this scenario wasn't appreciated by *mangaka* Himoru Arakawa (she complained when the threat of rape was introduced in relation to Rose Tomas in the early shows). Here, we have a gang rape situation – the no-goods cackle and leer at the girl, who's thrown to the ground. Edward hears her scream first, and hurls himself to her rescue, making mincemeat of the roughnecks. (This is the ugly side of romance, linking rape to the romantic melodrama surrounding Lust at the heart of this episode).

In amongst the to-ing and fro-ing of *Reunion of the Fallen*, and the multiple layers of time, Lust strides through it all like a she-devil, accompanied by her repulsive, squat, cannibal henchman Gluttony[6] (it's

---

5 Episode 1.35: *Reunion of the Fallen* also depicts the utter selfishness of the homunculi – in this case, Lust: Lujon is a doctor intent on healing other people, but Lust just thinks of herself.
6 Gluttony is scary because he is so powerful while being so child-like. To have that amount of force squashed into that grotesque body and slavering maw is terrifying. Gluttony's first question is always centred, as with children, around eating. Except that Gluttony's question – 'can I eat him?' – is meant literally! Fries and a cheese boiger won't do for Gluttony – he wants to chomp whole humans!

amusing how Lujon addresses her as 'Lust' – tho' in Japanese maybe her name means 'Strange Tattooed Witch-Lady In Black'). Of course, it can only end badly for Lujon, one of a number of guys taken in by Lust's man-eating, T. & A. appearance: she stabs him and kills him as they embrace in some woodland.

There is, yet again, a truly gruesome wastage of humanity in episode 35: *Reunion of the Fallen*, as if it doesn't matter how many people you kill in your quest for whatever it is you want (immortality, or endless riches, or real life, whatever). The scene with the mass of corpses at the end of 35: *Reunion of the Fallen* is tragic. As Lust, Envy and Gluttony move thru the world of *Fullmetal Alchemist*, they leave behind a trail of cadavers. They are psychotically destructive, out of control like insane kids with guns, with no regard whatsoever for human life (and as for caring for animal life or plant life, forget it!).

✳

The philosopher's stone is also to the fore in episode 35: *Reunion of the Fallen*, reminding us all of the centrality of this particular theme in the *Fullmetal Alchemist* series. For instance, as the homunculi convene and talk in a restaurant, chewing over recent events, a car crash outside includes Lujon healing a victim with the philosopher's stone he has in a ring (if the philosopher's stone is set in a ring, it can easily be included in most any kind of scene, as with Father Cornello in episode one).

As Lust and Envy view the town from a hill (with yet another of the customary glowing sunsets that *animé* simply can't resist depicting), they discuss the events: they are creating a wasting disease among humans specifically so they can force the humans to create more philosopher's stones, and even an Ultimate Philosopher's Stone (this is a version of using the whole of Amestris as a transmutation circle from the *manga*). Like gods, or Nazis – or governments, or politicians, or capitalists anywhere – the homunculi simply use humans for their own ends.

Episode 36. *The Sinner Within*

The next episode in *Fullmetal Alchemist*, 36: *The Sinner Within*, is jammed with very serious issues, which resonate in our contemporary world: refugees, political oppression, and the morality of killing within a military and political context. It's among the weightiest shows in the TV franchise.

Thankfully, this show focusses on our heroes once again. *The Sinner Within* is also a return to the grand, tragic aspects of *Fullmetal Alchemist*. That is, the series gets moving again, after drifting a little aimlessly for too long (yes, Big Fights *are* action, but not Great Action, if the fights lack dramatic or psychological impact, and are delivered in a rather routine fashion).

And as we are heading towards Ishbal, by far the most problematic region of the *Fullmetal Alchemist* world, with its fierce political and social conflicts, the character of Tattoo Man, Scar, is re-introduced. As Ed, Al,

Winry and co. head South to Ishbal (they've also picked up a couple of strays, the brothers Rick and Leo),[7] Ed discusses the possibility of killing Scar (well, this mass murderer and truly despicable psycho does need to be destroyed, by the lights and morality of *Fullmetal Alchemist,* at least). It's a lengthy scene which considers the ethics of death and murder, which're central to the *Fullmetal Alchemist* series. (Flashbacks to several important scenes in the series're included: Ed being unable to save the victims in the laboratory, Ed and the alchemist Majhal (that was an accident, Al insists), Ed and Barry the Chopper, etc).

Everybody's got their 'I mean business' + 'I am serious' + 'I am grim'[8] – frowns on again in ep. 1.36: *The Sinner Within.* At the close of the episode, super-cutie Winry Rockbell discovers some sinister news about the military (from Rick and Leo), which goes way back in the *Fullmetal Alchemist* series to the murder of the Rockbells, her parents (during the Ishbal rebellion). If the military is corrupt, then so is the government: in *Fullmetal Alchemist,* characters (particularly the younger ones) are continually being faced with the realization that the powers that be and their elders are not what they thought they were.

The depressing thing about *Fullmetal Alchemist* is the assertion that there is very little that can be relied upon in the adult world, in the social world, in the world where young people are expected to live when they grow up. Every social institution, including the military and the government, winds up being corrupt and aggressive.

What is the 'truth behind the truth'? In *Fullmetal Alchemist,* it is that individuals have to fare for themselves in the end. There is nothing and no one in the social fabric that can be relied upon. The State, in *Fullmetal Alchemist,* is built upon lies. (You have to work things out for yourself, Ed realizes).

Why is Winry Rockbell still hanging around? Both Ed and Al Elric voice the view that Winry-chan ought to return to Resembool. In the end, the writers opt to use the issue of the death of Winry's parents as a way of giving Winry her own quest: she decides to go to Central City (probably to confront Roy Mustang). So she asks to travel with Liza Hawkeye. Thus, episode 1.36: *The Sinner Within,* closes with another discussion evoking morality and how it relates to life-and-death issues, as Winry asks Hawkeye, while they sit on the train, if she has killed someone (Hawkeye is of course the assistant of Mustang – Hawkeye speaks of protecting someone special to her). When Winry visits the Hughes' family, and finds out that Hughes is dead (but he was Mustang's best buddy[9]), the tears fall (because she knows she must confront Mustang).

The discussions of life and death subjects are fundamental to the whole project of *Fullmetal Alchemist:* this is a series, too, where teenagers are earnestly and convincingly tackling such matters. And episode 1.36: *The Sinner Within* is exploring ethics and morality not only in the

7 The two kids are mirrors for Ed and Al, to the point where they even look like younger versions of the Elric brothers (even down to their hair).
8 In cel phone icons, it's :(
9 Seen in a family photograph.

characters of Winry, Ed and Al, but also in the wider political arena: in particular, Ishbal and the Ishbal Rebellion.

The evocation of refugees, and refugee camps, and people being displaced from their homeland, and civil wars created by aggressive regimes like Amestris, are strikingly sombre and complex issues in what appears to be a fantasy-adventure show aimed at a young audience. This is an animated TV show which has refugees being deported in trains – sinister images which inevitably hint at the treatment of Jews in WW2 (the Elrics hijack the train in order to ask the Ishbalians inside about philosopher's stones).

*

There is also a visit to an old, Ishbalian alchemist, who speaks of the 'Grand Arts', the Ishbalian term for alchemy (a version of the Ishbalaian alchemy of the *Fullmetal Alchemist manga*). It's yet another scene where the Elric brothers interview an old alchemist for the secrets of their art. Here the concept of creating a super-philosopher's stone by using not just one human but many is introduced (foreshadowing the finale of the *Fullmetal Alchemist* series).

There are scenes with the brothers Leo and Rick, whose plight echoes the Elrics (the brothers lost their mom – we see flashbacks of the brothers' mother, and the conflagration that engulfed her home, already shown in episodes 11 and 12, *The Other Brothers Elric*). And flashbacks to remind us of Scar, and the significance of Scar's arm, and his brother's experiments in alchemy.

The notion of social outcasts or defiled people is evoked (by Rick and Leo): in the religion of Ishbal, those who don't follow the societal orthodoxy become outcasts.

Most ominous of all, Scar is hauling a boulder on chains behind him, to dig a ditch for a giant transmutation circle (this is the first series' version of Sloth digging the tunnel around Amestris). The image has connotations with penance, and training,[10] and figures from the Middle Ages who carried crosses in *hommage* to Christ going to Golgotha.

Episode 37. *The Flame Alchemist*

Humour! Laughs! Comedy!

Thankfully, the *Fullmetal Alchemist* series takes a break from the doom and gloom and the perpetual down-turned mouths of *every* character for some goofing around. Split into two halves (over the commercial break – (*The Bachelor Lieutenant* and *The Mystery of Warehouse 13*), episode 37: *The Flame Alchemist*, focusses on the guys in Roy Mustang's office. In Part A, they find a date for officer Jean Havoc (Yuji Ueda), so he'll stop mooning about (Mustang has been effortlessly stealing his girlfriends – and everyone else's); and in Part B, the ghost story of the mysterious appearance at night of a 13th hangar in the military compound is told. Some of the material came from the *omake*

---

10 In *Silver Spoon*, horses in Hokkaido drag heavy sleds.

(extras) in the comic.

The show's played for comedy, with the filmmakers employing plenty of colourful, cutsie animation (some of it from *shojo manga*), to depict Havoc winding up at the Armstrong mansion to woo Major Armstrong's blonde, curvaceous sister Kathleen (voiced by Rie Kugimiya, who is Alphonse). The Armstrongs are very rich and inevitably very eccentric (and Kathleen turns down Havoc, preferring her men big and beefy, like her brother Alex).

The screenwriting in episode 37: *The Flame Alchemist* (by Katsuhiko Takayama) is pure TV sit-com material, delightfully fun and over-the-top, and also lighthearted to the point of being utterly pointless. But it does introduce some much-needed humour in a series which has had so many truly gruesome moments (mass murder in the previous few episodes, for instance. Of course, Alex Armstrong's sister in Himoru Arakawa's *manga* was very differently handled! The second *Fullmetal Alchemist* series followed the *manga* in portraying Maria Armstrong as the tough-as-nails military commander of Briggs Mountain).

In the prologue, Col. Mustang is comically monitored by his flunkeys, who find out that he goofs around a lot, spends much of his time reading the newspaper in his office while issuing orders to the team (who do the real work), and dating flower shop girls.

And there's even a sex scene, of a sort: Liza Hawkeye is in bed, murmuring in a sensual manner about someone or something tickling her and licking her (she might be imagining it's the lerrrve of her life, Roy Mustang) – she wakes to find her dog licking her feet (the mutt plays its biggest role in both *Fullmetal Alchemist* series here).

❁

Not all of the *Fullmetal Alchemist* on-going stories're left to one aside in episode 37: *The Flame Alchemist*: for instance, there's a scene where Sheksa's interviewed by Frank Archer, and later ordered to destroy the official documents about Maes Hughes; and Roy Mustang asks to join the party going East. (Mustang also visits Hughes' family briefly). Also, episode 37: *The Flame Alchemist* is significant in not featuring the Elric brothers on screen, and barely even mentioning them anywhere.

Episode 38. *With the River's Flow*

At last *shojo* Winry Rockbell gets Something Important To Do in *Fullmetal Alchemist*, in the next episode, 38: *With the River's Flow*, as she embarks on a quest (aided by the bookworm Sheska) to find out exactly what happened to Hughes-san, and the mysterious circumstances in which he died (Winry meets Sheska at Maes Hughes' gravestone – yet another cemetery scene in an *animé* – there was another in the previous episodes, when Dante was buried).

It's a welcome respite that a quest should be given to two of the non-crazy, non-villain, female characters, Winry and Sheska (the two young women are some of the very few well-meaning and non-ambiguous, non-corrupt, non-nasty charas in the entire *Fullmetal Alchemist* series). However, the scenes with Winry and Sheska in the library are far too talky and static (and over-written), as Sheska tries to convince Winry to support her quest to investigate Hughes' demise.

After all, what happened with Maes Hughes is the event that uncovers the corruption at the heart of the military (altho' Winry and Sheska overhearing Juliet Douglas talking on the phone helps). It takes a long time for all of this information to come out into the open, but it does mean that the military is being manipulated by not one but two homunculi (Führer Bradley and Sloth impersonating Captain Douglas). In the *Fullmetal Alchemist manga* (and the 2nd *animé* series), it's Colonel Mustang who takes up much of the questing of the mystery behind Hughes' murder, which is more convincing than having Sheska turn into Sherlock Holmes (but Mustang's characterization was altered for the first *Fullmetal Alchemist* series).

Our intrepid girls, Winry and Sheska, decide to sneak into the ducts below the military HQ to wire-tap the telephone of the sinister Captain Juliet Douglas (the officer who is also a homunculus).[11] The episode climaxes with a ghostly apparition which scares the bejesus out of our heroines (and seems to have the appearance of... Trisha Elric, the boys' mother, of all people. Only later do we find out who this spectral vision is. The filmmakers have given the homunculus-Douglas the ability to shape-change in the form of goopy ectoplasm).

✳

Meanwhile in episode 1.38: *With the River's Flow*, Elrics Ed and Al're on the way to Ishbal (yes, it *is* taking them a long time to get there, with many stops along the way – they seem to have started out for Ishabl in around 500 B.C.). The boys fall out over exactly what their quest is (yes, that old chestnut again!), and how to go about it (after breaking down in a tractor that Winry had obtained for them). This episode, 38: *With the River's Flow*, is thus a time to Take a Breather and to Reset the Quest: the issue raised is the classic one of a mid-movie scene (often in the second or third act of a film): what are we fighting for? Who are we fighting against? How are we going to achieve our goal?

The brothers Elric argue vehemently, the conflict escalating rapidly to an alchemists' slinging match, with the boys hurling alchemical trans-formations at each other (haven't you always wanted to trap your annoying brother in a giant stone hand?! Or an enormous steel cage? Or bury him waist-deep in the soil? If only!). The fall-out precipitates yet another flashback to the brothers' childhood (from Ed's point-of-view), and how Alphonse used to go to the river when he was sulking (which he does in the present tense, too – that's how Ed finds him. Now *that* is good screenwriting – tying a tough challenge (how to find someone in a strange area) to an emotional flashback, which further bonds the boys).

And, ah bless them!, the Brothers Elric make it up by the end of the *With the River's Flow* show (cue the liquiescent orange sunset, bathing

---

11 A version of the listening to General Hakuro in the comic.

everything in yellow and gold), and they are on their way again. (Martel also pops up, arguing with Alphonse over what to do about Scar and the homunculi, and re-appearing at the end, to offer the lads a ride).

Episode 39: *Secret of Ishbal*

Music!

You will notice right away that the music budget for episode 39: *Secret of Ishbal* (broadcast on July 10, 2004), goes thru the roof. The producers have told composer Michiru Oshima and the music producers, arrangers and orchestrators at Aniplex to GO NUTS! Spend what you like! Hire the orchestra and the number one recording studio in Tokyo for 20 days straight (no, only kidding! Two days! No, half a day!). So the stand-out element in *Secret of Ishbal* is that invisible, mysterious, but all-important, all-conquering ingredient (in any media): music.

The score in *Secret of Ishbal* is a sensational blend of high drama and piercing strings, as if Michiru Oshima and the team are trying to out-Shostakovitch Dimitri Shostakovitch (contemporary *animé* productions are especially fond of really trebly, zinging string sections, so the violas and violins really cut thru the dialogue and the sound effects to create tsunamis of sound. Yoko Kanno is a good example – her score for *Escaflowne* is razor-sharp. They are also fond of recording with Russian or Eastern European classical orchestras. Here, it's the Moscow International Orchestra).

It's gorgeous – the soundtrack of *Hagane no Renkinjutsushi* is top quality material, as if composer Michiru Oshima has one eye on the concert stage – as if she's preparing for a series of showcase gigs at some super-arena in Shinjuku as well as scoring an *animé* show for television.

Competing with the soundtrack of the episode *Secret of Ishbal* isn't easy for the filmmakers: the music is so strong on its own; because we are in another building-suspense-and-tension-and-drama episode. We are running up to Something Grand (and the anticipation is a good part of the whole pleasure of entertainment, isn't it? It's music as foreplay).

Secret of Ishbal builds and builds, thanks to the music. At this point in the first *Fullmetal Alchemist* series, all roads lead to Ishbal: Ishbal is where Something Horrible happened, something sinister and corrupt and downright dirty. It involved everybody, including the military (Edward Elric frames the question, repeatedly, in this episode: why would the military start a conflict in Ishbal? It is a very contemporary question, which is regularly fired in the media about the political situation in the real Middle East. What is the U.S.A. doing in the Middle East? What is Russia doing in the Middle East? What is Europe doing in the Middle East? And, as Ed finds out, there isn't an easy answer – or an answer he is going to like. Indeed, you know for sure that whatever Ed and Al find out, they are *not* going to like it, just as nobody likes what they find out about the motives, goals and operations of the military wings of Russia, North Amerika, Europe *et al* in the real Middle East).

Make no bones about it, *Fullmetal Alchemist* is deliberately raising many questions about the real, contemporary Middle East, and conflicts associated with the region (the oil issue, for instance, extends all over the globe), and also similar conflicts (throughout Africa, for instance). And the ideological and political issues raised in *Fullmetal Alchemist* can be applied to many other recent armed conflicts.

That is, underneath the silly humour, the ultra-violent imagery, the talking suits of armour, the magical transformations, the teenage, angst-ridden, blond J-pop heroes and the goofy, winsome babes in their micro skirts, there are very serious issues being presented to the audience.

Because episode 39: *Secret of Ishbal* contains a flashback which's gruesomely nasty in its depiction of a secret mission of a special military squad into Ishbal (in which Martel was involved – this is her flashback, as she explains to the Elrics in the desert what happened). There are numerous disturbing scenes of people being slaughtered left, right and centre, with the blood flowing like acid (in live-action, this would be 'R' rated). It's a show going out at 6.30 p.m. in Japan, but it has images of blood splattering on walls, blood dripping thru floors into the basement below, and numerous on-screen deaths. That this is a slightly altered vision of a Western power's special forces in the Middle East or Asia is clear to all.

But there is more: Martel also participated in the sinister military experiments which turned her into a (snake) chimera (along with others, like Roa). This part of the *Fullmetal Alchemist* series comes across as one of those origins stories in a superhero movie, with the montage stylized in North American comics colours and silhouettes (in the *Fullmetal Alchemist manga*, the gruelling experiments are conducted on Führer Bradley). In the experiments, victims are strapped to a bed in the shape of a cross – a simultaneous chimeraization and crucifixion (tho' many die in the process). Then they're thrown into a cell (naked).

Martel's flashback humanizes her, and makes her more of a victim of the military and the government. The first *Fullmetal Alchemist* series makes much more of Martel, and she is an appealing and sweet character (at least, with her tomboy, soldier attitude and her attractive design, she stands out from the many secondary charas in the Amestrisian military).

Edward Elric expresses the audience's anger for them, punching a wall with his automail arm, after he hears Martel's grim documentary. Ed demands to know what the military are up to in Ishbal – now as then.

✳

The rest of the action in *Secret of Ishbal* is rather perfunctory: there's yet another railroad trip, another scene of Ed and Al Elric in the desert, and more grumblings and rumblings in the upper echelons of the military. Ed and Al're brought in to see Col. Mustang (Jean Havoc and Heyman Breda discover them, then comically hide); Sheska and Winry're questioned by Maria Ross and Denny Brosh about what they were doing;

Frank Archer is lurking around smugly, creating more friction;[12] Ed opts to travel to Liore, alone (leaving Alphonse behind as insurance for the military, on Archer's orders), where Scar has been creating a giant, alchemical transmutation circle by dragging a rock behind him on chains (a bizarre and twisted take on carrying a cross). This act separates the brothers at a critical juncture (but in a more convincing manner than some of the separations in the *manga*, for instance). The deal that Ed makes with the military machine is an intriguing riff on the events in the *manga*.

It's Ed (after stuffing his face with food), who makes the crucial observation that Scar has been fashioning a transmutation circle across the whole city.[13]

Now Liore has been shifted into the desert, into Ishbal (remember, we first saw the brothers in this series in the desert?): the Elrics, the show reminds us that they are still seeking a philosopher's stone (they tell Martel), and they want to get any information about that out of Scar (even tho' he should the last person the Elrics ought to go to!). Other additions to the *Fullmetal Alchemist manga* include the amplification of alchemical powers using the State Alchemist pocket watches (conducted by Shou Tucker).

Episode 39: *Secret of Ishbal* draws to a close with a fantastic series of short, punchy scenes, as Michiru Oshima's music agitates the narrative to hyper-tense levels, and editor Hiroaki Itabe cuts to a bunch of characters from way back, including (A) Rose Tomas, from episode one (now revealed as the saintly 'Holy Mother' in a religious procession in the ruined streets of Liore, invented for the *animé*); (B) the homunculi Lust and Gluttony (looking from on high, and wondering about their next move); and (C) chief bruiser Scar encountering Ed.

Thus, the filmmakers have brought the audience to a thrilling, cliffhanger moment. Doesn't matter what happens next, or if the filmmakers can pay off this build-up of suspense, because the suspense and high drama is enough to be going on with.

Episode 40. *The Scar*

The Scar, episode 40, and the next episode, 41: *Holy Mother*, relate the epic sequence of the battle for Liore. The conflict in Liore is a replay of the Ishbal conflict, but it's happening in the present tense of *Fullmetal Alchemist* (the Ishbal rebellion had already occurred by the time the series began, tho' there are flashbacks to it in all versions of *Fullmetal Alchemist*, including extensive flashbacks here, centring this time around Scar).

For the screenwriters, these episodes are very complicated, because they are orchestrating a large number of characters, and groups of

---

12 That is Frank Archer's chief narrative function: to scupper plans within the military (and Roy Mustang's in particular). For example, in this episode, *Where's My Philosopher's Stone, Dude?*, Archer has hired the Crimson Alchemist Kimbley (and promoted him), much to the ire of Mustang and co. Archer was invented for the *animé*, partly to perform the role of Bradley plays in the comic.
13 There are State Alchemists present who could see that – such as Roy Mustang – but it has more dramatic impact if it's Ed who says it.

characters, each one with their own agendas, ways of working, personality traits, and issues to resolve (to see how difficult this can be, today's assignment is this: create 20 characters of your own and give them each something significant to do in 22 minutes, plus combine the storylines, develop the themes, advance the main plot, reveal mysteries and back-stories, etc. And give all of that a satisfying narrative structure and shape. Oh, and it must be entertaining).

So we have Ed Elric separated from Alphonse (he's gone undercover into Liore, in a natty, brown wig[14] and Ishbalian robes) • we have Al and Martel back with the military • we have Col. Mustang, Frank Archer and co. • we have Scar, Rose Tomas and Lyra • we have a number of homunculi (Lust and Gluttony form one group, Wrath is another) • we have Führer Bradley (who is another homunculus) • and we have the Crimson Alchemist, Zolf Kimbley. And other characters, too!

So it all gets a little complicated. Not only are there are different groups of characters, they are also different locations, and different time scales, because *The Scar, Holy Mother* and other episodes in this part of the first series of *Fullmetal Alchemist* are full of flashbacks which narrate the pasts of characters such as Scar and Rose.

If you can't follow it all closely, don't worry, because the filmmakers have also included tons of action, and a few high octane duels: Scar vs. Zolf Kimbley the Crimson Alchemist being one, Scar vs. Ed being another, Martel vs. the Führer Bradley is another, and Al + Martel vs. Kimbley is another, etc. (Kimbley comes across as a really venal villain, laughing with glee as he inflicts torment after torment on his victims in the Ishbal desert flashback. Will someone please rip this guy's head off?).

Unfortunately, the episodes in this part of the *Fullmetal Alchemist* series (*With the River's Flow, Secret of Ishbal, Holy Mother*, etc) have become incredibly violent. Very vicious: characters are shredded to pieces with an alarming regularity (with innocent bystanders being blown to bits by psychos such as the Crimson Alchemist). And Scar, one of the chief psychotics in the *Fullmetal Alchemist* series, is planning a wholesale massacre in order to create a philosopher's stone (out of an entire town).

Not only is *Fullmetal Alchemist* sickeningly violent, it is also morally dubious at many points (but not in the way it intends: that is, it is morally questionable outside of the characters and the scenarios). For instance, after Ed Elric has battled Scar in an alley (their duel is interrupted by the appearance of the weirdo homunculi duo of Lust and Gluttony), he talks with Scar, and Scar is further humanized with more flashbacks about his youth in Ishbal, his brother, his brother's relationship with Lust before she became a homunculus, the Ishbal rebellion and invasion, etc.

Yes, these flashbacks do illuminate how and why Scar came to be the way he is (set upon by Zolf Kimbley, tormented, and scarred with repulsive physical wounds), but they don't excuse the fact that he is a mass murderer! And he is planning to slaughter an entire town (yes, he'll allow the inhabitants of Liore to flee thru some tunnels, and to lure the military

---

14 The wig, covering one eye, makes Ed resemble the boy Wrath.

into the town, to use them as fodder for the creation of the philosopher's stone).

It doesn't matter what Scar's goals or motives are, if the means he employs is mass murder! He might promise world peace, but not at that price. He is a fascist, no better than Adolf Hitler, Josef Stalin, Pol Pot or any other dictator or mass murderer in history.

So to have Edward Elric standing there talking politely to Scar and listening to him and not doing much to stop him or get help in imprisoning him or even offer a strong verbal opposition to him is pretty hard to take. In fact, Ed is reduced to standing about quite a bit in these episodes, as the filmmakers (and *manga* creator Hiromu Arakawa) work out what Ed (and Al) can be doing, in amongst these large political events. Because Ed has to be a pro-active hero, has to be doing something all the time, but with so many characters in the mix now, and with so many conflicting goals and quests, it becomes increasingly difficult finding something that Ed and Al can do that fits their teenage status, fits in with their over-arching quest, puts them into the right contexts, with the right people – and, because they're the chief characters, something that's a final, decisive act. The obstacles are mounting up to a formidable level at this point in *Fullmetal Alchemist*, with political oppression seemingly unstoppable.

Thus, Scar has Rose Tomas with him, now in her Virgin Mary guise (she is called 'Holy Mother', wears the Madonna's wimple and costume, and even cradles a baby in her arms, with Lyra acting as her interpreter. Yes, the filmmakers've brought Lyra back – Lyra who is really the super-villain Dante, because Dante will benefit from Scar's town-sized transmutation ritual). Rose, wheeled in from the very first episode, *Those Who Challenge the Sun*, is now speechless (the reason hinted at is rape. Ed is shocked. And author Himoru Arakawa was not happy with that suggestion[15]). But Rose the 'Holy Mother' is a figurehead for the people, being manipulated by Scar (the Liore community is a parody of a religious community, first introduced following the false cult of the sun-god Leto and Priest Cornello in the first episode of *Fullmetal Alchemist*).

The Scar back-story mirrors the Elric brothers' story, of course: Scar's brother (Yuu Mizushima) was a dead-keen alchemist, who tried to bring his fiancée back to life (she was the woman who became, following the transmutation, the homunculus Lust – the woman who was also involved with Lujon in episode 35: *Reunion of the Fallen*). So Scar and his *nii-san* are another pair of siblings trying to create a philosopher's stone and resurrect the dead (it's something that brothers – and lovers – tend to do in *Fullmetal Alchemist*!).[16]

✳

Zolf Kimbley and Führer Bradley provide plenty of threat and obstacle in episode 40: *The Scar* – Kimbley's turning into the most

---

15 And it is rape by the military.
16 The complications of the philosopher's stone plot deepen – now we find out that Scar's brother created a philosopher's stone in his body, and parts of bodies (such as arms) were also included.

fearsome and psychotic opponent in *Fullmetal Alchemist* (he uses humans as bombs to attack his victims!). Meanwhile, the Führer reveals just how merciless he can be as he fights Martel then kills her (he also orders the death of Ed Elric). The death scene climaxes episode 40, with the horrific image of Alphonse Elric clutching his blood-stained armour, weeping for the dead Martel who hid inside him, stabbed to death by the Führer. No Western or Hollywood movie has done this to its teenage heroes!

There is some clunky scriptwriting in some of the duels. Martel, leaping on the back of Führer Bradley, instead of stabbing the sucker in the throat with the knife she holds there (which would prevent a lot of carnage, because Bradley is a repulsive homunculus), gives him time to react by telling him what she thinks of him. Oh dear. A fatal mistake – because not long after this Bradley walks up to Al, and stabs Martel inside the suit of amour. (as Deunan Knute says in Masamune Shirow's *Appleseed manga*, never talk in battle until you've won!).[17]

Episode 41. *Holy Mother*

This is a very busy but somewhat dissatisfying episode, despite all of its action, its two duels, and its to-ing and fro-ing. Structurally, it's somewhat misshapen, as it struggles to keep abreast of every character, scenario, goal and motive. Also, the grand themes of the military preparing to invade Liore, and the establishment of a philosopher's circle the size of the city (created by Scar), are sort of lost in the frantic action. It is also one of the grimmest, most downbeat shows in the first *Fullmetal Alchemist* series (there isn't a single moment of intentional humour in it).

For a time in episode 41: *Holy Mother*, Ed Elric goes along with Scar and his plans, tho' he has his own schemes (such as sending a letter back to the military). A defeated and depressed Edward is somewhat pitiful, but also, for us as an audience hankering after entertainment, not very appealing or interesting: we prefer our Ed feisty and chipper (romantic and nostalgic, too, yes, and melancholy and introspective at times too, yes – but not beaten down to the point of standing there morosely saying nothing).

So when Edward Elric, following the citizens of Liore along the brick tunnels out of the city (as commanded to do so by Scar), encounters a mysterious wall of goop that turns out to be the homunculus Sloth in the form of Juliet Douglas plus one of his arch-enemies, Wrath (Nana Mizuki), we are back with the fighting, kicking, yelling and alchemically-transmuting Edward Elric, the Fullmetal Alchemist.

The Edward-and-Wrath relationship is far more intriguing, dramatically and emotionally, than many of the other rivals' duels in the *Fullmetal Alchemist* series (such as between Ed and Scar, or Ed and Number 48 'Slicer', the resurrected, disembodied suit of armour, or between Scar and Zolf Kimbley). Because Wrath is the former offspring of

---

17 And when Ed Elric catches up with Scar and battles with him (as he vowed to do), he spends quite a bit of time telling Scar about the different metals he's had built into his automail, thus providing the villain with the means of defeating him! Oh dear.

Ed's *sensei*, Izumi Curtis (the *animé* flashes back to images from the fateful day when Wrath was created at the Gateway, using very rapid editing).

Now a twisted homunculus with wild, black spikey hair, a manic grin and very contemporary clothes, Wrath might be the lead guitarist for a metal, emo or J-pop band (his design clearly draws on Envy – ah, Envy! there is far too little of the insane diva Envy in the first *Fullmetal Alchemist* series! But the second series makes up for that!). Wrath is also, like Ed Elric, *very* quick to flare up, very temperamental, and full of antsy energy. Wrath, at least, is not a character that's going to stand about and mutter 'uhh', 'errr', or 'whatever, dude' (altho' he does, like many an emo or Goth personality, retreat into himself).

And in the Ed-Wrath duel in the tunnel in episode 41: *Holy Mother*, there is at last an inventive piece of scriptwriting: the baby that Rose, the 'holy mother', holds in her arms begins to cry, which incenses Wrath (the device's used twice, saving Ed both times). Wrath cries 'shut up!' And he advances on the baby with an evil look in his eye (the other eye, like so many characters in this and many other *animés*, being covered by floppy hair).

Great storytelling, because the baby's cries link to the primary plot of *Fullmetal Alchemist*, of recreating a dead life (and Rose Tomas stands there holding a baby – it's Wrath and his mom Izumi Curtis, and of course it's also Ed and his mom Trisha. When Douglas takes on the form of his dead mom, Edward screams). And when the *animé* inserts flashcuts showing the Gateway, Izumi, the magical rituals, and the mess of yuck that was the stillborn baby that became Wrath, the show achieves a far greater and deeper scale. Instead of action and stunts and endless, bitter assaults and violence, we have action plus drama and psychology and emotion.

A character smashing someone in the face might be exciting, but it can also be meaningless action. A character punching someone who is the weird, twisted mirror image of himself (and the resurrected stillborn son of his former teacher), is so much richer (if pretty bizarre!). And Wrath is still desperate to have a real body – to have Ed's body (as he yells at Ed).

Thus, compared to many of the homunculi and villains, such as Zolf Kimbley, Scar, Führer Bradley, Envy, Lust and Gluttony, the feral, maniacal Wrath is so much more interesting, because he is tied so directly to the central character of the whole *Fullmetal Alchemist* series, Edward Elric. And it's when the *Fullmetal Alchemist* series comes back to Ed – and Al – that it reaches its highest heights, and its deepest emotional resonances. But when it wanders off to Mustang-Archer-Kimbley-Scar-Lust-Envy and all the other secondary characters, it loses some of its oomph, its muchness, its alchemicalness.

There's a clever call-back, too, to the moment in the early episode where Edward Elric told Rose Thomas to get up and walk. Now Rose manages to find her voice so she can say the same to Ed, on the floor after being attacked by Wrath, and stunned by the appearance of Juliet Douglas looking uncomfortably like his mother.

Alphonse Elric voices a very reasonable idea, which has added impact because it comes from a teenager who's only a hollow suit of armour: *can everybody stop killing each other, please?* When Al says that, the many military types gathered around him look uncomfortable.

❋

The storytelling in *Fullmetal Alchemist* is coming thick and fast in the shows from episode no. 38 onwards. But is it me or is some of the animation (or the storyboarding) in these episodes of the *Fullmetal Alchemist* series lacking inspiration? Were the animator teams getting tired? For instance, in the Zolf Kimbley versus Scar duel in 41: *Holy Mother* (which goes on too long), the filmmakers employ simulations of circular tracking shots used in live-action (where the camera moves in a circle around a stationary actor, solely to provide some interest to a scene which is basically two guys standing there talking to each other. For the camera crew in live-action, it can involve building a circular track, and often the Steadicam device is employed).

Poor Alphonse Elric is not having a good time either, like his brother Edward: not long after a young woman is murdered inside his body, he wanders in to the midst of the Zolf Kimbley-versus-Scar duel, and it doesn't go well. Kimbley is finally defeated by Scar (using the recurring motif in fantasy *animé* of an arm thrust thru a torso like a sword), but tho' anybody else would be very dead, Kimbo remains alive enough to grab hold of Alphonse, in an attempt to turn him into a bomb (moments earlier, Kimbley had also transmuted Scar's arm, so that it's only moments before it will explode. And what does Scar do? Only cuts off his own arm! Yes, arms are a big deal in the *Fullmetal Alchemist* series!).

Any scene involving Kimbley is very nasty in *Fullmetal Alchemist* – this is a truly diseased individual. Here *Fullmetal Alchemist* delves into the psychopathic regions of the human heart, where murderous desires run unchecked, and there is no moral framework, no ethical blocks and no boundaries whatsoever. Kimbley is a S.O.B. who walks thru the streets of Liore killing people to the left and to the right, while he cackles and scorns the populace for being so weedy and not fighting back.

Also in ep. 41: Lyra is loitering about, not showing her true colours (as Dante) yet; we see flashbacks to the death of Martel; Alphonse tells the military officers that philosopher's stones are created using human lives (this revelation comes quite late in the series); the Führer holds off invading Liore (while Archer is gung-ho), but we do see lines of tanks rumbling thru the streets.

Episode 42. *His Name Is Unknown*

OK, grab your lightsabre, your ruling ring, your wizardly wand, your trusty broadsword, and gear up, because the *Fullmetal Alchemist* series finally takes flight into full-on dramatic, thematic, action-led and character-based territory in the sequence from episode 42: *His Name Is*

Unknown and 43: *The Stray Dog* thru episode 44: *Hohenheim of Light*. Big action, big music, big visual effects, but most of all, big conflicts, big issues, and big character-based scenes.

This is the point in an *animé* series where all of the effort laboured over the production pays off, when all of the groundwork of character-izations and relationships and plot points bears fruit, and where the audience is on the edge of their seat as the narrative gets its hooks in and won't let go.

There are surprises, revelations, plot twists and two determined, passionate kids at the heart of it all. Following his duel with Scar and then with Wrath, and then with Douglas/ Sloth, Edward Elric has his regained his zing, his Edwardness. Meanwhile, the writers find something amazing for Alphonse to do by making him into a bomb and then a philosopher's stone (another addition to the *Fullmetal Alchemist manga*).

Ed Elric does the fighting and the yelling in *Fullmetal Alchemist*, while Al is the conscience, the thought, the emotion, the point of it all. At least Ed has a body, despite having a metal arm and a metal leg. But poor Al, he's been a hollow suit of armour since forever! At least Ed gets to eat and sleep and do all the things humans can do (pretty much); but Al has to suffer having that clanky, cold, brittle body. No fun. (And for Al, first he's turned into a bomb by the super-sadist Zolf Kimbley, and now into a philosopher's stone by the equally deranged Scar!).

With these episodes – *His Name Is Unknown*, *The Stray Dog* and *Hohenheim of Light* (and the following ones), the *Fullmetal Alchemist* series is intensifying to a delightful degree, accelerating at a pace which's very enjoyable. It's still bone-crunchingly violent, it's still morally uncertain and very cynical, but the relationships and the quests and the themes are hurtling towards the climax.

And, best of all, Ed and Al Elric are absolutely at the centre of the mix, which's when *Fullmetal Alchemist* is at its most appealing. Not only that, their father, Hohenheim (Masashi Ebara), finally makes an appearance in the present tense of the story.

These episodes end on cliffhangers – freeze frames and smash cuts, accompanied by the music swelling to a pitch, before the fade to black and the end credits. When each episode closes with a cliffhanger, you're into storytelling as the Thrill Of The Chase, of What Happened Next, those magical chimera claws which dig into an audience and drag them to the next installment.

B4 he died, the Crimson Alchemist (Zolf Kimbley) had turned Al Elric into a bomb (what a creep, to do that to a teenager!).[18] Scar helps to save Al, but at a price – he transforms Al into a receptacle for philosopher's stones (Al springs tattoos all over his armour, and is wasting away as the effects of Kimbley's bomb-making take hold, collapsed on the ground and turning black). And a cost to Scar, too: he loses his arm (the other one was lost to Kimbley – another comment on the

---

18 At least Kimbley seems to die in this episode.

determination of political assassins – or terrorists, if you like – to sacrifice themselves to the Cause). It's all far-fetched nonsense, of course – and slinky *femme fatale* Lust, a cold-hearted homunculus if ever there was one – looks on pitilessly. She might look like the woman that Scar's brother fell in love with (and Scar may be harbouring repressed desires for), but now she's a homunculus she is far less than human (and she's ignored the commands of the homunculi's boss, Lyra-Dante).

Certainly the scenes featuring the psychotic bully and mass murderer Scar, the teenage boy who's a suit of armour, Al Elric, and the venal, cynical, black-haired woman-turned-homunculus, Lust, are unusual. These are not your everyday characters! And they are not in regular relationships with each other! These are the mightily-weird manifestations of a fantasy story nearing its finale.

✳

Meanwhile, Edward Elric is fighting his own battles in the tunnel, with Rose Thomas (and her bambino) at his side (Rose refuses to flee), and Wrath bouncing around the tunnel trying to kill him (Wrath again takes up some of the story points of Envy in the *Fullmetal Alchemist manga*). The *Holy Mother* episode closed with overtly comicbook-styled, freeze frame images of Ed hurling himself at Wrath, and Wrath hurling himself at Rose (both of them grimacing with hate, and enveloped with the speed lines of *manga* drawings. It's delightful when *animé* makes self-conscious *hommages* to the style of *manga*).[19]

The exciting, rapidly-cut duels in the tunnel relate directly to the central issue of *Fullmetal Alchemist:* Wrath, for example, is the botched outcome of Izumi Curtis's desperate bid to resurrect her stillborn son (and he took Ed Elric's arm and leg in the process). Ed wants those bits of his body back! (Understandably! Who wouldn't if they saw someone walking round with their arm and leg!).

But the revelation of just who the Führer's secretary (Juliet Douglas) is at this point offers even more dramatic fire power: she looks a lot like the Elric boys' mother Trisha. For good reason: she is a homunculus, and a homunculus is created when an alchemist tries to resurrect the dead. Douglas is in fact the offshoot of the calamitous experiment Ed and Al undertook to bring back their dead mother. (It is a tad confusing – when you have homunculi impersonating Führer Bradley, Juliet Douglas, Lyra/Dante, etc).

The revelation raises the stakes, and the jeopardy, and the interconnectedness of the heroes Alphonse and Edward Elric with their enemies in *Fullmetal Alchemist,* the homunculi. In the action-adventure genre (and in much of drama), the more psychological links you can make between the heroes and the villains, the juicier the mix.

Thus, in confronting Wrath and then Juliet Douglas, Ed Elric is facing his mistakes, his shadows, his failures, yet again. And his pride, his self-absorption, his selfishness (the heroes have committed the same 'sins' as the villains). It's this aspect of the *Fullmetal Alchemist* franchise that plays

---

19 But they draw the line of changing to black-and-white.

a huge part in making it so compelling. The moral and philosophical complexity of the Japanese, 2003-04 TV series adds so much to the eye candy of the adventures and the action, so it's not just about magical battles and transmutations. This animated series has real, genuine *weight*.

It's not resolved here, tho': despite Edward Elric triumphing over Wrath and Juliet Douglas in the Liore tunnel by using superior alchemy, they are not killed or even captured. Yes, we know that: this is episode 42 out of a 51-episode run. But it is a little lame when Ed simply walks off into the sunset with Rose Tomas, giving a complacent shrug, thinking he's just defeated two of the nastiest critters in the *Fullmetal Alchemist* universe. Come on, Ed, you *know* it's going to take more'n that to waste Wrath *and* Douglas/ Sloth! (And someone – Lyra – does tell him that).[20]

✳

Meanwhile, out on the streets of Liore, the philosopher's stone that Scar has created out of an entire town has to pay off, doesn't it? I guess. So it does: spectacular scenes filled with visual effects animation (and that all-important red glow), depict the equivalent in *Fullmetal Alchemist* of an atomic bomb blast (H-bombs haunt so many *animés*, and pretty much all sci-fi *animé*). (Is Scar dead, then? We might hope so – we last see him lying down in the trench he dug, to ignite the creation of the philosopher's stone. He's already been riddled with hails of bullets, twice, and lost both arms. But not much is made of his demise. And charas come back to life with a tireless regularity in the *Fullmetal Alchemist* cosmos, and also in fantasy *animé*).

Liore is razed flat. Utterly. Nothing left except a mound of sand buried under which is... Alphonse Elric.[21] Edward (having said *sayonara* to Rose Tomas and Lyra in some nearby ruins), races over to uncover him. It's one of their odder reunions, somewhat anti-climactic and dis-satisfying (it deserves to be played much bigger and more emotional). The lads soon discover that, yes, Al has become a philosopher's stone, as Scar intended (that is, Al is back to normal – back to his suit of armour, but with a glowing mass of scarlet inside his belly).

At this point, you might think that the Elric brothers would immediately try to fulfil their over-arching quest: to have their bodies brought back, using this new super-power. But they don't.

Why?

Why doesn't Ed Elric instantly cry, 'Al, let's transmute our bodies!' After all, they have a philosopher's stone at their disposal, and they're on their own in a desert, with nobody to stop them, no adult figures to tut-tut, shake their heads, and tell the Elrics to desist. (They might also be tempted to use the philosopher's stone as a weapon – after all, the military machine has been trying to create a philosopher's stone all this time. Indeed, Ed wonders if the military used the Ishbal rebellion to do just that, to use a whole city to produce a philosopher's stone).

But no, the story of *Fullmetal Alchemist* has got too big at this point: there are too many other plotlines to resolve, too many other characters to

---

20 Lyra is rather unconvincingly lurking on the edges of the story for a long time at this point.
21 A call-back to the first time we met the Elrics in this series.

follow up, too many issues to deal with, apart from the Elrics' yearning to have their bodies returned to them.

Also, that philosopher's stone has been created with thousands of lives. We have just witnessed the *Fullmetal Alchemist* equivalent of Hiroshima. So for the lads to use those deaths for their own, selfish ends is morally dubious.

And also they want to resurrect their mother, so they need one more thing: part of their mother's remains (another departure from the *manga*, where the Elrics only want their own bodies back). Hence they opt to travel back to their homeland, Resembool. (And they need a part of Wrath – so that Ed can retrieve his leg and arm; thus, he asks Izumi Curtis about that in episode 45: *A Rotted Heart*). Digging up their mother was part of the *Fullmetal Alchemist manga*, tho' given a different twist in the first *animé*.

So much story is jammed into episode 42: *His Name Is Unknown*, and yet some of it seems unsatisfying and rushed. However, for action and spectacle, *His Name Is Unknown* is plenty busy and eventful: apart from the deaths of three important secondary charas (Scar and Zolf Kimbley), this episode also includes a face-off between Roy Mustang and his cohorts and Frank Archer and Shou Tucker (plus a band of chimeras unleashed from cages); an invasion scenario (of deserted Liore), involving tanks and troops, overseen by Archer; and ruminations from Führer Bradley. (Archer also appears expire in the conflagration, but he returns).

Episode 43. *The Stray Dog*

Now with the Liore outing coming to a close, all roads turn towards Resembool (so that the Mongolian desert near Liore suddenly becomes the Alpine (= Hokkaido[22]) mountains of Resembool). The parallel action of this part of the *Fullmetal Alchemist* franchise depicts the more modest and domestic Resembool scenes by introducing 'Hohenheim of Light' – the father of the Elric boys. (Hohenheim might be the 'stray dog' of the episode's title, but Ed is also dubbed that, too – the stray dog is coming home. Himoru Arakawa wrote a *manga* called *Stray Dog*).

In the desert, an important plot point is introduced when Ed and Al Elric accidentally touch, and, because Al now seems to be a philosopher's stone, they have visions of the Gateway of Truth (the first *Fullmetal Alchemist* series leaves aside aspects of the other world and the Gate for long stretches, but the 2009-10 series rightly reminds the audience of those spiritual/ metaphysical elements often).

✶

Let's look at the return of the father: he is depicted using the classic trope of the Return of the Stranger (a guy coming back from a war is a typical example). He's first seen, as in the *manga*, at the railroad station (by Winry and Sheska, who're now transformed into goofy, comic relief twins). Now, in an *animé* series stuffed to the gills with surrogate fathers,

22 The settings of moorland and rocky, mountain streams surrounded by pine and fir trees are charmingly rendered.

false fathers, good father figures and bad father figures, and uncle types, and God types, and priests, and generals, and Führers, and older brothers – here, at last, in the foreground and present tense of the *Hagane no Renkinjutsushi* series, is the *real* father!

Enter van Hohenheim of Light (Masashi Ebara): he is a handsome man who appears to be in his late forties or early fifties (he still has the blond hair that he gave to Edward), and he looks like both boys. He doesn't say much, isn't given much of a personality, and has few unusual character traits, quirks or gestures.

Indeed, about the most striking thing about Hohenheim is his blandness. He seems friendly enough, calm enough, unassuming enough to fit in anywhere. Hohenheim is ultimately something of a mystery at this point – we actually know very little about him. We know he left the family years ago, we know he is the classic, absent father, and we know that Ed Elric in particular seethes with rage whenever his pa is mentioned. (Actually, Hohenheim is rather quirky – he spends the night at the grave-yard, for instance, because his home has been burnt down).

But we also know that Hohenheim of Light is an alchemist, and quite likely a very powerful alchemist (as well he might be with Ed and Al as his offspring). We have seen him engrossed in alchemical studies, ignoring his children in previous flashbacks. So we can guess that his travels have had something to do with alchemy (but we also realize that Hohenheim had to leave, and the mother had to die, because of the fundamental requirement of fiction with teenagers as the chief protagonists: you have to get rid of the parents!).

Hohenheim is introduced while the spectacular events in Liore are occurring, so that he is already established before Ed and Al Elric turn up (accompanied by a gaggle of the main secondary characters in the military, such as Colonel Mustang, Liza Hawkeye, and the four soldiers in Mustang's team).

Having Sheska and Winry Rockbell encounter van Hohenheim first (at the railroad station) is not necessary (but it gives them something to do). However, Winry is a stand-in for the Elric boys, emotionally, so the first meeting between Hohenheim and Winry does have some dramatic value. He mistakes her for her mother Sara, for instance. (Later, at the cemetery, for instance, it's Winry who talks with Hohenheim, while Pinako turns up then leaves without a word. Sheska, tho', has been dragged along to lighten the mood, it seems. Sheska has little to do except freak out over the slightest thing, in her intense, geeky way).

The journey from Liore to Resembool is not without incident, either (the *Fullmetal Alchemist* series rarely has characters going from one place to another without something mad happening). At this point, the screenwriters retain the key members of the military, so that Ed and Al aren't going to Resembool alone: Roy Mustang, Liza Hawkeye, Alex Armstrong and others are pursuing them (on the orders of Führer Bradley). Ed, importantly, vows never to be a 'dog of the military' again, and threatens to leave the institution (much to Col. Mustang's disgust –

Mustang is a military man thru and thru).

This part of the first *Fullmetal Alchemist* series isn't wholly satisfying narratively – it conjures up a false conflict between Roy Mustang and his team and the Elric brothers, for instance. False because Mustang has no intention of capturing or injuring the Elrics – so all of those alchemical battles in the stony river valley in the mountains amount to... nothing much.

Führer Bradley ordering Colonel Mustang to pursue and capture Edward and Alphonse plays into the homunculi's plans, of course – because they still need the Elrics to further their nefarious schemes. But the way that subplot plays out with rambunctious alchemical duels between Col. Mustang, Alex Armstrong, assorted officers and the Elric boys is somewhat dissatisfying.

However, there *is* an emotional pay-off, when Col. Mustang acknowledges that he killed Winry's folks, on the military's orders. Winry listens, slumped on the ground, in silence (Mustang has his back to her, a classic piece of staging you see everywhere in *animé*). This beat was transferred from Scar in the *manga*, in the scene where Winry confronts Scar in the street, holding a gun, while the Elrics looked on horrified. The producers changed the killer to Mustang perhaps to give more dramatic juice to Mustang's characterization. He is, after all, the Elrics' boss, and one of the 'good father' figures in *Fullmetal Alchemist*.

Episode 44. *Hohenheim of Light*

Broadcast on August 7, 2004, this is one of the most important episodes in the first *Fullmetal Alchemist* series. Even the author, Himoru Arakawa, makes an appearance herself – well, in the guise of her humorous stand-in, a black-and-white cow with glasses (dancing in big knickers in a comical skit involving Sheska the librarian, who is, like Winry and Izumi Curtis, one of Arakawa-san's stand-ins).

Because in episode 44: *Hohenheim of Light* much of the main plot of homunculi is revealed, and the Elrics' father Hohenheim finally meets his talented offspring. It's at this point, up in the mountains, next to a river, that the crucial information about Führer Bradley and Juliet Douglas being homunculi is exchanged (the Elrics, Winry Rockbell, Roy Mustang and members of the military're present). The question is raised here: what if the top man in an organization is corrupt? What if he's the top dog of the whole country? What if you've been working for an institution run by a madman? What if the people that're supposed to be protecting the whole nation – the military machine – are psychopaths? The questions're raised in a fantasy adventure animated TV series here, but they are valid questions! They are questions that have been asked throughout history, right into our contemporary era. You can see how *Fullmetal Alchemist* – and all fantasy literature – is completely of its time, completely contemporary, completely about *now*.

Meanwhile, Lyra has taken Rose Tomas and her child to... a rundown Cathedral (why are Cathedrals and churches always abandoned or in decline in Japanese animation? *Anime* never depicts Western religion as sparkingly new. Well, it's true that Christianity's origins go back 2,000 years). And to the customary secret passage (under the altar, naturally), to... the secret lair of the villains... the homunculi.

As they travel, Lyra muses on the dead religion that built this structure – one of numerous references to Xianity in the *Fullmetal Alchemist* series (and in *anime* in general). Yet Christianity is imported into *anime* often purely at the decorative or exotic level (angels, statues, stained glass, tolling bells), as something that looks intriguing, and is often portrayed as sinister (Christianity is quite often depicted as a menacing cult – exactly as the Xian religion throughout its history has viewed other cults!). Because Japan's religion is Shintoism (with Buddhism a key influence), and a tiny fraction of Japanese people follow Christianity.

*

I told you Lyra was a bad egg! She is: Lyra it turns out is really Dante in disguise, and the leader of the homunculi. Meanwhile, assorted homunculi are gathered in the swanky digs of the villains: Wrath, Gluttony, Pride and Lust (poor Lust is imprisoned – fixed to the wall in a crucifix pose by spikes – a function taken by Greed in the *Fullmetal Alchemist manga*). And it's li'l Lyra/ Dante who is running the show here (all of this departs from Himoru Arakawa's *manga*, tho' it keeps the essence of the homunculi as All-Time Bad Guys with a fearsome leader who lurk underground. However, portraying her as a young woman departs from Father in the *manga*, who takes his appearance from Hohenheim).

＊

Some of the screenwriting in the 1st *Fullmetal Alchemist* series in episodes 41 onwards is a little creaky and awkward at times. For instance, the writers're trying to keep track of all the secondary plots as well as the primary plots. Thus, the Winry-Mustang-parents plot, where Winry-chan is hot on the case of the man who killed her parents (Roy Mustang), is discussed right in amongst the confrontation scene between Mustang, Liza Hawkeye and the military and Ed and Al Elric (where Ed is going up against Mustang yet again in an alchemical duel involving plenty of rock-hurling, rain and fire vfx). Some of the dialogue scenes are messily handled, with characters suddenly appearing, overhearing conversations, then disappearing. At the Rockbells' house, for instance, one moment Sheska is there (popping up around a corner), the next it's Winry, or Grandma Pinako. Meanwhile, poor Hohenheim is relegated to sitting awkwardly outside the house, by a window (but over-hearing the conversation – there's an important point, tho', about Dante and Lyra, which sends him off the next morning to confront Dante). Later, he just happens to be sitting by a tree, handily adding to the conversation. Having charas simply popping up here and there for no convincing reason is just lazy screenwriting. In this episode, Hohenheim also has to sleep in a tent, instead of in the house (don't they have a couch free?! Despite what Ed says, Hohenheim is still the boys' father, and the husband of Pinako's daughter Trisha. We don't really get to find out why Hohenheim is not welcome at the Rockbells' crib. We know what Ed thinks of him!).

◆

Anyhoo, let's get to the long-awaited moment when Edward and Alphonse Elric finally meet their father, 'Hohenheim of Light': Al is overjoyed to see his pa, but – too late! – Ed is already dashing over to the man. Does Ed talk to him? Greet him? Hug him? Shake hands? No! He smashes his father in the face, sending the (far larger) man flying off the porch, onto the ground. And what does Hohenheim do? He just lies there! Like he expected nothing less from Ed (now he's in his Hopeless Dad persona).

The meeting of the family of alchemists is full of such odd moments (but if you know your Sigmund Freud, you know what's going on here! After all, the scene has Hohenheim flirting with Lt. Ross, with her blushing but enjoying it. And Ed mentions the flirting in his tirade against his absent father, as if it's yet another crime against his mother by his father. It's all textbook Freud and the œdipal complex).

And yet... somehow I expected more from the Final Meeting of the Elric boys with their pa. Playing Hohenheim for mystery means that so much of the subtext has to come out later. For instance, one key ingredient of Hohenheim's introduction is missing: his goals. What are his aims?

What does he want? Why has he come back to Resembool? (Surely not just to see if his old house is still there?!).

If you withhold that information about a new character, you keep the audience guessing. We already know that Elric senior is an ambiguous personality, but we don't know about his back-story, his goals, or his motives.

Intriguingly, Hohenheim camps out with Alphonse Elric in the tent. And in the morning he's gone. Where? To run down Dante and the homunculi in their under-the-Cathedral lair. Here is another alchemists' duel – between Dante and Hohenheim – who are the most powerful alchemists in the series (we see that Hohenheim is indeed a very strong alchemist, as he dispatches the clutch of chimeras that Dante sends against him – using, in a nice touch, warriors in the shape of his son Al). Hohenheim is given a Grand Entrance, too – he simply storms in to the villains' lair below the Cathedral, by blowing apart the doors.

The episode – 44: *Hohenheim of Light* – ends on yet another cliff-hanger, with the conflicts unresolved. But now we know plenty – about the homunculi, about Hohenheim (and we've seen his powers at last), and discovered who the Big Villain is who's behind everything (we also see that Hohenheim and Dante know each other).

We also have El and Al Elric hot on the trail of the central plot: this is the moment when the boys find out that Maes Hughes has died, which every other character knows (keeping this a secret this long does stretch belief – the revelation occurs much earlier in the *manga*). Ed in particular is livid that they have been kept in the dark (he focusses most of his ire on Col. Mustang, as expected).

There is much talk in episode 44: *Hohenheim of Light* of philosopher's stones (with the Elrics trying to keep the fact that Alphonse has been turned into a philosopher's stone hidden). There is action in episode 44: *Hohenheim of Light*, tho', despite the important conversations: Hohenheim versus Dante, for instance, Ed and his father, and a flashback to the Ishbal War (as the Elrics tell Sheska what really happened – a recycling of footage from episode 18: *Marcoh's Notes*).

There is so much going on in *Hohenheim of Light*, it can seem as if some of the scenes are a little rushed: it might've made the series weightier if some of the fluffier sections had been compressed somewhat, to allow more room for the dramatic scenes (even so, there is quita a bit of humour in *Hohenheim of Light*, too).

At the close of episode 44: *Hohenheim of Light*, we have the Victorian Gothic moment of Edward Elric digging up his mother's grave (in the second *Fullmetal Alchemist* series, this was given a much bigger treatment, with Pinako helping Ed shovel the soil in the rain).

Episode 45. *A Rotted Heart*

So, to episode 45 of the 2003-2004 *Fullmetal Alchemist* series, first broadcast in the Land of the Rising Sun on August 21, 2004, entitled *A*

Rotted Heart. As quite often in the *Fullmetal Alchemist* series, this excellent episode opens by backtracking a tad into the climax of the last episode, to remind us Where We Are. We are in the Big Confrontation Scene, between the heroes' dad and the chief villain: Hohenheim and Dante. (And, irritatingly, the episode also does something that all multiple-storyline *anime* shows do – it cuts away from this intense scene to other scenes (repeatedly). In this case, to Winry and Sheska cooking in the kitchen (!) in a wholly lightweight, throwaway, humorous scene).

OK, so Elric senior has entered the villain's lair to confront the arch baddie, Dante (or Dante in Lyra's body – keep up!). They stand 50 feet apart in the huge room, with Lust pinned to the wall on one side (for being a naughty girl, presumably), and Gluttony and Wrath lurking about somewhere (Sloth descends the stairs at the end of the sequence to imprison Hohenheim).

There is some talk first (what Big Confrontation Scene have you ever seen in the final act of an action-adventure series/ story/ movie that *doesn't* involve some talking? None). So they talk. Thankfully, to illustrate the all-important information, the filmmakers call upon the services of editor Hiroaki Itabe and his team of assistants at J. Film to produce two montages – one for the origins of the homunculi and the Dante-Hohenheim story, and one for Hohenheim's past with his family. These are some the finest moments in the whole *Fullmetal Alchemist* franchise, the montages depicting the back stories of Dante, Hohenheim, Trisha and the Elric boys (these are moments to rewind and watch again. Both Hohenheim and Dante narrate the montages).

This is magnificent. This is what filmmaking does best – storytelling without having a character standing there *telling* you the story. Instead, it's a flood of images, accompanied by a strong cue from composer Michiru Oshima. Each image is short, cut into a rapid flow of shots, going back much farther, the origins of it all...

...Turns out that Hohenheim and Dante go way back – four or five hundred years back, in fact. And they were lovers. Yes, it *is* a little disappointing that we're now into ever-lasting vampire territory, involving powerful people who want to live forever, and witchhunts, and magic spells to achieve immortality... Well, I guess it's worked for fantasy literature for 100s of years. I admit I was hoping for something a little juicier or more original than that (the ending of the *Fullmetal Alchemist* manga hadn't been published yet, and the second *anime* series was able to illustrate author Himoru Arakawa's much more satisfying ending, where the homunculus in the jar develops into a grandiose super-villain making a determined bid to become a god. However, altho' the *manga* wasn't published, Arakawa had likely thought out roughly how it would end).

On the other hand, the urge towards immortality – which can also be termed as the desire *not* to die – does play totally into the central issues of *Fullmetal Alchemist*, which're all about death and life and wanting people to come back from the dead (and, let's face it, we can all relate to a passionate desire NOT to die).

Yes, it *is* an old chestnut, a tired cliché, a much-used motif. And with such motifs – such as Finding True Love, or Achieving Happiness, or Rags To Riches, or Righting Wrongs – it's *how* you do them that counts. Can you deliver a cliché in a new way, or a poetic way, or a passionate way? Can you convince the audience that altho' they've Been Here a zillion times before, they're going enjoy Being Here again?

In *animé*, there is one filmmaker who can do this with an extraordinary facility – he is so good he makes it look easy – and that's Hayao Miyazaki, the grand master of Japanese animation. Miyazaki can take a whole junkyard full of tired, old narrative clichés and bring them back to life, make them breathe again, and encourage the audience to enjoy them all over again.

Maybe the filmmaking team at Studio Bones/ Enix/ Mainichi/ Aniplex, headed up by director Seiji Mizushima, are approaching the level of Hayao Miyazaki and Studio Ghibli (actually, Ghibli were involved in the production of the animation of *Fullmetal Alchemist*). Actually, several parts of *Fullmetal Alchemist* are the equal of Miyazaki's movies – the ambition, the themes, the action and the lead charas are worthy of comparison with Miyazaki's art.

The filmmakers do try: they have the heroes' father meeting the chief villain and the grand explication of the origins story, the whys and wherefores of the origins of alchemy back in the distant past. And it is marvellously achieved: selective (comicbook) colour is deployed (appropriately enough for the philosopher's stone motif, it's red, with dense black shadows, followed by orange and black. It looks really amazing).

And there's plenty of talk in episode 45: *A Rotted Heart* about souls and bodies – the metaphysical aspects of the living-forever storyline in fantasy literature. And the all-important bit of exposition – that both Dante and Hohenheim are at the end of their lives: you can't just go on creating philosopher's stones and fusing souls to new bodies (in the world of *Fullmetal Alchemist*, the soul seems to wear out, or the ability to fuse a soul to a body does). In the flashback sequence, we see Hohenheim (who's officiating as the chief priest-alchemist) collapsing in the philosopher's stone ritual, and Dante hurrying over to an onlooker to fuse Hohenheim's soul with his body (in a parallel of what Ed did with his brother Al).[1] In subsequent glimpses, we see the life that Dante and Hohenheim led (so that, altho' Hohenheim mentions his wife Trisha, he did spend quite a bit of time with Dante).

Dante is doing all she can to *not* die, even if that means using up any amount of philosopher's stones, or human bodies; but Hohenheim insists that, no, they are at the end of their life-span, even for super-intelligent, super-powerful alchemists. Hohenheim also asserts that he now has a wife (tho' she's dead), and that she (and his family) mean much more to him

---

1 Note that Dante fuses Hohenheim's soul with a guy: the concept of fusing male souls with female bodies or vice versa isn't part of *Fullmetal Alchemist* (that comes up in the gender-bending comedy version!).

than Dante. (Thus there is a strong undercurrent of erotic interplay between Dante and Hohenheim, and Dante is pretty miffed that Hohenheim is now downplaying their former relationship).

At the end of the sequence, Sloth appears in the form of Trisha, Hohenheim's wife, and the Elrics' mother, and imprisons Hohenheim (so we can guess that Daddy Elric is going be rescued by his sons, and will probably die in the finale). Hohenheim (like Ed in the tunnel earlier) is too stunned by the appearance of the Sloth-Trisha homunculus to react at first.

Then Dante orders the homunculi to go out on the quest for another philosopher's stone (and the implication is that it's all for her alone. Oh, movie villains are just so *selfish*, aren't they?! Lust is *not* happy about all this! In the end, the homunculi discover that they are mere slaves of Dante).

✳

The second flashback montage in episode 45: *A Rotted Heart* is edited to a stunning music cue by Michiru Oshima and her team, as the full orchestra (the Moscow International Orchestra) lets rip with a highly emotive piece of music. And when the music's this good, it makes everyone's life so much easier – music like this is a gift to an editor, who can happily arrange the images to the rhythm and flow of the symphonic sounds. And the music makes all of the animators' images and movements look great, too.

The second montage flashback gives us a potted history of Hohenheim and his family, their involvement in alchemy, and the childhoods of Ed and Al (but this time, from Hohenheim's point-of-view). These are the most erotic images, too, in either *Fullmetal Alchemist* TV shows – with several depictions of Hohenheim and Trisha in bed, naked.

The narrative information presented in the back-story montage is so juicy, it's a pity that the Elric brothers aren't there to witness it. But the filmmakers are saving that particular confrontation (and revelation) to climax the first *Fullmetal Alchemist* series.

✳

Meanwhile, just what is happening with Ed and Al Elric in episode 45: *A Rotted Heart*? Not too much, actually: what they are doing is preparation, rather than action or fulfilment (tho' there is a lot of to-ing and fro-ing for many of the characters in this show). So we see Ed returning to the Rockbells' place (following digging up his mother's remains), then leaving with Al, and yet another separation of Ed and Al, and Ed meeting his teacher Izumi Curtis. That Al is a philosopher's stone in himself is mentioned but doesn't bear fruit yet: it is being saved for later on in the finale episodes.

This new separation of the brothers seems artificial, and doesn't convince: the chief reason that Edward Elric gives his brother is that Alphonse can't go around practising alchemy, because he is a philosopher's stone. Because we know that *only Ed* will be the prime mover in making Al whole again, and that the *Fullmetal Alchemist* series will reach its finale with both brothers working together.

So we see Alphonse Elric slinking off when Ed's left to visit... Shou Tucker, of all people, the twisted murderer who killed his daughter and his wife in the pursuit of alchemical transformation: Al wants to learn how to use the philosopher's stone inside him.

That the younger Elric brother has selected Shou Tucker as a teacher is a very poor choice, a serious misjudgement, which stretches belief somewhat (and this late in the *Fullmetal Alchemist* series, too, after the heroes have seen/ done so much): this is a guy who used his spouse and kid (and the family dawg!) in his sick experiments! Would you go to someone like that for advice? (Roy Mustang or even Izumi Curtis would be far better choices, because they are clearly people with their hearts in the right place, and they care for the Elric boys, even tho' they've done some questionable things). But Tucker is a bona fide serial killer, as well as being a morally and ethically weak person.

Disappointing screenwriting, then (by Shou Aikawa). Yes: because in the next episode Edward Elric inadvertently hooks up with Lust. Well, sure, it does enhance the suspense if the boys're separated (we know they're stronger together), and it is a routine shift in plotting to have the heroes being forced to join up with (some of) the villains. But Al *chooses* to visit Tucker, as if he's forgotten everything that he and his brother Ed have been through.

The trouble with such plotting is that it announces to the audience: we're going to pretend that our characters have suddenly lost their senses, and don't know what they're doing, and they've forgotten what just happened, what you've just watched! It's at times like this that you wish Shou Aikawa and the other writers had spent a little more time in thinking thru just how the boys would were going to act in the final episodes of *Fullmetal Alchemist*.

☆

Even all of above storytelling isn't everything that's squeezed into episode 45: *A Rotted Heart* – there is also time for a tender scene between Winry-chan and Edward-kun (with Ed once again in the feminized role, partially-dressed in the bedroom, when Winry enters). Edward asserts his goals, again.

There are further modest scenes at Pinako's house which enhance the characterizations further: altho' Japanese animation is stuffed with action and incident, it is actually often the character-based scenes, and the emphasis on characterization, that really hit home. Meanwhile, the beats where the Elrics travel in disguise offer some comedy (Edward on stilts, with granny glasses and a long coat, for instance, and Alphonse having to travel inside a statue of naked Alex Armstrong in full, beefy glory).

Episode 46. *Human Transmutation*

Next up is episode 1.46: *Mine's a Cappuccino*. I mean: 46: *Human Transmutation*. It's another busy show, with twists and turns in the storytelling, plus many parallel scenes occurring at the same time. So Shou

Tucker and Alphonse Elric, an unlikely and uneasy pair, discuss what they're going to do with the philosopher's stone. Tucker proposes a deal ('equivalent exchange', one of the catchphrases of *Fullmetal Alchemist*): he'll show Al how to use the philosopher's stone if he can also use it to resurrect his daughter Nina (well, duh, don't kill her in the first place, *baka!*).

Well, we all know that this can't work, on any level. We know for good – for certain – for sure – for-ever-more – that there is *no way* that Nina – or anybody – can be resurrected from the dead in this particular show. We know (we have *always known*) that Ed and Al will *not* be able to bring their mom back from death (besides, her form is already wandering around the world and causing mischief in the person of Juliet Douglas, who turns up later in the episode).

And we also know for sure that the shady psychopath Shou Tucker is not going to be the character who demonstrates the full power of the philosopher's stone (and besides, that scuzzy basement, where Tucker's set up a tank of water for resurrection duties (a kind of birthing tank, with echoes of *Frankenstein*), is not the setting for the finale of a 51-episode series, either – we can guess that the philosopher's stone's unveiling will occur, as it so often does, in the villain's lair, which's usually the biggest set in a live-action action-adventure movie – and it's usually blown to bits in the process).

Well, Shou Tucker manages to bring some life back into the little, pitiful form of his daughter in the water tank (or he convinces himself that she is back from the dead; actually, she is inert, and lacks a soul). Al Elric has gotten himself into something more dangerous than he realized – especially when Juliet Douglas turns up to take control (deriding Tucker for creating a soulless doll).

✳

Meanwhile, Edward Elric is in a sullen mood, taking advice from Izumi Curtis again (she has a letter (how?) that hints that Hohenheim and Dante are lovers that go back some 400 years), back at Dante's place in the woods (haven't we already been in this mansion a few times already?). Hearing about Hohenheim's love life is already too much for Ed to bear! That he's aligned with a shady character such as Dante makes things even worse.

Far juicier in episode 1.46: *Human Transmutation* is the scene where Lust and Wrath pounce upon Edward Elric in the hotel room (Alphonse has left by now). Whenever the filmmakers put Wrath and Ed into the same scene, sparks fly and the energy level of the *Fullmetal Alchemist* series zings up to a higher (and far more entertaining) level. Because Wrath can't stay calm for more than 15/1,00ths of a second. The mere sight of Ed sends Wrath into apoplexy. And the mere sight of Wrath turns Ed into an aggressive tyke.

So, after two or three shots, Wrath has hurled himself at Ed Elric for yet another alchemical duel (*every* time Wrath and Ed meet they duel). The sexual subtext is made explicit when the filmmakers stage the scene by having Wrath pin Ed down on the bed (after his automail arm's been chopped up!). Like lovers locked in an embrace, Ed and Wrath hurl insults at each other with their faces inches apart (hell, why doesn't Lust leave the room and let them get on with it?!).

The struggle continues in an alley outside (after Ed Elric bursts thru the window); Edward brings along some of Lust's remains, which weakens her, but it's the argument between Lust and Wrath which dramatically alters the relationships (the locket is tossed around a lot in the duel). Lust wants to be human (as does Wrath), but Lust is out for breaking away from the homunculi pack (and their boss, the too-selfish Dante) and pursuing her goals alone. Wrath is having none any of that, and calls Lust a traitor; they tussle: Wrath is apparently killed. And then there's an uneasy and unconvincing teaming up of Edward and Lust (which, like putting Al with Tucker, doesn't convince).

▼

Episode 46: *Human Transmutation* also finds time, in amongst the hurried storytelling, to depict Roy Mustang and the Führer (troops're being sent North, to Briggs Mountain – which of course features much more prominently in the *manga* and the 2nd *animé*). Just when the TV series should be ramping up to real intensity and spectacle, as it races towards the end of its 51-episode run, too many of these scenes (with the military, with Roy Mustang, with the Führer, etc), are just too low key, too undramatic. The second *Fullmetal Alchemist* series was so much more satisfying in this respect, delivering spectacle and action, and also high drama (with quite a few scenes played at hysterical levels).

For instance, Envy finally makes a (welcome) re-appearance in episode 46: *Human Transmutation* – what a wonder Envy is in the *manga* and in the second TV series. In 1.46: *Human Transmutation*, Envy is allowed to let loose a little (ranting at Dante and Bradley, and attacking Bradley), but it's too short and too inconclusive. Dante reports that Hohenheim seems to be dead, or as near as dammit (tho' we can guess, having seen Hohenheim in action earlier, that he can't be done for yet).

Episode 47. *Sealing the Homunculus*

Episode 47 of *Fullmetal Alchemist* – *Sealing the Homunculus* – depicts a series of duels and struggles, between Al, Ed, Lust, Sloth and Wrath (with Shou Tucker lurking in the background). It's powerful stuff: now we are wholly into *Frankenstein* territory, Mary Shelley's astonishing 1820 novel of Promethean science run amok, and a creator being haunted (and tormented) by his creation. Here, it is Sloth, taking on the form of the Elric boys' mother Trisha, which adds familial and œdipal layers to the already rich thematic material (Sloth is a very different character in Himoru Arakawa's *manga* – there, Sloth is a lazy, simple-minded giant who spends most of the *Fullmetal Alchemist manga* digging the tunnel that circumvents Amestris).

Alphonse Elric is taken in by Sloth's apparent link to their mother

Trisha – to the point where he sides with her against Edward, and tries to protect her. Here the screenwriters (led by Shou Aikawa) have I think taken the sibling conflicts too far – not only has Alphonse gone to a known serial killer and downright nasty guy, Shou Tucker, for advice, he is now siding with a homunculus (Sloth) against his brother Edward.

It's one bust-up between the Elric brothers too many, maybe. However, it *is* a standard ploy of melodrama to put the heroes in conflict with each other. And, to justify it a little, Alphonse E. has become a philosopher's stone in himself, so who knows how that would affect him? Also, he is the younger brother, and much more inclined towards emotional tenderness. And, to be fair, Sloth does put on a pretty good impression of being the Elrics' mom. (This's also why you split the hero into two characters, which *mangaka* Himoru Arakawa did – so you can explore dramatic conflicts like this).

But Edward Elric puts it in a nutshell, as he is frantically defending himself against Sloth's repeated assaults: 'Al, this is the form our sin has taken!' Yes – that's the *Frankenstein* angle. Nobody has delivered it better than the young Mary Shelley in early 19th century England, in her unique novel, but it also works every time it's used. And cinema has mined *Frankenstein* so many times, because it's a brilliant concept.

That's why the battles in episode 47: *Sealing the Homunculus* of *Fullmetal Alchemist* have a dramatic as well as an action-led punch: because Edward Elric (as Viktor Frankenstein, the idealistic but mis-led scientist in *Frankenstein*) knows all too well that he is very much responsible for this mess. But he also pleads with Al to recognize that this creature that *looks like* mom is *not* their mom: 'mom would never hit me!', 'mom would never say that!', 'mom wouldn't do that!' (and this is a homunculus, which doesn't have a soul).

Alphonse Elric knows this, of course, deep down. He *knows* that this apparition in a svelte, purple dress can't be their mother (she never wore dresses like that, for a start!), that she's (or it's) a homunculus. Al is the conscience of the *Fullmetal Alchemist* series, stumbling at the last moment, doubting his brother, and hoping beyond hope that this creature might actually be their resurrected mother.

Also, it's not only that Sloth *looks* like their mother Trisha that makes the Elrics pause – it's that she can behave like her (after a fashion). Sloth also insists that she has memories, which were transferred to her from Trisha (begging the question: if a lifeform has memory, as well as autonomy and agency and independence, how different is it from being human? Japanese animation often addresses this question, and the homunculi are variations on aliens, cyborgs, robots, dolls, etc).

Luckily, Ed Elric is firing on all cylinders – and when Ed is hot, he is *very* hot! (Ed, indeed, is the only relatively sane and grounded character in this episode of *Fullmetal Alchemist*). Edward duels Lust, and Sloth, and

Wrath, taking them all on in extended, inventive battles.[2] And now we see why Ed took a piece of the remains from his mother's grave – *not* to bring their mother back to life (he realizes now that this is not going to be possible, because all the evidence he's seen about the philosopher's stone is pretty destructive).[3] And, besides, he is confronted with the result of his and Al's last attempt to resurrect his mother by the creature Sloth – who's right in front of him and trying to destroy him!

So part of the Elrics' mother's remains is used by Edward to (attempt to) seal up the homunculus Sloth – their 'sin'. But that's not going to be easy (nothing like defeating a major villain can at this point in the game (ep. 47 of 51 eps.) can be easy). The duels are fast and furious, and only let down for me by using the device of the undefeatable villain a few too many times (and a few too many resurrections from Sloth), which add up to reversals of fortune which stretch belief. Thus:

Edward attacks Sloth and wins.
But Sloth comes back to life.
Ed attacks again.
But Sloth slithers and gloops back to life again.
And so it goes on. And on.
Too many times.

The same approach is taken with Wrath (stabbed by Lust in the last episode, Wrath wriggles back to life).

Of course, a villain that won't die – or, rather, a villain that the hero/es can't vanquish for good – is not only part of the convention of this kind of action-adventure show, it also has a strong thematic point: that you can't get rid of a Big Problem with one quick, decisive act, that issues that're complex and multi-layered can't be swept aside easily, because there will always be elements of the issue that persist. Thus, you get rid of Sadaam Hussein but someone like Osama bin Laden or the Taliban or Al-Qaeda takes their place (and then you get into the more sinister reasons for just *why* Western powers *require* villains, and why the demonization of certain societies and communities and regimes occurs).

However, I don't think Sloth refuses to lie down and disappear for good is part of a Meaningful Statement on the part of the filmmakers of *Hagane no Renkinjutsushi* – it's just an aspect of the fantasy and action genre (especially when you have magical elements, and especially, too, when the show is all about life and death, and people coming back from death).

Yes – that issue is addressed head-on in episode 1.47: *Sealing the Homunculus*: Lust voices it: what does it mean to be human? Does she (it)

---

2 A side-note: Edward Elric alchemizes his broken automail arm using a piece of metal (from a gun, of course). In the *manga*, Ed has to travel back to Resembool to have Winry Rockbell do that.

Also, Ed alchemizes a machine gun, and uses it to attack Sloth. Himoru Arakawa was very conscious *never* to have Ed (or Al) firing a gun.

Incidentally, for no apparent reason, Winry-chan pops up at the end of the episode, looking dumbfounded (but it's actually Envy).

3 The detail of Wrath picking up the box containing the Elrics' mother's bones and absorbing it in his chest is intriguing – it pays off towards the end of 47: *Sealing the Homunculus* when Wrath literally bonds with Sloth, inside the magical circle.

want to become human just so she can die? Did she want to die in the first place, and end her existence as a homunculus? (The issue of longing for death is given a very Japanese inflection here – with its disturbing links to suicide).

▼

'Mama!' – episode 47: *Sealing the Homunculus* also has Wrath rushing around the place calling for his mother (Wrath is paralleling the Elrics' desire for their mother in a rather too-obvious fashion here). He seems to think that Sloth is his mom now (or does he have a severe mother fixation, aching to bond with any suitably maternal-looking woman?).

Poor Wrath! – is there a mama anywhere nearby who's going to wash those black shorts or comb that unruly, spikey hair? Is there no mama who's going to cook Wrath pizza and buy him new jeans and tuck him in bed at night and read him fairy tales about clever, little kids who work out how to live forever?

✳

One of the challenges filmmakers (and *mangakas*) face in the action-adventure genre is to create variety in the action set-pieces: unfortunately, too much of the action in episode 47: *Sealing the Homunculus* is somewhat samey. For instance, we see Sloth being tricked onto a transmutation circle on the ground, and partially sealed up by Edward, but the same circle is used for Lust (so episode 47: *Sealing the Homunculus* features the curious spectacle of two attractive women in their thirties being attacked by teenage kids! It's the revenge of teens on their moms!). And we see Sloth being seemingly vanquished into a blobby, watery mass, only to resurrect yet again.

The concept of someone leaping inside Al Elric's hollow suit of armour is also reprised (from Martel) – when Sloth dives inside his body, finding sanctuary in the philosopher's stone in there (poor Alphonse is destined in the *Fullmetal Alchemist* series to be invaded, operated from within, smashed up (repeatedly), dismantled and packed into wooden crates, travelling with sheep, turned into a bomb, and then into a philosopher's stone).

Meanwhile, the remains of the humans the homunculi once were are used twice (of Lust and Sloth). The cat-and-mouse games, in short, are extended just a little too much in the climactic episodes of the first *Fullmetal Alchemist* series, and too many of the duels and fights look like each other.

However, episode 47: *Sealing the Homunculus* is distinguished by depicting the deaths of two of the homunculi – Sloth and Lust. There is also an imaginative deployment of many flashbacks – we see Sloth's origins, for instance: how, following the botched transmutation of their dead mother, Sloth was rescued by Dante, and fed philosopher's stones, like a monster who is gradually turned into a human-ish form (this is a more grotesque variation on the *Frankenstein* mythology).

Lust thinks back to her life as an Ishbalian woman (with images of Scar's brother), further humanizing her (the *Fullmetal Alchemist manga* and the 2nd series had dispatched Lust long ago). Wrath remembers being at the Gate of Truth – rushing away from the grasping hands and the gleaming eyes in the doorway, and regressing in age to a baby, falling into the arms of a younger-looking Izumi Curtis). Wrath represents the Elrics at their most primal, fearful, vulnerable and hysterical – with his scarily intense desire for a mother figure (latching onto Curtis, and then Sloth/ Trisha).

Episode 48. *Goodbye*

The most important conversation in the 2003-2004 *Fullmetal Alchemist* series takes place in the next episode, 48: *Sayonara* (*Goodbye*, broadcast on September 11, 2004). It occurs between Edward Elric and Col. Mustang,[4] and comprises a passionate denunciation of war. Edward summarizes the situation of the whole *Fullmetal Alchemist* series: homunculi have been creating wars in order to produce philosopher's stones which they use to grant them longer lives. But everything is connected: Ed realizes now that the homunculi are themselves the consequence of alchemists attempting to resurrect the dead. So it's a vicious, murderous circle – from the State Alchemists to the wars (and the enormous cost in lives), to the philosopher's stones to the homunculi and back to the State Alchemists.

Not only that, Ed Elric also voices the moral and ethical stance of the *Fullmetal Alchemist* series, from the heroes' (and thus also the author's and filmmakers') point-of-view: those costs are *too high*. To create a war just so that a homunculus can live a little longer is beyond obscene. That his father Hohenheim is also involved in this abhorrent Holocaust (the term is strong but apt here), makes this scenario all the more horrific.

Episode 48: *Goodbye* also contains some parallel plots: one has Alex Armstrong up in the North (in/ near Drachma/ Briggs Mountain), with Jean Havoc in disguise posing as Roy Mustang (these narrative elements stand in for the Olivia Armstrong and Briggs Fortress sequences in the *manga*, which the second *Fullmetal Alchemist* series covered in depth). Armstrong announces his intention to rebel against the Führer (recalling Olivia Armstrong's views), much to the astonishment of the troops. Meanwhile, Mustang (aided by the ever-faithful Liza Hawkeye – will she ever have her affection reciprocated by this dashing womanizer?!), is setting about his own mission (again in disguise): to kill the Top Man, Führer Bradley.

Meanwhile (another 'meanwhile'), the Tringham kids, Fletcher and Russell (the ones who impersonated the Elric brothers), are brought back, in yet another case of mistaken identity). Why have the Tringham boys been re-introduced? They are minor characters, employed primarily to

---

4 They are on their way to the Führer's country residence – to assassinate him. Ed tells us what he's setting out to do – destroy the chief homunculus, and also the Führer. By this time, in a parallel story, we also know that Mustang also intends to kill the Führer (altho' he doesn't state that baldly).

reflect on the Elric brothers; it seems as if the writers are searching around for characters who can carry some 'heart' or 'conscience'; yet, in the final episodes of a big, action-adventure animated series, such diversions are distracting, and are not nailed to the primary plot. (The sequence where the Tringhams're captured when they impersonate the Elrics comes over as padding).

▼

The episode 48: *Goodbye* opens by reprising the cliffhanger from the previous episode, when Edward Elric faces off against Sloth, who's taken on the appearance of his beloved mother Trisha (and it doesn't help that Wrath is hopping about like the very irritating kid he is carping about his own 'mama'). Sloth is literally vaporized (but is she/ it really dead or gone? – you can never tell with fantasy shows like this!). Wrath is furious (what a surprise!). And Envy materializes (in the guise of the lovely Winry Rockbell – how dare he impersonate Winry-chan!), to steal away Al (by lifting him bodily!), to squirrel him back to the Homunculi's HQ.

Edward Elric, injured, isn't able to stop Envy capturing Alphonse (thus putting off the climax yet again, and once again placing Alphonse in the Fairy Tale Princess role, someone who has to be rescued). For no apparent reason, Izumi Curtis appears (with her downturned mouth, dreadlocks and white dress over black leggings). More duels occur, between Wrath, Envy, Curtis and Ed. The villains flee (why isn't Wrath stopped? Presumably Ed still wants his arm and leg back, and needs to keep Wrath close by. But Wrath is allowed to escape into the trees).

Later, Ed Elric and Izumi Curtis bump into Lt. Ross and Denny Brosh who've sprung the Tringham kids from jail (equivalents for the sequence in the *manga* where the Elrics're imprisoned in Briggs Fortress). Another chara from the past re-appears – Frank Archer, now part-machine (in the familiar metallic, cyborgized form of *animé*). Curtis stays behind to deal with Archer (meaning more alchemical duels), leaving Ed free to travel to the Führer and the homunculi's headquarters.

▼

The to-ing and fro-ing and the duels aren't that interesting (and many stretch belief). Episode 48: *Goodbye* does contain quite a bit of preparation and talk for the finale of *Fullmetal Alchemist,* but we know we're into the home lap, when all of the plot strands and issues are going to be paid off. And, with Al Elric captured by the villains, it's going to be up to Ed to single-handedly resolve everything (that's if Roy Mustang and Liza Hawkeye can deal with Führer Bradley).

Script-wise, and structurally, episode 48: *Goodbye*, like much of the last quarter of the first *Fullmetal Alchemist* series, is somewhat underwhelming: too many characters suddenly appear for no apparent reason (like Izumi Curtis or the Tringham kids), while others're brought back from the dead (such as Frank Archer – and Archer was invented for the first *animé* series). The military rebellion (by Alex Armstrong/ Roy Mustang) seems a side-story, with unclear goals. The Tringhams sub-plot adds little. Alphonse is captured too easily by the villains (again). Some of the settings are simply boring (the factory, for instance, the main location for these episodes).

Part of the problem is that the super-villain of the first *Fullmetal Alchemist* series, Dante, was initially conceived as a kindly grandmother figure, then reworked as Dante-in-Lyra's-body. But Dante is *talked about* far more than she is depicted in the foreground of the 2003-2004 TV show – especially when, in the final episodes, the villain/s really do need to be right in your face, creating merry hell.

Instead, the filmmakers rely on Edward Elric or Col. Mustang or someone talking darkly and gloomily about the homunculi and the villain who's behind them. It's true that in the *Fullmetal Alchemist manga* (which wasn't complete in 2004), the super-villain Father does stay in his underground bunker for much of the run, but he does get to act villainously now and then. Also, he is in direct contact with his many minions, such as the fearsome Pride, and has the heroes on the run many times.

Episode 49. *The Other Side of the Gate*

Three episodes to go: up next is episode 49: *I'll Do Anything, But I Won't Do That!* No, it's called: *The Other Side of the Gate*. Skinny, grim, determined – here comes Edward Elric in his black pants and black jacket and black boots and spiky, blond hair (does he have a change of clothes? Does the hero bother to change their clothes in any final act of any action-adventure show? No. Ah, but in the second series, Ed does – he alchemizes a new version of his famous red jacket before he heads out to take on the super-villain).

Edward Elric is leading the narrative of *Fullmetal Alchemist* at this point, because poor Al has been carted off to the villains' lair by the psycho Envy (whose favourite activity is kicking humans. If humans are in pain, Envy is happy). Which means – despite Al resisting and hurling himself at Envy, only to be overpowered – he is in the princess's role in fairy tales, the One Who Has To Be Rescued, and it's up to Ed to Save The Day. (The comic and the second series of *Fullmetal Alchemist* also tore the brothers apart).

There are a cluster of short, minor scenes: the Tringham boys help Ed with a page from their pa's journal;[5] Gluttony grieves over the death of Lust; Envy gloats over poor Alphonse, and kicks him; Wrath yelps for his 'mama' and generally gets in the way (much to Envy's annoyance); the Führer gives li'l Selim a tenth birthday present at his home; the girls, Sheska and Winry (safe and sound in sunny, rural Resembool), wonder what the boys are up to;[6] and the hapless and scarily passive Rose Tomas nurses her baby (when she should be running away as fast as possible). But she's under a spell – she's Dante's next victim (using her body as a vessel).

▼

---

5 In the *manga*, Scar's brother's notebook is the MacGuffin.
6 The writers do not solve just what to do with Winry Rockbell and Sheska.

So, finally, comes the confrontation between the hero and the villain, Edward Elric and Dante. It takes place in an empty opera house in the middle of the city that once was Central: there's a superb reveal of a whole city, which's buried underground, below the Cathedral. This is the city which was used to make a philosopher's stone 400 years ago: to hide the fact that the villains had killed all of the people to make that precious red stone, they buried it under the ground (as if to pretend it wasn't there at all! No, don't ask any awkward questions at this point, about capital cities that disappear overnight, just enjoy this *animé* show!).[7]

Whoever storyboarded this episode 49: *The Other Side of the Gate* should be told to try harder, and to do it again (it was Tamaki Nakatsu). Because the storyboarding is ropey and unimaginative. The confrontation scene is basically two people talking in a room. Yes, that is the fundamental scene of *all drama*. So, filmmakers sometimes try to liven things up a little, instead of delivering the usual two-shots and singles.

But what do the teams at Studio Bones and its *animé* affiliates do here, in the second half of episode 49: *The Other Side of the Gate*? They use (A) slow 360° pans, they use (B) the track-zoom effect from *Vertigo*, they use (C) the slowly-circling camera, they use (D) fish-eye camera close-ups, and they use (E) bird's-eye-view shots.

It's disappointingly dull – when this scene ought to be crackling with thrills, scares, and excitement. It's the finale scene (well, one of them), it's the hero coming face-to-face with the super-villain. But gimmicky camera angles or camera movements do not make up for lacklustre staging.

To be fair, there is *way* too much dialogue in this scene. I mean, villainous Dante witters on *and on* about – well, you know what she/ it blethers on about – *The History and Significance of the Philosopher's Stone*. It's the villain's Big Exposition Speech, but where was story editor Shou Aikawa while this was going on?! Did he leave the writing room and go shopping in Akihabara for three days straight? With all-night benders trawling every hostess bar in Akihabara? (Oh hell, no – Aikawa wrote all of the final episodes of *Fullmetal Alchemist*!).

Too much talking already! Way too much! And delivered in a really static scene. It takes ages for the action to flare up, when Dante conjures a monster to attack Ed Elric (it's one of the dragonish serpents that *animé* just loves – they crop up in the first *Fullmetal Alchemist* movie, too). Rose Tomas moons about on the sidelines and her baby is deployed as a potential victim (Dante is planning to use Rose's body for her next soul-to-body jump – this is ultimately the reason for the creation of the philosopher's stones – so that the villain can live forever. It's similar to Himoru Arakawa's *manga*, of course, tho' the finale of the *Fullmetal Alchemist manga* – and the second *animé* series – is more satisfying than this).

The scene lacks... *everything*. Where is the creepiness, the psychosis, the wit and the *threat* of the villain? Where is the imagination, the flair and the craziness in the duel? Unfortunately, Dante and Ed Elric seem to

7 In the second series, the city of Xerxes was conceived as an ancient world city (an Athens or Rome); in the first series, the city is more 17th or 18th century than 15th or 16th century.

be acting in different *animés*, while Rose Tomas, waltzing around the empty theatre with Ed,[8] is in yet another show – *The Rose of Versailles*, perhaps (the opera house, the empty city, and the ambience is reminiscent of the 1995 masterpiece *Memories* – the *Magnetic Rose* section).

▼

Only at the end, when the filmmaking assumes a wonderfully imagined subjective shot (with the camera *behind* Edward Elric's eyes, so we see an eye-shaped mask around the lens), does episode 49: *The Other Side of the Gate* soar. (This is Dante's scheme – to use Rosé Tomas's baby in a rite to send Edward to the other side of the Doorway of Truth).

Now we are in very strange territory: Ed Elric is not Ed Elric, or, as a mirror in the room reveals (and we step outside, into an objective view), he is a different Edward (he has a whole body, with his arm and leg back, and shorter hair), in… what appears to be Londinium during the First World War.[9] That is, London in 'our world'. And his father is there (or it seems to be Hohenheim), and daddy is yelling to Ed that they have to flee the building because there's an air raid. Ed and Hohenheim seem to be Brits, and that zeppelin that looms over the streets at night in the closing frames, is German (to accentuate the unreality, we hear the famous opening notes of Ludwig van Beethoven's *5th Symphony*). The war-torn city at night is reminiscent of Hayao Miyazaki's movies (such as *Howl's Moving Castle*), as well as *Hellsing Ultimate* (which also blasted apart London using German zeppelins).

So episode 49 answers the question in its title – *The Other Side of the Gate*. So the 'other side of the Gate' is not Heaven, or Hell, or limbo, as one might've expected, but another world, and a world that seems to look something like our world.

Episode 50. *Death*
Episode 51. *Laws and Promises (Munich, 1921)*

OK, here comes the Grand Finale of the 2003-2004 *animé* TV series *Hagane no Renkin Jutsushi*: episode 50: *Death* (broadcast Sept 25, 2004) and episode 51: *Laws and Promises (Munich, 1921)* (broadcast Oct 2, 2004).

Marvellous, moving, spectacular, and riveting, the climax of the 51 episodes of *Fullmetal Alchemist* does not disappoint. But it also ends in an intriguing place, with the brothers separated – by nothing less than being in two different worlds. Because the pay-off (or the price, as it's termed in the *animé*), has to be unusual and not entirely, 100% a Happy Ending. Indeed, it's an ending that remains open (for a sequel), while also at least paying off the bodily re-instatement of Alphonse Elric. I, for one, was glad to see that Al was made whole again, after spending four or so years as a hollow suit of armour! But there was a cost to Al's wholeness – and that

---

8 Who has the red cheeks of embarrassment – he's still a mid-teen, after all, and Rosé is a grown woman (he's pressed into her chest – which, as Dante caresses it in a previous scene, is ample).
9 The *manga* opens with Ed and Al in Liore – in 1914.

is the sacrifice that Edward made on the brink of death: to sacrifice himself so that Al should live, should be made entire (which he does in the second *Fullmetal Alchemist* series, too).

It's the Elric brothers who're at the heart of the *Fullmetal Alchemist* story, so it was wonderful that the finale chiefly involved them, and that Al Elric got to act, finally, after playing the Princess Who Has To Be Rescued (or the Philosopher's Stone That Nobody Can Touch). In the finale, it's not about Dante anymore, or the other homunculi (tho' they play their part), it's about Ed and Al – and their father, van Hohenheim.

✳

OK, let's go back to the start of the episode 50: *Death*: Edward Elric finds himself in another world, a strange world, where there is mechanical technology that creates flying machines in the sky, and mechanized warfare on a grand scale: welcome to Planet Earth, Ed!

Yes, this *is* London – London, England: there are several indicators, such as the photo on the wall of Ed's room of St Paul's Cathedral, the military recruitment posters, and we see Big Ben in the distance in the street scenes. That it's London in a time of *war* is significant (so it's no different from Amestris, then). That it's the Germans attacking the Brits is also significant (aligning the military in Amestris with the Germans, and the good guys – that's the Elrics, for a start – with the poor, put-upon, under-attack Brits).[10] Thus, *Fullmetal Alchemist* replays World War One from the West's Allies' point-of-view (as in most Anglo-American movies).[11] It's Us vs. Them, and the 'us' is the Allies (represented here by Great Britain. You might also align the heroes with the Japanese and the invaders, who're bombing the city to bits, with the North Americans in the Second World War. Japanese *animé* is sometimes set in Britain, and the characters are British, or identified with Brits. The link to WWII is emphasized when Hohenheim notes that in this world there is mechanized warfare which in the future will culminate in mass exterminations in the form of the atomic bomb. The *animé* includes a photograph of a nuclear explosion, the dreaded mushroom clouds which haunts so much of Japanese animation – and Japanese culture).

Yet, intriguingly, the whole *Fullmetal Alchemist* series closes with Ed Elric and his pa Hohenheim in Germany, after the War (in Munich in 1921). The *Fullmetal Alchemist* series is thus politically and ideologically wholly predictable, while also being unusual and ambiguous.

In episode 50: *Death*, we see Edward Elric in our world, trying to make sense of it: there isn't much time before he's killed by a crashing, burning airship (Edward 'dies' twice in this episode). But there is an important thematic conversation between father and son (as they join the crowds watching the devastated capital city from somewhere distant like Hampstead Heath): Ed guesses that the alchemy of the Amestrisian world draws on the souls of people from our world (as well as the victims in the alchemical world). Both Dante and Hohenheim are portrayed as heartless

10 And also the Ishbalians, who were invaded by Amestris.
11 However, some Japanese animations replay the war from the Axis powers' point-of-view, too; also, scenarios where the Germans win the war are a sub-genre of fantasy fiction in Japan.

vampires who feed off living people to create their extended lives.

This is one of *mangaka* Himoru Arakawa's key themes: that there is a price to magic (in Amestris) or to science (in our world), that the costs of alchemy (fantasy) and science (reality) are high. Yet Edward Elric counters his father's views in a crucial piece of monologue (which, curiously, is played as narration over scenes where father and son have parted – Hohenheim is in a car going to see one of Britain's commanders, Winston Churchill, and Ed is left in the dark countryside, in a state of anxiety as he wonders how to get back to Amestris).

Ed Elric voices the familiar 'don't give up'/ 'life is worth fighting for' views of someone moving forward, as Himoru Arakawa puts it, someone who won't give up. Optimism, utopianism – or at least, non-defeatism. Arakawa's message is crystal clear: while the older generation in Japan/ Amestris (embodied by Hohenheim) is on the point of caving in, that nothing can be changed, that idealism is mis-placed, that things can't or won't get better, Edward symbolizes the hope for the future, the urge to *do* something, to act, to 'move forward', as Arakawa asserts.

Thus, the *Fullmetal Alchemist* series vividly and elegantly expresses the tensions between middle-aged Japan and youthful Japan, between those who give up and give in, who add pessimism to their anxieties and depressions, and the youth of Japan, who haven't reached that point of the acceptance that nothing can be changed. Notice how Hohenheim is resigned to dying in England – he says he can't return thru the Gate (there is some rather confused information here about bodies being still in the Gate, but Hohenheim has moved thru the Gate, body, mind and soul). Anyhow, the upshot is, as Hohenheim tells Ed, that he can't get back to Amestris, but that Ed still has a chance (thus, Hohenheim hands over the mantle of power and alchemy to Ed).

And yet, the Edward in our world has to die so that the Amestrian Edward can travel thru the Gate again. (This is sort of explained by Ed realizing in Amestris that he 'used up' the body he inhabited as the price of travelling thru the Gateway).

◆

The Ed-Al Elric story in *Fullmetal Alchemist* plays out in a satisfying but unexpected fashion in the finale. I didn't think that the boys would regain their bodies, on the first viewing, before I'd read Himoru Arakawa's *manga* (but they would manage to triumph over the villains, of course, and they would destroy the philosopher's stone. Well, there was no way that Dante and the homunculi could ever be victorious).

However, the introduction of the *deus ex machina* scenario of the other world beyond the Gate was wonderful. Up until episode 49: *The Other Side of the Gate*, we didn't really know what was beyond that tall, imposing Gateway with its heavy, carved doors: all we saw was a mass of eyes, and Mr Tickle, extendible, black arms. It didn't look good, it didn't seem like there was much back there except unhappy, desperate, misshapen forms.

That you go thru the Gate into another world, and that world appears to be our world (tho' in a time period comparable with Amestris – the era of late 19th/ early 20th centuries), is a terrific invention by the filmmakers, taking the concepts *manga* author Himoru Arakawa and adding an unusual complication to the story, and to develop a way in which the brothers can be made whole yet also pay a price (with their separation). The first *Fullmetal Alchemist* movie, released shortly after the 2004 series finished (in 2005), continued the theme of two worlds.

Indeed, it does appear as if the producers were already working on the first *Fullmetal Alchemist* movie, and were pointing the TV series towards it: thus, the two-worlds theme continues; the re-uniting of the Elric brothers is a passionate desire to be made good; Edward and his father are in Germany (where the movie is set); and Envy slips thru the Gateway, too[12] (and also has a green, Chinese dragon form, which crops up in the movie. So it's a commercial hook – if you want to see the brothers re-united, see the movie!).

◆

The action in the final two episodes of *Fullmetal Alchemist* is far superior to episode 49: *The Other Side of the Gate*, where the Ed Elric vs. Dante confrontation resolved a whole lot of nothing (but involved page after page of talk – all to set up the final two episodes). Finding something for each homunculi to do was tough, but on the whole the two episodes 50 and 51 succeeded: Gluttony, still distraught over Lust's demise, becomes (at Dante's behest), an all-devouring machine (well, even more than he has been thru the entire series!). The poetic justice of that act bounces back on Dante, when it seems as if she is devoured by the crazed Gluttony in the elevator as she flees the underground city and the opera house (tho', as we don't see it (– we see an empty elevator – we don't know for sure, so Dante may well return. The series doesn't finish off Dante in a satisfying manner).

The revelation that Envy[13] is the homunculi that was created way back when van Hohenheim made an early philosopher's stone adds a further psychological dimension to proceedings. (So now Envy has an overweening desire to kill Hohenheim, and Hohenheim is kind of his father, too). This comes out as Edward Elric and Envy're duelling (Envy uses his familiar shape-changing routine to wind up Ed – turning into Maes Hughes, Dr Marcoh, Roy Mustang, Trisha and the young Hohenheim).

It's Envy who, in a striking turnaround, stabs and appears to kill Ed Elric at the end of episode 50: *Death* (meanwhile, in London, the Other Edward is killed when a zeppelin crashes on top of him, right after he's said *sayonara* to his father, who's hurrying off to see Winston Churchill, no less). Well, we've been here before many times in these climactic scenes to many a fantasy and action-adventure tale (that is, where heroes can die but come back to life in a myriad of ways). But for all intents and

---

12 For no particular reason other than to provide be a villain in the Germany of our world in the movie.

13 At times, Envy is the most irritating homunculi in terms of behaviour and attitude; the characterization of the spikey-haired freak is so much more satisfying in the second *Fullmetal Alchemist* series.

purposes, Ed is dead. Dead. Well, Rose Tomas thinks so (Dante hopes so), and Al, lying on his back in the middle of a transmutation circle, is finally roused to *act* (poor Alphonse spends all of episode 50: *Death* in the middle of an active transmutation circle, as Dante waits for the ritual to be complete, just so she can live a little longer).

In episode 50: *Death* we also see the insurrection led by Colonel Mustang, which includes Mustang and Liza Hawkeye entering the home of the Führer. It's a severely trimmed-down version of the uprising that Mustang leads in the *Fullmetal Alchemist manga* and the second *Fullmetal Alchemist* series, where it becomes an enormous action sequence.

Also in episode 50: *Death*, Frank Archer is still hurtling about in his mechanized state; and Izumi Curtis is helping the military (and Lt. Ross).

And in the final two episodes, 50: *Death* and 51: *Laws and Promises*, there were other sub-plots occurring in parallel: one involved Roy Mustang making good his previous dubious acts by assassinating the homunculus impersonating Führer Bradley (aided by the ever-faithful Liza Hawkeye). The Mustang vs. Bradley scenes were powerful action climaxes, which would be spectacular enough to close many *animé* series (they are very detailed scenes, involving many beats and gags. One of the curious elements has homunculus Bradley being scuppered by his adoring, young son Selim (Makoto Tsumura), when he gives him the key to his safe. In a *Hamlet* moment, Selim brings in his father's skull – the remains of a homunculus weakens them (a reprise of the scene btn Edward and Greed), enabling Mustang to reduce Bradley to fire and ash.

(To squeeze every second of air-time out of their broadcasting slot, the filmmakers at Bones & co. had scenes playing under the end credits (which occurs halfway thru the episode), and also dispensed with the opening credits, a common practice in the final episodes of an *animé* run, when there is so much story to tell. I love it when that happens – you know that the filmmakers and producers are really (and literally!) pushing at the boundaries of the time slot).

　　✶

Of course, no, *Fullmetal Alchemist* is not going to kill its hero. No way. However, the series has been exceptionally violent, and at times suicidally downbeat. Rather, Ed's death (or near-death) is there to inaugurate the final magical transformations: Alphonse is a whole philosopher's stone on his own, right? And the philosopher's stone can (supposedly) bring people back to life, right?

But no, it doesn't work out like that: there is a double trans-formation/ sacrifice/ switch occurring here, which pays off some of the key issues of *Fullmetal Alchemist* cleverly and emotionally: Ed Elric sacrifices himself in order to save Al, but Al acts by producing an alchemical transformation (using himself as the philosopher's stone) to return Ed, but Ed is sent (unconsciously perhaps) to the other side of the Gate, while Al is restored to his whole body. That both brothers attempt to save the other is perfectly in tune with the central relationship of the *Fullmetal Alchemist* series (it also gives Al a much more proactive role, after having played the victim/ princess to be rescued for too long).

But here is the climactic moment in the first *Fullmetal Alchemist* series: the awe-inspiring sight of Edward Elric standing alone inside a giant, alchemical circle in the empty opera house deep underground, about to transmute his own body and soul to save his brother.

This is certainly one of the greatest scenes in recent pop culture, West or East, depicting a hero acting as a true hero, embodying the themes of sacrifice and love.

The finale of *Fullmetal Alchemist* didn't quite have the emotional impact I thought (or hoped) it might, after that long journey thru the series (compared to some other *animé* series, such as *Escaflowne* or *Ghost In the Shell: Stand Alone Complex* or or *Fairy Tail* or *Moribito*). When you've watched an entire, long series, the emotional pay-off can be intense, as the emotion and suspense builds and builds. But not in the case of *Fullmetal Alchemist*; however, it does display a heightened feeling for poetic resolutions: that the brothers, the central relationship in the *Fullmetal Alchemist* series, are apart but yearning to be re-united. Now that *is* emotional: it's not lovers, it's not parents and children, it's not friends, it's two brothers. (On further viewings, the first series does come across as much more emotional).

In terms of pacing, I would've preferred to see a little less of the action in episodes 48 and 49, to allow more time for the climactic scenes in eps. 50 and 51. If this was *One Piece*, that climax would've been stretched out for at least ten shows!

But it's the score by Michiru Oshima that is perhaps the true star of the final episodes of *Fullmetal Alchemist* – a lovely piano-based cue for the transmutation and Gateway scenes, a plangent orchestral theme for the *dénouement* scenes, a reprise of the folk song, and a final cue in a major key featuring French horn and brass (that might be titled 'Hope'). The music really sends off *Fullmetal Alchemist* with a zing.

☆

The two final episodes of the first *Fullmetal Alchemist* series disappoint somewhat in comparison with both the *manga* by Himoru Arakawa and the second series of 2009-10. A key flaw, I think, was to neglect fully exploiting the possibilities of the Gate of Truth, that abstract, spiritual zone of life-and-death. For example, the climactic scenes featuring Alphonse's sacrifice to save Edward, and Edward's sacrifice to save Alphonse, were incompletely realized. Somehow, the filmmakers didn't quite find the images to accompany these highly emotional sequences.

Alphonse is depicted moving towards Ed lying on the floor in the opera house, as he glows all over with the red light of the philosopher's stone, discovering that Ed isn't dead, that he's still warm: really, this scene should've been played at a *very* grand, extremely emotional level. If there's any time for really letting rip with hysterical feelings, this is it! After all, this is Al's beloved brother, unconscious on the floor, blood spreading out from his body. The sequence also cried out for *huge* visual effects and barnstorming music – altho' the white-yellow tunnel effects and the monumental doorway were impressive, much more was required.

Similarly, Edward Elric's bid to rescue Alphonse, which's the last of the Important Acts in the first *Fullmetal Alchemist* series, was partly back-announced, so to speak, by Edward, after he's travelled thru the Gate to Germany in our world. Ed appears at the Gateway with Envy (so that Envy can appear in the sequel – the first *Fullmetal Alchemist* movie). But somehow the life-and-death issues aren't brought into the foreground in a vivid manner. As if admitting that they couldn't think of exactly what to do in the Gate of Truth sequences, the filmmakers and the writers simply had Edward appearing in Germany, after it had happened. But this is one event we really do need to see occurring in something like real time. This is, after all, where the entire *Fullmetal Alchemist* series has been heading, ever since the first episode, when the Elric boys tried to bring their mother back to life (where, for instance, were the crucial flashbacks to that first transmutation ritual? If there's any time for a re-cap of the whole *Fullmetal Alchemist* series, in the form of a montage of vivid flashbacks, this is it!).

So the finale of the first *Fullmetal Alchemist* series lacks elements which would really pay off everything we've seen, and satisfy at the emotional and spiritual as well as the visceral and visual levels. Some of the ingredients I've mentioned might've helped: a montage of flashbacks... incredible visual effects... out-size vocal performances... showing what's happening in real time... finding the right images to illustrate the issues and the conflicts...

But to see Ed Elric standing in that magical circle, covered himself in alchemical sigils (a great touch), is worth seeing. It's a spell-binding heroic moment.

However, you could say that the first *Fullmetal Alchemist* series was worth making because it meant that the next team having a go at Himoru Arakawa's *manga* (which included many of the same artists, actors and technicians) could develop it. They could see what worked, what didn't work so well – plus of course they could draw on much more of Arakawa's *Fullmetal Alchemist* story.

★

THE *DÉNOUEMENT*.

The *animé* plays out the *dénouement* in a teasing manner: it visits the restored Alphonse Elric, plus minor characters such as Winry, Rose, Pinako, Curtis, etc (now Rose plus baby appears to be living with the Rockbells), and also Col. Mustang (being tended in bed indulgently by Lt. Hawkeye, as he recovers from his ordeal with the Führer), before finally showing the audience what happened to Edward.[14] We are in Resembool, for what should be the Happy Ending, and the re-uniting of the key characters.

Now we switch to (something like) our world, leaping forward four

14 The *dénouement* scenes include short vignettes for many of the other characters – such as Armstrong and Breda; Sheska, Ross and Brosh; Winry and Sheska (at Hughes' grave, and Winry working); Tucker, etc.

or so years to 1921, and Munich, Germany, with Ed Elric living with his father van Hohenheim (the switch from England to Germany is intriguing). We see that Ed is back to his usual self (but not with automail: he's got an artificial arm and leg made in our world, and it doesn't work the same. Notice how his arm hangs uselessly, and how he limps on the street). Edward has a mission now: to find a way to get back to Amestris, and to find his brother Alphonse.

Like the *manga* and the second series, the first *Fullmetal Alchemist* series has Ed and Al Elric venturing out into the world again. Edward tells his father that he's going to see a rocket scientist (an American, Goddard), because he reckons that maybe by going into space he might find a way back to Amestris and Alphonse. Hohenheim is resigned to living in our world, in Germany (which's heading into the 1920s, the era of inflation and fascism).

Edward Elric packs his suitcase and leaves – on a train, of course! Always with the trains in *Fullmetal Alchemist*. And in Amestris, Alphonse is also riding the railroad – along with the Curtises (on his way to their place, to study alchemy again).

Izumi Curtis and her hubby appear in the closing scenes, and Al begs to become a pupil of the *sensei* again, to learn a way of re-uniting with his brother Ed. As Curtis remarks, nobody could resist those adorable eyes, as Al stares at Curtis intently and eagerly. Nobody knows what happened to Edward – he simply disappeared after he was transmuted by Alphonse.

The scenes featuring the restored Al Elric depict him playing with a dog by a river (where we had seen Al sulking earlier in the series), while Winry, Rose & co. look on (and discuss what happened; Pinako tells us how Wrath ended up). It's a scene of Innocence Restored (and for innocence to be regained; perhaps everything has to be forgotten, hence Al's amnesia).[15]

But soon Alphonse Elric is aching to be re-united with his blood brother – so the final scenes of the first *Fullmetal Alchemist* series (cut together in parallel), depict the two brothers in motion, heading towards some distant but hopefully achievable goal: they are both portrayed on a train, travelling towards that Grail. An intriguing motif has both brothers looking out of the train window, as if they're looking into the future, but also towards each other. They're in different worlds, but it's as if they are aware of each other, and could reach out and touch each other. And they do just that: the *animé* intercuts Edward reaching up to the sky with his automail arm, and Alphonse in Amestris doing the same (these are match cuts). Reaching up, reaching out – the image is a cliché, but it works – as an image of hope, of the future, of desire (of what Himoru Arakawa calls 'moving forward').

(Also, there is a montage of all of the characters, for their final bows and appearances, occurring in the last scenes of *Fullmetal Alchemist* – we see glimpses of Winry (automailing), Wrath, Selim and his mom,

15 There are curious elements to the finale, too: Al is restored to his whole body, but to a somewhat regressed state, with his memory impaired. He is also younger – ten, not 14 or 15.

Armstrong and Breda (as muscle-men), Tucker and his soulless daughter, etc.)

So the first *Fullmetal Alchemist* series closes on a note of emotional poignancy, with the central relationship of the show broken, but both brothers absolutely determined to bridge that gulf. And to keep the two Elric brothers apart, two people who're passionately loyal about each other, you need Something Big – it could have been death (well, it has been death, during the climax, as the brothers cross the thresholds between life and death). But if you're not going to kill one of the brothers (impossible, in terms of the genre and context of this series), then separating them in two different worlds is extreme and satisfies the themes and the story.

04

FULLMETAL ALCHEMIST

HAGANE NO RENKINSUTSUSHI

THE SECOND ANIME SERIES

INTRODUCTION.

It's a trend in Japanese animation to re-make a movie or TV show or Original Video Animation not long after it first aired. Why? For several reasons, but chief among them (as with any remake) is $$$$$ (sometimes they're called spin-offs, sequels, side-stories, re-boots, updates, 're-imaginings', whatever – it's still mining the franchise). Newer computer-aided techniques (such as colour and ink and paint and 3-D computer-aided graphics) have also contributed towards the recent Annie May remakes (that is, as another gimmick for flogging the same stuff to punters). Unfortunately, some of the remakes have been disastrous (*Legend of the Overfiend*, made over as *Urotsukidoji: New Saga* in 2004), or rather pointless, or very disappointing (the computer-aided animated *Appleseed* movies of 2004 and 2007) – above and beyond the overriding concerns of $$$$$.

The second, 2009-2010 series of *Hagane no Renkinjutsushi* (Apl 5, 2009 – Aug 25, 2010_ had one good reason for remaking the *manga* by Himoru Arakawa that had already been fully and spectacularly realized in Japanese animation in 2003 and 2004: it would tell the story much closer to the *manga* by Arakawa-sensei; the comic was nearly complete. Also, the 2003-04 fully-metal-and-fully-alchemical series had diverged from Arakawa-sensei's *manga* (particularly in the central section, and in the second half). And, let's not forget, the *Fullmetal Alchemist manga* series from publishers Square Enix had by this time been selling by the truckload.

The second *Fullmetal Alchemist* series can thus be seen as a remake and as a sequel, but featuring many of the same companies, many of the same voice cast (including the principals), many of the same personnel behind the camera, and adapted from the same comic.

Indeed, the second series replicates numerous elements from the first series, often using exactly the same shots and angles. And even when the second series alters many elements, it is still telling the same story (until the two series diverge. But even then many parts of the both series depict similar events).

The second series of *Fullmetal Alchemist* is 64 episodes long, delivered as five seasons in all (a season or *cour* in Japan is 10-13 episodes). Two seasons (26 shows) are followed by three seasons (37 shows), with a break after episode 26 (the finale of the first part, where Ed and Al finally meet face-to-face, in the Gateway of Truth). A re-cap/ clip show followed (ep. 27), and then the next three seasons began with the storming show, ep. 28.

Himoru Arakawa must've been very happy – to have not *one* marvellous *animé* series made from her *manga*, but *two*! And the tie-in *manga* sales and the merchandizing of *Fullmetal Alchemist* would've helped to make her rich.

Closer? Closer to the *Fullmetal Alchemist manga*? Actually, not entirely.[1] For a start, the second *Fullmetal Alchemist* series completely leaves out chapters 3 and 4 from Himoru Arakawa's *manga* – featuring the pulpy adventures on the railroad (ch. 3), and the story of the mining community and Loki (ch. 4) – which the 1st series had covered, after all. Instead, the 2nd *animé* series of *Fullmetal Alchemist* speeds from the Father Cornello-Liore episode to Shou Tucker the creepy alchemist. But it also has more time for flashbacks to the Elrics' childhoods, and also has more time to spend with Ed and Al in the present tense.

In addition, other elements were dropped for the second adaptation, such as Father reconstituting Gluttony; more of the Rockbells in the Ishbalian war; the Ishbalians being supplied with weapons from the country of Aerugo to the South; terrorists in Resembool, etc.

The second *Fullmetal Alchemist* series was given the title *Fullmetal Alchemist: Brotherhood* for overseas releases. In Japan, it's simply *Fullmetal Alchemist*. Which's preferrable. So we could call it *Fullmetal Alchemist 2*, or just the 2nd series of *Fullmetal Alchemist*.

❖

THE PRODUCTION.

The 2009-2010 *Fullmetal Alchemist* series (entitled *Hagane no Renkinjutsushi: Furumetaru Arukemisuto*) was headed up by a different team (tho' some in the crew, and many in the cast, were back): Hiro Maruyama, Nobuyuki Kurashige, Noritomo Yonai and Ryo Oyama were the producers, Hiroshi Onogi was chief writer, and the series director was Yasuhiro Irie. The companies behind the show were the same, however: Studio Bones, Aniplex, Square and Mainichi Broadcasting System. Thankfully, the two lead roles of Edward and Alphonse Elric were voiced by the same actors as the 2003-04 TV shows: Romi Pak and Rie

1 Altho' the second *Fullmetal Alchemist* series followed the story in the *manga* closer, it still departed from it many times. Only to be expected.

Kugimiya, two of the many wonderful *seiyu* in *anime* (it's difficult to imagine any other actresses being quite so impressive as Pak and Kugimiya as Ed and Al). In fact, many of the main characters were voiced by the same performers as the first *Fullmetal Alchemist* series, which helps enormously to give the second series a familiarity (meanwhile, Iemasa Kayumi (d. 2014) voiced both the narrator and Father – you'll recognize Kayumi in *One Piece* (Crocodile), *Nausicaä of the Valley of the Wind*, *Lupin III*, and *Ghost In the Shell* (the Puppeteer).

Hiroshi Ohnogi (b. 1959 – of the same generation as superstar Shoji Kawamori, with whom he has worked many times) was the chief writer on shows such as *Macross*, *Aquarion* (and the 2007 sequel), *Phantasy Star Online*, *Shangri-La*, *Seisen Cereberus*, *Kekkaishi*, *Birdy the Mighty Decode*, *Shugo Chara!* and *Noein*. Ohnogi also wrote for *Heat Guy J*, *Rahxephon*, *Gundam* (several series), *Eureka Seven* and *A.D. Police*. Many of those shows are superlative (*Kekkaishi* = *Barrier Hunter* is a charming comedy-action demon hunter series, and *Aquarion* is a 100% masterpiece).

Character design in *Fullmetal Alchemist* series two was by Hiroki Kanno; art direction was by Takeshi Satou; mechanical design was by Masahisa Suzuki; editing by Takeshi Sadamatsu; music by Akira Senju; music production by Hirohito Shinohara; art design was by Kazushige Kanehira; sound direction was by Masafumi Mima; sound fx by Shizuo Kurahashi; colour design by Satoko Nakao; and action animation director was Jun Shibata. Many, many animators worked on *Fullmetal Alchemist 2*: 32 animation directors and 138 2nd key animators, for example. Among the chief animation directors were: Chiyomi Tsukamoto, Hiroki Kanno, Hiroya Iijima, Jun Shibata, Kenichi Ohnuki, Masaru Oshiro, Ryousuke Sekiguchi, Sadakazu Takiguchi, Satoshi Ishino, Taichi Furumata, Tetsuya Kawakami, Tomokatsu Nagasaku (each of these directed the animation in four or more episodes). The chief storyboard artists of *Fullmetal Alchemist* (who all drew more'n 5 episodes each), were: Iwao Teraoka, Minoru Ohara, Shinji Ishihira and series director Yasuhiro Irie (there were 22 storyboard artists in total).

The director of the second *Fullmetal Alchemist* series, Yasuhiro Irie (b. 1971), was a veteran (by a young age) of numerous *anime* shows, including *Cowboy Bebop*, *Macross Plus*, *RahXephon*, *Wolf's Rain*, *Escaflowne*, *Soul Eater*, *Spriggan*, *Kabuto*, *Digimon*, *Dragon Slayer*, *Jin-Roh*, and *Gundam*, where he worked as key animator, storyboard artist, and also director (including parts of the first *Fullmetal Alchemist* series). (In *anime*, the series director or chief director oversees the series, while individual episodes often have their own director; sometimes there is a second director to run the production. There are 21 episode directors in *Fullmetal Alchemist 2*).

Among the numerous companies contributing to *Fullmetal Alchemist 2* were: Brains Base B.T.O., G.K. Entertainment, Production I.G, Sung San, Telecom Animation Film, Artemis, Asahi Production, Bird, D-Colors, F.A.I. International, Jinbun, M.S.J Musashino Production, Phoenix Animation, Studio Elle, Studio Gash, Studio Target, Triple A, T.Y.O.

Animations, Wish, Yong Chang Animation, A-1 Pictures, A.C.G.T., C2C, Rundock Studio, Studio Comet, Techno Sound, Kusanagi, Atelier Rourke 07, Green, Feng Animation, Team Elle, AI, Anime R., A.P.P.P., Arcturus, Bones Animation Dept., Bones Photography Dept., Def.c, Dogakobo, Hebaraki, Jumondo, Last House, Manglobe, Mook Animation, M.S.C., Noside, Picture Magic, Production Reed, Rising Force, Studio 4°C, Studio Izena, Studio Kyuma, Studio Liberty, Sunny Side Up, SynergyS.P., Wao World, Wombat, Yuhodo, Beijing Golden Pinasters Animation Company, Dayuan Animation, A.I., A.I.C., A.I.C. Takarazuka, Angle, Anime Spot, Anime Torotoro, A.P.P.P., Artland, Azeta Pictures, Beat Frog, Buyu, Code, Digital Network Animation, Diomedea, Domu, Fan Out, Front Line, Gonzo, I. S. Factory, J.C. Staff, Mushi Production, Oh! Production, P.A. Works, Sakura Create, Satelight, Snow Light Staff, Studio Ado, Studio Boomerang, Studio Cockpit, Studio Deen, Studio Fantasia, Studio Ghibli, Studio Gimlet, Studio Line, Studio Live, Studio Mark, Studio Mu, Studio Pastoral, Studio Pineapple, Studio Takuranke, Synergy N.S., Taikan Anime Kabushiki Kaisha, Tamazawa Dogasha, Tatsunoko Production, T.N.K., Ufotable, Tricycle Studio and Aoi Studio.

Thus, many well-known, celebrated studios worked on *Fullmetal Alchemist*, including Ghibli, Telecom, Cockpit, 4°C, Oh!, Mushi, Deen, Tatsunoko, Artland, A.-1, Satelight, etc.

Among the companies producing the outstanding backgrounds for the second series of *Fullmetal Alchemist* were Green, Kusanagi, Atelier Rourke 07, Feng Animation, Beijing Golden Pinasters Animation Company and Telecom Animation Film. A show like *Fullmetal Alchemist* is a major challenge for the background artists; they created a completely convincing fantasy world. One of the most charming elements of the background art is that brushstrokes were often retained, giving the images a handmade quality.

THE VOICE CAST.
The voice cast of the second *Fullmetal Alchemist* series included:

Romi Park – Edward Elric
Rie Kugimiya – Alphonse Elric
Iemasa Kayumi – Father and the Narrator
Megumi Takamoto – Winry Rockbell
Miyoko Asou – Pinako Rockbell
Minami Takayama – Envy
Shinichiro Miki – Roy Mustang
Fumiko Orikasa – Liza Hawkeye
Yoshino Takamori – Trisha Elric
Unshou Ishizuka – Van Hohenheim
Daisuke Namikawa – Van Hohenheim (Young)
Chika Fujimura – Sheska
Fumihiko Tachiki – Sloth
Hidekatsu Shibata – King Bradley
Hiroyuki Yoshino – Zolf Kimbley

Shoko Tsuda – Izumi Curtis
Yoko Soumi – Olivia Maria Armstrong
Yuichi Nakamura – Greed
Kaori Nazuka – Maria Ross
Mamoru Miyano – Ling Yao
Katsunosuke Hori – Fu
Kazuki Yao – Loki
Kazuya Nakai – Miles
Keiji Fujiwara – Maes Hughes
Kenji Utsumi – Alex Louis Armstrong
Kenta Miyake – Scar
Kikuko Inoue – Lust
Yuko Sanpei – Pride and Selim
Kinryuu Arimoto – Knox
Mai Goto – Mei Chang
Makoto Nagai – Shou Tucker
Masayuki Omoro – Tim Marcoh
Ryûzaburô Ôtomo – Buccaneer
Satsuki Yukino – Rose
Seizo Katou – Cornello
Takehito Koyasu – Scar's Brother
Takkou Ishimori – the King of Xerxes

THE OPENING AND CLOSING CREDITS.

The *Fullmetal Alchemist* series, like some other long-running, prestige *animé* series, have not one but a number of credits sequences (which usually run for 1m 30s). So the opening and closing titles sequences change as the series progresses. (Credits sequences are often produced by a separate team – tho' in collaboration with the producers, of course). As usual in *animé*, the credits sequences for *Fullmetal Alchemist* include Japanese pop songs playing like MTV pop promos over rapidly edited vignettes focussing on the major characters and themes, with short skits for the secondary charas.

The opening and closing credits of both *Fullmetal Alchemist* series are fantastic pieces of animation and television. A number of versions are employed of each set of credits, to offer some variation (the characters and the situations in the credit sequence also reflect their particular section of the series, as usual in *animé* series).

In the middle of the *Fullmetal Alchemist 2* series, for instance, Winry Rockbell gets a whole end credit sequence to herself.[2] Except now she's babed-out, with large, bouncy breasts and *Playboy* curves (the producers have a keen feeling for who their audience is).

The opening theme songs were performed by Yui ('Again'), Chemistry ('Period'), Nico Touches the Walls ('Hologram'), Sukima Switch ('Golden Time Lover') and Sid ('Rain'). The ending theme songs were performed by Sid ('Lie'), Miho Fukuhara ('Let It Out'), Lil' B ('Tied Hands'), Scandal ('Shunkan Sentimental'), Shoko Nakagawa ('Ray of Light'), Sid ('Rain')

---

2 Perhaps because Winry disappears from the story for a while, and putting her into the end credits is a way of keeping her in the loop. The same thing occurs with Sasuke in *Naruto*.

and Nico Touches the Walls ('Hologram').

NOTES ON THE SECOND SERIES.
Watching the second *Hagane no Renkinjutsushi: Furumetaru Arukemisuto* series is a curious experience, if you've already seen the first series, and also know Himoru Arakawa's *Fullmetal Alchemist manga* well. The gap between the two *Fullmetal Alchemist* series is so small – five years. Here are the same characters in the same situations, but all slightly (or very) different, with (slightly) different character designs (by Hiroki Kanno), (slightly) different dialogue, (slightly) different music (by Akira Senju), (slightly) different everything. Yet everything is also (almost) the same.

One of the challenges that the second *Fullmetal Alchemist* series faces is that it's a re-make/ sequel/ re-boot. No matter if it sticks closer to Himoru Arakawa's *manga*, the first *Fullmetal Alchemist* series of 2003-04 still got there first – with Ed and Al, with depicting alchemy, with portraying the homunculi and the vast cast of characters. Had the first series been a poor show, or badly received, so much better for the second series! But it wasn't – it was stunning. (And the second series might never have been made if the first one tankjed).

One of the chief appeals of the second *Hagane no Renkinjutsushi* series is to see characters from Himoru Arakawa's *manga* that were left out of the first *animé* series, some of them major figures, such as super-mysterious, almost-all-powerful Father, Pride as a monstrous boy, little martial artist Mei Chang and her pet panda, Envy in his full, manic glory, and super-bitch Major General Olivia Armstrong.

The filmmakers have a lot of fun with the tiny girl Mei Chang (Mai Goto) and her pet panda Xiao Mei. In Himoru Arakawa's *manga* Mei's a highly stylized Xingese (Chinese) girl of around ten or twelve years-old, with wild, black, braided hair (Arakawa loves Chinese martial arts and heroic figures – they feature in *Hero Tales*). Mei's at her best when she's furious (when those li'l eyebrows go diagonal), and when she has her passionate infatuations (for Al, and for Ed, when the *manga*, like the *animé*, shifts into major girliness – and her voice (by Goto-san) is also *very* girlie and *kawaii*). There are also humorous jealous rivalries between Mei and Winry over Al.

The screenwriters also included vivid flashbacks to the Renaissance era, back in Xerxes, when it all started (and let's not also forget the memorable flashback to van Hohenheim travelling in the deserts between Amestris and Xing, where Hohenheim is rescued by Xingese (Chinese) merchants riding camels).

The second *Fullmetal Alchemist* series employs several techniques which depart from the first series, such as split screens (which have an affinity, when there are several images in the frame, with *manga* panels), and extreme, colourful stylizations for the comical moments in Himoru Arakawa's *manga*. Sometimes a children's storybook approach was employed, using static or only partially animated scenes. Simulated newsreel, near black-and-white footage was used (additions to the *manga*, and very useful for delivering exposition and for the flashbacks).

◆

On the whole, the second *Fullmetal Alchemist* series was slightly lighter, mood-wise, than the first series (and the comedy helps with that). Himoru Arakawa's *manga* tended to be more light-hearted than the first *Fullmetal Alchemist animé*, or included more light-hearted or comical moments, which the *animé* dropped (which's often the way. Some *animé*, such as *Ghost In the Shell: Stand Alone Complex*, ditch 90% of the humour and goofing about in the *manga* – in this case, by Masamune Shirow).

Western fans still have a problem with the humour in *manga* and *animé*, especially when it's in the *middle* of serious or action scenes. Western/ North American TV shows and movies tend to place the humour *before* or *after* the serious or action-filled moments (typically, to lighten or diffuse tension and suspense). And the humour, in an action-adventure flick, is often a cool quip. But Japanese animations and comics go for over-the-top, super-deformed or cute comedy, and many (Western) fans clearly find it jarring or intrusive. It's another way in which drama and storytelling is fundamentally different in the two cultures.

As the *Fullmetal Alchemist* second series progressed, it continued – rightly – to include a lot of the humour of Himoru Arakawa's *manga*, while the first series tended to leave it behind (the *omake* (extras) in the *manga*, for example, are always humorous). One of the recurring gags which both series employed was of course Ed's sensitivity about his height. Even in the midst of heavy drama and high action, jokes about Ed's stature were included. Some episodes, such as the visit to Rush Valley (in episode 11), were largely humorous (this was the episode when spunky, black tomboy Paninya (Bunny – Akemi Okamura) steals Ed's State Alchemist watch, and when the Elrics and others witness the birth of a baby).

The character designs in the second *Fullmetal Alchemist* series (by Hiroki Kanno) tended to be similar to the 2003-2004 series (tho' leaning slightly more towards child-like or *kawaii* faces and eyes). Both series, tho', stick very closely to Himoru Arakawa's designs (they capture, for instance, Arakawa-sensei's penchant for using a single, black line, usually down-turned, for mouths. And the very amusing two diagonal lines for eyebrows when a character is angry).

The action keeps coming in the second *Fullmetal Alchemist* series at an exhilarating (but also exhausting) pace. The filmmakers never let up with their barrage of sword fights, gun fights, tank battles, and alchemical duels. One of the reasons why the filmmakers can keep the *animé* series so varied and stimulating is because of the sheer size of the production team. There are some 20 storyboard artists credited for the first *Fullmetal Alchemist* series, for instance (that's a lot!). These are the people who are given the script plus instructions from the producers, the animation directors, the episode directors, and of course the overall director, and they block the scenes by drawing each shot. Each storyboard artist has their own style, their favourite sort of shots,[3] and of course they will also be consulting the *manga* by Hiromu Arakawa (all of the key artists involved in the *animé* would have copies of the *manga* and they would've leafed thru it *hundreds* times).

In one respect the first alchemical fantasy series of 2003-04 was superior to the 2009-2010 remake, and that was the soundtrack. (It was performed by the Warsaw National Philharmonic Orchestra and the Warsaw Chorus, conducted by Mario Klemens. The Orchestra has been used for *animé* such as *Cowboy Bebop*, *Wolf's Rain*, *Aquarion*, *Escaflowne*, and *Hellsing*).

The second *Fullmetal Alchemist* series took a very different approach to the music: it was still generally orchestral, but it was less strident and in-your-face than Michiru Oshima's score for the first alchemical series (where often you couldn't ignore the music). The score for the first *Fullmetal Alchemist* series seems far weightier, more like serious classical music, while the second series' score, by Akira Senju, was more light-hearted, altho' it often launches into sombre straightness. (Also, some of the music for the second *Fullmetal Alchemist* series simply doesn't fit the visuals: the long, slow drones using violins and cellos, for instance,[4] and it is also allowed to putter too long underneath scenes, adding little. There are far too many episodes where the music is simply recycled: you get tired of hearing the high-pitched drones on violins and violas, for instance, or the string section of the orchestra rising in waves to a climax).

However, Akira Senju's score does reach true heights of musicality at times – in the Gluttony belly sequence, for instance, the choirs are unleashed, creating overwhelming washes of choral music worthy of any of the great composers in cinema of the present day (the Danny Elfmans, the Hans Zimmers, the Howard Shores of Western movies). And on repeated screenings, Senju's under-score gets better and better – his choral cues are terrific, and the rising cue of strident strings (used many times for the building of suspense) is very effective.

> As the oldest musical medium known to mankind [explained Akira Senju], choral music, to me, is the most expressive. Their range of expression is more expansive, able to express themes like destiny, love, and religious worldviews.

And let's not forget some of the humorous music cues – the funniest, perhaps, is the mock martial music, with a male choir, that accompanies the camp Alex Armstrong scenes when he's in full Muscle Man mode. The macho choral voices send up Communist songs from the 1920s-1930s – we might be marching through the streets of Moscow in a procession celebrating Russian military might.

Akira Senju composed the music from scratch, taking his inspiration from the *manga*, without looking at the first series:

---

3 You can see each storyboard artist blocking a scene in a different way.
4 For some reason, Japanese TV producers often demand piercing strings from *animé* composers, something like Dimitri Shostakovitch mixed with Soviet Minimalists like Arvo Pärt.

It was a thrilling experience, especially towards the second half, as the original story was written at the same time as the animation, which was a new experience for me.

Senju recalled that he would buy the *manga* in Spanish, English and French editions as he travelled around the world to keep up with it. He knew that the comic was now a global phenomenon when one of the members of the Warsaw Philharmonic Orchestra told him they were a fan.

◆

The more I watch *Fullmetal Alchemist* and think about it, the more it seems one of the great masterpieces of Japanese animation – at the same level as *Akira*, *Ghost In the Shell* and the movies of Hayao Miyazaki and Isao Takahata. Is *Fullmetal Alchemist* as good as *Akira*? Yes, I think it is: it goes to extraordinary places, its hits a very broad range of emotions (from ecstasy to despair, from happiness to depression), it conjures an enormous cast of compelling characters, and it explores fascinating themes (including all of the major ones, like love, death, family, memory, loss, war, desire, hope, fate and spirituality).

The *Fullmetal Alchemist* animations fly by so quickly, it's worth having a look at some of the screenshots and images from the two animated series to really appreciate just how impressive these shows are: for colours, for designs, for compositions, for poses of the body, for facial expressions, and for all of the technical aspects of drawing (such as the use of scale, viewpoint, contrast, perspective, shadows, lighting, etc).

ENVY.

Special mention should be made of the homunculus character Envy, one of many outstanding figures in the *Fullmetal Alchemist* universe, and given a cluster of remarkable scenes in the second *Fullmetal Alchemist* series.

Envy is one of *animé*'s insane divas, a character who's fantastically over-the-top, fiendishly nasty, yet somehow appealing in a sinister way – and even, well, cool (Envy is a gift to an animator as a character, full of complexities and contradictions, seething with resentments, possessing an extraordinary physical dynamism (yet he's also a coward!), and the animators at Bones, Aniplex, Mainichi, Square Enix *et al* fly far with him. And of course, Envy's voice actor, Minami Takayama, delivers one of the greatest performances in recent animation.)

Among the many sequences featuring Envy are: lording it over humans with Lust; acting as the homunculi's messenger; performing very nasty deeds (killing Hughes, inaugurating the Ishbal War); duelling Ed and Ling in Gluttony's belly; and battling with Alphonse, Scar, Mei and Dr Marcoh in the snowlands up North.

But it's the group of scenes in the tunnels below Central City that take Envy's characterization to sublime heights: duelling and chasing little Mei Chang; reviving back to his punk form; facing off against our heroes in the white hall; being hunted down by a malevolent Roy Mustang; and dying several times over in extraordinary conflagrations... The sequence culminates with a truly incredible death scene, when Minami Takayama steals the limelight from one of the strongest voice casts in all *animé*.

THE CRITICS.

'What truly separates *Fullmetal Alchemist: Brotherhood* from its original counterpart however is the way in which it explores profound philosophical themes. The level of depth in *Brotherhood*'s story is astounding', reckoned the *Nihon Review,* and 'the amount of detail and effort this show puts into characters is astonishing'.

For Anime News Network, the 2nd series possesses 'a sense of menace well beyond what the first TV series ever achieved and a tightness to the writing not as evident earlier in the series'.

'It's big and bold, and boy, does it deliver!' opined Mr Rhapsodist online in 2013. 'An outstanding series', wrote Anime Evo online in 2013.

05

FULLMETAL ALCHEMIST: THE SECOND *ANIME* SERIES: EPISODE GUIDE

Episode 1. *Fullmetal Alchemist*

The second *Fullmetal Alchemist* series was broadcast from April 5, 2009 until August 25, 2010. The first three episodes were scripted by head writer Hiroshi Ohnogi, a brilliant writer for *animé* (and also all of the final episodes; Ohnogi has writing credits on 24 of the 64 episodes. Ohnogi's credits as chief writer include *Macross, Aquarion, Heat Guy J, Rahxephon, Kekkaishi, Gundam, Noein, Shugo Chara, Phantasy Star Online, Shangri-La, Seisen Cerberus Ryukoku no Fatalie, Eureka Seven,* etc). One of the chief reasons why *Fullmetal Alchemist* is so good is Ohnogi's contribution. Series director Yasuhiro Irie storyboarded the opening two episodes (as well as 5, 8 and 63 and 64; thus, the director snagged the most significant shows in the series, the start and the end, as directors like to do if they can).

The producers opted to go all-out for their first *Fullmetal Alchemist* show, with tons of action and incidents, heaps of visual effects, goofy humour, and a vast cast of characters. And they would portray the two heroes, Ed and Al, in full flow, unleashing wave after wave of alchemical attacks.

The *Fullmetal Alchemist* series opens with an episode (*Hagane no Renkinjutsushi*) that does all of the things one would expect from an opening episode of a TV show, such as introducing the main characters, depicting their relationships, showing them in action, and introducing some of the primary themes (such as the Ishbal rebellion and the nefarious plans of the villains), some key motifs (transmutation circles and on-the-wing alchemical transformations), some props (a philosopher's stone), and the settings (Middle Europe *circa* 1910-1920). Plus of course showing off the amazing production values of this outstanding, expen$ive *animé* (including the lavish score), and delivering some very fine set-pieces and gloriously over-the-top superhero moments (including the mandatory comicbook icons of shadowy figures looming at the end of alleys, and figures in cloaks against the sky). Plus several examples of loony humour and *manga*-exaggerated characterizations (with Ed's paranoia about his stature a running gag); comedy is absolutely fundamental to the *Fullmetal Alchemist* series.

Episode 1: *Fullmetal Alchemist* introduced a huge number of characters (probably too many): the Elrics, Mustang, Hawkeye, Hughes (plus wife & daughter), Kimbley, Bradley, Armstrong, the military, etc. The focus is on the Elrics, of course, but they are sharing the show with a lot of other figures. When this second series starts up, for instance, the Elrics are already established as working for the military (and thus their journey from Country Boys to State Alchemists will come later). Indeed, the military officers are the principal secondary characters introduced here (Lust and Gluttony make a brief appearance).

However, episode one also departed from the *Fullmetal Alchemist manga* (and the first animated series of 2003-2004) by delaying the explanations of how Ed (Romi Pak) and Al (Rie Kugimiya) come to be how they are (putting it mainly into the second episode, *The First Day*). That was certainly one of the strong aspects of the first show of the first *Fullmetal Alchemist* series: it opened with Ed and Al and their taboo-breaking magical circle transmutation. In the second series' opener, that doesn't come until later, when Ed and Al are way up in the air, battling the villain-of-the-week, Isaac McDougal (played by the wonderful Koichi Yamadera), the 'Freezing Alchemist', a sort of Mr Freeze (as out of *Batman & Robin*, 1997), or Gray in *Fairy Tail*. McDougal is a combination of Scar and Kimbley. McDougal recognizes that these young alchemists have crossed the line into dealing with death, with their lost limbs and hollow suit of armour (he is given the exposition about their transmutation, when they talk atop one of the ice walls). Only then do we flashback to the primal scene of the *Fullmetal Alchemist* legend (cutting from close-ups of Edward remembering that fateful day to Ed aged ten, in the full trauma of the taboo ritual, with his leg severed. McDougal was invented as an explainer character).

There's a detail you might miss on the first viewing of the first episode, *Hagane no Renkinjutsushi*, of the second *Fullmetal Alchemist* series: two flashcuts to a big close-up of the super-villain of the whole series, Father. There isn't any explanation about who he is, he just suddenly appears. However, the heavy (Isaac McDougal), does hint to the Elric boys that something is happening in Amestris. And when we see the giant, aerial view of Central City, it depicts the creation of a transmutation circle (it is a *long* time in the series before any of this is fully explained). But a philosopher's stone does pop out of McDougal's corpse, followed by a cut to a cackling Crimson Alchemist (who supplied the stone, presumably). Showing the whole city as a transmutation circle is where the first *Fullmetal Alchemist* series *ended*: thus, this second series will go even bigger than that.

The first episode of *Fullmetal Alchemist 2* is a stops-all-out action and visual effects extravaganza, with multiple duels: the Elrics vs. McDougal (several times), Mustang vs. McDougal, Armstrong vs. McDougal, Bradley vs. McDougal, etc. The animation is outstanding by any standards, beautifully fluid, inventive, rapidly-cut, with glowing colours (and much of it is set at night, a tougher challenge for the colour designers, because everything can look muddy and indistinct).

So much is packed into ep. one! Of the many elements, Alex Armstrong certainly stands out. One of HimoruArakawa's beloved he-men rippling with muscles, Armstrong is a delightful send-up of the vaunted aspects of *shonen manga*, such as strength, fighting ability, determination and vanity. Col. Mustang's fire skills are seen for the first time, too, and the Führer's deadly talent with a sword (the scene where he dispatches McDougal employs the samurai freeze, where the participants hold a pose for a beat. Then blood gushes, and one of them collapses).

Notice, too, that some of the military's alchemists are undercut with humour: Armstrong blocks an advancing wall of ice, which turns 90° and smashes into buildings; Mustang, attempting to appear super-cool and debonair, is doused with water, which renders his flame alchemy useless.

Episode 2. *The First Day*

The second episode of the 2009-2010 *Fullmetal Alchemist* series (*Hajimari no Hi*) is probably the most densely-plotted of any show in either *Fullmetal Alchemist* series: it is stuffed with story and plot (hats off to writer Hiroshi Ohnogi for organizing and structuring this complicated show). In this installment, we receive the full explanation of just what the Elric kids did way back when. The narrative is actually more complex than a straight re-telling: it is framed by a railroad journey to Liore, with the Elrics reminiscing about their past (one of their first missions, when Ed had been newly-made a State Alchemist). Not only that, but the narrative structure also returns to the present day scenes to comment upon the past.

We also see the time when Roy Mustang visited the Rockbells' place in rural Resembool, to offer the dejected, exhausted Ed the possibility of becoming a State Alchemist (Pinako strongly resists); Pinako seeing the creature (related to Mustang – so this is a flashback-within-a-flashback); Hawkeye bonding with Winry (with some back-story of Winry's parents dying on the battlefield); the Elrics at their mother's graveside; arguments between Ed and Winry (and another argument at the cemetery); the kids coming home after school; the State Alchemist examination (overseen by the Führer); their years of studying alchemy, encouragements from their mom, and their determination to resurrect their mom; the fateful ritual; the boys learning alchemy from Izumi Curtis; Ed discussing having automail fitted; Ed and Al sparring after the operation; and Ed receiving his new name: *hagane no renkinjutsushi*.

How all of this is squeezed into 22 minutes is one of the marvels of

Japanese animation. And no wonder that Western television and movies seem *so slow* in comparison! *Fullmetal Alchemist* has *a lot to say*, and it knows *how to say it*.

In the childhood scenes in 2.2: *The First Day*, we see the scenario of the absent father, the boys learning alchemy from books (what scholarly, devoted kids!), their mother praising them, and the narration of the plague visiting the area and the primal scene: the death of the mother (this occurs off-screen. Instead, we cut to Al and Ed sitting by their parents' grave). Ed's fury over his father van Hohenheim's absence creates one of the deep rifts in the *Fullmetal Alchemist* series which, combined with the mother's death, gives it such psychological juice.

So when the 2009-2010 version of *Fullmetal Alchemist* portrays the botched ritual to Raise the Dead, it has a vivid poignancy, now we know more about the children before the sequence begins. However you edit the scenes, tho', it's still a very strong scene, whether you show it as the first *Fullmetal Alchemist animé* series did, or as Himoru Arakawa's *manga* did, or as the second series did.

In the flashbacks to the childhoods of Alphonse and Edward, the two lead voice actors deliver absolutely outstanding work. I mean Romi Pak and Rie Kugimiya, of course.[5] The animation, the script, the music and the visual effects are all doing a good deal of work in the transmutation of the dead sequence, but Kugimiya and Pak take the dramatic intensity to a whole other level.

The stand-out sequence in episode 2: *The First Day* is the alchemical ritual. The perspective stays with Edward Elric throughout, and immediately introduces us to elements that the first series left out: the giant eye, the grinning demon, the toll, and the cosmic trip Ed undertakes. We see many of the ingredients that appear later in Himoru Arakawa's *manga*, and are brought forward here – such as the concept of the toll/sacrifice, the imposing Gate of Truth, the demon introducing itself, and Edward bonding Alphonse's soul to the armour.

The supernatural ideas are marvellously visualized by the filmmakers – from the negative space of the godly demon and the white limbo of the Gateway to the unreal blue light and flashing, zigzagging energy around the transmutation circle.

As with episode one, episode two in the second *Fullmetal Alchemist* series has consciously stepped away from the portrayal of the same material in the first series. Whatever the first series did in its early episodes, the second series prefers not to simply repeat them, but to develop other forms of storytelling. You can see the second series thinking, well, that's already been done, so we'll do something else.

Even so, hundreds of narrative beats are inevitably repeated in the second *Fullmetal Alchemist* series (often exactly the same images). The second series works fine for people who haven't seen the first series, but it also adjusts the storytelling for the people who *have* seen the first series (by maintaining a balance between repeating the first series and doing

5 Other actors are used for the five year-old Elrics.

something new or different). After all, it's the same story adapted from the same *manga* made by the same companies and many of the same staff.

Episode 3. *City of Heresy*

The third episode of the 2009-10 series of *Fullmetal Alchemist* takes our heroes to Liore, a city under the spell of a false religion. It's an important aspect of the morality of *Fullmetal Alchemist* that organized religion is portrayed as dubious: the cult of the sun-god Leto is run by a charlatan (Father Cornello) who demonstrates bogus miracles using a fake (or impure) philosopher's stone. The fakery is simply an exaggeration, tho', of the suspicion that *Fullmetal Alchemist* has towards religion. Fake or not, organized spirituality is viewed with cynicism in *Fullmetal Alchemist.* In Liore, religion is being used as a cloak or decoration to hide political power: what Cornello really wants is to rule Liore. If he can do that by tricking people into believing in miracles, fine.

The issues are explored in the key discussion between Rose and Edward in the church – indeed, that conversation is central to the ideological project of *Fullmetal Alchemist,* and would be reason enough to include this section of Arakawa's comic.

That Christianity is chosen by Himoru Arakawa as the object of suspicion and investigation is intriguing: altho' Letoism is given a few attributes to distinguish it from Christianity, it is of course Christianity in essence. When Rose encounters Ed and Al, she is praying, and their conversation about false religions occurs right in front of the altar. (However, Christianity is also probably used for its exoticism and its otherness, as so often in Japanese *manga* and *animé*). Christianity for Japanese really is something truly 'other' and strange.

So there are only two significant new characters in the Liore episode: Rose (Satsuki Yukino) and Father Cornello (Seizo Katou). The animation follows the *Fullmetal Alchemist manga* closely, tho' I reckon more might've been made of Rose's hope that her devotion to Letoism might lead to her lover being brought back to life, at least visually, perhaps with some flashbacks. However, Rose's predicament is obviously introduced by *mangaka* Himoru Arakawa to throw light on the boys' taboo-breaking ritual (which's shown again in flashback). In Shintoism, nobody comes back fro the dead; when you're dead, you stay dead. Ed tells Rose this in jaded, weary tones, as if, as a mid-teenager, he has already Been There, Done That (tho' Rose doesn't want to hear it).

Meanwhile, Father Cornello is the second character so far in *Fullmetal Alchemist* (in only 3 eps.) to recognize that the maimed states of Ed and Al means they have committed the taboo that all alchemists know about (this introduces a motif that recurs regularly in the *Fullmetal Alchemist* series: characters see the heroes' incomplete bodies and put two and two together. Then they use this knowledge psychologically against them. Clever opponents always know how to exploit someone's weak points, and the weak points of Ed and Al are in plain sight. Notice that Ed tends to wears long-sleeved clothes, to hide his automail).

Stylistically, episode 3: *City of Heresy* employs a good deal of split-screens, placing, for ex, Edward and Rose together (partly to enliven the lengthy conflabs between the two). There are welcome comedic beats, in the *manga*-style (including more gags about Ed's height). Additions include Cornello's attack rebounding, so his body becomes enlarged, and the machine gun is welded into his arm, steam-punk-style (so he becomes an American-style superhero for a moment).

One addition to the *manga* was probably disliked by Himoru Arakawa: giving Rose a gun, which she aims at the Elrics not once, but twice. We know that Arakawa is acutely conscious of putting guns in the hands of her heroes (even tho', yes, firearms are everywhere in the *Fullmetal Alchemist manga*). In short, Arakawa doesn't want to do it, and neither Ed nor Al (nor Winry) fire a gun in *Fullmetal Alchemist* (and Edward only accepts the pistol that Liza Hawkeye hands him reluctantly. Actually, yes, Ed *does* use a gun – in the Gluttony belly sequence, but only as a means to extract a toll so they can escape through the Gateway of Truth, and the people he fires on are already dead. But he's very reluctant. Also, the actual moment is elided by Arakawa).

The first *Fullmetal Alchemist* series spent two episodes on this part of Arakawa-sensei's *manga*; by comparison, the version in the second series seems rushed. The show compresses two chapters of the comic, no less (about 100 pages, equivalent to four regular *manga* chapters).

Also, two whole adventures fly out of the window from the comic here: the Yousewell mining town adventure and the railroad hostage adventure.

Episode 4. *An Alchemist's Anguish*

The body count escalates in the *Fullmetal Alchemist* in this show, which includes not one but two serial killers, and opens with a murder, and ends with a quadruple killing. The Shou Tucker episode of the second *Fullmetal Alchemist* series was somehow even bloodier and sicker than the same story in the first animated series. Tucker (the 'Sewing Life Alchemist', played again by Makoto Nagai from the first series) came over as a really hopeless loser, one of the nastiest characters in the *Fullmetal Alchemist* series: transmuting his wife and then his daughter Nina (Sumire Morohoshi)[6] and dog is just so twisted.

This 4th episode of *Fullmetal Alchemist: Brotherhood* considers the concept of the chimera in more detail, a fake creature, a mockery of divine creation, and one that's so forlorn it wants to die (in the flashback to the time when Tucker transmuted his wife, we see the poor creature alone in inky blackness, and it says just one thing, 'I want to die'. So it stops eating, and wastes away).

And thus the scenes of Ed, Al, Nina and the dog are played very sweetly, almost too sweet, to make the pay-off in the transmutation scene,

---

6 A later *animé* star – *Heroman, Blue Exorcist, Tokyo Ghoul, Rage of Bahamut, Fairy Tail Zero*, etc.

and also when they're killed by Scar, even greater.

Ed's fury when he realizes what Shou Tucker has done is also shocking to witness – not only when he's punching Tucker repeatedly, until Al stops him from the killing the loser – but also Tucker's accusations that Ed and Al are also transgressors, by committing the taboo of transmutation. Attempting to bring someone back to life is not quite the same as killing two people, tho', is it?

What's striking about the *Fullmetal Alchemist* series is that is genuinely does explore giant moral and metaphysical issues. One reason it can achieve this so successfully is because it pins these big life-and-death issues to the two heroes (that is, Himoru Arakawa always finds a way of relating each issue or character that the heroes encounter on their journey thru the series to the heroes). The spiritual connectivity between the heroes and the issues and themes lends real dramatic electricity to the *Fullmetal Alchemist* series. It's brilliant writing by Arakawa, and by Ohnogi and the team.

And then you have Scar (Kenta Miyake), one of the most tortured and ambiguous charas in recent *animé*, introduced here in the *Fullmetal Alchemist* series stalking thru the story (episode four in the second series), as an angel of death, murdering people left, right and centre, and leaving behind a trail of blood and bodies, culminating with the death of Tucker and the chimera.

In the opening scene, Scar seeks out Basque Grand, a formidable State Alchemist (the 'Iron Blood' Alchemist), whose speciality is attacks with cannons and chains. The first *Fullmetal Alchemist* series gave more for Basque to do, but here he's finished off by Scar promptly. By the end of the show, Scar has killed at least four more people: he goes outside, looks up into the falling rain,[7] and intones pompously about God.

When the lads turn up at the Tuckers' home, it is of course raining, and a storm is brewing – suitably Gothic atmospherics for the revelation scene where Tucker confesses to transmuting his daughter, wife and dog. The colours in that scene in the lab are also washed-out, and the scene is played very straight, over huge close-ups of Ed and Tucker-san.

By comparison with the Scar and Tucker scenes, other scenes are more functional in episode 4: *An Alchemist's Anguish*: the Yousewell mining sequence, for ex, is left out, and boringly summarized in a dialogue scene instead (by Roy Mustang); and there's also an aftermath-of-Liore chat. (However, Yousewell is summarized in a later episode, 38: *Conflict At Baschool*, when Lt. Loki meets the boys, narrated in the style of silent movie comedy).

Episode 5. *Rain of Sorrows*

Episode 5 of the second Japanese, fully alchemical series is a very fine piece of animation and storytelling (it was written by Aya Yoshinaga – it's a rock-solid script). This show is nigh on perfect – look at the

7 Nonchalantly, with his hands in his pockets, in daylight.

storyboarding (by Shinsaku Sasaki), the selection of camera angles, the flow of action, the judicious use of music, the terrific voice work, the confident orchestration of a large ensemble of characters, and the introduction of important issues, such as Ishbal and the Ishbal War.

Consider how much ground this show covers in 22 minutes, how it has time for reflection on big issues (life, death, loss), time for action (two duels with Scar), time for back-story (to Resembool and Ishbal), time for explanations (including voiceovers), time for numerous character touches, and time for humour. And it also keeps the Elrics brothers in the foreground, tracking their gradual immersion in the politics of Amestris.

Shows like episode 5: *Rain of Sorrows* are marvels of conception and execution, and one of the reasons why *Fullmetal Alchemist* may be the greatest *animé* series of recent times, along with *Naruto* and *One Piece*. Edward Elric is the emotional focus of this show (there are lovely close-ups of the hero – some are right into the eyes), and Romi Pak delivers a powerful vocal performance.

Ed and Al find themselves out-matched by Scar, the Ishbalian who self-righteously takes revenge on all State Alchemists, on his Mission From God (the god Ishbala, not the Judæo-Christian God). Scar's attack on our heroes comes out of nowhere: they're sitting in a public park on the steps of a monument in the rain (where 1,000s of teens might hang out in real life), contemplating sadly on the deaths of li'l Nina and her dog Alexander (tho' not losing any tears over Shou Tucker!). Suddenly, Scar's right in their face, attacking them. They retaliate (there are many gags involving stone staircases), but they're out-classed and on the run (tho' they do, rather stupidly, hurry into an alley which of course happens to be a dead-end. But in *Fullmetal Alchemist*, narrow alleys are key settings, as they are in every action or thriller *animé* set in a city).

Scar's ruthless determination is disturbing. He is another of those opponents in Japanese animation who seem unstoppable and unkillable (even when he's surrounded by a squad of alchemists and guards, he can still out-dance their firepower. Yes, even Liza Hawkeye's two-gun assault! It's typical of *animé* to depict someone cornered with weapons aimed at him that he somehow manages to escape with just a scratch. *Lupin III* does it all the time).

The scene introduces the first of many instances where Lt. Liza (Riza) Hawkeye (played by the amazing Fumiko Orikasa)[8] saves Col. Mustang's butt (rain fizzles out Mustang's flame alchemy – but we see it in full effect in the Ishbal flashback). As Hawkeye told li'l Winry, she has someone to look after (and that's Mustang; this is one of the touching minor subplots in *Fullmetal Alchemist*). The big action scene in ep. 5 foregrounds Alex Armstrong duelling Scar (as in the *manga*), who, of course, strips off his

8 Fumiko Orikasa was also Lybia in the first series. The credits of Orikasa (born in Taito, Tokyo in 1972) include: the adorable Rukia in *Bleach*, Yuzuki in *Chobits*, Ruki in *Digimon Tamers*, Shirley in *Code Geass*, Kyubei in *Gintama*, Rumiko in *Higurashi no Naku Koro ni Rei*, Aki in *Inazuma Eleven*, Marion in *Kaleido Star*, Rinko in *Kinnikuman Nisei*, Satsuki in *Kuroko's Basketball*, Lotte in *Little Witch Academia*, Miss Valentine in *One Piece*, Kim in *Rahxephon*, Reiko in *Sket Dance*, Karin in *Stratos 4*, Kaaya in *The Tower of Druaga: the Sword of Uruk*, Shizuka in *Vampire Knight*, Meia in *Vandread*, and the wonderful Victoria Seras in both *Hellsing* series.

shirt to go into battle (as you do. Everyone looks on bemused). Meanwhile, Hughes (Keiji Fujiwara, who was also Hughes in the first series) wisely hides in the background.

Ep. 5 includes a very important message from Himoru Arakawa, delivered by Alphonse to Ed: live, live on, survive, never give up, and never, ever contemplate defeat or suicide. (This is expressed in the aftermath of Scar's attack).

Roy Mustang (Shinichiro Miki[9]) narrates the exposition in voiceover in episode 2.5: *Rain of Sorrows* (to the Elrics, in his office) about the Ishbal rebellion, explaining that Scar does have a reason for his one-man vengeance project. Ed's response to that is typical: *rubbish!* He reckons that Scar is simply using God and religion to hide behind. (Edward voices a common view of victims of terrorists: why does he have to involve innocents who have nothing to do with the issue?).

Over desaturated images simulating newsreel footage of WWII, we see the Ishbal War and the chaos that the State Alchemists wielded. This is one of Himoru Arakawa's most compelling themes in *Fullmetal Alchemist* – it's her version of WWI and WWII (some of the images might come directly from newsreels of WWII).

The level of ambiguity and complexity in *Fullmetal Alchemist* is impressive, because it doesn't type Scar as wholly evil (and therefore not so easy for the heroes to destroy). But as a zealot who imagines he's on a mission from God he is, like many religious psychopaths, very creepy and sinister. He has his reasons, sure, and he's raging against the oppressive State machine of Amestris, and he represents the guilt of Amestrisian aggression that won't go away – but he's also a mass murderer. (Meanwhile, Scar's very modern design – he might be a bodyguard in a hi-tech thriller set in Los Angeles – enhances the fact that he and his cause can't simply be dismissed, because it's happening right now).

✳

As well as introducing Scar, this jam-packed show also brings in Winry Rockbell (Megumi Takemoto), the workaholic automail engineer and chief female chara in *Fullmetal Alchemist*. And what is Winry doing when we first meet her? Only fixing automail at her workbench in the Rockbell home in Resembool – and at night (Winry is one of Himoru Arakawa's female hard-workers, a tough girl from the North, despite her blonde, *kawaii* design). To complement the introduction of Winry, the imagery comprises warm blues (for the night), and golden light.

And there's even more material in this show: the bickering among Mustang's team, for instance, plus the discussion of Scar with Hughes, and the discovery of the bodies of Tucker and the chimera (picking up the climax of the previous episode).

And we should mention – lest we're skewered in the skull with a pointy blade wielded by a psychopathic dominatrix – the homunculi, who pop up around this point in the *Fullmetal Alchemist* series, still causing

---

9 Among Miki's roles in *animé* is the marvellous Kisuke Urahara in *Bleach*. Casting Miki as Mustang, with his famously fey, enigmatic delivery, is perfect. Miki is also the headmaster in *Trinity Seven*, Creed in *Black Cat*, and Slader in *Seven Deadly Sins*.

trouble in Liore. And here comes Envy, one of the scene-stealers in this glorious TV series, introduced at first as a vain, unfeeling enigma, but who later develops into a monstrous diva.

Episode 6. *Road of Hope*

Another superb episode, with the filmmakers really getting into their stride. The show's split into two halves: an encounter with Dr Marcoh, an alchemist who represents the guilt and shame of war (and the Ishbal War in particular), as Scar does, in Part A, and a heart-warming trip home in Part B.

Following their calamitous encounter with super-brute Scar (in which Ed and Al Elric were badly mauled), the brothers head for their childhood home of Resembool, where their two mechanics Winry and Pinako Rockbell (Miyoko Asou, also Pinako in the 1st series) are able to fix them up. Accompanied by the towering, softie he-man Alex Armstrong (Kenji Utsumi), the episode is a welcome respite from the nefarious schemes and even the hi-octane action of the *Fullmetal Alchemist* second series so far.

On the way, Doctor Marcoh (the 'Crystal Alchemist' – Masayuki Omoro) is introduced, the guilt-ridden explorer of the sinister regions of alchemy (Marcoh's haunted by his mis-deeds in the Ishbal War). Marcoh narrates some more back-story about Ishbal (again using newsreel-style footage), which keeps that all-important issue of war buoyant.

For Ed and Al, tho', Dr Marcoh offers the possibility of edging closer to getting their hands on a philosopher's stone (when it appears, as red goop that plops out onto the table, it seems underwhelming. But not to Ed – we cut to a giant close-up as the boys react to this mythical substance. And the music cues us in that this is a Big Moment). Declining to hand over the secrets of his research, however, Marcoh instead later offers the brothers a clue of where to start (in a library, of course! Yes, libraries are *cool*, kids! Spend every waking hour in them, and you might end up an ace alchemist like Edward Elric!).

❈

Going Home in any narrative inevitably means back-story, catching up, and characterization. The *Road of Hope* episode focusses on Ed (Al is so beaten up he travels in a box, carried on Armstrong's shoulder), and introduces new perspectives on the Elrics (such as Pinako's account of their upbringing to Armstrong).

The most important new element, however, is Winry Rockbell: she's beautiful, she's blonde, she's a very hard worker, she's a genius with *mecha*... she is in fact the ideal girlfriend for any *animé* character, as well as being the dream girl of all *otaku* (however, the potential romance between Winry and Ed is never more'n a very minor side issue in the *Fullmetal Alchemist* tales. It's as if it's a no-brainer that Ed and Winry will get together in the end, so the filmmakers (like Himoru Arakawa) don't even bother with romantic subplots. They could've mined an erotic triangle between the Elric brothers and *kawaii* Winry but, no, it's just not important. Also, of course, there is so much happening in the narrative of *Fullmetal Alchemist*, there isn't time for romantic elements.)

Winry's introduced hard at work, and she pulls several all-nighters in order to get the rush job finished[10] (just like a dutiful animator![11]). She also coos comically over automail, takes pride in her workmanship, and gleefully adds up the fees.

And Winry-chan provides 'fan service' in both animated series: in this episode, she's introduced wearing overalls. Yes, but overalls pulled down to the waist, so she's essentially topless except for a boob tube. It seems like another instance of character designers shamelessly exploiting pretty, young things for the television audience, but no – this chara design is actually in Arakawa-sensei's *manga* (yes, Arakawa and her editor Yoichi Shimomura are very conscious of the demographic make-up of their market at Square Enix's *Monthly Shonen Gangen*, too).

We see Edward visiting the resting place of his mother, and also the ruins of his home (weather-wise, there are two options usually employed in *anime* for this sort of scene: 1. heavy rain, or 2. golden sunsets. This time, it's 2. In fact, skies of gold and gold light are everywhere in the Resembool scenes, the colour linked to Ed and Winry). Pinako provides the exposition of the Elrics' past (it's told to Alex Armstrong back in the house, and played as voiceover in sections. Pinako also talks about the loss of the Rockbells in the Ishbalian conflict).

The script for ep. 6 (by Natsuko Takahashi) is as neatly put together as Winry's lovingly-crafted automail. It portrays several segments of characterization and back-story – telling us more about the Elrics' background, as well as Winry's, and even Pinako's (she was a drinking buddy with Hohenheim,. for ex), and also allows for many humorous moments (such as Ed anxiously awaiting his automail, and Armstrong reacting weepingly and whimperingly to the hard luck story of the Elric boys. The prospect of burly Armstrong throwing off his shirt in order to embrace Edward all the firmer is indeed scary!).

Episode 6: *Road of Hope* also offers some gorgeous background art, with a lush, rural zone awash in greens and blues, and of course the mandatory super-glowing sunsets (there's no question that, of any art of any period of history, Japanese *anime* of 1963-to-today is the Supreme Emperor of Golden Sunsets). Resembool embodies the idea and the dream of 'home'. Yes, our heroes are kids from the sticks, with dinner, a dog, a grandma and a gorgeous babe waiting for them any time they want to return.

Episode 7. *Hidden Truths*

In episode 7 (entitled *Ed and Al Take Manhattan!*), we shift into *Sherlock Holmes* mystery territory, as the Elric brothers investigate the alchemical writings of Dr Marcoh (hidden in a since-destroyed recipe

10 Fio, the seventeen year-old plane engineer in *Porco Rosso* (1992) might be a reference point.
11 But many animators do *not* get paid for over-time.

book). Books, libraries, and studying – it's an episode which's a high school drama in all but name (as if the Elrics're studying and revising for an impossibly difficult exam at one of those tough, Japanese schools). As usual, Ed is at the forefront of the fevered pursuit of discovering the secrets of the philosopher's stone (Ed would've been a brilliant explorer in the Age of Explorers, from the 16th to the 19th centuries. Ed wouldn't give up until he's reached the North Pole – and stuck a snowman there, with a sprig of blond hair crowning it).

Himoru Arakawa introduces her silliest device in the *manga* here – even more unconvincing than philosopher's stones or alchemical transformations – the glasses-wearing nerd Sheska who can remember everything in every book she's ever read! Recognizing how dumb this idea is, the filmmakers cover it up with cartoony humour.

Apart from an encounter between Gluttony (Tetsu Shiratori)[12] and Scar in the sewers (where Scar escaped following his confrontation with the authorities) – in which Gluttony unfortunately fails to wolf down Scar, aided by Lust (Scar is no match for *two* homunculi, yet once again he survives) – there isn't much action in episode seven: *Hidden Truths* of series two. Instead, it's a thematic installment, exploring the background of the philosopher's stone, and just what philosophical-stone magic might be capable of. And it's also an exposition show, setting up future episodes.

The thematic climax of episode 7 is the depressingly scary revelation that the special ingredient required to create a philosopher's stone is living humans. This throws Al and Ed into a tailspin, so they take to sitting in their room frozen, in the dark. They've hit a major impasse, and have realized that the adult world is more complicated than they thought, and much nastier than they thought, and that the military and the government may also be involved.

To prove their theories, and to gather some more information, the brothers decide to investigate the city's fifth laboratory (supposedly closed down). The episode ends on a cliffhanger, as sinister presences with glowing red eyes close in on our heroes in the seemingly deserted building at night.

The general drift of episode 7: *Hidden Truths* follows Arakawa-sensei's *manga*, while streamlining the action. There are minor additions – such as the alchemical symbols which the brothers read in the recipe book.

Episode 8. *The Fifth Laboratory*

Dual fights at the sinister fifth laboratory comprise most of episode 8, with Ed and Al each tackling hollow suits of armour (Barry the Chopper and Slicer – both are serial killers!). The smart screenwriting (by head writer Hiroshi Ohnogi) combines (as with the first *Fullmetal Alchemist* series) more exposition about alchemy and the philosopher's stone with slam-bang action. There is actually a *lot* of information about the key themes of *Fullmetal Alchemist* parcelled out in this episode in between

---

12 He was Cain Furey in the first series.

scenes of Ed and Al hurling themselves at their steely, hollow opponents. Number 66 (played by Hideyuki Umez) is a delightfully vain, hysterical character. Barry the Chopper narrates the story of his serial killer days over children's storybook illustrations, with scarlet inevitably the dominant hue. Much more was made of Barry in the first *Fullmetal Alchemist* series: the second series often simply summarizes episodes that the first series explored in depth, or refers to them in dialogue.

Finally, in the climactic scene, Edward Elric comes face to face with the homunculi – Envy (Minami Takayama[13] – wonderful!) and Lust (Kikuko Inoue). It's striking that the screenwriters have delayed the meeting of the chief heroes and the chief villains for so long. When it occurs, Ed is exhausted and bleeding, and it's the homunculi who have the upper hand. You can't help noticing that the design (and attitude) of Envy is meant to echo (and satirize) Ed, nor that it's Envy who immediately starts to tease Ed (about being *chibi* – small), and also that it's Envy who's right in Ed's face. (Notice, too, that Envy is a coward, and doesn't like fighting, but as soon as Ed's automail arm fails, Envy springs forward to kick him).

At this point, Ed doesn't know exactly what's dealing with, only that these are fearsome opponents – Lust slices up the helmet of Number 48 (Dai Matsumoto and Kenji Nojima) – to stop him squealing about the philosopher's stone – and Envy kills the other half of Slicer (and this occurs right after Ed has refused to kill him/ them). Here, the audience is way ahead of Ed – we have already seen the very creepy and very dangerous homunculi in action. We have also seen that Envy can shape-change (impersonating Father Cornello), which makes the homunculi extra-threatening (because they could pretend to be anybody. And they do).

Indeed, surely one of the reasons that *Fullmetal Alchemist* is such a strong concept in either comic form or animated form is because the villains are so formidable. The homunculi are truly despicable, multi-talented (and richly-drawn) creatures – and they're only one kind of numerous villains and opponents and rivals in the *Fullmetal Alchemist* cosmos! Because you've also got rival alchemists, serial killers, condemned prisoners, and assorted monsters! Not to mention the God-like super-villain of them all, Father.

Style-wise, ep. 8 alters the visual approach a little – the storyboarding (by series director Yasuhiro Irie), for instance, favours many off-centre compositions, leaving plenty of space around the figures. And the fifth laboratory is a largely abstract space (i.e., to provide washes of colour as backgrounds for the busy fights). Unusual colours, too: instead of the expected gray, or black, the laboratory is dirty yellow (*anime* often plumps for unexpected colouration, as if someone has asked, why not have it yellow?[14]). The graphic approach of Japanese animation, with its

13 Minami Takayama (b. 1964) has done everything in voice work and then some: she is Kiki in a 100% classic, *Kiki's Delivery Service*, and one of her famous lead roles is Detective Conan. She was part of the pop act Two-Mix. Meanwhile, the insane Dilandu in *Escaflowne* is a clear forerunner of Envy.
14 The colour picks up with Ed's colour design – his blond hair and gold eyes.

decorative, flattened spaces, is simply a world away from Western animation.

The fifth laboratory scenes were milked too much in the first *Fullmetal Alchemist* series, with the dual duels continuing on for too long (no matter how much we enjoy seeing Ed leaping around like a monkey, and Al making mincemeat of the exasperated Number 66). Episode 8 is better paced, and feels shorter than ep. 20 in series one – partly because it has so much more story to cram in (and it's already left out whole chapters, such as the Yousewell mine, and the railroad adventure).

In a repeat of burning down the library, the homunculi blow up the laboratory. In the earthquake-like sequence outside, Al meets Lt. Ross (Kaori Nazuka) and Sgt Brosch (Yuuki Hayashi); and Envy, in an unexpected gesture, delivers the unconscious Edward to the group (this act reinforces the notion that the homunculi want to keep the *chibi* alchemist alive.

At the end of the show, Zolf Kimbley (Hiroyuki Yoshino)[15] is introduced – he's in jail, his hands are kept apart in wooden stocks, and he rejoices creepily at the sound of explosives – which tells us all we need to know about the Crimson Alchemist! (He appears at the end of the next ep., too).

Episode 9. *Created Feelings*

A show about emotions. The fall-out from the disastrous bust-up at the fifth laboratory takes up most of ep. 9 of the 2nd series of *Fullmetal Alchemist*, with Ed recovering in hospital, and Al doubting his own existence. The episode was all about characters and feelings: Ed and Al drift apart, Al broods, Maria Ross slaps Edward, Winry comes to fix Ed's arm, Winry visits Hughes-san and his family, and eventually the Elrics make-up (as boys do, with some scrapping on the roof). Winry is on hand to beat some sense into Al (with a spanner!), and to weep the tears the boys cannot or will not permit themselves to shed. Winry is the catalyst that enables the lads to express the feelings they've suppressed. (We have to suspend disbelief that Al would believe an opponent who's trying to kill him, who is a total stranger, who's also a hollow suit of armour made out of a convicted serial killer, and who looks like a really outlandish freak! But that's not the point – it's to remind us that Al is still a fourteen year-old kid, who's vulnerable and not sure of himself).

A charming exploration of relationships and the bonds between people, the lack of action in episode 9 (tho' it's glimpsed in flashbacks) isn't missed at all. Because the strength of *Fullmetal Alchemist* isn't wholly in its *shonen animé* action scenes: as with all the greatest *animé* (and *manga*), it's the *characters* that really make these things work.

But, note, episode 9 avoids the issue of the homunculi: Ed has just come face to face with some extremely powerful villains, but there's little discussion of them. Which the viewer might expect: instead, it's all about

15 Yoshi in *Kekkaishi*, Favaro in *Rage of Bahamut*, the Egg-Man in *Berserk*, Galina in *Yatterman Night*, and Meow in *Space Dandy*.

the relationship between the brothers, with the homunculi issue put off for the time being.

However, the episode does contain some elements of the grand narrative of *Fullmetal Alchemist*: Hughes and Mustang discuss Scar; and the show ends with a brief return of Scar, who's dreaming of the Ishbal conflict (in particular of Zolf Kimbley, introduced at the very end of the previous episode). Scar also remembers his fight with the homunculi in the sewers.

Being a relationships and emotions show, the filmmaking is kept simple and straightforward, in the main. Humour sweetens the deal, as ever, and there are several comedic moments (such as: the running gag of milk, of Ed being short, of Winry yelling at Ed, of Armstrong taking off his shirt – again!). And altho' we're watching animated drawings, there is a genuine emotional tug in *Fullmetal Alchemist* – beautifully done in the scene where Winry talks to Hughes, who tells her that boys hope their actions will speak in place of the words they can't find. (This is a great scene in both animated versions of Arakawa's comic).

Episode 10. *Separate Destinations*

This episode climaxes with the first really significant death in the second series of *Fullmetal Alchemist*: Maes Hughes. This is the guy who adores his wife and daughter so much he shows their picture to everyone, and who invites Winry to come stay with them. A doting family man, Hughes is too much of a busybody for his own good, and the villains are onto him, because he is onto them.

The episode opens with two visits to Ed in hospital: an ominous (and bewildering) one from the top man in the country, Führer (King) Bradley, in which he discovers that Alex Armstrong, Maes Hughes and the Elric boys in the room are investigating the fifth laboratory and the philosopher's stone. At this point, we don't know just who Bradley is, tho' we know that he is a crack swordsman (he cut off Ed's spear without Ed even realizing it), and that he is a gruff, formidable presence (later, we see that the Führer is one of the cruellest of the many villains in *Fullmetal Alchemist*). He was played once again by Hidekatsu Shibata.

But notice the blocking of the characters in the scene: Führer Bradley addresses himself mostly to Ed, yet his words are clearly also aimed at Maes Hughes and Alex Armstrong. When he leaves (via the window, to escape his lackeys, in a mock-comical manner), he has his back turned to Hughes, as if he's already decided there and then to dispatch him. (Prior to Bradley's arrival, Ed explains about the homunculi – a discussion delayed from episode 8).

The second visit in episode 10: *Separate Destinations* is from the delightful Winry-chan; the brothers are travelling to see their *sensei*, to ask her about the philosopher's stone. Winry begs to come along, because they'll be travelling through Rush Valley, which's Automail Heaven for her (cue some over-the-top *shojo manga* motifs as Winry raves about automail).

The air of foreboding in *Fullmetal Alchemist* thickens, after Maes Hughes has said goodbye to his family and Winry – this's the last time he sees them. Hughes is putting the puzzle together about the mysterious occurrences at the 5th laboratory, in Ishbal, and elsewhere. The *Fullmetal Alchemist* series' *femme fatale* Lust[16] corners Hughes in a dark office; she tells him, in that too-silky voice, that he has learnt too much; Hughes manages to bury a throwing knife in her skull, but she pierces him in the shoulder with her Edward Scissorhands. Hughes staggers into the hall, to make a call to Roy Mustang, then goes outside, to use a public call box (which's a red, English design). Here Envy (Minami Takayama) closes in, and Hughes doesn't have a chance: Envy takes on the guise of Lt. Ross then his wife Gracia (Tomoe Hanba).[17] Of course that makes him hesitate, and Hughes shoots (but a bullet, as we know, is not enough to stop any of the homunculi! Hesitation or not, Hughes is a dead man).

The demise of Maes Hughes in *Fullmetal Alchemist* is given the full funeral treatment – *animé* is especially fond of scenes in graveyards (with li'l Elicia (Misato Fukuen) weeping, setting off everybody else. The filmmakers draw the line at having it pouring with rain, though). After the service, Roy Mustang resolves to find out who killed his friend Hughes – this story-crammed installment even finds time to flashback to the Ishbal War (newsreel-style), at the beginning of the episode, showing Mustang delivering his flame alchemy, and talking with Hughes about going for the top job, of Führer). Hughes' burial is ironically counterpointed with Ed and Al and Winry on the train, in gold-red sunlight, laughing, carefree, happy to be on the move again. They mention Hughes-san and his wife's cooking (the dialogue is perhaps a little too obviously sweet and ironic, as it's intercut with the cemetery scenes).

Episode 10: *Separate Destinations* is certainly impressive for the sheer amount of information and story it contains (Michihiro Tsuchiya was writer). Not only that, it juggles a number of groups of characters, *and* also reminds us of the central themes, *and* even includes flashbacks, *and* keeps us up-to-date with other characters.

One of the greatest achievements of both *Fullmetal Alchemist animé* series is certainly the scripts – this is *way* beyond an action *shonen* cartoon, which depicts not much more'n endless fights between adversaries that barely alter from show to show.

As this is an installment where an important chara dies, the comedy is reduced, tho' there are still scenes where Ed and Al tremble over meeting their teacher, and the encounter with the Führer is partly played humorously. And Winry enthuses about automail.

---

16 Hughes draws attention to the ourosboros tattoo – well, yes, it *is* silly that Lust walks about with a giant tattoo between her breasts!
17 Taking his cue from a family photo that Hughes had which fell to the ground.

Episode 11. *Miracle At Rush Valley*

Winry Rockbell is the Star of the Week here: she takes centre stage in *Fullmetal Alchemist 2* in episode 11 (broadcast June 14, 2009). Winry is leading many scenes, and is given more to do than in any other episode.

So the Elrics and Winry stop at Rush Valley, paradise for automailers (Winry is in rapture! – it was her idea for detour here). As well as automail (discussed at length in this show), there are plots about giving birth (Winry leads this one), a re-affirmation of objectives (from Winry and Paninya – Bunny in the comic), a flashback to the Elrics burning their family home (with Winry prominent), and several new charas (including a flashback to childhood for Paninya).

In ep. 11: *Miracle At Rush Valley*, the filmmakers depict the humour in the *manga* of *Fullmetal Alchemist* at its broadest and silliest. Numerous visual stylizations are featured (*chibi* figures, flattened, comicbook-style images, heightened gestures, differences of scale and exaggerated, wavy dances of excitement), as well as comical sound effects and humorous vocal performances from the *seiyu*. The themes of *Fullmetal Alchemist* are still lurking in the background,[18] tho' episode 11 is much more about the characters and their relationships. (It is also a light-hearted episode, to counter the suspense and jeopardy in the previous episode).

The thief Paninya stealing Edward's State Alchemist's silver watch in a crowd of folks admiring Ed's automail offers the only comicbook action in this episode (with Ed in hot pursuit): Paninya leads our heroes to a household in the mountains where a young mom is about to give birth. (The alchemical transmutations that Ed and Al are performing now are scaled-up considerably). The chase is played entirely for laughs, and resembles a Harold Lloyd or Buster Keaton sequence from the 1920s, and of course *Lupin III* (it was much longer in the 1st series).

And then the birth: yes, alchemy may be amazing, but it's not a patch beside the miracle of giving birth. Ed, Al, Paninya, Winry and Sadila's husband Lear help out with the birth. The elements of awe and delight in a new life are uppermost for the Elrics: something this extraordinary puts their alchemy into perspective: 'Sugoi! Sugoi! Sugoi!' enthuses Edward. The episode also brings the brothers close to a mother, another stand-in for the mom they still miss deeply.

Episode 11 also thickens the relationship between Ed and Winry, the two most prominent figures in the *Rush Valley* show. When Winry discovers what Ed has scrawled inside his pocket watch, it reminds her of the really important things in life (like treasuring life itself). *Don't forget October, 1911,* Ed wrote – meaning the fateful time when he and Al tried to bring their mother back to life (there is a flashback to the day the Elrics burned down their home, before leaving).

Thus, Winry resolves to make better automail; Winry also helps Paninya to see the error of her crooked ways, and to give thieving a rest, and to get a job. There is also a minor plot about Winry begging the

18 There's a series of 'wanted' posters that includes Scar – but in the background; our heroes walked right past them, without noticing them.

automail engineer Dominic LeCoulte (Shozo Iizuka) to teach her. He refuses, but recommends her to an automailer in the town. So Winry stays behind in Rush Valley, conveniently leaving the Elrics to continue their adventures alone.

❖

In the *Fullmetal Alchemist* series around this point, the writers include images in more detail of the Elrics' father, van Hohenheim (Unshou Ishizuka – he is the voice of Jet Black in *Cowboy Bebop* and Guld in *Macross Plus*).[19] We see the poignant, virtually dialogue-less scenes of Hohenheim leaving the family home, in the early morning. He gives Ed a pointed look, as if he's blaming the child for something (for disrupting his life, perhaps?). He says nothing, he simply leaves.

So the father walks out on his family (into a door which opens onto white light) – an event that has scarred Edward, and he's never forgotten it (or forgiven Hohenheim). Because knitted together with the leavetaking scenes is the traumatic scene of the Elrics' mother Trisha (Yoshino Takamori, who was mom in the first series, too), collapsing to the floor.

Well, in many stories featuring young heroes, the parents are usually off-stage by the time the story begins. Many writers simply want to get on with giving their young characters adventures. And parents just get in the way. So they have to go! *Fullmetal Alchemist* is no different – in that the parents have already departed when the story starts. But there are numerous flashbacks to the mother-world and (later on) to the father-world. To the point where the loss of the mother and the loss/ absence of the father is worried over many times.

And also the actual moment of abandonment: *Fullmetal Alchemist* is Himoru Arakawa's version of *Hansel and Gretel*, the famous Brothers Grimm fairy tale published in *Children's and Household Tales*. Many times the Elrics seem to be re-living that agonizing moment when (1) their mother died, and when (2) their father left them. And the emotional and psychological scars of those times are very deep.

Episode 12. *One Is All, All Is One*

The filmmakers at Bones, Square Enix, Mainichi, Aniplex *et al* are really hitting their stride by this point in the *Fullmetal Alchemist* series. Just look at how much narrative information they pack into this emotional, satisfying episode, *One Is All, All Is One*. This is the one where the Elrics're travelling to Dublith, to meet their old *sensei* (teacher), Izumi Curtis (played by Shoko Tsuda, who was also Curtis in the first series), which triggers off the extended flashback to their training period with Curtis on Jack Island.

The second *Fullmetal Alchemist* series plays the Jack Island experience a little differently from the first series, tho' the essence of surviving in the wilderness and realizing the spiritual and physical inter-connectedness of all things is the same. It's explored in the brilliant 2001 *animé Earth*

19 Unshô Ishizuka (b. 1951) is a veteran of an enormous amount of *animé*, including *Samurai X*, *Gundam*, *Pokémon*, *Hellsing* and *Dragonball Z*.

Maiden Arjuna. This theme certainly comes from *mangaka* Himoru Arakawa's background on a dairy farm, where killing and eating occur all the time (it crops up in her later work, *Silver Spoon* – and the Curtises are of course butchers, and we see images of good, old-fashioned food like meat and milk). So li'l Ed and Al Elric learn how to hunt, and how difficult it can be at first to stab a rabbit so they can eat (especially when it's looking up at them with Cute Disney Eyes!).

Gone are charas in the first *Fullmetal Alchemist* series in the Jack Island sequence, such as the butcher's assistant spooking the kids in a mask, and the homunculus child that Izumi has, who lives on the island. (The first series staged Jack Island at episode 28: *All Is One, One Is All* – ep. 28 out of a 51-episode run. In the 2nd *Fullmetal Alchemist* series, it's ep. 12 out of a 64-episode run, because there's so much more story to tell).

Surviving in the wild is one thing, but it's actually the mystical apprehension of oneness that's really important here (and of course the concept of unity is linked to the idea of exchange in the form of alchemy invented for *Fullmetal Alchemist*). The philosophy of non-separation and non-duality (a.k.a. liberation) has become more popular in the West in the 1990s and 2000s. In the view of non-duality, there is no separation between you and everything else and everyone else (whereas Western philosophy and religion is founded on duality – us and them, good and evil, noodles or rice, Coke or Pepsi).

Himoru Arakawa is likely responding to current fashions in spiritual issues (and putting her own twist on them). However, the notions in religion of non-duality are ancient, too, and can be found in many Oriental religions, including Shintoism, the religion of Japan, and Taoism, Hinduism and Buddhism.

So you can see *Fullmetal Alchemist* as a sort of primer for youngsters about world religion – you have a number of religious paths explored, from the dualism, will-to-power and Frankensteinian and Faustian elements of alchemy (the Western way), to the ascetic, uncompromising, monotheistic religion of Ishbal, with its single god, Ishbal (the Middle Eastern approach), to the Taoist/ Shinto way of the oneness and the flow (the Oriental path).

Episode 12: *One Is All, All Is One* also includes more training sessions with Izumi Curtis – we see the Elric kids trying to land a kick or a punch on her while she reads aloud from a text book and effortlessly bats them away, like Kakashi and the heroic trio in *Naruto* (the image of a teacher as a brilliant martial artist). Cutting back and forth between the past and the present, when the Elrics arrive by railroad they come face to face with Curtis and her tough regime. The first thing she does it is to whack them. Very hard.

Throughout the episode, Izumi Curtis keeps her smile on upside-down, acting perpetually exasperated with the Elric boys (there is also a flashback to Curtis helping stem a river in flood with some alchemy, and the Elric boys begging to become her pupils; as in the *manga*, she rejects their pleas repeatedly, but then gives in). She is the teacher, they are the pupils (Curtis nixes this at the end of the next episode).

The confession about Izumi Curtis's weakened state (she vomits up blood – Japanese animation often goes for the obvious and the crude), leads to the revelations of just how Curtis also opened the gateway of death.[20] Her motives were very understandable – she was trying to bring back her still-born baby to life. The price she paid was that parts of her insides were taken away (it's not specified which parts, but presumably at least the womb).

The flashbacks in episode 12: *One Is All, All Is One* depicting Izumi Curtis using a transmutation circle are very similar to the staging of the Elric brothers trying to resurrect their mother at the top of the series. And in the middle of the circle is a writhing, black mass (bigger than a baby). It's an emotional evocation of the yearning and suffering of motherhood, of the fragility of life, and how close we all are to death, at every moment (even so, it doesn't stop Curtis whacking and kicking the Elric boys at every opportunity! But they were ten year-old kids! She was an adult! They should be whacking her! But never under-estimate the power of social hierarchies in Japanese society: Curtis is the boys' *sensei*, and will always remain thus. They always look up to her as their teacher and guide. These relationships are absolutely foundational in Japanese society, and you find them everywhere in *animé* and *manga*).

So when Izumi Curtis comes up to Ed and Al and gives them a hug (at the end of episode twelve), as they apologize, we half-expect her to step back mid-embrace and hurl them against the wall! (Curtis may be a teacher, but she'd be thrown out of every school in the civilized world for her brutal ways!).

But let's not forget one important thing: the chief teacher of the heroes in *Fullmetal Alchemist* is a woman. That's like Bruce Lee or John Wayne being taught by a woman (!). Well, perhaps not: you can't imagine the Duke or the Little Dragon taking the •••• that Izumi Curtis doles out!

But, yes, Curtis-sensei is a woman, and she's clearly an important figure for *Fullmetal Alchemist manga* creator Himoru Arakawa: because she is the chief mother stand-in for the heroes (that Curtis runs a butcher's shop is also significant – Arakawa grew up on a Hokkaido farm). With their mother dead, the Elrics are also on a mother quest as well as a father quest. And they find Curtis – she is the 'tough love' mother they desperately need.

As if this isn't enough, there are further scenes packed into episode 12: *One Is All, All Is One* – the flashbacks to the Elrics' childhood, for example. Here, the emphasis is on Hohenheim and him leaving the family. Some of the scenes expand on the *manga*. We also see the fateful moment, once more, of Trisha collapsing.

---

20 And scenes at the Gateway of Truth – seen this time from the perspective of Izumi Curtis.

Episode 13. *Beasts of Dublith*

This episode shifts the narrative focus considerably, as in the *manga*, by introducing a new set of situations, and a whole bunch of new characters in the fully alchemical universe, chief among them being the homunculus Greed (Yuichi Nakamura). This is our first, real, close-up look at a homunculus: Greed offers the exposition about just what a homunculus is and what powers they possess (to Ed and Al, tho' separately). He displays the ourosboros mark of the homunculi. Crucially, Greed demonstrates that he can resurrect after a blow to the head which smashes his skull to pulp (much to Al's shock!). And, whaddya know?, that All-Purpose Resurrection Ability will be used again and again in the rest of the *Fullmetal Alchemist* series.

Yes, there is a giant fight between Greed and Edward, but before that there's plenty of talk. For this reason (and others), Greed is given a rather affable characterization, so that he can deliver the explanations in a calm, rather weary manner – he might be your really cool, older brother who's bored by explaining everything to his younger siblings, or the guy at school who gets all the girls (his look, with the natty black, fake fur-lined jacket, the slicked-back hair and the cocky grin, exudes self-confidence, narcissism, fashion-sense, and boredom. He's an *animé* version of the Fonz from *Happy Days*. Greed is great value in both series and the comic – he's an instantly familiar characterization, and beautifully played by Yuichi Nakamura here, and Junichi Suwabe in the 1st series. The animators clearly enjoyed depicting him. In the *manga* he's introduced in the classic manner of a playboy *yakuza*: he's reclining on a couch with girls on each side. That's what you do when you've made it in *animé* and *manga* – you hold court in a hostess bar surrounded by women).

Story-wise, episode 13: *Beasts of Dublith* follows on directly from the previous episode, with the Elrics still at the Curtises' place, and talking over the revelations that Curtis also saw the door beyond death.

Izumi Curtis sends the Elric brothers packing, refusing to teach them anymore (in a scene drenched in sunset light). They are at the railroad station, tails between their legs, when man-of-few-words Sig (Seiji Sasaki, who was Sig in the first series, with his gloriously deep voice), reminds the lads that altho' Curtis has rejected being their *sensei*, that doesn't mean they can't talk anymore. Instantly – this is classic Ed! – Ed turns right around, and the boys hurry back to the butcher's store, demanding to know anything that Curtis can tell them about the philosopher's stone and getting their bodies back. The notion of recovering Al's memories is introduced (by Curtis).

The set-up of the Devil's Nest sequence is a little silly – it has Al wandering off on his own to an assignation with a bunch of strangers. That he doesn't tell Ed or Izumi where he's going, or that they don't go along with him, does stretch credibility quite a bit (but it does give Alphonse an adventure on his own). Bido (Yuji Ueda) the lizard spy has been slinking about several times (this departs a little from the comic, where both Ed and Al beat Bido up when their encounter him on the streets, heading home from the library).

So, anyway, we're introduced to Greed and his crew of misfit chimeras (they include Roa (Tetsu Inada), Bido, Martel, and Dolcetto (Anri Katsu)). One of whom – snake girl Martel (Takako Honda) – dives into Al so she can control him from inside. The *animé* doesn't quite capture the creepiness of that scene in the *Fullmetal Alchemist manga*).

What does Greed want? Why has he captured Al? The secrets to immortality (he says he's 200 years-old, but his body, when it's not transformed into a superhero shell, is normal. Yet Greed already seems weary of life: he craves immortality partly because he is, after all, the embodiment of the impulse of greed – so he wants women... money... and everlasting life!).

Poor Al (chained on the floor in the villains' den), confesses that he doesn't really know how to transmute a soul – it's his brother the bigshot State Alchemist they need to see. Episode 13: *Beasts of Dublith* duly instantly cuts to the Shrimp walking in the street, and he's soon confronting Greed and his shady mob at the Devil's Nest bar. Of course Ed isn't going to give away his secrets just like that! Ed's defiance of Greed and the bad guys is some of the most enjoyably OTT character animation in the 2nd *Fullmetal Alchemist*, with Romi Pak playing it maximum volume and hysteria (and no actors on Earth can do hysteria like Japanese voice actors!). Thus, in a reprise of the duel in episode 8: *The Fifth Laboratory*, there's a lengthy fight between Ed and Greed. Edward, nearly beaten, works out how to get the better of Greed (Ed uses alchemy a lot more here, compared to the 5th lab duel).

Izumi Curtis shows up to finish off Greed, with the dramatic entrance that artist Himoru Arakawa had wanted to use for a long time, when Curtis announces loudly: 'I'm a housewife!' The Devil's Nest scenes contain some of the finest duels in *Fullmetal Alchemist 2*, with writer Hiroshi Ohnogi, storyboard artist Michio Fukuda and episode director Keiko Oyamada coming up with some superbly accomplished gags.

❖

Meanwhile, in these densely-plotted, 22-minute animated shows, the audience is kept abreast of Scar and his recovery in an enclave of Ishbalians (following his explosive encounter with Gluttony and Lust). We meet an Ishbalian guru (Yuzuru Fujimoto), who wisely advises Scar to give up his project of vengeance against the State Alchemists, and a hapless loser called Loki (the 2nd series elided the chapters in the *manga* featuring Lt. Loki (Kazuki Yao) and the mining town, partly because the first *animé* series had already covered that ground in depth. But that also makes the highly unlikely pairing up of Scar and Loki too rushed. (Loki is still the same weasel, however, one of those people doomed to live in the shadow of others).

Another sequence cut down from the comic in this episode is the formation of Roy Mustang's team and the annoucement that they're transferring to Central City (the *manga* includes more of each character, adding some characterizations. Liza Hawkeye, for instance, is depicted at the firing range, as expected).

In the comic, Breda was playing *Shogi*; in a scene with General Grumman, a veteran general who also fancies the top job of Führer, Mustang and Grumann are playing chess.

Episode 14. *Those Who Lurk Underground*

This episode (*Chika ni Hisomu Monotachi* = *Those Who Lurk Underground*, broadcast July 5, 2009), follows directly on from the end of episode 13: it introduces us at last to the super-villain of the second *Fullmetal Alchemist* run, the homunculus Father, in a major set-piece; and Alphonse experiences a vision of the Gateway of Truth, in a marvellous montage of surreal imagery.

Much of episode 14: *Those Who Lurk Underground* is dominated by Führer Bradley, who is revealed as a super-nasty villain, a combination of Joseph Stalin (i.e., a corrupt dictator who abuses his power all the time), and the meanest samurai warrior ever. That Bradley is in control of the military *and* all of Amestris is very scary indeed (this is a military regime – no elected Prime Ministers or Presidents or officials to be found).

And then, in the final five minutes of episode 14: *Those Who Lurk Underground*, Führer Bradley is revealed to be second-in-command to the all-powerful Father. So if Bradley is a repulsively vicious villain, what does that make Father?! Thus, the *Fullmetal Alchemist* series waits until it's a quarter of the way thru its run b4 revealing the arch-villain behind it all.

In the second series of *Fullmetal Alchemist*, the raid on Greed's Devil's Nest operation plays differently: now characters such as the slinky snake-woman Martel are introduced and then dispatched with an alarming rapidity. In the first *Fullmetal Alchemist anime* series, the lovely Martel was kept around for longer, forming an uneasy alliance with the Elric brothers; they were never quite sure of her, though their destinations were the same at times, and they journeyed together. Martel was potentially a richer character than some in *Fullmetal Alchemist*, but she still ended up skewered by the psychopath Führer Bradley inside Al's armour (another of *many* grotesque murders in both *Fullmetal Alchemist* series).

The episodes featuring Devil's Nest (13: *Beasts of Dublith* and 14: *Those Who Lurk Underground*) are some of the most appallingly violent in either of the *Fullmetal Alchemist* TV series, with a truly alarming, even sickening amount of brutality and bloodshed. Führer Bradley enters the fray with his collection of razor-sharp swords and his lightning speed, and chops to pieces everyone in his path, including poor Martel, shut inside Al's hollow armour. Bradley doesn't only kill Martel, he also makes mincemeat of all of the other chimeras (for Al, a 14 year-old kid tied up and pinned to the ground, it must be really disquieting. Having someone killed inside you can't feel great).

The Devil's Nest episodes, however, redeem (some of) their sick violence by introducing a major character absent from the first *Fullmetal Alchemist* series, where his role was largely taken up by Dante: Father, played by Iemasa Kayumi (who also voices the narrator). From the outset, Father is introduced as a shadowy, ambiguous figure, all-powerful like an emperor, and the super-villain behind the homunculi and so much else that occurs in Amestris.

We don't know all of that yet, but we do know that Father is a very powerful character,[21] because all of the homunculi baddies defer to him. And also he is able to manipulate people and events without moving – one of the surest signs of power in cinema (and in real life). Father is a guy who doesn't have to lift a finger, he just thinks something and it happens. (Father is a character fans of the *Fullmetal Alchemist manga* have been eager to see in animation. He doesn't disappoint).

So we see that Greed has been captured by Führer Bradley, following the endless fight sequence where Bradley slashes Greed to bits numerous times (and he still doesn't die – that's one of the attributes of the homunculi, introduced by Greed in the previous episode). In the *Fullmetal Alchemist manga*, Greed is crucified in Father's lair: in the *animé*, that potentially offensive image (which was censored in the *manga* overseas), is dropped in favour of Greed being chained (offensive for overseas, that is, but not in Japan).

Also revealed in the Father episode *Those Who Lurk Underground* is that the homunculi are linked to Father, and also represent or embody aspects of himself (the connection being the chief MacGuffin in the *Fullmetal Alchemist* world, philosopher's stones). They are his children, aspects of his soul (the splitting up of Lord Voldemort's soul into seven parts in the *Harry Potter* series has affinities here). That he names them after the seven sins is another instance where Japanese artists use Western religion (the Seven Deadly Sins are Pride, Greed, Lust, Envy, Gluttony, Anger and Sloth), without necessarily taking up the context or meanings of those religious tropes (also used in the wonderful *Seven Deadly Sins manga* by Nakaba Suzuki and the *animé Sin: The Seven Mortal Sins*).

We were introduced to Lust and Gluttony first (one of *animé*'s odder couples!), and they are here now, deferring to Father; ditto with Envy (resentful and fretful as ever). And Führer Bradley, too: they are all pawns of Father. (We see images of Sloth, for about the first time, but the final homunculus, Pride, is being saved for later. However, Pride does appear at the end of episode 14: *Those Who Lurk Underground*, in its human form, as Selim).

When you introduce the major villain in an action-adventure fiction, you usually have him/ her doing something really nasty, that reveals their evil personality. So, Greed, after defying Father yet again (as he had done 100 years before), is lowered into a vat of something very hot and deadly

---

21 That he's depicted in hi-key lightning, not the expected gloom, enhances his ambiguity.

like lava and destroyed, his essence boiled up and condensed into a red liquid in a wine glass, which Father slurps down. The process somewhat resembles historical alchemy, tho' with live humans (or in this case, homunculi), as the substance which the alchemical process utilizes (as well as Viktor Frankenstein and the novel *Frankenstein*, the laboratory scene also evokes vampires (with the red, goopy philosopher's stone dripping into a wine glass at the end of the process) and cannibalism.) Greed was too good to cast aside, so Arakawa brought him back later.

Throughout the Father sequence, the super-villain leads the scene dramatically (as super-villains tend to do), issuing commands and admonitions, while the homunculi are gathered around him, all deferring to him (only Greed remains the rebel). The visual effects animation in the Father and Greed sequence is stunning.

❖

Episode 14: *Those Who Lurk Underground* is certainly a *tour-de-force* of action-based animation, yet the most energy and time (and Yen) was spent on the very impressive sequence (one of the finest in the whole series), involving Al flashing back to the moment when he lost his body (sparked off by the murder of Martel inside the suit of armour). The animators have been told by the producers: *go nuts!* And they do, serving up healthy doses of the ending of *Akira* and trippy visuals *à la 2001: A Space Odyssey*, with Al swirling and speeding thru an abstract, post-death realm with its ominous gateways, giant eyes, and grasping black hands and arms. The filmmakers stuff the sequence with numerous cinematic tricks and visual effects, including Al seeing his life zooming past him as a ribbons of celluloid, extreme differences in scale, panicking close-ups of Al, the grinning demon/ god/ presence as a negative shadow, images of Ed during the ritual, his mother, Al's body reaching out to his soul, and an inventive use of white space.

So episode 14: *Those Who Lurk Underground* is also an Alphonse Elric episode (as if making up for the previous episodes, where Edward Elric has dominated proceedings – understandably, as he's a major diva! But Ed does appear to help patch Al together afterwards, and they discuss what happened). And how weird is the *Fullmetal Alchemist* animé when you think about it: Al is a soul attached to a hollow suit of armour who's had a snake-woman stabbed to death *inside him* – killed by a homunculus who's also the Führer of all Amestris! – and it takes place after a giant battle in an underground sewer.

When you put all of the elements together in this scene – the suit of armour with a boy's soul fused with it + the chimera of a woman fused with a snake + the homunculus sadist and political tyrant + the fictional country of Amestris and the sewers + a major out-of-body spiritual experience – you have a pretty far-out example of fantasy. And this is of course only a tiny percentage of the genuine strangeness that the *Fullmetal Alchemist* franchise features!

Fullmetal Alchemist, the second TV series (2009-10).
This page and following pages.

鋼の錬金術師
FULLMETAL ALCHEMIST

see you next time

Episode 15. *Envoy From the East*

This is the Chinese episode, when four characters from Xing are introduced *en masse*. First up is little Mei Chang (a.k.a. May Chan), wonderfully played by Mai Goto, a cute moppet with a pet panda (Xiao Mei) on her shoulder (which everyone calls a cat in the comic – it's a common gag in *manga* to mis-identify animals). A bright, round face, giant, black eyes, long black hair (braided), and an irrepressible energy – Mei is certainly good value. *Mangaka* Himoru Arakawa puts sweet-natured Mei with Scar and Loki, instead of the Elrics as expected, so it's all about contrasts – the giant, hulking, taciturn man who's eternally bitter and bent on vengeance on an epic scale is paired with the sweet, little, Chinese girl. And what's the first thing that Mei does? She heals a wound[1] on Scar's thigh (using her alkahestry and her throwing stars). Mei is after the secret of Amestrisian alchemy and immortality, to take back to Xing (a familiar trope in Chinese legends), so pairing Mei up with Scar actually has thematic and motivational links.

The second bunch of Chinese (Xingese) characters introduced in episode 15: *Envoy From the East* are the young Prince-in-exile, Ling Yao (the brilliant Mamoru Miyano), and his bodyguards, Fuu (Katsunosuke Hori), an old, grey beard, and his granddaughter, Ran (Lan) Fan (Nana Mizuki, best-known in *animé* circles as Hinata in *Naruto*).[2] Mamoru Miyano (b. 1983) has appeared in many famous animations – he was Raito Yagami in *Death Note* (a truly remarkable performance in a masterpiece of animation), and the twin brothers in *Vampire Knight.*[3]

From the outset, Ling Yao irritates the hell out of Edward, with his nonchalant, carefree, whatever attitude: he's portrayed as a Chinese drifter, a well-meaning but seemingly dopey vagabond (he mooches off the Elrics – this is a running gag, and he latches onto the alchemists). But when Ling mentions the philosopher's stone, that gets the Elrics' attention right away, and they immediately walk away. (The Elrics have returned to Rush Valley to see Winry to have Ed's automail repaired; there are the inevitable scenes where Winry explodes in fury, yells 'baka!' lots of times, and sets to work. But Winry's delighted that she's got the opportunity to tag along to Central City. It's true that we have now gotten into repetitions of the Fixing The Automail motif by episode 15).

Thus, both Mei Chang and Ling Yao bring with them alchemical issues: Mei practises 'alkahestry', the Xinigese/ Chinese form of alchemy (which uses the *chi* in the natural world – linked to *feng shui* and the 'dragon lines' of Chinese geomancy). We see Mei healing Scar with a

1 We see Scar battling an old alchemist (Giolio Comanche, the 'Silver Alchemist') in the opening scene and killing him.
2 Nana Mizuki was Wrath in the first series. Mizuki (b. 1980) is a big music star in Nippon, selling out a week of concerts at the Budokan. Mizuki has huge credits in *animé*, including the voice of Cure Blossom in *Heartcatch Precure!*, Moka in *Rosario and Vampire*, Tsubasa Kazanari in *Symphogear*, Namo in *Love Hina*, and Fate Testarossa in *Magical Girl Lyrical Nanoha*. Mizuki specializes in cute, sweet, innocent and timidly-voiced characters, which she duly delivers here.
3 Miyano has also appeared in *Gundam, Hunter x Hunter, Pokémon, Yu-Gi-Oh!, Zipang, 009 Re; Cyborg, Soul Eater* (as Death the Kid), *Steins Gate, Wolf's Rain, Tekken, Star Driver, Bungaku Shojo, Nobunaga the Fool, Eureka Seven, Inazuma Eleven Go* and *Dog Days*. Miyano has also sung theme songs.

transmutation circle drawn on the ground, with throwing stars embedded at key points in the circle (this will be re-used a few times in the *Fullmetal Alchemist* series).

Mei Chang has travelled to Amestris to research alchemy; meanwhile, Ling Yao tells the Elrics that he has crossed the desert to Amestris for a similar purpose, tho' his quest is tied to helping his clan (Himoru Arakawa uses the old chestnut from a million Chinese, historical movies of the ailing Emperor and the quest for immortality. That is, Ling hopes to enrich his clan's prospects by discovering the secret of eternal life and gifting it to the Emperor).

❖

Enough with the back-story and the exposition! What about the drama and the action in episode 15: *Envoy From the East?!* Well, inevitably, the filmmakers stage giant fights for both Elric brothers as they're pitted against Lan Fan and Fu. (The pretext for the bust-up is swiftly forgotten (and it's flimsy anyway), and it's all-out, broad action as Ed and Al duel the masked, black-suited ninjas all over Rush Valley – busting it up in the process). The upshot is that both sets of Xingese characters tag along with our heroes, and all roads now are leading to Central City (where Col. Mustang and his crew are also headed – there is a brief couple of scenes involving Barry the Chopper attacking Liza Hawkeye (he's no match her), and being interrogated by Mustang and his cronies).[4]

As to the animation in episode 15: *Envoy From the East*, it's marvellous – the filmmakers are really stretching themselves by now in the run of *Fullmetal Alchemist* series, with some beautifully staged set-pieces and very inventive multiple imagery. For instance, the exposition about Xing (to the East), the clans and the Emperor, and Drachma (Russia) to the North (with Briggs Mountain prominent), and Ling Yao as a Prince, features some impressive montages of maps, landscapes and picturebook illustrations (with Edward and Ling providing the voiceover explanations).

Indeed, no one can miss that part of episode 15 is all about setting things up for future episodes with exposition and new characters. To counter the amount of talk and explanation, the duels with the Elrics are exaggerated. And the show opens with a furious duel at night by a river to re-introduce Scar, as he takes on the alchemist Giolio Comanchi.

Episode 16. *Footsteps of a Comrade-In-Arms*

This is the first episode in the second series of *Hagane no Renkinjutsushi* which seems less inspired and less involving than any of the previous episodes (on some viewings). It is a talky episode, with little action (much of it is about setting up the following eps.), which focusses on the aftermath and the consequences of the death of Maes Hughes. More than any other character, Hughes-san and his death is given a huge

---

4 In one of the warehouses – a nod to the ghost story in the first series and the *omake*.

amount of screen time. We see Winry, Ed and Al being stricken to the core by it (as they arrive back from Rush Valley, in Central City); and the Colonel lying about it to the Elrics (they find out from Lt. Ross – the sequence of events is altered from the *manga*).

However, so much running time is allotted to Maes Hughes' demise because it's the pebble in the pond that sets up the ripples of the beginnings of the investigation by Col. Mustang and his cohorts into the nefarious goings-on inside the military machine. Thus, there are scenes btn Mustang and Armstrong, Mustang and Hawkeye, Mustang and Sheska, Mustang and the Elrics, etc.

Meanwhile, the homunculi are infiltrating the military in Central City. Envy's ability to shape-change has him impersonating officers (such as Focker), and Lust's million-dollar feminine curves are employed to seduce lackeys close to Colonel Mustang (Lust appears in a restaurant as Jean Havoc's new girlfriend).

Meanwhile in episode 16: *Footsteps of a Comrade-in-Arms* (this is a very busy episode!), Vato Falman (Kenji Hamada) has the unenviable task of looking after the serial killer Number 66 – playing chess with him in a dingy backroom, when he'd much rather be out at night chopping people to pieces! And Ling Yao has gone missing; his *shinobi* bodyguards hunt him down (he winds up collapsed on the street, gasping for food – which's how the *manga* introduces him). The homunculi stir things up by having Lt. Ross arrested for Hughes' murder (this plot strand is one of the weaker parts of Himoru Arakawa's *manga* structurally).

The death of Maes Hughes is also employed to harden the resolve of the Elric brothers on their quest (we see selected flashbacks to Hughes' warmest moments). His widow Gracia tells the boys not to give up but to keep moving forward (that's writer Himoru Arakawa's over-riding *mantra* in the *Fullmetal Alchemist* series: *keep moving forward!*). Gracia tells them that if they give up now, Hughes will've died in vain. (Ed beats himself up for getting Hughes involved; but his wife says he was a meddler anyway).

Meanwhile, to reassure us that everything will be OK, that Hughes didn't die for nothing, the *anime* lavishes the goldenest, yellowest sunlight on our heroes for the scenes of them sinking into sorrow. Every scene is bathed in gold, including interiors. It's not raining, it's not grey, it's not overcast, it's not night, it's not shadowy. You could link this visual approach to the Japanese habit of finding beauty in everything, including in death and in melancholy (Japanese animation is full of beautiful deaths).

Episode 17. *Cold Flame*

As in episode 16: *Footsteps of a Comrade-in-Arms,* in episode 17: *Cold Flame* our heroes, Edward and Alphonse Elric, are *not* driving the action. Instead, they are *reacting* to events. Prime mover in these episodes of *Fullmetal Alchemist* is Roy Mustang. He's so hot on the tail of the killer of his friend Maes Hughes that he's manipulating people and incidents – keeping the Elrics in the dark, not telling Alex Armstrong or Liza Hawkeye more'n they need to know, and keeping his plans to himself.

Why? Because Colonel Mustang realizes that the enemy is within the military, and that blabbing to the wrong person might be dangerous. Someone is moving against the military, by instigating the Lt. Ross victim plot, and Mustang needs to out-manœuvre them. It's easy to see why Mustang is popular with fans of the *Fullmetal Alchemist* franchise – a handsome, canny operator with a cool alchemical technique (a wall of flame at the click of a finger!), the kind of guy that women around him love, who seems to sail thru life effortlessly. Only occasionally does Mustang let the arrogant, cool mask fall, and in private acknowledge that things are getting to him. Mustang is what Ed Elric might grow up to become if he stays in the military (they share many attributes – hence they are always bickering).

❖

The framing of Lt. Ross for the murder of Maes Hughes in episode 17: *Cold Flame* is given a little more screen time in the second alchemical series: now we see poor Ross being taken into custody and interrogated by Colonel Henry Douglas (but nobody asks the glaringly obvious question: *Why*? What is Ross's *motive* in killing Maes Hughes? It reveals the military to be as dumb as ever. Because Douglas *et al* are working under orders from higher-ups who in turn are commanded by Bradley and Envy). In the 2nd *Fullmetal Alchemist* series, Ross is a more sympathetic, less nagging and neurotic personality than she is in the first series.

Number 66's (Hideyuki Umezu) rescue mission of Lieutenant Ross from the jail is an amusing sequence (thankfully, he's had orders not to chop anyone up!). There's a lot more comedy in this part of the story in the second *Fullmetal Alchemist* series compared to the first series. Also, when Roy Mustang finally corners Ross in an alley and vaporizes her, we know now that there is some subterfuge going on, because throughout the episode Mustang has been acting oddly, orchestrating events behind the scenes (and Number 66 is a very unlikely rescuer for Ross, tho' this is partly why he's been retained in the story. He also sets Ling Yao free (he's been imprisoned for being an illegal alien.) Ling is soon mooching off Vato Falman, and sending smoke signals to summon his bodyguards).

Even so, when the Elrics stumble onto the scene, and see Col. Mustang standing there, apparently gloatingly, over Lt. Ross's charred remains, it's understandable that Edward, full of fury, hurls himself at the officer. Only later will it be revealed that Mustang has been pulling strings in the background to have Ross whisked off to safety.

Thus, the scene where Major Armstrong turns up at the hotel to hustle Edward Elric away is more plausible in the *animé* than in the *manga* (there's also a scene where Mustang says, 'good, now everyone's out of the way').

The *Fullmetal Alchemist* series explores interesting areas when it has the Elric lads stopped in their tracks, when they lose their *oomph*, when events seem too big for them to know what to do next. In ep. 17, they are depicted sitting around in their hotel room in Central City, stumped by the murder of Maes Hughes, and the destruction of the 5th laboratory. The ceiling fan turns… Ed lies on the bed, listless… It's great that the *Fullmetal Alchemist* series has enough time for such scenes of weariness and *ennui*, so it doesn't have to rush on to the next set-piece or action scene.

Having agreed to adapt the comic accurately (partly to distinguish itself from the 1st series), the second *Fullmetal Alchemist* series is sometimes scuppered by its ambitions. The subterfuge in the military involving Mustang, Ross and the faked death is probably something that an *animé* adaptation would alter in the journey to the screen. But it does the job of shaking up the narrative, and allowing dramatic changes of scene (such as the Eastern desert).

Episode 18. *The Arrogant Palm of a Small Human*

We are still enmeshed in the behind-the-scenes schemes of Colonel Mustang to weed out the people behind the murder of Maes Hughes, and the military's tiresome scapegoating of poor Lt. Ross for the crime. Which means our heroes are still *reacting* to events, and not pushing the story forward: they have lost their impetus, stricken into inertia by Hughes-san's demise. So Mustang is the primary motivator of these episodes, dramatically, with the homunculi counteracting with other tactics, such as sending in a henchman (the soul of Barry the Chopper in Number 66's body).

Dragged away from Winry and Alphonse (rather unconvincingly), Edward is taken to Resembool *en route* for the desert by Alex Armstrong, Heyman Breda (Biichi Satou), Fuu (Ling's bodyguard) and co.: the group visits Xerxes, one of the fabled origins of alchemy in *Fullmetal Alchemist*, and Lt. Ross is revealed to be alive and well (cueing the inevitable flashbacks to explain how Roy Mustang's ruse played out – now we see events from the perspective of Mustang *et al*).

What's impressive here, though, is the stupendous background art (by studios Green, Kusanagi, Rourke 07, Feng Animation, Beijing Golden Pinasters and Telecom), in particular in the evocation of Xerxes itself (as an Ancient Roman and Greek city fallen to ruin), and the desert, with hi-key colours of lemon yellow, blue and white.[5] The art of *Fullmetal Alchemist 2* is truly gorgeous to contemplate, with deeply saturated colours, and, towards the end of ep. 18, yet another red-orange-gold sunset (to tie in with the resurgence of our hero, Ed Elric – gold being his signature hue).

It makes sense that a trouble-maker like Edward E. would be whisked away from Central City – after his melancholy has worked thru, we know he would kick up a fuss with the Powers That Be (i.e., the military), until he got to the bottom of Maes Hughes' murder. (We find out later the signific-ance of this hall and alchemical circle).

5 Some of the images are taken right out of the *manga*, such as the iconic drawing of the ruined temple with its alchemical circle carved on the wall.

The second *Fullmetal Alchemist* series plays much of the *manga*'s story differently from the first *animé* series at this point. All sorts of characters (such as Ling Yao and his Xingese bodyguards) are included (so it's Fuu who takes Armstrong and Ed into the desert, and who crosses the desert to Xing with Lt. Ross, and it's Ling who explains about the deception to Winry and Al. It doesn't wholly make sense – we know that Fu, like Lan Fan, is absolutely devoted to the service of Ling; we can also guess that Ling would demand something in return for loaning out his bodyguard for an extended period).

Crucially, Ed Elric gets back his mojo, so to speak, his *oomph,* his Ed-ness, in Xerxes: he resolves (in a lengthy but important monologue) to keep moving forward (again with Himoru Arakawa's central *mantra*!). Gripping his robotic arm, he asserts his desire to fulfil what he started out to do with his brother Alphonse. Thus are the motivations and the goals of the central heroes of *Fullmetal Alchemist* affirmed again.

Good! The *Fullmetal Alchemist* series is much more entertaining when Edward Elric is in full flight and bursting with energy, and grabbing the dramatic reins, and not lying on the couch in darkness in a rented room like a depressed, teenage emo.

❖

Meanwhile, other narrative elements're included in episode 18: *The Arrogant Palm of a Small Human,* such as the appearance of some Ishbalians, and the revelation of the person who killed Winry Rockbell's Doctor parents: Scar. The serial killer, Barry the Chopper, is at large (let loose by the homunculi – now he's a crazed, Neanderthal ape), and Number 66, the hollow suit of armour, and Vato Falman, are also in the fray: there's an impressive sequence where Number 66 comes face-to-face with Barry the Chopper, realizing that the hulk has his body! The indignity of it sends Number 66 into a frenzy – he wants to chop Barry up (but the military won't allow that). Number 66 offers a reasonable argument: I should be able to cut up my own body, shouldn't I?!

So the homunculi and the military are closing in on each other, as the net tightens (on either side, with both sides thinking they've got the jump on the other). Episode 18: *The Arrogant Palm of a Small Human* climaxes with a classic cliffhanger, as Liza Hawkeye, operating her sniper rifle in a nearby tower, confronts the terrifying form of Gluttony looming out of the shadows behind her. She shoots. He collapses. But then, to Hawkeye's horror, the beast judders back to life... (This is not the last time that the Princess of the Military is threatened by a deadly enemy).

A busy, story-packed episode, then, aided by outstanding artwork and animation. Even if the Lt. Ross shenanigans stretch credibility in the *manga,* the animated adaptation keeps it lively with first-rate art and filmmaking. You could make a convincing argument for *Fullmetal Alchemist 2* being the most visually ravishing of *any* recent *animé* series, despite fierce competition from other TV shows.

Episode 19. *Death of the Undying*

Uwaaah!

This episode is one of the finest in the second *Fullmetal Alchemist* series, and one of the best in any recent *animé* series. It's got the lot: incredible action and visual effects, wonderful music, high drama, hysteria and screaming, goofy comedy, crucial revelations (about the homunculi), two deaths of minor charas, and even, to top the whole show, Ed Elric encountering Hohenheim in Resembool.

This show climaxes the hunting down Maes Hughes' killer sequence of the past few episodes, led by Roy Mustang. The episode is filled with big, very impressive action and duels, involving Lust vs. Jean Havoc and Roy Mustang, Number 66 vs. Barry the Chopper, Gluttony vs. Liza Hawkeye (and also Mustang and Cain Furey (Tetsuya Kakihara)), and Lust vs. Alphonse Elric and Hawkeye. One duel after another, featuring our heroes up against seriously psychopathic villains (Edward is away in Resembool, *en route* to Xerxes). Many of the scenes are played very loud and very passionately, with Hawkeye, Number 66, Mustang and Alphonse becoming operatically emotional. The scenarios, however, fully justify this shift up to the highest gear of the drama.

And the threat for the heroes is now life-or-death: this outing features the deaths of two characters, with our heroes only just managing to escape. The show features numerous attacks and repeated attempts to kill – guns are unloaded into homunculi and villains, and several characters are trying their darnedest to kill: Number 66, Barry the Chopper, Lust, Gluttony, Mustang, Havoc, Hawkeye, etc.

The second series of *Fullmetal Alchemist* dispatched the formidable villain Lust as per the *manga* by Himoru Arakawa. The filmmakers of the first animated series of *Fullmetal Alchemist* rightly saw Lust as an sub-stantial (and entertaining) opponent worth keeping around for most of the duration of the series. The second series plays it much closer to the *manga* by Arakawa, so Lust is kllled by Col. Mustang, as in the comic.

Well, one can understand Jean Havoc (Yuji Ueda) being enamoured of *femme fatale* Lust and her giant, bouncing boobs (in this serious, climactic face-off between the military and a major villain, the filmmakers still find time for goofy comedy – so they depict Havoc confessing manically that he loves big busts – and Lust happily bounces her *oppai* in response. The breasts gag functions to lighten the mood a tad, to soften up the audience before the very brutal violence and death scenes. It's a time-honoured device – you see horror movies using humour before scares and jeopardy all the time. For some fans, introducing comedy in the midst of highly dramatic scenes undermines them. Does it? Not here: the gag of breasts going *boing* doesn't detract from some really intense drama).

In this scene, Colonel Mustang fires repeatedly at Lust (yes, it's a man shooting at a woman at point blank range – he fires as soon as Lust quips that she'd wished she'd been the one to nail Mustang's friend Maes Hughes). In fury at Lust stabbing Jean Havoc, Mustang rips out the philosopher's stone from Lust's chest (which she foolishly shows him – will villains never learn?!), hoping to use its amplifying powers to revive Havoc (we don't see this, however, we cut away).

As for action, a striking moment occurs when Lust gloats over dispatching Liza Hawkeye's commanding officer, and Hawkeye, in teary frenzy, unloads every round in every weapon she possesses at the freak in the black dress that keeps coming back to life (to see Hawkeye, usually so calm and reserved, at this peak of hysteria is startling). Even more distressing, perhaps, is to see Hawkeye give up, collapsing to her knees; here, Al plays a significant role in encouraging Hawkeye to get up and flee. (Hawkeye makes a mistake that many heroes do when confronting an enemy – believing what they say. The rule in action-adventure movies and television is: don't listen to someone who's trying to kill you!).

In episode 19: *Death of the Undying* key figures from the military like Roy Mustang and Liza Hawkeye come face-to-face with the despicable homunculi for the first time. Alphonse informs Mustang and Hawkeye that they are dealing with homunculi (in the car). So when Havoc and Mustang see the ourosboros tattoo, they have an idea what they're dealing with (but it's still a huge learning curve for Mustang, Havoc and Hawkeye. They have to get to grips with a new very powerful threat which also appears to be unkillable).

Episode 19: *Death of the Undying* climaxes with an extraordinarily violent duel of fire and rage between Roy Mustang and Lust (Lust moves into the large transmutation chamber, to confront Alphonse and Hawkeye, assuming that Mustang is a goner – will bad guys never learn?!).

Not once does Roy Mustang ignite his alchemical fire to burn Lust alive, but many, many times (Alphonse Elric creates a large wall for him and Liza Hawkeye to shelter behind). The music is raging, Lust is screaming, the sound mixing team are adding twenty channels of fire, crackle, smoke and whooshing sound effects, the special effects crew add waves of orange, molten flames, and the scene becomes among the most apocalyptic in the whole *Fullmetal Alchemist* series – in *manga* or *animé* form. Well, I guess a major villain such as Lust does deserve a major send-off, but this becomes really intense, really vicious.[6] (Mustang will be consumed by a similarly hysterical fury when he tries to kill Envy in episode 53: *Flame of Vengeance*).

There's a minor but important beat in this part of the *Fullmetal Alchemist* series: Führer Bradley turns up at the laboratory. It's been revealed now that Bradley is a homunculus, and a *very* nasty piece of work. He's the sort of guy you'd cheer to see torn apart using ropes attached to horses then burnt to nothing with lava.[7] Bradley sneaks into the building, but hides around a corner while Lust is being incinerated by the Flame Alchemist. That Bradley *doesn't* go to her aid suggests the *limitat-ions* of the power of the homunculi (and also that Bradley probably

---

6 However, in the world of *Fullmetal Alchemist*, we know that dispatching one villain isn't going to do it! Because there are *loads* of villains! The demise of each homunculus, however, is always a *major* sequence.

7 Or decapitated by a guillotine. Repeatedly. Then burnt to ash.

wants to keep his identity secret from Mustang and co. Of course, he could kill Mustang,[8] Hawkeye and Al, but there's also the issue of the 'sacrifices', which Lust has hinted at a few times. Only much, much later will it be explained just what those 'sacrifices' will be).

Another minor scene, with its own sad significance, sees the serial killer Number 66 being chopped up by Lust, and then erased from existence by Barry the Chopper's near-dead body with its lab rat brain. It's a grotesque form of quasi-suicide, a twist on the *Frankenstein* mythology which Arakawa has mined many times.

❖

And then, at the end of this full-on, incendiary (literally!) episode of *Fullmetal Alchemist*, Edward Elric encounters someone unexpected... He's returned to Resembool from his sojourn in the desert and Xerxes, and goes to pay his respects to his mom in the graveyard on his own on a sunny afternoon (and probably to call on Pinako). And who should be standing there, in front of his mother's resting place? Only van Hohenheim, Ed's father!

'It can't be!' Ed mutters: the filmmakers cut in closer and closer to Ed's wide eyes and those tiny, golden irises. Stretching this important emotional moment out, the animators finish up with a slow turn from van Hohenheim, to look at his son (and the editors fold in some flashbacks to the last moment that Edward saw his pa, when he walked out of the family home on that fateful morning many years before.[9] So the episode ends on another cliffhanger – in its way, this is more gripping than the Gluttony vs. Liza Hawkeye duel in the previous episode, because we know that lovely Hawkeye isn't going to be sacrificed). Hohenheim's appearance also connects up with the previous trip to Xerxes – because Hohenheim is the 'golden man' who brings alchemy to Amestris.

Episode 20. *Father Before the Grave*

This is among the most satisfying episodes in the second *Fullmetal Alchemist* animé series, because it focusses mainly on Edward and Alphonse Elric, on their past, on their parents, on their taboo-breaking alchemical transmutation (and subsequent mutilation), and what they're going to do to set things to rights. In its way, *Father Before the Grave* (*Bozen no Chichi*, broadcast August 16, 2009), is the most important episode of the whole series, because of how it explores the characters of Ed and Al, and concentrates on their psychology and emotions. (This is very much a *writer's* show, too, an episode in which the writing takes precedence over every other element of the filmmaking, including the acting. It was written by Yoneki Tsumura).

So all of the stuff with homunculi and fearsome assailants like Scar and Führer Bradley, and Roy Mustang and the military, are put into the

8 Though Mustang, now in full flight with his flam alchemy, might be a challenge even for Bradley.
9 Van Hohenheim looks pretty much the same. We don't know at this point that Hohenheim has a very long life, stretching back to the Renaissance. The designers have ensured that father and son look very much alike.

background of the fully alchemical show for the moment, and the action and the fights're put on hold, too. The change of pace and tone from the previous episodes is striking – the Roy Mustang vs. Maes Hughes' killers storyline is played out (for the time being), and it's back to Ed and Al, who're absolutely the centre of this amazing fantasy, *animé* TV series.

The key scene in *Father Before the Grave* is where Ed and Al talk on the stairs of their hotel in Central City, in the final segment of *Father Before the Grave*: they are re-united in a common purpose: Alphonse has one of his longest speeches in the entire *Fullmetal Alchemist* series, as he tells Edward of his determination to regain his body (being relatively quiet for so long, it makes Al's monologue all the more powerful).[10] Thus their goals are re-stated.

The filmmakers also weave in some flashbacks to the moment when Alphonse Elric lost his body, and to Edward, maimed and bleeding, at the transmutation circle in Resembool. The enigmatic figure of Truth/ God/ Death/ whatever is there, too (he appears in a vivid nightmare Ed has – which also cleverly links to Al's worries, voiced to Winry, about his body – we go into the nightmare from Al's point-of-view but come out of it as a nightmare experienced by Ed).

The scenes between Edward Elric and his father van Hohenheim at his mother's graveside and later in the Rockbells' place are potentially among the most intriguing in the *Hagane no Renkinjutsushi* story. But Himoru Arakawa's *manga*, like the *animés*, doesn't quite know what to do with Hohenheim once he returns and confronts his son Edward. There are scenes where the father and son try to reconcile a little (well, Hohenheim does – like when he goes into Ed's bedroom, and seems to be about to stroke his head, but then pulls back).

Van Hohenheim confronts Edward and insists that in burning his house down he was trying to bury what he and Al and had done and was running away. That riles Ed no end! Because he knows that there's some truth in that.

In the second series, as in the *Fullmetal Alchemist manga*, there is an extended cemetery sequence (in Resembool) – with Ed digging up what he and Al transmuted as children, to check just who – or what – it is (he overhears in horror what van Hohenheim tells Pinako).[11] And there are more cemetery scenes – with Ed and Hohenheim at the graveside. And with Pinako and Ed standing in front of the Rockbells' resting place (where Ed also tells Pinako about the death of her offspring, the Doctors, in the Ishbal War).

As with most graveyard scenes in Japanese *animé*, these scenes are about back-story not horror, about family history, about the passing of time, about being haunted by the past, about the sadness of life itself. No matter what you *do*, you're going to end up like this: just a bunch of bones

---

10 The other characters – Winry, Ling, Lan Fan – listen intently but are rightly kept out of the scene.
11 There are also brief dips into the pasts of Hohenheim and Pinako – illustrated with photo-graphs.

in a forgotten cemetery. (*Animé* will use butterflies, fireflies, cherry blossom, flowers ✿✿✿ and flowing streams for the same poetic ruminations on time passing and mortality – it's called *mono no aware* = impermanence/ transience).

However, the sequence where Ed and Pinako dig up the remains of the thing the kids transmuted is played for full-on Gothika: a heavily overcast sky and hammering rain, with the colours of the heath dark and grimy (more fitted to *Wuthering Heights* or *Frankenstein*). Ed telephones Izumi Curtis and asks her a deeply unsettling question: is she sure that what she transmuted was her own child?

That Ed and Al didn't transmute their mother and bring her back to life, albeit in a botched state, but something else, is bitterly ironic. Ed laughs manically when he finds out (to Pinako's dismay): it's the insane laughter of someone who's come face-to-face with a terrible truth (characters often laugh wildly right in the middle of serious scenes in *animé*, alarming their companions).

Because Ed Elric realizes the simple truth: *no one comes back from the dead*. N-O-B-O-D-Y. As in Shintoism, when you're dead, you S-T-A-Y D-E-A-D. Yet this is also the realization that gives Ed the clue that Al will be able to get his body back: because Ed realizes now how the exchange of alchemy at the Gateway of Truth works.

The key thematic point is raised in ep. 20 that the bodies that were resurrected by the Elrics and by Izumi Curtis were not their loved ones: so they didn't kill them again. Because bringing someone back to life is impossible. So Al, Ed and Curtis feel very relieved (Alphonse was disturbed that he might have been involved in killing his mother a 2nd time).

Wonderful stuff! – this *animé* is highly operatic and extravagantly dramatic, and it has an emotional depth and a psychological truth which really hits home. One can imagine the authors of grandiose, tragic novels enjoying this life-and-death drama (such as Thomas Hardy, Emily Brontë and Alexander Dumas), or the composers of passionate operas (such as Giuseppi Verdi and Giacomo Rossini).

What makes episode 20: *Father Before the Grave* work is, fundament-ally, the concept, the characters and the scriptwriting. This is high quality television, and superb fantasy fiction. If you start with a very strong idea, and appealing characters, you are operating from a powerful place for whatever story you want to tell. *Fullmetal Alchemist* is so good, in either *manga* form or animated form, because the foundational concept is quite brilliant: the challenges that Ed and Al face are universal enough to appeal to a wide audience – it's all those fundamental metaphysical questions, the life and death issues – like: the costs of being alive, what it means to be alive, what life is, what counts as a 'good life', and how *doing* relates to *being*.

It's just sublime how *mangaka* Himoru Arakawa has dug into profound issues using quirky, even eccentric characters, and how beauti-fully the filmmakers at Bones/ Aniplex/ Square Enix/ Mainichi have brought them to life on celluloid.

The writing is smart and complex in *Father Before the Grave*: it weaves in nightmares, multiple flashbacks (in a variety of forms), philosophical speculations, telephone conversations, monologues and mysteries (and all in 22 minutes!). While the action and the visual effects and giant alchemical battles set the *Fullmetal Alchemist* on fire visually, and provide thrilling set-pieces, it's the depth and complexity of the psychology of the characters and their situations and relationships that gives *Fullmetal Alchemist* even more of an edge over the competition.

Another way of praising the *Fullmetal Alchemist* series for its conception and writing is to say this: it travels to some very interesting places in the human psyche. We are journeying with Ed and Al Elric far beyond 'children's' stories, or Saturday morning cartoons: this is very grown-up filmmaking, exploring issues on a par with the greatest cinema, such as the works of Carl-Theordor Dreyer, F.W. Murnau, Orson Welles, Ingmar Bergman and Pier Paolo Pasolini.

Is *Fullmetal Alchemist* really *that* good? Oh most definitely. In fact, it is more sophisticated and more profound than some of the movies by the filmmakers noted above. More profound than Bergman or Dreyer?! Surely not! But, actually, well, yes – *Fullmetal Alchemist is* more profound *and* more sophisticated than some of their works. *Fullmetal Alchemist* might not be filmed in contrasty black-and-white, it might not star Max von Sydow or Liv Ullmann (actually, it does! – it has two actors as good as Ullmann or von Sydow – Romi Pak and Rie Kugimiya), it might not have cameras drifting slowly over wintry landscapes or craggy, solemn faces (actually, it does!), it might not have classical music simmering in the background (actually, it does!), but it goes further into ambiguity, into complexity, and into sinister and twisted issues than many of the works by the great *auteurs* of cinema.

I've made my case! I could go on, with further arguments about how *Fullmetal Alchemist* delivers in terms of psychology > ambiguity> complexity > depth > profundity > philosophy > drama > emotion > spectacle > and style. Yes, and it explores the Big Themes of all great art: death + life + loss + transgression + identity + family + love + redemption + belief + politics + society + race + war.

Episode 21. *Advance of the Fool*

Part of this episode is set-up and preparation for future episodes, part is a catch-up and aftermath session (from the Roy Mustang vs. Lust sequence, and the discussions that Ed and Al Elric had), and part is furthering the story.

So the mystery of the homunculi deepens, and each side is skirting around the other... Ed and Al try to draw Scar out (and succeed), in order to force the homunculi to emerge from their lair[12] (these include some fun jokey scenes of the boys showing off)... Ling Yao and Lan Fan are hover-

---

12 They try to find a way in, but no dice.

ing on the sidelines (as ever), and run into Gluttony (pursuing the immortality of the homunculi)... Bradley stalks about grimly... Mustang curses being in hospital, unable to act (tho' he makes many phone calls to orchestrate his troops)... Liza Hawkeye remains as dutifully bound to Mustang as ever... Mustang creates multiple reports of sightings of Scar about town... Jean Havoc, paralyzed below the waist by Lust's Edward Scissorhands, wants to retire from military service... Breda visits Marcoh... Mustang chats to Doctor Knox (Kinryuu Arimoto)... Envy itches for some action (and complains to the Führer about why he let Mustang live after he'd toasted Lust)... Winry (who doesn't have much to do) gets angry about Ed breaking (or promising to break) his automail (again)...

Episode 21: *Advance of the Fool* keeps the plates of the *Fullmetal Alchemist* story spinning in the air with a skill that seems so easy (but it isn't!). The 2nd *Fullmetal Alchemist* series has generated a *very* large cast of charas by now, throwing up ever more challenges for the writers to keep everybody in the frame. (So that it's impressive that the producers and the writers didn't whittle down the cast, and do the usual adaptation thing of combining characters, or dropping them altogether. Because it takes *a lot* of writerly work to keep that many charas in the loop).

Episode 21: *Advance of the Fool* is thus one of the busiest episodes in the *Fullmetal Alchemist 2* series, with scenes kept short, dancing around a large of characters. The 'fool' of the title is Roy Mustang, advancing his plans to uncover the corruption higher up in the military government.

Episode 21: *Advance of the Fool* does not run to 22 minute of talk, however: the short scenes vary in tone and content, and the pacing is brisk. The final minutes ramp up to some storming action sequences: Ling Yao and Lan Fan against Bradley, and the Elrics versus Scar on the streets by day.

Episode 22. *Backs In the Distance*

This show is full of distressing, ultra-violent and hysterical scenes. The first half of *Backs In the Distance* (broadcast on September 6, 2009) flits around several groups of charas: Führer Bradley (and Glutters) pursuing Lan Fan and Ling Yao;[13] Winry and Gracia at Maes Hughes' graveside; and a flashback for Winry (in selective colour) to a scene from her childhood, when her parents left for Ishbal when she was a child (the last time she saw them). Why a flashback for Winry now? You will see very soon!

We follow Winry-chan walking thru the streets of Central City, hearing passers-by talking about the Elrics, and eventually stumbling upon Ed and Al duelling with Scar. Well, it *is* highly contrived (in both comic and cartoon form), right down to Winry having a pistol within easy reach on the ground (from some fallen soldiers).

This is the episode where Winry Rockbell gets to emote and yell and weep and become a more three-dimensional character (rather than having

13 A furious piece of swordplay, with Ling Yao at his finest, battling the Führer while carrying the injured Lan Fan.

the role of the on-off girlfriend of the hero). Of course, when Winry holds up the gun, she can't and won't fire it, even tho' Scar deserves, in the morality of fantasy adventure fiction, to have his head ripped off for committing countless murders – of State Alchemists, of Amestrian soldiers, of civilians, and of Winry's parents. (Megumi Takamoto steps up to the mark in voicing Winry in one of her key episodes).

The sight of their childhood friend holding a weapon and raising it at a victim unsettles El and Al more than almost anything they've encountered thus far. As if the Ishbal War and the military government have corrupted one of the people they hold dearest. Yes, even a sweet, decent soul like Winry can be poisoned by the rhetoric of political aggression.

Scar is a deeply ambiguous figure in the *Fullmetal Alchemist* universe – and he's kept alive and in the running precisely *because* he's so troublesome and so troubling. Using the standards of Western storytelling, with its fanatical adherence to the Western morality of the duality of good and evil, Scar should die or be punished for what he's done. But in this post-9/11, post-War On Terror fantasy series, absolute good and absolute evil don't exist (and have never been part of Japanese animation and comics anyway).

❖

The second half of this episode of *Fullmetal Alchemist 2* comprises an extended flashback to Scar's life in Ishbal, which leads up to a dramatic confrontation between Ed, Al, Winry and Scar in the present tense.

The flashbacks[14] to the Ishbal rebellion in the second *Fullmetal Alchemist* series are incredibly violent, with civilians being mowed down, and death and destruction on all sides (the 'Crimson Alchemist', Zolf Kimbley appears and creates mayhem; Kimbley becomes a much more prominent chara later in the series).

Scar is very much in the foreground of the Ishbal scenes – he is the character who embodies the trials and tribulations of the Ishbal nation. He also expresses what the Ishbalians would like to do in revenge. (The invading soldiers of Amestris are given *very* bright blue eyes, presumably a reference to the blond, blue-eyed Aryans of Nazi mythology – but also, this is the way that foreigners in *animé* are depicted – as *really* foreign, with their otherness – blond hair, for instance, or blue eyes – emphasized and/ or caricatured. For an island like Japan, which has never been colonized or invaded by a foreign power, until WW2, foreigners are often seen as *very* foreign).

So now we see the invasion of Ishbal by Amestris from the victims' point-of-view. It's Vietnam being invaded by the U.S.A., it's Iraq and the U.S.A., it's Afghanistan and the U.S.A., it's Israel and Palestine and – to even up the tally! – it's Japan invading China. (And, for H. Arakawa, it's the treatment of the Ainu people in Nihon).

In short, the Ishbal rebellion/ invasion/ war is something that *won't* go away. And the spectre of that calamitous event – Scar – comes to

14 The flashbacks are in pale, selective colour, close to black-and-white (again emulating a newsreel), and echoing the flashbacks of Winry.

Amestris to haunt it and to kill those he regards as evil. Alphonse tells Scar in this episode that he's using God as an excuse or pretext for his revenge. It doesn't *matter* anymore – God is just a word in the *Fullmetal Alchemist* world (as Ed explains, right at the start of the series: this is an *atheistic* series, in which *alchemy* is the magic or religion with real power, and organized religion (like the one in Liore) is a sham).

Unfortunately, the cycle of vengeance that Scar is embarked upon seems unbreakable. This guy goes on killing and killing, like a machine with no off-switch. Yet his acts of slaughter ultimately have no effect whatsoever on the powers-that-be or the status quo: because the military regime of Amestris can simply call up more'n more soldiers as cannon fodder.

We also see the moment when Scar kills Winry Rockbell's Doctor parents, in a blaze of fury when he wakes up in hospital (filmed subjectively, from Scar's p.o.v. in a hospital bed). We return to this moment in a later episode of *Fullmetal Alchemist*. This is the start of Scar's project of total revenge as total war: he comes round from his medical operation, sees the too-shiny, blue eyes of the two Rockbell Doctors, growls about Amestrisians (flashing onto images of the advancing soldiers), and kills them in an insane fury (the moment is also reminiscent of the horror genre, when the monster wakes up on the slab in the laboratory and immediately kills whoever's nearby. Arakawa has mined *Frankenstein* several times in her career as comic writer).

We also see that Scar was a fearsome warrior *before* he learnt alchemy (he is a religious monk – tho' he's a monk who has a giant, muscley body!). And we see Scar's brother (Takehito Koyasu), poring over his alchemical papers (much more monk-like): during the invasion by the Amestrisian forces, the Ishbalians hope that Scar's brother will have enough alchemical magic to defend the city. This motif is reminiscent of traditional tales in Japan of samurai warriors using the sword against the gun (or the motif in Chinese cinema of *kung fu* adepts during the Boxer Rebellion who hoped that Ancient Chinese magic could defeat foreign bullets, as seen in the *Once Upon a Time In China* movies).

So it's the old vs. the new, the tiny army vs. the massed army, ancient belief vs. modern science, religion vs. technology, etc.

Episode 23. *Girl On the Battlefield*

Ready for more action? Yes! – the following episode of the 2nd alchemical fantasy series, 23: *Girl On the Battlefield*, explodes with extended action scenes as the Elrics bravely take on Scar once again, and Führer Bradley pursues Ling Yao and Lan Fan (the action is mostly in the first half of ep. 23, reversing the usual structure of each show, and a typical action *animé* show). In this episode, we see story elements not included in the first *animé*, such as the capture of Gluttony in a bundle of cables by the quick-thinking Ling; Mei Chang launching into action; and Lan Fan's injury, among others.

By now the writers (Hiroshi Onogi *et al*) were juggling a whole slew of parallel storylines – they even found time for very modest scenes like Winry's customers calling her up and begging her to return and fix their automail. There were scenes between Liza Hawkeye and Roy Mustang; Winry talking with the Elrics; a railroad farewell for Winry-chan; Al and the panda Xiao Mei; Mustang and Hawkeye manning the radios; Lan Fan being patched up by Doctor Knox – and all of this was squeezed into 22 minutes!

Fullmetal Alchemist's episode 23 continues the action and events of episode 22 directly, keeping a number of groups of characters and plotlines running beside each other. So we see Bradley and Gluttony hunting down Ling Yao and Lan Fan; Ed Elric with Winry Rockbell; Scar fighting Al (then Ed and Al battling Scar); the arrival of Mei Chang; Ling capturing Gluttony; Liza Hawkeye and Ling squirrelling Gluttony away in a car, and so on.[15]

Chases along rooftops, alchemical battles at railroad sidings – episode 23: *Girl On the Battlefield* sustained the balance between action and discussion, forward movement and thoughtful reflection, as well as keeping the animation bright and clear, and providing all of the main characters to have their moment to shine. (Some of the action in *Girl On the Battlefield* is a little clunky, tho' – for instance, Lan Fan, badly wounded, cuts off her own arm in order to put Führer Bradley off the scent. Bradley's followed the trail of drip of blood as Ling Yao carries his faithful servant Lan Fan away. But cutting off your arm is going to create an enormous amount of blood! However, that was in Himoru Arakawa's *manga*, and it's there to show how desperate events are becoming. Also, adhering to 'realism' is jettisoned wholesale at times: for ex, Ling is able to leap from a fifth storey window, carrying Lan on his shoulder, and he can land on the ground and scamper away).

It's sad that a sweet girl like Mei Chang should be aligned in *Fullmetal Alchemist* with Scar and Loki, and only later to team up with the Elrics. But of course, that is precisely her purpose – to bring some healing, some softer words, some feminization and humanity to the vengeful, perpetually melancholy and grim Scar (after comically launching herself at the Elrics, Mei spirits Scar away and heals him).

Winry Rockbell is the 'girl on the battlefield' of the title of this *Fullmetal Alchemist* episode: the story brings her into the thick of things by having her overhearing Ed Elric and Scar discussing the death of Winry's parents. Then Winry-chan confronts Scar with a gun. Like Mei Chang and Pinako Rockbell, Winry's function in the *Fullmetal Alchemist* series is partly to act as the heart, the conscience, and to remind the heroes what they're fighting for. In the 'girlfriend of the hero' role (well, at this point Winry's not yet Ed's girl), Winry is inevitably on the periphery of events

---

15 But those action scenes were mere tasters for the truly awesome action when the Elrics faced off against Gluttony, now on a hysterical rampage for Lust's death, while Ling duelled with the homunculus Envy. These were further scenes dropped from the first*animé* version of *Fullmetal Alchemist*, and it was a delight to see them here, in the 2009-2010 version.

(until the *Fullmetal Alchemist* series brings her into the foreground, such as with the death of her parents plotline).

Winry Rockbell is also Ed's mechanic, of course, but in any story that's only a minor role, offering support and checking-in: indeed, Winry makes the obvious statement of all girlfriends-of-the-hero characters everywhere: do I just have to *wait*? Is *waiting* what I have to do? That's not Winry talking, that's the author, Himoru Arakawa! Is this what secondary charas have to do in stories, especially if they are the girlfriends?!

Luckily, help is at hand when her devoted customers back in Rush Valley beg Winry Rockbell to return and fix their automail limbs (in a phone call – a *very* over-cooked scene of sentimentality). So off Winry goes, having a legitimate reason for exiting the story at this point (altho' it is, like the scene of Winry overhearing the conversation about the death of her parents, rather awkwardly contrived. Truth is, the filmmakers want Winry to be part of the story, but not part of the action; they don't want to put Winry in the line of fire. An obvious ploy, which Himoru Arakawa in her *manga* – and the writers of the series – must've considered, would be to have the homunculi capturing Winry).

On the train, Winry-chan wonders if she's falling in love with Ed. Come on, girl, we guessed that ages ago! Winry is given a series of flashbacks, which illustrate her time with Edward. Winry's send-off at the station is exploited for big emotions (complete with a stirring orchestral music cue and the mandatory gold-yellow light). The farewell is significant, because it's the last time that we see Winry for some time.

At the end of *Girl On the Battlefield* that Führer Bradley may also be a homunculus is revealed to the group gathered in the forest, in the abandoned house[16] (which includes the Elrics, Roy Mustang, and Ling Yao).[17] The idea is shocking, because it means that the entire social and governmental system, from the top down, is debased. Not only is the top man corrupt (we expect politicians to be crooks, don't we?!), but a dangerous psychopath! And not only a psycho, he's also armed and vicious! (Here, Glutters, hearing the name 'Roy Mustang', seethes with malice, bursting out of his bonds, which provides the show's climax).

Episode 24. *In the Belly*

The homunculi are becoming much more prominent in the *Fullmetal Alchemist* series by now, with no less than four appearing in *In the Belly* (*Hara no Naka*, broadcast September 20, 2009) (and Father and Lust are referred to in the dialogue): Gluttony, Wrath (Bradley), Envy and a new character, Pride (heard but not seen yet).

The meat of episode 24: *In the Belly* concerns our heroes, the Elric *kyoudai*, and the group assembled around them: Col. Mustang, Lt. Hawkeye, Lan Fan, Ling Yao and the Doctor (Knox) brought in by

---

16 We return to this locale several times, including for the grand heroes vs. Pride and Gluttony sequence.
17 It's rather silly that they discuss such dangerous matters right in front of the prisoner (Gluttony) they have bound in a room.

Mustang to help out with Lan Fan's injury (two characters are injured now – Mustang and Lan Fan). They've got a homunculus (Gluttony) cornered and bound, but these are fearsome opponents – some of the most inventive and deadly baddies in recent *anime*. Gluttony explodes in rage – literally – with his/ its body splitting apart to reveal... one of *mangaka* Himoru Arakawa's disturbing designs: an unblinking eye set with a black, vaginal hole, surrounded by bones (ribs) which form teeth. This symbol is the toothed vagina of Freudian castration (the devouring mother), *plus* the all-seeing eye, *plus* it's enclosed by a psychopathic cannibal! (And it leads to Hell!).

Mouth->vagina->womb->tomb->Hell[18] – the homunculus Gluttony opens up to reveal a nightmarish vision of Hell, a sea of blood and decay and skeletons and rotting nothingness.

And the score by Akira Senju rose to the occasion, too, with a marvellously effective use of the Warsaw Chorus (you wonder if it was the sheer intensity of the imagery that inspired Senju to write powerful choral cues that would match the visuals, although composers in *anime* often compose after reading the script). This is where the budget for the music and music arranging, orchestration, production and mixing is well-spent.

The 2nd *Fullmetal Alchemist* series becomes impressively operatic and baroque in sequences like this, when the filmmakers render action set-pieces which have powerful symbolic and thematic ingredients.

❖

There's a crucial scene mid-way in episode 24: *In the Belly* of *Fullmetal Alchemist 2* when the adults hand over the baton to the children: Col. Mustang's injured, and Lan Fan too, and they have to admit they are no match for Gluttony (the monster simply devours Mustang's signature fiery alchemy – and it's chomped Hawkeye's weaponry). So they flee in a car, leaving Ed, Al and Ling Yao to battle two homunculi, because Envy joins Gluttony.

By this point, the filmmakers at Bones/ Aniplex/ Mainichi/ Tokyo Broadcasting System/ Square Enix *et al* are delivering state of the art visual effects and highly imaginative animation in their action set-pieces. The duel between Ling Yao and Envy is marvellously fierce (with, once again, swords as a chief weapon – all animators in Japan are serious sword fanatics!), as both participants bait each other with arrogance and speed. (Hurrah for the return of Envy, one of the great characterizations of the *Fullmetal Alchemist* universe: things are never dull when Envy is around – he's a delightfully contradictory mix of vanity and cowardice, fury and uncertainty, brutality and madness).

Elsewhere, in a colonnade at night, Führer Bradley has a sinister conversation with an unseen but creepy voice[9] (the revelation of the owner of that voice is saved for later – but when Pride is fully revealed, it is one of *mangaka* Himoru Arakawa's finest monsters. Meanwhile, the scene is

---

18 The symbolic links are positively Shakespearean.
19 A spider catching a moth is included as the psychological counterpoint in the conversation (a common trope in Japanese *anime*).

also foreshadowing for the amazing sequence where Liza Hawkeye encounters Pride in the same colonnade). And there's a tease in the following scene, at the family dinner table, where the Bradley's 'son' Selim reads aloud a sickeningly syrupy letter he wrote in class about his so-wonderful daddy. Sick, because we know by now that Bradley/ Wrath is a repulsive character and one of the chief villains in *Fullmetal Alchemist 2* (and it becomes even sicker later when it's revealed that Selim is in fact the homunculus Pride, who turns out to be a mass murderer – as all of the homunculi are).

Some time later, Roy Mustang, trying to set up some allies he can rely on in the battle against the corruption of the military government, finds himself well and truly out-manœuvred, when the officer he's courting (General Raven – Katsuhisa Houki) leads him right into the lions' den – a high level political meeting involving the Führer and high-ranking officials.

Episode 24: *In the Belly* climaxes with Ed waking up in hell, the interior of Gluttony's infinite body which's one of the most effective depictions of a netherworld in recent fantasy. This is a place you really *don't* want to be.

Episode 25. *Doorway of Darkness*

In *Yami no Tobira* (= *Doorway of Darkness*), the filmmakers let loose with hugely impressive visual effects and action sequences which culminate with a street punk, skater kid turning into a giant dog-dinosaur. The sequence in the *Fullmetal Alchemist manga* where Ling Yao, Ed Elric and Envy're swallowed by Gluttony in his super-size nastiness was brilliantly realized in the 2009-10, *animé* show. The disturbing image of an endless, dark realm awash with blood is given the full, Gothic treatment by the filmmakers (they can use plenty of red, for a start, where the *manga* relies on black-and-white and screen tone). The flickering flames (from Roy Mustang's explosions), the ruined pieces of Classical architecture, the bits of earth and detritus, a car, Al's hand, and of course the skeletons – this was a vivid and imaginative portrayal of a deathly, dangerous limbo.

Ed and Ling try running but never reach a wall; they make a well-sized hole (which proves bottomless when they hurl a flaming torch down it); Ling collapses, and Ed carries him.

Nothing to eat, nothing to drink – it was a macabre take on the action-adventure staple of being marooned on the ocean, surrounded by undrinkable salt water. (In the end, Ed cooks his own boots!,[20] telling Ling Yao that he survived his alchemy training, a call-back to Jack Island, and he's not going to stop surviving now. Besides, his thoughts immediately fly to Alphonse, and how they're definitely going to get their bodies back).

When Envy turns up (after Ed Elric and Ling Yao have finished their meal and are wondering how to escape from this Hell), before the (inevit-

---

20 So those familiar chunky black boots get used!

able) fight begins, Envy relates some of the back-story of Ishbal from *his* point-of-view. It's not pretty. At all. (See below).

Envy, who is often reluctant to fight Ed Elric (or Ling Yao) – he talks ominously about 'sacrifices' (and orders Gluttony not to kill the Elric brothers) – is taunted to the point of deciding to fight. Now he reveals his true nature: a giant, green monster (somewhat dog-shaped) with a long, dragonish tail and cadavers absorbed into its body that bubble and scream in a chaotic, creepy mass of heads, eyes and mouth. Handily, Ed can transmute some weaponry out of the iron[21] in the flood of blood at his feet (*Fullmetal Alchemist* is like having a science lesson – hey, blood contains iron, folks!), and battle commences.

It's a wild, full-on action sequence, with the filmmakers calling upon everyone in the huge team behind this incredible *animé* show to deliver big time. *Fullmetal Alchemist* is an outstanding action series, by any standards, and the equal of anything in *animé*, including all of the celebrated examples from *Astro Boy* to *The Wind Rises*.

Yet in amongst the slashing, slavering, leaping, hollering and beat-me-senseless action, the filmmakers include all manner of simultaneous stories and plot points in this middle episode of 2009-10's *Fullmetal Alchemist*. Such as:

• Liza Hawkeye is ordered to become the Führer's assistant;
• li'l Mei Chang (a.k.a. May Chan) recalls her origins in Xing (and that of her pet panda Xiao Mei) in a cute-tender flashback;
• the revelation that Führer Bradley is a homunculus reaches more ears;
• the generals in a meeting discuss how to use to create a Doorway;
• Roy Mustang is embroiled in the military in Central City, and realizes that the corruption is wider than he thought;
• Envy recounts how the Ishbal Civil War started;
• Scar broods on Ishbal again;
• and Al persuades Gluttony to take him to his father.

This is, in short, very dense storytelling, with the screenwriters (headed up by Hiroshi Onogi) keeping track of a number of parallel storylines, which intertwine with a striking complexity. And the editor (Takeshi Sadamatsu) is right on top of each story strand (as challenging as the *writing* of *Fullmetal Alchemist* is, the *editing* also requires a good deal of concentration and effort). For instance, when Envy finishes his diabolical tale of shooting dead a very young girl at point blank range (the act which ignites the civil strike in Ishbal), the *animé* cuts to a big close-up of Scar (the character who embodies the Ishbalian side of the issue).[22]

Much of this is performed at the script stage and when the script is storyboarded (animation is pre-planned in minute detail, with every shot carefully considered before it's even animated), but it requires a great editor to make it fly.

---

21 Reminiscent of Sasha in *The Qwaser of Stigmata*, who resembles Ed.
22 There are several other poetic cuts in this ep. – such as from Ed in the bloody limbo to Al in a sunny forest with a blue sky.

Mei Chang's back-story is illustrated using Chinese landscape paintings, a delightful choice (of course, Japanese *manga*, with their roots in woodblock art of the 19th century, also drew on Chinese landscape art). So we see li'l Mei finding the tiny, abandoned panda and taking care of it (the filmmakers even include scenes where Mei practices martial arts with the panda, now flying. Certainly, the character of Mei really inspired the filmmakers, allowing them to indulge in their love of *kung fu* movies – Japanese filmmakers are *major* fans of Chinese action movies! If you're stuck with how to stage some action, just have a look at a Tsui Hark or Tony Ching Siu-tung movie – it's all there!).

Episode 25: *Doorway of Darkness* also includes a brief scene of the Führer and Roy Mustang: now it's explained why Bradley hasn't had Mustang quietly taken care of (it seems too that the Führer wants to teach him a lesson). Bradley also disbands Mustang's serving officers, further weakening his influence (and we know how significant teams are in Japanese *animé*).

❖

Yes, the *Fullmetal Alchemist animé* does illustrate visually the ruthless psycho Envy (in the guise of an Amestrisian soldier) killing the five year-old girl – a scene you very rarely see (or want to see) anywhere. You won't see it in almost any Hollywood movie. It's true that the filmmakers do cloak the flashback sequence with a stylized, archive footage approach (desaturated colours, shaky camera, scratched film), and the image of the murder occurs as a long shot. But that stylization doesn't hide the dramatic impact of the scene.

The flashback sequence should mean instant death for Envy, in a typical action-adventure flick. Killing a five year-old girl! An unarmed girl, and with no provocation (and smiling insanely before it's done). But *animé* series which stretch on for 50-plus episodes have to *wait* to punish their characters, and can't dispatch them halfway thru.[23] Nevertheless, Envy's gloating tale is more than enough to incite Edward Elric to attack him (yet again) in blind fury (and surely, by now, Ling Yao <u>plus</u> Ed are enough to triumph over Envy? But no: Envy doesn't even flinch, and transforms into his monstrous guise. As we see later, it takes *a lot* to finally dispatch the homunculus Envy (he's reduced to a tiny, snail-like creature, then roars back to life again), and his demise is a truly spectacular, operatic end).

In *Fullmetal Alchemist*, it seems that no matter what the heroes do, no matter how hard they try, the villains can *not* be made to pay for the abominations they perpetrate (it will take more than catching a few Nazis or Islamic terrorists to solve complex issues, *Fullmetal Alchemist* says). Ishbal is fomented into civil war, children are slain, civilians are mown down – the Japanese *animé* depicts all of this – but there is no retribution, no punishment, no one is called to account (instead, the villains smirk, and pour even more scorn on mere humans).

The *Fullmetal Alchemist animé* (and the *manga*) is reluctant to sacrifice

---

23 Envy survives quite some time.

its villains as well as its heroes. Lust dies, and Maes Hughes dies, and minor characters such as Tucker, Nina, Tucker's wife, and Barry the Chopper die, but still Bradley, Envy, Gluttony, Pride, Greed and other villains thrive (and some villains're even brought back to life to continue their rampages!).

Certainly the *Fullmetal Alchemist manga* is unbelievably savage, as homunculi and humans are torn to shreds (and the *animé* depicts a five year-old girl being shot in the face in the Ishbal flashback). It's true that *mangaka* Hiromu Arakawa does reserve the most vicious images for the villains (such as the homunculi and the 'immortal' puppets). That is, it's OK for the evil homunculi to be sliced 'n' diced. However, there is *so much* violence, it goes way beyond the dramatic or narrative requirements of the story, to become a creepy and disturbing dwelling on suffering. A pornography of savagery, you might say, like you also see in movies such as *Black Hawk Down* (2001) or *Sin City* (2005) or *Saving Private Ryan* (1998) or *The Lord of the Rings* (2001-03). Those movies are not only physically and visually violent to a psychotic degree (you could argue that the depiction of horror and physical abuse reaches clinically insane levels), they are also *ideologically* aggressive (with their repulsive pro-military, pro-right-wing and pro-Amerikan politics). Some of those movies are virtually commercials for the North Amerikan war machine: *Amerika Über Alles*, I call it.

Well, shoot, there's no getting around the fact that altho' *Fullmetal Alchemist* is *critical* of the military, of the military-industrial complex, of proto-fascism, of the politics and ethics that create the military in the first place, and of the ideology that sustains the military, it is also celebrating the military, and getting off on some of the military's acts. That is, altho' *Fullmetal Alchemist* admirably explores the moral and ethical conflicts of going to war and killing people (as when Roy Mustang and Maes Hughes, for instance, debate what they're doing in Ishbal), you can't deny that the *Fullmetal Alchemist manga* is also wallowing in it, that it is also enjoying depicting violence and horror on a *massive* scale (and the *animés*, too). The same ambiguous attitude to war crops up in the greatest *animé* filmmaker, Hayao Miyazaki (as he acknowledges).

We see scenes where Roy Mustang, Maes Hughes, Liza Hawkeye *et al* are killing unarmed civilians (in a few episodes' time). Even lovely, quiet, meek Hawkeye takes up her sniper rifle and shoots people from a tower (pretty cowardly). Yes, the camera stays on her bewildered face, as she contemplates what she's done, but she's still a willing cog in the military machine – that is, a participant in barely-disguised modern fascism. (Hawkeye, in the scene with Winry, asserts her belief in using arms to protect what she deems important).

Fullmetal Alchemist wants to have it both ways (as art always does, as filmmakers always want to do!): it wants to depict the heroes as lovable, heroic, brave, liberal, caring and sweet people, yet they are also stand-ins for Amerikan fascists, German fascists, Italian fascists, Japanese fascists, British fascists, Chinese fascists, Russian fascists, and other fascists of the modern era. Heroes who fire on unarmed civilians are not 100% heroes with tiny flaws, nor are they 'ambiguous' characters: they are villains. If the *Fullmetal Alchemist manga* retains aspects of ambiguity, the *animé* is clear and unequivocal: it portrays the State Alchemists and the Amestrisian soldiers as Nazis.

Episode 26. *Reunion*

This is a transcendentally wonderful show in the second *Fullmetal Alchemist* series – and therefore one of the finest episodes in any recent *animé*. It's the equal of the greatest fantasy director – Hayao Miyazaki – and any top-class animation.

This is the climax of the first half of the series (two seasons of 13 episodes in length), before the recap (clip show) episode, 27: *Interlude Party*. So in *Saikai* (*Reunion*), broadcast in Japan on October 4, 2009, the filmmakers at Bones, Mainichi, Aniplex, Square Enix *et al* go all out. As filmmaking, this episode is riveting. It is stuffed with inventive action, with visual effects, with dramatic confrontations, and with rich thematic material (Michihiro Tsuchiya was writer and Takahiro Ikezoe was storyboard artist).

Reunion is a very satisfying episode too because it goes to the heart of the *Fullmetal Alchemist* series, and the predicament of Edward and Alphonse Elric, and their quest to get their bodies back whole. It's an episode that resets the series before the recap show, and reaffirms the goals of the brothers. And it brings the brothers face-to-face – although in the abstract, spiritual, beyond-life realm of the Gateway of Truth.

This is one of the Ed's greatest moments in the *Fullmetal Alchemist* franchise, when he really demonstrates just why he's such an impressive hero. It's thrilling to watch Ed take control of the situation, clambering out of Envy's body, ordering the monster to gather the Xerxes stones, drawing a transmutation circle, and performing a miraculous act of alchemy. This scene really works on every dramatic level – it's exciting in terms of action and spectacle, for sure, but it also possesses deeply resonant psychological and emotional levels, and it works up to a majestic pay-off, in the Doorway of Truth.

How are Ed and Ling Yao going to get out of the endless Hell of Gluttony's stomach (which's a false Gateway of Truth)? It takes Ed being pushed to his limit (swallowed alive inside the Envy-monster) to work out how to do it. The solution plays right into the central theme of the *Fullmetal Alchemist* series: to open the Doorway of Truth using alchemy, to go to the borders of life and death.

But the means of escape also requires making an uneasy alliance with a fearsome enemy: Envy. For the first part of the *Reunion* episode, Ling Yao and Edward Elric are duelling the Envy-dog-monster, and finding it very difficult to trounce him (the action and gags are absolutely incredible). Sheer force isn't going to defeat Envy. Ed is going to have to play the clever, resourceful hero of folk tales, and discover another way of doing it.

Envy's body is filled with screaming, groaning heads and torsos that implore Ed Elric, 'Kill me!', 'Let me die!' (And they are also children – 'play with me!', 'Mommy!', 'Daddy!'). In the sea of blood surrounding them are the remains of buildings from Xerxes, including part of the wall mural of the transmutation circle that Ed saw on his trip to the desert (it's a very smart piece of writing from Himoru Arakawa). Like the quick-witted boy in fairy tales, Edward realizes that the corpses trapped inside the Envy-demon's body are the people from Xerxes who were used to make a philosopher's stone (we see flashbacks of that extraordinary sequence – we will see the whole thing not far ahead in the seres).

This foreshadows how the whole *Fullmetal Alchemist* shebang will end: Ed realizes that someone used the population of Xerxes to create a philosopher's stone (which's why the city is now deserted, and why the inhabitants seemed to vanish over-night). The over-arching plot of the villains in the *Fullmetal Alchemist* story is to create another philosopher's stone, but a much bigger one, by using the entire country of Amestris.

How clever is the screenwriting (by Michihiro Tsuchiya) in this episode, *Reunion*? Because the story doesn't simply put our heroes in a snakepit situation (which're staples of the action-adventure genre), but into a scenario which plays not only into the larger political and religious themes of the *Fullmetal Alchemist* series, but also the personal predicaments of the two heroes. Because to find a way out of this horrific place, they have to employ the forces of life and death (and also make bargains with enemies).

And yet – this is stunning conceptually – all of that action and spectacle of escaping from the belly of Hell is a mere preamble to the real crux of the episode: Edward Elric emerging at the Gateway of Truth. Here he comes face-to-face with the enigmatic self/ other/ presence/ god/ soul and, unexpectedly, yet emotionally logical, Alphonse, his dear brother (Al is facing another doorway).

This is an extraordinary finale to the first half of the 2009-10 *Fullmetal Alchemist* animated series: Edward sees Alphonse (his body, at least), naked, thin, turning towards him. As he fights to close the distance between them, the little, black arms of alchemical transmutation explode from the Doorway of Truth, dragging him back. Ed, at the point of hysteria and intensity, screams that he will be back for Al (as he punches thru the doors after they've closed). Ed hasn't seen his brother in the flesh for many years.

A scene like this is one of the key reasons why the *Fullmetal Alchemist* series, in any of its forms, is one of the most compelling creations of recent Japanese popular culture. And the filmmakers do the material full justice, with absolutely fantastic animation, visceral action, piercing music, vivid colours and designs, a beautifully judged tonal/ emotional quality, and an incendiary vocal performance from voice actress Romi Pak (Pak is simply astonishing as Ed).

✣

And yet this is not all in episode 26: *Reunion*: there is also the back-story of Führer Bradley, related by Bradley to Roy Mustang in his office in Central City. Now we see that Bradley underwent one of those Nazi-like, governmental, eugenic experiments (reminiscent of many superhero comicbooks, and *manga* such as *Akira*), in which test subjects are trained to become Adolf Hitlers (culminating with the extremely painful injection of a philosopher's stone). We see the training of Bradley, the winner in amongst an army of would-be Hitlers.[24]

Meanwhile, all roads are leading underground, to the lair of the super-villain of the *Fullmetal Alchemist* universe: Father. There are two groups of characters travelling towards the arch nemesis underneath Central City (and both sets of characters are uneasy pairings: Scar and Mei Chang, and Gluttony and Al (plus Xiao Mei the pet panda).)[25]

No trip to meet the super-villain is an easy stroll across the park to buy a newspaper and a cuppa coffee. Oh no – it means martial arts battles with numerous monsters[26] (Mei Chang shines here). And in the distance, Father glowers, as the two groups approach. (Now the stakes are getting much higher – it's not one chimera to fight, but a whole battalion of them).

Episode 27. *Interlude Party*

Episode 27: *Interlude Party* of the second *Fullmetal Alchemist* series was a clip show: many *animé* shows include an assembly of previous material, sometimes with a wraparound story of additional animation. Here the framing device was van Hohenheim remembering much of the story-so-far. We see the two Hohenheims (Hohenheim and Father), a younger Pinako Rockbell (played by Mami Koyama – she was Kei in *Akira*),[27] and the Elrics' future mom Trisha as a youngster.

With the new animation framing the clips, *Interlude Party* gets away with being a clip show. Because now the story is seen from van Hohen-heim's (and from Pinako Rockbell's) point-of-view. Hohenheim expresses the weary, cynical opinion of humanity and its petty struggles; Pinako embodies the indomitable spirit of keeping going and striving (Himoru Arakawa's 'moving forward' mantra). So Hohenheim is for giving up, or accepting fate; Pinako is for fighting and saying 'no'.

The setting for the summary show is van Hohenheim dreaming of being at a party – a dance around a large bonfire in somewhere like Resembool. Hohenheim and the young Pinako Rockbell share a drink[28]

24 The Man With the Gold Tooth is here – but he would be very old in the present day scenes (unless he too has prolonged his life).
25 That Al has taken up Mei Chang's pet is a minor plot point – but it plays into the friendship that develops between the two.
26 One of the chimeras is an *hommage* to the *Berserk manga* by Kentaro Miura (the character Nosferatu Zodd, in fact).
27 Mami Koyama's credits include: *Sailor Moon, Detective Conan, Black Lagoon, Rainbow, Dragon Ball* (playing Lunch), *Gundam, Ayakashi – Samurai Horror Tales Appleseed, Millennium Actress, Metropolis, Magical Princess Minky Momo* (the lead role), *Lupin III* (playing Fujiko), *X, Gunnm, Goku Midnight Eye, Case Closed, Shaman King, Ninja Scroll* (TV), *Silent Möbius, Riding Bean, Urusei Yatsura, Vampire Princess Miyu, City Hunter, The Dagger of Kamui, Doraemon, Lensman, Harmageddon* and *Dr Slump*.
28 The label on the liquor is 'Stray Dog' – a reference to Himoru Arakawa's *manga*, and also Hohenheim's status as a 'stray dog'.

and reminisce, while teens and children dance round the fire. The filmmakers edit together montages of the best bits of the *Fullmetal Alchemist* series up to this point. When you see everything slammed together like this, you realize just how much storytelling the filmmakers have crammed into this outstanding fantasy series, and just how good the filmmaking is.

Fullmetal Alchemist is so impressive because the *concept* and the *script* are rock solid, unusual, compelling and deeply moving (in contrast to most animation and filmmaking). And because of the way the characters and the stories are delivered, with a remarkable imagination and flair.

Why did the filmmakers chose van Hohenheim as the figure for the framing story for this catch-up episode in *Fullmetal Alchemist 2*? Ed and Al Elric, his sons, would be the obvious choices, or perhaps, at a pinch, Winry Rockbell. Maybe because not only does Hohenheim feature more prominently in future episodes, and not only is he at the heart of how and why the homunculi came into being, and not only because he is the father of the heroes, but because he is one of the very few figures with a God-like view of the whole story, someone who can see the flaws and weaknesses of both sides, of the heroes and the villains (and he was there at the start of it all).

Van Hohenheim acts like someone who has lost everything, and who has taken to wandering the surface of this beautiful planet with no home, no family, nowhere to rest his head (other than a dead, fallen tree in the wilderness). Someone who had everything, then lost it. So he doesn't want ties anymore, and prefers to be alone.

So at the end of episode 27: *Interlude Party*, many of the characters in this magical 2009-10 animated story are lined up in front of van Hohenheim, smiling at him (all except Edward Elric, who frowns!). *This*, the filmmakers suggest, is what it is all about, this is what is at stake, and this is what makes life worth living: family, children, friends... in short: *humanity*.

Meanwhile the new credit sequence appearing in episode 27: *Interlude Party* teases us with many new charas and places, such as Briggs Mountain and the formidable Olivia Armstrong (which we haven't seen yet).

Episode 28. *Father*

The *Fullmetal Alchemist* comes roaring back following the catch-up clip show (episode 27: *Interlude Party*) with one of the greatest shows in recent *animé*. Episode 28: *Father* (= *Oto-sama*) is one of the finest installments in either *Fullmetal Alchemist* series, too: it has so much packed into it: (1) the reunion of the Elric brothers (absolutely crucial); (2) the full introduction of Father; (3) the meetings of many charas (the Elrics with Scar, Mei Chang, etc); (4) an encounter with Scar and Alphonse in the sewers; (5) Father nixing alchemy; (6) the transformation of Ling Yao into a homunculus (plus a spiritual fusion with Greed); (7) *shojo* humour and

Mei Chang's fury over Ed; and (8) massive battles (Ed versus Envy, Ed and Al versus Father, Ed versus Ling Yao, Scar versus Father, Scar versus chimera, Mei Chang versus Gluttony, etc). For action, this show is astonishing.

One of the pluses of having another run at the *Fullmetal Alchemist manga* is that the audience gets to see lots of elements dropped from (or not available to) the 2003-04 *animé* series. One of the most significant is the shadowy, ambiguous and extremely dangerous figure of Father, introduced in full following the clip show, episode 28: *Father* (*Oto-sama*).

Gluttony takes Alphonse Elric to see his 'father': underneath Central City, Father lives like a giant spider in the middle of a web, controlling everything from a distance (recalling Dornkirk in Sunrise's *Escaflowne* series). A huge, cavernous lair filled with steel and pipes. The design of Father tells you all you need to know about him: he was left unpainted, so he looked like a *manga* drawing, just a black outline over white (with minimal colours added, such as for his beard). That is, Father is a nonperson, a non-human, an unfinished creature (creepily human but not human, as Mei Chang puts it. Chang is rightly terrified of Father, as is her pet panda. He has killed literally hundreds of thousands of people).

When the second *Fullmetal Alchemist animé* reaches the character of Father, we are in a very interesting place: here, after all, is one of the origins of the whole story, the man/ creature/ god/ presence who created the homunculi, and who is orchestrating much of what's happening in the series (including the Ishbal invasion and the catastrophe of Xerxes). The filmmakers rapidly bring in some of the others charas – principally Edward Elric (so his scheme of escaping from Gluttony's belly worked), accompanied by Envy (in his monster form) and Ling Yao. And also turning up soon are Scar and li'l Mei Chang.

Among the many dramatic beats presented in this episode *Father*, the most entertaining are those concerning Ed, Al and Father. Ironically, not only does Father look like their real father, van Hohenheim, and even behaves like him, he also acts like a parent: the first thing he does is fixes Alphonse's hand, and Edward's injuries (and he also acts – for the only time in the *animé* – with a little eccentric humour. It seems the homunculus in the glass jar featured in the back-story of Xerxes lost his wicked, taunting sense of humour).

But as Edward and Alphonse find out more about Father, and not liking what they hear, they join battle with him (tho' there's no way a major, all-powerful figure like Father can be defeated as soon as he's been intro-duced – despite the Elrics, Mei Chang and Scar having a go).

That both Al and Ed mistake Father for being their own father van Hohenheim is terrific storytelling: it tells us that, despite everything, they are still missing him, and still hoping to meet him (as well as the disturbing link of their father to this strange super-villain). The filmmakers help this along by designing Father in this episode to closely resemble van Hohenheim (this's also why Hohenheim was included as the main character in the previous clip show).

We also see in this scene Ling Yao making a Faustian pact with Father to become a homunculus (the new Greed), an important plot twist, vividly depicted by the animators as an encounter between Ling and Greed against an abstract, flowing red background (of screaming souls), while Ling confers with a giant, grinning demon.

It's this kind of storytelling – intense, dynamic, colourful, and very weird – that puts Japanese filmmaking far in advance of Western cinema. One of the wonderful aspects of Japanese animation is how it can suddenly switch into a very abstract form of filmmaking, into a spaceless, emotional, or psychological (or spiritual) realm, and yet retain the storytelling elements. (Both voice actors – Mamoru Miyano and Yuichi Nakamura – are exceptional as Ling Yao and Greed; they really sell the concept of a battle of wills inside Ling's body).

Later, in episode 45: *The Promised Day*, the filmmakers render the Jekyll and Hyde conflict within Ling Yao in a fantastic, hyper-active manner, combining shaky flashbacks in Ling's mindscreen (of the people in Ling's life) with the avatar of Ling sitting in the abstract red and black interior confronting the demon face that represents Greed. Depicting at least three layers of psychological material within a single character is brilliantly achieved – and it's done *so fast*. Compared to Western filmmaking, which lumbers along like an old dinosaur on its last legs, Japanese animation is zinging and zigzagging with a ferocious rapidity. (And there's no equivalent in Western TV and animation for multiple psychological and spiritual layers).

The Ling-Greed sequence in episode 28: *Father* alone is quite brilliant, but episode 28 is also a full-on action episode, with multiple fights occurring all over the place: Ed and Al attempt to attack Father (and so do Scar and Mei Chang), with no effect at all; Ling duels with Ed; Al and Mei battle chimeras in the corridor...

This is without question some of the finest action filmmaking in recent animation from Japan. It's on a par with any of the classic and revered *animé* outings. And it's very labour-intensive, too – just look at the vast array of visual effects animation here. (The filmmaking is outstanding, with the visual effects team conjuring a torrent of amazing images in vivid reds and crackling blues. The use of deep red lighting is especially impressive – drenching all in scarlet, with shadows in deep black. One should also note the tremendous music, in particular a pounding, percussive cue).

In the midst of it all, crucial dramatic points are made: how Father is able to disarm Ed and Al's considerable alchemical powers, but Mei Chang and Scar, using a different system, can deploy theirs (this perplexes Father – hence these charas return for the finale of the whole series). When Father disarms the Amestrisian form of alchemy, it creates a wave of energy that moves outward from Central City all the way to van Hohenheim, walking in the distant mountains.

Girlie humour, too, arrives in full effect during the encounter between

Mei Chang and the Elrics: little Mei has built up Edward as a handsome Princeling from *shojo manga* in her heart, only to find he's a short, grubby grain of rice. The filmmakers put Mei's outraged responses in 4-*koma* style, as rapid gags. (The outrage of Mei leads, improbably, to the release of Ed and Al from under Envy's paws, when she unleashes her magic).

Episode 29. *Struggle of the Fool*

As well as a clip show (episode 27), the second *Fullmetal Alchemist animé* also included one of my favourite formats in Japanese animation: the set-up show, the chess pieces show, where every character is included in very short scenes, as the writers move all of the counters in the game into position (this is very much a writer's show – Seishi Minakami was the author). We are reminded about the characters, who they are, what they do, where they are, and they re-assert their goals.

This means some of episode 29: *Struggle of the Fool* is rather talky, as the writers set up new plots, and remind us of the existing ones (and include plenty of recycled animation used for flashbacks). It seems talky partly because it follows such an incendiary episode; there is also plenty of humour, to lighten the proceedings after the 28: *Father* show.

Some of this is necessary, of course: we should note that *Fullmetal Alchemist* is a TV series which runs over a period of months (up to a year for *Fullmetal Alchemist 1* and over a year for the 2nd series), so it needs to update the stories from time to time (same with any long-running *manga* or Annie May series). The credits sequence also acts as a summary, with its mini-character sketches, and the trailer for the next episode, following the end credits, adds further plot material. When you watch the *Fullmetal Alchemist animés* on DVD, video, Blu-ray, the web, download, wherever, you are outside of the initial broadcast context of *Fullmetal Alchemist*, where it would be sandwiched in between all of the material that television churns out 24 hours a day: commercials, 100s of other shows, continuity announcements, trailers, promos, news, etc.

One of the intriguing scenes in episode 29: *Struggle of the Fool* is where Envy takes the Elric brothers up in an elevator to see the homunculus Wrath, who's revealed to be... Führer Bradley! Don't you just hate it when the leader of your country turns out to be a psychotic freak created by black magic?! It's intriguing because there's the Führer sitting on his own, with no bodyguards, in a room with our heroes, plus Roy Mustang. Each of them in interior monologue wonders if they could take the Führer – and they probably could. But, as we're only halfway thru the *Fullmetal Alchemist* series, and as sitting down a nice cup of tea in a small office isn't the setting for a major smackdown, it isn't going to happen, and nobody tries anything.

❖

For the rest of episode 29: *Struggle of the Fool*, there're talk-driven scenes which set up future developments; Ed tries to resign from the military, only to be rejected by the Führer (instead, he creepily threatens the Elrics with harming Winry Rockbell); the Elrics call Winry to check she's OK (resulting in another embarrassed/ cute Ed-+-Winry moment); Al gives Lan Fan a message from Ling Yao (who's inside Greed, or vice versa), and of course Lan Fan, severely wounded, reacts badly (she always does where her beloved Prince Ling is concerned – she instantly becomes manically protective); Lan Fan asks Al for automail; Dr Knox looks after Mei Chang and Lan Fan; in a comic exchange, Lan Fan and Mei glower at each other and throw daggers; Ed takes a shower; Ed fixes some damaged buildings; Edward ponders on why he and Alphonse had their alchemical powers subdued earlier, tho' Scar and Mei Chang didn't; and the word about the Führer being a homunculus spreads (Alex Armstrong is stunned that the military he has devoted his life to turns out to be corrupt from the top down, and proving that the Ishbal invasion, which he abhorred being a part of, was also an unjust conflict. The flashback of Armstrong holding a dead child in his arms and weeping is employed again).

Episode 30. *The Ishbalan War of Extermination*

Another outstanding animated show (30: *The Ishbalan War of Extermination*), packing a whole movie into 22 minutes. Expertly written by Hiroshi Ohnogi, storyboarded by Shinji Ishihira, directed by Ikuro Sato and edited by Takeshi Sadamatsu (tx Nov 1, 2009), this is masterful storytelling orchestrating multiple flashbacks and two framing stories. (This episode stuffs the running time with a staggering amount of information).

And the visuals are breathtaking – ep. 30: *The Ishbalan War of Extermination* delivers a completely convincing depiction of genocide in a Middle Eastern setting (in a documentary style, avoiding the bombast of many war movies).

In this middle-of-the-series-run episode of *Fullmetal Alchemist*, we revisit the Ishbal rebellion (and of course the filmmakers re-use some of the earlier footage); but this time it's narrated from Liza Hawkeye's point of view, and also Dr Marcoh's (while Ed Elric listens. He's gone to Hawkeye's *aparto* to return her pistol, which he wasn't able to use. Ed is not a killer, but Hawkeye tells him she has killed many people. And we see her doing it here).

For voice actress Fumiko Orikasa, this is her Big Episode in *Fullmetal Alchemist*'s second run, as she has more dialogue to deliver than all of the other episodes put together (Orikasa plays Lt. Hawkeye very quiet and restrained). For those fans who love Hawkeye with her giant, *kawaii* eyes and neat, blonde hair, this is her shining episode (it's also the moment when Hawkeye is depicted nude in a 'fan service' shower scene – justified because it reveals that she too is tattooed with alchemical info, like Scar). *The Ishbalan War of Extermination* also intercuts scenes of Scar interrogating Dr Marcoh, whom's he stumbled upon in the bowels of Central City (the Doctor's a prisoner of the homunculi).

The imagery of the seven-year Ishbal War is truly horrific – altho' *Fullmetal Alchemist* is a high fantasy *animé* series, the portrayal of the massacres clearly draws on 20th century atrocities. We see the State Alchemists wading into the territory, using philosopher's stones to accentuate their destructive powers (Zolf Kimbley), or burning people alive (Roy Mustang), or alchemizing themselves into iron chain weaponry (Basque Grand), or creating stone walls to round up civilians like cattle so the soldiers can dispatch them with rifles (Alex Armstrong), and even picking off lone Ishbalians with a sniper gun (Liza Hawkeye).

This is 'R' rated violence and bloodshed – it's reminiscent of later movies of World War Two and the Vietnam War like *Saving Private Ryan*, or *We Were Soldiers*, or *The Windtalkers*. Gruesome, bloody, and in some images repulsive. (This is fully-armed soldiers firing upon unarmed civilians, including women and children, with no apparent strategic purpose other than extermination).

Do we really *need* to see so much horror and suffering? Yes and no. *Yes* for all the obvious reasons. And *no* for all the obvious reasons. It's a balance, isn't it? You want to show how catastrophic war and oppression and conflicts can be (or actually are), but you also don't want to alienate the audience, or over-state your case, or to wallow in violence to a gratuitous or sick degree.

We also see Mustang talking with Maes Hughes (about the morality of war), and with Hawkeye. Mustang also mentions his ambition to lead the nation. (We are thus examining armed conflict from several perspectives).

On a different tack (tho' just as downbeat as the Ishbalian War scenes), we go back in episode 30: *The Ishbalan War of Extermination* to Roy Mustang's youth, in a scene (which opens the episode) between him and his dying alchemist *sensei*. Now we find out that Mustang's teacher's daughter is Liza Hawkeye, and her pa is Berthold Hawkeye (Atsuki Tani). He has inscribed some of the secrets of his form of alchemical power on her body in the form of tattoos (!).[29] Don't ask, *why*? Don't think, hell, that *is* creepy! Don't say, why do people in Himoru Arakawa's *Fullmetal Alchemist* series use *people's bodies* as notebooks?! Don't they have the $$$ for a cheap notepad from Staples?! Couldn't they inscribe their alchemical findings in the margin of *Weekly Shonen Jump*?! Why do they spend hours (inflicting incredible pain!) tattooing their own children or brothers?!

Well, anyhoo – we do find out that Liza Hawkeye has been gooey for Roy Mustang since way back (1905 is the date of Berthold Hawkeye's demise, so at least ten years). And, responding to her father's request that he look after her, Mustang assigns her the post of his assistant, on his journey to the Top Job in the country. (The Hawkeye-Mustang flashback also includes an obligatory cemetery scene).

In the other framing story, Dr Marcoh tells Scar about some of the

29 Which justifies the inevitable 'fan service' images of Liza Hawkeye in the shower, nude, so we can see those alchemical tattoos!

very nasty things that the Amestrisian militia did: creating philosopher's stones, for ex, using Ishbalians as victims (and then deploying those very stones to massacre the Ishbalians in their own country). Representatives from Ishbal attempt to end the conflict by offering themselves up (no dice). Kimbley scorns the liberal notions of Mustang and co.

There's even time for a short scene between Mei Chang and Alphonse Elric, when our pint-sized, Xingese ninja discovers the guy in the suit of armour's true identity (and instantly transfers her affections for *chibi* Ed to much-taller Al).

❖

Add up all of the narrative information in ep. 30: *The Ishbalan War of Extermination* and you can't believe it's all crammed into 22 mins: a long Ishbal flashback, ruminations on the ethics of war, Mustang and Hughes bonding, Mustang and his *sensei*, Mustang and Hawkeye at the graveside, Mustang commissioning Hawkeye to watch his back, Marcoh and the transmutation of the stone, Alphonse and Mei Chang, and Edward talking about Winry.

Episode 31. *The 520 Cens Promise*

Episode 31: *The 520 Cens Promise* (surely 'cents'?) is a somewhat bitty, unsatisfying episode – if you regard it as a stand-alone piece. It's one of those *animé* episodes which keep the plot simmering, keep the major characters in the frame, and feature exposition to set-up later episodes. There isn't a single stand-out sequence in *The 520 Cens Promise*: rather, there are numerous very short scenes, many of which are re-caps (and many of which recycle animation).

So episode 31: *The 520 Cens Promise* is similar to episode 27: *Interlude Party* in being something of a clip show. However, it isn't a clip or recycled show, it does advance the plot of *Fullmetal Alchemist*. For instance, we see Ed and Al Elric on the hunt for Mei Chang and her pet panda; we see Scar springing Doctor Marcoh from prison; we see Mei re-uniting with Scar and Loki; we see Ed taking his leave of Liza Hawkeye; we see Doctor Knox being haunted by his nefarious past (including his involvement in dodgy, alchemical experiments); we see Envy springing the Crimson Alchemist (Kimbley) from jail; we see Lan Fan castigated by their grandfather Fuu for losing her arm; we see Roy Mustang gathering intelligence, and saying farewell to his officers; we see the Elric brothers re-uniting with Mustang, and Mustang re-affirming his ambition to become the leader of the country (which's linked to the title of the show – the money that Mustang reluctantly lent to Edward).

So, there's a lot of narrative information packed into *The 520 Cens Promise*, but most of it is a preparation for future episodes. However, there is an important aspect to this episode, *The 520 Cens Promise*, and that is to deepen the characterizations. Certainly it's the *characters* that're one of the reasons for the high impact of Japanese animation: that is, these are three-dimensional characters, and each one is given their own hopes and dreams. After all, over the course of a long run, the audience spends *a lot* of time with the characters (this series is 64 episodes). Understanding their fears and desires enriches them as characters, so that they are not merely pawns in a giant game of chess.[30]

Zolf Kimbley receives a fuller character exploration in this show, with a flashback to his time in the Ishbal War. In the present day, he's been hired by the homunculi to help them create mayhem in Amestris and forge a new transmutation circle (all of their efforts, all of their torture and genocide, remember, are so that one guy can become a God).

Mei Chang makes a mistake here by hurrying back to the miserable bunch of people led by Scar: which's why Himoru Arakawa put her there in the comic. In this show, Scar affirms that they will head North – a foreshadowing of the next big chunk of story in *Fullmetal Alchemist*.

Another of Scar's hideous acts occurs now: with no warning, he grabs Dr Marcoh by the face and transforms it so he won't be recognized. How would that feel? Extremely painful! Darn, what's wrong with the good, old dark glasses and a moustache disguise? Even terrorists know how to disguise themselves without burning your face to shreds!

Instead of decapitating Scar on the spot, Dr Marcoh of course humbly, guiltily, shamefully, masochistically accepts it all – because this man embodies the Guilt of the Ishbal War. Mei and Yoki react in fear, but Mei doesn't flee.

Episode 32. *The Führer's Son*

Another episode which focusses on characterization as much as story development, 32: *The Führer's Son* depicts a number of quests/ chases: the military police (led by Zolf Kimbley) are hunting for Scar (and Dr Marcoh), and discover them a few times, only to have them escape. Siblings Ed and Al are searching East City for Xiao Mei, Mei Chang's pet panda (which they think is a cat – they have a terrible drawing to show people, one of the satires on *manga* art from the *Fullmetal Alchemist* comic). The brothers end up in the library (so you know they're doomed, libraries being the worst place to look for anything in *animé*!).[31]

However, the Elric brothers do find something they don't really want to encounter in Central Library: little Selim Bradley, the son of the Führer, one of the very nastiest characters in all *animé*. The portrayal of Selim in an over-the-top comic style (a *kawaii* kid in bright colours with a girlie voice – by Makoto Tsumura), is a vivid subversion of expectations; because later this li'l tyke who worships the State Alchemists turns out to be the murderous son-of-a-gun homunculus Pride.

There is a thematic point to the very uncomfortable, embarrassing scene in *The Führer's Son* where Ed and Al Elric are persuaded to take tea with Selim Bradley and his parents: and that is the contrast of Führer

---

30 The chess motif is employed a few times in *Fullmetal Alchemist*. *The 520 Cens Promise* is rather like the first moves of a chess game, before the action becomes complicated.
31 However, they are also researching alkahestry in the library (and of course find nothing useful in the books).

Bradley and his 'family' (whom he apparently dotes on), and the Elrics' family. Ed especially finds it *very* disturbing that a psychopathic homunculus like Bradley should be talking about the importance of the family and ruffling his child Selim's hair, right in front of him (there are flashcuts in Ed's mind to Pinako, Winry and the pre-armoured Alphonse).

One of the Führer's unsettling attributes is how he keeps insisting that he, too, should be allowed to have a family and a home life. Maybe – but he's a war criminal and mass murderer with thousands of deaths on his hands.

There is also a dramatic reason for the awkward Selim and Führer scenes: because after this, we are travelling North to Briggs, with the Elrics, leaving Central City and East City far behind. So it's important to have the heroes spend some time with the father and (adopted) son, because they feature prominently later on (and also in the Roy Mustang and Liza Hawkeye subplots).

Meanwhile, General Grumman (Rokuro Naya) has turned up for a meeting with Colonel Mustang in disguise as an old woman. Poignantly, their rendezvous is at the graveside of Maes Hughes (whom Mustang is determined to avenge). Plotting, scheming, more plotting: the middle episodes of *Fullmetal Alchemist* aren't always heavy on action and spectacle: instead, they're keeping the audience informed about movements which're taking place behind-the-scenes, as well as exploring the characters a little more.

Episode 32: *The Führer's Son* keeps the juggling balls of drama high in the air as it flits around a large ensemble of characters. No easy task: consequently, every scene is short, and often intercut with other scenes in parallel action. *The Führer's Son* also employs plenty of flashbacks within characters' speeches, to remind us of things that've happened (as well as to cut down on new animation).

Looming behind the to-ings and fro-ings in episode 32: *The Führer's Son* is the next destination in the *Fullmetal Alchemist* saga: the North (Himoru Arakawa's fantasy version of Hokkaido). Ed and Al are heading North, for Briggs Mountain, as are Scar and his band of misfits (and Zolf Kimbley and others soon follow). Railroad stations and trains are a recurring motif in the *Fullmetal Alchemist* series, as in the cinema of Hayao Miyazaki (reflecting the real Japan, of course, where millions take to the rails every single day). Characters are always getting on or stepping off trains, or leaping onto trains (as Scar and Dr Marcoh[32] do in *The Führer's Son*), or riding in trains and contemplating their lives. There's a restlessness to *Fullmetal Alchemist* (with Edward the most restless of all): it is a series of movements, travels, borders and boundaries.[33]

You could say that it is a weakness of the structure of the story of *Fullmetal Alchemist* created by Himoru Arakawa that she felt she had to

---

32 Dr Marcoh is a middle-aged man who looks like he has trouble getting out of a chair, but here he's leaping onto trains and racing through forests. Actually, it's revealed to be Loki pretending to be Marcoh; but Loki isn't Jet Li, either.
33 Characters also consult maps at length, as Kimbley does in *The Führer's Son*.

keep her characters in constant motion (but that is part of the format of weekly/ monthly *manga*, where action and movement are mandatory). It is also certainly a key thematic ingredient in the *Fullmetal Alchemist* world of being in exile (or of feeling like an exile, an outsider), of being a foreigner or an immigrant, of crossing borders, of never feeling at home,[34] and of being restless. That is thoroughly modern (and postmodern), an Existential condition of the contemporary era where borders are in constant dispute, where no one feels wholly at home, where travel and movement are the norm.

Elrics Ed and Al, in a way, embody that feeling of not having a home. Or, even tho' Winry and Pinako Rockbell insist that Resembool is their true home, not really feeling that it is their home (not, that is, while the story is in progress). Home for Ed and Al is wherever they happen to be: that comes over very strongly in *Fullmetal Alchemist*. These are teenagers who live perpetually in hotel rooms, in friends' houses, or in establishments like military academies or barracks. Their parents are absent, and they have nothing like a regular home life (with a bedroom, the teenager's sanctuary, to call their own).

This is all part of the adventure genre, of course, where the first thing you do is to get your heroes on the move, and have them leaving home. But in the *Fullmetal Alchemist* universe there is more to it than that: the feeling of uprootedness, of being a drifter or traveller, is fundamental to the series.

According to French philosopher Julia Kristeva, we are all exiles, outsiders, strangers: being an exile helped Kristeva see both her own country (Romania) and her adopted country (France) more clearly. Her experience of displacement was an ingredient in her idea of the 'cosmopolitan' individual, the 'intellectual dissident'. As Kristeva knows, strangeness or otherness (being a foreigner) is fundamental to being human: as Kristeva put it, *étrangers à nous-mêmes* (we are strangers to ourselves). In *Strangers To Ourselves* Kristeva describes the foreigner as the 'cold orphan', mother-less, a 'devotee of solitude', a 'fanatic of absence', alone even in a crowd, arrogant, rejected, yet oddly happy (4-5). The stranger is always in motion, doesn't belong anywhere, to 'any time, any love' (7).

Episode 33. *The Northern Wall of Briggs*

All roads lead to the North in episode 33 of the 2009-10 series of *Fullmetal Alchemist*, entitled *The Northern Wall of Briggs*. Ed and Al're on their way via railroad and cart and walking boot to the shivering cold of the mountainous borderland with the vast country of Drachma (drawing on Russia, of course). The tough climate, a realm of fearsome bears and survival against the odds are evoked as the Brothers Elric enter the snowlands (an extensive (and expensive) amount of visual effects animation depicts hurricane winds, fog, and of course falling snow). The

---

34 The Elrics symbolically torched their home!

animé really sells the cold – you feel it as the brothers traverse deep snow in the mountains on their way to Briggs, and as the trains carrying Scar and co. fly through dense pine forests covered in snow. It's Arakawa's fantasy version of Hokkaido.

There is time too for some reminiscing from the Elrics (a key ingredient of the *Fullmetal Alchemist* universe), as they think back to their childhoods, when snow fell heavily one year in Resembool (and they played in the snow, and made snowmen using alchemy). It's sweet when the boys are on their own, without being hassled by parental surrogates, or being attacked by grizzled guys, or being ordered about by the numerous authorities in the *Fullmetal Alchemist* cosmos (scenes like this're some of the tenderest in the *Fullmetal Alchemist* saga).

❖

Two action scenes are featured in 33: *The Northern Wall of Briggs*. The second one has the Elrics coming face-to-face with a mountain bear, in the form of Captain Buccaneer (Ryûzaburô Ôtomo), a formidable soldier (a Russian Bear), another of Himoru Arakawa's hulking warriors who're tough and gruff on the outside, but whose heart is in the right place. Buccaneer takes on Ed and Al, with his giant chainsaw for an automail arm going up against Ed's regular automail (automail not working in the intense cold is one of Arakawa's many Hokkaidoan details). As the snowstorm clears, the Elrics discover that they are standing at the foot of a colossal wall, a metal and concrete dam across a valley, built by the military of Amestris to guard the dangerous border with Drachma: the Wall of Briggs Mountain (it has a very mid-20th century, WW2-look. There's little that's exaggerated here: border walls have been part of human history for millennia).

The Elrics look up in awe at Briggs Fortress, and we're introduced to some new charas – chief among them is super-bitch Olivia Maria Armstrong (Yoko Soumi), the commander of the North Wall, the take-no-prisoners, I'll-challenge-anyone-to-a-fight sister and counterpart from hell to super-butch, I'll-strip-off-my-shirt-now Alex Armstrong (wonderfully voiced by Kenji Utsumi). Yoko Soumi as Olivia's voice is great, and Olivia's design (as a blonde, Nordic Brunhilde) is close to Himoru Arakawa's *manga*, but, despite the yellowy, blonde hair locks and the 1960s, pink lipstick, she's not quite as compelling visually as in the *manga*. However, she sure is formidable! And she takes no •••• from anybody, least of all the Elric brothers! This is one lady Edward *won't* be able to charm! (Olivia is basically another version of harsh but fair *sensei* Izumi Curtis).[35]

The first action sequence in *The Northern Wall of Briggs* is the climax of Zolf Kimbley's pursuit of Scar and Dr Marcoh: this has been portrayed as the middle act of a spy movie made in the 1960s, or a World War Two adventure of men on a mission somewhere like Finland, Switzerland or

---

35 And Curtis appears briefly in a flashback in the next episode – because the *sensei* survived life in the icy mountains as part of her alchemical training. And it wasn't quite in the wilderness, because she stole supplies from Briggs Fortress. (Ed mentions Curtis's survival as they approach Briggs, but he and Al don't know the details).

Czechoslovakia.[36] There are railroad cars hurtling thru snowy nights, rushing past pine forests, with military squadrons dressed like German soldiers in pursuit (recalling movies such as *Where Eagles Dare* and *On Her Majesty's Secret Service*; the racing trains also recalls movies such as *Runaway Train*, the 1985 action film scripted by Akira Kurosawa). The *animé* really captures the textures and excitement of rapid movement through a snowy night – even before the action begins, it's a stunning sequence.

When Zolf Kimbley comes face-to-face with Scar in an empty carriage, with the full moon illuminating them against the snow (a great, classic *animé* touch – when Scar realizes who Kimbley is), the smackdown is intense and spectacular. The filmmakers make up for some of the underwhelming passages in the previous couple of *Fullmetal Alchemist* episodes with a return to vicious duels. Scar and Kimbley have a history going back to the Ishbalian War (seen in brief flashbacks), when Kimbley attacked Scar and his brother, which adds psychological fire to their fight.

But the filmmakers don't sacrifice Scar or Zolf Kimbley just yet – the duel closes on a stalemate, with Kimbley apparently fatally injured (a pipe thru the torso), and Scar left behind on a carriage separated from the rest of the train, in a gag that goes back to the days of silent cinema (we know that Scar can't be dispatched just yet, and not by Kimbley, either).

The Scar-Kimbley duel is rendered with technically impressive animation, bold storyboarding and angles, a seamless integration of backgrounds with characters in movement, and a suitably old-fashioned, adventure serial score by Akira Senju.

Episode 34. *Ice Queen*

The first half of the episode 34: *Ice Queen* (*Kori no Joo*) involves the usual exposition of a new, major location, complete with a tour of Fort Briggs, in order to set up the geography of the place for the subsequent episodes of *Fullmetal Alchemist*, when the action explodes. The second half of 34: *Ice Queen* introduces the dumb, giant homunculus Sloth (Fumihiko Tachiki – not seen in the first *animé* series of *Fullmetal Alchemist*), with broad, slamming action scenes as Sloth runs amok and nothing the tough soldiers at Briggs throw at him (including multiple tank shells) has any effect (you'll recognize the voice of Sloth – Fumihiko Tachiki: he played the amazing Zaraki Kenpachi in *Bleach*). The struggle with Sloth continues into the next episode, again following Himoru Arakawa's *manga* closely, while also adding plenty of material to it. (The action filmmaking is clear, coherent and punchy – every cut is easy to read, and the use of space is remarkable. You forget that these are animated drawings made on desks, paper, tablets, computers and cameras, and are sucked into the drama).

There are two new characters to introduce in episode 34: *Ice Queen*, as well as the dumb, perpetually fed-up monster Sloth: we see much more of

36 Notice that we pore over maps, and contemplate vistas of snowy mountains, all of which explores the new setting of the Amestrisian North.

Olivia Maria Armstrong, the 'Ice Queen' of the show's title, and her lieutenant, Miles (the very wonderful Kazuya Nakai – best-known as Zoro in *One Piece*[37]).

Ms. Armstrong is another of Himoru Arakawa's tough-as-nails warrior women, a commanding officer who strides around Briggs Mountain brandishing a sword (which she flourishes at any opportunity, challenging anyone who opposes her). That she despairs of her brawny (and camp) brother is expected (but amusing), that she is dangerously serious about everything is also expected, that she might've stepped out of Richard Wagner's *Ring* opera, as a blonde Brunhilde, is wonderful. Japanese pop culture is very fond of Valkyrie figures (for fighting girls or for *mecha*).

The most dramatic juice in episode 34: *Ice Queen* is squeezed out of the encounter between the Elrics and the Icy Maiden, when she demands information from them, and they refuse to give it (this sort of scene is a regular exercise for budding actors in drama school: one actor wants something, and the other actor refuses to give it up). Ed is certainly ballsy here in ep. 34: *Ice Queen*, as he faces off against a stern commanding officer who might chuck him and his bro' outside in the cold, or in a cell on a whim (which she does, actually!).

Edward Elric is full of *chutzpah* in the second character-led scene, when he and Alphonse talk with Miles while walking along a corridor. Ed questions Miles about the regime at Briggs Mountain, and the brothers discover that Miles is partly an Ishbalian. Miles is brought into the mix to remind the audience of the significance of the Ishbal War, a time of immense conflict when the State Alchemy system of the Amestrisian military displayed its corruption for all to see, and when the whole civil war was concocted for the purpose of creating philosopher's stones and magical weaponry. (Once again flashbacks depict parts of Miles' back-story, including his encounter with the Ice Maiden – the flashbacks thus also describe the new character of Maria Armstrong).

One reason that the Briggs Mountain episodes are satisfying is because they centre once again upon the Elric brothers. This always brings us back to the central themes and quests of the *Fullmetal Alchemist* world. There are a *huge* number of characters to keep track of in the *Fullmetal Alchemist* series, and keeping the audience up-to-date with them means that the narrative has to step away from the central duo.[38] But when it comes back to them, it always energizes the story, re-states the quests and the themes (as well as including some welcome light-hearted fooling around and humour).

Also impressive is the background art and the storyboarding: the filmmakers create a completely convincing interior for Briggs Fortress – it's a combination of WW2 hangers and military bases, a power station, and communication centres. Armstrong is stockpiling a bunch of weap-

37 Nagai was Jan in *Hellsing* (2002), Alexander in *Nobunaga the Fool* (2014), and Mugen in *Samurao Champloo* (2004-05).
38 The jam-packed screenwriting (by Shôtarô Suga) also manages to reference charas not seen, to keep them in the loop – such as Winry, Alex Armstrong, the Führer, etc.

onry and resources to fight against Drachma (one reason she is going to help the Elrics is because she wants to get hold of Mei Chang's Xingese alchemy).

Episode 35. *The Shape of the Country*

As the Briggs Mountain sequence continues, a number of parallel stories are introduced: one is the resolution of the Sloth subplot, with the team at Briggs Fortress nailing the *oni* by shoving it outside using tanks and dousing it in fuel which helps to freeze it.

Another is the odd couple of li'l Mei Chang (and her pet panda Xiao Mei) and the disgraced and disfigured Doctor Marcoh, who're holed up in a remote, snowbound house not far from Briggs, discussing Xingese and Amestrisian forms of alchemy (called Rentan Jutsu in Xing, or 'alkahestry' in the 2nd *Fullmetal Alchemist anime*). Marcoh has got hold of Scar's brother's notes on alchemy (which he hid there), and is deciphering them with Mei in the house; Mei demonstrates how Xingese (Chinese) alchemy works, with the 'dragon pulse' that employs the rivers of energy in the Earth (the 'dragon lines' or *chi* of Chinese *feng shui*).

Another plot strand is the arrival of the Crimson Alchemist Zolf Kimbley and General Raven[39] (and a sinister-looking Doctor With the Gold Tooth who works for the government), plus the centrepiece of the show – the conversation between Raven and Major Olivia, overheard by Al, Ed & co., which introduces more of the concept of the whole country as a giant foundry for making philosopher's stones and immortal armies.

This is introduced in the key scene in 2.35: *The Shape of the Country*, where Olivia Armstrong takes the Elrics and Vato Falman into the tunnel Sloth carved out to question them about Father, the homunculi, Sloth and everything else. Here Ed cleverly works out that the enemies are setting about producing an enormous alchemical transmutation circle – so large it takes in the whole country.[40] This is the grand scheme that helps to give the *Fullmetal Alchemist* fantasy story such a hard political edge, because the powers-that-be have created the nation of Amestris itself specifically for the purpose of producing a colossal philosopher's stone. They are not using the country as it exists, they founded the country in the first place with this nefarious goal in mind.

It's fitting that it's our heroes, Ed and Al Elric, who solve the puzzle of the tunnel and the government's acts of the past four hundred years: the villains' scheme begins in the late 16th century (around 1588), when they orchestrated armed conflicts in order to create causalities which would feed the production of philosopher's stones, and the giant philosopher's stone to beat all others. In each incident, the army from Central was sent in, and always made matters worse. (This is also Himoru Arakawa's critique of when the Western world began to decline into political and social corruption, after the Renaissance. Arakawa's nostalgia is clearly

---

39 Last seen in ep. 24: *In the Belly.*
40 The cutting pattern links the ruminations of Marcoh with those of Ed, as they both reveal the concept of a country-sized transmutation circle.

for a Renaissance world, or a pre-Renaissance/ mediæval world, before mercantile capitalism, and before colonialism and imperialism on a grand scale).

The audience of *Fullmetal Alchemist* doesn't know for certain yet that it's the homunculus Father who's behind all of this, or just what the villains are trying to achieve, but that doesn't matter. What counts is that our heroes have uncovered a terrifying truth ('the truth behind the truth', as Dr Marcoh puts it): that the government of Amestris has used the military (and State Alchemists) to instigate civil wars and armed conflicts. Each time an uprising or incident occurs, the government in Central City sends in its troops with the over-arching intention of making things worse.

There is, then, a passionate anti-war, non-violent ethics at the heart of the *Fullmetal Alchemist* enterprise, with Himoru Arakawa attacking war-mongers, politicians, political systems and corruption of all kinds. The irony is that she has used very violent storytelling to get her pro-peace, anti-war morality across (you have to keep remembering that the *Fullmetal Alchemist* story was produced in the 2000s, and it very much reflects that era).

Artwork for the Fullmetal Alchemist animé

Episode 36. *Family Portrait*

Family Portrait (= *Kazoku no Shozo*) opens with the character of van Hohenheim, one of the most enigmatic figures in the whole *Fullmetal Alchemist* enterprise. Exactly *who* van Hohenheim is remains something of a mystery, even to the end of the *Fullmetal Alchemist* series, when he is fighting alongside his sons to defeat the homunculus Father.

But when the *Fullmetal Alchemist* series includes van Hohenheim in any scene, it's always interesting (his character's a combination of issues such as origins, ancestry, authority, fatherhood, families, alchemy, history and mystery). The van Hohenheim section of *Family Portrait* is constructed along a flashback pattern, so we have Hohenheim in the present tense thinking back to his earlier life as a family man and father of two young sons (back in Resembool). Hohenheim narrates this part of the *Fullmetal Alchemist* series in voiceover, allowing us access to his thoughts. (This section of the *Fullmetal Alchemist* series reprises elements from the episodes 11: *Miracle at Rush Valley* and 19: *Death of the Undying*, where we saw Hohenheim in the foreground, and also the catch-up episode 27: *Interlude Party*).

The flashback of thirteen years, to the childhoods of the Elric boys, narrated from the viewpoint of van Hohenheim, is very intriguing. Again following the *Fullmetal Alchemist* manga pretty closely, we see the home life of the Elric family, with Hohenheim as the aloof, unapproachable and rather cold father who keeps everybody at a distance (including his wife Trisha). The flashbacks further humanize Hohenheim, tho' he insists that he is a monster, with an immortal body. He is ageless, but his children (and his wife Trisha) are growing older by the day.

The flashbacks in *Family Portrait* include the Elric sons at a young age, then a little older. There are vignettes of the family: Hohenheim fixing the kids' swing on a tree; Ed peering in to see his father working in his study on alchemical research (we see Hohenheim drawing a trans-mutation circle on a piece of paper, apparently working out what the homunculus Father is up to); Trisha organizes a photo shoot for the family (which again emphasizes the issue of ageing and mortality, one of the fundamental aspects of photography – and cinema: they are full of dead people).

Van Hohenheim regrets that he has to leave, and weeps, but he still goes. Hohenheim is a portrait of the workaholic father, the salaryman dad who becomes so absorbed in his work or things outside of the home, he is compelled to leave (only later is it revealed that Hohenheim has been maimed and cursed by his encounter with the homunculus Father, and that he in fact has half a million souls inside him! That's got to affect your mood a little!).

Family Portrait explains a little about why Edward has such a chip on his shoulder about van Hohenheim abandoning his family (early in the morning Hohenheim departs, and the kids are awake to see him leave; he stares at them, steeling himself to leave, and they glare back with reproachful expressions. Notice, tho', that Trisha doesn't get hysterical, or even admonishes Hohenheim for leaving his family. The leavetaking scene is all the more poignant for avoiding hysterics and melodrama. Instead, Trisha gently chides Hohenheim for not being more openly affectionate with his children. When he tells her he has to leave, and to wait for him, she assents).

Back in the present day, van Hohenheim is all alone, sitting around an open fire in a wilderness, clutching the photograph (taken from chapter 68: *Portrait of a Family* in the *Fullmetal Alchemist manga*). But he is doing something now about the homunculus behind all of the strife in Amestris, Father: this is the first really magical/ alchemical thing we've seen Hohenheim do: he reels off some names of people, pulls open his shirt, and digs his hands into his chest. Red goop falls to the ground, and each drop wriggles into it – presumably this red stuff is some kind of manifestation of the people or their souls which reside inside Hohenheim, and they appear to be going searching. None of this is explained yet, and there is plenty about Hohenheim that is always mysterious.

✳

The giant tunnel constructed by Sloth is another subplot introduced in the over-long Briggs Castle sequence, which continues in episode 36: *Family Portrait*: we see our first glimpse of the terrifying, grinning demon of darkness that Pride becomes when he/ it is on the attack (those eyes, white in the *manga*, are of course red in the *anime*). The filmmakers at Studio Bones, Aniplex, Mainichi, Square and the associated companies were clearly inspired by the characterization of Pride in his demonic aspect, as a barrage of grasping, black hands, pointed, ravenous claws, glinting, red eyes and grinning, devilish mouths.[1] And the way that Pride in its/ his monster form slides around walls, floors and ceilings, like venal shadows. The animation of Pride is one of the outstanding elements of the 2009-10 *Fullmetal Alchemist* series; the sound team give the monster wonderfully evocative slithering, grating sound effects. Pride demolishes the search party of soldiers on horseback in the tunnel, including an outrider, Smith, who gallops back to safety (only his arm is found afterwards! Probably the finest use of monsters who are created out of shadows occurs in *Vampyr*, the 1932 classic horror movie directed by Carl-Theodor Dreyer).[2]

Family Portrait is full of reversals and surprises: *Family Portrait* includes General Raven coming to Briggs Fortress to meddle; Zolf Kimbley, now made anew (courtesy of philosopher's stones),[3] strutting around the stronghold in his white, European suit; Ed and Al being put in prison (twice); Scar and Yoki re-uniting with Dr Marcoh and Mei Chang in the snowbound hovel; Raven trying to make a deal about an immortal

---

1 The *Hellsing manga* by Kohta Hirano, and in particular the transformations of the arch vampire Alucard, might be influences here.
2 As critics have noted, *Vampyr* is one of the great films of light and shadow. A movie in which shadows literally come alive and have a life of their own. Few movies transform shadows into something spiritual and metaphysical, but *Vampyr* does. These are shadows which interact with the characters, as characters in themselves, but also personify the forces of evil and dread.
3 And the first appearance of the Doctor With the Gold Tooth.

army with Olivia Armstrong; Raven ordering the homunculus Sloth back to work in the tunnel; and Miles stalling Kimbley while Armstrong dispatches the old coot with her sword (and pushing him into the wet concrete that's closing up the fissure in the tunnel).

We know that Major Olivia Armstrong is seething underneath her long, blonde tresses and pouty, pink lips, as she listens to General Raven's sinister approaches (and enduring his fumbling caresses), and we know that it's merely a matter of time b4 she explodes and runs the old lech thru with the sword she always carries (women should always carry swords for precisely this sort of situation! If a guy's bothering you, simply stab him right through the arm).

Family Portrait is a strong, tightly-written piece of television (by Michihiro Tsuchiya), advancing the story with confidence and intelligence (and also an unusual use of voiceover – we hear characters thinking in the middle of scenes: Ed Elric, Olivia Armstrong, Hohenheim, Miles, etc). The technique is only used occasionally (so you can see how episodes in long-running *animé* are often written and storyboarded by separate teams: some writers will use voiceover, say, while others will try to tell the story visually, without dialogue. Meanwhile, storyboard and layout artists have their own styles: some will go for tricky, show-off shots, like fish-eye lenses or worm's-eye-views, while others will stick to standard singles, two-shots and over-the-shoulder angles). Meanwhile, there is some vivid performance animation in this show: look at how Edward shifts uncomfortably, restlessly forwards and backwards as he sits on the bed in the jail.

Family Portrait closes with a cliffhanger – the arrival of the only other feminine presence for many episodes in the *Fullmetal Alchemist* series:[4] Winry Rockbell. Now that Zolf Kimbley has been let off the leash (with the death of General Raven), and is acting on direct orders from Führer Bradley, he has brought Winry-chan to the North. The lads are in prison, their hands chained into wooden stocks (so they can't perform alchemy), and they are shocked and furious that Winry materializes in Briggs (she, innocently, thinks she's been brought there to adapt Ed's automail to the cold, not realizing that Kimbley is manipulating her, and that Briggs already has technicians who can manufacture cold-weather automail. But the Elrics know straight away what Kimbley is up to).

It's great screenwriting – inspired by Arakawa's comic, an unexpected reversal. Now we have a legitimate reason for Winry to be brought back into the story. Not because she needs to fix or adapt Ed's automail, but because the villains are exploiting her relationship with the Elrics.

Episode 37. *The First Homunculus*

Cinema's greatest special effect is invisible: editing. In *The First Homunculus* (*Hajimari no Homun-kurusu*), the 37th episode of the second

---

4 Bar Mei Chang, of course.

animé series of *Fullmetal Alchemist*, parallel cutting is employed to link up the homunculus Pride in his/ its fearsome, devilish guise with Selim Bradley as Pride, the little, well-spoken, well-behaved son of the Führer of all Amestris. Thus, when the rescue party in the tunnels at Briggs Mountain (led by burly bear Buccaneer) seems about to be attacked by the slashing arms of darkness that is Pride, the monster is called away by the arrival of Liza Hawkeye at the family mansion back in Central City (thus, Pride also extends in monster form for 100s of miles!). In the *Fullmetal Alchemist manga*, scenes in two different places but happening at the same time can be put side by side on the page, but in animation you can cut from one to the other, to accentuate even further the simultaneity of the action (and the music and sound fx help, too).

Thus, when we cut back to Pride as Selim Bradley, the fact that he's depicted as small boy who seems to have been awoken by Liza Hawkeye's late visit to the Bradley mansion is all the more creepy, because we've just seen some of the toughest soldiers at Briggs Fort preparing for an assault from an unknown monster.

The subsequent scene in *The First Homunculus*, when Selim/ Pride corners Hawkeye as she leaves the mansion, is brilliantly scripted and staged: in the *Fullmetal Alchemist manga*, it's a *very* creepy scene, with Selim/ Pride lurking in the shadows and terrifying the bejesus out of Hawkeye. In the *animé*, the setting, a moonlit colonnade (note the eclipse image of the moon, which looks forward to the finale of the whole *Fullmetal Alchemist* series), enhances the creepiness even further. And when Hawkeye freezes, and those little, black arms and hands slither over her body, it's a genuinely nasty scene of threat (not least because it's a ten year-old boy, in form at least, threatening a woman, who is also a hard-ass professional soldier, with his hands all over her).

Talking about editing: you'll notice right away that the editing and pacing of *The First Homunculus* episode has a different rhythm from the previous episodes, with the shots much shorter in length. Meanwhile, the storyboard artist for this episode (Iwao Teraoka) has altered the look and style of *Fullmetal Alchemist* once again, by introducing a host of unusual camera angles and extreme wide angle lenses. Which all enhances the aura of nervy suspense in *The First Homunculus*. It also renders the conversations in *The First Homunculus* fascinating – between Ed and Kimbley, Pride and Hawkeye, Ed and Winry, etc.

✳

This episode – 2.37: *The First Homunculus* – also contains plenty of comedy, as Winry Rockbell arrives at Briggs Mountain to offer some humorous scenes which lighten the somewhat dour middle episodes of the 2009-10 *animé* series of *Fullmetal Alchemist* (as well as an important feminine presence). The funniest moment has Ed topless, lying on his back, while Winry administers to his automail: the sexual subtext is pushed into the foreground as comical farce, as Ed wills himself not to get flustered (by reciting a list of chemicals from the Periodic Table, a variation on baseball players in a Woody Allen movie). The *Fullmetal Alchemist* series likes to feminize Ed-kun, and also to reverse the gender roles, so that Ed is passive, at Winry-chan's mercy, and partially undressed, on the bed, while she is in control of the situation.

Winry Rockbell is re-introduced in *Fullmetal Alchemist* to deepen the threat, of course – now the Elric boys have to look after Winry as well as themselves. Al spends much of his time in a prison cell (in this and previous episodes), so that it's Ed who's driving this part of the plot forward.

Meanwhile, Zolf Kimbley is trying to manipulate the three kids, by playing them off against each other. He offers Ed a Faustian pact – ordering him to be the State Alchemist again and to work for the Führer. Kimbley uses the one thing that could *really* motivate Ed – a philosopher's stone (which he places on the table in front of Ed). But the three teens are finding ways to out-smart Kimbley (with Ed and Al secretly bringing Winry up to speed). They play along with Kimbley, but have their own agendas.

Placing the brothers next to a philosopher's stone re-states the central quest of the Elric boys again, bringing this giant, animated series of 2009-10 with its huge cast of characters back to the central teenage duo and their overriding quest: of finding their bodies/ wholeness/ identity/ peace.

And back in East City, the Flame Alchemist is gathering intel on what's happening in the North of Amestris (with the customary flirty, romantic setting of flowers and women as the social context for the scenes, to the irritation of Mustang's co-workers). Even these rather talky scenes are kept light and entertaining with breezy editing and inventive story-boarding.

Yes, it's true that this episode is a little too talky – it's a set-up show, laying the foundations for future installments. But at the end of the episode, the Elrics are on the move again – with Briggs having exhausted much of its potential as a setting. But let's not forget that this show also features one of the great scenes in *Fullmetal Alchemist*, where Lt. Hawkeye is threatened by a boy-monster.

Episode 38. *Conflict At Baschool*

The level of comedy and goofing around in the *Fullmetal Alchemist* series reaches a peak in episodes like *Conflict At Baschool*. For Western fantasy and action fans who don't like the comedy in Japanese animation that's inserted into the midst of 'serious' action scenes, this sort of episode rankles, spoiling the drama and the suspense. For audiences who enjoy the wacky mix of wild comedy with high drama, the *Fullmetal Alchemist* series is wonderful. (And anyway, why does a TV series have to stick to the same tone throughout?).

There are numerous comical scenes in 2.38: *Conflict At Baschool*: Mei Chang meeting with Ed and Al Elric and going lovey-dovey over Al (and having a hissy fit when Winry Rockbell clambers out from inside Al's suit of armour – who is this hussy?! Mei demands); Yoki relating his sorry life after the events in the mining town when he met the Elrics, and the brothers ran rings around him (this chapter of the *manga* (4) wasn't included in this second animated series, but instead is summarized here); and Ed and Al reacting to the chimeras.

Episode 2.38: *Conflict At Baschool* opens with Liza Hawkeye reeling from her terrifying encounter with the homunculus Pride (with the disturbing realization that he/ it let her live). Tying Hawkeye to Col. Mustang occurs again with a well-timed phone call, and Mustang sensing that something has upset his trusty assistant Hawkeye. (The show opens unusually – with a big close-up of Hawkeye).

The scene shifts to Baschool (after spending a *long* time at Briggs Mountain). Baschool is a former industrial town down on its luck and nearly abandoned (a favourite sort of location in Japanese animation – in *Fullmetal Alchemist*, Baschool has very detailed background art depicting derelict and decayed industrial buildings deep in snow, recalling *anime* such as *Cowboy Bebop*[5] and *Wolf's Rain*, and, for a Japanese audience, very evocative of Russia, and parts of Northern Japan). Now Scar is the centre of attention, as Zolf Kimbley and his underlings search for the Ishbalian terrorist. Ed and Al slip away from their minders (the chimeras), and encounter Dr Marcoh, Mei Chang and Yoki (and Scar a little later).

Having added Winry Rockbell to the mix, the filmmakers at Bones/ Aniplex/ Square/ Mainichi *et al* make two expected narrative moves: the first is to have Winry confront the killer of her parents again: Scar. The second is to have Winry being kidnapped (so she can be rescued by the heroes again). After all, if you put a teenage girl in this harsh, cold, industrial environment in the midst of warring soldiers and villains, she's there primarily as a Princess To Be Rescued (as well as to act as the conscience for the Elric brothers, and offer some lighter-toned beats).

The capture of Winry-chan provides the cliff-hanger to 38: *Conflict At Baschool*, with Scar appearing out of smoke atop a building, holding the unconscious girl (the image is reminiscent of 100s of superhero comics, and it also reverses the Ishbal flashback, when Zolf Kimbley was on top of the building). Exactly *how* Scar manages to snaffle Winry Rockbell out from under the noses of both Ed and Al Elric is glossed over here with the simple device of a cut to another scene (a long shot of Baschool and a distant explosion). We find out later how a deal was struck among the group.

Back at Briggs Fortress, the search party returns from the tunnel, with the two spooked survivors (Buccaneer is grateful). It's one thing after another for Olivia Armstrong, as she sees a convoy from Central City approaching – she has to face the consequences of dispatching General Raven.

Meanwhile, the centrepiece of episode 38: *Conflict At Baschool* action-

5 The *Jupiter Jazz* episode in *Cowboy Bebop* is a city that's seen better times (it's reminiscent of Detroit or Toronto for me), and also mining colonies and the snowbound industrial towns of Alaska or Northern Russia (and if we're in Russia, we're in a country with numerous historical rivalries with Japan).

wise is a giant duel between Scar and the chimeras Jerso and Zampano swiftly followed by the Elrics vs. the chimeras. The action follows many of the beats of the *manga* by Himoru Arakawa, and it also captures how the artist depicts fights as very rapid, racing movements across large spaces, with compositions that emphasize diagonals and asymmetrical framing. So in the *Fullmetal Alchemist manga* characters tilt their bodies forward, heads and chins pushing forwards, with one knee raised not far underneath, and the other leg thrust behind. Both animated series of *Fullmetal Alchemist* translate that ferocious feeling for movement and penetrating, stabbing moves into stunningly dynamic smackdowns.

Stylistically, episode 38: *Conflict At Baschool* of *Fullmetal Alchemist* is all over the place: there's rapidfire duelling and smackdowns (where Ed, Al and Scar battle the chimeras); there's *shojo* hearts and flowers and cuteness (where Mei Chang coos over her beloved boyfriend-to-be-in-armour, Alphonse); there's 1940s *film noir* menace with Hitchcockian camera angles in the scenes involving Liza Hawkeye and Roy Mustang; and there's an extensive parody of numerous animated styles in the Yoki flashback (including shaky black-and-white newsreel footage from 1914; sepia-hued montages; still frames like children's storybooks; and *very* cartoony, very exaggerated poses. This all plays without dialogue, in a lengthy *hommage* to silent cinema).

The Yoki flashback expands upon the *manga* considerably: first we see what happened in chapter 3: *The Mining Town* of the *manga*, with the Elrics out-witting the hapless, vain, foolish and selfish Yoki (portrayed in grainy b/w footage from 1914, complete with silent movie intertitles); we see Yoki trying his hand at burglary, gambling, and other jobs to raise funds (depicted in the pale colours of early colour film); and there's an insert of the Armstrong family (including the beautiful, blonde daughter), when Yoki burgles the Armstrong mansion. (The kicker is that, at the end of Yoki's flashback, nobody is listening to him).

Episode 39. *Daydream*

This is an important and cleverly-written episode (by Seishi Minakami), in which the motivations and goals of the chief characters are laid out and re-presented once again.[6] Winry Rockbell confronts Scar over the murder of her parents; Ed and Al Elric encounter the two chimeras and discuss getting their bodies back; Miles speaks to Scar about trying to make a positive difference politically in Amestris, as an Ishbalian; Dr Marcoh and Mei Chang show up to revive the alchemy/ alkhahestry (and Save Amestris) plot; Alphonse confronts his body in the netherworld; and Father schemes and plots in God-like fashion.

2.39: *Daydream* is a crucial episode of *Fullmetal Alchemist* because it reminds the audience just what our heroes are fighting for, what they are up against, what they want, and what is motivating them. The smart use of flashbacks (such as of Scar with his tribal leader, in b/w), introduces

6 *Animé* series are produced in seasons of 13 episodes, in runs of 13, 26, 39 or 52 episodes – so episode 39 is a typical place to re-boot the series.

one of the key themes of the whole *Fullmetal Alchemist* series: not to forgive, but to abide injury and injustice. Don't forgive, says the leader, but live with it (rather like living with a curse, as Hayao Miyazaki put it in relation to the hero of *Princess Mononoke*, the Prince Ashitaka).[7]

Structurally, episode 2.39: *Daydream* takes the unusual step of moving back in time from the cliffhanger of the previous episode, *Conflict At Baschool,* to explain how it came about that Scar was standing on top of the building with the unconscious Winry-chan as his hostage. So the two scenes, of Scar and Winry, book-end the lengthy discussion inside the building, where Miles, Scar, Winry, Alphonse and Edward ponder on what they're going to do with Scar, how they're going to evade Zolf Kimbley and his soldiers, and bigger issues, such as what is going to happen to Briggs Fort, and what is bubbling underneath (literally) Amestris.

The writer (Seishi Minakami) gives each character their bit to say or do in episode 39: *Daydream* of *Fullmetal Alchemist* series two. So Alphonse gets to offer some sympathy to the two tied-up chimeras, encouraging them not to give up hope that they can get their real bodies back. Winry Rockbell gets to come up with the hostage plan, aided by Al (which, you have to admit, is full of things that could go wrong, and that Winry herself would think of the idea is not convincing). Scar gets to contemplate issues such as empathy and compassion, as Winry binds his wound, and Miles berates him as a red-eyed Ishbalian brother about how to right the wrongs of the civil war in Ishbal, and Scar thinks back to his ethical discussion with the tribal chief. Yoki has his moment of glory, too, when he shows off his knowledge of mining towns, and works out how they can escape back to Briggs Fortress along the mine tunnels.[8]

Dr Marcoh and Mei Chang turn up late in the episode to re-introduce the theme of Amestrian alchemy vs. Xingese alkahestry (and the chief MacGuffin in this section of *Fullmetal Alchemist*, the notebook of Scar's brother. Yes, folks, that li'l notebook is over-used by the writers, and there is also the unconvincing side to the notebook MacGuffin that so many characters seem to think that Scar's brother holds the secrets of alchemy. Notice that the one guy who could tell them everything – van Hohenheim – is absent). Mei muses on the notion of immortality, and how philosopher's stones shouldn't be used if they require corpses for their creation (Mei also reminds us of Chinese Emperors who would kill any number of people in their pursuit of eternal life).

Of all the characters, it is Edward Elric who has to undergo the largest turnaround, as the goals and motivations of the charas are re-set. Ed-kun has to grit his teeth and accept that Winry-chan will buy them some time to escape if she pretends to be Scar's hostage. Ed isn't happy at all having to make deals with a mass murderer such as Scar. What

---

7 Hayao Miyazaki explained in 1997 of his movie *Princess Mononoke*: 'Ashitaka was cursed for a very absurd reason. Sure, Ashitaka did something he should not have done – killing Tatari Gami. But there was enough reason to do so from the humans' viewpoint. Nevertheless, he received a deadly curse. I think that is similar to the lives of people today. I think this is a very absurd thing that is part of life itself.'

8 The series (and the *manga*) occasionally uses Yoki – as when he rescued the heroes in the car.

ultimately persuades him is the promise of deciphering Scar's brother's notebook, plus Winry challenging him face-to-face in close-up, when they try to out-scowl each other.

All of this talk and argument consumes most of episode 39: *Daydream* of *Fullmetal Alchemist 2*. But there are a cluster of short but fascinating scenes at the end of the show: in one, Alphonse is trudging thru the snow back to Briggs Mountain (to warn the others that Olivia Armstrong has been replaced, and has been sent to Central City). As Al stumbles into a white-out snowstorm, he has a vision, as out of snow-blindness or the cold, of his body in the other-world of the Gateway of Truth. Al, the soul in the suit of armour, reaches out to his body, with its skinny frame and long finger nails, who is waiting for him. The scene is mysterious, but reminds the audience of the big issues at stake for our heroes (as well as a setting that will form a much larger part in the final episodes of *Fullmetal Alchemist*).

Episode 39: *Daydream* closes with the arch villain of the whole series, the homunculus called Father, back in his underground bunker in Central City. He's playing events from his perspective as a grand chess game. On top of a drawing of the alchemical transmutation circle of the whole of Amestris, Father places chess pieces (with Tim Burtonesque, Hallowe'en designs of skulls, and a little of *Death Note*), while he ruminates in super-villain style about how everything is going his way.

Episode 40. *Homunculus (The Dwarf In the Flask)*

Episode 40: *Homunculus (The Dwarf In the Flask)* (= *Homunkurusu*), broadcast on January 17, 2010, is one of the reasons why Japanese animation is the finest in the world, why Japanese filmmakers are the greatest fantasy filmmakers in the world, and why *Fullmetal Alchemist* really rocks as one of the most magnificent television series of recent times.

Everything in episode 40 of the 2nd *Fullmetal Alchemist* series is working at 100%, from the script (by head writer Hiroshi Ohnogi), to the story-boarding (by Yoshimitsu Ohashi), to the animation (Tetsuya Kawakami was animation director), editing, cinematography, sound editing, direction (Shuji Miyahara was the episode director), and vocal performances.

So in the Xerxes flashback the origins of the whole alchemical/ homunculus story are revealed. It's one of the most entertaining elements of the *Fullmetal Alchemist manga* (it's in chapter 74: *The Dwarf In the Flask* = *Furasuku no Naka no Kobito*) and of the 2009-10 *animé* series: we see the young van Hohenheim (Daisuke Namikawa) as a modest, nameless slave, Number 23), encountering the tiny, smoky homunculus in a glass jar.

The scenario in the flashback takes up the *Frankenstein* mythology and reworks it in an alchemical context in the European Renaissance epoch (plus a little *A Thousand and One Nights*, with the homunculus as the Genie-In-the-Bottle, and Hohenheim as the hapless Aladdin, succumbing to the Genie's powers). We see van Hohenheim as a slave assisting his

Master, an alchemist, who's working for the King of Xerxes (Takkou Ishimori), searching for immortality (echoing the Xingese/ Chinese Emperor in the present day of *Fullmetal Alchemist*).

The homunculus is given a mocking, sarcastic voice, as he/ it effortlessly manipulates van Hohenheim and then the Master Alchemist and the King of Xerxes. The animation perfectly captures the eccentric designs by *mangaka* Himoru Arakawa of the homunculus (and Pride too) as a little, black cloud of a demon in a glass jar with a single eye and a grinning mouth.

Now we see the full extent of the evil of alchemy – when giant trenches are constructed in the soil throughout Xerxes (which the people think are going to be irrigation canals. 'The Emperor even thinks of us poor people', they say). Then comes the bloodshed – whole villages are torched and villagers are cut to ribbons as the King of Xerxes requests a holocaust in order to gain eternal life.[9] (This all lays the ground-work for what's going to happen in Amestris in the present tense of the *Fullmetal Alchemist* series, of course, with those giant tunnels built by the homunculus Sloth, and the murderous conflagrations created by the government around the nation).

Thousands of Yen are spent on an impressive battery of visual effects as the King of Xerxes orders up a grandiose ritual to promote immortality, overseen by the tricksy, little homunculus in the glass jar. Scenes filled with magic, action, cataclysms, visions and visual effects are one of the things that Japanese animation is simply amazing at delivering, and the 2nd series of *Fullmetal Alchemist* doesn't disappoint. The immortality ritual has the filmmakers at Studio Bones, Aniplex, Mainichi, *et al* working at their height (they're also trying all sorts of unusual ideas, such as tilting the camera way over, so the long shots of Xerxes on fire at night are tipped nearly upside-down).[10]

The images of the grand ritual going horribly wrong, as the homunculus opens the Gateway, letting out the writhing, black arms and that creepy, giant eye, are really spectacular. The scale of the visuals is enormous – the Eye of the Gateway opens up below the centre of the magic circle, bulging up like the mushroom cloud of an atomic bomb to engulf the city of Xerxes.

Nobody, absolutely *nobody*, does apocalyptic visions like the incredible animators and filmmakers in contemporary Japan. When it comes to devastation on a truly colossal scale, and to depicting catastrophe in vivid, highly unusual ways, Japanese filmmakers rule supreme. The images of giant moons, vast eyes, fires, electrical energy, grinning demons, screaming victims, swirling vortexes of evil are one of the hallmarks of Japanese animation when it really lets rip. (Yoshimitsu Ohashi's storyboards skillfully create transitions from scene to scene, such as the homunculus in the jar dissolving to the round, full moon. Throughout this episode circular motifs are everywhere).

9 It takes time, too, as the King notes. Also, he is ill in bed when the transmutation circle is finally ready, suggesting that months have passed.
10 The colours and the cinematography too are marvellously handled, with crisp, saturated hues (here's where you can let the colour run wild in a big, visual effects scene).

The storytelling in episode 40 of *Fullmetal Alchemist*'s 2nd series is remarkable, filled with dread on an epic scale. We see how a tiny creature in a glass jar is able to orchestrate absolute mayhem across the entire nation without moving from a jar on a shelf. The King of Xerxes and the master alchemists are convinced that the homunculus knows the secrets of eternal life – it's the terror of dying that drives the Lord of the land onward, to the point where he will sacrifice everyone in the nation. (The fear of dying mobilizes many a fantasy outing, from the *Earthsea* books of Ursula Le Guin to the *Twilight Saga* by Stephenie Meyer. And of course, *Frankenstein* is the Ur-text behind/ underneath it all).

The climax of the Xerxes flashback in episode 40: *Homunkurusu* is astonishing: van Hohenheim comes round from unconsciousness in the temple, swiftly realizing that everybody, including the King of Xerxes, is dead. He staggers outside, calling names, but all he finds are corpses. It's a scenario we have seen a few times – when the sole survivor of some cataclysm wakes up to find no one left alive. Typically it's a sci-fi trope, following a war/ invasion/ plague/ catastrophe. But in *Fullmetal Alchemist*, it seems so much more gruesome and horrific in being a conscious act by a demon to destroy everybody for the sole purposes of making itself immortal. (And the victims are also now inside Hohenheim).

The staging and performance of the finale of the Xerxes flashback of episode 40: *Homunculus* is brilliantly achieved: this is truly great filmmaking. After the noisy mælstrom of the alchemical ritual, there is an eerie silence... van Hohenheim's bewilderment as he stumbles his way out of the temple to see all of Xerxes silent as the grave... the country has become one vast cemetery... and behind him looms the homunculus, who has, bizarrely (but somehow appropriately), taken on the form of Hohenheim himself... (A great touch has Hohenheim kneeling, thinking at first that the homunculus is King Xerxes; and then the homunculus also kneels).

Then the dwarf in the flask reveals the repulsive truth: that in order to achieve an immortal form, he/ it has consumed all of the souls of Xerxes: half reside inside the homunculus, and half inside van Hohenheim. It's a dramatic twist with a huge thematic punch, and of course it sickens Hohenheim to the core. (The camera pulls back rapidly as Hohenheim screams).

*

The Xerxes flashback is the one of the outstanding sequences in the two *Fullmetal Alchemist* series: yet episode 40: *Homunculus* also contains an important sequence in the present day: we cut from van Hohenheim in agony in the city of Xerxes four hundred years ago to van Hohenheim on a train (always with the trains in *Fullmetal Alchemist*!). He has been daydreaming (or nightmaring) about that horrible time. He runs into, of all people, Izumi Curtis (one of Himoru Arakawa's author surrogates), and her big, burly husband Sig.

As the three people leave the railroad station and walk in a back alley of a city (that might be Dublith), Izumi Curtis collapses. Van Hohenheim comes to her aid by guessing that Curtis has also seen 'the Truth' (the Gateway). Curtis confesses that she tried to bring back her dead baby. Hohenheim, using alchemy, rearranges her internal organs (by grotesquely thrusting his hand into her belly). Hohenheim then admits that he is no ordinary man, but a philosopher's stone in the form of a man. The scene demonstrates that Hohenheim tries to heal and help using his alchemical powers, the opposite of Father.

There's another narrative ingredient in episode 40: *Homunculus*, involving Liza Hawkeye and Roy Mustang: they meet at lunch and use code to exchange news (that Selim Bradley is a homunculus – decoded by Mustang in the English language on a piece of paper in the men's room). Mustang also encounters Olivia Armstrong, on her way to meet the Führer (there is no love lost between them – but then, Armstrong looks down on almost all males). The Führer has one up on Major Armstrong, guessing that she had General Raven taken care of (Armstrong is gambling on being able to act within Central HQ, the Briggs bear amongst the Central City tigers. Bravely, Armstrong tells the Führer what she knows about the homunculi – Bradley might slice her up there and then).

Episode 41: *The Abyss*

In episode 41: *The Abyss* we return to the main narrative spine of the *Fullmetal Alchemist* 2 series – back to our heroes, the Elric brothers, plus charas such as Winry Rockbell, Yoki, Scar, Dr Marcoh, Mei Chang and Miles. We are back in the North of Amestris, in the snowy environs of Baschool and the ice-bound Briggs Mountain (and back to mine tunnels and derelict mining buildings). So it's a world of cold, metallic, uncomfortable spaces – and nowhere to get a decent cup of coffee and warm up. As it comes after the incredible Xerxes flashback, the events in *The Abyss* come across as bittier. But the episode does climax with a terrific moment: the hero's gravely wounded (perhaps fatally).

One of the stand-out scenes in the 2009-10 *Fullmetal Alchemist* series is where Ed E. goes up against two powerful chimeras (Darius and Heinkel, Shinpachi Tsuji), and that truly nasty military alchemist, Zolf Kimbley (who has philosopher's stones to help him gain the upper hand). The cat-and-mouse games between Miles and Kimbley and their associates ends with Edward injured with a steel girder right thru his side (another Christ-like wound). Ed heals himself with the help of the two chimeras who earlier were trying to capture/ kill him (he saves them by lifting the debris they're trapped under).

Actress Romi Pak provides some powerful, painful screams to express the intense pain that Ed experiences as the metal girder is pulled out of his body. These are just images on a screen, but you really feel Ed's agony. (And once again, Pak demonstrates why she is one of the top *seiyu* in *animé*. The more I watch *animé*, the more I recognize that Japan has the finest voice actors in the world: they do everything voice performers have to do, but they also do so much more. Their non-verbal and effort sounds, for example, are marvellously effective).

Meanwhile, the filmmakers milk the scene for every ounce of emotion: we see Edward badly injured in giant close-ups of his eyes and face (which also dip in and out of focus). Visual effects animation enhances the pang of the Faustian pact (with the customary zigzags of alchemical energy). As the girder is drawn out and Ed seals the wound using alchemy (using his own life or soul as payment), he has a vision of the Gateway, and there's a brilliant piece of parallel action: we cut to Alphonse in the snow near the entrance to the mine, collapsing as he realizes that his soul is pulling away from his body in the Gateway (we glimpse Al's body at the Gate).

It takes *a lot* out of Edward to heal himself (he collapses afterwards), but the incident leads to another re-setting of the central quest of the *Fullmetal Alchemist* series – about the brothers and their bodies. Edward uses some of his life-span to repair his body (which demonstrates how the stakes are getting higher). Meanwhile, Al has only just been reunited with Winry and co. in the snow when he collapses.

Prior to the duel with Zolf Kimbley, Edward Elric has a crucial discussion with Miles about his determination *not* to be a killer. Miles puts out the order that Kimbley and his men must be taken out: Edward insists to Miles that, no, he is *not* going to be a killer.[11] This is an important theme in the *Fullmetal Alchemist* cosmos, and it's not only because the heroes are teenagers. Author Himoru Arakawa doesn't want to promote heroes who actively seek out violence and death. Her heroes are not war-mongers (tho' they find themselves thrown into a world where pretty much everybody is aggressive and violent). The counterpoint to the pacifist, idealist argument is put forward by Miles to his men: he voices the practical, realist approach: sometimes it's better to take life than let it continue.

Episode 42. *Signs of a Counterforce*

This episode (written by Shôtarô Suga) begins with a re-grouping scene involving the motley crew headed up by Winry Rockbell, Alphonse Elric and Scar. They have taken refuge in yet another ruined dwelling (which're handily everywhere in fantasy and adventure *animé*), and focus on deciphering the alchemical notebook of Scar's brother. Dr Marcoh and Mei Chang, aided by a (dismantled) Alphonse, decode the book by taking it apart and rearranging its pages according to key alchemical phrases (such as 'gold' and 'immortality'). It reveals... the transmutation circle that is being formed across the whole of Amestris. Al has the idea to turn the pages over, which depict the counter-measure, a circle based on Xingese alchemy (alkahestry). Thus, thankfully, all of that work put in by Mei Chang or Marcoh pays off.

11 Miles discusses the issue later with his soldiers: they are grown-ups, cynics, who see now that murder is sometimes the only way of shifting a problem. But *Fullmetal Alchemist* does not endorse that view.

Meanwhile, we follow a host of characters and groups of characters (but note the absence of Edward Elric in this episode – his fate (last seen near death) is left open): Sloth has been digging the tunnels under Amestris and joins up with his starting-point. Now the tunnel's complete, we cut to Father brooding in his bunker, announcing that the end is in sight. Minor charas such as Heyman Breda, Vato Falman and others get in touch by phone (there's a vivid flashback of Cain Furey in a WWI scenario fleeing in trenches from a bombardment; his buddy, Thomas, expires, and Furey escapes, screaming that he will live). Back at Briggs Fort, Miles returns with news of death and disaster.

Zolf Kimbley, wandering in the mines beyond Baschool, stumbles on the tunnels that Sloth has created and encounters the homunculus Pride, who pretty much orders Kimbley to stage an attack on Briggs Mountain (this will form one of the last 'crests of blood' (a genocide) that Father needs to complete his transmutation circle across the whole Amestris nation).

Pride appears again in the finest sequence in episode 42: *Signs of a Counterforce*, featuring van Hohenheim going up against the homunculus in the tunnels under Liore, a city we haven't visited for some time (prior to this episode, we see a character from way back in the Liore episodes – Rose. Now she's acting as a mother of the people, ladling out soup to the needy, who queue up for their hand-outs. This is how Hohenheim is introduced, crawling in the dirt and begging for food).[12] The first series spent more time in Liore.

Van Hohenheim is taken to the basement of the (now ruined) Church[13] of Leto by Rose and the café owner. Now we see Hohenheim taking the initiative, and moving into action. He strides into tunnel flooded with toxic water (using a magical bridge) and soon encounters the homunculus Pride.

The animators (led by animation director Kiyomitsu Sato) let rip with some startlingly inventive and very rapid action, portraying Pride splitting into multiple arms, claws and maws, pursuing Hohenheim along the tunnel (the sound effects editing is very fine this sequence). The animation vividly captures the hurtling, vicious quality of Himoru Arakawa's *Fullmetal Alchemist manga*, and how death is mere feet away (one slip and it's curtains for van Hohenheim).

When it's/ he's unleashed in full effect, the homunculus Pride is pretty much unstoppable (we saw in episode 36: *Family Portrait* how it cut a party of tough Briggs soldiers to ribbons). Except we know now that van Hohenheim is a majorly talented alchemist, who has no less than half of the souls of the population of a whole country inside him. Van Hohenheim tries a few alchemical blocks, but Pride smashes through them. The filmmakers like to portray Hohenheim as an extremely powerful alchemist, but also a little klutzy and clumsy (which's in the *manga*) – so

12 In the first *Fullmetal Alchemist* series, Rose appeared as a Virgin Mary figure, called 'Holy Mother'.
13 It was demolished during the duel between Cornello and Ed in the third episode, *City of Heresy*.

it's appropriate that he stumbles into the side tunnel seemingly by accident. Here he discovers that Pride has to stick to the shadows and to the tunnel that Sloth's dug.

The layouts of the scenes involving the homunculus Pride in *Fullmetal Alchemist 2* are quite brilliant: the designers flatten Pride into frontal views and side views, and allow the black, grinning demon to abstractly consume all of the frame, so that it/ he seems about to swallow everything in its/ his path (there are also several fades to/ out of black here). In the reverse angles, we see Hohenheim (and Zolf Kimbley) standing against a vast background of sliding, quivering mouths, teeth, claws and red eyes. Pride really is a masterpiece of design and animation – all taken from Himoru Arakawa's conception and drawings in the *manga*, of course, a genuinely creepy, venal villain.

But van Hohenheim has the measure of Pride now – he's the 'first homunculus', split off from Father and created in the image of the black blob in the glass jar of 400 years ago in Xerxes (Hohenheim delivers the exposition about the homunculi being created as parodies of the Seven Sins of Western religion: we see freeze frames of each one). Hohenheim gives Pride a message to take back to Father along the tunnels: a Declaration of War.

Episode 42: *Signs of a Counterforce* closes with a Big Dramatic Scene, as the forces of Drachma (= Russia) close in on Briggs Fortress, with columns of marching soldiers and heavy artillery (and led by Zolf Kimbley, fulfilling his orders from the homunculus Pride). The alarm sounds in Briggs and it's battle stations, with everyone hurrying to man the guns as the barrage begins. By this time, *Fullmetal Alchemist: Brotherhood* has attained an unstoppable momentum as a masterpiece of animation and fantasy/ adventure storytelling.

Episode 43. *Bite of the Ant*

This is an Envy episode – which means it's going be shouty and over-the-top and full of diva hissy fits. (Envy cries out for an *animé* series of his own! How he would love it! Unfortunately, you couldn't have Envy winning all of the time!).

This is also a stupendous show for performative animation and for visual effects animation. It is technically dazzling,[14] as the animators find themselves truly inspired by Envy in his three chief guises: as the cocky, young, spiky-haired punk, as the formidable dragon-dog monster, and as the pathetic, shrimp-like creature.

In episode 43: *Bite of the Ant*, Envy has been lured to the North by Zampano: here's the welcome return of the insane villain Envy, tho' he's soon at the mercy of our heroes as he stumbles into their trap of alkahestry mines (operated by Mei Chang and Alphonse nearby).

The second *animé* series of *Fullmetal Alchemist* delivered a fantastic duel between the group of misfits (who include Scar, Dr Marcoh and

---

14 The storyboarding (by Iwao Teraoka) is excellent, featuring an exceptional use of close-ups.

Alphonse Elric) and Envy in the snow in the North, which was a highpoint of the *Fullmetal Alchemist manga*. The filmmakers went way beyond Himoru Arakawa's comic in producing grotesque transformations for Envy, and a suitably hollerin', screamin' demise for the homunculus (here Doctor Marcoh, caught in the Envy-monster's giant, brown tongue, performs one of his most significant acts in the *Fullmetal Alchemist* series, destroying the philosopher's stone inside Envy). The visual effects animation ramps up the battle with the Envy-monster to a grandiose, operatic level: when the action lets rip in the *Fullmetal Alchemist* series two, it really is astounding. (Marcoh, Scar, Mei – they all get their chance to attack the likably unlikeable Envy).

But Envy isn't dead, of course – he becomes, in the final gasp of his death throes (splurging out of his third eye! and a series of heads erupting from gaping mouths), a tiny, green, snail-like thingie. And again, the filmmakers at Studio Bones, Aniplex, Mainichi & co. are inspired to squeeze plenty of comedy out of Envy's new, ignominious state, as the group taunt him, flick him with their fingers, rattle him around in a glass jar,[15] and ignore him when he latches onto (the neck of) poor, hapless Yoki, hoping to take him hostage (the comedy here is terrific, as the group shrugs their shoulders over the fate of the weasel Yoki. As the *Fullmetal Alchemist manga* showed, this wasn't the end of Envy! He is simply too good not to bring back again. But the fact that he's been bested by a bunch of humans infuriates Envy probably more than anything!).[16]

✳

Following the stand-out action sequence in episode 43: *Bite of the Ant* (all of the scenes seem anti-climactic after this!), the group discusses what to do next, leading to a parting of the ways (at a symbolic crossroads in snowy fields). Mei Chang is packed off to Xing (China), with the remains of the homunculus Envy in a jar; Scar lopes away with Doctor Marcoh in tow to do something grim and serious (every scene featuring Scar is grim and serious). Which leaves Winry Rockbell and Alphonse Elric and the others musing on Envy's news that Edward has possibly been injured.

The invasion of Briggs Fortress by the forces of Drachma (which formed the cliffhanger of the previous episode), involves a fierce artillery bombardment (in the manner of movies about the First World War), closing with the Drachman army decimated. Zolf Kimbley stands alone and smug in the white snow dotted with shell craters and pools of red blood.

✳

Smaller, more modest scenes in episode 43: *Bite of the Ant* include a discussion between Liza Hawkeye and Führer Bradley about the homunculi (where Bradley is humanized a tad when he says that altho' he was a pawn of higher-ups, he chose his own wife). A minor scene depicts the lizard-like Bido, one of Greed's henchmen, spying on Amestrisian soldiers who're looking for Izumi Curtis at her butcher's shop (we don't

---

15 In one amusing beat, Envy rocks on his back, nonchalant, like a child who knows he'll get his own way in the end.
16 Even though it would be better for them if they'd stepped on the critter and finished him off.

know why yet, but later we discover it's because Father is searching for candidates to help him create the ultimate philosopher's stone). We see Olivia Armstrong being re-united with her brother Alex in Central's military HQ (she constantly puts him down as a cowardly weakling, even tho' Armstrong has the stature of an eight-foot tall, professional wrestler).

Episode 43: *Bite of the Ant* closes with another teaser, as Olivia Armstrong is escorted by a flunkey down to the catacombs below Central City's military government, where he reveals the army of immortal soldiers hung in rows (upside-down). It's a creepy, unsettling moment. Once they've been revealed, we know that the filmmakers will be using them later on (when they become a formidable obstacle for many of our heroes).

Episode 44. *Revving At Full Throttle*

The title of this episode – *Revving At Full Throttle* – refers to Edward Elric. The *chibi* hero of the *Fullmetal Alchemist* franchise returns with a vengeance in this episode, waltzing along a corridor with his arms and gob stuffed with food. Episode 44: *Revving At Full Throttle* teases the audience for some time about (the imminent arrival of) Edward, with assorted charas talking about him (including Alphonse, Winry, Rose, Hohenheim, Zampano, Jerso and others), and the identity of the unseen assailant at the Doctor's surgery. The first half of the episode builds up to the introduction of Edward, now fully restored and, as he announces, 'revving at full throttle!'

Ah, it's good when Edward Elric is back in the saddle at the centre of the *Fullmetal Alchemist* franchise. Sweet and thoughtful as Alphonse is, it's just not *Fullmetal Alchemist* unless Ed is in the thick of things, going nuts when people call him *chibi*, being his usual restless self, stuffing his face with candy, and reminding everybody of his overriding goal of attaining his body.

Episode 44: *Revving At Full Throttle* is a character-based installment in the 2009-10 *Fullmetal Alchemist* series, gently stopping to explore the characters and their motivations while also advancing the plot (but not forgetting to add several action scenes). We begin with a husband and wife team of dodgy Doctors[17] who patch Edward back together. The authorities are close on their heels, however, and after a stand-off in the Doctors' scuzzy dwelling (with Ed beating up assorted militia), there's an amusing car chase along Old European streets (with Edward alchemic-ally transforming the car into what he thinks is a cool design – a cross between something out of *Batman*, *The Road Warrior* and *Dick Tracy*. And in full colour, it's purple!). Ed now has one chief goal: to be re-united with his brother Al (but he needs intel – they stop at a roadside, and the Fullmetal Alchemist ponders his next move.

Meanwhile, in Liore, Alphonse-kun, Winry-chan, Yoki-san and the others meet up with Rose-chan at the café seen way back in the third

---

17 They are the back streets counterparts of the Rockbells.

episode of *Fullmetal Alchemist 2* (where they broke a radio, which is referenced here). The plot takes an unusual turn now by introducing van Hohenheim as working with the citizens of Liore in physically rebuilding their town. So, instead of continuing his fight against Father and the homunculi, which he announced so boldly to the homunculus Pride at the end of episode 42: *Signs of a Counterforce*, the Elrics' father has become a builder (partly because he's biding his time until 'the Promised Day', which he mentions to Al).

The meeting between father and son is awkward at first – they haven't seen each other for years, and Hohenheim is the classic absent (and somewhat distant) father (he exits clumsily after their initial meeting). Soon, tho', Alphonse has sat and listened to Hohenheim's story of the creation of the homunculi and how he became a philosopher's stone (the setting is, appropriately, the church blasted apart in the battle with Cornello in episode three – we cut to the statue of the god Leto several times, which a reminder of how Ed transmuted it).

Van Hohenheim reminds us of the principal plot involving the villains in *Fullmetal Alchemist 2*, and how a Big Event is approaching rapidly. He also warns that they are up against formidable foes, including the homunculus Pride. (Al says he is going to investigate the tunnel in Liore, but Hohenheim warns him away).

Other modest scenes include one where Winry takes a bath at Rose's apartment: as in the *manga* by Himoru Arakawa, it is an unashamed 'fan service' moment, with Winry naked (and carefully posed). It's typical of long-running TV shows to put the female characters in a hot spring or in bikinis at the beach; *Fullmetal Alchemist* doesn't do that – this is as much 'fan service' of that kind that you'll find. The girls discuss events, their thoughts turning inevitably towards the *chibi* alchemist (Rosie re-affirms that altho' Edward was somewhat blunt, he inspired her).

*

There's a lengthy sequence in episode 44: *Revving At Full Throttle* involving the skulking spy Bido the lizard-man, one of Greed's men, overhearing the moment when Olivia Armstrong sees the immortal soldiers (neatly linking up the two subplots, but also tracking back in time a little). Hurrying away in panic (along the ubiquitous underground tunnels and pipes of countless *animé* adventures), Bido encounters the renewed Greed inside the body of Ling Yao. Ordered to dispatch all intruders underground by Father, Greed slays Bido, only to find the memory of the former Greed coming back to haunt him, provoking an incredible scene of guilt and self-torture. (The memory flashes are visualized as stabs of video static).

The imagination and staging of the 2nd *Fullmetal Alchemist* series now ramps up many notches for another of the stunning scenes right inside the body – or rather, the soul – of Ling Yao. Against that flickering, red-and-black space of abstraction and speed and howling faces, Ling argues with the re-born, demon-shaped Greed, calling him to account for murdering Bido, one of his followers. Once again, the filmmakers deploy a very successful, highly operatic approach, with out-sized but brilliant voice acting from Yuichi Nakamura (as Greed) and Mamoru Miyano (as Ling). This is incredibly inspired filmmaking, with virtually no equivalents in the West. The vivid Jekyll and Hyde approach to Greed/Ling continues in the following episode (and will continue to be milked right up to the final scenes, when Greed attacks the super-villain Father, and Ling tells him what he really wants is real friends).

Episode 45. *The Promised Day*

Greed returns in the next two episodes of *Fullmetal Alchemist: Brotherhood*, for an incredibly rapidly staged duel with Führer Bradley (swords flailing all over the place, and the characters leaping with Jet Li speed), followed by an outstanding and imaginative representation of the psycho-spiritual conflict raging with the body of Ling Yao between Ling and Greed. This plus the other ingredients make ep. 45 one of the finest in the series.

Following this strong opening sequence, *The Promised Day* shifts to the comical scene of the Armstrong siblings Olivia and Alex fighting over ownership of the family mansion (the Armstrongs have been persuaded to leave by their won't-take-no-for-an-answer daughter). In the *manga* by Arakawa-sensei, the sister-brother relationship is played for laughs (until they encounter the homunculus Sloth), with Olivia continually berating her brother for being such a wuss.

The third scene in Part A of ep. 45 concerns Edward Elric and the chimeras in the abandoned house in the Kanama forest near Central City (there are a *lot* of handily abandoned buildings in the *Fullmetal Alchemist* series. Being on this kind of adventure means holing up in crummy dwellings). This is where Ed reckons Al will return to (not having a cel phone or telepathy creates problems in the world of *Fullmetal Alchemist*, so that Ed simply doesn't know where Al is. Now, come on, we could pedantically point out that Ed could leave messages with a host of friends and colleagues, and ask them to pass along a note if they see Al or know where he is! Mustang does that all the time. Indeed, the finale of this episode portrays exactly that – the message about the 'Promised Day' being sent all over Amestris).

Anyhoo, not long after Ed Elric reaches the empty, woodland house, Greed/ Ling Yao staggers in and collapses (like Ed, Greed/ Ling, or Ling as he is for the mo', is perpetually hungry. So Ed knows that it's Ling). The exchange which follows is curiously ambiguous: Greed/ Ling is a loose cannon, but Ed craftily makes a deal with him, to act as their leader (for the time being). Greed/ Ling is suspicious, but also a little flattered, tho' he wants to rule the world (no less – well, he *is* Greed, after all!). That Ed and the chimeras team up with Greed/ Ling is one of many unexpected twists in the story of *Fullmetal Alchemist* that is typical of Japanese animation and *manga*. (Once again, the voice work by Yuichi Nakamura and Mamoru Miyano bring Greed and Ling Yao forcefully to life, and express the battle of wills inside Ling brilliantly – and comically).

*

Chibi Mei Chang, bless her dreadlocks, is heading home to Xing – she moves through the snow in Yousewell. Here we encounter a bunch of charas which we met in the *first Fullmetal Alchemist* series, but in this one the Yousewell mine scene was referenced only in dialogue (and a silent movie flashback from Yoki). Overwhelmed by the kindness of strangers (who offer her food, bed, rest, etc), and persuaded by Envy's clever argument, Mei about-turns and hurries back to Central City (so that she will be part of the finale of *Fullmetal Alchemist*). Ah, Envy is a powerful opponent, even when he's reduced to being carried around in a jar as a three-inch critter. Of all the homunculi, Envy is the finest at manipulating the weaknesses of humans. He discovers their vulnerabilities instantly, and exploits them.

*

By this time, the second series of *Fullmetal Alchemist* is flitting around an enormous cast of characters – it's with Ed Elric and the chimeras in the old house in the forest; it's with the Armstrong brother and sister and their hilarious fight for the family mansion; it's with Mei Chang trudging home to Xing and discovering the kind-hearted folk of Yousewell (plus Envy's evil schemes); it's with Roy Mustang and Liza Hawkeye, exchanging information via secret codes, and getting ever closer to unravelling what's happening behind the scenes in Amestris; it's with van Hohenheim and Alphonse, when they roll up in Liore; and it's with the hapless, lizard-man sidekick Bido, encountering his former boss Greed in the form of Ling Yao (among other plotlines).

Juggling them all is quite a feat – as well as advancing the central storylines, plus providing plenty of action and conflict, not to mention the all-important ingredients of humour (thus, the knockabout brawl between the Armstrong brother and sister, where Olivia trounces Alex (and smashes up the country house in the process), is played for comedy, and comes right after the much more serious Greed vs. Bradley duel in the Bradleys' home). For chief writer Hiroshi Ohnogi, and the team, earlier episodes in *Fullmetal Alchemist 2*, such as the visit to Liore were a cinch, because they were largely self-contained stories involving a much smaller number of charas, and relatively simple narrative through-lines.

Episode 45: *The Promised Day* of *Fullmetal Alchemist* closes with Al Elric and others spreading the news about the fateful day when Father and the homunculi will strike their allies (to prepare them for what's coming from the villains, and to promote their support). So the episode ends with a brisk and very impressive montage of numerous charas, including Liza Hawkeye, Jean Havoc, Roy Mustang, the Curtises, Rebecca Catalina (Naomi Shindoh), General Grumman, and the Armstrongs (the ways they use to exchange intel are right out of the spy genre – messages rolled up in cigarettes, for instance, as well as the more usual means of telephones). Part of this is mechanical narrative stuff, to get characters into the right place for the story to develop (which continues in the next show), but look at how the filmmakers have given each scene its own design and staging.

Episode 46. *Looming Shadows*

In *Looming Shadows*, the 46th episode of the 64 episodes of the second *Fullmetal Alchemist* series, the narrative is split into a huge number of parallel stories. Keeping track of this enormous cast and their motivations, goals and personalities is no easy task (chief writer on the series, Hiroshi Ohnogi, makes a valiant effort at juggling 2,000 apples). So the scenes in 2.46: *Looming Shadows* tend to be short and crisply edited. There's no time in twenty-two minutes for wastage.

Thus, we flit like a restless moth (or a restless, pint-sized alchemist) from scenes of Winry-chan and Edward-kun in Resembool; to Alphonse alone on a train; Führer Bradley and General Grumman over-seeing a military show; the Führer and co. being attacked in a train on a bridge by a bomb; Roy Mustang meeting Olivia Armstrong (uneasily delivering more intel);[18] Armstrong in the government HQ; Liza Hawkeye meeting up with Denny Brosh and Cain Furey; and Scar and Dr Marcoh encountering some of their buddies in Liore (and some Ishbalians later on). (It is the day before the Promised Day). Part of this episode is preparation, with characters being moved around like pieces on a chessboard.

The scenes between Winry Rockbell and Edward Elric are given the very familiar comic/ erotic undertone of *manga* and *animé* (when Winry turns round as she's stripping off her top, revealing her breasts, to find Ed there, stuffing his face again).[19] She explodes in fury, and kicks out the other guys who come to see what the commotion is (Winry is sexualized in a number of ways in the later *Fullmetal Alchemist* episodes – she is often the only female presence for many minutes. In the previous episode, for instance, there's a fan service sequence where Winry takes a bath,. The designers also emphasize her curves in the later episodes – the three kids from Resembool are growing up, and Winry might be 16 now).

Winry and Ed are depicted as the classic bickering, possible lovers, not agreeing on anything, with Edward just too restless to keep still for long (and being blind to Winry's affection). The conversation between them is vital in reminding us of the central motivations of the heroes in *Fullmetal Alchemist*, and their goals (when Alphonse is absent, Winry acts as the conscience of the series; in a typical scene, Winry talks with Ed, then blows up, hurling a spanner at him, then she goes quiet, and whispers something emotional).

A key scene occurs later in 2.46: *Looming Shadows* when Ed Elric leaves Winry Rockbell in Resembool, to head for Central City (all roads lead to Central City at this point in *Fullmetal Alchemist*, which's where the finale takes place). Ed is leaving Winry yet again, and this time he is firm that she must stay behind, and he must go off to fight the villains. He

18 A bunch of hyacinths, which Olivia hurls on a fire.
19 Why is Ed in Winry's bedroom and not in the kitchen? Because he's in hiding (hence the closed drapes).

reminds her that when he returns, it will be with with his body fully restored. And he's right: the would-be lovers don't meet until the end of the series.

The scenes of the military exercises in *Fullmetal Alchemist 2* are impressive (armies and navies and air forces around the world perform exercises all the time – nothing has changed in 100s – nay, 1,000s of years). The production team capture the flavour of the military manœuvres – the canvas tents, the rows of cannons, and the top brass in their viewing platform (Shinji Aramaki – *Appleseed, Ghost In the Shell 2045* – designed the training camp). And even tho' Grumman and co. seem to get the better of the Führer (blowing him up in a train on a bridge after feeding false intel to General Hakuro), we know that this ruthless homunculus won't be dispatched like this.

In the action finale of 2.46: *Looming Shadows*, Al is captured by the homunculi Gluttony and Pride. Complicated as this episode is script-wise, the writers don't quite offer a convincing explanation for Alphonse travelling on his own in a railroad carriage (especially when Winry tells Edward that Al is down at the Resembool station in a train waiting to move off). Al is separated from the others for obvious reasons (such as to increase the jeopardy, and so he can have more visions of his soul in the other world).

Episode 47. *Emissary of Darkness*

Among the finest action sequences in the *manga* of *Fullmetal Alchemist* are those in nighttime forests near the poor Kanama suburb involving Edward Elric, Ling Yao/ Greed, Lan Fan, Fuu and the homunculi Gluttony and Pride. *Mangaka* Himoru Arakawa was inspired by the scenario of staging duels in total darkness,[20] and the filmmakers at Bones, Aniplex, Square Enix *et al*, led by director Yasuhiro Irie, responded with some of their greatest action set-pieces in the whole second series. The characterization of Pride as the ultimate in Jekyll and Hyde – a sweet, well-behaved, young boy who is also a deadly monster with multiple claws, fingers, hands, tendrils, teeth and eyes – makes for hugely entertaining battles in both the 2001-2010 *manga* and the 2009-10 *animé* of *Fullmetal Alchemist*.

The filmmakers deliver extraordinary scenes, in which Japanese animation once again demonstrates why it is the greatest fantasy cinema in the world, as well as the greatest cinema in delivering action and spectacle. There's no question that the two *Fullmetal Alchemist* series are among the masterworks in the entire history of animation (even including all of the masterpieces of animation from 1895 to 2009-10) – and this episode is a good example of just why.

Everybody in the enormous filmmaking team in Japan rises to the challenge of these big, sensational scenes, with the visual effects and

---

20 The filmmakers employ one of the simplest devices to indicate the darkness: a fade up from black (coupled with reduced saturation in the colour design – animation typically uses hues with greys and black added, to suggest low light levels).

cinematography departments excelling themselves, aided by a formidable battery of sound effects, razor-sharp editing, and a thunderous score from Akira Senju and the Warsaw National Philharmonic Orchestra.

Dramatically, the forest action sequence is also strong, because we have both of our heroes wrestling with the villains in the midst of it all. Ed Elric goes up against the shooting spikes 'n' claws of Pride, while Al is captured and manipulated by Pride (while his soul is elsewhere – in the other world of the Gateway).

The forest action sequence is built in sections: there's the preamble between Edward Elric, Greed/ Ling Yao, the chimeras and the first appearance of Al's armour (with a very creepy/ horror movie build-up); followed by the initial duels; clever Ed puts out all of the lights, and the fight continues, with the chimera Heinkel battling the little boy Selim Bradley; the appearance of Gluttony ups the stakes considerably, especially when Gluttony opens up his belly to reveal that terrifying maw and eye (where Ed and Ling were swallowed earlier in the series); the switch of Greed for Ling is an interesting twist (because Ling's Xingese martial arts can detect where Gluttony is in the darkness),[21] which prepares the audience for the *deus ex machina* arrival of the renewed, Xingese bodyguard and super-ninja, Lan Fan, whom Ling recognizes with delight (she leaps to the rescue, slicing up Gluttony into pieces. We know, tho', that it takes more'n that to waste a homunculi!).

Captured by the enemy, Alphonse Elric experiences another out-of-armour trip to the other-world, the white-on-white limbo of the Gateway of Truth. Here we see an arm reaching out to Al (teasingly, it appears to be his body, but then it becomes Pride; the clever screenwriting also uses the voice of Al turning into Pride to enhance this wrong-footing of the audience). Again, the writers (here it's Seishi Minakami) deploy Al and his visions of the other-world to remind us that this is going to be a major location in the finale of the second run of *Fullmetal Alchemist*.

The preamble to the fight is another of the imaginative sequences employing the monster Pride: the filmmakers emphasize the shadows from the low angle lighting all thru the sequence as they evoke the genuine creepiness of Pride and its/ his arms and claws of shadows. (And it's when Ed looks down to see Pride's deep black shadows moving across his own slightly paler shadow that he works out to combat the homunculus).

A creature that can suddenly explode into a tangle of shooting black arms (clearly drawing on Hong Kong fantasy movies such as *A Chinese Ghost Story* and *The Bride With White Hair*, where a witch's giant tongue or long hair becomes a vicious, super-fast weapon), that can blow up to the size of a blue whale in milli-seconds (and change shape instantly), that can also slink around slyly and slowly (with a low, eerie voice), is a gift to the animators, and every scene involving Pride is simply marvellous in *Fullmetal Alchemist* series 2.

Ed Elric has no idea what he's going up against here – but the

21 Himoru Arakawa is very fond of Chinese martial arts (like so many fantasy writers in Japan); she employs them in detail in *Hero Tales*.

audience knows what's coming! Ed's genius idea of extinguishing all of the lamps and lights in the village and its environs manages to stop Pride momentarily: the action shifts into memorable evocations of characters acting in total darkness, with the chimeras using their sense of smell to hunt and tackle Selim Bradley.

The filmmaking in episode 47: *Emissary of Darkness* is as all-out as the brutal duels it's depicting, and immensely satisfying on all levels. And, rightly, the fighting is allowed to run on much longer than many of the previous action sequences (this is one sequence that storyboard artists would be clamouring to be commissioned to draw).

The climax, the un-looked-for-but-welcome appearance of Lan Fan, is glorious – a blurred whirlwind in black, Lan Fan zips around Gluttony, dicing the freak to pieces (tho' he still doesn't die!). The visual effects animation, working over-time in ep. 47, delivers wild, scarlet zigzags of energy and rapid lighting changes.

✳

Prior to the forest action sequence in 2.47. *Emissary of Darkness*, there is a crucially important psycho-emotional scene where Edward Elric encounters his father, van Hohenheim. His companions take a back seat as Edward has an uneasy meeting with his pa (first off is to punch his old man, so that he's sprawled on the ground). Hohenheim tells them the whole history of the homunculi and what's going to happen tomorrow, on the Promised Day (the setting is once again with the charas sitting around an open fire, already used several times in *Fullmetal Alchemist*, and one of the primal images of storytelling, going back probably tens of thousands of years).

As Edward Elric leaves, he delivers Pinako Rockbell's message from Trisha to van Hohenheim. With the aide of a soft, plangent piano cue by composer Akira Senju, the scene shifts into high melodrama territory, as Hohenheim weeps (Ed is taken aback). Ed walks away, and Hohenheim is left haunted by his memories (this will play into the very final moments of the whole 2009-10 series).

The *Fullmetal Alchemist* series alters its narration now, moving into a flashback sequence: here it's all about Hohenheim being the absent father, leaving his family unwillingly, and regretting it. Once again, the prop of the Elric family photo is made to do more dramatic work (as Hohenheim stares at it in despair), and the filmmakers recycle the childhood scenes from the early episodes yet again. [22]

This scene is vital in preparing the audience for the bigger role that van Hohenheim will play in the finale of *Fullmetal Alchemist*'s second series (and also for his appearance in the following episode, where he helps to save Ed and his chums from the nasty attacking homunculi).

---

22 Tho' with the voices echoey – it's a memory of a memory.

Episode 48. *The Oath In the Tunnel*

Another truly remarkable show.

In episode 2.48, entitled *The Oath In the Tunnel*, the narrative stays with two groups of characters: the continuing fight between Edward Elric, Ling Yao/ Greed, Lan Fan and the chimeras versus the homunculi Gluttony and Pride in Kanama Forest, and Roy Mustang and his followers. The plot strands contrast each other vividly: one is all noise, speed, visual effects and ultra-violence (explosive fantasy and action), and the other is calm conversation and grim resolve in tunnels and bars (a WW2 spy movie).

It's not over yet! Oh no – the filmmakers at Studio Bones, Aniplex, Square Enix, Mainichi *et al* are milking everything they can from the intense and bitter duelling between the homunculi Pride, Gluttony, Ling/ Greed[23] and our heroes in the forest. All sorts of the additions and complications are thrown into the mix to even up the fight, and also to push our heroes to the edge: Lan Fan's automail isn't broken in; Ling Yao still has Greed inside him; Pride manages to set alight the trees and bushes, so he can deploy his stabbing, hurtling claws and pincers; and the heroes counter with flash bombs of dazzling light.

The filmmaking in *Fullmetal Alchemist: Brotherhood* is quite extraordinary, and all the more so because this was an era – 2009-10 – when audiences had probably pretty much seen *everything*. And then some! Yet the Japanese filmmakers manage to conjure up incredible action and fantasy sequences which, altho' they run on for many minutes past their dramatic requirements, are absolutely thrilling.

So Ling Yao and Lan Fan have got Gluttony on the run, hurtling thru the trees ninja-style, and slicing up the fat, child-like monster into pieces (repeatedly – because homunculi have the irksome habit of regenerating themselves, even when their hands have been cut off). Blood gushes from Gluttony's body again and again, and his body grotesquely re-animates itself. Edward flashes his carbon-strong arm against the onslaught of Pride's multiple arms, and the chimeras do their best against fearsome monsters (Heinkel pounds Selim's skull into the ground, but the demon still won't die).

The ten year-old boy in all of us – male, female, dwarf or vampire – is going to love this sort of visceral, high impact, state-of-the-art filmmaking. The forest action sequence in episode 48: *The Oath In the Tunnel* reaches numerous climaxes and regroupings (with Edward rightly at the forefront of proceedings): in the most gruesome moment, Pride eats Gluttony in order to absorb his energy and abilities (and we know how much power Gluttony has! – there's a whole hell-zone of blood and corpses inside that infinite belly!). Our heroes look on in horror – you yell at your team mates, you stalk off in a huff, but you don't eat them! (Cannibalism marks out the homunculi as very base creatures – altho', as we know, cannibals have existed at every stage in human history, going

---

23 Greed cheers on Ling from inside his soul.

back 3 million years).

Once again, the filmmakers have found Pride an endlessly inspiring monster – in every shot they find new ways of presenting this fearsome antagonist. When it/ he swallows Gluttony, for instance, the homunculi becomes dragon-shaped, recalling chomping the hapless lawyer Gennaro in half like the T-rex out of *Jurassic Park* (1993), then attacking the pulsing, red philosopher's stone beating inside it/ him with stabbing daggers of black shadows (which smother the screen in black).

Our heroes look on in disgust, forgetting their fight for the moment as they can't believe that one of the homunculi has turned on one of its kind and eaten it (but we, the audience, know that these homunculi are nothing but mere servants for the granddaddy monster who's driving all events towards the Promised Day in *Fullmetal Alchemist* – Father). So that even ferocious assailants like Gluttony are mere pawns in the super-villain's grand scheme of things. (Poor Alphonse has little to do in 48: *The Oath In the Tunnel* 'cept be a pawn for Pride to manipulate (luckily, Al's soul is elsewhere), until Ed, Fuu and Darius manage to squirrel him away). Ed and Fuu orchestrate the flash bombs with amazing results.

Throughout the forest fight sequence, the animation is simply astounding. No, the history of animation is *not* bottom-heavy, and the 'golden age' was *not* 1937-42 (Walt Disney), and it was *not* the 1920-30s (*avant garde*, silent films), and it was *not* the 1960s (experimental films), the 'golden age' is *now*, it's the 2000s and 2010s, it's all the time – at least, the 'golden age' is all the time when the Japanese movie and television industries are producing TV shows like *Fullmetal Alchemist*. (And *One Piece*, and *Aquarion*, and *Ghost In the Shell* and 100s of others).

Look at the moments of abstraction in the forest battle scenes – how the filmmakers have a screen teeming with black arms which froth and fret until they consume the screen; how the zigzags of red, alchemical energy flash in close-up; how the screen is full of sliding eyes and mouths. The flash bombs inspire incredible pieces of animation – such as Selim trying to drag his shadows on the ground back with his feet, as if he's pulling at some unseen force (which is light itself).

Yes, the motif of light (how Pride operates) is a gift to filmmakers, who love to play about with light and shadow as much as anything.

❋

By contrast, the Roy Mustang plot in episode 48: *The Oath In the Tunnel* seems positively tame and pedestrian after the Kanama Forest action sequences. It involves the Flame Alchemist gathering intel from Madame Christmas (apparently his foster mom), in her downtown bar. Here we find out that Selim Bradley has been around for a long time in the form of a twelve year-old boy (depicted in some creepy b/w photographs from 50 years ago, like the final shot of *The Shining*, 1980).

Col. Mustang leads these scenes, as he literally goes underground, by climbing into the sewers (always with the tunnels in spy stories and action-adventures yarns! Indeed, the colour palette, of mid-browns, greys and greens, is a delightful evocation of the WWII period). The bar has to be destroyed, because government heavies have tailed them there. Here is the 'oath in the tunnel' of the title of this episode, as Madame Christmas and Mustang vow to succeed in their schemes, including Mustang becoming the Führer of Amestris.

So, from now on, Roy Mustang has abandoned his post as a State Alchemist, and is now working as a political rebel, aided by his loyal followers – Liza Hawkeye, Heyman Breda and Cain Furey. When he meets them, in a side tunnel, he commands them: 'don't die', at the end of one of those Grim Resolve speeches, facing the camera in a medium shot (and accompanied by a militaristic cue from composer Akira Senju).

'Don't die!' is good, general advice for life. In *One Piece*, Luffy orders Jimbei: 'even if you die, don't die!'

Episode 49. *Filial Affection*

The extraordinary battle between the homunculus Pride and our heroes forms the action-packed crux of this episode, *Filial Affection* (broadcast in Nippon on March 21, 2010). *Filial Affection* conforms perfectly to the *mantra* of Japanese comics aimed at young boys and teens: action... action... ACTION! Yes, and when you've delivered *one* scene of pure action, deliver *another* one! And the filmmakers at Bones/ Aniplex/ Mainichi/ Square Enix/ F.A. Project *et al* do just that.

The action sequences in the forest in *Filial Affection* featuring super-ninja Lan Fan, and our heroes Ed and Al Elric, and Greed/ Ling, and assorted chimeras and survivors, are as accomplished as any you'll find in the whole history of animation. Again and again, the monster Pride inspires the storyboard artists and the animators to greater heights: there's a storming, stops-all-out speed and ingenuity to the action sequences that leaves the audience breathless (as well as a remarkable use of screen space – Pride stabs those claws/ arms everywhere). Pride is a *meeeean* villain, and the filmmakers go to the toppermost tops of their imaginations with a series of battering, slamming action beats. The filmmakers use Arakawa-sensei's *manga* merely as a template, going beyond it with superb sound effects, dazzling camera angles, and a vertiginous movement of the camera. But they never lose sight of the characters and what they are fighting for.

Rightly, the filmmakers push the jeopardy to the maximum, and have the homunculus Pride cornering all of our heroes, and it seems like it's the end for them (they are surrounded by a sea of black shadows). As in the *Fullmetal Alchemist manga*, van Hohenheim finally steps in to perform some alchemy of his own now[24] (as suggested by his son Alphonse): to encase Pride and his battery of gnashing, slicing teeth, claws and hands in a giant stone mound. To show just how powerful Hohenheim is, he produces the alchemy with his hands in his pockets, strolling along, as if he's simply chatting to the furious Edward Elric standing next to him (it's a common motif in *animé* and comics – guys that're so cool relaxed and

24 After calling Alphonse back from the limbo-land of the Gateway.

cool, they have their hands in their pockets like it's nothing). Here Ed sees his pa performing alchemy up close – and it's very impressive. (Ed isn't happy that Alphonse, now come back to the world, is imprisoned with Pride in the earth dome. Hohenheim reminds him that it was Al's idea, anyway. The two brothers talk on either side of the walls of the mound).

❊

The smaller scenes in episode 49: *Filial Affection* involve playing catch-up with some of the characters that we haven't seen for some time: Zolf Kimbley, for instance, getting into place for the Promised Day (by doing what he does a lot of in *Fullmetal Alchemist 2* – slaughtering Ishbalians); Scar, Dr Marcoh and co. turn up and exchange news; Greed/Ling Yao bounces off to Central City with *Naruto*-ninja-speed to begin his own bid for ruling the world (which continues right up to the very final moments); Pride is given a slice of flashback (in sepia hues), in which the homunculus marvels at the compassion of humans (when Mrs Bradley rescued him); at the end of episode 49: *Filial Affection*, some of the groups of characters meet up (Ed, Scar, Marcoh, Heinkel, and Hohenheim), with Ed unhappy that poor Alphonse is cooped up with the monster Pride in the earth mound.

There are discussions about what to do about Father and the Promised Day: so that these conversations don't spoil what's coming up, the filmmakers cleverly stand back, and we don't hear the words, but see the group from the chimeras' point-of-view nearby (it's yet another chat around an open fire at night – there's a lot of sitting around fires in *Fullmetal Alchemist*; maybe it's something that Himoru Arakawa did a lot of up growing up in rural Hokkaido).

Ep. 49: *Filial Affection* closes with Ed suiting up in his familiar red jacket, as dawn breaks on the Promised Day (cue the music! cue Edward looking grim and heroic!).

THE FINAL EPISODES OF THE SECOND *FULLMETAL ALCHEMIST* SERIES.

From the forest scenes onwards, as in the *Fullmetal Alchemist manga* by Himoru Arakawa, the action ramps up in theAnnie May to full steam ahead. We are now firmly in the third act of the piece: everything is in place for a roaring, stops-all-out finale: (A) all of the characters have been introduced; (B) all of the motivations, goals[25] and flaws have been outlined; (C) the rivalries and resentments are simmering along nicely; (D) the characters are all converging on Central City; and (E) the much-anticipated (and advertized) 'Promised Day' is upon us. (Even so, there will be *plenty* of twists and turns in the storytelling, including *many* surprises, such as characters coming out of nowhere to seriously affect the trajectory of the narrative).

The final dozen episodes or so of the 2009-10 *Fullmetal Alchemist* series are an example of why and how a long *animé* series can deliver such stupendous entertainment. The finest *animé* series build and build as they

---

25 We don't know quite yet that Father intends to become God, or steal God's power!

progress, introducing more'n more charas, complicating the issues and themes, interweaving the plotlines, until they have all of the elements necessary in place, and they can let themselves *fly*. *Escaflowne*, *Ghost In the Shell: Stand Alone Complex*, *Cowboy Bebop*, *Moribito* – these 26 or 52-episode *animé* series thicken and deepen all the way along, so that their finales deliver richer, pacier and mightier finales than a two-hour movie or a short series.

When you reach the climaxes of the two incredible *Ghost In the Shell: Stand Alone Complex* series, for example, or the truly astonishing *Cowboy Bebop* ('*three, two, one – let's jam!*'), you're on the edge of your seat, watching the greatest filmmakers in the world *soar*. Because in the finales, the animation teams don't have to slow down, to stop and explain things, to introduce new characters, or to introduce new settings or motifs.

The producers at Bones, Square Enix, Mainichi, Aniplex *et al* have instructed the filmmaking team to *go nuts* in the finale of the second series of *Fullmetal Alchemist*, to deliver a wall-to-wall action extravaganza, a thrill ride that will top everything that happened before, including the first *Fullmetal Alchemist* series.

Altho' the *manga* is the template for the finale of the second *Fullmetal Alchemist* series, the filmmakers in Tokyo have completely updated it, rewritten it, and re-imagined it. There are numerous inspired moments – the filmmakers have the confidence to let the screen go completely black, for instance, or they use splinters of white light (to evoke Alphonse Elric coming back to this world from his time in the Gate limbo), or they employ a brilliant light moment drawn from the opening of the mothership's doors in *Close Encounters of the Third Kind* (for the scene where Captain Buccaneer and the Briggs Mountain crew emerge from the Armstrong cellars).[26]

The Japanese filmmakers are also fully in control of every element of storytelling – we are in the hands of masters here: these guys really know what they're doing. For instance, look at the way the form of the narration shifts from the lengthy action sequence in the forest by the slums into an epic form of narration, where the *animé* is now drawing together a huge number of characters, as the conflict explodes all over Central City and its environs.

In the finales of the juiciest *animé* series there's a breathlessness to the storytelling: the filmmakers are trying to squeeze in as much story and incident as possible (notice how the animation pushes into the closing credits, for instance – there's a wonderful use of the closing music (by Sid, Shoko Nakagawa and Nico Touches the Walls) over each show's animation. And in the later *Fullmetal Alchemist* episodes, the sound editors mix in the theme songs, to form a new kind of background music). The filmmakers are showing us so many things occurring simultaneously – look! – there's Olivia Armstrong pinning down two guys John Woo-style, with a sword and a gun! Here's Ed and Ling/ Greed flying thru the air and tumbling over and over as they escape from Pride's deadly claws!

---

26 Speed lines are employed many times in the final confrontations of *Fullmetal Alchemist: Brotherhood*, as if in *hommage* to the *Fullmetal Alchemist manga* by Himoru Arakawa.

And here's super-cool Colonel Mustang clicking his fingers and creating explosions in yet another back alley in Central City!

Oh boy, *Fullmetal Alchemist* is Total *Animé* Heaven! *Hagane no Renkinjutsushi* has *everything* you could want or hope for in animation... in Japanese filmmaking... in fantasy television... in filmmaking of any kind anywhere!

Episode 50. *Upheaval In Central*

Once the ominous 'Promised Day' dawns, the action is breaking out all over Amestris, and every group of characters is involved in some action, in another stupendous piece of filmmaking: blonde bombshell Olivia Armstrong is facing off against jittery officers in the board room of the government; Ed Elric, Al Elric, van Hohenheim and the chimeras have finished battling Pride, and are heading towards Central City (tho' Al remains cooped up with Pride in the earth mound); Roy Mustang, Liza Hawkeye and their faithful followers embark on their programme of causing maximum mayhem in Central without killing anyone; Captain Buccaneer and the burly bears from Briggs Mountain are let loose on the streets of Central City...

Part A of episode 50: *Upheaval In Central* presents the conflict that breaks out in skirmishes all over downtown Central City, as Col. Mustang, Lt. Hawkeye and their colleagues start their plan to destabilize the military government, now that the Führer is lost in a railroad accident (but we know he'll be back!). In this modest but effective military rebellion, the tiny gang of dissidents manages to nobble many soldiers (but wounding them, not killing them), and the military are unable to stop them (the military's own State Alchemists are notably absent, for instance).

Characters from way back are re-introduced – including Denny Brosh and Lt. Maria Ross (and Rebecca Catalina slews into the fray to deliver ammo and weaponry inside, of all things, an ice cream truck, just as the rebels're running out of rounds). The episode depicts a military-led insurgency, as one group of professional soldiers attacks another group of professional soldiers. It's a civil war, a battle for control of the leadership of the country of Amestris. (Civil wars are very common in Japanese *animé* – no need for Russians, Chinese or Americans (the usual three nations) when there are fellow Japanese to fight).

✳

In Part B of episode 2.50: *Upheaval In Central*, the story shifts to other groups of characters. There's li'l Mei Chang, for example, spotted hurrying along the streets (still carrying the Envy-creature in the jar), and disappearing in an alley (with Envy hinting at the immortality secrets that Father will unleash – words designed to keep Mei under his influence). Poor Al Elric is still trapped inside the mound of earth, along with the homunculus Pride, who persists in tapping Al's armour helmet.

Chief among the characters is Edward Elric – along with van

Hohenheim, he's leading the group (which includes Scar, Yoki, Doctor Marcoh and the chimeras) to Central City. They try one entrance, then use the third laboratory to access (yet another) underground tunnel, which'll lead them to the super-villain, Father. At the end of episode 50: *Upheaval In Central*, the charas have split up, with Hohenheim and Lan Fan heading off on their own, until Hohenheim gets rid of the female ninja by allowing her to go in search of her beloved Prince Ling Yao.

✳

There's a huge amount of to-ing and fro-ing in episode 50: *Upheaval In Central*, with the film editors staying with one group of characters often for a very short time, cutting back and forth between them. Some of this is functional screenwriting, to get the characters in place for the showdown. The pace is breakneck – and almost every scene takes place (or seems to) in a new location (once again, hats off to the truly remarkable work of the background artists, having to keep up with storytelling that's zipping about as fast as one of Roy Mustang's flame alchemical attacks).

And there is some very fine filmmaking here, too: for instance, the face-off between Major Armstrong and the two generals, where she pins one in the arm with her sword and holds the other at gunpoint (and then she shoots him in the head, where he tumbles out of the Führer's meeting room).[27] In Himoru Arakawa's philosophy, women can be just as tough as men, even when they're housewives (Izumi Curtis). In this scene, for instance, Armstrong kills a man at point blank range – right after lecturing him and his colleague that Central's military men are too soft (not like her Briggs Mountain troops, who, she boasts, have been trained to carry on without her).

Speaking of which, the *animé* releases Buccaneer and the boys from the basement at the Armstrong mansion with an *hommage* to the scene in *Close Encounters of the Third Kind* (1977) when the doors of the mothership open at Devil's Tower, unleashing the famous Spielbergian light (which has been copied numerous times ever since). So with Mustang's lads on one side and the Briggs boys on the other, Central City's military is being soundly beaten, and none of the authorities seem able to counter-attack (much to the irritation of the commanding officers). This is an important plot point, because it explains how Mustang & co. are able to gain the upper hand in Amestris's government.

The fiftieth episode of *Fullmetal Alchemist 2* climaxes with the creepy scene of the immortal soldiers being activated, using liquid philosopher's stones, and letting out an almighty, hysterical shriek, a very unholy sound (how did the sound designers find that sound?! Because it really is unlike any other sound in TV or cinema!).

Sound is also employed very cleverly in the sequence in episode 50: *Upheaval In Central* which introduces Father deep underground,[28] and the enormous shifts in *chi* (energy) which the Xingese charas can sense (as well as dogs in Central City – they bark at the ground in the street): from

---

27 He's the general who showed O. Armstrong the immortal army down below, and he's shot in the forehead, in the same spot as the immortal soldiers' single eye.
28 He's just a homunculus in a bigger jar, Hohenheim points out.

the labyrinth of pipes snaking along the tunnels, the grating thuds echo outwards, until we reach the mound of earth far away, and the sound mixes with the reverb sounds to become the tapping of the stick that Pride uses to hit Alphonse's helmet.

And while we're talking about sound – how about the score by Akira Senju? He and the music producers have hired the Warsaw Chorus again for this episode, to create two wonderful cues which fully embody the might of the military. There is a brassy, shiny cue to accompany the heroic images of the heroes gathering together to destabilize the Central City authorities.

What also comes across strongly in episode 2.50: *Upheaval In Central* is how masterful and confident the storytelling in *Fullmetal Alchemist: Brotherhood* is – you really feel that you are in the hands of people who *really* know what they're doing. There is plenty of action for action fans, there is genuine creepiness for horror fans (in the immortal army), there are rich thematic and political issues for intellectuals, and there are many character-based moments and bits of humour for the rest of us.

Episode 51. *The Immortal Legion*

In the next episode, the moments of *Animé* Bliss keep coming: stand-outs include:

(1) Edward Elric, Scar and the chimeric lads taking on a swarm of the zombie-like, immortal soldiers in front of a colossal doorway;[29]

(2) Li'l Xingese alchemist Mei Chang duelling a horde of immortal soldiers with rapidfire martial arts movies (blink and you miss them), while balancing, the glass jar containing mini-demon Envy on her head, Jackie Chan-style, *and* conducting an argument with the petulant homunculus in the jar!

(3) The re-birth of Envy, consuming all of the immortal army;

(4) Bad-ass Olivia Armstrong duelling dim-wit hulk Sloth;

and (5) Alphonse Elric and Heinkel fighting back against Pride and Zolf Kimbley at the stone mound in the forest.

In short, *animé* doesn't get any better than this. Virtually every shot in episode 2.51: *The Immortal Legion* is a visual effects shot, the camera is rarely still, the sound effects're blasting away, the music brings in the Warsaw Chorus as well as simple piano rhythms, and the filmmakers're trying every technique the (high) budget will allow. (That this is expensive filmmaking can be gleaned from any frame). In particular, the storyboarding (by Minoru Ohara[30]) and the screenwriting (by Seishi Minakam), is superb, balancing moments of moral reflection (Al Elric and Heinkel contemplating using a philosopher's stone, knowing full well that it was created with people's lives), with outrageous and brilliantly conceived and staged action sequences. (Notice how the voice cast is also playing the scenes at a higher hysterical level, as virtually every episode in the last section of *Fullmetal Alchemist 2* is climactic and delivered at fever

---

29 A visual reminder of the Gateway of Truth.
30 According to the show itself, Shinji Ishihara was storyboard artist.

pitch).

Fullmetal Alchemist 2 is also very beautiful – there are so many luminous colours here, and exquisitely-framed compositions, reminding us that one of the beauties of animation is that it is drawn, that it is constructed in layers (with each layer being designed to fit with the others), and that it carefully composed, for each individual shot.

There is so much going in episode 2: 51. *The Immortal Legion* that it's awe-inspiring: the re-animation of the immortal soldiers follows directly on from the end of episode 50 (*Upheaval In Central*): a fan of *Frankenstein* (she has produced her own version in *manga*, in 2005's *Raiden 18*), Himoru Arakawa has the zombies attacking their creators right off the bat (a general and a scientist), in scenes out of zombie movies from *Night of the Living Dead* onwards (and lit by the dangerous scarlet of philosopher's stones bobbing in glass tubes – a superb addition to Arakawa's comic).

Pretty soon, the immortal soldiers are rampaging everywhere in the government building (screaming, 'it hurts!', 'big brother!' and 'mama!'): Mei Chang, carrying Envy in a glass jar, duels the zombie soldiers in a corridor, using stunning, Chinese *wushu* moves. Look at the animation here – how the animators have the glass jar spinning above little Mei's head, and Envy inside, being hurled about (and how Mei is able to tap it or flick it above her, to stop it smashing, even as she battles the mannequins).

But in the second section of the corridor sequence, the team at Bones, Aniplex, Mainichi, Square Enix *et al* deliver one of those scenes which cinematic animation seems to have been invented for: a jaw-droppingly wild transformation scene, in which the three-inch-long homunculus Envy gets eaten by one of the immortal soldiers, only to take over its body and use it to consume all of the others in rapid succession. Soon Envy is back to his giant, green dragon-dog-monster form, then gloops into human form from the monster's forehead, emerging as the wicked, antsy, rebellious youth with the mad, spikey hair and Akihabara fashion. (Look at the in-between states that Envy undergoes, when he's part-zombie, part-Envy and part-dragon-dog-monster. It's *incredible!*).

The character acting that is captured (created) in the animation is simply outstanding, conveying the naughty, creepy joy of Envy's rebirth, and his crazed arrogance and his gloating over the tiny, Chinese girl quaking in front of him (once again, Minami Takayama impresses with her scarily good voice work as Envy).

❋

Outside a colossal doorway with an alchemical motif painted on it (as if, with those white walls and that giant door, we are already in the Gateway of Truth limbo), Edward Elric, Scar and the chimeras are duelling more undead: that these zombies were manufactured using philosopher's stones (i.e., people's lives), adds a rich, thematic layer to the action sequence (that is, it's not just good guys beating up bad guys). Edward in particular is incensed at the notion that the government has forged this army of mutants (that are linked to the people inside Envy).

Notice, however, the important humorous beat before the mannequins attack: Ed goes to the door to open it: the others assume he's going to use some cool alchemical trick: no, he tries to pull the doors apart! The animators deliver some OTT facial expressions for Edward – thus is the suspense cleverly deflated before rising rapidly as the zombies rush in and start attacking our heroes.

Staging her one-woman coup, Major Armstrong has taken one of the generals hostage in order to force the military to back off from her Briggs Mountain forces. Ms. Armstrong is always good value in the world of *Fullmetal Alchemist*, and watching her take on the macho, patriarchal dominion of the military machine and the all-male government of Amestris is very satisfying. If anyone can make a dent in the testosterone-drenched realm of the militarized government in *Fullmetal Alchemist*, it is Major Armstrong.

However, the sudden appearance of the homunculus Sloth ups the stakes somewhat: the action sequence depicting Olivia Armstrong going up against the dumb but persistent giant Sloth is gloriously broad and energetic. And what rankles most of all for Major Armstrong is that she has to be saved from being squished to jelly in Sloth's fists by her brother Alex (who, true to form, strips off in a jiff, amidst sparkly stars and body-building heroics, and a martial music cue).

Meanwhile, back at the mound of earth in the countryside, Alphonse Elric gets to do something more'n sit there and listen to Pride bashing his steel helmet (Heinkel alerts him to Pride using Morse code, but just then Zolf Kimbley arrives, and it's too late). So an action scene swiftly follows featuring Al versus *both* Pride and Kimbley; the MacGuffin of the *Fullmetal Alchemist* universe, a philosopher's stone (picked up by Heinkel), is introduced at this point to thicken the plot a little (and to give our heroes more of an advantage – now that Al's legs have been cut off after being snaffled by Pride). There is a crucial scene where Alphonse debates with himself whether to use the philosopher's stone: when he decides to, it provides the climax of the episode.

Also near Central City, Roy Mustang, Liza Hawkeye & co. are staging their own programme of rebellion – they're trying to keep out of the way of the military, after hearing reports of their rebellion. Mustang decides that it's time to enter Central, somehow.

EDITING.
The editing in the final episodes of the 2009-10 *Fullmetal Alchemist* series (by Takeshi Sadamatsu) is very fine indeed. Look at all of those simultaneous duels and battles, springing up all over the place, and how the filmmakers have orchestrated them in time and space. This is where a really good editor proves their worth: we've all seen climactic acts of action and fantasy movies and TV shows which botch the pacing and the editing. *Fullmetal Alchemist* achieves a remarkable balancing act between juddering, screaming action taking place all over Amestris, and slower, quieter moments, or scenes where vital information is exchanged (these

are very short, however).

A movie might have three or four different characters or groups of characters to keep juggling in the climax of a 90-minute adventure/ action film (for instance: (1) the hero and sidekick, (2) the super-villain, (3) a henchman vs. secondary chara duel and (4) unexpected help for the last-minute rescue) – but *Fullmetal Alchemist* has an enormous cast.

Editor Takeshi Sadamatsu rightly stays for one-to-two minutes with each duel and action scenario, rather than splintering them up too much. So when the narrative switches to a new action scene, the flow of the drama isn't broken up too much. It's tempting to flit around the multiple action scenes again and again, but Sadamatsu rightly resists that.

This is masterclass editing, on a par with anything in the history of TV or cinema. Look at the balancing of the *tempos*, how a fast-tempo scene (Ed & co. vs. the zombies) is balanced with a dialogue scene with Mustang *et al* (animators are always talking about *tempo* – the rhythm and timing of a scene, the mixing of tempos, etc).

It's all pay-off – one action scene after another, coming thick and fast, playing out the goals, motives, relationships and personalities of the huge ensemble of characters. It's something of a *tour-de-force* by artist/ writer Hiromu Arakawa in the *Fullmetal Alchemist manga*, to be sure, and it's a *tour-de-force* in the 2009-10 *animé*, too. And director Yasuhiro Irie and the filmmakers don't let everything become *too* serious or *too* blood-soaked[31] – they allow time for breathers, and air for pauses, and they allow moments to be savoured by the audiences: three-foot Mei Chang in one of her marvellous martial arts poses... Roy Mustang arriving at a key moment to snap his fingers and explode another fire-bomb... Olivia Armstrong recovering herself on the floor after being smashed yet again by the giant Sloth ('dying is such a bother', complains Sloth), and grudgingly thanking her brother Alex...

Episode 52. *Combined Strength*

There are few new plot points or story elements in episode 52: *Combined Strength* – instead, the episode continues and develops the four or so action sequences and duels established in episode 51: *The Immortal Legion*. At last, Alphonse Elric is allowed to have a giant action sequence all of his own: it opens episode 52 with some of the fastest and most furious of all the action scenes in *Fullmetal Alchemist 2*, as Al takes on two formidable opponents – Pride the homunculus and Zolf Kimbley, the psychotic, maverick alchemist (tho' Al now has the help of a philosopher's stone).

Comprising about about 45 shots, the animation is at its broadest and most inspired in action sequences such as this, depicting a teenager trapped in a suit of armour versus a monster who's part-multi-headed dragon and part-small boy, and a man who's coked up with philosopher's stones (yes, this is Japanese animation!). They are letting fly

---

31 Several characters expire in front of us.

at each other with explosions, billowing dust and smoke, transmuted piles of earth, and deadly sharp claws. In a moment of genius, Al manages to encase Pride again in a mound of dirt. A lengthy discussion ensues, between Al and Kimbley, as the man plays devil's advocate with Al, asking teasing questions about the morality of using philosopher's stones. (Alphonse is a mid-teen, and no match for the truly depraved soul of Kimbley; yet Al's ethical purity wins thru).

And then the action starts up again all of a sudden (this plot strand is intercut with the others), and Pride is on the loose again. Who's going to come to the rescue of Alphonse now, when Pride's fangs and claws are slithering towards him like a Hydra? – only the most unexpected rescuer of all – the hapless Yoki, in his most heroic moment in the whole series, driving into the fray in a car. Al also has help from fellow alchemist Dr Marcoh, and the lion chimera Heinkel (who chews on Zolf Kimbley's neck, inflicting a mortal wound).

The culmination of the forest sequence in episode 52: *Combined Strength* has Zolf Kimbley near-death, while the homunculus Pride stands over him, gloating (Pride spends a lot of time gloating – well, he is called Pride, after all!). Lying on the ground (in a cruciform position, a recurring motif in *Fullmetal Alchemist*), unable to speak because his throat's been chomped, Kimbley's demise is given a grandiose music cue of eerie choir by Akira Senju, as Pride decides to swallow him whole. (This is Pride at his creepiest, and the visuals match his cannibalistic insanity. For ex, there's a Pride-point-of-view shot, as the dying Crimson Alchemist is raised on Pride's multiple arms up to his maw (it's a bitter spoof of a religious ascension to Heaven, perhaps, or a send-up of an injured victim being gently lifted by helping hands to safety). The final crunching bite takes place, as usual in *Fullmetal Alchemist*, over black. Too gruesome to show? No – it's over black because the audience can visualize the grisly death for themselves!).

✳

Meanwhile, the Armstrong *kyodai* (brother A. and sister O.) have another homunculus as their foe, the giant Sloth, in the command centre. The action's pretty much non-stop, with the extra twist of Sloth suddenly developing præternatural speed, so that the s-l-o-w homunculus who grumbles incessantly 'what a bother' ('what a bother' it is to die, even), becomes a blur of motion, unstoppable. The added complication of the immortal army bursting into the hall ups the stakes yet again (as well as the Central City soldiers insisting on carrying out their order to shoot and kill Major Armstrong – this recurs, too, as other groups of soldiers persist in following their call of duty to arrest O. Armstrong,[32] even tho' the place's full of zombies and monsters!). In addition, Olivia Armstrong is wounded.

Altho' we are watching nothing but bits of celluloid and digital ink and paint, and drawings (plus voices, and sound fx, and music, of course), the filmmakers at Bones, Aniplex, Mainichi, Square *et al* manage to infuse

---

32 Armstrong pulling the officer's gun to her forehead and yelling at him to choose between her and the monsters, stretches credibility. Acting suicidally like that is not in Armstrong's nature.

the filmmaking in *Fullmetal Alchemist 2* with a visceral, pulverizing impact. So that you can really feel those punches, or the pain that Olivia Armstrong feels when she's hurled against a wall. The effects of action in *Fullmetal Alchemist* is *really* sold by the filmmakers.

Another meanwhile: Ed Elric, Scar and the chimeras are still beating off hordes of immortal soldiers in the grand hall somewhere below the Command Centre in Central City. They take to chopping off the freaks' legs, tho' even that doesn't stop the creatures crawling along the floor and grabbing our heroes. Things are lookin grim for the Fullmetal Alchemist and his chums – but they are saved at the last moment by the Flame Alchemist, Roy Mustang, backed by Lt. Hawkeye and the others.

Yet another meanwhile: Mei Chang is duelling the reborn homunculus Envy in an underground tunnel. How many of the filmmakers at Aniplex, Square Enix, Mainichi, Bones *et al* are avid fans of martial arts movies? Of Hong Kong action movies? *All of them*, I would guess! (aren't we all?!) – because they have included many martial arts moves in the Mei Chang scenes (she is a pint-sized Jet Li or Jackie Chan, with flailing plaits and huge eyes who can move faster than Bruce Lee).

Altho' Mei Chang is three foot six, she is one of the fiercest warriors in the *Fullmetal Alchemist* series – but even she is no match for Envy when he's gobbling up immortal soldiers and absorbing their life-force to become even more powerful. So she flees (pondering, in a galloping close-up, on the nature of the immortal soldiers being fuelled by philosopher's stones, and more determined than ever to take back the secret of eternal life to her clan in Xing/ China).

Fullmetal Alchemist costume play, including Amanda Leite from Brazil, 2013 (top right),

Episode 53. *Flame of Vengeance*

Envy has to die – he's a homunculus, his body is full of dead (tortured) souls, he killed Maes Hughes and many others, and he helped to start the Ishbalian War by shooting a 5 year-old girl in the face. But Himoru Arakawa focussed not on the demise of Envy (altho' that consumes much of the *manga* and the *animé*), but rather on the psychological/ moral *effect* of killing Envy on the Flame Alchemist, Roy Mustang. Slaughtering Envy becomes an ethical quandary for Mustang, and for those around him. So Liza Hawkeye becomes very concerned that Mustang is being eaten away by vengeance, and even Edward Elric (who has no special love for the irritatingly arrogant and always-right Mustang), is worried that the urge for revenge is damaging Mustang's soul (actually, that does strike a false note – would Ed really be bothered that much about whether Mustang is going to be psychologically scarred by killing Envy? Wouldn't Ed simply be glad that the homunculus is going to be destroyed? Besides, therre is a much more pressing job to be done here – saving all of Amestris from the catastrophic effects of a nationwide transmutation circle. Rescuring Mustang's soul from Hell is all very well, but millions of lives are also at stake!).

It's an interesting switch in the focus of the final episodes of *Fullmetal Alchemist* 2, so that killing the villains isn't a simple act (as in most action-adventure yarns, where the heroes're always in the right, and the villains 'deserve' or ' must' be destroyed), but is given a moral and ethical element.

How it works narratively in episode 53: *Flame of Vengeance* is that Mei Chang is fleeing Envy in the underground tunnels (a giant action sequence of its own); using her throwing stars she creates a fissure, and the two charas fall thru to the grand hall below, where Edward, Scar, the chimeras, Roy Mustang and Liza Hawkeye are battling the immortal soldiers (Mustang has arrived just before to find Ed, Scar & co. struggling to beat down the killer puppets. There's a scene where he uses his alchemy to burn all of the immortal soldiers to cinders. The visual effects animation of the conflagration is truly awesome).

Roy Mustang assumes control of the situation (as he always tends to do when he arrives on any scene), tho' Envy gloats at foolish humanity for a long time. Minami Takayama brilliantly articulates Envy's fleeting changes of emotion, veering from scorn and arrogance, to spluttering disbelief and finally yelled outrage. Oh, humans never cease to delight/ confuse/ frustrate/ irritate/ anger Envy!

Roy Mustang stubbornly refuses to budge, and confronts Envy with a single question, treating him like a naughty child: *who killed Maes Hughes?* (Mustang is relentless in his questioning of Envy).

The character design of Roy Mustang alters as he descends into a mælstrom of hatred – his eyes become sunken and ringed with black. Mustang is leading the action in this section of the 2009-10 *Fullmetal Alchemist* series (the other characters have been told to leave and head for the centre of the underground complex, and Father. We know that the Colonel has the alchemical firepower to take on Envy single-handed, altho' it took a *lot* to best Lust). Mustang attacks Envy, and the homunculus transforms into his dog-dragon form, the better to dispatch Mustang (but Mustang burns his eyes before Envy has even had the time to flaunt his power some more – Envy loves to flaunt and boast and gloat in *Fullmetal Alchemist*. It's one of the things that makes him such an entertaining character!).

Episode 2.53: *Flame of Vengeance* delivers an astonishing cat-and-mouse sequence in the tunnels below Central City, as Col. Mustang has Envy on the run and being repeatedly incinerated: the screen flashes to white and yellow, Envy is a stick insect silhouetted in black, and he screams (again and again). The dramatic level is hysterical, operatic, very over-the-top – and absolutely thrilling.

The animation is extreme in its performances and poses, approaching near-abstraction many times. And it's *very* rapid, hurtling from pose to pose with lightning-quick poses in-between. Only a team of veteran animators can deliver this sort of animation this well – it's a *lot* of work. But all of that effort pays off.

This remarkable show ends on a cliffhanger, as Envy impersonates either Roy Mustang or Liza Hawkeye in a dark tunnel, and Hawkeye holds a gun to Mustang's head.

❊

However, *Flame of Vengeance* opens with a lengthy sequence involving the possible *coup d'état* in Central City, as Mrs Bradley goes on the radio to talk about her kidnapping and her husband, Führer Bradley (the radio was established in the first episode as an important presence in people's lives, and one of the chief ways in which authorities communicate with the populace). It's a reprise of the sequence in episode 3: *City of Heresy*, where the Elrics exposed the fraud Father Cornello and his fake religion of the Sun God Leto (using the media – radio – to broadcast the truth to the masses). Well, in *Fullmetal Alchemist*, the device of changing people's minds using a radio broadcast is supremely simplistic (tho' it is true that one of the first things an occupying or invading force does in a new territory is to take control of the media). Himoru Arakawa is fond of scenes where the general population are embroiled in the story, so it's not just something that happens to the heroes, the villains, and the characters caught in between them.

So there are lots of scenes of Joe Public listening to the radio broadcast in episode 53: *Flame of Vengeance*, and reacting to it. Some Ishbalians help to spread the word about the disappearance of Führer Bradley in a railroad accident. The Central City forces are unable to shut down the broadcast (there is some comedy with the radio manager pretending to be under attack on the phone to the exasperated general (Cremin – Kiyoshi Katsunuma) in the government command centre). Meanwhile, the soldiers from Briggs Fortress begin their assault on the command centre, using a tank (ah, how animators in Japan love their tanks! Three of the greatest artists of recent times, Hayao Miyazaki, Masamune Shirow and Katsuhiro Otomo, are crazy tank fans).

This form of storytelling in animation is unusual, and very ambitious. It's unusual partly because it's very time-consuming in creating all of those vignettes, which are only on screen for moments. These are characters that're only seen in these short scenes, but they have to drawn from scratch (and individualized). The ambition aims to encompass a whole city within the scope of the narrative (and then to extend that to a whole country). So *Fullmetal Alchemist* really does feel like an *animé* show that covers an entire nation – the vignettes include all sorts of people.

This creative work was undertaken also to help the finale of *Fullmetal Alchemist* to pay off: Father's obscene act is to attempt to kill a whole country in order to feed his ego. Thus, it makes Father's crime all the greater because we've met many of the victims already, throughout the series in these crowd scenes and montages of vignettes of everyday folk.

Episode 54: *Beyond the Inferno*

The *Fullmetal Alchemist* animated series is a work of genius, and this episode (air date: April 25, 2010) is one of the reasons why. This show encapsulates the moral-philosophical themes of the *Fullmetal Alchemist* enterprise in an intensely vivid fashion – it may be the most sigfnificant show in the series. It also features one of the greatest death scenes in recent pop culture, live-action or animation.

The first half of the episode comprises a lengthy discussion about one of the central themes of the *Fullmetal Alchemist* series: what does it mean to be a human being? But this section of episode 54: *Beyond the Inferno* is no simple talky scene: it is driven by a strong dramatic concept, majorly important themes, a crackling script, and an incendiary performance by Minami Takayama as the homunculus Envy. And if that isn't enough, it also includes yet more action sequences, as Envy is hunted down and burnt alive. Indeed, there is so much action and conflict squeezed into the final episodes of the 2nd *Fullmetal Alchemist* series, it's startling to hit a lengthy talky scene.

In these connected episodes the screenwriters (they are all written by Hiroshi Ohnogi, tho' this one was scripted by Shôtarô Suga), milk the character of Envy and his demise to the max: so it's Envy pitted against the Flame Alchemist. We get to see flashbacks of both Liza Hawkeye's and Roy Mustang's lives (to the Ishbal civil war, for instance), and how Hawkeye has the secrets of flame alchemy tattooed onto her back (by her father (Atsuki Tani) – *ouch*, that must've hurt! thanks Dad!). We see Hawkeye begging Mustang to burn the tattoo off her back so that no one else can pursue the alchemy of fire (there are better ways of erasing a tattoo!). We see the unspoken (and unexpressed) romantic relationship between Mustang and Hawkeye at its most intimate. We see Mustang dissolving into a cauldron of hatred as he battles Envy, using billowing walls of fire to incinerate the homunculus time after time. We see Ed Elric – and even Scar – offering their own views on the pursuit of vengeance, which's eating up Mustang alive (after they had turned back).

Meanwhile, the filmmakers and screenwriter Shôtarô Suga have given a huge amount of dialogue to Envy, and voice actor Minami Takayama rises to the challenge (encouraged by sound director Masafumi Mima), delivering a terrific series of mean, sarcastic, murmured, whimpered and also yelled monologues, as Envy scorns humanity, cackles over it, and finally pleads for his life. Something about seeing a very powerful villain being reduced to a little, green creature the size of a kitten fascinates both the animators and the scriptwriters, because they give an enormous amount of time to Envy and his death throes in *Fullmetal Alchemist 2*.

It's true that the filmmakers of both *Fullmetal Alchemist* series like to exploit the death of each homunculus to their full potential, because these are such major villains. With Envy, they really go to town with the repeated battery of fiery alchemy unleashed by Roy Mustang, and with the suffering that Envy undergoes. The violence and horror enacted upon Envy seems to go on and on – way beyond the necessities of drama. (Envy is furious that of all people it's Edward Elric who should've understood him best of all – how he secretly desires friends and a family, and is jealous of humans. Ling Yao tells Greed the same thing, in the penultimate show).

This really is a *tour-de-force* performance by Takayama-san, one of the finest examples of voice work in recent Japanese animation. It's like watching a great, Shakespearean actor play a death scene – and it's even more exceptional because Takayama plays the last part of the soliloquy in the high-pitched voice of the tiny Envy, and that Envy is delivering his speech from an inch off the ground!

Episode 54: *Beyond the Inferno* is all about morality and ethics: Envy voices some key points of moral philosophy here: that the humans are co-operating with each other: Scar is there, for instance, the sworn enemy of both Roy Mustang and Liza Hawkeye... Scar is also the murderer of Edward Elric's friend's parents (and has attacked Ed and his brother Al many times)... Envy appeals to each of them in turn – this is brilliant scriptwriting by Shôtarô Suga.

Voice actor Minami Takayama escalates her performance to a hysterical pitch, as Envy cries, 'why?... how come?' How can these humans work together when they have so many reasons for loathing each other? He urges them to remember their resentments and betrayals and to start arguing and killing each other.

And lurking behind episode 54: *Beyond the Inferno* is the disturbing issue of suicide: Roy Mustang and Liza Hawkeye hint at suicide (Hawkeye says she would follow Mustang in death if he killed himself by burning up Envy and himself). And then, squeezing his *chibi* form from out of Edward's grasp, Envy plops to the floor and stages his dramatic, prima donna suicide. He finds it unbearably humiliating to be understood best by the pipsqueak Fullmetal Alchemist (that he is, fundamentally, jealous of humans, and would like to be human himself).[1] Envy's disgust at humanity masks a corrosive jealousy, and also a self-hatred at his own inadequacies.

It's a remarkable scene, at once pitiful and blackly amusing, with the vocal performance by Minami Takayama reaching amazing heights of emotion, accompanied by terrific actorly animation (and a plangent cue from composer Akira Senju – the choral cue accompanying the images from Mustang's life is especially impressive). The producers (Hiro Maruyama, Nobuyuki Kurashige, Noritomo Yonai and Ryo Oyama) must've been very pleased with this episode, because the production teams really did come up with the goods.

✻

So that when episode 54: *Beyond the Inferno* cuts to some of the other stories in the *Fullmetal Alchemist* series, it's almost a let-down from the high drama and high emotion of the first half of the show. Follow that! You can't – in fact, this might well be the highpoint of the *Fullmetal Alchemist* run, even though there is plenty of action and thrills to come.

To counter the more static but totally compelling Envy Death Scene, the episode is filled with some wild action animation, as the Armstrongs continue to battle against the giant Sloth and the immortal puppets in the corridors of power (aided by more Central soldiers, who're still under orders to kill Armstrong). Alex A. recovers enough to show off his boxing prowess (with a reprise of the very funny martial choral music).

Elsewhere, Briggs soldiers enter the command centre (led by Captain Buccaneer); their tank bombards HQ's gates; and housewife Izumi Curtis arrives to save the day (announcing herself as an alchemist). And over the credits we see van Hohenheim coming face to face with the homunculus in the jar, Father, in the bunker.

Episode 55. *The Adults' Way of Life*

In these episodes of *Fullmetal Alchemist: Brotherhood* we are into the full-on battle for control of Central City: Ed and Al are sidelined almost entirely, as the Japanese TV series focusses on the civil war between the factions of soldiers from Central and from Briggs, the *coup d'état*, the Radio Capital broadcasts (featuring Mrs Bradley), and duels between Bradley and Buccaneer, Bradley and Greed, the Armstrongs vs. Sloth (who finally expires), plenty of soldiers vs. the immortal legion of zombies, and last but not least, Hohenheim vs. Father. (Consequently, this is a *very* busy episode, with few scenes lasting longer'n a minute).

Ed Elric appears early on in episode 55, but only to offer some light-hearted banter with Roy Mustang (to wrap up the high drama of the previous episode with some humorous *dénouement* scenes), and Al is seen helping with a car that's stuck (Alphonse is with Dr Marcoh, Yoki and Heinkel, on their way to the command centre).

---

1 The first *Fullmetal Alchemist* series drew on this envy for being human.

Among the stand-out sequences in these episodes of *Fullmetal Alchemist* included the continuation of the duels featuring the Armstrong brother and sister going up against Sloth and an army of the undead. Especially memorable was the last-minute rescue and arrival of Hiromu Arakawa's favourite housewife alchemist, Izumi Curtis,[2] and her loyal husband Sig, who help the Armstrongs to finally dispatch the unkillable Sloth (Akira Senju reprises the wonderfully over-the-top, comic and camp Germanic-Soviet choral cue to accompany the muscle-man heroics of Alex Armstrong and Sig[3]). Curtis also gets to show off more of her martial arts moves, dispatching many immortal mannequins, and punching Central City officers.

In episode 55: *The Adults' Way of Life*, Sloth finally expires, after putting up a staunch fight.[4] So with Envy buying it in the previous episode (54: *Beyond the Inferno*), and Sloth in this episode, that's two tough homunculi out of action: thus, a new villain is required, and he duly turns up in the midst of the revelry as Briggs Mountain soldiers celebrate taking control of the command centre. Well, we knew Führer Bradley couldn't have been destroyed by the railroad explosion (we know too that we are nearing the end of this incredible animated series, with only three major villains surviving: Bradley, Pride and Father, plus the wild card, Greed).

The re-introduction of the Führer is one of Himoru Arakawa's wish-fulfilment set-pieces: that a king would return to claim his kingdom by simply walking[5] to the fortress as a one-many army is a crowd-pleasing if ridiculous moment (like how Bradley happens to be able to intercept the transmission to the troops about the Briggs victory to announce his homecoming).

Elsewhere in the Central City HQ, we see Olivia Armstrong entering the throne room, then leaving with no desire to assume command of the military machine[6] (and also another pretender to the throne, who's soon chomped by more of the immortal soldiers as he reaches for the hallowed Chair of Command). Buccaneer and his cronies are swiftly taking control of the HQ, securing every gate.

Meanwhile, Father (Iemasa Kayumi) is finally introduced in super-villain mode in the 2nd *Fullmetal Alchemist* series (continuing from the end credits in the previous episode), after a lengthy time hovering on the margins as a character (or a presence) much discussed (or sensed). So the two characters face each other in the underground complex: Father and van Hohenheim (they are two sides of the same coin, linked by the blood that Hohenheim gave to the dwarf in the jar): note that Hohenheim doesn't threaten Father at first, he merely states that something needs to be done about Father, the former homunculus from Xerxes. It's Father, rather, who

---

2 Curtis, in her casual attire, looks as if she's just popped out of the kitchen in the middle of preparing a nice *ramen* supper.
3 Accompanied by gleaming stars.
4 The title of this episode, *The Adults' Way of Life*, is explained by Olivia Armstrong: the adults must carry on, to offer an example to youngsters.
5 We see a pair of feet walking past Alphonse & co. by the car.
6 La Armstrong tends to regard the people running Amestris as fools, and has no desire to be the boss of a bunch of weak men. Tho' she would no doubt be the first lady leader of Amestris.

threatens to absorb Hohenheim.

And it's Father who attacks first – hurling stone fists and darts at van Hohenheim, who dodges them or escapes from stone prisons with a casual ease (yet also humorously awkward. Hohenheim is not a fighter – like Envy; tho' he can when he must). Out comes the extraordinary visual effects animation, with the zinging red bolts of energy which perfectly capture the look and the feel of Himoru Arakawa's *Fullmetal Alchemist manga*.

The Father vs. Hohenheim duel is basically a wizards' duel, and it's marvellously staged (similar duels will crop up in the very last episodes). It adheres to the thematic basis of the *manga*, too, by keeping the goals of both characters in plain sight: Father professes his aim to become a perfect being (i.e., a god), and Hohenheim is determined to put a stop to Father's schemes (Father insists that he doesn't want to become human; Hohenheim asserts that he does, and that what he really wanted was a family. Hence why he created the homunculi). The two characters are light and dark, the hero and his shadow (in a way, the seven homunculi representing the Seven Sins are a summary of all of Hohenheim's flaws – pride, sloth, gluttony, wrath, etc – and the faults at the heart of all humans).

But Hohenheim informs Father that he is unable to steal the philosopher's stone from inside his body (when Father disappears into the ground and emerges to thrust his arm right into Father's torso),[7] because he lacks one thing. (Father is the classic villain in lacking humanity, compassion, and – as Hohenheim astutely judges – a true family. Father is above all a lonely, disconnected character, utterly friendless, with no companions other than the ones he creates himself – the homunculi – and whom he treats as slaves).

So when episode 55: *The Adults' Way of Life* leaves the wizards' duel unfinished, we know we are going to come back here probably several times. We know that because each of the homunculi in *Fullmetal Alchemist* has taken *a lot* to destroy them, so the chief homunculus is likely going to be *extremely* difficult to subjugate (and he/ it is!).

Notice that at this point in the proceedings, the Elric brothers have not been depicted dispatching any of the homunculi, though they bave battled them many times: Mustang defeats Lust (with the aid of Havoc) and Envy (with the aid of Hawkeye); the Armstrongs trounce Sloth (with the aid of the Curtises); and Pride eats Gluttony. The Elrics are being saved for the battle with Father.

Episode 56. *The Return of the Führer*

Broadcast on May 9, 2010, this episode continues the *tour-de-force* masterwork that is series two of *Fullmetal Alchemist*. For action and spectacle, *Fullmetal Alchemist* is hard to beat: and it's partly the *variety* of action on offer that's so impressive. Instead of duel followed by duel, we have all sorts of action, including fire-fights, a sword vs. tank duel, knife

---

7 It's a move that occurs in other *animés*, such as *Legend of the Overfiend*.

fights, and so on.

The show opens with an intriguing flashback to 400 years ago, when van Hohenheim fled the destruction of Xerxes (which we last saw quite some time ago, in episode 40: *Homunculus*). Lost in the desert that spreads between Amestris and Xing, Hohenheim wanders, a lone figure on the sand dunes who collapses (a familiar action-adventure motif – the first *Fullmetal Alchemist* series introduced the Elric brothers first in a similar scene, with Ed gasping for water). A group of Xingese merchants on camels discover him (forging the legend of the Golden Man from the East – it's Hohenheim who brings alchemy to Amestris).

When episode 56: *The Return of the Führer* cuts to the present day, we are back with van Hohenheim confronting Father in the labyrinth below Central City. Van Hohenheim offers some explanation here about the souls buried inside him, how he has conversed with each one of the half a million people, one by one, person by person, and how they are going to help him bring down Father. There are charming vignettes of each soul that Hohenheim names, one after another (which thus continue the flashbacks of Xerxes – and of the young Hohenheim in the city. Carpenters, slaves, rivals, flower girls, etc).

Once the explanation is over (Father listens attentively – this is all news to him, he's never considered humans on an individual basis), the dead souls infiltrate Father's body, again using the internal views unique to Japanese animation, achieved here with abstract red lines and shapes over black. The thousands of floating, red blobs, in an extraordinary piece of visualization, coalesce and force a blackened stump or horn out of Father's forehead, from the *inside*. Which would kill any mortal human. Father breaks off the horn: the souls try again: they pin him with black stakes (which erupt again from the inside). It's another action sequence which vividly depicts the long-awaited face-off between van Hohenheim and the homunculus he let out of the jar 400 years earlier, the little critter who now goes by the name of Father. Out spritzes the visual effects animation (plenty of zigzag zaps of red, alchemical magic, fire, smoke, falling debris), and that eternal stand-by of animators everywhere: bodily transformations.

There is blood and guts a-plenty here, and Father is divested of his skin and clothes, which lie in a heap on the floor. Van Hohenheim imagines that It Ends Here (when a body is now nothing but a leather bag), but no, no – Father isn't done yet!

Once again, the filmmakers at Bones, Square Enix, Mainichi, Aniplex *et al* added numerous ingredients to the already-stuffed-full *Fullmetal Alchemist manga* by Hiromu Arakawa, staging incredibly visceral destructions and reanimations for the chief villain, Father. Here, a black creature climbs out of the ruins of the leather bag of Father's body (which was always only a shell/ vehicle for the homunculus in the jar), emerging this time as a black, humanoid shape fitted with Pride-like eyes and mouths and Hohenheim realizes what we already knew: that it would take more'n this to waste this super-villain!

*

The rest of episode 56: *The Return of the Führer* is straight down-the-line action of the World War Two movie variety. There are a few magic or fantasy elements (from the Führer, Greed and from the ninja Fuu), but most of the action is 'real world' stuff – guns, tanks, swords, daggers, etc. And it's Boy Heaven in ep. 56, as heroes and villains slug it out the old-fashioned way, with brute strength.

So Führer Bradley arrives at Central City's military HQ as a One-Man Army, with only a sword (and a grenade) as his weapons: this is a terrific riff on the Return of the King trope, when a monarch returns to take back his throne.

The *Fullmetal Alchemist manga* included a lengthy series of duels for the Führer outside the main gate of the HQ; the *animé* added numerous elements (as well as dropping action beats in the comic). One of the marvellous additions was the battle between King Bradley and a tank reversing back up the diagonal shaft that leads up from street level to the main gate: it seems like a dream of an *otaku* to stage a duel between a man armed with swords and a main battle tank. The sequence is rightly played at full chaos level, and full speed. It is very reminiscent of *Akira* (in both *manga* and animated form), where film director and *manga* artist Katsuhiro Otomo exploited the diagonal elevator shaft to the underground Akira complex to the full. (And the shaft to the main gate in *Fullmetal Alchemist* is similarly milked for its potential, with gun battles, a ninja sprint, and that tank duel).

The battles and feuds in *Fullmetal Alchemist* keep coming – the action is simply divine, some of the finest in recent *animé*. Everybody in the production team is delivering some magnificent work – this is big, broad, supremely confident filmmaking, which utilizes a huge number of animators and a vast array of companies (check out the credits! Every pair of hands in Tokyo seems to have worked on *Fullmetal Alchemist*, including numerous famed companies, such as Production I.G, Studio Deen, Studio Ghibli, Telecom, Tokyo Animation Center and Asahi Production. If you are an *animé* fan, you will have seen 100s of hours of animation produced by these groups of workaholics in Tokyo, a city where it seems nobody sleeps).

The brutality of *Fullmetal Alchemist* doesn't let up in the final episodes of the 2009-10 TV series, with gouts of blood flying across the screen with astonishing rapidity and volume. From single drops of blood dripped onto a character's cheek to whole bodies exploding with blood (all 8 pints of it), *Fullmetal Alchemist* is excessively, irredeemably, unashamedly violent.

The Führer in particular is portrayed chopping up numerous victims who stand in his way, including attacking Captain Buccaneer until the Russian Bear is severely crippled. Greed/ Ling Yao enters the fray (first he gloats from his usual superhero perch on high), taking on Bradley single-handed, and is joined later on by Fuu,[8] the *shinobi* from Xing still devoted

---

[8] Like the tank duel, Fuu is also given a remarkable sequence in the diagonal shaft leading up to the main gate, as he slices his way thru many Central soldiers.

to his master Ling Yao (while Vato Falman does his bit in trying to prevent the Central City soldiers climbing up the diagonal shaft).

Episode 56: *The Return of the Führer* depicts a siege and defence scenario in a thrilling manner, as the Briggs Fortress soldiers and the Central City forces battle for control of the city and its government. There are a huge number of characters to orchestrate in many locations – while the tussle for the government HQ is playing out, for instance, the 2010 episode also finds time to visit the radio station where Bradley's wife is being interviewed live (and Lt. Ross and Cain Furey outside in the corridor discuss their options, as events accelerate and threaten to overwhelm them – it's moving that the *Fullmetal Alchemist* series finds time for modest scenes involving minor characters, reminding us that big political events affect regular soldiers as well as the people at the top).

The *Fullmetal Alchemist* story spends a *lot* of time, in both *manga* and *animé* forms, on the military forces battling for control of Amestris – and there is nothing fundamentally fantastical or magical about all of this: it's not about alchemy or monsters, it's very familiar from the history of recent times. Central City might be Prague, Paris, Berlin, Sarajevo or Moscow (author Himoru Arakawa clearly has recent Middle Eastern conflicts in mind, centring on cities such as Baghdad, Tehran and Beirut, and also the Balkans in the 1990s).

Episode 57. *Eternal Leave*

The fights against the Führer continue apace in this episode, as Fuu and Captain Buccaneer and Greed/ Ling Yao try to nobble the psycho. Both Fuu and Buccaneer are mortally wounded (spraying blood everywhere), but they keep coming back, hurling themselves against Bradley repeatedly (but even when Fuu hurtles at him armed with bombs strapped to his waist, the Führer is still able to trounce him, by cutting off the fuses, and wounding Fuu in the process). In a daredevil and painful move, Buccaneer thrusts his sword *through* Fuu in order to stab the Führer (not even his homunculus eye could foresee that).

Meanwhile, Lan Fan is scampering thru the underground tunnels of Central City, and, over-hearing some soldiers, she changes course, hurrying to the roof of the gateway, to witness her grandfather's demise.

In another part of Central City, Alphonse and his chums (Yoki, Dr Marcoh *et al*), have reached the stricken capital (their car crashed).[9] But no sooner has Al appeared, than the transmutation circle for Father's 'sacrifices' reduces Al to pieces.

Major Armstrong, Izumi Curtis, Sig and their group decide what they're going to do, now that Sloth and the mannequins have been destroyed. They have captured one of the generals and forced him to tell them about the government's plans. The discussion is important, because it outlines some of the conflicts – between the loyal and the corrupt wings of the military, for instance, and between the 'ordinary people' of

9 It did take Al and co. a *long* time to enter the battleground – the writers have overlooked them in favour of the many other groups of charas.

Amestris (represented by the Curtises) and the government. Both Armstrong and Curtis are furious to hear about the government's plans – Curtis takes off her shoe to belt the general around the face (like a mother with a naughty child).

The discussion continues as the party enters the vast staircase lit by torches that leads down from the Führer's office to the bowels of Central City and Father's lair. Interestingly, it's Izumi Curtis and Olivia Armstrong who lead the scene here, not the big, burly men surrounding them (Sig, Armstrong, the soldiers of Briggs and Amestris): where she can, *mangaka* Himoru Arakawa likes to place women in roles usually inhabited by men (however, the Armstrongs, injured after fighting Sloth, should really be in hospital! Actually, almost all of the characters should be either collapsed in agony on the floor or dead by now!).

The conversation turns to the Elric brothers, and how they relate to the key issue of transmutation and bringing back the dead in the *Fullmetal Alchemist* series; Armstrong talks up Edward, reminding us of the hero, and Curtis tells Armstrong what happened to her. We already knew this, but the scene functions as a catch-up summary for the audience, and it's also vital in re-asserting the major themes and goals of the series.

✳

Underneath Central City, we return to another bunch of heroes – Edward Elric, Roy Mustang, Liza Hawkeye and Scar (it's a welcome return for the hero of the *Fullmetal Alchemist* series). They encounter the Doctor With the Gold Tooth and the square glasses – he is a Nazi in all but name (i.e., Josef Mengele), who conducts sick experiments on humans in trying to breed the perfect fighting machine. The Doctor relates part of the back-story of the creation of Führer Bradley (tho' Mustang provides the voice) – how a group of men were trained and injected in the familiar but repulsive pursuit of producing a super-human. We see glimpses of this in a montage flashback format, intercut with scenes of our heroes battling the Führer rejects, who materialize at the Doctor's command; all dressed alike, all with grim, blank faces, they are formidable swordsmen – so that Scar, Mustang, Hawkeye and Ed're really having to work hard to avoid being sliced to pieces. (This is a essentially replay of the heroes vs. the zombies scenario: battling overwhelming odds in an underground chamber, and it further delays our heroes from reaching Father).

The climax of episode 57: *Eternal Leave* is a *tour-de-force* of imagination and realization: the Gold-Toothed Doctor finishes creating a transmutation circle on the ground in chalk and, using five of the Führer cast-offs as fuel (i.e., payment), he ignites an alchemical transformation which also unites the other alchemical laboratories in Central City. Out come the blue zigzags of magical energy, the unreal, violet glow, the visual effects animation, a loud, solemn, choral cue, and ærial images of the capital of Amestris lit with alchemical fire.

The aim of this particular alchemical transmutation is to ferry the remaining 'sacrifices' to Father underground: we see our heroes crumbling into tiny pieces, with the eye of the Gateway of Truth opening below them. Exactly what the purpose of this transmutation isn't made clear yet, but the action's intense and wild enough for the audience to realize that whatever it is, it's painful and extreme, and might well be the death of the heroes.

The action climax of episode 57: *Eternal Leave* is a very powerful piece of high drama, delivered in the compelling, grand opera manner of the *Fullmetal Alchemist* series, which brings together each of the plot strands that the episode has been following: so we see Izumi Curtis being snatched away from the staircase, in the middle of talking to Olivia Armstrong and her group, Alphonse dissolving in the streets of Central City, and Ed too, in vivid, yelling close-ups.

The visual effects animation is quite brilliant – how the bodies dissolve in tiny squares (from the *manga*), as if they're just hollow dummies, but they also have scarlet energy lines underneath. And how the transmutation roils through Edward's body, disintegrating it, ending up on his face, which rumbles, until just his golden eye remains, then that goes, too (and, throughout, each character is screaming).

The conception by Himoru Arakawa is genius – it's a marvellous way, in a series based around alchemy, for the super-villain to gather his hostages, rather than the usual ways we've all seen 1,000s of times before (such as: being captured at gun-point, or knocked unconscious, or lassoed, or rounded up, etc).

Episode 58. *Sacrifices*

Much of the first half of this incredible, incident-jammed episode of the second *Fullmetal Alchemist* series comprises the battle for the gate of the government HQ. We are back with Führer Bradley as a one-man army beating off Ling Yao/ Greed, Captain Buccaneer and Fuu. The Führer is impossible to kill, impossible to stop: but eventually the heroes manage to drop the Führer into the moat surrounding the HQ, in a literal cliffhanger (but we can bet we haven't seen the last of him! Anyway, he'd already survived the attempt on his life on the train on the bridge. Super-villains falling into water never dispatches them. But it does take away the threat of Bradley, leaving the way clear for death scenes and moral resolve scenes).

The Russian Bear, Captain Buccaneer, dies, uttering his final words to Ling Yao – to defend the gate as he promised his queen, Major Armstrong. His final vision is of the clear, cold skies above Briggs Fortress. The soldiers guarding Buccaneer look on solemnly. Now the deaths are piling up as we near the end of *Fullmetal Alchemist* (there are only six episodes to go after this): Sloth, Envy, Fuu and now Buccaneer.

Mamoru Miyano as Ling Yao delivers some loud, tortured vocals here as the Xingese prince mourns Fuu – bringing back some of Raito Yamagi's remarkable madness that Miyano performed in the finale of 2006's *Death Note*.

So Ling Yao calls upon the powers of Greed the demon inside him, and goes on the rampage – in some of the finest superhero-style mayhem in the *Fullmetal Alchemist* series (after all, the design of Greed in his shield guise is very superhero-ish). The sloping approach to the gate from ground level is employed again for more pandemonium, with Ling-Greed as a one-man army (a favourite motif with action movie writers), demolishing all the Central forces who have remained (he gives them the chance to leave if they have families). And his frenzy continues outside (such as stabbing a truck's engine thru the radiator so it blows up).

*

But what happened to the Elrics and Izumi Curtis, eaten and dissolved by the black hands in the previous episode? The filmmakers make us wait before revealing that they have travelled thru a beyond-life realm (of abstract spaces and lightning bolt energy), ending up in the subterranean labyrinth of the super-villain, Father. Again, the focus is on eyes – a giant close-up of Edward's gold eye as he awakens after that tortuous trip through the worm-hole of death and beyond.

Ed Elric leads the scene, as the heroes encounter the bizarre form of Father, now a vaguely anthropomorphic, bulbous shape with multiple eyes and mouths sliding over purple-black skin. And, in a classic design particular to Japanese popular culture, van Hohenheim is embedded in the monster's body, with his head protruding from its belly (as if the demon has devoured Hohenheim but not quite digested him). Handily, having Hohenheim poking out of Father means that he is able to explain something of what's happening (and, crucially, to identify the monster standing before them as the bearded guy they met earlier). Unfortunately, Alphonse remains unresponsive, lying on the ground nearby, seemingly unconscious (we find out what happened with Al in the next episode).

A moving scene takes place on the staircase leading from the Führer's office to Father's bunker, where Sig Curtis is looking for his wife, and the Armstrongs hear of the fate of the Briggs take-over of the HQ. Here Olivia A. is told of the death of her staunchest supporter, the Bear of Briggs, Buccaneer: no tears are shed by the Ice Queen, of course (instead, there's one of the oft-used close-ups in all *animé* – a shot of her hand tightening its grip. If he died with a smile on his face, we won't mourn him, she asserts).

The second series of *Fullmetal Alchemist* is following the *manga* by Himoru Arakawa very closely (tho' always adding 1,000s of elements of its own). Now comes one of the most gruesome scenes in the *manga*, in an animated series that has never held back from depicting an extraordinary barrage of horrors: the sacrifice of Liza Hawkeye in a hostage scenario, having her throat slit.

Now, in the action and adventure genre, the hero/ine might be threatened, taunted, beaten and tortured, but not often do they have their throat slit open, so that they are bleeding to death in front of the heroes! Even tho' we know that this is a high fantasy series, and that there are MacGuffins such as philosopher's stones that can possibly reverse dying (tho' not usually death), the scene is still extreme.

So the hateful Gold-Toothed Doctor, still running the show in this part of *Fullmetal Alchemist*, stands over Lt. Hawkeye as she bleeds on the stone floor, lying in a transmutation circle, while the heavies have Col. Mustang and Scar held at swordpoint. The degree of bloodshed and violence in the *Fullmetal Alchemist* series is striking – and it's also a feature of many *animés* and *mangas* (blood is spraying and sloshing everywhere in this part of *Fullmetal Alchemist 2*).

What the Doctor wants is a fifth sacrifice – and he commands Roy Mustang to perform that duty by opening the Gateway, and undertaking human transmutation (also dangling a philosopher's stone in front of him, which could possibly bring back Hawkeye if she expires). This dilemma forms a suitably high drama cliffhanger to episode 58: *Sacrifices,* another absolutely thrilling installment in what might be the greatest *animé* series ever (if *One Piece* didn't exist!).

Episode 59. *Lost Light*

Another rapturous episode.

As the installments of *Fullmetal Alchemist 2* approach the Grand Finale, thankfully we see more of Elrics Ed and Al (Alphonse returns: I found his meeting with his body in the non-space of the Gate moving: how his soul talks to his body in that spiritual limbo; and, as he leaves to help fight the villain, he tells his body he'll be back!). And once Al is back with the land of the living (tho' trapped with the others inside the belly of Father), the fireworks can begin (or rather, continue – because they haven't stopped for the past few episodes!).

Much of episode 59: *Lost Light* plays out the confrontation between Roy Mustang, Liza Hawkeye, Scar and their foes – the Gold-Toothed Alchemist, the Führer cast-offs and – turning up as the embodiment of political corruption and coercion that will simply never go away, and never die (just like in real life) – the Führer himself (a flashback[10] shows how he survived the high fall from the battlements of the government HQ – somewhat redundant, this, because we know already that the Führer is virtually unkillable!). And Pride joins the party, too.

Col. Mustang plays for time, refusing to perform human transmutation, and help arrives in the form of the chimeras (Jerso, Zampano, and Darius) and li'l Mei Chang (they break their way in from above). It's to-and-fro here, cat-and-mouse – because no sooner has aid arrived for our heroes, than Führer Bradley stalks into the fray, followed by Pride. In the chaos, Mei is able to staunch the bleeding from Lt. Hawkeye's throat wound (Mei chooses healing over obtaining the philosopher's stone, as it's kicked in a little phial around the chamber), and Scar takes on Bradley.

The upper hand switches rapidly to the villains again with the arrival of Pride, the extraordinary schoolboy-cum-monster (he has a grand entrance, with a full build-up), who hurries along the villain's schemes by having Wrath pin Roy Mustang to the ground with swords stabbed into the Colonel's palms (another crucifixion image in *Fullmetal*

---

10 Within a white vignette, silent movie-style.

Alchemist). Using the Gold-Toothed Alchemist as the means of performing transmutation (a suitably gruesome demise for him),[11] there's another spectacular magical sequence, and Mustang is taken into the belly of the super-villain, Father, the original homunculus, via the Gateway of Truth.

There are thus two scenes in the beyond-life limbo of the Gate – for Roy Mustang and for Alphonse Elric. Again, we see the ominous images of the giant doors, the white limbo, the enormous, staring eye, the tiny, black hands, and the grinning form of Hubris/ Truth/ God/ whatever. Mustang's eye-sight is the price for travelling thru the Gate: we follow Mustang to the belly of the homunculus beast, where Edward Elric and Izumi Curtis are astonished to see the Colonel fall from the ceiling (using another birth-like trope, with red goop). To add to the cast of characters assembled for the finale, Himoru Arakawa included Mei Chang (the Xingese form of alchemy, alkahestry, is employed as a spiritual counterpoint to the Amestrian/ Western form of alchemy, and Mei is an interesting and quirky character to add to the ensemble).

Meanwhile, Scar stays behind to battle the Führer – which leads, finally, to the demise of both of them. It's apt that it's Scar, the embodiment of the race issue, the Ishbal War, and the victim of the Amestrisian government, who should be the one to take down Bradley.

＊

Episode 59: *Lost Light* climaxes with the emotional reunion of Alphonse Elric – as he experiences a true out-of-body trip to the Gateway of Truth – with his own body. It's a body and a soul – *mangaka Himoru Arakawa* certainly conjured up some unusual and memorable motifs to depict an after-life/ beyond-life/ spiritual limbo: colossal doors, giant eyes, grasping, black hands, a grimacing demon/ non-demon, and a white-on-white space that is literally nowhere.

Alphonse Elric finds his body in an emaciated state – he needs more strength than that to fight the enemy ('it's not enough!' he wails). So – extraordinarily – he opts to leave his body behind, to *not* be reunited with it – but to come back for it later (which paves the way for the amazing finale of *Fullmetal Alchemist*). Meanwhile, actress Rie Kugimiya delivers a scorching performance as Al at the borders of life and death.

This is brilliant storytelling, using recognizable motifs and themes, but coming up with its own, unique spin on them, and its own, vivid way of manifesting them. The mythology of life and death that Himoru Arakawa created for the *Fullmetal Alchemist* series is formidable. And there is nothing else quite like this.

This is another stunning show, with the action and the drama evolving logically out of the characters and the emotions: it's a key reason for the success of the *Fullmetal Alchemist* series as a whole. This isn't simply action for action's sake or spectacle for spectacle's sake (tho' with

11 Pride absorbs the Gold-Toothed Doctor, which means he is now able to perform alchemy. It's kind of a get-out clause, because only Father among the homunculi can use alchemy. However, we have seen Pride absorb Gluttony and his sense of smell. (You could argue that the ability to perform alchemy is of a different order from soaking up a creature's senses)

animation this incredible, that would certainly be enough!). It's the solid base of the characters' emotions, motives, goals, flaws and hopes that gives *Fullmetal Alchemist* such power.

And when that depth and complexity is coupled with some of the most imaginative and skilful animation of recent times, the effect is quite majestic.

MORE ON THE FINAL SCENES OF *FULL-METAL ALCHEMIST*.

As it continues, and particularly in the finale episodes (from episode 50-ish onwards), you watch each show of *Fullmetal Alchemist* in awe and joy: as each show finishes, you are floating: this is Animé Bliss, this is really is outstanding filmmaking at every level. The high budget and the 1,000s of hours of work pay off. (Hiroshi Ohnogi, chief writer on the *Fullmetal Alchemist* series, is the writer of all of the episodes from 58 to the last one, 64, as well as 53, 55 and 56).

The very high quality of the animation in the finale episodes of *Fullmetal Alchemist*'s 2nd TV series is apparent everywhere. Yet the filmmakers are not afraid to use literally hundreds of freeze frames. Now, in some animated shows, a still frame can draw attention to itself as a money-saving device. Not in shows like *Fullmetal Alchemist*, where static shots are employed alongside sound effects, dialogue and music to create so many vivid moments. You don't need to see a sword swinging in motion if you have a marvellous still drawing of the action. It's all storytelling, whether the animation contains movement or not, and the stylization of the freeze frame works wonders (as also in shows such as *Samurai Champloo, Cowboy Bebop, Dominion: Tank Police* and *Escaflowne*). It's one cinematic tradition that simply doesn't exist at all in Western film (which sometimes reverts to slow motion, which has different effects).

When an *animé* show crowds its storytelling into the closing credits, you know they have a lot of story to pack into those crucial 22 minutes. Towards the end of the 2nd *Fullmetal Alchemist* series, the filmmakers're using the credits as well as the show to tell the story (sometimes fading down the theme music, but often using non-dialogue scenes to continue the story).

The final episodes of *Fullmetal Alchemist* do everything you could wish for in cinema and animation: thrills, chills, plenty of magic and spectacle, some humour, and some emotion. In fact, as each episode only lasts for 22 minutes, and they are so good, I tend to make the final episodes of the finest *animé* series last, by not watching them all at once. You don't want to rush to the end with shows like *Fullmetal Alchemist* or *Cowboy Bebop* or *Ghost In the Shell: Stand Alone Complex* or *Escaflowne*.

Can the filmmakers at Aniplex, Square Enix, Mainichi and Bones *et al* top themselves with each episode? Well, like the best animation teams, they have a really good try. In fact, this is one of the aspects of Japanese animation that impresses me a good deal: in the finest series (*Aquarionflowne, Macross Plus, Rage of Bahamut, Naruto, One Piece*, and *Ghost In the Shell: Stand Alone Complex*), the level of filmmaking gets higher and higher as the series hurtle towards their finales. It's pretty incredible to see filmmaking teams *start* at very high levels of storytelling and animation, but then go *even higher* as they reach the final episodes.

The folks in Tokyo at Aniplex, Square Enix, Mainichi and Bones & co. do that in *Fullmetal Alchemist*: they start *high*, then they go *nuts*, and go *really high!* The animation simply *soars* in the final ten episodes of the second *Fullmetal Alchemist* series. Some of it is so brilliant it burns up the screen.

Once again, watching the finale episodes of *Fullmetal Alchemist* is like watching *every* action-adventure movie you've ever seen, *every* cliffhanger thriller serial, *every* big fantasy epic movie, and *every* blockbuster movie of any kind from any part of the planet. This occurs with the finest *animé* series (*Moribito*, *Overfiend* and *Hellsing 2*), and with the works of *animé* masters such as Katsuhiro Otomo, Shoji Kawamori and Hayao Miyazaki.

In episode 60: *Eye of Heaven, Gateway of Earth*, for instance, the filmmaking reaches new visceral heights, where visual effects are zinging across the screen with a blissful openness and freedom. In this kind of filmmaking, *anything* really does seem *possible*. The filmmakers are *really* letting themselves go wild, as arch-villain Father's plans reach their fulfilment.

Episode 60. *Eye of Heaven, Gateway of Earth*

We are now in *Animé* Bliss.

This episode of *Fullmetal Alchemist 2* contains some of the most spectacular visual effects animation you will ever see. The scenes where Father opens the 'Gate' of the planet itself, and clambers out above the Earth as a colossal, black demon, are fantastically well-achieved. The storyboard artists (Iwao Teraoka in this episode), have captured the feel of the *manga* perfectly at this gobsmacking moment in the *Fullmetal Alchemist* series, but they also go beyond it, adding all sorts of elements of their own.

Blasts of magical energy in red flames, enormous eyes opening in our heroes' bellies (and in the sky above), grasping black hands and arms, and domes of white light (with the inevitable and actually *mandatory* references to the atomic bombs dropped on Japan) – it's simply magnificent. The colours are wild – crimsons, blacks, deep blues (the colour design by Fusako Nakao and Soko Nakao is sensational) – and there's Father as a deity who cackles and booms with his electronically-altered voice – reaching up to the moon and the sun (the eclipse), drawing down God itself. And Akira Senju delivers a hi-voltage music score featuring choirs. And everybody in Amestris faints to the ground, enabling the filmmakers to cut to many characters we haven't seen for a while (we revisit the lovely Winry-chan, for instance, who hasn't been a part of the finale episodes for a *long* time. Of course, as she expires on the floor, near Pinako,[12] she whimpers Ed's name. But the Winry-Ed romance plot is definitely a minor plot – the big love story in *Fullmetal Alchemist* is between the Elric brothers).

Intense is one word for the final episodes of *Fullmetal Alchemist,* as waves of crackling, scarlet, magical energy sizzle across the screen. The battles and the action are some of the most intense you'll see. The animation is truly unrestrained – even if the animation teams weren't paid loads of money (we *know* they weren't!), I hope the producers at least gave them plenty of praise. Because they deliver *extraordinary* filmmaking, by any standards.

And the sound team (Masafumi Mima, Tomoko Nakajima, Yuri Ichimura and the folk at Techno Sound) are also delivering big time in the final episodes of *Fullmetal Alchemist* – filling 60 channels of sound with roars, hums, hisses, whooshes and yells. The soundtrack of *Fullmetal Alchemist* is very dense, as thickly multi-tracked as a Hollywood blockbuster movie.

❋

And yet episode 60: *Eye of Heaven, Gateway of Earth* actually opens with a call-back to the scenarios and charas we haven't seen for a while in *Fullmetal Alchemist 2,* such as the conflicts between the factions of the military, including a teary reunion for Denny Brosh and Lt. Ross (one of the minor but touching romances in *Fullmetal Alchemist*).

From that modest (tho' weepy) reunion, of two people in a foyer, this show ramps up to two gods battling it out above the planet – this is why we *love animé*!.

Other scenes in episode 60: *Eye of Heaven, Gateway of Earth* include the continuing fight between Scar[13] and Führer Bradley (which steps up the brutality to an awesome level); Bradley's wife at the radio station; the citizens of Central City observing the eclipse (reminders of what is at stake – ordinary people); some Ishbalians laying the groundwork for a counter-transmutation circle (this also links to the tattoo on Scar's arm, which Scar shows Bradley); and the chimeras left behind in the tunnel wondering what's happening below.

But the central section of episode 60: *Eye of Heaven, Gateway of Earth* of the second *Fullmetal Alchemist* – the part that really compels our attention – concerns our heroes trapped inside the belly-realm of Father: the Elrics are there, along with Izumi Curtis, the blind Roy Mustang, Hohenheim and Mei Chang. They are all exhausted and stretched to the limit. Father, meanwhile, is the character who dominates this part of the *Fullmetal Alchemist* TV series: he's in the form of a black/ purple blobby creature with evil eyes and grinning mouths on his skin (the homunculus Pride lurks nearby, reduced to a humble magician's assistant role). This is the face-off that the whole *Fullmetal Alchemist 2* series has been building up to (and Father is so powerful now, even the late arrival of Greed can't

---

12 Pinako's last words are to mutter that if she sees van Hohenheim again, she'll wring his neck (Pinako realizes that this catastrophe has something to do with Hohenheim!).
13 Scar became somewhat sidelined, from the Briggs Fortress scenes onwards. Often, he is tagging along with other characters.

stop him).

The writers and filmmakers, headed up by director Yasuhiro Irie and chief writer Hiroshi Ohnogi, have followed the logical progression of events in Himoru Arakawa's *manga* closely (as well as adding all sorts of elements of their own): so from the collection of the 'sacrifices', the television *animé* moves on to attacks from Mei Chang, Ed and Al Elric on the villains, followed by regrouping; the 'sacrifices' are pinned down on the floor by Father; van Hohenheim lets out a blast of energy, which engulfs Father, who seems for a moment beaten; but Father reconstitutes himself (to Hohenheim's dismay); then the eclipse reaches totality, and the super-villain's ritual begins; gleefully, Father slams his hand down on the chessboard drawing of the transmutation circle (which we saw him contemplating throughout the series), howling with hysterical delight as the power surges thru him from the five 'sacrifices', who're physically connected to him via elongated arms. The citizens of Central City and all of Amestris are stricken, as their souls're reaped for the opening of the Gate of the Earth and the Gate of Heaven. Purple-black liquid, a deadly flood (a great touch), rises throughout the HQ and into the surrounding streets, as an enormous swamp of energy and darkness, swallowing up people, and helping to form the giant doors that stretch across the entire country of Amestris. There is a poetic logic to the sequence of events here, with the narrative becoming grander and wilder with each passing minute.

Thus, having gathered his 'sacrifices', Father is keen to begin the proceedings. But first, our heroes have a go at battling him: here is Mei Chang's finest moment in the *Fullmetal Alchemist* series, perhaps, as she single-handedly launches herself against Father, desperate to get her hands on the secrets of immortality (Mei takes her duty of finding immortality for her Chinese clan *very* seriously!). Van Hohenheim, still trapped inside Father's belly, knows she hasn't got a hope, and warns her away (before Father shoves him back inside). Mei is repelled and thrown aside by Father, landing in a bloody heap (the filmmakers replay this horror – so that we really feel Mei's suffering – this is the villain beating up a teenage girl. But if you watch a lot of *animé*, violence against young girls is as common as violence against pretty much anybody).

✳

Meanwhile, Elrics Ed and Al have taken on the homunculus Pride: Ed's noticed that Pride is crumbling a little at the edges (one of the signs that a homunculus is weakening, that they are no longer immortal). Alphonse tends to Mei Chang on the ground, and Edward attacks Pride repeatedly. It's *very* pleasing to have the Elric brothers back in the narrative, leading the scenes, and taking the offensive. This is the *Fullmetal Alchemist* series at its best, when Ed is all about hurling himself at the bad guys to kick some butt.

The staging, storyboarding, layouts and visual effects of the animation in 2.60: *Eye of Heaven, Gateway of Earth* are simply staggering. Just look at how the filmmakers use space, point-of-view, cutting, sound effects, selective colour, interactive lighting, scale and movement. It is a masterclass in animation-without-boundaries, using every frame to its maximum potential.

Now you can see why it took a whole battery of animation companies centred in Tokyo to produce this super-dense extravaganza! And a *lot* of man and woman hours. And a *lot* of planning, organization, and Yen – plus some all-nighters for some people in the 100s of crew, I bet, and some probably stayed over and slept on the floor of the animation studio.

You can see from episode 60: *Eye of Heaven, Gateway of Earth* that this animation could only have been produced by workaholics – people who're so into animation and filmmaking they will stop at nothing to deliver outstanding work. (And it could only have been produced in one place: Japan. Nowhere else on Earth can regularly achieve this level of genius animation).

✳

The scenes of duels and chaos inside Father's belly are so intense, they demand that the filmmakers cut away from them from time to time. So the *Fullmetal Alchemist* series step away to include many of the secondary characters, as the ominous eclipse reaches fulfilment.

The staging of the opening of the Gate of the Earth sequence in *Fullmetal Alchemist* is truly remarkable, with a genuinely epic feeling for colossal scale and extraordinary vistas that take in the entire country. Circles are a key motif (the circles of the eyes in the bellies, of the transmutation circle, of the sun behind the moon). The colours and designs employ dark purples and blacks as the signature look to embody the insanity and hubris of Father's scheme to become a god (a common colour design in fantasy *animé*).[14] The filmmakers employ a huge number of cinematic devices: fish-eye lenses; giant close-ups of eyes; crash zooms; choral chanting; roaring sound effects; electronically-treated voices; very bright bolts of energy zipping across the screen; very unusual camera angles; selective colour; and views of Earth from outer space. Throughout the sequence, the camera is shaking, evoking earthquakes and atomic bombs (Japan is very earthquake-prone).

In short, this episode of *Fullmetal Alchemist* is a masterpiece of jaw-dropping filmmaking, imaginatively conceived and brilliantly staged. You have to admire the conceit of this piece – where a villain can become enlarged to the scale of a giant-god clambering out of the doorway of the planet, and how it uses the souls of the entire population of the nation to achieve that. So we have the familiar trope of a villain sucking up the life/ energy/ souls of the whole population, but with a religious/ spiritual context and goal (Father's aim is partly simply power for power's sake).

The *Fullmetal Alchemist* series is making many narrative leaps here, but because it has been delivered in *stages*, and has a perverse (and horrific) *logic* to it, we go along with it. The events, as astonishing and spectacular as they are, develop out of the *characters* and the *situations*, so they are very satisfying dramatically and thematically.

---

14 The colour design resembles the climax of *Princess Mononoke*.

It's a superbly achieved combination of ancient folklore with contemporary visual effects, of Biblical-scale events combined with very modern animation techniques, of archaic dramatic elements mixed with smart pop culture. The dramatic and narrative elements have been around for millennia: the will to power, the urge to dominate, to be a god (for the villains), set against the heroes' motives and goals: family, friendship, liberty and love.

Also, the finale of the second *Fullmetal Alchemist* is a work of genius because it is founded on very *strong* and *solid* narrative concepts and dramatic elements. All of that wild animation and frenetic movement and howling sound and religious chanting would rapidly become mere noise and chaos and meaningless motion if it wasn't locked completely into a convincing and compelling drama.

Episode 61. *He Who Would Swallow God*

The magnificent filmmaking and storytelling continues: the final episodes of *Fullmetal Alchemist 2* are a barrage of truly stupendous scenes which can rival any animated product in any era of film or television history in any part of the Solar System.

In *He Who Would Swallow God* (*Kami o Nomi-komishi Mono*), Father has achieved his goal of becoming a god by absorbing the power of God in the heavens. The episode begins with still frames of the collapsed characters all across Amestris, underneath the opening credits, to emphasize the extreme cost of an extreme act (the filmmakers are now using the credits for extra space in which to cram in more storytelling). There's a brief replay of the climactic sequence of the previous episode (60: *Eye of Heaven, Gateway of Earth*), to remind us how Father in his spectral form clambers up to the celestial realm, to snatch the power of Godhead for himself.

When the fizzing, crackling, roaring visual effects animation abates, there's a pause, a moment of silence, as our heroes (fallen to the floor) wake from their near-death experience, to see... a new-born god, sitting on a stone throne. Father is now embodied in the form of a handsome, white man in his twenties with the chiselled looks of both van Hohenheim and his son Edward Elric. He wears a white robe around his waist, is bare-chested, sports blond locks, and might've stepped from the grassy, sunny field of the first ever Olympic Games in Greece, *circa* 500 B.C., as the star athlete.

And of course Father gloats – as all super-villains must! – to find that his insane scheme of becoming a god has been successful. But now van Hohenheim takes control of the storytelling of *Fullmetal Alchemist*, facing Father grimly with the other heroes arranged behind him (it's Hohenheim who first sees the Father-youth, with a suitably eye-popping reaction in C.U.). Oh no, Hohenheim informs the god-like Father, no, no, no – he is not a god, because already the heroes' counter-measure is operating. Years ago, Hohenheim realized that the dwarf in the glass jar might try something like this. So he set a plan in motion which would work against Father and his mad desires, creating the means where the souls of the people of Amestris (some 50 million folk) are returned to their bodies. (We see the shadow of the moon as a second, counter-alchemical circle, and we see flashbacks of Hohenheim letting loose some of the souls from his chest – so that mysterious image from much earlier is now explained. We also hear the souls of ancient Xerxes discussing helping the Amestrisian souls to return to their bodies; the souls are visualized as glowing, red dots. In the *manga*, their voices were represented abstractly, as speech bubbles over black).

Well, this is pretty abstract, spiritual/ religious material – souls and bodies, becoming a god, stealing God's power, etc – but Himoru Arakawa in her *Fullmetal Alchemist manga* and the filmmakers in this astonishing animated series have developed methods of visualizing it all in drawings and colours and sounds and motion. So we witness the mind-boggling images of 50 million souls trapped inside Father's body exploding out and up in a tornado of blood-red energy, and spiralling outwards from the government HQ all over Amestris, returning to their bodies as burning red flames.

The first denizen of Amestris to awaken is, appropriately enough, a baby in a buggy on a street. Soon we see many of the secondary charas in *Fullmetal Alchemist* struggling back to life, including, in the premier position, Winry and Pinako Rockbell in Resembool (and wondering just what the hell happened).

Back in the underground lair of the super-villain in Central City, Father is deeply irked that his plan of becoming a god has back-fired (because now he can't draw on the power of the 50 million souls of Amestris), and that van Hohenheim has stolen his moment of divine glory. Retribution on both sides is instant and fantastically violent: our heroes are hurtling energy blasts at Father, and he is deflecting them and retaliating with assaults of his own devising. (The Father-god had disabled our heroes' alchemical powers (as his first act), but they come back to life following the reversal of the souls).

Everybody (except blind Roy Mustang)[15] is given their moment to shine: Izumi Curtis has transformed the stone in the lair into a giant crossbow and bolt, for instance; Mei Chang aids the heroes by creating a defensive bubble to protect the heroes from Father's relentless attacks; and Ed and Al Elric help their father Hohenheim repel Father's magic (again, in these scenes, Edward is the character who's used most as the audience's identification figure: the *animé* rightly puts Ed at the centre of proceedings, cutting back to him repeatedly. There are some moving images of all three of them in the same shot, too, working together).

With Father no longer god-like (he can't contain the Eye of God without the power of the 50 million Amestrisian souls), the two sides are

[15] Note that with Roy Mustang losing his sight, the remaining sacrifices comprise two teenage boys (the heroes), their father, and their female teacher. So it's a family and a friend of the family that Himoru Arakawa selects as the final group to take on the super-villain Father (with Izumi Curtis as a clear authorial stand-in, and a mother figure to the boys), tho' also with the help of plenty of other charas.

evened up (we saw way back, for instance, that the homunculus in the jar and van Hohenheim had roughly the same number of the souls from Xerxes trapped in their bodies. Father should've given himself the advantage!). Clever Hohenheim placed souls from Xerxes in secret spots around Amestris, to help him counter Father's schemes (the *anime* includes abstract, unusual images of tiny, red dots in amongst rocky mountains to portray the souls lying in wait. This really is astonishing storytelling).

✳

We return to the underground lair in a moment, because there is a *vast* amount of storytelling going on in ep. 61: *He Who Would Swallow God!* Including the deaths of two homunculi: Pride and Wrath.

The Scar-Führer fight, for example, is still raging, and there is a direct link to the explosive face-off in the underground bunker between our heroes and Father: Scar and the Ishbalians have been busy laying the ground-work for an alchemical circle which will work against the effects of Father's transmutation circle.

With simple colour symbolism – red for Father/ homunculi, and blue for the Ishbalians – and using the entire country as a battleground (via vistas seen from space) – the filmmakers portray the alchemical/ spiritual power struggle for control of Amestris and its 50 million souls.

It's a classic clock or countdown device – the alternative transmutation circle can only be activated once Scar has defeated Führer Bradley (a character we know is practically unwasteable!). However, at the end of a lengthy, highly exaggerated and poundingly brutal conflict, Scar manages to cut off Bradley's arms (when Bradley's blinded by the return of the sun following the eclipse, as he has Scar pinned down. But he manages to stab Scar with a sword held in his teeth, a classic samurai gag). Lan Fan appears to witness the Führer's final moments – and even tho' Bradley/ Wrath has been a supremely evil and vicious antagonist, the filmmakers still humanize him in his death scene, by having him talk about his wife (and in the process he's also making digs at Lan Fan, who worships Prince Ling).

✳

Back to the underground lair: when Scar manages to activate the Ishbalian transmutation circle, our heroes are able to fight back at Father with extra vigour. The visualization of the waves of energy, the alchemical attacks, and the repelling of magical forces, is sublimely achieved by the filmmakers. In super-rapid cuts, the screen is awash with saturated colours, multiple elements of energy, and truly inspired staging and storyboarding. Even the Big Three, among *anime* series of this 2000s-2010s era (*Naruto*, *Bleach* and *One Piece*), are trumped by this level of animation.

Once again, Father seems to have been defeated (smothered in the vat of burning lava that drowned Greed), only to emerge yet again. This time, Father ascends on a pillar of fire, all the way up and out of his subterranean base, flying out into the daylight of Central City (the movement of the villain enables the filmmakers to have a change of scene, involve new characters, and take the fight into a bigger arena. But there is a reason for the villain suddenly fleeing the battle – he needs more souls to create another philosopher's stone, now that he is not a god but a sort of enhanced homunculus. And he sets about absorbing the soldiers standing near the fissure).

So our heroes pursue Father out of the underground labyrinth on rising columns of stone (this allows for the reunion of two of the romantic couples in the *Fullmetal Alchemist* world: Liza Hawkeye and Roy Mustang, and Izumi and Sig Curtis, who've been waiting in the lower levels of the government HQ).

But Edward Elric stays behind to deal with the one remaining homunculus servant of Father's: Pride (Greed is still at large, however, tho' he is no friend of Father's anymore! He arrives to see that Wrath/Bradley has already expired). The action is staged with Selim Bradley standing to one side, while his shadowy claws and maws are hurled at Ed, who stands opposite him, deflecting every assault with his automail blade. Being a street punk himself, Ed knows a few moves, and is able to anticipate what Selim-Pride is going to do (he uses the good, old headbutt at one point. And it works! – punching a hole in Pride's skull).

For a time, it seems as if Selim-Pride has the upper hand, pinning Ed by his limbs on the ground with his black, octopus hands. Pride intends to steal Ed's body. Pride clutches his face as it crumbles (then gives up, and reveals the gaping wound, with the dead souls inside. The character design enhances the severity of Pride's degeneration with an ugly amalgam of mouths, eyes and pointed claws).

And then the battle shifts, incredibly, to the *interior* of Selim-Pride, as a *deus ex machina* appears: Zolf Kimbley! (Pride swallowed him up in episode 52: *Combined Strength*). It's a surprise, to say the least, but Kimbley's presence is enough to destabilize Selim-Pride, allowing Ed to literally enter Selim-Pride (as a philosopher's stone), and finally nobble him. Outside, the homunculus's body falls back in a puff of black dust (which's all that's left of homunculi when they finally expire – and that goes for all of us. We're all just dust in the end. *Dust*).

As with the homunculus Envy, there is a true, inner form to Selim-Pride hidden inside the homunculus's fearsome outer shell: it's a tiny, foetal form which bleats 'mama!' In death, in the world of *Fullmetal Alchemist*, we revert to primal forms, like foetuses, or babies – we become small, fragile, vulnerable and powerless. Edward Elric is not depicted as a killer in *Fullmetal Alchemist* – so he lays the inch-long foetus of Pride on his famous red coat, and leaves to join the others.

Episode 62. *A Fierce Counterattack*

This episode continues from the end of the previous episode, as all of the action in the finale of *Fullmetal Alchemist* series two is strung together. Episode 62: *A Fierce Counterattack* opens with the antagonist still creating merry hell in the courtyard of the government's central headquarters, the centre of political power in Amestris. Father's goal is to create another philosopher's stone, using fresh souls, in order to defeat our heroes, who're intent on stopping him at whatever cost (this is, then, the primary structure of all action-adventure narratives: the villain acts, and the heroes react to that).

Most of the *Fierce Counterattack* episode comprises loud, wild battle scenes, as everybody who's still standing in the *Fullmetal Alchemist* series has a go at flattening Father. Very little of any assault has any effect on him at all – he barely breaks a sweat, as Alex Armstrong mutters in astonishment.

Van Hohenheim leads the heroes in the attacks and counter-attacks, as the play of power and energy moves between the heroes to the super-villain. Father has a few surprises left in him, however – literally *inside him*, as he manifests the souls trapped from the Xerxes catastrophe that we saw way back in episode 40: *Homunculus (The Dwarf in the Flask)*. This occurs after Hohenheim has derided the homunculus for not being able to create, so he can't be regarded as a deity. Now King Xerxes and others erupt screaming from Father's torso, in yet another grotesque parody of birth; zombie-like, they stumble towards our heroes (note that a baby tugs at Izumu Curtis's shins, and children cluster around Alphonse, clamouring for his body). The filmmakers cast this sequence in the lurid pink-purple light that *animé* reserves for spiritual or fantastical events (indeed, the lighting is adjusted throughout these finale shows, to depict the eerie half-light of the eclipse, for example, or the sun-blocking effects of billowing smoke).

Only van Hohenheim can put a stop to this abomination (and only Hohenheim truly understands what it feels like to have half a million souls trapped inside your body! Hohenheim also recognizes some of the souls who materialize). Father sends out a colossal blast of energy which destroys half of the government HQ. Alphonse Elric and Hohenheim protect Izumi Curtis, Ed and Mei Chang by standing in front of them with their arms held wide (unfortunately, this also seriously harms father and son, rendering them less able to continue the fight).

Luckily, there are plenty of people in the vicinity who're keen to have a go at nailing Father, too: the Briggs Mountain soldiers assemble to launch mortar shells and fire guns, the remaining alchemists like Edward, Izumi Curtis and Alex Armstrong hurl stone and steel bolts at Father, and Roy Mustang is also back in play, with his ever-faithful assistant Liza Hawkeye to guide his flame alchemy now that he's blind.

*

Yet in among the roaring, slamming action scenes of the final three episodes of the 2009-10 series of *Fullmetal Alchemist*, extraordinarily, the filmmakers often pause – but not only for the Big Emotional Scenes (such as those between Ed and Al Elric in the climactic moments, when Al sacrifices himself in order to defend Ed from Father), but also for significant exchanges between minor characters. For instance, there's a moving conversation between Olivia Armstrong and her colleagues: she is desperate to carry on fighting (she is a lifelong professional soldier), but Greed & co. persuade her that she is too injured; on the radio, her officers assure her that Briggs soldiers can continue the fight without her. To have Major Armstrong stand down and step out of the battle is wholly against her military ethics. *Fullmetal Alchemist* displays its very *Japanese* quality by including such scenes, which're about loyalty to one's colleagues, to the community, and to one's job.

The scene, set in the lower levels of the government headquarters, sees Greed taking command, explaining that Father is a super-human foe beyond the capabilities of even State Alchemists. So Major Armstrong steps down, as well as others who're injured (or who are, like Sig, merely human). But Roy Mustang is determined to keep fighting, now with Liza Hawkeye to aid him. There is also a quiet beat where Major Armstrong contemplates the corpse of Führer Bradley nearby (with a call-back to Captain Buccaneer, who inflicted a wound on him). And Scar is also revealed to be out for the count (yes, even these two amazingly tough charas, Armstrong and Scar, are going to wait out the finale!). These scenes are not wholly necessary, to be sure, and they partly arise from the mechanics of keeping a large cast of characters in the loop (and they do acknowledge the contributions that Scar and Armstrong and others made to the battle against Father and the homunculi – because we don't see many of these secondary characters from now to the end of the 2nd *Fullmetal Alchemist* series).

✻

Back in the courtyard of the government's HQ, every character is hurling themselves at the half-god-all-villain Father, including Edward Elric, Lan Fan, Izumi Curtis, Roy Mustang and the chimeras. The filmmakers create gags and stunts for every character to perform, accompanied by a sound effects track and a music track that's mixed very high. So that the battle scenes are full of cracking, crunching, explosive sounds.

Greed appears too, zooming down from his usual superhero perch atop a tower, to smash his fist right into Father's face – into his eye, in fact. Greed is like Father in miniature – both are power-mad; the confrontation ends with Father weakened but Greed not successful either.

By this point, Father has been attacked so many times, in so many different ways, he is finally weakening, and losing control of his power: van Hohenheim notices that he uses his arm to deflect a flying martial arts kick from Edward Elric (instead of his usual alchemical magic, where he simply stands and fumes and frowns while everything bounces off him).

The shift in the balance of power leads to the climax of episode 62: *A Fierce Counterattack*: Father explodes again with a blast of energy, which knocks out some of our heroes. The key remaining characters are arranged in space around Father in a hierarchical order: Edward Elric is closest to Father, with van Hohenheim and Alphonse nearby (these three charas will be the most prominent from now on; the others are further away).

Father, reduced to a feeble, zombie-like state, lurches towards the nearest human, to suck up their life-energy vampirically: his would-be victim is, of course, the hero of the *Hagane no Renkinjutsushi* world, the pint-sized Fullmetal Alchemist himself, Edward Elric. With everybody seriously injured or unconscious, and only Alphonse, Mei Chang and van Hohenheim nearby to help, the narrative drive of the *Fullmetal Alchemist* series hones in on the central duo, Ed and Al, and their quest to regain their whole bodies.

Great filmmaking and great storytelling, this – it works powerfully at a dramatic level, a thematic level, a cinematic and visual level, an emotional level, and even a spiritual and religious level: clever Alphonse Elric realizes that he can use a sort of reverse alchemical transmutation to help his brother Edward, by returning his flesh-and-blood arm (we saw Father destroying Ed's automail arm in a slow motion shot earlier, a motif already used in *Fullmetal Alchemist*, and a *hommage* perhaps to Tetsuo in *Akira*).

The heroic sacrifice is a marvellous moment in this 100% masterpiece of contemporary filmmaking: aided by Mei Chang's Xingese alkahestric magic (and her throwing stars), Alphonse Elric sacrifices himself so that his brother Edward can regain his real arm and fight back. The other characters realize what he's doing and yell and weep (because they understand the cost of what Alphonse is attempting).

It is a brilliant, high drama and highly emotional scene. The film-makers cut to extreme close-ups of Edward Elric as he twigs what his brother is going to do: 'YOU IDIOT!' Alphonse claps his hands for the last time... the lights dim in Alphonse's eyes... Edward's arm is reborn... Ed manages to wrench himself free of the metal spike embedded in his arm (yet another crucifixion motif), and, using alchemy immediately, he attacks the zombie-version of Father (with a volley of stone slabs).

With a completely satisfying turn of events, that combines the central quest of the entire *Fullmetal Alchemist* series with narrative twists, and grand themes like heroic sacrifice, the filmmakers at Bones/ Aniplex/ Mainichi/ Square *et al* (following *mangaka Himoru Arakawa*) are able to have the hero defeating the super-villain. It's a *tour-de-force* of screen-writing and filmmaking – and because the hero's been split into two, into two brothers, one brother is able to 'die' and sacrifice himself, while the other brother is able to kick the super-villain's ass.

The next beat in Episode 62: *A Fierce Counter-attack* – of having every single character cheering on Edward Elric as he thumps and kicks Father into jelly – is another genius dramatic move. So that it's not just an individual defeating the super-villain Father, it's *everybody*. And of course all of these characters have interacted with Edward, and some of them know him very well – and some of them are his friends.

This is one of the greatest moments in recent animation.

(Another thematic point is made in the finale of *Fullmetal Alchemist*: as Edward Elric repeatedly bombards Father with blows, we cut several times to close-ups of Greed. Inside Greed, Ling Yao tells Greed that what the homunculus really desires is friends, like the ones who're cheering on

Edward. The same view was made of Envy earlier – that the homunculi lack humanity, the passions and emotions which make humans human. It is something the homunculi scorn, and never fully understand).

Ah, this is simply *magnificent storytelling*! So imaginative, so free, so wild – there's a *fearlessness* to this kind of filmmaking, when you see an outstanding team of filmmakers really letting rip, and letting *nothing* hold them back!

◆

Episode 62: *A Fierce Counterattack* could end there, but it doesn't: it follows Alphonse Elric to the non-place limbo that everyone goes when they perform alchemical transmutation: the Gateway of Truth. Here is the endless, white space, the forbidding door, the grinning demon/ alter ego/ other... but only one thing draws our attention: the body of Alphonse, waiting patiently for the return of his soul...

Now Alphonse Elric is ready to be united with his body, and the body and the soul clasp hands. Al's armour disappears in the familiar tiny, square pieces, which blow away on the breeze. The ghostly demon wonders if Edward will come to reclaim his brother... Al is certain. '*Zettai*', he asserts, in a big close-up, to-camera. The ghostly other replies, 'I can't wait to see what he sacrifices'.[16]

Episode 63. *The Other Side of the Gateway*

Broadcast on June 27, 2010, episode 63: *The Other Side of the Gateway* (*Tobira no Muko gawa*) is a masterpiece of animation (like all of the climactic shows here). It is all pay off in this show where the grand story ends (the next show is the *dénouement* show): Father expires, Greed dies, Hohenheim falls into the Big Sleep, and Edward saves his brother Alphonse from the other world. Every part, every minute – nay, *every second* of this show is outstanding.

The Other Side of the Gateway brings the long *Fullmetal Alchemist* TV series to a grand and ravishing finale. The emotion whipped up in the climax of the *animé* of *Fullmetal Alchemist* is more intense and finer played than in the *manga* by Himoru Arakawa. For me, at least. Defeating the villain Father is incredibly spectacular, with Edward Elric leading the way. That scene doesn't disappoint – yet it is not the true highpoint of the series, nor the psychological or emotional climax. That occurs with the trio of Ed, Alphonse and Hohenheim. (Which automatically has *Fullmetal Alchemist* elevating itself higher than your average action-adventure or fantasy story, where defeating the villain usually means the end of the piece: because once Sauron/ Darth Vader/ Joker's dead, we can pack up and go home, right?). Indeed, this show, and this series, is one of the greatest pieces of animation in history.

The fight between Edward Elric and Father continues directly from the end of episode 62: *A Fierce Counterattack:* Father is severely weakened, to the point where he can be beaten up with punches thrown by Ed in his

16 Note that the grinning demon has Edward's arm and leg attached to it.

full-on, two-fisted[17] fighting mode. Nevertheless, the final demise of Father includes the intervention of the last remaining homunculus, Greed, who steps in to wrest power from Father.

Inside Ling Yao/ Greed, the filmmakers stage a marvellously thrilling (and final) exchange between Ling Yao, who's been trapped inside Greed while Greed takes over his body for quite some time. Father has thrust his hand inside Greed's belly (a move that often occurs in fantasy *anime*), to snatch his philosopher's stone. Inside Greed, in that abstract, crimson, rushing soul-space, Ling grabs onto the demon face of Greed, with Father's fist on the other end, pulling the other way. It's a remarkable visualization and physical manifestation of a tug-of-war occurring in a spiritual, psychological and metaphysical realm (how *do* you visualize characters fighting over souls or spirits? Well, Japanese animators know how to show it! As no other filmmakers can).

That Greed turns on Father again, at the last moment, adds an ironic twist to the demise of the super-villain of the *Hagane no Renkinjutsushi* series (Father thinks he knows Greed, because he created him, but his own avarice clouds his vision). The villains in this 2009-10 series, as usual in drama, are mirrors and shadows of the heroes – and so too the offspring of the super-villain are shadows of himself.

Visually, the tussle between Father and Greed in episode 63: *The Other Side of the Gateway* involves some grotesque imagery – Father with an eye in his maw, and with Greed's grinning demon mask in his mouth, too, which he yanks out and bites off, like chewing off a slab of meat. Greed is given a lengthy death scene, with his demon mask floating above the astonished gathering, with close-ups of Edward Elric and Ling Yao most prominent. As with the other homunculi, it's a death scene like no other in fantasy cinema or television – very abstract, yet also moving (because Greed, as amazingly voiced by Yuichi Nakamura, has been an appealing adversary, with his mocking, sarcastic, world-weary attitude and tone. And both Nakamura and Miyano play the spiritual tussle inside Ling Yao at a hysterical pitch, which's very satisfying).

Enclosed in the flaky, carbon carapace donated by Greed as his parting gift to his Father and Creator, the super-villain homunculus is now feeble to the point of expiring. Edward Elric lunges in and punches a hole right thru his torso. With a scream, Father is broken, and the last of the thousands of souls erupt in a torrent of red and black colour into the air, finally free from the monster that imprisoned them for 100s of years.

Father collapses: it's the final end for the homunculus when the tiny, black hands from the other side of the Gateway emerge and take hold of Father, reducing his form in a rapid transformation down to nothing. With a *ziiiip* (of beautiful visual effects animation), Father is gone.

✳

The narrative in episode 63: *The Other Side of the Gateway* now shifts to the Gateway of Truth (for the first of two visits – one to vanquish the super-villain, the other to rescue the hero), where Father is now back in his

---

17 Now he has both arms.

tiny, soot-ball form as the dwarf in the glass jar. The filmmakers and the writer (Hiroshi Ohnogi wrote these masterful episodes) make this last appearance by the homunculus a very memorable one, as the creature pleads for its life – from its opposite number, the grinning, floating thing which is its mirror, or the World, or God, or the All, or the One, or the Truth – whatever you want to call it. (That the grinning demon takes on the form of the dwarf in the flask makes perfect sense).

When Father becomes the tiny sphere of black dust, with nothing but an eyeball and a mouth (and an arm added for gestures), he/ it is sort of sympathetic. Is it so wrong, it/ he pleads, to be curious, to want to know about the world? The homunculus's appeals are understandable,[18] but he is begging to the wrong person!

The storyboard and layout artists conjure marvellous angles and compositions of a scene that is nothing more'n two floating, talking balls in a white space. Iemasa Kayumi as the homunculus adds a great voice track, and the editors go back thru the *Fullmetal Alchemist* 2nd series to intercut short flashes of memorable scenes (which they do throughout the final episodes of the TV show). Director Yasuhiro Irie storyboarded the final two episodes of *Fullmetal Alchemist 2* – and the first two (it's typical for the chief animation director to snag the best episodes!).

✳

The finale of *Fullmetal Alchemist* is beautifully scripted (by Hiroshi Ohnogi): Alphonse Elric sacrifices himself to save his beloved brother Ed (and succeeds); both Ed and van Hohenheim realize what he is attempting (with the aid of the non-Amestrisian alchemy of little Mei Chang), but they can't stop him. Al's heroic gift brings him to the limbo of the Gate, to be reunited with his body. But back in the real world, Al's suit of armour falls to the ground, lifeless (and in pieces).

Renewed (with his real arm back), Edward Elric is able to finish off the homunculus Father. In the end, that's all Father ever was: a homunculus in a jar. These scenes are hugely impressive, and deliver plenty of heat dramatically. But the defeat of the villain is *not* the triumph it should be. Roy Mustang, who can't see, asks Liza Hawkeye, 'did we win?' We did, Liza replies, but we lost Al (in a high angle shot, we see the characters gathered forlornly around the empty shell of Alphonse's armour).

Now the *Fullmetal Alchemist animé*, like the *manga*, comes full circle, with Ed Elric making good the loss and separation of their initial alchemical transmutation, back at the start of the 2009-10 series – over a year ago in broadcasting time (and the *manga*). The *emotional* catharsis, so important in a great, epic series like this, comes from the family relationship: van Hohenheim (supported by Izumi Curtis), offers to use up his life to save Al. The *animé* cuts, as one would expect (and demand), to close-ups of father and son. Ed, weeping, tells his pa that he promised Al he wouldn't use human transmutation anymore. (Ed also rejects the offer of a philosopher's stone from Ling Yao).

18 Notice that as he expires in Central City, Father says similar things, and Hohenheim is struck by them – because he's felt the same things.

We shift into interior monologue, as the filmmakers and writers milk this sequence for its maximum emotion: Edward Elric berates himself repeatedly to think, think, think. *There must be a way!* The *Fullmetal Alchemist* series makes Edward a full and true hero by having him (1) defeat the super-villain (tho' aided by others, of course), and (2) saving his brother from death.

Over anguished close-ups of Edward Elric, and an Oscar-worthy vocal performance by Romi Pak (earning every Yen of her fee!), the *Fullmetal Alchemist* series draws out this Most Important Moment. You can't bring someone back to life, but you can pull them back from the limbo they've exiled themselves to. By sacrificing something of yourself.

So when Edward Elric decides that, in the end, only *he* can bring back his beloved brother Alphonse Elric, by offering him something precious of himself, it's very moving. The ending of *Fullmetal Alchemist* hits all the right buttons – it really is superlative stuff, and has the grandeur of great opera or a tragic play. Is it that good? Oh yes, it most definitely is! (In fact, one can imagine the celebrated authors of Elizabethan tragedies or even Ancient Greek tragedies enjoying this climactic drama). And when you add to the mix simply *sensational* animation and filmmaking, plus a plangent score by Akira Senju, you have a very powerful, persuasive mix of elements.

Everyone looks on in silent expectation or confusion or growing fear as Edward Elric works out what to do. Van Hohenheim realizes what Ed is going to attempt (as he draws a transmutation circle on the ground with a broken pipe), and he yells, 'no'. But, in a final close-up – smiling grimly, to-camera – Ed announces the final alchemical transmutation of Edward Elric.

It's a brilliantly realized, grandly sublime moment, one of the emotional highs that audiences get hooked on. We *love* moments like this! When the hero makes the fearless plunge into the abyss... when the hero leaps into battle for the final time...

Edward Elric's final alchemical transmutation takes him, as expected, to the Gateway of Truth limbo, and a meeting with his alter ego, his spiritual self, the grinning, blank creature (who also, of course, has his own voice). It's just wonderful stuff, this 2009-10 Japanese *anime*, how it plays with life and death issues in such a flamboyant, vivid and also abstract and metaphysical manner. When Ed willingly gives up his alchemical powers to save his brother Alphonse, and reminds the grinning spirit – and us – that he was always human, that he is still himself, that he still has his friends, still has all of the people in his life (they are heard in voiceover all crying 'Ed!' – a marvellous touch, with no need to add their faces),[19] it's perfect. (His shadow soul says yes, that was the correct answer. It's actually a profound truth – that you *already have* everything you could possibly need).

This is the Big, Emotional Finale that makes the finest *anime* work wonders. It satisfies on many levels, and it's as if the *Fullmetal Alchemist*

---

19 Winry has pride of place as the last voice.

animé (and the *manga*) could have ended only this way and no other. Of course, you could complain that nobody of significance dies,[20] that only the villains expire, that Ed losing his alchemy isn't really that big a price. But, hell, you can't be complaining now, honey, not after 63 episodes of Pure *Animé* Bliss!

Edward Elric turns about in the Gateway of Truth, and there, waiting for him, is his brother Alphonse (after he transmutes his own Gateway of Truth, which vanishes). Their meeting, now restored to their full bodies, is beautifully played. The reunion scene, back in the courtyard of the government HQ in Amestris, is rather short – and that's perfect, too; it doesn't need to be a long, protracted scene. There are some weeping reunions as the principal characters stand in a group around the restored Al, lying on the grass under a coat (Mei Chang hurls herself at Alphonse-sama, for instance). And Alphonse utters a simple but moving phrase, said whenever the Japanese come home: *tadaima* (= 'I'm home').

The main narrative of *Fullmetal Alchemist* is now over: the brothers have regained their bodies, Amestris is saved from annihilation, and the super-villain is no more.

✳

The 2nd series of the *Fullmetal Alchemist animé* shifts rapidly to a lone figure, standing in the empty courtyard: van Hohenheim. The following scenes are so simple, dramatically and staging-wise, but they do the trick: Alex Armstrong arrives to remind Hohenheim that without his sons Amestris would have been destroyed. (Both men bow to each other, with polite 'thank yous', reminding us that this series was always about Japan).

So the emotion wells up; van Hohenheim weeps, and leaves for Resembool, a solitary figure on the railroad. The *animé* has one all-powerful ingredient that the *Fullmetal Alchemist manga* didn't have in evoking the wellsprings of emotion: *music*. If anything can get to you emotionally, out of *all* the arts, it is *music*. Oh *yes* – music gets there quickest, and often deepest, and no matter what barriers you put up, even giant walls of alchemically-generated stone, while you sulk and complain behind them, music will blow them down!

The *animé* of *Fullmetal Alchemist* gives van Hohenheim the closing scene in the penultimate episode of the 2009-10 series, *The Other Side of the Gateway*. Rightly so. It's right, too, that the filmmakers give Hohenheim a moving speech for his dying words, as he sits before his wife Trisha's grave in sunny Resembool. It's skillfully judged – not too long, not too mawkish, not over-written (well, really, it comprises mainly of 'thank yous' – thank you to his wife Trisha, to his family, to life itself).[21] And he too says, *tadaima*, as Alphonse did. This delivers the crucial emotional catharsis which was a little lacking in the *manga*.

And the filmmakers deliver an *hommage* to van Hohenheim over the

---

20 Actually, significant charas do expire, such as Hohenheim.
21 Van Hohenheim is also implicated in the rise to power of the dwarf in the glass jar – he reminds us here that he gave the homunculus some of his blood. So Hohenheim has to die, in terms of the adventure genre. In other ways, he is the older generation giving way to the younger generation, to his children.

closing credits, with a montage of Hohenheim-related moments from the series.

Can cartoons move you? People doubted that a feature-length cartoon was even possible, when the Walt Disney Studios embarked upon 'Disney's Folly', *Snow White and the Seven Dwarfs* in the 1930s. Well, yes, animation can certainly be full of feelings – and when the animation is as magnificent as *Fullmetal Alchemist,* emotions are evoked all over the place.

Episode 64. *Journey's End*

Episode 64 is the final installment of this extraordinary, grandiose, operatic, humorous, over-the-top, intelligent, political, moving and tragic animated series. Maybe 'perfect' is the wrong word – but you wouldn't change a thing in *Fullmetal Alchemist 2.* It'so good, as soon as it's over, you'll want to start watching it all again.

Journey's End comprises, like half of the previous episode, *dénouement* scenes. Because we've already seen the super-villain being defeated, and Ed and Al being restored (tho' with the price paid for the final transformations).[22] But there are some subplots to pay off, and a few 'what happened next?' questions need to be answered. (Structurally, the show goes back to the immediate aftermath of the villain's defeat, plus two months later, and then two years later).

One is the Ed-Winry romantic subplot, which closes episode 64: chief writer Hiroshi Ohnogi has decided to tie up the secondary charas first, before moving onto the central duo, Edward and Alphonse Elric (so they take pride of place, and book-end the *Fullmetal Alchemist* series).

The final episode of *Fullmetal Alchemist 2* bowties many subplots, such as Roy Mustang regaining his eyesight (using a philosopher's stone, courtesy of Doctors Marcoh and Knox), and addressing the Ishbalian problem, on his way to becoming Führer (there is much debate about setting Ishbal to rights – before Mustang becomes the Führer). Mustang's team is re-united (at the hospital bedside of Mustang and Liza Hawkeye), and there's a suggestion too that the crippled Jean Havoc will be cured (Mustang promises that the philosopher's stone will be used on Havoc first – Havoc was injured way back, when they were fighting Lust).

The homunculus-Pride-as-a-tiny-foetus motif pays off with Selim Bradley now grown into a child anxious about injured birds he's found in the garden (this occurs two years later). General Grumman pays a visit to the Bradleys' country estate, to take tea with the ex-Führer's widow. That the homunculus has been allowed to live at all is a tribute to the ambiguity and moral complexity of *Fullmetal Alchemist* – because Selim is a war criminal who's personally murdered 100s of people (including many Amestrian soldiers. No one would've shed any tears if that tiny creature had been eaten by a dog. But Edward Elric of course saves him).

In another tie-up scene, Scar agrees to work with the authorities in the

---

22 Notice how both Ed and Al are hobbling as they walk up the last stretch of the trail to the Rockbell residence. Al is still weak from his body spending so much time in limbo, and Ed was injured in the climactic duels, plus he hasn't maintenanced his automail leg.

rejuvenation of Ishbal – Major Armstrong has squirrelled Scar away in her family mansion to work for her, along with Miles (also an Ishbalian). Thus, despite his numerous evil deeds and his untold killings, Scar is also allowed to live by the *Fullmetal Alchemist* series (but only if he promises to help restore Ishbal).

In a flashback (the last episode of *Fullmetal Alchemist* is not plotted in a simple A-to-B fashion), we see Ling Yao, Lan Fan and Mei Chang talking to Ed and Al Elric and all three resolving to return to Xing. Ling offers to look after Mei's clan, and Mei (predictably) blubbers (there is a *lot* of weeping in the final scenes of the 2009-2010 *Fullmetal Alchemist!* – as the emotions run high, from abject despair up to hysteria and ecstasy). There is also a scene where Al visits Gracia Hughes (which honours the deceased Hughes-san).

✻

We cut now to the Brothers Elric, at last: Alphonse is back to his pre-transmutation form (tho' still weak): both boys look older (Al is now a mid-teen), but relaxed, happy to be going home to Resembool. Winry Rockbell is re-introduced after a *long* spell away in the metal alchemist series (it must've been tempting for the producers to include Winry-chan in the finale of *Fullmetal Alchemist* – she would be perfect as one of the 'sacrifices', for instance. But the producers stuck to the plot of Himoru Arakawa's *manga*, and kept Winry as the stay-at-home, girl-next-door type for this part of the *animé* series).

The viewpoint in episode 64: *Journey's End* switches to Winry Rockbell, as the Elric lads approach the Resembool house (again it's a sunny day): the filmmakers milk the reunion for all they can: there's a s-l-o-w build-up as Winry walks to the front door, followed by a slow motion dive on top of the boys (Akira Senju's music is working over-time throughout the episode).

It's Ed and Al Elric who're re-positioned at the centre of things in the final installment of *Fullmetal Alchemist,* with their decision to leave Resembool after two years (the episode shifts forwards two years, as does the *Fullmetal Alchemist manga*), as they stand on the roof at the Rockbells' place in Resembool, looking out at the wide, wide world like fairy tale characters. As Winry-chan remarks, they are the kind of guys who can't keep still for long (a man who stays too long in one place is boring, she says). The lads' research is undertaken to right the wrongs that alchemy has created, but it's also implied that Ed's alchemical powers could be restored (relatively easy to do in a fantasy series like this, which has already shown us ten million crazy things!).

Having Elrics Ed and Al close the series on the move is an illustration of one of *mangaka* Hiromu Arakawa's primary moral messages in *Fullmetal Alchemist:* you must keep moving forward. All things change, and attempting to stay put like a stick in the mud isn't going to work. *You must move,* Arakawa insists. (One wonders if Arakawa had been influenced by the ending of the first *Fullmetal Alchemist* TV series, which put the boys in motion).

Alphonse Elric is now the leader is his own little group, as he visits the chimeras Zampano and Jerso (in a café, where they're eating like wild animals), and tells them he's going to Xing, and they opt to go along with him (they have been inspired by Al to get their real bodies back – another manifestation of the 'never give up!' philosophy of *shonen manga*).

As the Elric brothers decide to leave, one going East, the other going West (so their alchemical research will combine – notice that Ed heads towards Europa, where he ended up in the first *Fullmetal Alchemist* movie), the Winry-Edward romance plot is resolved. It is a sweet, embarrassed and coy scene, and follows the *Fullmetal Alchemist manga* largely (down to the clichéd setting of the railroad station just as Ed is about to board the train). Ed plucks up courage, asking Winry to marry him in his own awkward, pink-cheeked fashion (using the terms of the equal exchange of alchemy). Of course Winry agrees (blushing up); cue our hug.

The 2009-10 *animé* of *Fullmetal Alchemist* makes the other romantic subplot – of Alphonse Elric and Mei Chang – more emphatic than the *manga* does (altho' the *manga* does include a photograph of Al and Mei, and we know that Al is going to travel East to Xing, to study Xingese alchemy. And Mei was of course devoted to Al, calling him 'Alphonse-sama').

The final scene of *Fullmetal Alchemist: Brotherhood* is of the central hero, Edward Elric, alone on the train. He delivers the final speech (in voiceover), with the familiar moral message of Himoru Arakawa's *manga* (about no pain = no gain, about having to sacrifice something to gain something).

✳

Stylistically, episode 64: *Journey's End* of the 2nd *Fullmetal Alchemist* employs a slower, gentler animation style, with many lap dissolves (from a face to another face, for instance, or a face to a sky and the camera tilts up wistfully into the heavens several times). There are many images of verdant landscapes and Miyazakian blue skies (the world is now in perpetual Summer – and every single scene is set, appropriately, in full daylight; there are no night scenes). Meanwhile, composer Akira Senju delivers some very sweet orchestral cues, highly emotional but tender, too, running underneath most of the episode (music is once again the secret weapon in *animé*).

▼

The 2009-10 *Fullmetal Alchemist animé* dropped the epilogue of the *manga* – rightly, I think: you can't have *dénouement* scenes dragging on too long! (The *manga*'s epilogue included scenes where Alphonse Elric's armour is returned in a crate, and Al decides to have it turned into automail parts). But the *animé* did retain the common filmic device of still photographs to illustrate some further plot developments running under the closing credits (*animé* uses this ploy a lot – of course, *animé* makes extensive use of freeze frames anyway. The films of Hayao Miyazaki are masterclass examples of taking the *dénouments* into the end credits – and

Fullmetal Alchemist has been at least half Miyazakian). So we see Ling Yao as the Xingese emperor, Roy Mustang in Führer mode with Liza Hawkeye; an aged Scar with Miles, etc (and even, in a very Arakawan moment, the Rockbell's dog having puppies).

And, most memorable of all, our heroes with their girls: Edward Elric and Winry Rockbell, now with a couple of kids in their arms, and Alphonse and a grown Mei Chang standing behind them. So sweeeet! ♥♥♥ Big, big smiles!

Yes, but, come on, after all of that prolonged and very excessive violence and bloodshed in the *Fullmetal Alchemist* finale, a cutie scene of the heroes becoming lovers and also parents is welcome. Indeed, children're often included in the final freeze frames of many an *animé* – for all of the obvious reasons. That children are the future is a platitude that's often thrown about. But it's true! Children are without question the most important thing in the human world (and far more important than people beating the hell out of each other, or going to war, or corrupting whole countries with their nefarious, fascistic schemes).

The very last images in the whole of *Fullmetal Alchemist* series two, are of Edward Elric, alone, standing next to a train: a young man going out into the world to do amazing things. It's a smiling portrait of Hope, of the Future, of Potential, of Idealism. This is a hero – someone who can overcome setbacks, suffering, and agonies that would flatten many of us. Edward is the embodiment of Himoru Arakawa's *mantra* of 'moving forward', and her greatest creation. Edward's determination, his inner strength, his sense of justice, and his unstoppable energy are simply staggering. This is a boy who never gives up!

Part Four

Fullmetal Alchemist

Hagane no Renkinjutsushi

鋼の錬金術師

Movies and Original Video Animations

01

FULLMETAL ALCHEMIST: CONQUEROR OF SHAMBALLA

GEKIJOBAN HAGANE NO RENKINJUTSUSHI: SHANBARA WO YUKU MONO

INTRO.

The first *Fullmetal Alchemist* movie, subtitled *Conqueror of Shamballa* (in Japanese: *Gekijoban Hagane no Renkinjutsushi – Shanbara wo Yuku Mono*), was released on July 23, 2005 in Japan. It was scripted by Shou Aikawa (chief writer for the TV series) and directed by Seiji Mizushima (who also directed the TV show). The ten producers were: Arimasa Okada, Haruhito Yamazaki, Hiro Maruyama, Kenji Komatsu, Masahiko Minami, Nobuyuki Kurashige, Ryo Oyama, Seiji Takeda, Tsuyoshi Yoshida and Yukio Yoshimura. It was produced by Anime Film/ Aniplex/ Buyu/ Dentsu Inc./ Falcon Inc./ Mainichi Broadcasting System/ Production I.G./ R.I.C./ Shochiku Co. Ltd/ Square Enix/ Studio Elle/ Studio Wood/ Trans Arts Co. Key animator was Yashuhiro Kato, art director was Kazuo Ogura, Yoshiyuki Ito was character designer, Hiroshi Osaka was animation director, sound director was Masafumi Mima, music by Michiru Ôshima, editing by Hiroaki Itabe, Susumu Fukushi was DP, and *mecha* design was by Jin Fukuchi (the backgrounds were by Studio Bones, Kusanagi, Moon Flower and Studio Fuga). Released 2005.7.23. 105 minutes.

Many in the voice cast were from the *Fullmetal Alchemist* TV series, including Rie Kugimiya as Alphonse Elric and Romi Park as Edward Elric. The cast included: Hidekatsu Shibata, Kazuko Katou, Kenji Utsumi, Masane Tsukayama, Megumi Toyoguchi, Michiko Neya, Miyuu Sawai, Rikiya Koyama, Shun Oguri, Toru Ohkawa, Keiji Fujiwara and Masashi Ebara.

Some movies spun off television series (in live-action or animation) can be disappointing: sometimes they don't have time to give everything and everybody in the TV series a satisfying presentation; or they are for fans only, assuming that the audience knows the TV show; or they replay the same plots as the TV series without adding much that's new. But *Fullmetal Alchemist: Conqueror of Shamballa* is one of the best.

The 2005 *Fullmetal Alchemist* movie was set in two worlds – the Munich and Germany of the 1920s in something like our world and the alternative/ parallel world of Amestris. The brothers (or a brother and their double/ alter ego) exist in both worlds. In the Amestris, alchemy is a real science (rather as it was regarded as a science for centuries in Europe). All you got to do is to clap and use those hands! (a Japanese form of praying). So there are transformations, magic circles (and portals), and spells, and of course the philosopher's stone.

Why did the producers opt to use a parallel worlds plot? Because the *Fullmetal Alchemist* series ended with Edward Elric being sent to our world, after saving Alphonse (a heroic sacrifice motif). Himoru Arakawa's *manga*, of course, finished with Edward giving up his alchemical powers in order to save his brother.

If you've seen the first *Hagane no Renkinjutsushi* series, which the 2005 movie continues and to a degree resolves (or resolves further), there is even more to enjoy in *Fullmetal Alchemist: Conqueror of Shamballa*. The 2004-05 *animé* series, for instance, climaxed with the separation of Ed and Al Elric in two different worlds, separated by that scary Gateway of Truth[1] (the *Fullmetal Alchemist manga* hadn't been completed at the time – it finished in 2010. The decision was taken before committing to the TV series that the show would diverge from the comic, and Himoru Arakawa was happy with that).

Fullmetal Alchemist: Conqueror of Shamballa exploited the concept of parallel worlds to the max,[2] adding all sorts of charas and elements from the world of Amestris, which viewers were by now familiar with, and giving them a new spin in the Germany of the 1920s:[3] Maes Hughes, for instance, turns up as a stick-in-the-mud, racist policeman on the beat, having an unspoken longing for local florist Gracia – who's his wife in the *animé* series; Dante/ Lyra appears briefly as a waitress; there's another melancholy, young woman – Noah (Miyu Sawai), the movie's version of Rose Tomas from the *animé* series; Führer Bradley (Hidekatsu Shibata) in the *animé* show turns up in a different guise in the 2005 movie – now he's not a nasty homunculus who looks like Adolf Hitler or Joseph Stalin, but a guy chasing dragons, who identifies himself as a Jew.[4] The guy calls

---

1 The Gate and crossing between the two worlds is used a few too many times in *Fullmetal Alchemist: Conqueror of Shamballa*, I reckon, which diminishes its power as a threatening, mysterious entity.
2 Evoking Philip Pullman's *His Dark Materials* books – where there are numerous crossovers between Lyra's world and our world.
3 However, some of the mirroring of the two worlds is not only confusing – there are dates such as 1917, 1921 and 1923 in the captions, so the events aren't occurring in parallel – some of it also doesn't quite make sense. But then, a parallel world plot isn't going to make complete sense – which's partly why you use it!
4 Edward teams up with Lang, and they visit the Bavarian castle twice (the second time in a bi-plane, with Ed diving into a tower, and down to the transmutation chamber! A fall which would kill a human but, hell, this is *animé*!).

himself Mabuse (another German Expressionist cinema reference, from the series of movies that Fritz Lang directed), before identifying himself as Lang (as if Lang is a filmmaker looking for a real dragon to use in a movie – evoking the mechanical dragon in *Die Niebelungen*).[5]

So in *Fullmetal Alchemist: Conqueror of Shamballa*, Alphonse and Edward Elric are re-united at last. For me, the scene, which occurs in the middle of a loud, chaotic confrontation (halfway thru act two of four acts), simply wasn't big enough or emotional enough – to pay off the 51-episode *animé*, anyway. It's a smart move, tho', to have Alphonse in his suit of armour appearing as one of the soldiers sent from our world to Amestris by the Germans (so that, when he returns with the rest of the (dead) warriors, he can be re-united with Ed (yes, it takes quite a bit of finagling by the filmmakers to make it work narratively – you can bet they didn't find the solution immediately. For instance, the doorway between the worlds has to be opened on both sides, so Ed in Germany completes the transmutation circle with some chalk, and uses his blood to activate it).[6]

But at least Al's re-introduction meant that some more comedy could occur; and, importantly, it gives Ed hope that he can make it to Amestris – Al, too, tells Ed that he knows a way they can do it (however, before he can tell him, Al is spirited away back to Amestris, because his soul can't exist too long on the other side of the Gate yet. And, dramatically, the brothers need to be kept apart to act as one of the emotional engines in their relationship.

THE SCRIPT.

Fullmetal Alchemist: Conqueror of Shamballa is an elegant two worlds script, cleverly evoking both worlds, with the charas echoing each other. At the level of details, too, *Shamballa* is impressive: Ed, for instance, can't do alchemy in our world of 1923 (he claps his hands and nothing happens), but he still has an automail arm, and pulls on a wire inside it, to activate it.

The rhymes and chimes are neatly worked-out in this superb screenplay: the charas dream of each other, and of other worlds; in Amestris, Wrath battles Gluttony and is chomped in a shower of blood; soon after that, Hohenheim is killed by the dragon Envy; in Amestris, Alphonse is asleep (in Resembool), waking when his counterpart does in Germany; instead of oppressed Ishbalians, the movie has Jews and gypsies.

To counter some of knots in the plotting in the two worlds, *Fullmetal Alchemist: Conqueror of Shamballa* has characters forgetting their former lives.

Fullmetal Alchemist: Conqueror of Shamballa evokes several fascinating elements and themes: two worlds and doubles; alchemy vs. science; Germany in the 1920s; the occult pursuits of the German aristocracy,

---

5 He has the famous Langian monocle instead of the black eyepatch that Führer Bradley wore in the *animé* series. Here, it's Roy Mustang who has an eyepatch.
6 Though really it shouldn't activate.

which parallel the scientific and rocket research of Germany; the rise of Nazism; the demonization of an under-class (the gypsies); and a compelling visit to the Universum Film Aktiengesellschaft Studios.

One wonders if the double worlds device in the first *Fullmetal Alchemist* series was devised solely so that this movie could be made. Certainly, *Fullmetal Alchemist: Conqueror of Shamballa* is one of the most elegant evocations of Germany in the first half of the 20th century in *animé* (including the run-up to World War Two), which is a sub-genre of Japanese animation: *Jin-Roh* and *Hellsing*.

Japanese animators enjoy travelling back to Germany when it was aligned politically with Japan in the 1920s and 1930s, and they also like to muse on alternative histories (if Germany had won WWII, for example). Of course, Himoru Arakawa drew heavily on German history and its military in creating *Fullmetal Alchemist*.

The 2005 *Fullmetal Alchemist* movie takes place some time after the end of the TV series: now Edward Elric is deep into his pursuit of ways of getting back to Amestris (yet also being disenchanted with ever achieving his goal; he has realized, perhaps, that rockets aren't going to propel him back to his homeland). Ed has managed to fashion some automail, or have some manufactured for him (he has a whole pile of legs in his bedroom, which's how he makes a living, but he dreams of Winry-chan, his automail expert). Meanwhile, his pa, Hohenheim, has disappeared somewhere.

When we meet Edward Elric in the present tense of *The Conqueror of Shamballa*, he is part of a troupe which puts on displays of rocket science at country fairs. Yet, for all his friendliness and laidbackness, Ed is also still an outsider, looking at life from outside. He lacks – well, we know what he lacks! – his brother, Al. Edward, in short, can never be whole not only recovering his leg and his arm, but by being re-united with his brother.

One of the striking aspects of the movie is that Ed Elric is fed up, or, at least, he's not quite his usual self. Why? It's suggested that he's been pursuing several projects in our world (such as developing prosthetic limbs). But his idea of flying into space to explore ways of travelling back to Amestris seems to have run into set-backs; when we meet Ed and a rocket, for example, it's at a country fair, rather than the cutting edge of scientific research in one of the facilities in Germany. At the end of the *Fullmetal Alchemist* series, Ed had announced that he would take up rocket science, as this world (our world) doesn't have alchemy.

So Ed Elric is a little dejected – it's been some time (two years is hinted at) that he's been stranded in our world. The real reason for his melancholy is missing his brother Alphonse, of course.

Not only does *Fullmetal Alchemist: Conqueror of Shamballa* deliver a very fine parallel worlds premise, it is also one of the most convincing portrayals in animation of the rise of Nazism. Not only is the movie doing that, it's also telling a *Fullmetal Alchemist* story.

The *Fullmetal Alchemist* movie is developing, continuing and paying off the plots of the TV animated series, as well as the incomplete *manga*.

The TV series departed from the spine of the comic, and the movie follows that up.

Intriguingly, altho' the *manga* by Himoru Arakawa wasn't finished when this movie was released in 2005, it took the events beyond the end of the comic. Thus, we see an older Winry, a dead Izumi Curtis (in an after-life scene, at the Gates of Truth), and Alphonse living in Amestris but he's forgotten what happened after he and Ed transmuted their mother (the loss of memory comes from the *Fullmetal Alchemist manga*, tho' used in a slightly different way).

The mirroring and doubling extended to Alphonse and Edward Elric, too: thus, in 1920s Germany Edward has a friend called Alphonse Heiderich (Shun Oguri) who's the spitting image of his real brother Al (he met this new Al in Romania). Ed is still trying to find a means to return to Amestris, and is investigating rockets and space travel: the Al in our world is a scientist (the equivalent of an alchemist in Amestris). The idea of flying in a rocket to another world is a perfect science fiction correspondence with a magical journey to another realm (Fritz Lang refers to science fiction when he meets Ed).

These are technologies which of course chime with historical events in Germany – particularly during and after WW 2. Uranium and the atom bomb, cited briefly at the end of the *animé* series (and the beginning of this movie), are just around the corner, as so often in *animé*, with all of their ominous echoes for Japanese viewers. (Japan is still the only country which has suffered the use of nuclear weapons in a war). Atomic power is evoked in many *manga*, such as *One Piece, Akira, Fire Force* and *Naruto*.

Of course, being a good guys versus bad guys action-and-fantasy narrative, there are numerous clichés in *Fullmetal Alchemist:* the bad guys are truly evil, for instance (anyone who teams up with the Nazis are), and they are led by a cold, nasty woman, Dietlinde Eckhart (Kazuko Kato).[7] There are other heavies, too, such as Rudolf Hess (Rikiya Koyama) and Karl Haushofer (Masane Tsukayama). But the main characters, in particular Edward Elric, and the gypsy girl, Noah, whom he teams up with, are quirky and unusual enough to make you forget about all the action and fantasy genre clichés.

Certainly the script for the 2005 *Fullmetal Alchemist* movie (by Shou Aikawa) is fascinating and intricate. It's far superior, for example, to the *Indiana Jones* movies (which cover a similar period, and include Nazis as Ultimate Villains). And the other worlds concept is as elegantly evoked as in *His Dark Materials* by Philip Pullman (the books, not the awful TV series). It's no surprise that the first drafts of the screenplay came in too long, and had to be trimmed down. Because *Shamballa* is *stuffed* with ideas and scenarios (enough for a whole *animé* series of its own). Especially impressive is the evocation of historical politics following World War One, and the clever intermingling of the two worlds – our world and Amestris.

The second and third act (using the 4-act model) of the Japanese

---

7 It's yet another case of a female villain – *manga* sensei Himoru Arakawa is especially fond of them.

fantasy movie are the most intriguing – here the screenplay is shuttling back and forth btn Amestris and our world, creating all sorts of rhymes and contrasts. The Alphonse Heiderich in our world, for instance, falls into deep sleep when Alphonse Elric travels btn the two worlds, in his suit of armour body, and is re-united with the real Edward. So it's not only Noah who had presentiments of the other world (Fritz Lang, for instance, discusses the possibility with Ed at U.F.A. Studios).

As the 2005 film switches back and forth from Amestris to our world, there are numerous short scenes which bring in many of the secondary charas of the *Fullmetal Alchemist* world. Some of these are unusual, and look like they have been cut down drastically. In one scene, Breda and Havoc visit a dejected Roy Mustang, who's now living in a lowly, snowbound hovel in the wilderness (and ruminating on his past war crimes as the Flame Alchemist – now he can't even light a match). In another scene, we learn that Izumi Curtis, one of the key secondary charas, has died (unfortunately, for viewers who haven't seen the *Fullmetal Alchemist* series, Curtis's death doesn't carry any weight whatsoever. Yet for *mangaka* Himoru Arakawa it would be a Major Event, and of course it *doesn't* occur in the *Fullmetal Alchemist manga* – not least because Curtis is a chara that Arakawa-sensei is very fond of). In another, Winry-chan (Megumi Toyoguchi) and Sheska (Naomi Wakabayashi) visit a cemetery (to Curtis's grave), and Winry converses with Alphonse (where they talk of Ed, inevitably). In a clever parallel, Edward and Fritz Lang head for Berlin, and Winry makes for Central City. Liza Hawkeye also pops up, as do Alex Armstrong (now helping to revitalize Liore, with a comical use of his alchemizing, turning the food stall into a gleaming edifice topped by a golden statue of Armstrong in a he-man pose. One imagines that Arakawa delighted in these riffs on one of her favourite characters).

STYLE.

With its dark, brooding Bavarian castles, its big action scenes involving dragons being shot at by a phalanx of bi-planes (a nod to *King Kong*), its intense magical rituals, and its broad, historical sweep, *Fullmetal Alchemist: Conqueror of Shamballa* comes over, like the best *animé* works, as grandiose as opera at times. Many of the finest *animé* outings have this magical ability to open up, bigger and bigger, from small beginnings, until the scale of the events become operatic and visionary: *Escaflowne, Moribito, Ghost In the Shell: Stand Alone Complex, Overfiend, Aquarion* and *Akira*. Yet they also never lose sight of the characters – it's another reason why I reckon the Japanese film industry delivers the finest fantasy cinema in the world.

The settings in *Fullmetal Alchemist* are hugely impressive – the background and layout artists (at Bones, Kusanagi, Moon Flower and Fuga) have earned their Yen with intricate and finely-researched vistas of German castles and Bavarian forests, and the townscapes of Munich and Berlin. The background art and the art direction is truly exquisite in *Fullmetal Alchemist: Conqueror of Shamballa* (look at the scene where Ed and Al sit on the banks of a river in Munich). Somehow, Japanese animators are incredibly good at picturing 20th century Europe – the cinema of Hayao Miyazaki is without question the most accomplished at this, but you also see it in the *Black Butler* series, in *Steam-boy,* in *Spirit of Wonder,* in *Hellsing,* etc. (The colour design of the German scenes, for instance, is marvellous, with browns, beiges and greens for the clothing, and a more restrained approach to colouration, as if the scenes were filmed with an early form of colour film technology).

The visual style, the animation, the storyboarding and angles, the pacing and timing, the visual effects – all are topnotch in *Fullmetal Alchemist: Conqueror of Shamballa.* By the time the movie was in pre-production (from March, 2004),[8] the filmmakers had already delivered many sensational episodes in the *Fullmetal Alchemist* TV series. When it comes to spectacular action and inventive staging, the filmmakers at Anime Film, Aniplex, Buyu *et al* are masters. *Fullmetal Alchemist: Conqueror of Shamballa* is as fine as anything in *animé.* There are sequences, for example, which shift into visual abstraction (which moves Asian animation far away from Western animation).

The music composed by Michiru Oshima (the first *Fullmetal Alchemist* series' composer) is a grand, symphonic score, and played by the Moscow International Symphony Orchestra (so maybe the strains of Dimitri Shostakovitch come thru). L'Arc-en-Ciel were back from the TV series performing the opening and closing theme songs.

THE PROLOGUE.

The prologue of the *Fullmetal Alchemist* movie doesn't connect completely with the rest of the piece in narrative terms, but it does feature many of the motifs of the *Fullmetal Alchemist* franchise: principally, our two heroes, depicted here in action, plus tropes from the series such as mad scientists/ alchemists, human transmutation, our teen heroes vs. middle-aged guys, some humour (btn the brothers), the steam-punk world, the Gate, and a big, loud action scene (because after the prologue, it is a *long* time – in action-adventure *animé* terms, that is – until the next Big Action Sequence, which's the appearance of the dragon Envy in the castle, around the 27 minute mark. There are smaller action scenes, however, such as Ed taking on the heavies sent to collect Noah at the travelling fair).

The prologue of *Shamballa,* which turns out to be a story that Edward in our world tells the Alphonse he met in Romania (it's set in 1914 in Amestris), illustrates a time when the Elric brothers were working together. In the *Fullmetal Alchemist* TV series, we know they were separated, so portraying them together also illustrates Ed's deepest desires – to be reunited with his brother Al.

The prologue depicts our teen heroes battling an alchemist who's

---

8 The *Fullmetal Alchemist* movie went into pre-production in March, 2004 (about halfway thru the *animé* series).

produced a uranium-based device,[9] typing him as an especially bad baddie in Japanese popular culture (he has also used some innocent victims in the pursuit of this ultimate weapon, echoing the way the military in *Fullmetal Alchemist* exploit civilians for nefarious ends).

Of course, the Elrics manage to defeat Huskisson – Unsho Ishizuka (after an all-out battle), sending him to the limbo of the Gateway of Truth, where Huskisson's fate (plus the uranium ball) is to be swallowed by the creatures in the Doorway.

NAZISM.

One of the first things that the 2005 *Hagane no Renkinjutsushi* movie has to do is to create a bunch of new villains, as the *animé* series of *Fullmetal Alchemist* had dispatched most of the existing ones (tho' charas such as Gluttony re-appear). And, in grand style, the filmmakers at Anime Film, Buyu, Mainichi Broadcasting System, Production I.G. *et al* go for the Big One – the Nazis. But – and this is the really interesting aspect of *Fullmetal Alchemist: Conqueror of Shamballa*, and of the *Fullmetal Alchemist* franchise as a whole – they don't drop our heroes straight into 1940, with the Nazis in full flight and the war already raging. Instead, they go back to the origins of political fascism in Germany in the 1920s, beginning with scenes of rising inflation, dissatisfaction with foreigners and aristocrats, and the years of economic instability (once again, the parallels between Europe in the 1920s and Japan just after World War Two, and in the 1990s and 2000s, hardly need to be pointed out). This intelligent script includes references to the Jewish issue and the Communist Party.

In the 2005 *Fullmetal Alchemist* movie, real figures such as Adolf Hitler, Fritz Lang, Rudolf Hess and Karl Haushofer appear, cleverly interwoven with fictional characters (Hermann Göring is referenced in the dialogue). This is one of the most intriguing aspects of *Fullmetal Alchemist* – its political and ideological elements (it is certainly an intricate and meticulously researched script by Shou Aikawa).

Adolf Hitler, Nazism and Germany/ Europe in the 1920s and 1930s have proved to be fascinating for Japanese filmmakers: the period crops up in many *animés*, as well as the figure of the Führer. As if Japanese animators are exploring Japan's own bleaker times in the Thirties, when it leaned heavily towards right-wing ideology, but thru the lens of modern, European history (and often fantasy – fantasy, that is, on top of the fundamental unreality of *animé*). For instance, the *Legend of the Overfiend* series explores the occult obsessions of National Socialism, and also has a magical ritual of opening portals to other dimensions and summoning dragons (the writer of the 2005 *Fullmetal Alchemist* movie, Shou Aikawa,

---

9 The uranium weapon is a small, metal ball which derives from the glass sphere containing the dangerous red water from the 1st series (ep. 12). It also seems to consciously evoke the steam ball in 2004's *Steam-boy*. (Other elements echo *Steam-boy*, such as the giant crane which attacks the brothers, the vast, circular interior, and the metal troopers in suits of armour). However, films take a long time to produce, so it's not simply a case of one set filmmakers being directly influenced by another group. Katsuhiro Otomo began developing *Steam-Boy* from the mid-1990s.

was one of the writers on the *Urotsukidoji* series).[10]

In *Hagane no Renkinjutsushi*, the emergence of fascism becomes an important issue: *Fullmetal Alchemist* handles this Big Issue in a sensitive and subtle manner. *Fullmetal Alchemist* is not afraid to foreground Jewish and gypsy characters and the political oppression they face – not only from the authorities (like suspicious policemen), but also their fellow citizens (in fact, *Fullmetal Alchemist: Conqueror of Shamballa* spends quite a bit of its first act depicting the oppression and suspicion that Noah suffers amongst the townspeople of Munich. Early on, the movie identifies Jews and gypsies as persecuted people – they take the place of the Ishbalians in the *Fullmetal Alchemist* TV series. However, the gypsies are introduced initially as a jolly, singing bunch. In fact, there's a lengthy musical interlude early on in *Fullmetal Alchemist: Conqueror of Shamballa* when Ed and (the other) Alphonse hitch a ride with a cartload of gypsies (all women) heading for town. And they start to sing).[11]

Noah isn't merely a token female character introduced to bump up the female quotient in this boysy movie of a *shonen manga*. Noah carries some of the plot (in being one of the first people to recognize that Ed Elric comes from another world, for instance. There were other characters who played a role in this part of the plot, but they were dropped from the final script).

Noah is also one of the oppressed characters that form a key ingredient of the *Fullmetal Alchemist* universe. Also, not only do the townspeople regard Noah with wariness because she's a gypsy, the villains are also seeking her out (for her clairvoyant powers – part of the Nazis' pursuit of occultism). This is a script device, of course, to put Noah together with Edward – when he rescues her from the heavies, who've come for her (so they're on the run together, both people without a home). Aligning Ed with Noah also puts him on the side of the underdogs, being pushed around by the ruling powers in Germany. (Noah is also a motherly figure, as Rose Tomas was in the TV series – in a detail typical of *anime* but rare in the West, Noah has the dead Al's blood staining her dress – and it's right over her belly and womb, another of several birth images in *Fullmetal Alchemist: Conqueror of Shamballa*).

Noah is also an exposition character, of course: she's there to deliver some of the explanations about the world of 1920s Germany for the audience (from the point-of-view of ostracized folk, the gypsies). Later, Fritz Lang takes up that role, when Ed Elric teams up with him on the way to the Bavarian castle.[12]

The parallels between 1920s Germany and 1930s Japan, as well as 2000s Japan, are continually evoked (for example, the Germans lament being defeated in WW I and suffering the ignominy of the Treaty of

10 However, the ritual in *Urotsukidoji* is a little more extreme than the one in *Fullmetal Alchemist*: it involves an infernal machine out of Hieronymous Bosch and the Marquis de Sade which uses women in bondage gear having their life energy sucked out of them. Well, Toshio Maeda is the author of *Urotsukidoji*!
11 But for some reason Ed and Al, surrounded by gorgeous, young women, look as miserable as kids locked in a three-hour theology exam. Cheer up guys, this is the Happy Bit before the movie gets all 'dark' and 'brooding' and 'sinister'! Or are they simply very embarrassed?
12 That's a rather unconvincing scene, as Ed waylays Lang and his driver in their car in a forest at night.

Versailles – clear parallels with what happened to Japan after WW 2).

This is classy, clever scriptwriting, in which out-there fantasy ingredients, like giant, fearsome dragons and magical portals to other worlds, are integrated seamlessly with real, historical elements, like 1920s Munich or Nazism. Unlike many fantasy and action outings which evoke Nazism and Germany in the 1920s-30s, *Fullmetal Alchemist* has real political points to make.

UNIVERSUM FILM AKTIENGESELLSCHAFT.

In the 2005 *Fullmetal Alchemist* movie, there's a delightful trip to the famous Universum Film Aktiengesellschaft Studios in Berlin, where F.W. Murnau, Fritz Lang and G.W. Pabst worked on classics of German Expressionist cinema such as *The Last Laugh, Faust, The Cabinet of Dr Caligari* and of course *Metropolis*.

The 2005 fully alchemical movie goes overboard on depicting the Universum Film Aktiengesellschaft Studios (during the making of *Die Niebelungen*), right down to the Wagnerian scenes (including Brunhilde, Siegfried *et al*), and the famous, mechanical dragon that Siegfried fights (there's a comparison between this film-with-a-film dragon and the green serpent that crashes into Edward Elric earlier (a new form for Envy in Himoru Arakawa's *manga*), and the live dragon is designed like the beast in the *Niebelungen* film).

The whole Universum Film Aktiengesellschaft sequence is also rather indulgent (at an *otaku*, film geek level), because dramatically it consists of a conversation between Fritz Lang and Edward only (on a sound stage with a castle and rainbow back-drop, reminiscent of mediæval manuscript illuminations). But director Seiji Mizushima and the team, like so many filmmakers, can't resist paying a visit to a film studio. And we've visited Hollywood studios in their heyday many times (in movies such as *Singin' In the Rain, Sunset Boulevard* and *The Bad and the Beautiful*), but how often do you get to go to the U.F.A. Studios in its prime? (And in full colour?!). This really is an absolutely marvellous sequence.

Thus, it's Fritz Lang who tells Edward Elric the story of one of the most infamous periods in recent history – the rise of Nazism in modern Germany. Lang also lays out his own involvement (the story of how Lang fled to the U.S.A. in 1933, rather than work for the Nazis, is well-known. The film even cites Lang's wife, and her different attitude towards the Nazis[13]).

However, what *Fullmetal Alchemist: Conqueror of Shamballa* doesn't ram home quite hard enough is the bitter irony that the military in Amestris and in the *Fullmetal Alchemist* series as a whole (including the State Alchemists) is also distinctly right-wing (and close to fascistic),

---

13 Tho' it doesn't mention her name: Thea Gabriele von Harbou (1888-1954) was one of the stars of German silent cinema, the writer of *Metropolis, Die Niebelungen, M, Spy, Dr Mabuse, The Testament of Dr Mabuse, Phantom* and *Das Wandere Bild*. Von Harbou wrote for Carl Dreyer, E.A. Dupont and F.W. Murnau as well as Lang. Von Harbou famously stayed in Germany after the Nazis came to power, but Lang fled (they married in 1922 and divorced in 1934; Lang was her 2nd of 3 spouses). Von Harbou continued to write scripts and novels, and she also directed (*Hanneles Himmelfahrt* and *Elisabeth und der Naar*).

with numerous parallels to Germany in the 1920s and 1930s (there are obvious affinities between the State Alchemists and its cult of alchemy in Amestris and the occult wings of Nazism.[14] Indeed, *Fullmetal Alchemist: Conqueror of Shamballa* evokes the right-wing Thule Society, a real group).

But instead, the filmmakers of *Fullmetal Alchemist: Conqueror of Shamballa* have focussed on the parallels between Nazi Germany and the present political climate (and to Japan in particular: Fritz Lang shows Edward a book which discusses Japan and its island status (as a nation that retains its racial 'purity', having not been invaded or colonized, prior to WW2, when the movie takes place). Meanwhile, Germany, he points out, is surrounded by countries on all sides, and Germans are in many parts of the globe).

FRITZ LANG.

I wonder what Fritz Lang would make of his appearance in *Fullmetal Alchemist*? I imagine it might amuse him greatly – certainly it's not something he could have predicted! One of the giants of German cinema, Lang (1890-1976) directed, among other films, the ground-breaking sci-fi epic *Metropolis* (1928),[15] still the greatest vision of a future city in cinema, and still for many *the* great science fiction movie, the *Dr Mabuse* films,[16] *Die Niebelungen* (1927), quoted here, *The Spiders* (1919-20), *The Master of Love* (1919), *Der Müde Tod* (1921), the influential man-hunt movie *M* (1932), starring Peter Lorre, *Fury* (1937), *You Only Live Once* (1938), *You and Me* (1940), *Western Union* (1943), *Man Hunt* (1943), *The Woman In the Window* (1945), *The Ministry of Fear* (1945), *Cloak and Dagger* (1948), *Secret Beyond the Door* (1948), *House By the River* (1950), *Clash By Night* (1953), *Rancho Notorious* (1953), *The Blue Gardenia* (1953), *The Big Heat* (1954), *Human Desire* (1954), *Moonfleet* (1955), *While the City Sleeps* (1956), *Beyond a Reasonable Doubt* (1956), *Der Tiger von Eschnapur* (1959), and *Das Indische Grabmal* (1961).

As that list (not complete) of Fritz Lang's movies as film director shows, he was a formidable filmmaker, with some bona fide classics to his name. Pretty much everyone agrees that Lang's silent German epics *Metropolis* and *Die Niebelungen* are among the finest of the period, and that Lang was brilliant at adapting to the move from the German to the North American movie business (Lang mentions that he's going to the U.S.A. in *Fullmetal Alchemist: Conqueror of Shamballa*).

Fritz Lang's influence on subsequent cinema is enormous (solely in terms of *Metropolis*, let alone his other works). Lang's mark crops up all over the place. Ken Russell has delivered comic *hommages* to *Die*

14 Nazism's fascination with occultism has been employed a few times in *animé* – most notoriously in the *Legend of the Overfiend* series.
15 Japanese animation, for instance, is profoundly influenced by *Metropolis* (as is every futuristic science fiction movie from *Blade Runner* and *Akira* to *The Matrix* and *Minority Report*). *Metropolis* was remade in 2001 as a Japanese animated movie, produced by Madhouse and Tezuka Production, written by Katsuhiro Otomo and directed by Rintaro (it was partly based on Osamu Tezuka's *Metropolis manga* – a comicbook which Tezuka, the superstar of Japanese fantasy, based on the German Expressionist movie, which he hadn't seen – he'd seen an article in a magazine).
16 *Dr Mabuse*, 1924, *The Last Will of Dr Mabuse*, 1933, and *The Thousand Eyes of Dr Mabuse*, 1961.

Niebelungen, for example, in movies like *Mahler* (1974). The filmmakers at Anime Film, Aniplex, Buyu & co. are clearly big fans – there's a ton of research in *Fullmetal Alchemist: Conqueror of Shamballa* – it's on show as Lang and Edward walk thru the Universum Film Aktiengesellschaft Studios.

DRAGONS AND FATHERS.

The designs in *Fullmetal Alchemist* (by Yoshiyuki Ito and Jin Fukuchi, and art direction by Kazuo Ogura and Tomoaki Okada) are very impressive, as is the staging. For instance, the dragon[17] (which Ed identifies as Envy – we saw him pass thru the Gate at the end of the series, tho' Envy isn't revealed in his usual form), is employed in an unusual manner: it's looped around the circular gateway machine and magic circle to the other world, inside the dome (the 'Serpent Room') of a Bavarian castle (if you know about the symbolism of dragons, which includes notions such as eternity, the cycle of life, circles and trans-formation, as well as snakes and dragons looping around to eat themselves, like time itself, it makes perfect sense. Dragons and snakes eating themselves were also part of the *Fullmetal Alchemist* animé series – the homunculi wear` *ourosburos* tattoos).

Equally unusual in *Shamballa* is the introduction (and unveiling) of Edward Elric's father van Hohenheim: he's caught alive in the jaws of the dragon,[18] and stays around long enough to have a brief chat with his son before sacrificing himself as the serpent chomps him in two with an explosion of blood (which chimes with the death of Wrath in Amestris – the final act of the movie contains many rhymes and echoes between the worlds). It's strange. But not really: *Fullmetal Alchemist* is very much about the Sins of the Fathers, about the uneasy, ambiguous and tense relationship between the older generation and the younger generation, embodied in fathers and sons – which's a recurring theme in Japanese animation. And Edward Elric is surrounded by all sorts of shady father figures and father surrogates, as he was in the *animé* series: indeed, *Fullmetal Alchemist* is about, on one level, young boys negotiating the complex world of adults, their behaviour and their politics. (If you've seen the *animé* series of *Fullmetal Alchemist*, you'll know that the last we saw of Envy was hurtling into the Gateway, intent on murdering his 'father', who's also Ed's father, Hohenheim. The dragon as Envy thus pays off that plotline).

It's not a wholly satisfying inclusion in the film for Hohenheim because it's so short – but then, in a movie of regular length, there simply isn't time for explore every character in depth. But it does feature the central notion of sacrifice – of Hohenheim sacrificing himself for his son, just as his son sacrifices himself for his brother (twice).

◆

One of the intriguing turns of events in *Fullmetal Alchemist: Conqueror*

---

17 It's a Chinese dragon, however, not the dragon of Western mythology.
18 In the TV series, the filmmakers added the notion that Envy was a homunculus created by Hohenheim as the result of making a philosopher's stone.

of Shamballa is to have Alphonse Elric play scenes of regret at a hysterical level – when he realizes that in opening the Gate from the Amestris side, he has inadvertently allowed the invasion of the Germans into Central City (Al is the conscience of the *Fullmetal Alchemist* franchise, and always the first one to say sorry). Thus, the German military act as the villains in two worlds. It takes a firm talking to from Edward before Al realizes that it's not all his fault, that they won't give up, that nobody wants war but they're not going to lie down and admit defeat, and with that short, curt nod and an exchange of determined looks (which you see often in Japanese animation), the Elric brothers are back on track. (This is the key speech in the movie, a riff on Himoru Arakawa's mantra of *move forward*).

◆

When you consider *Fullmetal Alchemist: Conqueror of Shamballa* as a whole, it was a tough challenge for the screenwriter (Shou Aikawa) to juggle all of the plotlines from the fully alchemical *animé* television series and all of those characters – to give everybody Something To Do. And, importantly, Something To Achieve. And to deliver some great action, explore the key themes of the series, and also to weave in some surprises and twists.

As the 2005 *Fullmetal Alchemist* movie is so much shorter than the TV series (or even a group of five episodes), and has a compressed narrative style, it has to crack on at a rapid pace. Not much time for longueurs or lyricism, and no time at all for side-stories. (Yet secondary charas, such as Noah and Mabuse/ Lang, do have a character trajectory, as do the villains).

THE FINALE.

The climax of *Hagane no Renkinjutsushi* inevitably shifts into big action sequences involving military invasions, war, planes, rockets, a mobile suit army, gun battles, and travel between worlds (the big, operatic action is reminiscent of two animated Japanese movies of 2004: *Steam-boy* and *Howl's Moving Castle*, and the invasion recalls the Tolmekian forces in 1984's *Nausicaä of the Valley of the Wind*). Characters are viciously bumped off one by one as the fascists use the powers of the other world to take political control of Germany (Hess shoots Al, Dietlinde Eckhart shoots Noah, then Ed). There are numerous disturbing images – such as Adolf Hitler at a political rally of National Socialists holding a revolver above his head and firing it. What's impressive about *Fullmetal Alchemist* is that it doesn't evoke such horrors for cheap effects, but uses them seriously and thoughtfully.

There is *a lot* of tricksy scriptwriting by Shou Aikawa and co. to get everybody in the right place for the finale of *Fullmetal Alchemist: Conqueror of Shamballa:* how Winry Rockbell and Sheska just happen to fall hundreds of feet into the subterranean city, so that Winry can be one of the people who first meets Edward Elric when he finally returns to his home world (crashlanding in the rocket plane – and to fix his automail, of course). Indeed, when the Gate of Truth is opened (on both sides), the storytelling is incredibly rapid: Hohenheim has a brief chat with Ed before allowing Envy to chomp him to bits so he can be a sacrifice to send his son back to Amestris; Ed has no time (5 seconds) to mourn the passing of his father in a spray of blood, because Eckhart shoots him, then he comes round in the cockpit of a plane. Another very short chat occurs between the Alphonse in our world and Ed, before the plane's launched, and Al is killed by Hess.

The script doesn't only deliver full-blown action sequences, it also includes plenty of narrative reversals, surprises and twists. iIt is not an A-to-B-to-C action climax. This helps to render the finale even more satisfying – such as the surprise of having Ed decide to return to the other world, not long after he's just arrived and been re-united with his chums.

Incidentally, Wrath (Nana Mizuki) is given a different characteriz-ation in the *Fullmetal Alchemist* movie from the TV *animé* – now he gives himself up in a sacrifice (in the jaws of the super-size Gluttony), so that Alphonse is able to open the Gate in the sunken city (this's one of the outstanding action beats in *Fullmetal Alchemist: Conqueror of Shamballa*, with Wrath being hurled about by the octopoid Gluttony in the under-ground town). And thus, in death, Wrath achieves his longed-for reunion with his momma – the dead Izumi Curtis[19] (they embrace, naked, in the Gateway; this kind of resolves the way that Wrath was depicted in the first *Fullmetal Alchemist* series).[20] But in Arakawa-sensei's *manga*, Wrath is King Bradley. (It also means that Al transmutes Wrath to open the Gate, something that the Elrics have been very reluctant to do. In order to persuade, Wrath yells at Al repeatedly while he's being chomped to death in Gluttony's jaws, which mirrors the sacrifice of Hohenheim in our world).

The emotional and psychological climax of the first *Fullmetal Alchemist* series *and* the *Shamballa* movie occurs in the midst of the busy-busy invasion sequence: as Miyazakian behemoths from our world emerge from the Gateway of Truth (aircraft covered in the blackened detritus of the black arms of the Gate – a great touch, because there's always a price to visiting the Gate), and Central City is exploding and under attack from armoured stormtroopers, Edward and Alphonse Elric meet. Yes, *this* is the most significant reunion of the 2005 movie – and it resolves the *Fullmetal Alchemist* series, too: because this is Ed and Al being re-united in the flesh (i.e., Al isn't in his suit of armour guise).[21] And yet, incredibly, it is another Big Dramatic Scene that is severely under-played by the filmmakers.

◯

In the climactic scenes of *Shamballa*, which turn into a stops-all-out battle between the heroes and the villains, Dietlinde Eckhart turns into the blood-crazed super-villain of a million *animés* (with her mad cackle and scary intensity, she is reminiscent of Dilandu in the *Escaflowne* series).[22]

19 Izumi Curtis is already dead by the time of the movie (which also contains cemetery scenes).
20 But not the issue of Wrath having Ed Elric's limbs!
21 Another great touch has Al now dressed as Ed, in the familiar red coat and black pants. As if Alphonse can now be a State Alchemist.
22 Even her first name, Dietlinde, echoes Dilandu.

Roy Mustang redeems himself during the climax of *Fullmetal Alchemist: Conqueror of Shamballa*, when he returns from his self-imposed exile in a snowy wilderness (dwelling too long on his failures), and starts to kick ass (in the familiar, super-cool manner of simply clicking his fingers and unleashing walls of fire. Mustang is given a dramatic introduction). Indeed, Mustang as the Flame Alchemist is promoted to the chief ally for our heroes, the Elric brothers, when he helps them take on the villains (leaving Ed free for the inevitable showdown with the key baddie, Eckhart, in the cockpit of the aircraft, a scene very reminiscent of the cinema of Hayao Miyazaki).

For fans of the 2003-2004 *animé* series, the finale of *Fullmetal Alchemist: Conqueror of Shamballa* pays off many of the minor plotlines of the TV *animé*, while also discovering clever solutions to the challenges of finding the multiple heroes something for each of them to do (thus, altho' it's Ed Elric who goes up against master villain Dietlinde Eckhart, it's Alphonse who is also instrumental in defeating her, using the mobile suits). Even Winry Rockbell and Sheska get to do their bit (Winry by fixing Ed's armour, when he crashlands in the underground city (she just happens to be carting around a brand new arm and a leg in a suitcase!). And Winry muses, how long is he going to keep me waiting? – for ♥ lerrrve).

After defeating the villain (but not quite – Dietlinde Eckhart makes one final appearance, in a scary *mecha* suit), Ed and Al Elric are separated yet again. It's rather artificial, this last split, but the reason for it is solid enough: Edward takes himself off to deal with the German invaders, to haul them back thru the Gate of Truth, and to destroy it from the other side. The scene is a replay of Ed performing the ultimate sacrifice (though the *manga* hadn't shown that yet). The plot twist pushes the Elrics apart again, so that we can have another emotional reunion in the final minutes of *Fullmetal Alchemist: Conqueror of Shamballa*, as the Elrics're re-united again (when Alphonse stows away in his suit of armour, an inventive use of the recurring gag in *Fullmetal Alchemist* of characters jumping into Alphonse's suit. To have Al himself do it is very clever). So the 2005 movie ends with the boys in our world, in Germany of the 1920s (not the best place to be, perhaps. And not in their homeworld of Amestris, either – they can't perform alchemy in our world).

02

FULLMETAL ALCHEMIST:
THE SACRED STAR OF MILOS

HAGANE NO RENKINJUTSUSHI:
MILOS NO SEI-NARU HOSHI

The second *Fullmetal Alchemist* movie, *Fullmetal Alchemist: The Sacred Star of Milos* (= *Hagane no Renkinsutsushi: Milos no Sei-Naru Hoshi*, 2011), was created by the seven producers as a stand-alone story set in a new area of Amestris. The movie was produced after the second *Fullmetal Alchemist* series was complete, so there was no need to tie up storylines associated with the series (altho' there are numerous links to the 2009-10 TV series). The producers wanted an *Indiana Jones*-style action-adventure tale of the order of *The Castle of Cagliostro* (the 1979 *Lupin III* movie, directed by the biggest name in all *animé* – Hayao Miyazaki, that's often cited as a near-perfect template for an adventure caper involving action, mystery, suspense, romance, exotic settings, humour, stunts, *mecha*, appealing characters and a rapid pace. The influence of Miyazaki-sensei is all over this movie, as it is over everything in the *Fullmetal Alchemist* universe).[23]

Fullmetal Alchemist: The Sacred Star of Milos was produced by Aniplex/ Bones/ Dentsu Inc./ Mainichi Broadcasting System/ Shochiku Co. Ltd./ Square Enix/ Tokyo Broadcasting System. The producers were Arimasa Okada, Fumi Teranishi, Hiro Maruyama, Masahiko Minami, Nobuyuki Kurashige, Ryo Oyama and Shin Furukawa. Released: 2011.07.02. 110 minutes.

Yuichi Shinpo was commissioned to write the script, and first-timer Kazuya Murata (a former trainee at Studio Ghibli)[24] was hired to direct the 2011 movie. Tara Iawashiro wrote the music; Kenichi Konishi was character designer and chief animation director; Kazuo Ogura and

---

23 It's one of Steven Spielberg's favourite movies.
24 Enhancing the Miyazakian links. Both the movie's Murata and Konishi were apprentices at Studio Ghibli.

Tomoaki Okada were art directors; Kumiko Sakamoto was editor; Masafumi Mima was sound director; Yoshiyuki Takei was DP; and *mecha* designer was Shinji Aramaki (director of the *Appleseed* movies and *Ghost In the Shell: 2045*).

Many of the same cast and crew worked on *Fullmetal Alchemist: The Sacred Star of Milos* as on the TV series, including the all-important *seiyu*, Romi Pak and Rie Kugimiya, who played Ed and Al Elric (tho' the producers considered replacing them with new actors. Thankfully, they didn't. Ed and Al can only be Romi Pak and Rie Kugimiya for me).

There is an entertaining 'making of' documentary which outlines the production of the second *Fullmetal Alchemist* movie (included on the home releases). It's a good demonstration of how movies and television work: it's the *producers*, not the director, or the writers, or the actors, or the composers, or the cameramen, or the animators, who originate the idea for making the piece. As the 'making of' *Fullmetal Alchemist: The Sacred Star of Milos* demonstrates, the producers decided they wanted to make a movie (no doubt encouraged by the reception of the TV series, and also by Square Enix); they'd kicked around some ideas, *then* they hired the writer, and as the script was being written, *then* they hired the director. In Japan, movie-making is dominated by studios and producers, just as it is in Hollywood; Japan has a similar studio system to the U.S.A. (Unfortunately, there is one person missing from the documentary – author Himoru Arakawa – the famously shy *mangaka* seldom appears in public, but we'd love to see and hear what she thinks of the animated versions of *Fullmetal Alchemist*).

The second *Fullmetal Alchemist* movie introduces a bunch of new characters: chief among them is Julia Crichton (played by Maaya Sakamoto),[25] the young (sixteen year-old), independent, and attractive woman who is the Winry/ Rosie character (tho' her design, by Kenichi Konishi, consciously moves away from the usual *Fullmetal Alchemist* woman, with ginger-red hair[26] and blue eyes, and a colour palette heavy on oranges and reds – the colour palette extended to all of the Milos scenes)[27] Julia is given a brother figure, the ambiguous, wayward Ashleigh (Hidenobu Kiuchi), and the sister-brother relationship of course acts as a mirror to the Ed and Al brotherhood, which forms the emotional core of the entire *Fullmetal Alchemist* franchise. Other new charas include Miranda (Sakiko Tamagawa), the slinky leader of the rebels, chief villain Melvin Voyager (Toshiyuki Morikawa), Mrs. Crichton (played by Major Motoko Kusanagi herself, Atsuko Tanaka), the chimera Peter Soyuz (Hideyuki Umezu), Pedro (Kiyotaka Furushima), Graz (Kouji Ishii),

---

25 Maaya Sakamoto (b. 1980) was Hitomi in *Escaflowne*, Makuri in *Naruto*, Deunan Knute in the *Appleseed* remakes, Merlin in *Seven Deadly Sins*, and the young Motoko in *The Laughing Man*, the *Ghost In the Shell* movie and TV series (and Motoko in the *Arise* series). Sakamoto's other credits include: *Clover, Black Butler, Death Note, Cowboy Bebop, Evangelion, The Heroic Legend of Arslan, Hellsing 2, Kanon, .hack, Macross Frontier, Mushishi, Gundam, Persona 3, RahXephon, Record of Lodoss War, Saint Seiya, xxxHolic, Star Driver, Tsubasa* and *Wolf's Rain*.
26 However, in the *Fullmetal Alchemist* artbook, early designs for Rose gave her ginger hair. And ginger is after all a classic look for late Victoriana (popularized in art of the Pre-Raphaelites). And it's Miyazaki's favourite colour for hair in female charas.
27 Julia has the mini-skirt, tho' of Winry Rockbell.

Santos (Ryuichi Kosugi) and Alan (Takanori Hoshino).

○

The filmmakers of *Fullmetal Alchemist: The Sacred Star of Milos* drew heavily on the two *Fullmetal Alchemist* TV series (which many in the production team had worked on), adding a few new elements of their own. The setting, for a start, was a conscious shift away from Amestris. Now it's a border zone, in between Amestris and Creta, in the West of Amestris (aligning Creta, as the name suggests, with Greece). In the middle of the two nations is the homeland of Milos, which has been taken away from the denizens by the reigning powers (of course, our heroes're aligned with the repressed rebels. After the action scenes of the first act, both Al and Ed travel down to the valley floor – tho' separately).

The dramatic set-up of *Fullmetal Alchemist: The Sacred Star of Milos*, however, isn't really introduced until the start of act two. And it takes a *lot* of talky scenes to lay it all out (there's so much exposition, it threatens to bog the movie down). The background context is a replay of Ishbal again, with a community ousted from their homeland, political repression, a rebellion, and all of that takes ages to explain to the audience in the movie's act two and act three scenes. But if you want a political story, it often takes some time to set out the communities and the conflicts, as well as to put a *Fullmetal Alchemist* spin on things, to give it those Hiromu Arakawan touches.

This's partly because the filmmakers of *Fullmetal Alchemist: The Sacred Star of Milos* opted for such a lengthy chase and action sequence for the second half of act one (if you fill act one with action, you have to slow down the movie to explain things later – it's a trade-off). Certainly the chases, the fights, the stunts, the action and the alchemical exchanges were incredibly impressive, as ever in *Fullmetal Alchemist*: the filmmakers exploited the chase to introduce each area of their new setting of Milos (and the multi-level aspects of it, too – the high railroad bridges, the deep, circular canyon below, and the domes and towers of the city).

It is some four minutes b4 we are introduced to the heroes of the *Fullmetal Alchemist* universe, Ed and Al Elric: before we meet them, the movie first depicts the early life of the Crichtons – opening in Milos, we see the Crichton children fleeing with their parents to Creta (the point-of-view stays with Julia Crichton, aged about seven – she's 16 in the rest of the movie, about the same age as Ed). The following scene, in the Crichtons' home, is devastating: it depicts the slaughter of the parents in pools of blood (they're hung upside-down like animal carcasses).

When we shift to the present day, during harvest festival celebrations (amid fireworks), we are rapidly introduced to Edward and Alphonse Elric (Ed's asleep, surrounded by alchemical books – it's his default position, to be studying, as a good Japanese boy should do, but he's also falling asleep).

The inciting event of the 2nd *Fullmetal Alchemist* movie is the break-out of the criminal Melvin Voyager (Toshiyuki Morikawa): he's an alchemist using a form of alchemy the boys don't recognize (at this point,

Voyager evokes Scar most of all – he even has scars on his neck). The action sequence on the streets of Central City depicts some terrific gags as the Elrics find themselves out-matched by Voyager. The prison break-out is couched in a mystery format – with the Elrics working with Roy Mustang and his crew to uncover what's behind it. Thus, the Elrics're dispatched to Milos (by Mustang) to discover what's going on (Mustang – and Hawkeye – remain in Central City).

The railroad action sequence in *Sacred Star* is one of the longest continuous action scenes in the *Fullmetal Alchemist* franchise.[28] It draws heavily on Himoru Arakawa's *manga* – the duel between Kimbley and Scar on the train at night in the snow, for instance, or the *animé's* episode 5: *The Man With the Mechanical Arm (Dash! Automail),* where Ed and Al foil Bald's gang that's taken a train hostage.

The railroad sequence contains numerous narrative elements, all delivered at a lightning pace, as if you're watching every silent comedy that ever used a steam engine, compressed into ten minutes. For instance, one of the villains appears to be a chimera in the form of a wolf; the military are on board, rounding up political undesirables (who flee); armed, flying terrorists on wings (called Black Bats) complicate matters; and Ashleigh Crichton also happens to be on his way to Milos (in another train), and encounters the Elrics. Multiple confrontations occur, using alchemy, guns, nets, etc. There is also plenty of bloodshed: the action scenes in the first act contain many on-screen deaths (Ashleigh Crichton is depicted killing, too – which marks him out for a bloody death at end of the piece – because he isn't Ashleigh, he's really Melvin Voyager).

O

Among the many ingredients wheeled in from the *Fullmetal Alchemist* universe for this second movie were the chimeras, Roy Mustang and Liza Hawkeye, Winry Rockbell, human transmutation, an underground city, an oppressed people, an uprising, earrings,[29] a new form of alchemy, a new energy source (magma), and of course the philosopher's stone, created using a whole city (it can't be *Fullmetal Alchemist* without a philosopher's stone or twenty in there somewhere, can it?).

Altho' the character designs (by Kenichi Konishi) had changed slightly,[30] nothing much was different in *Fullmetal Alchemist: The Sacred Star of Milos.* This movie has all of our favourite characters back in their usual place. Indeed, *The Sacred Star of Milos* recalled the early episodes of both the *manga* and the *animés* – with the boys travelling to some distant place to investigate a mystery or incident, which quickly becomes more complicated and difficult than they envisaged; soon, Roy Mustang, Liza Hawkeye *et al* have to travel from Central City to sort out the trouble the lads are causing.

---

28 The action in act one seems to be almost continuous, from the time that Ed and Al Elric encounter Ashleigh Crichton (or the man posing as him) to the lengthy railroad chase and the arrival in Milos.

29 Earrings are used as a token of the relationship between the Crichtons (taken from the 2nd *animé*).

30 Ed's eyes, for instance, aren't the bright gold of previous *animés,* but slightly paler (yet somehow shinier).

O

In *Fullmetal Alchemist: The Sacred Star of Milos* the designers have opted to visualize the oppression of Milos and its people literally: so they have to live at the bottom of a deep valley, in shabby hovels, while the people of Creta and Amestris live above, in the light.[31] (Hey, the scenario of the Haves and the Have-nots, upper and lower, worked for *Metropolis. Fullmetal Alchemist: The Sacred Star of Milos* is a kind of *Metropolis* with magic. *Metropolis*, a much-revered movie in Japan, had of course appeared in the first *Fullmetal Alchemist* movie, and been remade in 2001 in a high fantasy, *anime* style). The valley was carved out in the pursuit of the MacGuffin of the *Fullmetal Alchemist* cosmos – a philosopher's stone.

So the people of Milos became pawns in a political struggle power between Creta and Amestris, with the prospect of obtaining philosopher's stones being the real motive for the conflicts. And the price of philosopher's stones is the same: living humans. (The filmmakers expand on the concepts of mining for philosopher's stones, a key element in the *Fullmetal Alchemist manga*, by including lava and volcanoes. The natural forces of the Earth chime with a Japanese audience, of course, because Japan is a highly volcanic region, and visually lava and fire matches up perfectly with red philosopher's stones, with fiery rituals in underground caves, and with alchemical magic).

The emphasis on verticality in *Fullmetal Alchemist: The Sacred Star of Milos* has a narrative purpose, too: the philosopher's stone here (called 'the Star of Fresh Blood') is generated by the flow of blood thro' a vast series of brass tubes. It's truly grotesque, but in keeping with the notion of Hiromu Arakawa's that a power so great and sinister like a philosopher's stone can only be manufactured with an abhorrent sacrifice – that of humans. *Fullmetal Alchemist: The Sacred Star of Milos* re-stages the Holocaust, then, with the people of Milos as the victims. (It's a variation on the ending in the *manga*).

O

Often Ed and Al Elric are in the midst of the action, helping out, battling oppressors, chasing villains, etc. But just as often they put on their teenage sleuth hats, and pursue the mystery of Milos and the philosopher's stone (for example, scenes where the brothers investigate the towers of Milos, and the underground chambers. There's yet another church, and yet another hidden city under the surface). Also, the boys are there to offer the audience's views of events: Ed, in particular (and as usual) is the sceptical, doubting one. He and Al observe what the Milosian rebels are trying to do (re-establishing their 'holy land'), and finds it mis-guided, and founded on untruths.

In the important scene in the sacred chamber of the Milosian activists, which explores the morality and ethics of the struggles in the film, Ed Elric derides their goals of using a philosopher's stone to overthrow their oppressors in Creta and Amestris. For Ed, the Milosians' goal is flawed, and the means (using the philosopher's stone) is definitely wrong. Julia,

---

31 And they dump their garbage in the valley.

finding her views and ideas being rapidly eroded throughout the movie, is caught in the middle of the conflict. (The scene threatens to derail the movie, however: it's far too long and too static).

Here the *Fullmetal Alchemist* franchise is more sophisticated than your average action-adventure yarn, is insisting that, no, there are no quick and easy solutions to big political and social issues. You can't kill a bunch of people (the villains) and find yourself miraculously victorious, with all your problems vanquished. No – life is much more troublesome than that.

○

Fullmetal Alchemist: The Sacred Star of Milos resurrects the notion of tattoos and skin (of Scar and his brother): so Julia Crichton has part of an alchemical secret tattooed on her skin, and so does her brother (a vile sadomasochistic way of hiding a secret). The skin motif is also food for some Gothic horror moments: the villain, Melvin Voyager, for instance, rips off Ashleigh's face, so he can pass himself off as Julia's brother (so the real Ashleigh takes to wearing a white Phantom of the Opera mask). During the finale of *The Sacred Star of Milos*, there's blood flowing all over the place, as Voyager betrays and slaughters Milosian rebels, and skin's being ripped off bodies (Voyager has the Scar role and Zolf Kimbley from the TV series and *manga*).

Indeed, *Fullmetal Alchemist: The Sacred Star of Milos* is fantastically, grotesquely violent. During the creation of the philosopher's stone sequence, people are dying all over the place: Miranda is stabbed by Voyager, as he reveals his true colours. His Cretan aide meets the same fate. Miranda's blood. gushing from a wound, spills down a pipe which connects to others in Milos. This inaugurates a truly remarkable piece of animation and visualization – the production designers have certainly earned their pay in coming up with intricate machines, pipework, columns, towers and couplings to depict the fiendish and repulsive scheme of slaughtering whole squadrons of soldiers[32] in order to generate the necessary flow of blood to create just one (tiny) philosopher's stone. We see entire battalions of the soldiers falling to their doom in enormous bowls which guide and collect the rushing flow of blood.

It's one of the aspects of Japanese animation which goes way, way beyond anything in Western animation (or live-action): when blood flows in Japanese pop culture, it *really* flows! So *animé* Original Video Animations such as *Legend of the Overfiend* portray awesomely nasty rituals where women in fetish gear are sexually assaulted on a colossal, circular 'rape machine', while pipes suck our their life's essence – overseen by Nazis and the Führer himself in a castle near Berlin (all to summon up a dragon-sized god). Well, OK, *Fullmetal Alchemist* doesn't have naked women being raped, but it has everything else (including Hitlerian psychos).

Fullmetal Alchemist: The Sacred Star of Milos doesn't hold back on depicting super-violent scenes: the 2011 movie opens with the bloody

32 Unlike the ending of the *manga*, it is mainly soldiers who're used as fodder.

death of the parents, continues with many soldiers dying in the action sequence in act one, and, in one beat, a guy who's helping Ed Elric, Pedro (Kiyotaka Furushima), is killed right in front of him. *Fullmetal Alchemist: The Sacred Star of Milos*, however, does show the consequences of aggression: there is a moving funeral sequence, where the corpses of Pedro and others who've died in the conflicts are decorated with flowers, then cremated.

One of the challenges of *Fullmetal Alchemist: The Sacred Star of Milos* is giving everybody something to do: this is another movie with plenty of characters. Luckily, the 2011 movie keeps Ed and Al Elric in the foreground, as well as the two new main charas, Julia and Ashleigh Crichton. Unfortunately, altho' Winry, Hawkeye and Mustang turn up in Table City, they don't have much of significance to do, in the end. The finale, for instance, concerns the Elrics, Julia and Ashleigh. (Winry fixes Ed's automail arm – yet again! – but, with the focus on Julia, she has nothing much else to perform. And Winry is introduced rather lamely in act one, turning up unannounced in Mustang's office. Often the adapters of *Fullmetal Alchemist* don't know quite what to do with Winry. Mustang, meanwhile, helps to heal Julia's wound, and rounds up the errant militia in Milos, but there are no big action scenes for him).

O

The finale of *Fullmetal Alchemist: The Sacred Star of Milos* had Ed and Al battling the bad guys, aided by Julia Crichton. There are two characters in disguise – a man poses as Ashleigh Crichton, but he's really Melvin Voyager, a Cretan soldier (a.k.a. Atlas) intent on obtaining a philosopher's stone for himself. And, this being Japanese animation, some of the villains were not out-and-out villains (for instance, Julia's brother Ashleigh, thought to be dead, re-surfaces as Lieutenant Colonel Herschel, presiding over the military from atop a tower). Voyager has a moment of god-like arrogance during the lava-filled climax, talking about creating a new world using the philosopher's stone. Well, Ed's having none of that!, and he duels with Voyager, as does Julia. Injured and near-death, Julia uses the philosopher's stone she's ingested to save her brother Ashleigh (but sacrificing her leg in the process, aligning her with Ed). Julia thus manages to bring her brother Ashleigh back from the brink of (1) death and (2) evil.

The villain, meanwhile, is Melvin Voyager: after the Crichtons were murdered (in a grotesque scene, where the parents are strung up and their children see them (with their bodies seen reflected in pools of their blood)[33] – Julia, understandably, faints), he schemes to obtain a philosopher's stone for himself. So the finale of *Fullmetal Alchemist: The Sacred Star of Milos* combines the creation of the philosopher's stone with a rebellion by the Milosians to take back their land. Ashleigh/ Herschel, meanwhile, unleashes a flow of lava from a volcano, which adds a spectacular obstacle to the ones our heroes already face. (There are two villains, then, orchestrating a flow of red stuff in Table City – blood and

---

33 Recalling the murder of the Rockbells, Winry-chan's parents.

lava).[34]

The finale of *Fullmetal Alchemist: The Sacred Star of Milos* thus combines multiple battles, a lava flood encroaching upon the Milosians in the sunken valley, and our heroes trying to stop Melvin Voyager and Ashleigh/ Herschel. Out come the bolts of red lightning and the blue zigzags of numerous alchemical transformations, which are so much a part of the *Fullmetal Alchemist* franchise. Combined with abstract, 3-D cross-sections of the pipes of blood in Table City, a vigorous orchestra-'n'-choir score by Tara Iawashiro, and 1,000 channels of sound effects, the finale of *Fullmetal Alchemist: The Sacred Star of Milos* is certainly action-filled and vivid.

The visual effects animation is truly remarkable in *Fullmetal Alchemist: The Sacred Star of Milos*, on a par with anything in the history of Japanese animation. Even if there are no surprises whatsoever in the plotting, which follows the action-adventure model very closely (the producers wanted an *Indiana Jones*-style movie, and that's what they got), doesn't matter. The use of light and shadow, of high contrast, of flashed frames, of space and viewpoint, combines to make the duels in *Fullmetal Alchemist: The Sacred Star of Milos* some of the finest in recent animation. The filmmakers have got the action-adventure scenes of magical bolts of energy zinging back and forth between fierce, frowny participants down to a 'T', which, situated in the middle of the unstoppable flow of lava in the narrow valley (which provides the necessary countdown to disaster), combine to deliver a really exciting showdown.

Every *Fullmetal Alchemist* outing in *animé* is especially accomplished at going *all-out*, at providing *really* extreme action and spectacle.

O

In the end, however, *Fullmetal Alchemist: The Sacred Star of Milos* doesn't quite have the impact of either the first *Fullmetal Alchemist* movie (of 2005), or the two *Fullmetal Alchemist animé* series. Part of the problem is that we have already seen pretty much everything before. After all, *Fullmetal Alchemist: The Sacred Star of Milos* has to follow two long and incredible *animé* series (of 51 and 64 episodes). Perhaps if *The Sacred Star of Milos* had been released first, it would've impressed the audience much more.

On the down side, *Fullmetal Alchemist: The Sacred Star of Milos* has some patchy pacing. Not in the action scenes, which are, as one would expect from an animation team this talented, absolutely splendid. No, it's in the quieter scenes, the talky scenes, that *Fullmetal Alchemist: The Sacred Star of Milos* comes unstuck. The *dénouement* scenes, for instance, are too long and too talky (there are scenes where Mustang *et al* discuss the future of Milos, where the Elrics talk with Julia, where Julia talks with Vatanen (Yusaku Okura), the leader of the Milosian rebellion – way, way too much talk! Ten minutes of talk after the we've seen the big, loud action finale, plus our heroes Saving The World).

Also, the emotional catharsis doesn't come. Part of the problem is that

34 *Sacred Star* also complicates the finale by having the oppressed people of Milos staging a rebellion – another version of the ending of the *Fullmetal Alchemist* manga.

altho' Julia Crichton is changed, and her brother Ashleigh too, the Elrics aren't: they are the same as when they arrived in Table City. Ed speaks darkly of Julia's use of the philosopher's stone, and announces that they (the Elrics) will continue their search for answers (i.e., to regain their bodies).

The trouble with the finale of *Fullmetal Alchemist: The Sacred Star of Milos* is that it concentrates too much on the brother-sister relationship of Julia and Ashleigh. And, fine as they, they are *not* our heroes in the *Fullmetal Alchemist* franchise. Yes, we know they offer mirrors to our heroes, of sibling love, of the problems of familial relationships, and of using philosopher's stones to bring people back to life (Ed niggles over this issue – technically, Ashleigh wasn't quite dead).

The departure was announced at the start of this 2011 movie – which opened not with Ed and Al Elric, but with Julia and Ashleigh Crichton – so we knew, from the start, that *Fullmetal Alchemist: The Sacred Star of Milos* was going to be shifting the dramatic viewpoint slightly away from the Elrics and onto a new pair of kids (the *Fullmetal Alchemist* franchise has used other sibling pairs from time to time).

And, in the end, Julia C. is a rather smug, too-good character – and rather humourless (even when she's voiced by *animé* superstar Maaya Sakamoto). Give me Edward and Alphonse Elric any time!

03

THE *FULLMETAL ALCHEMIST* ORIGINAL VIDEO ANIMATIONS

A series of short Original Video Animations spun off *Fullmetal Alchemist* were produced by the same team as each *animé* series.

The first series Original Video Animations (*Hagane no Renkin-jutsushi: Premium Collection*, 2004) were directed by Seiji Mizushima, written by Shou Aikawa, with ani. dir. by Yoshiyuki Ito. Music: Michiru Oshima. Produced by Bones/ Aniplex/ Square Enix/ Mainichi Broadcasting System.

The O.V.A.s comprised *Alchemists vs. Homunculi*, *Kids*, *Reflections*, *Chibi Party* and *Live Action*.

• The 6 minute *Chibi Party* was set after the filming of the *Conquest of Shamballa* movie, featuring many of the best-known charas from the *Fullmetal Alchemist* universe in *chibi*/ super-deformed style. It was a humorous outing based in a restaurant, where the characters, appearing as actors in *Fullmetal Alchemist*, retire for the wrap party after a hard day's filming. There are jokes about the tyrannical director (which anyone who's worked in the TV industry can identify with!), the tiring day, the extras (often secretly scorned in showbiz by the production and the main actors), the costumes, Hawkeye deriding Mustang, Envy spoofing a diva, Lust and Scar as angry extras,[35] Gluttony eating people, etc (there's an open mic session, which Hawkeye commandeers. The characterization of Hawkeye as a bossy tycoon is excellent). A drunk and jealous Winry berates Edward for his bedroom scene with Noah in the *Shamballa* movie (culminating in Winry taking out her automail tools to attack Ed).

• *Kids* is a touching, largely dialogueless piece of about three minutes long. It features the great-great-grandchildren of Edward Elric: the two boys and a girl resemble Al and Ed and Winry very closely. They move thru a modern city,[36] young, happy, carefree: their destination is to visit their great-great-grandfather on his birthday – Edward E. (only

---

35 A great gag has Scar ripping off his trademark scar and using it as a throwing star to attack the Elrics.
36 That the city is distinctly Japanese confirms what we always knew: Amestris, the nation in *Fullmetal Alchemist*, is Japan.

glimpsed in profile, and looking like Hohenheim. He lives in a modern apartment block). A caption tells us that Ed was 100 in 2005. (The city contains several ads for *Fullmetal Alchemist* – a billboard for the series, *Fullmetal Alchemist* merchandize, etc. Some of the other modern-day charas resemble *Fullmetal Alchemist* characters).

• The *Seven Homunculi vs. State Alchemists* portrays a battle between the rivals in the *Fullmetal Alchemist* universe, overseen by Führer Bradley, Roy Mustang and the military. The Original Video Animation employs the gimmick of subjective camera to put the viewer into the position of a new recruit among the State Alchemists (which comes across as an interactive/ video game sort of device, which's in tune with one of the companies behind *Fullmetal Alchemist*, Square Enix).

The action is based around the finale of the first *Fullmetal Alchemist* series, in the underground lair of the homunculi, including the ballroom. Greed and Envy are prominent among the homunculi, and the Elrics and Mustang among the heroes. *Seven Homunculi vs. State Alchemists* is like an alternative take on the first series' finale episodes. The action gags are wild and rapid, so that *Seven Homunculi vs. State Alchemists* comes across as a climactic short film, as if you're watching all of the final episodes condensed into five minutes.

• *Reflections* was a lyrical musical montage featuring the Elric boys as children, focussing on their relationship with their mom. Some voiceover was added of the older Elrics remembering their past. *Reflections* concluded with the death and the funeral of the mother.

◆

For the second *Fullmetal Alchemist* series Original Video Animations, Hiroshi Ohnogi was writer, Yasuhiro Irie was director, and char. des. by Hiroki Kanno. Released: 2009.8.26.

The episodes were *The Blind Alchemist, Simple People, The Tale of Teacher,* and *Yet Another Man's Battlefield*.

The Original Video Animation episodes ranged from a few minutes to 14 or so minutes long. Ed and Al appeared in the first episode, *The Blind Alchemist,* and popped up in later episodes, which focussed on (1) Izumi Curtis (her famous, month-long, training session at Briggs Mountain, in the depths of Winter); (2) a brief, OTT *shojo* episode of Curtis's first meeting with her future husband, Sig; (3) Roy Mustang and Maes Hughes during the training days of their youth, and (4) later in the Ishbal rebellion; and (5) Winry and Liza Hawkeye (with Ed and Al returning to Resembool for more repairs).

The 2009 *Fullmetal Alchemist* Original Video Animations were on the whole light-hearted, containing spoofs of the characters, as well as send-ups of *animé* formats (the mock-serious opening credits of action-adventure movies, for instance). But the Roy Mustang/ Maes Hughes segment, with its topic of the Ishbal civil war, was much more serious – the subject is racial genocide, no less, and the Hawkeye-Rockbell episode confronted the issue that Liza has to kill people in her job as military sniper.

• *The Blind Alchemist* had the Elric brothers visiting a famed alchemist who lives in the plush surroundings of a Northern European mansion and garden. Once again the topic under discussion is that one close to the Elrics' hearts: human transmutation – bringing a dead child (Rosalie) back to life.

Doesn't work. Never does, does it? Nope.

The daughter of the family in *The Blind Alchemist* remains very dead – but is kept in a children's den as a skeleton, fully dressed, surrounded by heaps of cuddly toys (echoes of Mrs Bates in *Psycho*, and one of *anime's* major works, the *Magnetic Rose* sequence in *Memories*, 1995).[37] The family adopt an orphan (Emi) to act as Roselie in her stead. The cost of the human transmutation is multiple – for the alchemist, it's his sight.[38] The husband is also dead. The wife and mother lives on in an uneasy truce with fate.

Ed Elric gets the creepy picture of the rich family very quickly (and he's more unforgiving than Al, true to his personality, as we saw when he met the loser alchemist Shou Tucker). *The Blind Alchemist* is yet another instance in *anime* of people hanging onto the past, or being unable to escape the past, or unwilling to let go.

• In the Winry Rockbell and Liza Hawkeye episode (*Simple People*), the friendship between Hawkeye and Winry is uppermost, along with Ed repeatedly breaking his automail (Hawkeye has her hair long, emulating Winry, and Winry pierces her ears after seeing Hawkeye). The subtext is the unspoken romance between Winry and Ed, symbolized by the brother's gifts of earrings, plus the usual comical, argumentative outbursts.

• 18 year-old Izumi Curtis is the subject of *The Tale of Teacher*, taken largely from the *Fullmetal Alchemist* manga, relating Curtis's famous month-long survival ordeal in the snowy wastes near Briggs Fortress (which she subjects the Elric boys to, but on Jack Island). It's a story of surviving against the odds in a Hokkaido-like Winter, of snow, building fires, killing animals, and punching out the mountain guards from Briggs to raid their rations. Curtis, one of Arakawa-sensei's very favourite characters in *Fullmetal Alchemist*, emerges as a tough,[39] no-nonsense young woman who never gives up. Which makes the following skit, where Curtis meets her future husband, Sig, a welcome change of emphasis: now Curtis is a girlie girl in a *shojo manga* spoof.

• The story of the young (18 year-old) Roy Mustang, in *Yet Another Man's Battlefield*, depicted how he met Maes Hughes. The friendship is formed in a classic motif of *anime*: young soldiers. Training camp scenes showed the two youths dealing with the harsh regime, focussing on their encounter with macho racism, as a bunch of upper classmen set upon a lone Ishbalian at the military academy.

37 *Magnetic Rose* is an *anime* masterpiece, 43 or so minutes of pure genius. The opulence of the animation and imagery is rarely equalled in filmmaking, West or East. The filmmakers have thrown *everything* into the mix, and it works. *Magnetic Rose* is a hyper-dense, mega-layered animation, where every cut is crammed with incident, movement, colour, texture, light, shadow, visual effects and pure imagination.
38 The facial wound evokes Scar's famous scar.
39 Curtis takes out an adult bear as if it's nothing, and carries it back into town on her shoulder.

The bonding between the Isbalian and the Amestrisians is an important prelude to the second section of the Mustang-Hughes sequence, which portrayed the grim scenario of the Ishbal War. Now Hughes has to drag Mustang into the field, to perform his military duties as a State Alchemist. Where, inevitably, he encounters the Ishbalian he met at the military academy, resulting in Hughes killing the man as he attacks Mustang. Once again, Hughes expresses the practical, honest view of war: he wants to survive, to meet his girl (Gracia), and he doesn't waste time agonizing over the morality of warfare, so he does what is necessary to survive.

◆

FULLMETAL ALCHEMIST 4-KOMA.

As well as two major *animé* series and two big *animé* movies, there were other animated entries in the *Fullmetal Alchemist* franchise: some spin-off Original Video Animations (2009), and a series of short skits. The *Fullmetal Four-Panel Comic Theater* included sixteen short pieces comprising several shorter gags (most were 1.5 to 2.5 minutes long) in a comical, super-deformed style, using the notion of a theatrical performance as the frame. The skits parodied well-known scenes from both *animé* series (such as Roy Mustang's pomposity, for example, or Ling Yao's perpetual hunger). The approach had already been employed throughout both *Fullmetal Alchemist animé* series, and in the *manga* (Hiromu Arakawa appeared in the skits; no, not directly, but in her cow image).

Fullmetal Four-Panel Comic Theater drew on the 4-*koma* jokes that Himoru Arakawa included in the *Fullmetal Alchemist manga* (published at the back of the collected volumes). The sixteen short films added many elements and gags not in Arakawa's 4-*koma*. They followed the narrative spine of the *Fullmetal Alchemist* series.

04

FULLMETAL ALCHEMIST –
THE LIVE-ACTION MOVIES

Firstly, there is a mistaken assumption that animation is somehow inferior to live-action. And the mistake is applied to live-action remakes of animated works. Mamoru Hosoda (*Wolf Children, The Girl Who Leapt Through Time*) derides the whole concept of making live-action movies from animated movies:

> I have gotten asked if I want to turn any of my films into live action, but I simply think that's just meaningless... I actually do get frustrated about live action versions of animation because the general concept, probably, is that live action films are superior to animation. So by making a live action version, they think they are trying to improve the animated movie. No, that's not true. Or people think live action may be better for being accepted by a general audience. I don't think that's true. It's all about good stories, good movies.[40]

In addition, the live-action version wasn't a remake of a rubbish animated show, but of two masterpiece series.

Live-action versions of *animé* and *manga* tend to be very disappointing: *Ghost In the Shell, Appleseed, Alita: Battle Angel, Death Note,* and Arakawa's own *Silver Spoon.* (However, the Hong Kong action versions can be entertaining: *City Hunter, Wicked City, Initial D,* etc).

There is one way in which live performers can really enhance a comic or an *animé* – musical theatre. The live shows of *Bleach* and *Naruto,* for example, are great fun, with songs, dances, comedy, special effects, audience participation, etc. The ten or so *Rock Musical Bleach* shows in particular are remarkable (and worth tracking down).

○

The live-action version of *Fullmetal Alchemist* appeared in 2017.[41] Executive produced by Kazuya Hamana, Makoto Takahasi, Masami Takahashi, Keiichi Yoshizaki, Osamu Aranami, Julie Fujishima, Yoshiro

---

40 Hosoda in J. Slater-Williams, *The Skinny,* Oct 26, 2018.
41 Principal photography ran from May to August, 2016.

Hosono, Nobuo Miyazaki, Eiji Ohmura, Hajime Inoue, Atsuhiro Iwakami, Toshiaki Kawai and Katsuyoshi Matsura, plus seven line/ associated producers[42] for Oxybot/ Square Enix/ Netflix, released thru Warners in Nippon, scripted by Fumihiko Sori and Takeshi Miyamoto, directed by Fumihiko Sori, music by Reiji Kitazato, DP: Keiji Hashimoto, art dir. by Takeshi Shimizu, editing by Chieko Suzaki, and sound effects by Koji Kasamatsu. Released: Dec 1, 2017. 135 mins.

Visual fx houses for all three movies included Oxybot, Annex Digital, DigiCast, Sultamedia, Stealthworks, Omnibus, Zinou Pharmaceutics, Griot Groove, Padoga, Garyu, N-Design, Studio Picapixels, Crescent, Morie, Safe House, D/Visual, Finewave, Codelight, Raylight, Sequence U, Megalis and Mini Engine.

In the cast were: Atom Mizuishi as Alphonse Elric, Ryosuke Yamada as Edward Elric, Dean Fujioka as Roy Mustang, Fumiyo Kohinata as General Hakuro, Jun Kunimura as Dr. Tim Marcoh, Kanata Hongo as Envy, Kenjiro Ishimaru as Cornello, Misako Renbutsu as Riza Hawkeye, Natsuki Harada as Gracia Hughes, Ryuta Sato as Maes Hughes, Shinji Uchiyama as Gluttony, Tsubasa Honda as Winry Rockbell, Natsuna as Maria Ross, Yasuko Matsuyuki as Lust and Yo Oizumi as Shou Tucker.

Himoru Arakawa was delighted with the cast of the live-action version, from Ryosuke Yamada on down: 'it was a truly a magnificent cast', she said. Arakawa's attitude towards the live-action movie was positive: she was intrigued to see what the filmmakers would do with the comic. Instead of focussing on the differences between the *manga* and the movie, Arakawa recognized that an adaptation was a new work in itself ('an adaptation is a new challenge in the first place'). And of course one of the benefits of new adaptations is the new attention that the *manga* would receive.

The *Fullmetal Alchemist* live-action movie brings out the ethnic slant of Japanese cinema and television again: the principal cast was played by Japanese actors, but the films were partially filmed in Italy,[43] and were set in a vaguely European country (which is, of course, a fantasy version of Japan).

It's a wholly *Japanese* enterprise: the three productions filmed in Italy, but they hired Japanese extras to fill out the streets, characters bow to each other, they drink *saké* from saucers, and the street signs are in Japanese.

Most of *Fullmetal Alchemist* is drawn from the first volumes of the comic, but parts of the finale come from much later – the army of zombies, and the nefarious schemes of the military and the homunculi. Shou Tucker is brought back as a villain (who captures Al), and General Hakuro is an obstacle along with the homunculi.

There's no need to draw attention to the cuts made to Himoru Arakawa's comic in trimming down the story to a two-hour movie. The script made the usual changes to a long-running story (deletions,

---

42 No, I don't know why movies of recent times require *thirteen* executive producers! And seven more producers!

43 The production visited Volterra and Siena in Tuscany. Other locations included Tokyo, Kobe City and Wakayama City (the Porto Europe theme park at Wakayama Marina City was used).

combinations of characters and events, dialogue summaries of too-expensive scenes, etc).

○

The live-action adaptation of *Fullmetal Alchemist* suffered from many of the flaws of similar live-action versions made in Japan and aimed at a Japanese audience of popular *manga*: it followed a spectacular *animé* series (two series, in fact – and a couple of great movies, too); it didn't live up to the comic; it didn't capture the things we love about *Fullmetal Alchemist* (the characters, the story, the themes, the world, etc); it employed a similar tone and mood in too many scenes; it lacked a coherent and powerful cinematic style of its own; it sped thru the material – it's a 'greatest hits' version of *Fullmetal Alchemist*, but it's too hurried; it floundered under a too-low budget; and it squandered the possibilities of the original material.

This is *Fullmetal Alchemist* we're talking about!

This sort of material demands a stops-all-out approach to film-making. Instead, we were offered a watered-down, decidedly under-whelming interpretation of a scorchingly hot *manga*.

Rather than fiery Ed Elric tearing up the screen, we get a muted, polite teenager. Of course, Ed is impossible to cast – no 15 year-old actor can embody or play this character (but was Ryosuke Yamada really the best choice available in Japan in 2017?). The homunculi, meanwhile, should be a fearsome and creepy presence lurking in the shadows: the movie stumbled here, too. These are very lame adversaries, despite Arakawa-sensei offering all you need for scary opponents.[44]

In an effort to bump up the low female character count, Winry Rockbell comes along for the adventures with the lads – but she has very little to do other than to stand there, wring her hands and react (fear, awe, surprise, etc).

Himoru Arakawa conceived the *manga* of *Fullmetal Alchemist* as a rollicking fantasy adventure outing – she is a fan of *Star Wars* and *Indiana Jones*. The two animated series delivered that but, alas, the live-action version of *Fullmetal Alchemist* interprets the material as a ponderous, stodgy drama about angst-ridden teenagers. The *manga* is filled with slambang action in pretty much every chapter – it's a *shonen manga*, and an action *manga*, after all. But the movie, following the kids' botched rite and the exciting monster fight in Liore (a.k.a. Reole) in act one, gets bogged down with repetitious scenes of people talking in rooms.

The climax of *Fullmetal Alchemist* is a face-off between the heroes and the homunculi (chiefly, Lust and Envy). It is very disappointing, if you know the *Fullmetal Alchemist animé*, and doesn't resolve the key issues (leaving a 'To Be Continued' hanging in the air. But there's little desire to see any more of this particular take on the *Fullmetal Alchemist manga*).

Style-wise, *Fullmetal Alchemist* lacked the grandeur and spectacle of Himoru Arakawa's astonishing *manga*. Arakawa-sensei paints *big* on a

---

44 Lust, who should be an insanely murderous dominatrix with a va-va-voom body, is played like a sorceress from a cheap, *jidai geki* TV show, and Envy, the astonishingly over-the-top diva and super-cruel fiend of the *manga*, is frustratingly pathetic.

huge canvas, but the movie didn't deliver that. Altho' we can look at pretty Italian towns[45] for hours on end, this certainly wasn't the richly imagined world that Arakawa created. (The budget looked stretched everywhere, with art director Takeshi Shimizu struggling to conjure up a vast alternative universe with only 20 Yen to spend).[46]

It's a movie, but it looks like a made-for-TV drama. This happens so often when Japanese *anime* are adapted – the incredible visuals that the *mangaka* slaved over are jettisoned. Many theatrically-released movies these days are filmed using digital video systems; but they *look* like films made celluloid, because the filmmakers carefully emulate the appearance of celluloid. Many Japanese movies don't – they look like TV video movies. Similarly, the acting style is completely wrong – it's TV soap opera acting, which brings everything down to the level of just any other TV show.

The direction of the actors is poor: the production has sets and costumes and lighting and actors and all (i.e., everything it needs), but it just doesn't come alive. The performers look as if they're going thru the motions of clocking off 2 pages of the script per day. Passion doesn't come from actors yelling from time to time. A live-action version of material as good as *Fullmetal Alchemist* should be burning off the screen, but not even Colonel Mustang's flame alchemy can ignite this baby.

★

Two sequels to the 2017 film appeared in 2022: *Fullmetal Alchemist: The Revenge of Scar* (*Hagane no Renkinjutsushi: Kanketsu-hen – Fukushusha Scar*, 2022) was prod. by Ryuji Abe, Juli Fujishima, Kazuya Hamana, Yoshiro Hosono, Hiroyuki Ikeda, Atsuhiro Iwakami, Kei Morita, Shinji Nakano, Masami Takahashi, Mitsuru Uda and Yumiko Yoshihara, scripted by Fumihiko Sori and Takeshi Miyamoto and dir. by Sori. Released: May 20, 2022. 125 mins.

Fullmetal Alchemist: Final Transmutation (*Hagane no Renkinjutsuschi: Kanketsu-hen – Seigo no Rensei*, 2022) shared the same credits. Released: June 24, 2022. 142 mins.

Ryosuke Yamada was back as Ed Elric, with Atom Mizuishi as Alphonse, Dean Fujioka as Col. Mustang and Tsubasa Honda as Winry Rockbell. Among the new cast in the two films of 2022 were Mackenyu Arat as Scar,[47] Seiyo Uchino as Hohenheim, Toshio Kakei as Fuu, Jun Fubuki as Pinako, Hiroshi Tachi as the Führer, Yuta Hiraok as Miles, Haruchi Ryoga as Izumi, Tomomi Maruyama as Buccaneer, Chiaki Kuriyama as Major Armstrong, Yuina Kuroshima as Lan Fan, and Keisuke Watanabe as Ling Yao.

The two *Fullmetal Alchemist* sequel movies followed the example of

---

45 Curiously empty of all people – not the Italy we know!

46 Every room looked like all of the modern items had been carried outside for a day, to be replaced by the too few props that the budget allowed for. This look occurs all the time in productions battling a low budget – locations are hired, but the budget doesn't stretch to dressing and lighting them fully.

47 The characterization of Scar is a gift to an actor in live-action. He's tormented, he's driven, he's charismatic, and he's very dangerous. For much of the first sequel, *Fullmetal Alchemist: The Revenge of Scar*, the Ishbalian assassin is a major obstacle and antagonist. But Mackenyu Arata failed to come up to the mark.

the first film, and made the same kind of excisions, additions, and combinations of the narrative. As with the first installment, there is little excitement to compel here, and the movies are pushing against the budget throughout.

Fullmetal Alchemist: Conqueror
of Shamballa (2005).

Fullmetal Alchemist: The Sacred Star of Milos (2011),
this page and over.

Fullmetal Alchemist, live-action movie (2017).

FILMOGRAPHY

FULLMETAL ALCHEMIST

FIRST SERIES. 2003-2004. 51 episodes.

CREW

Production – Aniplex/ Bones/ Mainichi Broadcasting System/ Square Enix
Broadcaster – Animax, Bandai Channel, Mainichi Broadcasting System, Tokyo Broadcasting System
Executive producers – Hideo Katsumata, Kouji Taguchi, Seiji Takeda
Producers – Hiro Maruyama, Masahiko Minami, Ryo Oyama
Director – Seiji Mizushima
Original creator – Hiromu Arakawa
Chief writer – Shou Aikawa
Written by Akatsuki Yamatoya, Aya Yoshinaga, Jun Ishikawa, Katsuhiko Takayama, Manabu Ishikawa, Natsuko Takahashi, and Toshiki Inoue
Director of Photography – Susumu Fukushi and Toru Fukushi
Editing – Hiroaki Itabe (J Film)
Music – Michiru Oshima
Music Production – Aniplex
Character Design – Yoshiyuki Ito
Art Director – Kazuyuki Hashimoto
Art Design – Hideo Narita
Additional Production Design – Takefumi Anzai
Animation – Studio Bones
Background Art – Green and Kusanagi
Paint – Asahi Production
Color Coordination – Shihoko Nakayama
Sound Director – Masafumi Mima
Recording Studio – Studio Aoi
Sound Effects – Soundbox
Sound Production – Techno Sound

VOICE CAST
(Main characters only)

Rie Kugimiya – Alphonse Elric
Romi Pak – Edward Elric
Masashi Ebara – Hohenheim Elric
Megumi Toyoguchi – Winry Rockbell
Houko Kuwashima – Rose Tomas

Michiko Neya – Liza Hawkeye
Miyoko Asou – Pinako Rockbell
Toru Ohkawa – Roy Mustang
Keiji Fujiwara – Maes Hughes
Kenji Utsumi – Alex Armstrong
Hidekatsu Shibata – Fuhrer King Bradley and Pride
Junichi Suwabe – Greed
Nana Mizuki – Wrath
Mayumi Yamaguchi – Envy
Yuuko Satou – Lust
Yasuhiro Takato – Gluttony
Yoshino Takamori – Juliet Douglas/ Sloth, and Trisha Elric
Yumi Kakazu – Lyra
Makoto Nagai – Shou Tucker
Naomi Wakabayashi – Sheska
Ryotaro Okiayu – Scar
Shoko Tsuda – Izumi Curtis
Asami Mukaidono – Bradley's Wife
Daisuke Gouri – Dominique
Eriko Kawasaki – Rick
Jin Horikawa – General Hakuro
Kazue Komiya – Revy
Kazuki Yao – Lieutenant Yoki
Kentarou Itou – Barry The Chopper
Kinryuu Arimoto – Priest Cornello
Kotono Mitsuishi – Gracia Hughes
Kouji Ishii – Baldo
Kouji Totani – Tim Marcoh
Kousuke Okano – Russell Tringham
Kyoko Hikami – Paninya
Makoto Tsumura – Selim
Masaaki Tsukada – General
Masane Tsukayama – Karl Haushofer
Masao Harada – Denny Brosh
Mayumi Yoshida – Elicia Hughes
Miho Shiraishi – Clara/ Psiren
Minako Arakawa – Fletcher Tringham
Mitsuaki Madono – Cain Furey
Mitsuki Saiga – Maria Ross
Motoko Kumai – Elisa
Nobuyuki Furuta – Lemack
Rintarou Nishi – Wilson
Romi Pak – Alex Armstrong's mother
Rie Kugimiya – Kathleen Armstrong
Rumi Kasahara – Martel
Rumi Ochiai – Marin's Mama
Satomi Koorogi – Nina Tucker
Seiji Sasaki – Sig Curtis
Shin Aomori – Basque Grand
Sho Hayami – Frank Archer
Takaya Hashi – Majhal
Takayuki Godai – Magwall
Takehito Koyasu – Lujon
Tetsu Shiratori – Cain Furey
Tomoyuki Shimura – Heyman Breda
Tomoko Kawakami – Kayal

Toshihiko Seki – Belshio
Youji Ueda – Agohige
Yuji Ueda – Zolf Kimbley
Yuriko Yamaguchi – Sara Rockbell
Yuu Mizushima – Scar's Brother

FULLMETAL ALCHEMIST

SECOND SERIES. 2009. 64 episodes.

CREW

Production – Aniplex/ Bones/ Mainichi Broadcasting System/ Square Enix
Broadcaster – Animax, Bandai Channel, Mainichi Broadcasting System and
T.B.S.
Producers – Hiro Maruyama, Nobuyuki Kurashige, Noritomo Yonai and Ryo
Oyama
Original creator – Hiromu Arakawa
Director – Yasuhiro Irie
Chief writer – Hiroshi Ohnogi
Written by Michihiro Tsuchiya, Seishi Minakami, Shôtarô Suga, Yoneki
Tsumura
Music – Akira Senju
Character Design – Hiroki Kanno
Art Director – Takeshi Satou
Mechanical Design – Masahisa Suzuki
Art Design – Kazushige Kanehira
Sound Director – Masafumi Mima
Action Animation Director – Jun Shibata
Color Design – Fusako Nakao
Guest Character Design – Mitsuyasu Takekoshi, Naomi Kaneda
Sound Production – Techno Sound
Special Effects – Masataka Ikegami, Satomi Ryukaku

VOICE CAST
(Main characters only)

Romi Park – Edward Elric
Rie Kugimiya – Alphonse Elric
Iemasa Kayumi – Father and the Narrator
Megumi Takamoto – Winry Rockbell
Minami Takayama – Envy
Shinichiro Miki – Roy Mustang
Unshou Ishizuka – Van Hohenheim
Ai Satou – Mrs. Bradley
Akemi Okamura – Paninya
Anri Katsu – Dolcetto
Atsuki Tani – Berthold Hawkeye
Biichi Satou – Heyman Breda
Chie Satou – Grandma
Chika Fujimura – Sheska
Dai Matsumoto – Slicer (Older brother)
Kenji Nojima – Slicer (Younger brother)
Daisuke Namikawa – Van Hohenheim (Young)
Fumihiko Tachiki – Sloth
Fumiko Orikasa – Liza Hawkeye
Hidekatsu Shibata – King Bradley
Hiroyuki Yoshino – Zolf Kimbley
Kaori Nazuka – Maria Ross

Katsuhisa Houki – Raven
Katsunosuke Hori – Fuu
Kazuki Yao – Yoki
Kazuya Nakai – Miles
Keiji Fujiwara – Maes Hughes
Tomoe Hanba – Gracia Hughes
Misato Fukuen – Elicia Hughes
Kenji Hamada – Barry the Chopper and Vato Falman
Hideyuki Umezu – Barry the Chopper (armor body)
Kenji Utsumi – Alex Armstrong
Kenta Miyake – Scar
Kikuko Inoue – Lust
Yuko Sanpei – Pride and Selim
Kinryuu Arimoto – Knox
Kiyoyuki Yanada – Henschel
Koichi Yamadera – Isaac
Mai Goto – Mei Chang
Makoto Nagai – Shou Tucker
Mamoru Miyano – Ling Yao
Masao Komaya – Bose
Masayuki Omoro – Tim Marcoh
Masayuki Shouji – Damiano
Mitsuru Ogata – Mick
Miyoko Asou – Pinako Rockbell
Nana Mizuki – Lan Fan
Naomi Shindoh – Rebecca Catalina
Noriko Uemura – Shan
Rokuro Naya – Grumman
Romi Park – Mrs. Armstrong
Ryûzaburô Ôtomo – Buccaneer
Satsuki Yukino – Rose
Sayuri – Satera
Shoko Tsuda – Izumi Curtis
Seiji Sasaki – Sig Curtis
Seizo Katou – Cornello
Shin Aomori – Basque Grand
Shinpachi Tsuji – Heinkel
Shozo Iizuka – Dominic
Shuuhei Sakaguchi – Mason
Sumire Morohoshi – Nina Tucker
Takako Honda – Martel
Takanori Hoshino – Gustav
Takehito Koyasu – Scar's Brother
Takkou Ishimori – the King of Xerxes
Tetsu Shiratori – Gluttony and Han
Tetsuya Kakihara – Cain Furey
Tokuyoshi Kawashima – Ridel
Tora Take – General Hakuro
Yoko Soumi – Olivier Mira Armstrong
Yoshino Takamori – Trisha Elric
Youko Matsuoka – Madam Christmas
Yuichi Nakamura – Greed
Yuji Ueda – Bido and Jean Havoc
Yuuki Hayashi – Denny Brosh
Yuri Amano – Sara Rockbell
Yuzuru Fujimoto – Scar's Master

FULLMETAL ALCHEMIST: CONQUEROR OF SHAMBALLA

2005. 105 minutes.

CREW

Production – Anime Film/ Aniplex/ Buyu/ Dentsu Inc./ Falcon Inc./, Mainichi Broadcasting System/ Production I.G./ R.I.C./ Shochiku Co., Ltd/ Square Enix/ Studio Elle/ Studio Wood/ Trans Arts Co.
Producers – Arimasa Okada, Haruhito Yamazaki, Hiro Maruyama, Kenji Komatsu, Masahiko Minami, Nobuyuki Kurashige, Ryo Oyama, Seiji Takeda, Tsuyoshi Yoshida and Yukio Yoshimura
Director – Seiji Mizushima
Script – Shou Aikawa
Key Animator – Yashuhiro Kato
Animation Director – Hiroshi Osaka
Art dDrector – Kazuo Ogura
Art Design – Hideyasu Narita
Character Designer – Yoshiyuki Ito
Mechanical Design – Jin Fukuchi
3D Director – Hiroaki Matsuura
Sound Director – Masafumi Mima
Music – Michiru Ôshima, Hirohito Shinohara and Tadahito Kimura
Editing – Hiroaki Itabi
DP – Susumu Fukushi
Color Design – Shihoko Nakayama
Backgrounds – Studio Bones, Kusanagi, Moon Flower and Studio Fuga

VOICE CAST
(Main characters only)

Rie Kugimiya – Alphonse Elric
Romi Park – Edward Elric
Hidekatsu Shibata – Mabuse/ Fritz Lang
Kazuko Katou – Dietlinde Eckart
Kenji Utsumi – Alex Armstrong
Masane Tsukayama – Karl Haushofer
Megumi Toyoguchi – Winry Rockbell
Michiko Neya – Liza Hawkeye
Miyuu Sawai – Noah
Rikiya Koyama – Rudolf Hess
Shun Oguri – Alphonse Heiderich
Toru Ohkawa – Roy Mustang
Atsushi Kakehashi – Better
Eiji Miyashita – Munich Soldier
Keiji Fujiwara – Officer Hughes
Kotono Mitsuishi – Gracia
Keiji Hirai – Munich Soldier
Houko Kuwashima – Rose Tomas
Makoto Nagai – Slave Trader
Masao Harada – Denny Brosh
Masashi Ebara – Hohenheim Elric

Mayumi Yamaguchi – Envy/ Dragon
Mitsuki Saiga – Maria Ross
Miyoko Asou – Pinako Rockbell
Nana Mizuki – Wrath
Naomi Wakabayashi – Sheska
Seiji Sasaki – Sig Curtis
Shoko Tsuda – Izumi Curtis
Takehiro Murozono – Vato Falman
Tetsu Shiratori – Cain Fuery
Tomohisa Asou – Liore Bartender
Tomoyuki Shimura – Heyman Breda
Toshio Furukawa – Erik Jan Hanussen
Unsho Ishizuka – Huskisson
Yasuhiro Takato – Gluttony
Yasunori Matsumoto – Jean Havoc
Yoko Nishino – College Student
Sayuri – Gypsy
Yuka Komatsu – Gypsy
Yumi Kakazu – Actress

FULLMETAL ALCHEMIST: THE SACRED STAR OF MILOS

2011. 110 minutes.

CREW

Production – Aniplex/ Bones/ Dentsu Inc./ Mainichi Broadcasting System/ Shochiku Co., Ltd/ Square Enix/ T.B.S.
Director – Kazuya Murata
Original creator – Hiromu Arakawa
Screenplay – Yoichi Shimpo
Producers – Arimasa Okada, Fumi Teranishi, Hiro Maruyama, Masahiko Minami, Nobuyuki Kurashige, Ryo Oyama and Shin Furukawa
Storyboard – Kazuya Murata
Unit Director – Shingo Natsume
Music – Taro Iwashiro
Character Design – Kenichi Konishi
Art Directors – Kazuo Ogura and Tomoaki Okada
Chief Animation Director – Kenichi Konishi
Sound Director – Masafumi Mima
Mechanical Design – Shinji Aramaki
3D Director – Koki Ota
Color Design – Fumiko Numahata
Editing – Kumiko Sakamoto
Director of Photography – Yoshiyuki Takei
Background Art – Basara and Kusanagi

VOICE CAST
(Main characters only)

Rie Kugimiya – Alphonse Elric
Romi Park – Edward Elric
Toshiyuki Morikawa – Melvin Voyager and Atlas
Maaya Sakamoto – Julia Crichton
Fumiko Orikasa – Liza Hawkeye
Hidenobu Kiuchi – Ashleigh Crichton
Kenji Utsumi – Alex Armstrong
Megumi Takamoto – Winry Rockbell
Sakiko Tamagawa – Miranda
Shinichiro Miki – Roy Mustang
Atsuko Tanaka – Mrs. Crichton
Biichi Satou – Heyman Breda
Gô Shinomiya – Elderly Gentleman
Hidenobu Kiuchi – Lieutenant Colonel Hershel
Hideyuki Umezu – Peter Soyuz
Hisao Egawa – Sizzler
Kensuke Satou – Cretan Officer
Kiyotaka Furushima – Pedro
Kouji Ishii – Graz
Kousuke Takaguchi – Warden
Minami Tanaka – Train Station Announcer
Nao Toyama – Karina
Nobuyuki Kobushi – Engineer

Ryohei Kimura – Ashleigh Crichton (young)
Ryuichi Kosugi – Santos
Shinji Kawada – Tony
Takanori Hoshino – Alan
Takashi Yoshida – Carlos
Tsuguo Mogami – Wolf Chimera
Yuki Hayashi – Wolf Chimera 2

FULLMETAL ALCHEMIST (LIVE-ACTION)

2017. 135 minutes.

CREW

Production – Oxybot/ Square Enix/ Netflix
Executive producers – Kazuya Hamana, Makoto Takahasi, Masami Takahashi, Keiichi Yoshizaki, Osamu Aranami, Julie Fujishima, Yoshiro Hosono, Nobuo Miyazaki, Eiji Ohmura, Hajime Inoue, Atsuhiro Iwakami, Toshiaki Kawai and Katsuyoshi Matsura
Director – Fumihiko Sori
Script – Fumihiko Sori and Takeshi Miyamoto
Original creator – Hiromu Arakawa
Music – Reiji Kitazato
DP – Keiji Hashimoto
Editing – Chieko Suzaki
Art Director – Takeshi Shimizu
Sound Effects – Koji Kasamatsu
Visual Effects – Oxybot, Pagoda, Stealthworks, Sultamedia, Garyu, Zinou Pharmaceutics, Griot Groove/ Animaroid, Omnibus Japan, Mozoo

CAST

Atom Mizuishi – Alphonse Elric
Ryosuke Yamada – Edward Elric
Dean Fujioka – Roy Mustang
Fumiyo Kohinata – General Hakuro
Jun Kunimura – Dr. Tim Marcoh
Kanata Hongo – Envy
Kenjiro Ishimaru – Cornello
Misako Renbutsu – Liza Hawkeye
Natsuki Harada – Gracia Hughes
Ryuta Sato – Maes Hughes
Natsuna – Maria Ross
Shinji Uchiyama – Gluttony
Tsubasa Honda – Winry Rockbell
Yasuko Matsuyuki – Lust
Yo Oizumi – Shou Tucker

FULLMETAL ALCHEMIST: THE REVENGE OF SCAR

2022. 125 minutes.

CREW

Executive producers – Ryuji Abe, Juli Fujishima, Kazuya Hamana, Yoshiro Hosono, Hiroyuki Ikeda, Atsuhiro Iwakami, Kei Morita, Shinji Nakano, Masami Takahashi, Mitsuru Uda and Yumiko Yoshihara

Scripted by Fumihiko Sori and Takeshi Miyamoto
Director – Fumihiko Sori
Music – Rejiji Kitasato, Yasuhiro Maeda and Tetsuya Takahashi
DP – Keiji Hashimoto
Editing – Chieko Suzaki
Art Director – Takeshi Shimizu
Set Decoration – Mami Ishida and Takeshi Iwai
Costumes – Rie Nishihara
Casting – Jun Kanaizuka and Eri Nagao
Sound Designer – Koji Kasamatsu
Visual Effects – Sultameda, Annex Digital, Megalis, Griot Groove/ Animaroid, Omnibus Japan, N- Design, Zinou Pharmaceutics, Oxybot, Modeling Bros., Pica-pixels, Mini Engine, Crescent, Morie, Finewave, Codelight, Rayliught, Pagoda, C.G.S. Lab, Newpot, DigiCast, D/Visual

CAST

Atom Mizuishi – Alphonse Elric
Ryosuke Yamada – Edward Elric
Dean Fujioka – Roy Mustang
Misako Renbutsu – Liza Hawkeye
Kanata Hongo – Envy
Yuina Kuroshiima – Lan Fan
Keisuke Watanabe – Ling Yao
Kokoro Terada – Selim
Shinji Uchiyama – Gluttony
Monroe Ron – Mei CHang

FULLMETAL ALCHEMIST: FINAL TRANSMUTATION

2022. 142 minutes.

Credits same as above.

HIMORU ARAKAWA

MANGA WORKS

Stray Dog, Monthly Shonen Gangen/ Square Enix, 1999
Ghost Demons of Shanghai (Shanghai Yomakikai), Monthly Shonen Gangen, 2000
Fullmetal Alchemist (Hagane no Renkinjutsushi), Monthly Shonen Gangen, 2001-2010
Fullmetal Alchemist, VIZ Media, 2005
Raiden 18, 2005-2013
A Bat In Blue Sky (Soten no Komori), 2006
Hero Tales (Jushin Enbu), Gangen Powered/ Square Enix, 2006–2010
Noble Farmer (Hyakusho Kizoku), 2006, *Wings*
Silver Spoon (Gin no Saji), Weekly Shonen Sunday/ Shogakugan, 2011-2019
The Heroic Legend of Arslan (Arusuran Senki), Bessatsu Shonen Magazine/ Kodansha, 2013–
Daemons of the Shadow Realm, Square Enix, 2021-

BIBLIOGRAPHY

OTHERS

Animage. *The Art of Japanese Animation*, Tokuma Shoten, 1988-89
—. *Best of Animage*, Tokuma Shoten, 1998
J. Beck, ed. *Animation Art*, Flame Tree Publishing, London, 2004
D. Bell & B. Kennedy, eds. *The Cybercultures Reader*, Routledge, 2000
E. Bell *et al*, eds. *From Mouse To Mermaid: The Politics of Film, Gender and Culture*,
    Indiana University Press, Bloomington, IN, 1995
J. Berndt, ed. *Global Manga Studies*, Seika University International Manga Research
    Center, Kyoto, 2010
C. Bloom, ed. *Gothic Horror*, Macmillan, 1998
D. Bordwell & K. Thompson. *Film Art: An Introduction*, McGraw-Hill Publishing Company,
    New York, NY, 1979
—. *Narration In the Fiction Film*, Routledge, London, 1988
—. *The Way Hollywood Tells It*, University of California Press, Berkeley, CA, 2006
F. Botting. *Gothic*, Routledge, 1996
—. *Sex, Machines and Navels: Fiction, Fantasy and History In the Future Present*,
    Manchester University Press, Manchester, 1999
J. Bower, ed. *The Cinema of Japan and Korea*, Wallflower Press, London, 2004
S. Brewster *et al*, eds. *Inhuman Reflections: Thinking the Limits of the Human*, Manchester
    University Press, Manchester, 2000
P. Brophy, ed. *Kaboom! Explosive Animation From America and Japan*, Museum of
    Contemporary Art, Sydney, 1994
S. Bukatman. *Terminal Identity: The Virtual Subject In Postmodern Science Fiction*, Duke
    University Press, Durham, NC, 1993
J. Butler. *Gender Trouble: Feminism and the Subversion of Identity* , Routledge, 1990
—. & J.W. Scott, eds. *Feminists Theorise the Political*, Routledge, 1992
—. *Bodies That Matter*, Routledge, 1993
D. Cartmell *et al*, eds. *Alien Identities: Exploring Differences In Film and Fiction*, Pluto, 1999
D. Cavallaro. *The Cinema of Mamoru Oshii: Fantasy, Technology and Politics*, McFarland &
    Company, 2006
—. *The Animé Art of Hayao Miyazaki*, McFarland, Jefferson, NC, 2006
C. Chatrian & G. Paganelli, *Manga Impact!*, Phaidon, London, 2010
Tom Chetwyd. *A Dictionary of Symbols*, Collins, London, 1982
J.E. Cirlot. *A Dictionary of Symbols*, Routledge, London, 1981
J. Clarke. *Animated Films*, Virgin, London, 2007
J. Clements & H. McCarthy. *The Animé Encyclopedia*, Stone Bridge Press, Berkeley, CA,
    2001/ 2006/ 2015
—. *The Development of the U.K. Anime and Manga Market*, Muramasa Industries, London,
    2003
—. *Schoolgirl Milky Crisis*, Titan Books, London, 2009
—. *Anime: A History*, British Film Institute, London, 2013
C. Clover. *Men, Women and Chain Saws: Gender In the Modern Horror Film*, Princeton
    University Press, N.J., 1992
J. Collins *et al*, eds. *Film Theory Goes To the Movies*, Routledge, N.Y., 1993
I. Condry. *The Soul of Anime*, Duke University Press, Durham, NC, 2013
D.A. Cook. *A History of Narrative Film*, W.W. Norton, New York, NY, 1981, 1990, 1996

B. Creed. *The Monstrous-Feminine*, Routledge, 1993

C. Degli-Esposti, ed. *Postmodernism In the Cinema*, Berghahn Books, N.Y., 1998

C. Desjardins. *Outlaw Masters of Japanese Film*, I.B. Tauris, London, 2005

J. Donald, ed. *Fantasy and the Cinema*, British Film Institute, London, 1989

P. Drazen. *Animé Explosion*, Stone Bridge Press, Berkeley, CA, 2003

Mircea Eliade. *Shamanism: Archaic Techniques of Ecstasy*, Princeton University Press, Princeton, NJ, 1972

—. *Myths, Dreams and Mysteries*, Harper & Row, New York, NY, 1975

—. *From Primitives To Zen: A Sourcebook*, Collins, London, 1977

—. *The Forge and the Crucible*, tr. Stephen Corrin, University of Chicago Press 1978

—. *Ordeal By Labyrinth*, University of Chicago Press, Chicago, IL, 1984

—. *Symbolism, the Sacred and the Arts*, Crossroad, New York, NY, 1985

Johannes Fabricus: *Alchemy: The Medieval Alchemists and Their Royal Art*, Aquarian Press, London, 1989

George Ferguson. *Signs and Symbols In Christian Art*, Oxford University Press, Oxford, 1961

J. Ferguson: *An Illustrated Encyclopaedia of Mysticism*, Thames & Hudson, London, 1976

D. Fingeroth. *The Rough Guide To Graphic Novels*, Rough Guides, 2008

H. Garcia. *A Geek In Japan*, Tuttle, North Clarendon, VT, 2011

Fred Gettings. *The Hidden Art: A Study of the Occult Symbolism in Art*, Studio Vista, 1978

P.C. Gibson & R. Gibson, eds. *Dirty Looks: Women, Pornography, Power*, British Film Institute, 1993

J. Goodwin, ed. *Perspectives On Akira Kurosawa*, G.K. Hall, Boston, MA, 1994

B.K. Grant, ed. *Planks of Reason: Essays On the Horror Film*, Scarecrow Press, N.J., 1984

—. ed. *The Dread of Difference: Gender and the Horror Film*, University of Texas Press, Austin, 1996

P. Gravett. *Manga*, L. King, London, 2004

—. ed. *1001 Comics You Must Read Before You Die*, Cassell, London, 2011

E. Grosz. *Sexual Subversions*, Allen & Unwin, 1989

—. *Volatile Bodies*, Indiana University Press, Bloomington, 1994

—. *Space, Time and Perversion*, Routledge, 1995

J. Halberstam. *Skin Shows: Gothic Horror and the Technology of Monsters*, Duke University Press, Durham, NC, 1995

James Hall. *A Dictionary of Subjects and Symbols In Art*, John Murray, 1984

D. Haraway. "A Manifesto For Cyborgs", *Socialist Review*, 15, 2, 1985

—. *Primate Visions: Gender, Race and Nature In the World of Modern Science*, Routledge, 1989

—. *Simians, Cyborgs, and Women*, Routledge, 1991

E.R. Helford, ed. *Fantasy Girls: Gender In the New Universe of Science Fiction and Fantasy TV*, Rowman & Littlefield, Lanham, MD, 2000

H. Hitoshi. *Mecha World*, in *Appleseed Databook*, 1990

Tze-yue Hu. *Frames of Anime*, Hong Kong University Press, HK, 2010

J. Hunter. *Eros In Hell: Sex, Blood and Madness In Japanese Cinema*, Creation Books, London, 1998

C.G. Jung. *Mysterium Coniunctionis*, Routledge & Kegan Paul, London, 1955

—. *Memories, Dreams, Reflections*, Collins, 1967

—. *Psychology and Religion: East and West*, Routledge & Kegan Paul 1977

E. Ann Kaplan, ed. *Psychoanalysis and Cinema*, Routledge, 1990

B.F. Kawin. *Mindscreen: Bergman, Godard and First-Person Film*, Princeton University Press, N.J., 1978

—. *How Movies Work*, Macmillan, N.Y., 1987

R. Keith. *Japanamerica*, Palgrave Macmillan, London, 2007

Sharon Kinsella. *Adult Manga*, University of Hawaii Press, Honolulu, 2002

P. Kramer. *The Big Picture: Hollywood Cinema From Star Wars To Titanic*, British Film Institute, 2001

J. Kristeva. *Desire In Language: A Semiotic Approach To Literature and Art*, ed. L.S. Roudiez, tr. T. Gora *et al*, Blackwell, Oxford, 1982

—. *Powers of Horror: An Essay On Abjection*, tr. L.S. Roudiez, Columbia University Press, N.Y., 1982

—. *The Kristeva Reader*, ed. T. Moi, Blackwell, Oxford, 1986

—. *Tales of Love*, tr. L.S. Roudiez, Columbia University Press, N.Y., 1987

—. *Black Sun: Depression and Melancholy*, tr. L.S. Roudiez, Columbia University Press, N.Y., 1989

—. *Strangers to Ourselves*, tr. L.S. Roudiez, Harvester Wheatsheaf, 1991

A. Kuhn, ed. *Alien Zone: Cultural Theory and Contemporary Science Fiction*, Verso, London, 1990

—. ed. *Alien Zone 2*, Verso, London, 1999

F. Ladd & H. Deneroff. *Astro Boy and Anime Come To the Americas*, McFarland, Jefferson, NC, 2009

T. Lamare. *The Anime Machine*, University of Minnesota Press, Minneapolis, MN, 2009

T. Ledoux & D. Ranney. *The Complete Animé Guide*, Tiger Mountain Press, Washington, DC, 1997

—. ed. *Anime Interviews*, Cadence Books, San Francisco, CA, 1997

T. Lehmann. *Manga: Masters of the Art*, HarperCollins, London, 2005

J. Lent, ed. *Animation in Asia and the Pacific*, John Libbey, 2001

A. Levi. *Samurai From Outer Space: Understanding Japanese Animation*, Open Court, Chicago, IL, 1996

P. Macias. *The Japanese Cult Film Companion*, Cadence Books, San Francisco, CA, 2001

—. & T. Machiyama. *Cruising the Anime City*, Stone Bridge Press, CA, 2004

L. Maltin. *Of Mice and Magic: A History of American Animated Cartoons*, New American Library, New York, NY, 1987

—. *The Disney Films*, 3rd ed., Hyperion, New York, NY, 1995

A. Masano & J. Wiedermann, eds. *Manga Design*, Taschen, 2004

G. Mast *et al*, eds. *Film Theory and Criticism: Introductory Readings*, Oxford University Press, New York, NY, 1992a

—. & B. Kawin. *A Short History of the Movies*, Macmillan, New York, NY, 1992b

H. McCarthy. *Anime! A Beginner's Guide To Japanese Animation*, Titan, 1993

—. *The Animé Movie Guide*, Titan Books, London, 1996

—. & J. Clements. *The Erotic Animé Movie Guide*, Titan Books, London, 1998

—. *Hayao Miyazaki: Master of Japanese Animation*, Stone Bridge Press, Berkeley, CA, 2002

—. *500 Manga Heroes & Villains*, Barron's, Hauppauge, New York, 2006

—. *500 Essential Anime Movies*, Collins Design, New York, NY, 2008

S. McCloud. *Understanding Comics*, Harper, London, 1994

—. *Reinventing Comics,* Harper, London, 2000

—. *Making Comics*, Harper, London, 2006

H. Miyazaki. *Points of Departure, 1979-1996*, Tokuma Shoten, Tokyo, 1997

—. *Starting Point, 1979-1996,* tr. B. Cary & F. Schodt, Viz Media, San Francisco, CA, 2009

—. *Turning Point, 1997-2008,* tr. B. Cary & F. Schodt, Viz Media/ Shogakukan, San Francisco, CA, 2014

T. Moi. *Sexual/ Textual Politics: Feminist Literary Theory,* Methuen, 1985

K. Morrissey. "Interview: *Fullmetal Alchemist* Composer Akira Senju", Anime News Network, June 2, 2022

S. Napier. *Anime: From Akira To Princess Mononoke*, Palgrave, New York, 2001

—. "Excuse Me, Who Are You?", in S. Brown, 2006

S. Neale & M. Smith, eds. *Contemporary Hollywood Cinema*, Routledge, London, 1998

C. Odell & M. Le Blanc. *Studio Ghibli: The Films of Hayao Miyazaki and Isao Takahata*, Kamera Books, Herts., 2009

—. *Anime*, Kamera Books, Herts., 2013

A. Osmond. *Spirited Away*, British Film Institute, London, 2003a

—. "Gods and Monsters", *Sight & Sound*, Sept, 2003b

—. *Satoshi Kon*, Stone Bridge Press, San Francisco, 2009

—. "Masahiko Minami", Manga UK, 2020

D. Peary & G. Peary, eds. *The American Animated Cartoon*, Dutton, New York, NY, 1980

G. Poitras. *The Animé Companion*, Stone Bridge Press, Berkeley, CA, 1999

—. *Animé Essentials*, Stone Bridge Press, Berkeley, CA, 2001

N. Power. *God of Comics: Osamu Tezuka and the Creation of Post-World War II*, University of Mississippi Press, 2009

K. Quigley. *Comics Underground Japan*, Blast Books, New York, NY, 1996

D. Richie. *The Films of Akira Kurosawa*, University of California Press, Berkeley, CA, 1965

C. Rowthorn. *Japan*, Lonely Planet, 2007

B. Ruh. *Stray Dog of Anime: The Films of Mamoru Oshii*, Palgrave Macmillan, 2004

K. Sandler. *Reading the Rabbit: Explorations In Warner Bros. Animation*, Rutgers University Press, Brunswick, NJ, 1998

R. Schickel. *The Disney Version: The Life, Times, Art, and Commerce of Walt Disney*, Pavilion, London, 1986

M. Schilling. *The Enclyclopedia of Japanese Pop Culture*, Weatherhill, Boston, MA, 1997
—. *Contemporary Japanese Film*, Weatherhill, New York, NY, 1999
F. Schodt. *Manga! Manga! The World of Japanese Magazines*, Kodansha International, London, 1997
—. *Dreamland Japan: Writings On Modern Manga*, Stone Bridge Press, Berkeley, CA, 2002
—. *The Astro Boy Essays*, Stone Bridge Press, CA, 2007
C. Shiratori, ed. *Secret Comics Japan*, Cadence Books, San Francisco, CA, 2000
T. Smith. "Miso Horny: Sex In Japanese Comics", *Comics Journal*, Apl, 1991
E. Smoodin. *Animating Culture: Hollywood Cartoons From the Sound Era*, Roundhouse, 1993
—. ed. *Disney Discourse: Producing the Magic Kingdom* , Routledge, London, 1994
V. Sobchack. *The Limits of Infinity: The American Science Fiction Film*, A.S. Barnes, N.Y., 1980
—. *Screening Space: The American Science Fiction Film* , Ungar, N.Y., 1987/ 1993
G. Stewart. *Between Film and Screen: Modernism's Photo Synthesis*, University of Chicago Press, Chicago, IL, 1999
J. Stieff & A. Barkman, eds. *Manga and Philosophy*, Open Court, Chicago, IL, 2010
J. Thompson. *Manga: The Complete Guide*, Del Rey, New York, NY, 2007
K. Thompson & D. Bordwell. *Film History: An Introduction*, McGraw-Hill, New York, NY, 1994
—. *Storytelling In the New Hollywood*, Harvard University Press, Cambridge, MA, 1999
P. Wells. *Understanding Animation*, Routledge, London, 1998
Colin Wilson. *The Occult,* Granada, 1971
—. *Mysteries,* Granada, 1979
C. Winstanley, ed. *SFX Collection: Animé Special*, Future Publishing, London
J. Wolmark. *Aliens and Others: Science Fiction, Feminism and Postmodernism*, Harvester Wheatsheaf, 1993
—. ed. *Cybersexualities: A Reader On Feminist Theory, Cyborgs and Cyberspace*, Edinburgh University Press, Edinburgh, 1999
T. Woods. *Beginning Postmodernism,* Manchester University Press, Manchester, 1999
J. Zipes, ed. *The Oxford Companion To Fairy Tales*, Oxford University Press, 2000
—. *The Enchanted Screen: The Unknown History of Fairy-tale Films*, Routledge, New York, NY, 2011
—. *The Irresistible Fairy Tale*, Princeton University Press, Princeton, NJ, 2012

WEBSITES

Website for Himoru Arakawa:

arakawanews.tumblr.com

Fullmetal Alchemist websites:

ginnodangan.wordpress.com
fullmetal-alchemist.com
Michiru Oshima: michiru-oshima.net
Wikia.com is excellent for guides to the *Fullmetal Alchemist* universe.

Animé

manga.com
animenewsnetwork.com
anipike.com
koyagi.com
jai2.com
otakunews.com
midnighteyec.com

JEREMY ROBINSON has published poetry, fiction, and studies of J.R.R. Tolkien, Samuel Beckett, Thomas Hardy, André Gide and D.H. Lawrence. Robinson has edited poetry books by Novalis, Ursula Le Guin, Friedrich Hölderlin, Francesco Petrarch, Dante Alighieri, Arseny Tarkovsky, and Rainer Maria Rilke.

Books on film and animation include: *The Akira Book* • *The Art of Katsuhiro Otomo* • *The Art of Masamune Shirow* • *The Ghost In the Shell Book* • *Fullmetal Alchemist* • *Cowboy Bebop: The Anime and Movie* • *The Cinema of Hayao Miyazaki* • *Hayao Miyazaki: Pocket Guide* • *Princess Mononoke: Pocket Movie Guide* • *Spirited Away: Pocket Movie Guide* • *Blade Runner and the Cinema of Philip K. Dick* • *Blade Runner: Pocket Movie Guide* • *The Cinema of Donald Cammell* • *Performance: Donald Cammell: Nic Roeg: Pocket Movie Guide* • *Pasolini: Il Cinema di Poesia/ The Cinema of Poetry* • *Salo: Pocket Movie Guide* • *The Trilogy of Life Movies: Pocket Movie Guide* • *The Gospel According To Matthew: Pocket Movie Guide* • *The Ecstatic Cinema of Tony Ching Siu-tung* • *Tsui Hark: The Dragon Master of Chinese Cinema* • *The Swordsman: Pocket Movie Guide* • *A Chinese Ghost Story: Pocket Movie Guide* • *Ken Russell: England's Great Visionary Film Director and Music Lover* • *Tommy: Ken Russell: The Who: Pocket Movie Guide* • *Women In Love: Ken Russell: D.H. Lawrence: Pocket Movie Guide* • *The Devils: Ken Russell: Pocket Movie Guide* • *Walerian Borowczyk: Cinema of Erotic Dreams* • *The Beast: Pocket Movie Guide* • *The Lord of the Rings Movies* • *The Fellowship of the Ring: Pocket Movie Guide* • *The Two Towers: Pocket Movie Guide* • *The Return of the King: Pocket Movie Guide* • *Jean-Luc Godard: The Passion of Cinema* • *The Sacred Cinema of Andrei Tarkovsky* • *Andrei Tarkovsky: Pocket Guide.*

'It's amazing for me to see my work treated with such passion and respect. There is nothing resembling it in the U.S. in relation to my work.'
(Andrea Dworkin)

'This model monograph – it is an exemplary job, and I'm very proud that he has accorded me a couple of mentions… The subject matter of his book is beautifully organised and dead on beam.'
(Lawrence Durrell, on *The Light Eternal: A Study of J.M.W. Turner*)

'Jeremy Robinson's poetry is certainly jammed with ideas, and I find it very interesting for that reason. It's certainly a strong imprint of his personality.'
(Colin Wilson)

'*Sex-Magic-Poetry-Cornwall* is a very rich essay... It is a very good piece… vastly stimulating and insightful.'
(Peter Redgrove)

MEDIA, CINEMA, FEMINISM and CULTURAL STUDIES

J.R.R. Tolkien: The Books, The Films, The Whole Cultural Phenomenon
J.R.R. Tolkien: Pocket Guide
The *Lord of the Rings* Movies: Pocket Guide
The Cinema of Hayao Miyazaki
Hayao Miyazaki: *Princess Mononoke*: Pocket Movie Guide
Hayao Miyazaki: *Spirited Away*: Pocket Movie Guide
Tim Burton : Hallowe'en For Hollywood
Ken Russell
Ken Russell: *Tommy*: Pocket Movie Guide
The Ghost Dance: The Origins of Religion
The Peyote Cult
Cixous, Irigaray, Kristeva: The *Jouissance* of French Feminism
Julia Kristeva: Art, Love, Melancholy, Philosophy, Semiotics and Psychoanalysis
Luce Irigaray: Lips, Kissing, and the Politics of Sexual Difference
Hélène Cixous I Love You: The *Jouissance* of Writing
Andrea Dworkin
'Cosmo Woman': The World of Women's Magazines
Women in Pop Music
HomeGround: The Kate Bush Anthology
Discovering the Goddess (Geoffrey Ashe)
The Poetry of Cinema
The Sacred Cinema of Andrei Tarkovsky
Andrei Tarkovsky: Pocket Guide
Andrei Tarkovsky: *Mirror*: Pocket Movie Guide
Andrei Tarkovsky: *The Sacrifice*: Pocket Movie Guide
Walerian Borowczyk: Cinema of Erotic Dreams
Jean-Luc Godard: The Passion of Cinema
Jean-Luc Godard: *Hail Mary*: Pocket Movie Guide
Jean-Luc Godard: *Contempt*: Pocket Movie Guide
Jean-Luc Godard: *Pierrot le Fou*: Pocket Movie Guide
John Hughes and Eighties Cinema
Ferris Bueller's Day Off: Pocket Movie Guide
Jean-Luc Godard: Pocket Guide
The Cinema of Richard Linklater
Liv Tyler: Star In Ascendance
Blade Runner and the Films of Philip K. Dick
Paul Bowles and Bernardo Bertolucci
Media Hell: Radio, TV and the Press
An Open Letter to the BBC
Detonation Britain: Nuclear War in the UK
Feminism and Shakespeare
Wild Zones: Pornography, Art and Feminism
Sex in Art: Pornography and Pleasure in Painting and Sculpture
Sexing Hardy: Thomas Hardy and Feminism

The Light Eternal is a model monograph, an exemplary job. The subject matter of the book is beautifully
organised and dead on beam. (Lawrence Durrell)
It is amazing for me to see my work treated with such passion and respect. (Andrea Dworkin)

CRESCENT MOON PUBLISHING
P.O. Box 1312, Maidstone, Kent, ME14 5XU, Great Britain. www.crmoon.com

cresmopub@yahoo.co.uk   www.crescentmoon.org.uk